DICTIONARY OF

MARKETING

third edition

A. Ivanovic MBA
P.H. Collin

BLOOMSBURY

A BLOOMSBURY REFERENCE BOOK

658 . 8003

Originally published by Peter Collin Publishing

Third edition published 2003
Second edition published 1996
First edition published 1989

Bloomsbury Publishing Plc
38 Soho Square
London W1D 3HB

British Library Cataloguing-in-Publication Data

A catalogue record for this book is available from the British Library

ISBN 0-7475-6621-6

Text computer typeset by Bloomsbury Publishing
Printed in Italy by Legoprint

PREFACE TO FIRST EDITION

This dictionary provides the user with a comprehensive vocabulary of terms used in marketing. It covers such aspects of the subject as market research, advertising, promotional aids and selling techniques.

The main words are explained in simple English, and, where appropriate, examples are given to show how the words are used in context. Quotations are also given from various magazines and journals, which give an idea of how the terms are used in real life.

The Supplement at the back of the book gives some further information which may be of use to the user.

We are particularly grateful to Margaret Jull Costa and Stephen Curtis for valuable comments which they made on the text.

PREFACE TO SECOND EDITION

Business terminology changes rapidly, and this second edition includes a variety of new terms and expressions which have come into use since the first edition was published. We have also included new examples and quotations from recent magazines.

Also included is a pronunciation guide for the main entry words.

PREFACE TO THIRD EDITION

This third edition of the dictionary takes into account the many new terms that have come into marketing with the growth of e-commerce and the Internet. The supplement at the back of the book has also been comprehensively updated.

We are grateful to the following for their valuable comments on the text: Ian Linton, Georgia Hole, Dinah Jackson and Sandra Anderson.

Pronunciation

The following symbols have been used to show the pronunciation of the main words in the dictionary.

Stress has been indicated by a main stress mark (') and a secondary stress mark (,). Note that these are only guides as the stress of the word changes according to its position in the sentence.

Vowels		*Consonants*	
æ	back	b	buck
ɑː	harm	d	dead
ɒ	stop	ð	other
aɪ	type	dʒ	jump
aʊ	how	f	fare
aɪə	hire	g	gold
aʊə	hour	h	head
ɔː	course	j	yellow
ɔɪ	annoy	k	cab
e	head	l	leave
eə	fair	m	mix
eɪ	make	n	nil
eʊ	go	s	save
ɜː	word	ʃ	shop
iː	keep	t	take
i	happy	tʃ	change
ə	about	θ	theft
ɪ	fit	v	value
ɪə	near	w	work
u	annual	x	loch
uː	pool	ʒ	measure
ʊ	book	z	zone
ʊə	tour		
ʌ	shut		

A

ABC method /ˌeɪ biː ˈsiː ˌmeθəd/ noun a sales method, where the customer's attention is attracted, the salesperson then shows the benefits of the product to the customer, and finally closes the deal. Full form **attention, benefit, close**

ABCs abbr Audit Bureau of Circulations

above-the-fold /əˌbʌv ðə ˈfəʊld/ noun the part of a webpage which is seen first without having to scroll, and so is preferred for advertising

above-the-line advertising /əˌbʌv ðə laɪn ˈædvətaɪzɪŋ/ noun advertising for which a payment is made and for which a commission is paid to the advertising agency, e.g. an advertisement in a magazine or a stand at a trade fair. Compare **below-the-line advertising** (NOTE: as opposed to direct marketing)

absenteeism /ˌæbs(ə)nˈtiːɪz(ə)m/ noun staying away from work for no good reason ○ the rate of absenteeism or the absenteeism rate always increases in fine weather ○ Low productivity is largely due to the high level of absenteeism. ○ Absenteeism is high in the week before Christmas.

'…but the reforms still hadn't fundamentally changed conditions on the shop floor: absenteeism was as high as 20% on some days' [Business Week]

absolute /ˈæbsəluːt/ adjective complete or total

absolute advantage /ˌæbsəluːt ədˈvɑːntɪdʒ/ noun an advantage enjoyed by an area of the world which can produce a product more cheaply than other areas ○ For climatic reasons, tropical countries have an absolute advantage in that type of production.

absolute cost /ˌæbsəluːt ˈkɒst/ noun the actual cost of placing an advertisement in a magazine or other advertising medium

absolute monopoly /ˌæbsəluːt məˈnɒpəli/ noun a situation where only one producer or supplier produces or supplies something ○ The company has an absolute monopoly of imports of French wine. ○ The supplier's absolute monopoly of the product meant that customers had to accept his terms.

absorb /əbˈzɔːb/ verb to take in a small item so as to form part of a larger one □ **overheads have absorbed all our profits** all our profits have gone in paying overhead expenses □ **to absorb a loss by a subsidiary** to write a subsidiary company's loss into the group accounts □ **a business which has been absorbed by a competitor** a small business which has been made part of a larger one

absorption /əbˈzɔːpʃən/ noun making a smaller business part of a larger one, so that the smaller company in effect no longer exists

absorption costing /əbˈzɔːpʃən ˌkɒstɪŋ/ noun costing a product to include both the direct costs of production and the indirect overhead costs as well

accelerated depreciation /əkˌseləreɪtɪd dɪpriːʃiˈeɪʃ(ə)n/ noun a system of depreciation which reduces the value of assets at a high rate in the early years to encourage companies, as a result of tax advantages, to invest in new equipment

accelerator /əkˈseləreɪtə/ noun the theory that a change in demand for consumer goods will result in a greater

change in demand for the capital goods used in their production

accept /ək'sept/ *verb* **1.** to take something which is being offered □ **to accept delivery of a shipment** to take goods into the warehouse officially when they are delivered **2.** to take something which is being offered or to say 'yes' or to agree to something ○ *to accept an offer of employment* ○ *she accepted the offer of a job in Australia* ○ *he accepted £2000 in lieu of notice* **3.** to agree formally to receive something or to be responsible for something

acceptable /ək'septəb(ə)l/ *adjective* which can be accepted ○ *Both parties found the offer acceptable.* ○ *The terms of the contract of employment are not acceptable to the candidate.*

acceptance /ək'septəns/ *noun* □ **acceptance of an offer** agreeing to an offer □ **to give an offer a conditional acceptance** to accept an offer provided that specific things happen or that specific terms apply □ **we have his letter of acceptance** we have received a letter from him accepting the offer

acceptance against documents /ək,septəns əgenst 'dɒkjʊmənts/ *noun* a transaction where the seller takes charge of the shipping documents for a consignment of goods when a buyer accepts a bill of exchange ○ *Acceptance against documents protects the seller when sending goods which are not yet paid for.*

acceptance sampling /ək'septəns ,sɑːmplɪŋ/ *noun* testing a small sample of a batch to see if the whole batch is good enough to be accepted

accepted bill /ək,septɪd 'bɪl/ *noun* a bill of exchange which has been signed, and therefore accepted by the buyer

acceptor /ək'septə/ *noun* a person who accepts a bill of exchange by signing it, thus making a commitment to pay it by a specified date

access /'ækses/ *noun* □ **to have access to something** to be able to obtain or reach something ○ *She has access to large amounts of venture capital.* ■ *verb* to call up data which is stored in a computer ○ *She accessed the address file on the computer.* ◇ **access to the market** **1.** the legal right to sell in a particular market **2.** the ability to reach a market by promotion and distribution

Access /'ækses/ a credit card system formerly operated by some British banks, part of the MasterCard network

accessibility /ək,sesɪ'bɪlɪti/ *noun* the ability of a market to be reached by promotion and distribution ○ *There is much demand in the market, but, because of the great distances involved, accessibility is a problem.* ○ *We must analyse the geographical aspects in assessing the market's accessibility.*

access time /'ækses taɪm/ *noun* the time taken by a computer to find data stored in it

accommodation bill /ə,kɒmə-'deɪʃ(ə)n ,bɪl/ *noun* a bill of exchange where the person signing (the 'drawee') is helping another company (the 'drawer') to raise a loan

account /ə'kaʊnt/ *noun* **1.** a record of financial transactions over a period of time, such as money paid, received, borrowed or owed ○ *Please send me your account* or *a detailed* or *an itemized account.* **2.** (*in a shop*) an arrangement which a customer has to buy goods and pay for them at a later date, usually the end of the month ○ *to have an account* or *a charge account* or *a credit account with Harrods* ○ *Put it on my account* or *charge it to my account.* □ **to open an account** (*of a customer*) to ask a shop to supply goods which you will pay for at a later date □ **to open an account** *or* **to close an account** (*of a shop*) to start or to stop supplying a customer on credit □ **to settle an account** to pay all the money owed on an account □ **to stop an account** to stop supplying a customer until payment has been made for goods supplied **3.** □ **on account** as part of a total bill □ **to pay money on account** to pay to settle part of a bill □ **advance on account** money paid as a part payment **4.** a customer who does a large amount of business with a firm and has an account with it ○ *Smith Brothers is one of our largest accounts.* ○ *Our sales people call on their best accounts twice a month.* **5.** □ **to keep the accounts** to

write each sum of money in the account book ○ *The bookkeeper's job is to enter all the money received in the accounts.* **6.** STOCK EXCHANGE a period during which shares are traded for credit, and at the end of which the shares bought must be paid for (NOTE: On the London Stock Exchange, there are twenty-four accounts during the year, each running usually for ten working days.) **7.** a notice □ **to take account of inflation** *or* **to take inflation into account** to assume that there will be a specific percentage of inflation when making calculations **8.** an arrangement which a company has with an advertising agency, where the agency deals with all promotion for the company ○ *The company has moved its $3m account to another agency.* ○ *The small agency lost the account when the company decided it needed a different marketing approach.* ○ *Three agencies were asked to make presentations, as the company had decided to switch its account.* ■ *verb* □ **to account for** to explain and record a money transaction ○ *to account for a loss* or *a discrepancy* ○ *The reps have to account for all their expenses to the sales manager.*

accountancy /əˈkaʊntənsi/ *noun* the work of an accountant ○ *They are studying accountancy* or *They are accountancy students.* (NOTE: American English is **accounting** in this meaning)

accountant /əˈkaʊntənt/ *noun* **1.** a person who keeps a company's accounts ○ *The chief accountant of a manufacturing group.* **2.** a person who advises a company on its finances ○ *I send all my income tax queries to my accountant.* **3.** a person who examines accounts

account book /əˈkaʊnt bʊk/ *noun* a book with printed columns which is used to record sales and purchases

account director /əˈkaʊnt daɪˌrektə/ *noun* a person who works in an advertising agency and who oversees various account managers who are each responsible for specific clients

account executive /əˈkaʊnt ɪgˌzekjʊtɪv/ *noun* an employee who looks after customers or who is the link between customers and the company

account handler /əˈkaʊnt ˌhændlə/, **account manager** /əˈkaʊnt ˌmænɪdʒə/ *noun* a person who works in an advertising agency, and who is responsible for a particular client

'...we have moved the account because we thought it would be better suited in a smaller agency' [*Marketing Week*]

accounting /əˈkaʊntɪŋ/ *noun* the work of recording money paid, received, borrowed or owed ○ *accounting methods* or *accounting procedures* ○ *accounting system* ○ *accounting machine*

'...applicants will be professionally qualified and have a degree in Commerce or Accounting' [*Australian Financial Review*]

accounts department /əˈkaʊnts dɪˌpɑːtmənt/ *noun* a department in a company which deals with money paid, received, borrowed or owed

accounts manager /əˈkaʊnts ˌmænɪdʒə/ *noun* the manager of an accounts department

accounts payable /əˌkaʊnts ˈpeɪəb(ə)l/ *noun* money owed by a company

accredited agent /əˌkredɪtɪd ˈeɪdʒənt/ *noun* an agent who is appointed by a company to act on its behalf

accurate /ˈækjʊrət/ *adjective* correct ○ *The sales department made an accurate forecast of sales.* ○ *The designers produced an accurate copy of the plan.*

accurate description /ˌækjʊrət dɪˈskrɪpʃən/ *noun* an honest and true description of a product or service in an advertisement or catalogue ○ *As the advertisement was clearly not an accurate description of the product, the company had to pay a fine.* ○ *It is not an accurate description of the product to state that it gives out more light than the sun.*

accurately /ˈækjʊrətli/ *adverb* correctly ○ *The second quarter's drop in sales was accurately forecast by the computer.*

achiever /əˈtʃiːvə/ *noun* a person who is successful or who tends to achieve his or her objectives ○ *It was her reputation as a high achiever that made us think of headhunting her.* ♦ **VALS**

acknowledge /ək'nɒlɪdʒ/ *verb* to tell a sender that a letter, package or shipment has arrived ○ *He has still not acknowledged my letter of the 24th.* ○ *We acknowledge receipt of your letter of June 14th.*

acknowledgement /ək-'nɒlɪdʒmənt/ *noun* the act of acknowledging ○ *She sent an acknowledgement of receipt.* ○ *The company sent a letter of acknowledgement after I sent in my job application.*

ACORN /'eɪkɔːn/ *noun* a classification of residential areas into categories, based on the type of people who live in them, the type of houses, etc., much used in consumer research ○ *ACORN will help us plan where to concentrate our sales visits.* Full form **a classification of residential neighbourhoods**

acquire /ə'kwaɪə/ *verb* to buy ○ *to acquire a company* ○ *We have acquired a new office building in the centre of town.*

acquirer /ə'kwaɪərə/ *noun* a person or company which buys something

acquisition /ˌækwɪ'zɪʃ(ə)n/ *noun* **1.** something bought ○ *The chocolate factory is our latest acquisition.* **2.** the act of getting or buying something □ **data acquisition** *or* **acquisition of data** obtaining and classifying data **3.** the action of acquiring new customers, as opposed to retention, which is keeping the loyalty of existing customers

acronym /'ækrənɪm/ *noun* a word which is made up from the initials of other words ○ *The name of the company was especially designed to provide a catchy acronym.* ○ *BASIC is an acronym for Beginner's All-purpose Symbolic Instruction Code.*

across-the-board /əˌkrɒs ðə 'bɔːd/ *adjective (of an advertisement)* running for five consecutive days from Monday to Friday

action shot /'ækʃən ˌʃɒt/ *noun* a scene with movement either in a film or on TV

activity sampling /æk'tɪvɪti ˌsɑːmplɪŋ/ *noun* an observation of tasks and their performances, carried out at random intervals ○ *Activity sampling*

was carried out to see how fast the machinists worked. (NOTE: no plural)

ad /æd/ *noun* same as **advertisement** (*informal*) ○ *We put an ad in the paper.* ○ *She answered an ad in the paper.* ○ *He found his job through an ad in the paper.*

Ad-A-Card /'æd ə kɑːd/ *noun US* a type of perforated card bound into a magazine which a reader can tear off and return to the advertiser

adapt /ə'dæpt/ *verb* to change something a little to fit in with changing circumstances ○ *This product must be adapted in line with recent technological developments.* ○ *The device has been adapted for use on board aircraft.*

adaptation /ˌædæp'teɪʃ(ə)n/ *noun* **1.** a small change ○ *With a few minor adaptations, the machine will cut square holes as well as round ones.* **2.** something which has been adapted ○ *This machine is an adaptation of our original model.*

adaptive control model /əˌdæptɪv kən'trəʊl ˌmɒd(ə)l/ *noun US* a model for planning advertising expenditure in line with changes in consumer responses to advertising

ad banner /'æd ˌbænə/ *noun* same as **banner**

ad click /'æd klɪk/ *noun* same as **click-through**

ad click rate /'æd klɪk ˌreɪt/ *noun* same as **click-through rate**

added value /ˌædɪd 'væljuː/ *noun* an amount added to the value of a product or service, being the difference between its cost and the amount received when it is sold. Wages, taxes, etc. are deducted from the added value to give the profit. ♦ **Value Added Tax**

add-on sales /'æd ɒn ˌseɪlz/ *noun* the sale of items which complement items being bought, e.g. washing powder sold with a dishwasher

address label /ə'dres ˌleɪb(ə)l/ *noun* a label with an address on it

ad hoc /æd 'hɒk/ *adjective* 'for this particular purpose' ○ *They run ad hoc surveys to test customer reaction when products are launched.* ○ *Shipping by*

airfreight was an ad hoc arrangement initially.

ad hoc research /ˌæd hɒk rɪˈsɜːtʃ/ *noun* research carried out for a particular client or in a particular market

ad impression /ˈæd ɪmˌpreʃ(ə)n/ *noun* same as **ad view**

adjacency /əˈdʒeɪs(ə)nsi/ *noun* a commercial which is run between two TV programmes

adjust /əˈdʒʌst/ *verb* to change something to fit new conditions ○ *to adjust prices to take account of inflation* ○ *prices are adjusted for inflation*

'...inflation-adjusted GNP moved up at a 1.3% annual rate' [*Fortune*]

'Saudi Arabia will no longer adjust its production to match short-term supply with demand' [*Economist*]

'...on a seasonally-adjusted basis, output of trucks, electric power, steel and paper decreased' [*Business Week*]

adman /ˈædmæn/ *noun* a man who works in advertising (*informal*) ○ *The admen are using balloons as promotional material.* (NOTE: plural is **admen**)

administer /ədˈmɪnɪstə/ *verb* to organise, manage or direct the whole of an organisation or part of one ○ *She administers a large pension fund.*

administered channel /ədˌmɪnɪstəd ˈtʃæn(ə)l/ *noun* a distribution channel in which there is cooperation between businesses

administered price /ədˈmɪnɪstəd praɪs/ *noun* US a price fixed by a manufacturer which cannot be varied by a retailer (NOTE: the British equivalent is **resale price maintenance**)

administration /ədˌmɪnɪˈstreɪʃ(ə)n/ *noun* the running of a company in receivership by an administrator appointed by the courts

administration costs /ədˌmɪnɪˈstreɪʃ(ə)n ˌkɒsts/ *noun* the costs of management, not including production, marketing or distribution costs

administrative /ədˈmɪnɪstrətɪv/ *adjective* referring to administration ○ *administrative details* ○ *administrative expenses*

administrator /ədˈmɪnɪstreɪtə/ *noun* **1.** a person who directs the work

of other employees in a business ○ *After several years as a college teacher, she hopes to become an administrator.* **2.** a person appointed by a court to manage the affairs of someone who dies without leaving a will

adopt /əˈdɒpt/ *verb* to agree to something or to accept something

adopter /əˈdɒptə/ *noun* a customer who adopts a particular product

adoption /əˈdɒpʃən/ *noun* the decision to buy or use a particular product ○ *More promotion was needed to speed up adoption of the product.* ○ *Widespread adoption of its new shampoo range has made the company the market leader.*

adoption curve /əˈdɒpʃən kɜːv/ *noun* a line on a graph showing how many consumers adopt or buy a new product at various time periods after the launch date ○ *The adoption curve shows that most people who buy the product do so at a fairly late stage.*

Adshel /ˈædʃel/ *noun* a trademark for a poster site for advertisements in a bus shelter

adspend /ˈædspend/ *noun* the amount of money spent on advertising

ad transfer /ˈæd ˌtrænsfɜː/ *noun* same as **click-through**

ad valorem duty /ˌæd vəˈlɔːrəm ˌdjuːti/ *noun* the duty calculated on the sales value of the goods

advance /ədˈvɑːns/ *noun* **1.** money paid as a loan or as a part of a payment to be made later ○ *to receive an advance from the bank* ○ *to make an advance of £100 to someone* ○ *to pay someone an advance against a security* ○ *She asked if she could have a cash advance.* ○ *We paid her an advance on account.* ○ *Can I have an advance of £100 against next month's salary?* **2.** an increase ○ *an advance in trade with Eastern European countries* ○ *an advance in prices* **3.** □ **in advance** early, before something happens ○ *freight payable in advance* ○ *prices fixed in advance* ■ *adjective* early ○ *advance booking* ○ *advance payment* ○ *Advance holiday bookings are up on last year.* ○ *You must give seven days' advance notice of withdrawals from the account.* ■ *verb* **1.** to

lend ○ *The bank advanced him £100,000 against the security of his house.* **2.** to increase ○ *Prices generally advanced on the stock market.* **3.** to make something happen earlier ○ *The date of the AGM has been advanced to May 10th.* ○ *The meeting with the German distributors has been advanced from 11.00 to 09.30.*

advance freight /əd'vɑːns freɪt/ *noun* freight which is payable in advance

advance man /əd'vɑːns mæn/ *noun US* a person who publicizes a performance and sells tickets for it before the performers arrive

advert /'ædvɜːt/ *noun GB* same as **advertisement** (*informal*) ○ *to put an advert in the paper* ○ *to answer an advert in the paper* ○ *classified adverts* ○ *display adverts*

advertise /'ædvətaɪz/ *verb* to arrange and pay for publicity designed to help sell products or services or to find new employees ○ *to advertise a vacancy* ○ *to advertise for a secretary* ○ *to advertise a new product*

advertisement /əd'vɜːtɪsmənt/ *noun* **1.** a notice which shows that something is for sale, that a service is offered, that someone wants something or that a job is vacant **2.** a short film on television or a short announcement on the radio which tries to persuade people to use a product or service

advertisement manager /əd-'vɜːtɪsmənt ˌmænɪdʒə/ *noun* the manager in charge of the advertisement section of a newspaper

advertisement panel /əd-'vɜːtɪsmənt ˌpæn(ə)l/ *noun* a specially designed large advertising space in a newspaper

advertiser /'ædvətaɪzə/ *noun* a person or company that advertises ○ *The catalogue gives a list of advertisers.*

advertising /'ædvətaɪzɪŋ/ *noun* the business of announcing that something is for sale or of trying to persuade customers to buy a product or service ○ *She works in advertising* or *She has a job in advertising.* ○ *Their new advertising campaign is being launched next week.*

○ *The company has asked an advertising agent to prepare a presentation.* □ **to take advertising space in a paper** to book space for an advertisement in a newspaper

advertising agency /'ædvətaɪzɪŋ ˌeɪdʒənsi/ *noun* an office which plans, designs and manages advertising for other companies

advertising appeal /'ædvətaɪzɪŋ ə-ˌpiːl/ *noun* the appeal of an advertisement to the intended audience

advertising appropriation /'ædvətaɪzɪŋ əprəʊpriˌeɪʃ(ə)n/ *noun* money set aside by an organisation for its advertising ○ *The marketing director and the chief accountant have yet to fix the advertising appropriation.* ○ *We cannot afford as large an advertising appropriation as last year.*

advertising brief /'ædvətaɪzɪŋ briːf/ *noun* basic objectives and instructions concerning an advertising campaign, given by an advertiser to an advertising agency ○ *The brief stressed the importance of the market segment to be targeted.* ○ *The advertising brief was not detailed enough and did not show what sort of product image the advertiser wanted to create.*

advertising budget /'ædvətaɪzɪŋ ˌbʌdʒɪt/ *noun* money planned for spending on advertising ○ *Our advertising budget has been increased.*

advertising campaign /'ædvətaɪzɪŋ kæmˌpeɪn/ *noun* co-ordinated publicity or advertising drive to sell a product

advertising control /'ædvətaɪzɪŋ kənˌtrəʊl/ *noun* legislative and other measures to prevent abuses in advertising ○ *If voluntary advertising control doesn't work, then the government will step in with legislation.*

advertising department /'ædvətaɪzɪŋ dɪˌpaːtmənt/ *noun* the department in a company that deals with the company's advertising

advertising expenditure /'ædvətaɪzɪŋ ɪkˌspendɪtʃə/ *noun* the amount a company spends on its advertising

advertising hoarding /ˈædvətaɪzɪŋ ˌhɔːdɪŋ/ *noun* a billboard or wooden surface onto which advertising posters are stuck ○ *Advertising hoardings have been taken down in the town since the council banned posters.* ○ *Giant advertising hoardings were placed in fields on either side of the road.*

advertising jingle /ˈædvətaɪzɪŋ ˌdʒɪŋg(ə)l/ *noun* a short and easily remembered tune or song to advertise a product on television, etc.

advertising manager /ˈædvətaɪzɪŋ ˌmænɪdʒə/ *noun* the manager in charge of advertising a company's products

advertising medium /ˈædvətaɪzɪŋ ˌmiːdiəm/ *noun* a type of advertisement, e.g. a TV commercial ○ *The product was advertised through the medium of the trade press.* (NOTE: plural for this meaning is **media**)

advertising message /ˈædvətaɪzɪŋ ˌmesɪdʒ/ *noun* whatever a company is trying to communicate in an advertisement ○ *Bad copywriting made the advertising message unclear.* ○ *The advertising message was aimed at the wrong target audience and therefore got little response.* ○ *The poster does not use words to get its advertising message across.*

advertising rates /ˈædvətaɪzɪŋ reɪts/ *noun* the amount of money charged for advertising space in a newspaper or advertising time on TV

advertising space /ˈædvətaɪzɪŋ speɪs/ *noun* a space in a newspaper set aside for advertisements

advertising specialities /ˌædvətaɪzɪŋ speʃiˈælɪtiz/ *plural noun* special items given away as part of an advertising campaign, e.g. T-shirts, mugs, umbrellas, etc.

Advertising Standards Authority /ˌædvətaɪzɪŋ ˈstændədz ɔːˌθɒrəti/ *noun* the independent body which oversees the system of self-regulation in the British advertising industry. Abbr **ASA**

advertising time /ˈædvətaɪzɪŋ taɪm/ *noun* the time on television or radio set aside for advertising ○ *Advertising time is cheapest in the afternoon.* ○ *They spent a month selling advertising* time over the telephone. ○ *How much advertising time does this programme allow for?*

advertising weight /ˈædvətaɪzɪŋ weɪt/ *noun* the amount of advertising given to a brand

advertorial /ˌædvəˈtɔːriəl/ *noun* text in a magazine which is not written by the editorial staff but by an advertiser

'The objective of advertising for new products differs from that of advertising for improved products' [*International Journal of Advertising*]

'…in 1987, the advertising expenditure total was £6,264m' [*Precision Marketing*]

'…as media costs have spiralled, more financial directors are getting involved in the advertising process' [*Marketing Week*]

advice /ədˈvaɪs/ *noun* a notification telling someone what has happened □ **as per advice** according to what is written on the advice note

advice of dispatch /ədˌvaɪs əv dɪˈspætʃ/ *noun* communication from seller to buyer stating that goods have been sent, specifying time and place of arrival ○ *We have paid for the goods but as yet have received no advice of dispatch.* ○ *The advice of dispatch informed the buyer that the goods would arrive at Southampton on the morning of the 10th.*

ad view /ˈæd vjuː/ *noun* the number of times an advertisement is downloaded from a webpage and assumed to have been seen by a potential customer

advise /ədˈvaɪz/ *verb* to tell someone what has happened ○ *We have been advised that the shipment will arrive next week.*

advocacy advertising /ˈædvəkəsi ˌædvətaɪzɪŋ/ *noun* advertising by a business that expresses a particular point of view on some issue ○ *Because of its prestige as a producer, the company's advocacy advertising had great influence.* ○ *The food company's advocacy advertising condemned unhealthy additives in canned produce.* ○ *Advocacy advertising has changed the public's attitude to smoking.*

aerial advertising /ˌeəriəl ˈædvətaɪzɪŋ/ *noun* advertising displayed in the air from balloons or planes or in smoke designs ○ *Aerial advertis-*

ing proved to be an effective gimmick. ○ *Aerial advertising was used to attract the attention of people on the beach.*

affiliate /əˈfɪlieɪt/ *noun* a local TV station which is part of a national network

affiliated /əˈfɪlieɪtɪd/ *adjective* connected with or owned by another company ○ *Smiths Ltd is one of our affiliated companies.*

affiliate directory /əˌfɪliət daɪˈrektəri/ *noun* a directory that lists websites belonging to affiliate programmes (NOTE: Affiliate directories provide information both to companies that want to subscribe to a programme and to those who want to set up their own affiliate programmes.)

affiliate marketing /əˈfɪliət ˌmɑːkɪtɪŋ/ *noun* marketing that uses affiliate programmes

affiliate partner /əˈfɪliət ˌpɑːtnə/ *noun* a company which puts advertising onto its website for other companies, who pay for this service

affiliate programme /əˈfɪliət ˌprəʊɡræm/ *noun* a form of advertising on the web, in which a business persuades other businesses to put banners and buttons advertising its products or services on their websites and pays them a commission on any purchases made by their customers

affinity card /əˈfɪnɪti kɑːd/ *noun* credit card where a percentage of each purchase made is given by the credit card company to a stated charity

affluent /ˈæfluənt/ *adjective* very rich ○ *We live in an affluent society.* □ **the mass affluent** people with large sums of money in liquid assets

affluent society /ˌæfluənt səˈsaɪəti/ *noun* a type of society where most people are rich

affordable method /əˈfɔːdəb(ə)l ˌmeθəd/ *noun* a method of budgeting how much can be spent on marketing and promotion, which is based on what you can afford, rather than what you want to achieve ○ *Affordable method appeals to accountants, but won't help us achieve a high enough market share for the product.*

after-date /ˈɑːftə deɪt/ *noun* a reference on a bill of exchange to the length of time allowed for payment after a specific date ○ *The after-date allowed the buyer three months in which to pay.*

after-sales service /ˌɑːftə seɪlz ˈsɜːvɪs/ *noun* a service of a machine carried out by the seller for some time after the machine has been bought

after-sight /ˈɑːftə saɪt/ *noun* a type of bill of exchange which is due to be paid on a specific day after acceptance

agate /ˈæɡət/ *noun US* a measurement of advertising space in a newspaper, equal to one-fourteenth of an inch

age group /ˈeɪdʒ ɡruːp/ *noun* a category including all people whose ages fall between two established points ○ *What age groups is this product meant to appeal to?* ○ *Research shows an increase in smoking among the 18–20 age group.*

age limit /ˈeɪdʒ ˌlɪmɪt/ *noun* the top age at which you are allowed to do a job ○ *There is an age limit of thirty-five on the post of buyer.*

agency /ˈeɪdʒənsi/ *noun* **1.** an office or job of representing another company in an area ○ *They signed an agency agreement* or *an agency contract.* **2.** an office or business which arranges things for other companies

agency commission /ˈeɪdʒənsi kəˌmɪʃ(ə)n/ *noun* the commission charged by an advertising agency

agency mark-up /ˌeɪdʒənsi ˈmɑːkʌp/ *noun* an amount added by an advertising agency to purchases, which forms parts of the agency's commission

agency roster /ˈeɪdʒənsi ˌrɒstə/ *noun* a group of different advertising agencies all working for a large company

agent /ˈeɪdʒənt/ *noun* **1.** a person who represents a company or another person in an area ○ *to be the agent for IBM* **2.** a person in charge of an agency ○ *an advertising agent* ○ *The estate agent sent me a list of properties for sale.* ○ *Our trip was organised through out local travel agent.*

agent's commission /ˌeɪdʒənts kəˈmɪʃ(ə)n/ *noun* money, often a percentage of sales, paid to an agent

aggregate /ˈægrɪgət/ *adjective* total, with everything added together ○ *aggregate output*

aggregate demand /ˌægrɪgət dɪ-ˈmɑːnd/ *noun* total demand for goods and services from all sectors of the economy, such as individuals, companies and the government ○ *Economists are studying the recent fall in aggregate demand.* ○ *As incomes have risen, so has aggregate demand.*

aggregate supply /ˌægrɪgət sə-ˈplaɪ/ *noun* all goods and services on the market ○ *Is aggregate supply meeting aggregate demand?*

aggregator /ˈægrɪgeɪtə/ *noun* a website which collects news from other websites, allowing rapid syndication of information

AGM *abbr* annual general meeting

agree /əˈgriː/ *verb* **1.** to approve ○ *The auditors have agreed the accounts.* ○ *The figures were agreed between the two parties.* ○ *We have agreed the budgets for next year.* ○ *The boss has agreed your prices.* ○ *The terms of the contract are still to be agreed.* **2.** to say yes to something that is suggested ○ *It has been agreed that the lease will run for 25 years.* **3.** □ **to agree to/on something** to approve something ○ *After some discussion he agreed to our plan.* ○ *The bank will never agree to lend the company £250,000.* ○ *We all agreed on the need for action.* □ **to agree to do something** to say that you will do something ○ *She agreed to be chairman.* ○ *Will the finance director agree to resign?* □ **to agree on something** (*of a group of people*) to come to a joint decision about something ○ *They have finally agreed on a new marketing strategy.* ○ *Can we agree on a date for the new product launch?*

agreed /əˈgriːd/ *adjective* which has been accepted by everyone ○ *We pay an agreed amount each month.* ○ *The shop is leased on agreed terms.* ○ *The agreed terms of employment are laid down in the contract.*

agreed price /əˈgriːd praɪs/ *noun* a price which has been accepted by both the buyer and seller

agreement /əˈgriːmənt/ *noun* a spoken or written contract between people or groups which explains how they will act ○ *a written agreement* ○ *an unwritten or verbal agreement* ○ *to draw up or to draft an agreement* ○ *to break an agreement* ○ *to sign an agreement* ○ *to witness an agreement* ○ *to reach an agreement or to come to an agreement on something* ○ *an international agreement on trade* ○ *a collective wage agreement* ○ *a marketing agreement*

'…after three days of tough negotiations the company has reached agreement with its 1,200 unionized workers' [*Toronto Star*]

agreement of sale /əˌgriːmənt əv ˈseɪl/ *noun* a written contract that sets out in detail the terms agreed between the buyer and the seller when a property is sold

agree with /əˈgriː wɪð/ *verb* **1.** to say that your opinions are the same as someone else's ○ *I agree with the chairman that the figures are lower than normal.* **2.** to be the same as ○ *The auditors' figures do not agree with those of the accounts department.*

aid /eɪd/ *noun* something which helps ■ *verb* to help

AIDA *noun* a model showing stages in the effects of advertising on consumers, i.e. you attract their Attention, keep their Interest, arouse a Desire and provoke Action to purchase. Full form **attention, interest, desire, action**

aided recall /ˌeɪdɪd rɪˈkɔːl/ *noun* a test to see how well someone remembers an advertisement by giving the respondent some help such as a picture which he or she might associate with it ○ *Even aided recall brought no reaction from the respondent.* ○ *Aided recall has shown that we must make our advertising more striking.* (NOTE: also called **prompted recall**)

aid-to-trade /ˌeɪd tə ˈtreɪd/ *noun* a service which supports trade, e.g. banking and advertising ○ *The recession has affected aids-to-trade and the industries they support and supply.* ○ *At that time,*

advertising was the fastest expanding aid-to-trade.

aim /eɪm/ *noun* something which you try to do ○ *One of our aims is to increase the quality of our products.* □ **the company has achieved all its aims** the company has done all the things it had hoped to do ■ *verb* to try to do something ○ *Each sales rep must aim to double their previous year's sales.* ○ *We aim to be No. 1 in the market within two years.*

air /eə/ *noun* a method of travelling or sending goods using aircraft ○ *to send a letter* or *a shipment by air*

air carrier /'eə ˌkæriə/ *noun* a company which sends cargo or passengers by air

air forwarding /'eə ˌfɔːwədɪŋ/ *noun* the process of arranging for goods to be shipped by air

air freight /'eə freɪt/ *noun* a method of shipping goods in an aircraft ○ *to send a shipment by air freight* ○ *air freight tariffs are rising*

airfreight /'eəfreɪt/ *verb* to send goods by air ○ *to airfreight a consignment to Mexico* ○ *We airfreighted the shipment because our agent ran out of stock.*

air letter /'eə ˌletə/ *noun* a special sheet of thin blue paper which when folded can be sent by air mail without an envelope (NOTE: American English is **aerogramme**)

airline /'eəlaɪn/ *noun* a company which carries passengers or cargo by air

airmail /'eəmeɪl/ *noun* a way of sending letters or parcels by air ○ *to send a package by airmail* ○ *Airmail charges have risen by 15%.* ■ *verb* to send letters or parcels by air ○ *We airmailed the document to New York.*

airmail envelope /'eəmeɪl ˌenvələup/ *noun* a very light envelope for sending airmail letters

airmail transfer /'eəmeɪl ˌtrænsfɜː/ *noun* sending money from one bank to another by airmail

airtight /'eətaɪt/ *adjective* which does not allow air to get in ○ *The goods are packed in airtight containers.*

air time /'eə taɪm/, **airtime** *noun* the time set aside for advertising on television or radio ○ *How much air time do we need for this commercial?* ○ *We should look for air time on the new radio station.* ○ *All the air time in the world won't sell this product.*

aisle /aɪl/ *noun* a space or passageway between the shelves of products on display in a supermarket

à la carte /ˌæ læ 'kɑːt/ *noun* a system whereby advertisers use the services of a whole range of businesses rather than relying on one agency over a long period

all-in rate /ˌɔːl ɪn 'reɪt/, **all-in price** /-ˌɔːl ɪn 'praɪs/ *noun* a price which covers all items in a purchase such as delivery, tax and insurance, as well as the goods themselves

allowable expenses /əˌlauəb(ə)l ɪk'spensɪz/ *plural noun* business expenses which can be claimed against tax

allowance /ə'lauəns/ *noun* money removed in the form of a discount ○ *an allowance for depreciation* ○ *an allowance for exchange loss*

'...most airlines give business class the same baggage allowance as first class' [*Business Traveller*]

'...the compensation plan includes base, incentive and car allowance totalling $50,000+' [*Globe and Mail (Toronto)*]

alpha activity /'ælfə æk,tɪvɪti/ *noun* the measurement of a person's brain activity as a way of measuring their reaction to an advertisement

alternate /ɔːl'tɜːnət/ *adjective* different from what is actually used

alternate media /ɔːl,tɜːnət 'miːdiə/ *adjective* forms of advertising which are not direct mailing, e.g. TV commercials, magazine inserts, etc.

alternative close /ɔːl'tɜːnətɪv kləuz/ *noun* an act of ending a sales negotiation by asking the customer to choose something such as a method of payment

ambient media /ˌæmbiənt 'miːdiə/ *noun* advertising media outdoors, e.g. posters, advertisements on the sides of buses, etc.

ambush marketing /ˈæmbʊʃ ˌmɑːkɪtɪŋ/ *noun* the linking of a promotion campaign to an event such as a sporting contest which is sponsored by another manufacturer without paying a fee

analyse /ˈænəlaɪz/, **analyze** *verb* to examine someone or something in detail ○ *to analyse a statement of account* ○ *to analyse the market potential*

analysis /əˈnæləsɪs/ *noun* a detailed examination and report ○ *a job analysis* ○ *market analysis* ○ *Her job is to produce a regular sales analysis.* (NOTE: plural is analyses)

analyst /ˈænəlɪst/ *noun* a person who analyses ○ *a market analyst* ○ *a systems analyst*

ancillary-to-trade /ˌænˌsɪləri tə ˈtreɪd/ *noun* a service which supports trade, e.g. banking and advertising ○ *The recession has affected ancillaries-to-trade and the industries they support and supply.* ○ *Advertising was the fastest expanding ancillary-to-trade at that time.*

animatic /ˌænɪˈmætɪk/ *noun* a rough outline version of a television commercial shown to the advertiser for approval ○ *The animatic was sent back to the agency with several criticisms.* ○ *The animatic impressed the advertiser because it put the message over stylishly.* ○ *If the animatic is approved, the creative team will begin work on the final product.*

animation /ˌænɪˈmeɪʃ(ə)n/ *noun* a cartoon film, a film made from drawings

annual /ˈænjuəl/ *adjective* for one year ○ *an annual statement of income* ○ *They have six weeks' annual leave.* ○ *The company has an annual growth of 5%.*

'...real wages have risen at an annual rate of only 1% in the last two years' [*Sunday Times*]

'...the remuneration package will include an attractive salary, profit sharing and a company car together with four weeks annual holiday' [*Times*]

annual accounts /ˌænjuəl əˈkaʊnts/ *plural noun* the accounts prepared at the end of a financial year ○ *The annual accounts have been sent to the shareholders.*

annual depreciation /ˌænjuəl dɪpriːʃiˈeɪʃ(ə)n/ *noun* a reduction in the book value of an asset at a particular rate per year. ♦ **straight line depreciation**

annual income /ˌænjuəl ˈɪnkʌm/ *noun* money received during a calendar year

annual report /ˌænjuəl rɪˈpɔːt/ *noun* a report of a company's financial situation at the end of a year, sent to all the shareholders

anonymous product /əˌnɒnɪməs ˈprɒdʌkt/ *noun* a product with no apparent brand name, used in advertisements to highlight the product being promoted ○ *Brand X is the anonymous product which never gets your washing completely white.* ○ *No one watching the commercial would believe the anonymous product was as bad is it seemed.* ○ *What happens if the respondent chooses the anonymous product instead of ours?*

anti- /ænti/ *prefix* against

anti-dumping /ˈænti ˈdʌmpɪŋ/ *adjective* intended to stop surplus goods being sold in foreign markets at a price that is lower than their marginal cost

anti-inflationary measure /ˌænti ɪnˈfleɪʃ(ə)n(ə)ri ˌmeʒə/ *noun* a measure taken to reduce inflation

anti-trust /ˌænti ˈtrʌst/ *adjective* attacking monopolies and encouraging competition ○ *anti-trust laws* or *legislation*

any other business /ˌeni ʌðə ˈbɪznɪs/ *noun* an item at the end of an agenda, where any matter can be raised. Abbr **AOB**

AOB *abbr* any other business

appeal /əˈpiːl/ *noun* being attractive

apperception /ˌæpəˈsepʃən/ *noun* ◊ **thematic apperception test**

application form /ˌæplɪˈkeɪʃ(ə)n fɔːm/ *noun* a form to be filled in when applying for a new issue of shares or for a job

appraisal /əˈpreɪz(ə)l/ *noun* a calculation of the value of someone or something

'…we are now reaching a stage in industry and commerce where appraisals are becoming part of the management culture. Most managers now take it for granted that they will appraise and be appraised' [*Personnel Management*]

appraiser /ə'preɪzə/ *noun US* a person who estimates how much money something is worth

appro /'æprəʊ/ *noun* same as **approval** □ **to buy something on appro** to buy something which you will only pay for if it is satisfactory

approach /ə'prəʊtʃ/ *noun* getting in touch with someone with a proposal ○ *The company made an approach to the supermarket chain.* ○ *The board turned down all approaches on the subject of mergers.* ○ *We have had an approach from a Japanese company to buy our car division.* ○ *She has had an approach from a firm of headhunters.* ■ *verb* to get in touch with someone with a proposal ○ *He approached the bank with a request for a loan.* ○ *The company was approached by an American publisher with the suggestion of a merger.* ○ *We have been approached several times but have turned down all offers.* ○ *She was approached by a headhunter with the offer of a job.*

appropriation /ə,prəʊpri'eɪʃ(ə)n/ *noun* the act of putting money aside for a special purpose ○ *appropriation of funds to the reserve*

appropriation account /ə,prəʊpri-'eɪʃ(ə)n ə,kaʊnt/ *noun* the part of a profit and loss account which shows how the profit has been dealt with such as how much has been given to the shareholders as dividends, how much is being put into the reserves etc.

approval /ə'pruːv(ə)l/ *noun* **1.** agreement ○ *to submit a budget for approval* **2.** □ **on approval** a sale where the buyer only pays for goods if they are satisfactory ○ *to buy a photocopier on approval*

approve /ə'pruːv/ *verb* **1.** □ **to approve of something** to think something is good ○ *The chairman approves of the new company letter heading.* ○ *The sales staff do not approve of interference from the accounts division.* **2.** to agree to something officially ○ *to ap-prove the terms of a contract* ○ *The proposal was approved by the board.*

APR *abbr* annual percentage rate

area /'eəriə/ *noun* **1.** a subject ○ *a problem area* or *an area for concern* **2.** a part of a country, a division for commercial purposes ○ *Her sales area is the North-West.* ○ *He finds it difficult to cover all his area in a week.*

area code /'eəriə kəʊd/ *noun* a special telephone number which is given to a particular area ○ *The area code for central London is 0207.*

area manager /,eəriə 'mænɪdʒə/ *noun* a manager who is responsible for a company's work in a specific part of the country

arithmetic mean /,ærɪθmetɪk 'miːn/ *noun* same as **average**

armchair research /,ɑːmtʃeə rɪ-'sɜːtʃ/ *noun* looking for information that has already been compiled and published in reference books such as directories ○ *Most of our armchair research can be done in libraries.* ○ *If we cannot find all the data through armchair research, we shall have to do a market survey of our own.* (NOTE: also called **desk research**)

arrears /ə'rɪəz/ *plural noun* **1.** money which is owed, but which has not been paid at the right time ○ *a salary with arrears effective from January 1st* ○ *arrears of interest* ○ *to allow the payments to fall into arrears* ○ *salary with arrears effective from January 1st* ○ *We are pressing the company to pay arrears of interest.* ○ *You must not allow the mortgage payments to fall into arrears.* **2.** □ **in arrears** owing money which should have been paid earlier ○ *The payments are six months in arrears.* ○ *He is six weeks in arrears with his rent.*

art director /'ɑːt daɪ,rektə/ *noun* a coordinator of creative work in advertising ○ *The art director briefed the copywriter and illustrator on the main points of the campaign.* ○ *After three years as an agency photographer, he was made art director.*

article /'ɑːtɪk(ə)l/ *noun* **1.** a product or thing for sale ○ *to launch a new article on the market* ○ *a black market in lux-*

ury articles **2.** a section of a legal agreement such as a contract, treaty, etc. ○ *see article 8 of the contract*

article numbering system /ˌɑːtɪk(ə)l ˈnʌmbərɪŋ ˌsɪstəm/ *noun* a universal system of identifying articles for sale, using a series of digits which can be expressed as bar codes

artificial obsolescence /ˌɑːtɪfɪʃ(ə)l ɒbsəˈles(ə)ns/ *noun* the practice of deliberately making old models seem out of date by bringing out new ones with changes and additional features which will attract the customer ○ *Artificial obsolescence is making our products seem cheap and disposable.* ○ *Artificial obsolescence means that no product can be fashionable for very long.*

artwork /ˈɑːtwɜːk/ *noun* an original work to be used for an advertisement, e.g. drawings, layouts, photographs

ASA *abbr* Advertising Standards Authority

asking price /ˈɑːskɪŋ praɪs/ *noun* a price which the seller is hoping will be paid for the item being sold ○ *the asking price is £24,000*

assay mark /ˈæseɪ mɑːk/ *noun* a mark put on gold or silver items to show that the metal is of the correct quality

assembly /əˈsemblɪ/ *noun* **1.** the process of putting an item together from various parts ○ *There are no assembly instructions to show you how to put the computer together.* ○ *We can't put the machine together because the instructions for assembly are in Japanese.* **2.** an official meeting

assembly line /əˈsembli laɪn/ *noun* a production system where a product such as a car moves slowly through the factory with new sections added to it as it goes along ○ *She works on an assembly line* or *She is an assembly line worker.*

assessment /əˈsesmənt/ *noun* a calculation of value ○ *an assessment of damages* ○ *a property assessment* ○ *assessment of damages* ○ *a tax assessment*

asset /ˈæset/ *noun* something which belongs to a company or person, and which has a value ○ *He has an excess of*

assets over liabilities. ○ *Her assets are only £640 as against liabilities of £24,000.*

'…many companies are discovering that a well-recognised brand name can be a priceless asset that lessens the risk of introducing a new product' [*Duns Business Month*]

asset stripping /ˈæset ˌstrɪpɪŋ/ *noun* the practice of buying a company at a lower price than its asset value, and then selling its assets

asset value /ˌæset ˈvæljuː/ *noun* the value of a company calculated by adding together all its assets

associate programme /əˈsəʊsiət ˌprəʊɡræm/ *noun* same as **affiliate programme**

assortment /əˈsɔːtmənt/ *noun* a combination of goods sold together ○ *The box contains an assortment of chocolates with different centres.*

assumptive close /əˈsʌmptɪv ˌkləʊz/ *noun* an act of ending the sales negotiation by assuming that the customer has agreed to buy, and then asking further details of payments, delivery, etc.

asterisk law /ˈæstərɪsk lɔː/ *noun* a law which prevents telemarketing agencies from trying to sell to people who have indicated that they do not want to be approached by telephone salesmen by putting an asterisk against their names in the phone book

ATM *abbr* automated telling machine

'Swiss banks are issuing new cards which will allow cash withdrawals from ATMs in Belgium, Denmark, Spain, France, the Netherlands, Portugal and Germany' [*Banking Technology*]

'…the major supermarket operator is planning a new type of bank that would earn 90% of its revenue from fees on automated teller machine transactions. With the bank setting up ATMs at 7,000 group outlets nationwide, it would have a branch network at least 20 times larger than any of the major banks' [*Nikkei Weekly*]

atmosphere /ˈætməsfɪə/ *noun* **1.** the general feeling in a shop or shopping area **2.** the effect that the medium itself through which an advertisement is presented has on the audience

atmospherics /ˌætməsˈferɪks/ *noun* **1.** a way of encouraging customer interest by using the senses such as smell and sound **2.** creating an overall image of a

company through the design of its premises and products

ATR *noun* a model showing stages in the effects of advertising on the consumer, where the customer becomes aware of the product, buys it once to try it and then buys it again when he finds it is satisfactory. Full form **awareness, trial, repeat**

atrium /'eɪtriəm/ *noun* a very large open space in a building, usually with a glass roof, fountains and plants, which acts as a central meeting point, linking shopping and office areas and restaurants

attention /ə'tenʃən/ *noun* careful thought or consideration

attitude /'ætɪtjuːd/ *noun* the way in which a person behaves or thinks □ **a person's attitude towards an advertisement** a person's reaction to an advertisement

attitude measurement /'ætɪtjuːd ˌmeʒəmənt/, **attitude testing** /'ætɪtjuːd ˌtestɪŋ/ *noun* the act of ascertaining the way in which a person views something by assigning scores to various factors ○ *Attitude measurement has given us a good idea of how consumers view our product.* ○ *Will attitude testing lead to the redesigning of these heaters?*

attitude research /'ætɪtjuːd rɪˌsɜːtʃ/, **attitude survey** /'ætɪtjuːd ˌsɜːveɪ/ *noun* **1.** the act of carrying out a survey to discover people's attitudes to products, advertisements or the companies producing them **2.** research that attempts to discover whether people's feelings about something, such as the company they work for, are positive or negative

attitude scale /'ætɪtjuːd skeɪl/ *noun* a device which measures or tests attitudes by analysing a subject's responses

attrition /ə'trɪʃ(ə)n/ *noun* a decrease in the loyalty of consumers to a product, due to factors such as boredom, desire for a change ○ *We must adapt our products if we are to avoid attrition.* ○ *Attrition showed the company that brand loyalty could not be taken for granted.*

auction /'ɔːkʃən/ *noun* a method of selling goods where people make bids, and the item is sold to the person who makes the highest offer ○ *The equipment was sold by auction* or *at auction.* ○ *Their furniture will be sold in the auction rooms next week.* ○ *They announced a sale by auction of the fire-damaged stock.* □ **to put an item up for auction** to offer an item for sale at an auction ■ *verb* to sell something at an auction ○ *The factory was closed and the machinery was auctioned off.*

auctioneer /ˌɔːkʃə'nɪə/ *noun* the person who conducts an auction

auction house /'ɔːkʃən haʊs/ *noun* a company which specialises in holding auction sales, especially of items such as antiques or paintings

auction mart /'ɔːkʃən mɑːt/ *noun* US auction rooms

audience /'ɔːdiəns/ *noun* **1.** the number of people who watch a TV programme or listen to a radio programme **2.** the number of people who are exposed to an advertisement

audience accumulation /ˌɔːdiəns əkjuːmjʊ'leɪʃ(ə)n/ *noun* the building up of an audience by repeating advertisements over a period of time

audience composition /ˌɔːdiəns kɒmpə'zɪʃ(ə)n/ *noun* the way an audience is made up, i.e. the age range, sex, lifestyles, etc.

audience research /ˌɔːdiəns rɪ'sɜːtʃ/ *noun* research into the attitudes of an audience to an advertising campaign

audimeter /'ɔːdɪmiːtə/ *noun* an electronic device attached to a TV set, which records details of a viewer's viewing habits

audiovisual /ˌɔːdiəʊ 'vɪʒuəl/ *noun* media that can be seen and heard, e.g. a TV commercial ○ *The exhibition was devoted to the latest in audiovisual equipment.*

audit /'ɔːdɪt/ *noun* the examination of the books and accounts of a company ○ *to carry out the annual audit*

Audit Bureau of Circulations /ˌɔːdɪt ˌbjʊərəʊ əv sɜːkjʊ'leɪʃ(ə)nz/

noun an organisation which verifies and publishes the circulation of magazines and newspapers. Abbr **ABCs**

augmented product /ɔ:g,mentɪd ˈprɒdʌkt/ *noun* a product with added benefits such as warranties or installation service etc.

aural signature /,ɔ:rəl ˈsɪgnɪtʃə/ *noun* musical sounds used as a signature to identify a product or service

automatic /,ɔ:təˈmætɪk/ *adjective* which works or takes place without any person making it happen ○ *There is an automatic increase in salaries on January 1st.*

automatic merchandizing /,ɔ:təmætɪk ˈmɜ:tʃəndaɪzɪŋ/, **automatic selling** /,ɔ:təmætɪk ˈselɪŋ/, **automatic vending** /,ɔ:təmætɪk ˈvendɪŋ/ *noun* selling through a machine ○ *Automatic selling is popular because of the low labour costs involved.*

automatic telling machine /,ɔ:təmætɪk ˈtelɪŋ məˌʃi:n/ *noun* a machine which gives out money when a special card is inserted and special instructions given

automatic vending machine /,ɔ:təmætɪk ˈvendɪŋ məˌʃi:n/ *noun* a machine which provides drinks, cigarettes etc., when a coin is put in

automation /,ɔ:təˈmeɪʃ(ə)n/ *noun* the use of machines to do work with very little supervision by people

availability /ə,veɪləˈbɪlətɪ/ *noun* **1.** being easily obtained □ **offer subject to availability** the offer is valid only if the goods are available **2.** the time and number of advertising slots which are available to be used

average /ˈæv(ə)rɪdʒ/ *noun* **1.** a number calculated by adding several figures together and dividing by the number of figures added ○ *the average for the last three months* or *the last three months' average* ○ *sales average* or *average of*

sales **2.** □ **on average** in general ○ *On average, £15 worth of goods are stolen every day.* ■ *adjective* **1.** the middle of a set of figures ○ *the average figures for the last three months* ○ *the average increase in prices* ○ *the average price* ○ *The average cost per unit is too high.* ○ *The average sales per representative are rising.* **2.** not very good ○ *The company's performance has been only average.* ○ *He's only an average worker.*

'…a share with an average rating might yield 5 per cent and have a PER of about 10' [*Investors Chronicle*]

'…the average price per kilogram for this season to the end of April has been 300 cents' [*Australian Financial Review*]

average cost pricing /,æv(ə)rɪdʒ ˈkɒst ,praɪsɪŋ/ *noun* pricing based on the average cost of producing one unit of a product

average due date /,æv(ə)rɪdʒ dju: ˈdeɪt/ *noun* the average date when several different payments fall due

average frequency /,æv(ə)rɪdʒ ˈfri:kwənsi/ *noun* the average number of times a consumer will see a particular advertisement ○ *We will have to buy a lot of advertising time to attain a high average frequency.* ○ *What average frequency do we need to get this advertisement across to the target audience?*

average out /,æv(ə)rɪdʒ ˈaʊt/ *verb* to come to a figure as an average ○ *It averages out at 10% per annum.* ○ *Sales increases have averaged out at 15%.*

average quarter-hour figure /,æv(ə)rɪdʒ ,kwɔ:tər aʊə ˈfɪgə/ *adjective* the average number of people watching a TV programme during a 15-minute period

awareness /əˈweənəs/ *noun* the state of being conscious of an advertisement's message or of a brand's existence and qualities ○ *The survey after the campaign showed advertising awareness had remained low.* ♦ **ATR, maximal awareness**

B

B2B /ˌbiː tə ˈbiː/ *adjective* referring to advertising or marketing that is aimed at other businesses rather than at consumers (NOTE: The word is most commonly used of business-to-business dealings conducted over the Internet.)

B2B auction /ˌbiː tə biː ˈɔːkʃən/ *noun* a web marketplace where supplier companies bid against one another to offer the lowest price for a particular product or service, while the buyer company waits until the sellers have reduced the price to one that it can afford (NOTE: Businesses have to register to take part in B2B auctions by providing their credit-card information and shipping preferences, and also have to agree to the site's code of conduct.)

B2B commerce /ˌbiː tə biː ˈkɒmɜːs/ *noun* business done by companies with other companies, rather than with individual consumers

B2B exchange /ˌbiː tə biː ɪksˈtʃeɪndʒ/ *noun* same as **exchange**

B2B web exchange /ˌbiː tə biː ˈweb ɪksˌtʃeɪndʒ/ *noun* same as **exchange**

B2B website /ˌbiː tə biː ˈwebsaɪt/ *noun* a website that is designed to help businesses trade with each other on the Internet

B2C /ˌbiː tə ˈsiː/ *adjective* referring to advertising or marketing that is aimed at consumers rather than at other businesses (NOTE: The word is most commonly used of business-to-consumer dealings conducted over the Internet.)

B2C website /ˌbiː tə siː ˈwebsaɪt/ *noun* an online shop that sells products to consumers via its website

baby boomer /ˈbeɪbi ˌbuːməz/ *noun* a market composed of people born during the period from 1945 to 1965, when the population of the UK and the USA increased rapidly

back /bæk/ *noun* the opposite side to the front ○ *Write your address on the back of the envelope.* ○ *The conditions of sale are printed on the back of the invoice.* ○ *Please endorse the cheque on the back.* ■ *adjective* referring to the past ○ *a back payment* ■ *verb* □ **to back someone** to help someone financially ○ *The bank is backing us to the tune of £10,000.* ○ *She is looking for someone to back her project.*

'…the businesses we back range from start-up ventures to established companies in need of further capital for expansion' [*Times*]

back cover /bæk ˈkʌvə/ *noun* the back of a magazine cover, which can be used for advertising

backdate /bækˈdeɪt/ *verb* to put an earlier date on a document such as a cheque or an invoice ○ *Backdate your invoice to April 1st.* ○ *The pay increase is backdated to January 1st.*

backdoor selling /ˌbækdɔː ˈselɪŋ/ *noun* the practice of bypassing an organisation's bureaucracy and selling direct to the chief decision-maker in it ○ *If we did not resort to backdoor selling the right department might never hear of us.* ○ *The chairman was asked out for a meal by the sales director of the other company to try a little backdoor selling.*

backer /ˈbækə/ *noun* **1.** a person or company that backs someone ○ *He has an Australian backer.* ○ *One of the company's backers has withdrawn.* **2.** □ **the backer of a bill** the person who backs a bill **3.** a piece of publicity material placed at the back of a display or stand

background /ˈbækɡraʊnd/ *noun* past work or experience ○ *My back-*

ground is in the steel industry. ○ *The company is looking for someone with a background of success in the electronics industry.* ○ *She has a publishing background.* ○ *What is his background?* or *Do you know anything about his background?*

background music /ˈbækɡraʊnd ˌmjuːzɪk/ *noun* music played over the tannoy in a shop, supermarket, atrium etc., as a means of calming potential customers

backing /ˈbækɪŋ/ *noun* financial support ○ *He has the backing of an Australian bank.* ○ *The company will succeed only if it has sufficient backing.* ○ *Who is providing the backing for the project?* ○ *Where does the backing for the project come from?*

'…the company has received the backing of a number of oil companies who are willing to pay for the results of the survey' [*Lloyd's List*]

backload /ˈbækləʊd/ *verb* to make sure that most of the costs of a promotional campaign come in the later stages, so that they can be regulated according to the response received. The campaign can then be cut back if the response rate is inadequate – this is opposed to frontloading, where most of the costs are incurred in the early stages. Compare **frontload**

backlog /ˈbæklɒg/ *noun* work which has piled up waiting to be done, e.g. orders or letters ○ *The warehouse is trying to cope with a backlog of orders.* ○ *We're finding it hard to cope with the backlog of paperwork.*

back of book /ˌbæk əv ˈbʊk/ *noun* the last pages of a magazine containing advertisements

back-of-the-house services /ˌbæk əv ðə haʊs ˈsɜːvɪsɪz/ *plural noun* services which are in the back part of a shop

back orders /ˈbæk ˌɔːdəz/ *plural noun* orders received and not yet fulfilled, usually because the item is out of stock ○ *It took the factory six weeks to clear all the accumulated back orders.*

back payment /ˈbæk ˌpeɪmənt/ *noun* paying money which is owed

backup /ˈbækʌp/ *adjective* supporting or helping ○ *We offer a free backup service to customers.* ○ *After a series of sales tours by representatives, the sales director sends backup letters to all the contacts.*

backup ad /ˈbækʌp æd/ *noun* an advertisement designed to accompany editorial material in a publication

backup copy /ˈbækʌp ˌkɒpi/ *noun* a copy of a computer disk to be kept in case the original disk is damaged

backward integration /ˌbækwəd ˌɪntɪˈɡreɪʃ(ə)n/ *noun* a process of expansion in which businesses which deal with different stages in the production or sale of the same product join together, i.e. a business becomes its own supplier ○ *Buying up rubber plantations is part of the tyre company's backward integration policy.* ○ *Backward integration will ensure cheap supplies but forward integration would bring us nearer to the market.* Compare **forward integration** (NOTE: also called **vertical integration**)

bad debt /bæd ˈdet/ *noun* a debt which will not be paid, usually because the debtor has gone out of business, and which has to be written off in the accounts ○ *The company has written off £30,000 in bad debts.*

baggage cart /ˈbæɡɪdʒ kɑːt/ *noun* US a metal holder on wheels, on which baggage can be placed to be moved easily in an airport, train station, etc.

bait /beɪt/ *noun* an article which is sold at a loss to attract customers ○ *This is an attractive enough product to use as bait.* ○ *The shop's best bargains were displayed in the window as bait.*

bait ad /ˈbeɪt æd/ *noun* an advertisement for low-priced goods, used to attract customers into a shop

bait and switch /ˌbeɪt ənd ˈswɪtʃ/ *noun* a sales technique where the salesperson offers what looks like an attractive bargain and then says at the last minute that it is not available and replaces it with something inferior

balance of payments /ˌbæləns əv ˈpeɪmənts/ *noun* a comparison between total receipts and payments arising from

a country's international trade in goods, services and financial transactions

balance sheet /'bæləns ʃiːt/ *noun* a statement of the financial position of a company at a particular time such as the end of the financial year or the end of a quarter showing the company's assets and liabilities ○ *Our accountant has prepared the balance sheet for the first half-year.* ○ *The company balance sheet for the last financial year shows a worse position than for the previous year.*

COMMENT: The balance sheet shows the state of a company's finances at a certain date; the profit and loss account shows the movements which have taken place since the end of the previous accounting period. A balance sheet must balance, with the basic equation that assets (i.e. what the company owns, including money owed to the company) must equal liabilities (i.e. what the company owes to its creditors) plus capital (i.e. what it owes to its shareholders). A balance sheet can be drawn up either in the horizontal form, with (in the UK) liabilities and capital on the left-hand side of the page (in the USA, it is the reverse) or in the vertical form, with assets at the top of the page, followed by liabilities, and capital at the bottom. Most are usually drawn up in the vertical format, as opposed to the more old-fashioned horizontal style.

balloon /bə'luːn/ *noun* a loan where the last repayment is larger than the others

balloon payment /bə'luːn ˌpeɪmənt/ *noun* the last payment, usually much larger than the others, that is made when repaying a balloon loan

band /bænd/ *noun* a strip of paper or plastic or a rubber ring put round articles to attach them together

banded /'bændɪd/ *adjective* attached with a band

banded offer /ˌbændɪd 'ɒfə/ *noun* a type of sales promotion involving the offer of an additional item along with the main one ○ *The banded offer consisted of a full-sized bottle of shampoo along with a small bottle of hair conditioner.*

banded pack /ˌbændɪd 'pæk/ *noun* a pack which includes two items attached to form a pack, or with an additional dif-

ferent item bound along with the main one ○ *These banded packs have been specially designed for our sales promotion drive.*

bandwidth /'bændwɪdθ/ *noun* a measurement of the capacity of a fibre-optic cable to carry information to and from the Internet (NOTE: The higher the bandwidth, the faster information passes through the cable.)

bangtail /'bæŋteɪl/ *noun US* a type of folded mailer, with a pocket for an information card or reply coupon and a flap that tucks in

bankable paper /ˌbæŋkəb(ə)l 'peɪpə/ *noun* a document which a bank will accept as security for a loan

bank account /'bæŋk əˌkaʊnt/ *noun* an account which a customer has with a bank, where the customer can deposit and withdraw money ○ *to open a bank account* ○ *to close a bank account* ○ *How much money do you have in your bank account?* ○ *If you let the balance in your bank account fall below £100, you have to pay bank charges.*

bank base rate /bæŋk 'beɪs reɪt/ *noun* a basic rate of interest on which the actual rate a bank charges on loans to its customers is calculated

bank bill /'bæŋk bɪl/ *noun* **1.** *GB* same as **banker's bill 2.** *US* a piece of printed paper money

bank card /'bæŋk kɑːd/ *noun* a credit card or debit card issued to a customer by a bank for use instead of cash when buying goods or services (NOTE: There are internationally recognised rules that govern the authorisation of the use of bank cards and the clearing and settlement of transactions in which they are used.)

bank charges /'bæŋk ˌtʃɑːdʒɪz/ *plural noun* charges which a bank makes for carrying out work for a customer (NOTE: American English is **service charge**)

bank credit /'bæŋk ˌkredɪt/ *noun* loans or overdrafts from a bank to a customer

bank draft /'bæŋk drɑːft/ *noun* an order by one bank telling another bank,

usually in another country, to pay money to someone

banker /ˈbæŋkə/ *noun* a person who is in an important position in a bank

banker's bill /ˈbæŋkəz bɪl/, **bank bill** /ˈbæŋk bɪl/ *noun* an order by one bank telling another bank, usually in another country, to pay money to someone

bank giro /ˈbæŋk ˌdʒaɪrəʊ/ *noun GB* a method used by clearing banks to transfer money rapidly from one account to another

banking account /ˈbæŋkɪŋ ə-ˌkaʊnt/ *noun US* an account which a customer has with a bank

bank manager /ˈbæŋk ˌmænɪdʒə/ *noun* the person in charge of a branch of a bank ○ *He asked his bank manager for a loan.*

bank transfer /ˈbæŋk ˌtrænsfɜː/ *noun* moving money from a bank account to another account

banner /ˈbænə/ *noun* **1.** material stretched between two walls or buildings, carrying an advertising message ○ *There were banners across the street advertising the charity run.* **2.** an online interactive advertisement that appears on a webpage, usually at the top or bottom, and contains a link to the website of the business whose products or services are being advertised (NOTE: Banner ads often use graphics images and sound as well as text.)

banner advertising /ˈbænə ˌædvətaɪzɪŋ/ *noun* a website advertising which runs across the top of a webpage, similar to newspaper headlines

banner exchange /ˈbænə ɪks-ˌtʃeɪndʒ/ *noun* an agreement between two or more businesses, in which each allows the others' advertising banners to be displayed on its website

banner headline /ˌbænə ˈhedlaɪn/ *noun* a headline set in very large black type, running across a page

bar chart /ˈbɑː tʃɑːt/ *noun* a chart where values or quantities are shown as columns of different heights set on a base line, the different lengths expressing the quantity of the item or unit

bar code /ˈbɑː kəʊd/ *noun* a system of lines printed on a product which, when read by a computer, give a reference number or price

bar coding /ˈbɑː ˌkəʊdɪŋ/ *noun* the process of attaching an identifying label, written in machine-readable code and able to be read by a scanner, to a product or container (NOTE: Bar codes are useful for stock control and order picking and can be used to trace a product through every stage of a transaction from packaging to customer delivery.)

bargain /ˈbɑːgɪn/ *noun* **1.** an agreement on the price of something ○ *to strike a bargain* or *to make a bargain* □ **to drive a hard bargain** to be a difficult person to negotiate with □ **it is a bad bargain** it is not worth the price **2.** something which is cheaper than usual ○ *That car is a (real) bargain at £500.* ■ *verb* to discuss a price for something ○ *You will have to bargain with the dealer if you want a discount.* ○ *They spent two hours bargaining about* or *over the price.* (NOTE: you bargain **with** someone **over** or **about** or **for** something)

bargain basement /ˌbɑːgɪn ˈbeɪsmənt/ *noun* a basement floor in a shop where goods are sold cheaply □ **I'm selling this at a bargain basement price** I'm selling this very cheaply

bargain hunter /ˈbɑːgɪn ˌhʌntə/ *noun* a person who looks for cheap deals

bargaining /ˈbɑːgɪnɪŋ/ *noun* the act of discussing between two persons or groups, to achieve a settlement, usually wage increases for workers

bargaining position /ˈbɑːgɪnɪŋ pə-ˌzɪʃ(ə)n/ *noun* the statement of position by one group during negotiations

bargaining power /ˈbɑːgɪnɪŋ ˌpaʊə/ *noun* the strength of one person or group when discussing prices or wage settlements

barrier /ˈbæriə/ *noun* anything which makes it difficult for someone to do something, especially sending goods from one place to another □ **to impose trade barriers on certain goods** to restrict the import of some goods by

charging high duty ○ *They considered imposing trade barriers on some food products.* □ **to lift trade barriers from imports** to remove restrictions on imports ○ *The government has lifted trade barriers on foreign cars.* □ **barrier to entry into a market** something which makes it difficult for a company to enter a new market, e.g. start-up costs

'...a senior European Community official has denounced Japanese trade barriers, saying they cost European producers $3 billion a year' [*Times*]

'...to create a single market out of the EC member states, physical, technical and tax barriers to free movement of trade between member states had to be removed. Imposing VAT on importation of goods from other member states was seen as one such tax barrier' [*Accountancy*]

barrier to entry /ˌbæriə tʊ ˈentri/ *noun* a factor that makes it impossible or unprofitable for a company to try to start selling its products in a particular market (NOTE: Barriers to entry may be created, for example, when companies already in a market have patents that prevent their goods from being copied, when the cost of the advertising needed to gain a market share is too high, or when an existing product commands very strong brand loyalty.)

barrier to exit /ˌbæriə tʊ ˈegzɪt/ *noun* a factor that makes it impossible or unprofitable for a company to leave a market where it is currently doing business (NOTE: Barriers to exit may be created, for example, when a company has invested in specialist equipment that is only suited to manufacturing one product, when the costs of retraining its workforce would be very high, or when withdrawing one product would have a bad effect on the sales of other products in the range.)

barter /ˈbɑːtə/ *noun* 1. a system in which goods are exchanged for other goods and not sold for money 2. a system in which advertising space or time is exchanged for goods from the advertiser ■ *verb* to exchange goods for other goods and not for money ○ *They agreed a deal to barter tractors for barrels of wine.*

'...under the barter agreements, Nigeria will export 175,000 barrels a day of crude oil in

exchange for trucks, food, planes and chemicals' [*Wall Street Journal*]

bartering /ˈbɑːtərɪŋ/ *noun* the act of exchanging goods for other goods and not for money

base /beɪs/ *noun* 1. the lowest or first position ○ *Turnover increased by 200%, but started from a low base.* 2. a place where a company has its main office or factory, or a place where a businessperson's office is located ○ *The company has its base in London and branches in all the European countries.* ○ *He has an office in Madrid which he uses as a base while travelling in Southern Europe.* ■ *verb* to set up a company or a person in a place ○ *a London-based sales executive* ○ *The European manager is based in our London office.* ○ *Our overseas branch is based in the Bahamas.*

'...the base lending rate, or prime rate, is the rate at which banks lend to their top corporate borrowers' [*Wall Street Journal*]

'...other investments include a large stake in the Chicago-based insurance company' [*Lloyd's List*]

base line /ˈbeɪs laɪn/ *noun* the part of promotional material that contains basic information about the organisation such as its name and address

basement /ˈbeɪsmənt/ *noun* a section of a shop which is underground

base year /ˈbeɪs jɪə/ *noun* the first year of an index, against which changes occurring in later years are measured. ♦ **database**

basic /ˈbeɪsɪk/ *adjective* 1. normal 2. most important 3. simple, or from which everything starts ○ *He has a basic knowledge of the market.* ○ *To work at the cash desk, you need a basic qualification in maths.*

basic commodities /ˌbeɪsɪk kəˈmɒdɪtiz/ *plural noun* ordinary farm produce, produced in large quantities, e.g. corn, rice, sugar, etc.

basic discount /ˌbeɪsɪk ˈdɪskaʊnt/ *noun* a normal discount without extra percentages ○ *Our basic discount is 20%, but we offer 5% extra for rapid settlement.*

basic industry /ˌbeɪsɪk ˈɪndəstri/ *noun* the most important industry of a country, e.g. coal, steel or agriculture

basic necessities /ˌbeɪsɪk nəˈsesɪtiz/ *plural noun* the very least that people need to live, e.g. food and clothing ○ *Being unemployed makes it difficult to afford even the basic necessities.*

basic price /ˌbeɪsɪk ˈpraɪs/ , **basic rate** /ˌbeɪsɪk ˈreɪt/ *noun* the price of a product or service that does not include any extras ○ *This is a rather high basic price.* ○ *Please make clear whether £1,000 is the basic rate or whether it is inclusive of spare parts.*

basic product /ˌbeɪsɪk ˈprɒdʌkt/ *noun* the main product made from a raw material

basics /ˈbeɪsɪks/ *plural noun* simple and important facts ○ *She has studied the basics of foreign exchange dealing.* □ **to get back to basics** to consider the main facts again

basis /ˈbeɪsɪs/ *noun* **1.** a point or number from which calculations are made ○ *We forecast the turnover on the basis of a 6% price increase.* **2.** the general terms of agreement or general principles on which something is decided □ **on a short-term** or **long-term basis** for a short or long period ○ *He has been appointed on a short-term basis.* ○ *We have three people working on a freelance basis.*

basket of currencies /ˌbɑːskɪt əv ˈkʌrənsiz/ *noun* a group of other currencies used to establish the value of a particular unit of currency

batch /bætʃ/ *noun* a group of items which are made at one time ○ *This batch of shoes has the serial number 25–02.* ■ *verb* to put items together in groups ○ *to batch invoices* or *cheques*

batch number /ˈbætʃ ˌnʌmbə/ *noun* a number attached to a batch ○ *When making a complaint always quote the batch number on the packet.*

batch production /ˈbætʃ prəˌdʌkʃən/ *noun* production in batches

battle /ˈbæt(ə)l/ *noun* a fight □ **battle of the brands** competition in the market between existing product brands ○ *This battle of the brands will lead to dramatic price-cutting.*

Bayesian decision theory /ˌbeɪziən dɪˈsɪʒ(ə)n ˌθɪəri/ *noun* a method for helping decision-making, often applied to new product development. The decision-maker is aware of alternatives, can work out the probable advantages or disadvantages of the alternatives, and makes up his or her mind according to the value of the best alternative.

BDI *abbr* brand development index

behavioural segmentation /bɪˌheɪvjərəl segmənˈteɪʃ(ə)n/, **behaviouristic segmentation** *noun* the segmentation or division of the market according to customers' buying habits and usage of a product ○ *Behavioural segmentation will mean there are several distinct target audiences for our product.*

behind schedule /bɪˌhaɪnd ˈʃedʒuːl/ *noun* late ○ *The agency is way behind schedule with the promotional material.*

believer /bɪˈliːvə/ *noun* in the VALS lifestyle classification, someone with conventional values and strong principles who buy traditional, well-known products

bells and whistles /ˌbelz ənd ˈwɪs(ə)lz/ *plural noun* every possible feature that has been included in an advertising campaign

below-the-line advertising /bɪˌləʊ ðə laɪn ˈædvətaɪzɪŋ/ *noun* advertising which is not paid for and for which no commission is paid to the advertising agency, e.g. work by staff who are manning an exhibition. Compare **above-the-line advertising**

below-the-line expenditure /bɪˌləʊ ðə laɪn ɪkˈspendɪtʃə/ *noun* **1.** payments which do not arise from a company's normal activities, e.g. redundancy payments **2.** extraordinary items which are shown in the profit and loss account below net profit after taxation, as opposed to exceptional items which are included in the figure for profit before taxation

benchmark /ˈbentʃmɑːk/ *noun* **1.** a standard used to measure performance (NOTE: A benchmark was originally a

set of computer programs that was used to measure how well a particular computer performed in comparison with similar models.) **2.** a point in an index which is important, and can be used to compare with other figures

'…the US bank announced a cut in its prime, the benchmark corporate lending rate, from 10½% to 10%' [*Financial Times*]

'…the benchmark 11¾% Treasury due 2003/2007 was quoted at 107 11/32, down 13/32 from Monday' [*Wall Street Journal*]

benchmarking /'bentʃmɑːkɪŋ/ *noun* the testing of an audience's response using a benchmark

benchmark measure /'bentʃmɑːk ˌmeʒə/ *noun* the measure of a target audience's response at the beginning of an advertising campaign which is then compared to responses at the end of the campaign to test its efficiency

benefit /'benɪfɪt/ *noun* the way in which a product or service will improve the quality of life of the purchaser, as opposed to 'features' which highlight the particular important aspects of the product or service itself

'…what benefits does the executive derive from his directorship? Compensation has increased sharply in recent years and fringe benefits for directors have proliferated' [*Duns Business Month*]

'…salary is negotiable to £30,000, plus car and a benefits package appropriate to this senior post' [*Financial Times*]

'California is the latest state to enact a program forcing welfare recipients to work for their benefits' [*Fortune*]

'…salary range is $54,957 – $81,189, with a competitive benefits package' [*Washington Post*]

benefit segmentation /ˌbenɪfɪt segmənˈteɪʃ(ə)n/ *noun* the division of a market into segments according to the types of benefit obtained by the customer from a product such as ease of availability, light weight

berth /bɜːθ/ *noun* the place in a harbour where a ship can tie up ■ *verb* to tie up at a berth ○ *The ship will berth at Rotterdam on Wednesday.*

berth cargo /'bɜːθ ˌkɑːɡəʊ/ *noun* cargo carried at especially low rates ○ *If we do not send the goods as berth cargo we will have to charge the buyer more.*

bespoke /bɪˈspəʊk/ *adjective* made to order or made to fit the requirements of the customer

bespoke tailoring /bɪˌspəʊk ˈteɪlərɪŋ/ *noun* the making of clothing for customers, to fit their individual measurements or requirements

best-before date /ˌbest bɪ ˈfɔː deɪt/ *noun* the date stamped on the label of a food product, which is the last date on which the product is guaranteed to be of good quality. ♦ **sell-by date, use-by date**

best-in-class /ˌbest ɪn ˈklɑːs/ *adjective* more effective and efficient, especially in acquiring and processing materials and in delivering products or services to customers, than any other organisation in the same market or industrial sector

best practice /ˌbest ˈpræktɪs/ *noun* the most effective and efficient way to do something or to achieve a particular aim (NOTE: In business, best practice is often determined by benchmarking, that is by comparing the method one organisation uses to carry out a task with the methods used by other similar organisations and determining which method is most efficient and effective.)

best-selling /ˌbest ˈselɪŋ/ *adjective* which sells very well ○ *These computer disks are our best-selling line.*

best value /ˌbest ˈvæljuː/ *noun* a system adopted by the UK government to ensure that local authorities provide services to the public in the most efficient and cost-effective way possible (NOTE: Best value, which came into force with the Local Government Act 1999, replaced the previous system of compulsory competitive tendering (CCT). It requires local authorities to review all their services over a five-year period, to set standards of performance, and to consult with local taxpayers and service users.)

Better Business Bureau /ˌbetə ˈbɪznɪs ˌbjʊərəʊ/ *US* an organisation of local business executives that promotes better business practices in their town

bias /'baɪəs/ *noun* favouring one group or person rather than another ○ *A postal*

survey will do away with bias. ○ *The trainee interviewers were taught how to control bias and its effects.*

bid /bɪd/ *noun* **1.** an offer to buy something at a specific price □ **to make a bid for something** to offer to buy something ○ *We made a bid for the house.* ○ *The company made a bid for its rival.* □ **to make a cash bid** to offer to pay cash for something □ **to put in a bid for something** *or* **to enter a bid for something** to offer to buy something, usually in writing **2.** an offer to sell something or do a piece of work at a specific price ○ *She made the lowest bid for the job.* ■ *verb* □ **to bid for something** (*at an auction*) to offer to buy something □ **he bid £1,000 for the jewels** he offered to pay £1,000 for the jewels

bidder /'bɪdə/ *noun* a person who makes a bid, usually at an auction ○ *Several bidders made offers for the house.* □ **the property was sold to the highest bidder** to the person who had made the highest bid or who offered the most money □ **the tender will go to the lowest bidder** to the person who offers the best terms or the lowest price for services

bidding /'bɪdɪŋ/ *noun* the act of making offers to buy, usually at an auction □ **the bidding started at £1,000** the first and lowest bid was £1,000 □ **the bidding stopped at £250,000** the last bid, i.e. the successful bid, was for £250,000 □ **the auctioneer started the bidding at £100** he suggested that the first bid should be £100

big box store /ˌbɪg bɒks 'stɔː/ *noun* a large retail superstore that sells a very wide range of merchandise from groceries to refrigerators or televisions

big business /bɪg 'bɪznɪs/ *noun* very large commercial firms

big idea /bɪg aɪ'dɪə/ *noun* the main new idea behind an advertising campaign, the aim of which is to attract potential customers

big picture /bɪg 'pɪktʃə/ *noun* a broad view of a subject that takes into account all the factors that are relevant to it and considers the future consequences of action taken now (*informal*)

big-ticket /ˌbɪg 'tɪkɪt/ *adjective* costing a lot of money

big ticket item /ˌbɪg 'tɪkɪt ˌaɪtəm/ *noun* a large expensive item, e.g. a car, washing machine, etc.

bilateral /baɪ'læt(ə)rəl/ *adjective* between two parties or countries ○ *The minister signed a bilateral trade agreement.*

'…trade between Japan and China will probably exceed $30 billion this year to mark a record high. Ministry of Finance trade statistics show that bilateral trade in the first half of the year totalled $16.60 billion, up 29.7% from a year earlier' [*Nikkei Weekly*]

bilateralism /baɪ'læt(ə)rəlɪz(ə)m/ *noun* a system whereby a country balances its trade with another ○ *With luck, bilateralism will put an end to the trade war.*

bill /bɪl/ *noun* **1.** a written list of charges to be paid ○ *The sales assistant wrote out the bill.* ○ *Does the bill include VAT?* ○ *The bill is made out to Smith Ltd.* ○ *The builder sent in his bill.* ○ *She left the country without paying her bills.* **2.** a list of charges in a restaurant ○ *Can I have the bill please?* ○ *The bill comes to £20 including service.* ○ *Does the bill include service?* ○ *The waiter has added 10% to the bill for service.* **3.** a written paper promising to pay money □ **bills payable (B/P)** bills, especially bills of exchange, which a company will have to pay to its creditors □ **bills receivable (B/R)** bills, especially bills of exchange, which are due to be paid by a company's debtors **4.** *US* a piece of paper money ○ *a $5 bill* (NOTE: British English is **note** *or* **banknote**) **5.** a draft of a new law which will be discussed in Parliament **6.** a small poster □ **'stick no bills'** a notice prohibiting unauthorised sticking of posters ■ *verb* to present a bill to someone so that it can be paid ○ *The plumbers billed us for the repairs.*

billboard /'bɪlbɔːd/ *noun* **1.** a poster site of double crown size (30 x 20 inches) **2.** *US* a large outdoor poster site (measuring 12 x 25 feet) ○ *The railway track was lined with billboards specially set up for election propaganda.* ○ *A shortage of billboards has led to an increase in press advertising.* **3.** a short

announcement which identifies an advertiser at the beginning, end, or in the breaks of a broadcast

billing /'bɪlɪŋ/ *noun US* the writing of invoices or bills

bill of entry /ˌbɪl əv 'entri/ *noun* the written details of goods that have to go through customs

bill of exchange /ˌbɪl əv ɪks-'tʃeɪndʒ/ *noun* a document signed by the person authorising it, which tells another to pay money unconditionally to a named person on a certain date (usually used in payments in foreign currency) □ **to accept a bill** to sign a bill of exchange to show that you promise to pay it □ **to discount a bill** to buy or sell a bill of exchange at a lower price than that written on it in order to cash it later □ **to retire a bill** to pay a bill of exchange when it is due

bill of lading /ˌbɪl əv 'leɪdɪŋ/ *noun* a list of goods being shipped, which the transporter gives to the person sending the goods to show that the goods have been loaded

bill of sale /ˌbɪl əv 'seɪl/ *noun* a document which the seller gives to the buyer to show that the sale has taken place

bill poster /'bɪl ˌpəʊstə/ *noun* a person who sticks up small posters. ♦ **fly poster**

bin /bɪn/ *noun* **1.** a large container **2.** a separate section of shelves in a warehouse

Bingo card /'bɪŋgəʊ kɑːd/ *noun* a printed card bound into a magazine, with a squared grid of numbers and letters which a reader can mark. The numbers refer to products advertised in the magazine, and the card is returned post free to the publisher, who passes the card to the advertiser for further response.

bipolar scale /ˌbaɪpəʊlə 'skeɪl/ *noun* a scale used in questionnaires which contains two extreme points between which an interviewee can choose an answer

birth rate /'bɜːθ reɪt/ *noun* the number of children born per 1,000 of the population

black /blæk/ *adjective* □ **in the black** in credit ○ *The company has moved into the black.* ○ *My bank account is still in the black.* ■ *verb* to forbid trading in specific goods or with specific suppliers ○ *Three firms were blacked by the government.* ○ *The union has blacked a trucking firm.*

black economy /blæk ɪ'kɒnəmi/ *noun* goods and services which are paid for in cash, and therefore not declared for tax

black list /'blæk lɪst/ *noun* a list of goods, people or companies which have been blacked

blacklist /'blæklɪst/ *verb* to put goods, people or a company on a black list ○ *Their firm was blacklisted by the government.*

black market /blæk 'mɑːkɪt/ *noun* the buying and selling of goods or currency in a way which is not allowed by law ○ *There is a flourishing black market in spare parts for cars.* □ **to pay black market prices** to pay high prices to get items which are not easily available

black-market economy /blæk 'mɑːkɪt ɪˌkɒnəmi/ *noun* an economy, or part of an economy, that functions by illegally trading goods that are normally subject to official controls

blank cheque /blæŋk 'tʃek/ *noun* a cheque with the amount of money and the payee left blank, but signed by the drawer

blanket agreement /ˌblæŋkɪt ə'griːmənt/ *noun* an agreement which covers many different items

blanket branding /ˌblæŋkɪt 'brændɪŋ/ *noun* giving a whole group or line of products the same brand name ○ *Blanket branding will make the brand a household name.*

blanket coverage /ˌblæŋkɪt 'kʌv(ə)rɪdʒ/ *noun* advertising to the general public with no particular target audience in mind ○ *We will go for blanket coverage first and then see what kind of people buy the product.*

blanket insurance (cover) /ˌblæŋkɪt ɪn'ʃʊərəns ˌkʌvə/ *noun*

insurance which covers various items such as a house and its contents

blanket refusal /ˌblæŋkɪt rɪ-ˈfjuːz(ə)l/ *noun* a refusal to accept many different items

bleed /bliːd/ *noun* an illustration or text which runs right to the edge of the printed page ■ *verb* to allow advertising space to run to the edge of a printed page

blind offer /ˌblaɪnd ˈɒfə/ *noun* a premium offer which is hidden away in an advertisement so as to find out how many readers read the advertisement

blindside /ˈblaɪndsaɪd/ *verb* to attack a competitor unexpectedly and in a way which it is difficult to respond to

blind testing /blaɪnd ˈtestɪŋ/ *noun* the practice of testing a product on consumers without telling them what brand it is

blister pack /ˈblɪstə pæk/, **bubble pack** /ˈbʌb(ə)l pæk/ *noun* a type of packing where the item for sale is covered with a stiff plastic cover sealed to a card backing

blitz /blɪts/ *noun* a marketing campaign which starts at full pressure, as opposed to a gradual build-up

blow-in /ˈbləʊ ɪn/ *noun US* a postcard-size advertising card inserted in a magazine

blue-hair /blu: ˈheə/ *adjective US* referring to elderly women

blue-sky thinking /blu: ˌskaɪ ˈθɪŋkɪŋ/ *noun* extremely idealistic and often unconventional ideas

blur /blɜ:/ *noun* a period in which a great many important changes take place in an organisation very quickly

blurb /blɜ:b/ *noun* a brief description of a book, printed in a publisher's catalogue or on the cover of the book itself

body copy /ˈbɒdi ˌkɒpi/ *noun* the main part of the text of an advertisement ○ *The body copy is OK, though the company's address needn't be included.* ○ *The body copy on the poster is too long for passers-by to read it all.*

body language /ˈbɒdi ˌlæŋgwɪdʒ/ *noun* gestures, expressions, and movements which show what somebody's response is to a situation ○ *Trainee salesmen learn how to interpret a customer's body language.* ○ *The interviewer of prospective marketing managers observed the body language of the candidates very carefully.* ○ *The candidate claimed to be very confident about taking the job, but her body language was saying the opposite.*

bogof /ˈbɒgɒf/ *noun* the practice of giving free gifts to customers, e.g. one free item for each one bought. Full form **buy one get one free**

boilerplate /ˈbɔɪləpleɪt/ *noun* a basic standard version of a contract that can be used again and again

bonded warehouse /ˌbɒndɪd ˈweəhaʊs/ *noun* a warehouse where goods are stored until excise duty has been paid

bonus /ˈbəʊnəs/ *noun* an extra payment in addition to a normal payment

bonus offer /ˈbəʊnəs ˌɒfə/ *noun* a special offer, especially one to launch a new product, which includes a bonus or free gift

bonus pack /ˈbəʊnəs pæk/ *noun* a pack with extra contents or extra items for which no extra charge is made ○ *We are offering bonus packs in order to attract new customers to the product.*

bonus size /ˈbəʊnəs saɪz/ *noun* an extra large size of pack sold at the usual price as a form of sales promotion ○ *Bonus size packs are 20% larger, but are sold at the normal price.*

bonus spot /ˈbəʊnəs spɒt/ *noun* a free television or radio spot offered to an advertiser as part of an advertising package

book /bʊk/ *noun* a set of sheets of paper attached together □ **a company's books** the financial records of a company

book club /ˈbʊk klʌb/ *noun* a group of people who pay a small subscription and buy books regularly by mail order

booking /ˈbʊkɪŋ/ *noun* the act of reserving a room or a seat etc. ○ *Hotel bookings have fallen since the end of the tourist season.*

booking clerk /'bʊkɪŋ klɑːk/ *noun* a person who sells tickets in a booking office

booking office /'bʊkɪŋ ˌɒfɪs/ *noun* an office where you can book seats at a theatre or tickets for the railway

bookmark /'bʊkmɑːk/ *verb* to make a special mental note of somebody or something so that you remember them in future ■ *noun* a software tool in a web browser that enables users to select and store webpages that they want to look at often and to access them quickly and conveniently

book sales /'bʊk seɪlz/ *plural noun* sales as recorded in the sales book

book token /'bʊk ˌtəʊkən/ *noun* a voucher bought in a shop which is given as a present and which must be exchanged for books

book value /'bʊk ˌvæljuː/ *noun* the value of an asset as recorded in the company's balance sheet

boom /buːm/ *noun* the time when sales, production or business activity are increasing ○ *a period of economic boom* ○ *the boom of the 1970s* □ **the boom years** years when there is an economic boom ■ *verb* to expand or to become prosperous ○ *business is booming* ○ *sales are booming*
  '…starting in 1981, a full-blown real estate boom took off in Texas' [*Business*]

boom industry /'buːm ˌɪndəstri/ *noun* an industry which is expanding rapidly

booming /'buːmɪŋ/ *adjective* which is expanding or becoming prosperous ○ *a booming industry* or *company* ○ *Technology is a booming sector of the economy.*

boom share /'buːm ʃeə/ *noun* a share in a company which is expanding

Boston Box /ˌbɒstən 'bɒks/ *noun* a system used to indicate a company's potential by analysing the relationship between its market share and its growth rate (NOTE: The Boston Box was devised by the Boston Consulting Group in the 1970s to help companies decide which businesses they should invest in and which they should withdraw from. In this system businesses with a high

market share and high growth rate are called stars, businesses with a low market share and low growth rate are called dogs, businesses with a high market share and a low growth rate are called cash cows and businesses with a low market share and a high growth rate are called question marks.)

Boston matrix /ˌbɒstən 'meɪtrɪks/ *noun* a type of product portfolio analysis, in which products are identified as stars, question marks, cash cows or dogs (NOTE: the full name is the **Boston Consulting Group Share/Growth Matrix**)

bottle hanger /'bɒt(ə)l 'hæŋə/ *noun* an advertisement in the form of a card which hangs round the neck of a bottle

bottleneck /'bɒt(ə)lˌnek/ *noun* a situation that occurs when one section of an operation cannot cope with the amount of work it has to do, which slows down the later stages of the operation and business activity in general ○ *a bottleneck in the supply system* ○ *There are serious bottlenecks in the production line.*

bottom /'bɒtəm/ *noun* the lowest part or point □ **the bottom has fallen out of the market** sales have fallen below what previously seemed to be the lowest point □ **rock-bottom price** the lowest price of all ■ *verb* to reach the lowest point

bottom line /ˌbɒtəm 'laɪn/ *noun* the last line on a balance sheet indicating profit or loss

bottom price /'bɒtəm praɪs/ *noun* the lowest price

bounce back /ˌbaʊns 'bæk/ *verb* (*of emails*) to be returned to the sender because the address is incorrect or the user is not known at the mail server

bounce-back coupon /ˌbaʊns 'bæk ˌkuːpɒn/ *noun* a coupon offer made to existing customers in order to persuade them to continue purchasing the brand

boutique /buːˈtiːk/ *noun* **1.** a small specialised shop, especially for up-to-date clothes ○ *a jeans boutique* ○ *a ski boutique* **2.** a section of a department store selling up-to-date clothes

box 27 **brand image**

box /bɒks/ *noun* a cardboard, wooden or plastic container ○ *The goods were sent in thin cardboard boxes.* ○ *The watches are prepacked in plastic display boxes.* □ **paperclips come in boxes of two hundred** paperclips are packed two hundred to a box

boxed /bɒkst/ *adjective* put or sold in a box

boxed set /ˌbɒkst 'set/ *noun* a set of items sold together in a box

box store /'bɒks stɔː/ *noun* a supermarket like a warehouse, with not much service or promotion, where goods are sold from their original packing cases ○ *The school bought stationery in large quantities from the box store.* ○ *With low overheads, box stores can offer cut-rate prices.*

boycott /'bɔɪkɒt/ *noun* a refusal to buy or to deal in certain products ○ *The union organised a boycott against or of imported cars.* ■ *verb* to refuse to buy or deal in a product ○ *We are boycotting all imports from that country.* □ **the management has boycotted the meeting** has refused to attend the meeting

BRAD *abbr* British Rate and Data

brainstorming /'breɪnˌstɔːmɪŋ/ *noun* an intensive discussion by a small group of people as a method of producing new ideas or solving problems

brainstorming session /'breɪnˌstɔːmɪŋ ˌseʃ(ə)n/ *noun* a meeting to thrash out problems, where everyone puts forward different ideas

branch /brɑːntʃ/ *noun* the local office of a bank or large business, or a local shop which is part of a large chain

branch manager /brɑːntʃ 'mænɪdʒə/ *noun* a person in charge of a branch of a company

'…a leading manufacturer of business, industrial and commercial products requires a branch manager to head up its mid-western Canada operations based in Winnipeg' [*Globe and Mail (Toronto)*]

branch out /ˌbrɑːntʃ 'aʊt/ *verb* to start a new but usually related type of business ○ *From car retailing, the company branched out into car leasing.*

brand /brænd/ *noun* a make of product, which can be recognised by a name

or by a design ○ *the top-selling brands of toothpaste* ○ *The company is launching a new brand of soap.*

'…the multiple brought the price down to £2.49 in some stores. We had not agreed to this deal and they sold out very rapidly. When they reordered we would not give it to them. This kind of activity is bad for the brand and we cannot afford it' [*The Grocer*]

'…you have to look much further down the sales league to find a brand which has not been around for what seems like ages' [*Marketing*]

'…major companies are supporting their best existing brands with increased investment' [*Marketing Week*]

brand awareness /'brænd əˌweənəs/ *noun* consciousness by the public of a brand's existence and qualities ○ *How can you talk about brand awareness when most people don't even know what the product is supposed to do?* ○ *Our sales staff must work harder to increase brand awareness in this area.*

brand building /'brænd ˌbɪldɪŋ/, **brand development** /'brænd dɪˌveləpmənt/ *noun* the expansion of the total awareness and sales of a brand in a given market

brand champion /'brænd ˌtʃæmpiən/ *noun* an executive who is passionate about a brand and promotes it vigorously worldwide

brand development index /ˌbrænd dɪ'veləpmənt ɪnˌdeks/ *noun* an index that compares the percentage of a brand's total sales in a given market to the percentage of the total population in the market. Abbr **BDI**

branded goods /ˌbrændɪd 'gʊdz/ *plural noun* goods sold under brand names

brand equity /'brænd ˌekwɪti/ *noun* the extra value brought to a product by being a brand, both value as seen by the customer as well as financial value to the company

brand extension strategy /ˌbrænd ɪk'stenʃən ˌstrætədʒi/ *noun* the applying of an existing brand name to a new product

brand image /brænd 'ɪmɪdʒ/ *noun* an opinion of a product which people associate in their minds with the brand name

branding /ˈbrændɪŋ/ *noun* the act of giving brand names to products

'...marketing and branding are becoming more important in the hotel and restaurant business. There is increasing competition in hotels and reviews of brand image are commonplace' [*Marketing Week*]

brand leader /brænd ˈliːdə/ *noun* the brand with the largest market share

brand life cycle /ˌbrænd ˈlaɪf ˌsaɪk(ə)l/ *noun* stages in the life of a brand in terms of sales and profitability, from its launch to its decline

brand loyalty /brænd ˈlɔɪəlti/ *noun* the feeling of trust and satisfaction that makes a customer always buy the same brand of product

brand management /brænd ˈmænɪdʒmənt/ *noun* directing the making and selling of a brand as an independent item

brand manager /brænd ˈmænɪdʒə/ *noun* the manager or executive responsible for the marketing of a particular brand ○ *The brand manager and the production manager met to discuss changes to be made to the company's leading brand of soap.*

brand name /ˈbrænd neɪm/ *noun* a name of a particular make of product

brand positioning /brænd pəˈzɪʃ(ə)nɪŋ/ *noun* the practice of placing a brand in a particular position in the market, so that it is recognisable to the public ○ *Intensive television advertising is a key part of our brand positioning strategy.* (NOTE: also called **product positioning**)

brand recognition /ˌbrænd rekəgˈnɪʃ(ə)n/ *noun* the ability of the consumer to recognise a brand on sight

brand switching /ˈbrænd ˌswɪtʃɪŋ/ *noun* the practice of changing from buying one brand to another, showing little brand loyalty ○ *We can't rely on steady sales with such a lot of brand switching going on.* ○ *Brand switching makes shopping more fun for consumers.*

brand value /ˈbrænd ˌvæljuː/ *noun* the value of a brand name

brand wagon /ˈbrænd ˌwægən/ *noun* the tendency for marketers to see branding as the only way to promote a product

brandwidth /ˈbrændwɪdθ/ *noun* the amount of customer recognition which a brand enjoys

brand X /brænd ˈeks/ *noun* the anonymous brand used in TV commercials to compare with the named brand being advertised

breach /briːtʃ/ *noun* a failure to carry out the terms of an agreement

breach of contract /ˌbriːtʃ əv ˈkɒntrækt/ *noun* the failure to do something which has been agreed in a contract

bread-and-butter line /ˌbred ən ˈbʌtə laɪnz/ *noun* a range of items which are found in all stores of one category, and which provide a solid basis of continuing sales

break /breɪk/ *noun* a pause between periods of work ○ *She keyboarded for two hours without a break.* ■ *verb* (NOTE: **breaking- broke- has broken**) □ **break bulk** to split into small quantities for retail sale after having bought a large quantity □ **break even** to balance costs and receipts, but not make a profit ○ *Last year the company only just broke even.* ○ *We broke even in our first two months of trading.*

breakeven analysis /breɪkˈiːv(ə)n əˌnæləsɪs/ *noun* **1.** the analysis of fixed and variable costs and sales that determines at what level of production the breakeven point will be reached ○ *The breakeven analysis showed that the company will only break even if it sells at least 1,000 bicycles a month.* **2.** a method of showing the point at which a company's income from sales will be equal to its production costs so that it neither makes a profit nor makes a loss (NOTE: Breakeven analysis is usually shown in the form of a chart and can be used to help companies make decisions, set prices for their products and work out the effects of changes in production or sales volume on their costs and profits.)

breakeven point /breɪkˈiːv(ə)n pɔɪnt/ *noun* a point at which sales cover costs, but do not show a profit

breaking bulk /ˌbreɪkɪŋ 'bʌlk/ *noun* the practice of buying in bulk and then selling in small quantities to many customers

break up /ˌbreɪk 'ʌp/ *verb* to split something large into small sections ○ *The company was broken up and separate divisions sold off.*

break-up value /'breɪk ʌp ˌvæljuː/ *noun* **1.** the value of the material of a fixed asset ○ *What would the break-up value of our old machinery be?* ○ *Scrap merchants were asked to estimate the tractors' break-up value.* **2.** the value of various parts of a company taken separately

bricks-and-mortar /ˌbrɪks ən 'mɔːtə/ *adjective* conducting business in the traditional way in buildings such as shops and warehouses and not being involved in e-commerce. Compare **clicks-and-mortar**

bridge /brɪdʒ/ *verb* to print an advertisement across the centre of a double-page spread in a magazine

brief /briːf/ *verb* to explain something to someone in detail ○ *The sales staff were briefed on the new product.* ○ *The managing director briefed the board on the progress of the negotiations.*

briefing /'briːfɪŋ/ *noun* telling someone details ○ *All sales staff have to attend a sales briefing on the new product.*

British Rate and Data /ˌbrɪtɪʃ ˌreɪt ən 'deɪtə/ a regular publication which lists British newspapers and magazines, giving all relevant information about their circulation, rates, frequency and other advertising services offered ○ *You should consult BRAD first to find the most suitable newspaper to carry our advertising.* Abbr **BRAD** (NOTE: the comparable American publication is **Standard Rate and Data Service**)

broadband /'brɔːdbænd/ *noun* a data transmission system that allows large amounts of data to be transferred very quickly

broadcast /'brɔːdkɑːst/ *noun* a radio or TV programme ■ *verb* to send out on radio or TV

broadcasting media /-'brɔːdkɑːstɪŋ ˌmiːdiə/ *plural noun* media such as radio or TV

broadsheet /'brɔːdʃiːt/ *noun* a large size of newspaper page (as opposed to tabloid). Compare **tabloid**

broadside /'brɔːdsaɪd/ *noun* US a large format publicity leaflet

brochure /'brəʊʃə/ *noun* a publicity booklet ○ *We sent off for a brochure about holidays in Greece* or *about postal services.*

brochureware /'brəʊʃəweə/ *noun* a website that provides information about products and services in the same way as a printed brochure (NOTE: The word is often used negatively to refer to electronic advertising for planned but nonexistent products.)

broken lot /ˌbrəʊkən 'lɒt/ *noun* an incomplete set of goods for sale ○ *We'll give you a discount since it is a broken lot, with two items missing.*

broker /'brəʊkə/ *noun* **1.** a dealer who acts as a middleman between a buyer and a seller **2.** □ **(stock)broker** a person or firm that buys and sells shares or bonds on behalf of clients

brokerage /'brəʊkərɪdʒ/, **broker's commission** /ˌbrəʊkəz kə'mɪʃ(ə)n/ *noun* payment to a broker for a deal carried out

brown goods /'braʊn ɡʊdz/ *plural noun* electrical equipment for home entertainment, e.g. television sets, hi-fi equipment. Compare **white goods**

browser /'braʊzə/ *noun* a piece of software that enables computer users to have access to the Internet and World Wide Web

bubble card /'bʌb(ə)l kɑːd/, **bubble pack** /'bʌb(ə)l pæk/ *noun* a type of packaging, where the item for sale is covered by a stiff plastic sheet sealed to a card backing

bubble wrap /'bʌb(ə)l ræp/ *noun* a sheet of clear plastic with bubbles of air in it, used as a protective wrapping material

bucket shop /'bʌkɪt ʃɒp/ *noun* **1.** an firm of brokers or dealers that sells shares that may be worthless **2.** a firm

that sells cheap airline or other travel tickets

'...at last something is being done about the thousands of bucket shops across the nation that sell investment scams by phone' [*Forbes Magazine*]

budget /ˈbʌdʒɪt/ *noun* **1.** a plan of expected spending and income for a period of time ○ *We have agreed the budgets for next year.* **2.** □ **the Budget** the annual plan of taxes and government spending proposed by a finance minister. In the UK, this is the Chancellor of the Exchequer. ○ *The minister put forward a budget aimed at boosting the economy.* □ **to balance the budget** to plan income and expenditure so that they balance ○ *The president is planning for a balanced budget.* **3.** (*in shops*) cheap □ **budget prices** low prices ■ *verb* to plan probable income and expenditure ○ *We are budgeting for £10,000 of sales next year.*

'...he budgeted for further growth of 150,000 jobs (or 2.5 per cent) in the current financial year' [*Sydney Morning Herald*]

'...the Federal government's budget targets for employment and growth are within reach according to the latest figures' [*Australian Financial Review*]

budget account /ˈbʌdʒɪt əˌkaʊnt/ *noun* a bank account where you plan income and expenditure to allow for periods when expenditure is high, by paying a set amount each month

budgetary /ˈbʌdʒɪt(ə)rɪ/ *adjective* referring to a budget

budgetary control /ˌbʌdʒɪt(ə)ri kənˈtrəʊl/ *noun* controlled spending according to a planned budget

budgetary policy /ˌbʌdʒɪt(ə)ri ˈpɒlɪsi/ *noun* the policy of planning income and expenditure

budgetary requirements /ˌbʌdʒɪt(ə)ri rɪˈkwaɪəmənts/ *plural noun* the rate of spending or income required to meet the budget forecasts

budget department /ˈbʌdʒɪt dɪˌpɑːtmənt/ *noun* a department in a large store which sells cheaper goods

budgeting /ˈbʌdʒɪtɪŋ/ *noun* the preparation of budgets to help plan expenditure and income

budget surplus /ˌbʌdʒɪt ˈsɜːpləs/ *noun* a situation where there is more revenue than was planned for in the budget

budget variance /ˌbʌdʒɪt ˈveəriəns/ *noun* the difference between the cost as estimated for a budget and the actual cost

building materials /ˈbɪldɪŋ məˌtɪəriəlz/ *plural noun* materials used in building, e.g. bricks and cement

building permit /ˈbɪldɪŋ ˌpɜːmɪt/ *noun* an official document which allows someone to build on a piece of land

build-up approach /ˈbɪld ʌp əˌprəʊtʃ/ *noun* a method of calculating the budget for promotion by determining the tasks that have to be carried out and estimating the costs of performing them

built-in /ˈbɪlt ɪn/ *adjective* forming part of the system or of a machine ○ *The PC has a built-in modem.* ○ *The accounting system has a series of built-in checks.*

built-in obsolescence /ˈbɪlt ɪn ɒbsəˌles(ə)ns/ *noun* a method of ensuring continuing sales of a product by making it in such a way that it will soon become obsolete

bulk /bʌlk/ *noun* a large quantity of goods □ **in bulk** in large quantities ○ *to buy rice in bulk*

bulk buying /bʌlk ˈbaɪɪŋ/ *noun* getting large quantities of goods at low prices

bulk carrier /bʌlk ˈkæriə/ *noun* a ship which carries large quantities of loose goods such as corn or coal

bulk discount /bʌlk ˈdɪskaʊnt/ *noun* a discount given to a purchaser who buys in bulk

bulk rate /ˈbʌlk reɪt/ *noun* a cheap rate offered to advertisers who take large amounts of advertising space

bulk shipment /bʌlk ˈʃɪpmənt/ *noun* a shipment of large quantities of goods

bulky /ˈbʌlki/ *adjective* large and awkward ○ *The Post Office does not accept bulky packages.*

bulldog /'buldɒg/ *noun* the first edition of a daily newspaper

bulletin /'bulətin/ *noun* a short note, newsletter or report, issued regularly ○ *Bulletins were regularly sent to the sales force.* ○ *The bulletin contained sales figures for the month.*

bulletin board /'bulitin bɔ:d/, **notice board** *noun* a website that allows members of an interest group to exchange emails, chat online, and access software

bumper sticker /'bʌmpə ˌstikə/ *noun* an advertising sticker put onto the bumper of a car

bundle /'bʌnd(ə)l/ *verb* to market a package that contains various products or services at a special price

bundling /'bʌndliŋ/ *noun* putting several items together to form a package deal, especially offering software as part of the purchase of computer hardware

buppies /'bʌpiz/ *plural noun* young professional people with relatively high incomes (NOTE: Short for **Black Upwardly-Mobile Professionals**)

burst /bɜːst/ *noun* a large number of advertisements for a product placed over a short period ○ *Shall we go for a burst or for a more prolonged campaign?*

business /'biznis/ *noun* **1.** work in buying or selling ○ *business is expanding* ○ *We do a lot of business with Japan.* ○ *Business is slow.* ○ *Repairing cars is 90% of our business.* ○ *We did more business in the week before Christmas than we usually do in a month.* ○ *Strikes are very bad for business.* ○ *What's your line of business?* □ **to be in business** to run a commercial firm □ **on business** doing commercial work ○ *He had to go abroad on business.* ○ *The chairman is in Holland on business.* **2.** a commercial company ○ *He owns a small car repair business.* ○ *She runs a business from her home.* ○ *He set up in business as an insurance broker.* **3.** affairs discussed ○ *The main business of the meeting was finished by 3 p.m.*

business address /'biznis əˌdres/ *noun* the details of number, street and town where a company is located

business agent /'biznis ˌeidʒənt/ *noun* US the chief local official of a trade union

business call /'biznis kɔːl/ *noun* a visit to talk to someone about business

business card /'biznis kɑːd/ *noun* a card showing a businessperson's name and the name and address of the company they work for

business case /'biznis keis/ *noun* a statement that explains why a particular course of action would be advantageous or profitable to an organisation (NOTE: A business case depends on the preparation and presentation of a viable business plan and is intended to weed out ideas that may seem promising but have no real long-term value to an organisation.)

business centre /'biznis ˌsentə/ *noun* the part of a town where the main banks, shops and offices are located

business class /'biznis klɑːs/ *noun* a type of airline travel which is less expensive than first class and more comfortable than economy class

business community /'biznis kəˌmjuːniti/ *noun* the business people living and working in the area

business computer /'biznis kəmˌpjuːtə/ *noun* a powerful small computer programmed for special business uses

business correspondence /'biznis kɒriˌspɒndəns/ *noun* letters concerned with a business

business correspondent /'biznis kɒriˌspɒndənt/ *noun* a journalist who writes articles on business news for newspapers

business cycle /'biznis ˌsaik(ə)l/ *noun* the period during which trade expands, slows down and then expands again

business efficiency exhibition /ˌbiznis iˈfiʃ(ə)nsi eksiˌbiʃ(ə)n/ *noun* an exhibition which shows products such as computers and word-processors which help businesses to be efficient

business environment /ˌbɪznɪs ɪn-'vaɪrənmənt/ *noun* the elements or factors outside a business organisation which directly affect it, such as the supply of raw materials and product demand ○ *The unreliability of supplies is one of the worst features of our business environment.*

business equipment /'bɪznɪs ɪˌkwɪpmənt/ *noun* the machines used in an office

business expenses /'bɪznɪs ɪkˌspensɪz/ *plural noun* money spent on running a business, not on stock or assets

business game /'bɪznɪs geɪm/ *noun* a game, often run on a computer, in which individuals or teams compete to do business in an imaginary market ○ *Students on management courses are often asked to take part in business games to improve their decision-making skills.*

business gift /'bɪznɪs gɪft/ *noun* a present received by a customer, either attached to a product bought or given to him by the retailer or producer on proof of purchase of a minimum quantity of goods

business hours /'bɪznɪs aʊəz/ *plural noun* the time when a business is open, usually 9.00 a.m. to 5.30 p.m.

business intelligence /'bɪznɪs ɪnˌtelɪdʒ(ə)ns/ *noun* information that may be useful to a business when it is planning its strategy

business letter /'bɪznɪs ˌletə/ *noun* a letter which deals with business matters

business mailing list /ˌbɪznɪs 'meɪlɪŋ lɪst/ *noun* a list of names and addresses of businesses

businessman /'bɪznɪsmæn/, **businesswoman** /'bɪznɪsˌwʊmən/ *noun* a man or woman engaged in business

business park /'bɪznɪs pɑːk/ *noun* a group of small factories or warehouses, especially near a town ○ *He has rented a unit in the local business park.*

business plan /'bɪznɪs plæn/ *noun* a document drawn up to show how a business is planned to work, with cash flow forecasts, sales forecasts, etc., of-ten used when trying to raise a loan, or when setting up a new business

business portfolio analysis /ˌbɪznɪs pɔːt'fəʊliəʊ əˌnæləsɪs/ *noun* a method of categorising a firm's products according to their relative competitive position and business growth rate in order to lay the foundations for sound strategic planning

business publication /'bɪznɪs ˌpʌblɪkeɪʃ(ə)n/ *noun* a magazine or newspaper which is only concerned with business matters, e.g. trade journals

business-to-business /ˌbɪznɪs tə 'bɪznɪs/ *noun* full form of **B2B**

business-to-business advertising /ˌbɪznɪs tə 'bɪznɪs ˌædvətaɪzɪŋ/ *noun* advertising aimed at businesses, not at households or private purchasers

business-to-consumer /ˌbɪznɪs tə kən'sjuːmə/ *noun* full form of **B2C**

business transaction /'bɪznɪs trænˌzækʃən/ *noun* an act of buying or selling

business unit /'bɪznɪs juːnɪt/ *noun* a unit within an organisation that operates as a separate department, division or stand-alone business and is usually treated as a separate profit centre

busy season /'bɪzi ˌsiːz(ə)n/ *noun* the period when a company is busy

buy /baɪ/ *verb* to get something by paying money ○ *to buy wholesale and sell retail* ○ *to buy for cash* ○ *He bought 10,000 shares.* ○ *The company has been bought by its leading supplier.* (NOTE: **buying- bought**) □ **buy one get one free** giving free gifts to customers such as one free item for each one bought. Abbr **bogof**

buy back /ˌbaɪ 'bæk/ *verb* to buy something which you sold earlier ○ *She sold the shop last year and is now trying to buy it back.*

buy-back agreement /'baɪ bæk əˌgriːmənt/ *noun* an agreement that a producer will buy back goods from a distributor on a specific date if the distributor has not been able to sell them

buy classes /'baɪ ˌklɑːsɪz/ *plural noun* categories of buying based on how much the purchasing decisions of an or-

ganisation have changed from the time of the previous purchase

buyer /'baɪə/ *noun* **1.** a person who buys □ **there were no buyers** no one wanted to buy **2.** a person who buys stock on behalf of a trading organisation for resale or for use in production **3.** in B2B selling, a person who has made a commitment to buy, but has not finalised the deal

buyer expectation /ˌbaɪə ekspek-'teɪʃ(ə)n/ *noun* same as **customer expectation**

buyer's guide /'baɪəz gaɪd/ *noun* a book or pamphlet which gives advice to purchasers on the prices, availability and reliability of products or services

buyer's market /'baɪəz ˌmɑːkɪt/ *noun* a market where products are sold cheaply because there are few people who want to buy them (NOTE: the opposite is a **seller's market**)

buyer's risk /ˌbaɪəz 'rɪsk/ *noun* the risk taken by a buyer when accepting goods or services without a guarantee

buyer's surplus /ˌbaɪəz 'sɜːpləs/ *noun* an extra margin generated when an item is bought at a higher discount than usual ○ *When the brand manager realised how great the buyer's surplus was, she decided to lower the price of the product.*

buy forward /baɪ 'fɔːwəd/ *verb* to buy foreign currency before you need it, in order to be sure of the exchange rate

buy grid /'baɪ grɪd/ *noun* a method used for objective assessment of com-

peting products, especially when purchasing industrial supplies

buy in /ˌbaɪ 'ɪn/ *verb* (*of a seller at an auction*) to buy the thing which you are trying to sell because no one will pay the price you want

buying /'baɪɪŋ/ *noun* the act of getting something for money

buying agent /'baɪɪŋ ˌeɪdʒənt/ *noun* a person who buys for a business or another person, and earns a commission ○ *Our buying agent is presently looking for materials in Portugal.* ○ *The buying agent knows a whole network of suppliers round the country.*

buying department /'baɪɪŋ dɪ-ˌpɑːtmənt/ *noun* the department in a company which buys raw materials or goods for use in the company

buying habits /'baɪɪŋ ˌhæbɪts/ *plural noun* the general way in which some people select and buy goods

buying power /'baɪɪŋ ˌpaʊə/ *noun* the ability to buy ○ *The buying power of the pound has fallen over the last five years.*

buying service /'baɪɪŋ ˌsɜːvɪs/ *noun* an agency which buys advertising space or time for its clients

buy phases /'baɪ ˌfeɪzɪz/ *plural noun* phases in the buying of industrial products. The main phases are the recognition of a want, the identification of a product, comparison with other competing products on the market, evaluation of possible courses of action and final decision-making.

by-line /'baɪ laɪn/ *noun* the journalist's name which appears before a newspaper report

C

C2C commerce /ˌsiː tə siː ˈkɒmɜːs/ same as **consumer-to-consumer commerce**

CA *abbr* Consumers Association

cabinet /ˈkæbɪnət/ *noun* a display case for goods for sale, especially frozen food

cable television /ˌkeɪb(ə)l telɪˈvɪʒ(ə)n/, **cable TV** /ˌkeɪb(ə)l tiːˈviː/ *noun* a television service which a viewer receives via a cable from a particular station and pays for on subscription

caging /ˈkeɪdʒɪŋ/ *noun* the handling of cash and cheques in a direct-mail operation

call /kɔːl/ *noun* a visit ○ *The sales reps make six calls a day.* ■ *verb* □ **to call on someone** to visit someone ○ *Our sales people call on their best accounts twice a month.*

call bird /ˈkɔːl bɜːd/ *noun* a low-priced product advertised to attract customers to the point-of-sale where they can then be sold more profitable goods ○ *We need a call bird to bring round more customers.*

call centre /ˈkɔːl ˌsentə/ *noun* a department or business that operates a large number of telephones and specialises in making calls to sell products or in receiving calls from customers to helplines or information or after-sales services (NOTE: A call centre often acts as the central point of contact between an organisation and its customers.)

call cycle /ˈkɔːl ˌsaɪk(ə)l/ *noun* the time between a salesperson's visits to the same customer ○ *Because we now have more customers to deal with, call cycles are getting longer.*

call divert *noun* a telephone facility in which calls are automatically switched from one number to another

call frequency /ˈkɔːl ˌfriːkwənsi/ *noun* the number of times a salesperson visits a specific customer during a period of time

call in /ˌkɔːl ˈɪn/ *verb* **1.** to visit ○ *Their sales representative called in twice last week.* **2.** to telephone to make contact ○ *We ask the reps to call in every Friday to report the weeks' sales.*

calling line identification /ˈkɔːlɪŋ laɪn aɪdentɪfɪˌkeɪʃ(ə)n/ *noun* ◊ **computer telephony integration**

call letters /ˈkɔːl ˌletəz/ *plural noun* US a series of letters used to identify a radio station

call rate /ˈkɔːl reɪt/ *noun* the number of calls per day or per week which a salesperson makes on customers

call report /ˈkɔːl rɪˌpɔːt/ *noun* a report made by a salesperson after a visit to a customer ○ *In his call report, the sales rep explained why he was experiencing sales resistance.* ○ *The call reports have to be handed in each week to the sales manager.*

call to action /ˌkɔːl tʊ ˈækʃ(ə)n/ *noun* a prompt which encourages a potential Internet purchaser to do something such as click to see a range of colours

camp /kæmp/ *verb* □ **to camp on the line** to have to wait on hold for a long time until someone answers your telephone call

campaign /kæmˈpeɪn/ *noun* a series of co-ordinated activities to reach an objective

cancellation clause /ˌkænsə-ˈleɪʃ(ə)n klɔːz/ *noun* a clause in a con-

tract which states the terms on which the contract may be cancelled

cancellation date /ˌkænsəˈleɪʃ(ə)n deɪt/ *noun* the final date by which an advertisement must be cancelled if the advertiser does not wish to proceed

canned presentation /ˌkænd prez(ə)nˈteɪʃ(ə)n/ *noun* a standard sales presentation which some salespeople use all the time ○ *When trainee sales reps are not sure how to approach customers they fall back on canned presentations.* ○ *The sales manager feels that the artificiality of canned presentations makes them ineffective.*

cannibalisation /ˌkænɪbəlaɪˈzeɪʃ(ə)n/, **cannibalization, cannibalism** /ˈkænɪbəlɪz(ə)m/ *noun* a situation where a company launches a new product which sells well at the expense of another established product ○ *Though the new product sold well, the resultant cannibalisation damaged the company's overall profits for the year.* ○ *Cannibalism became a real problem because the new product made the existing line seem obsolete.*

canvass /ˈkænvəs/ *verb* to visit people to ask them to buy goods, to vote or to say what they think ○ *He's canvassing for customers for his hairdresser's shop.* ○ *We've canvassed the staff about raising the prices in the staff restaurant.*

canvasser /ˈkænvəsə/ *noun* a person who canvasses

canvassing /ˈkænvəsɪŋ/ *noun* the practice of asking people to buy, to vote, or to say what they think ○ *door-to-door canvassing* ○ *canvassing techniques*

capital /ˈkæpɪt(ə)l/ *noun* **1.** the money, property and assets used in a business ○ *a company with £10,000 capital* or *with a capital of £10,000* □ **capital structure of a company** the way in which a company's capital is made up from various sources **2.** money owned by individuals or companies, used for investment □ **movements of capital** changes of investments from one country to another □ **flight of capital** the rapid movement of capital out of one country because of lack of confidence in that country's economic future

'...issued and fully paid capital is $100 million, comprising 2340 shares of $100 each and 997,660 ordinary shares of $100 each' [*Hongkong Standard*]

capital account /ˈkæpɪt(ə)l əˌkaʊnt/ *noun* an account of dealings such as money invested in or taken out of the company by the owners of a company

capital allowances /ˈkæpɪt(ə)l əˈlaʊənsɪz/ *plural noun* the allowances based on the value of fixed assets which may be deducted from a company's profits and so reduce its tax liability

COMMENT: Under current UK law, depreciation is not allowable for tax on profits, whereas capital allowances, based on the value of fixed assets owned by the company, are tax-allowable.

capital assets /ˈkæpɪt(ə)l ˈæsets/ *plural noun* the property, machines, etc., which a company owns and uses but which the company does not buy and sell as part of its regular trade

capital city /ˈkæpɪt(ə)l ˈsɪti/ *noun* the main city in a country, where the government is located

capital gain /ˈkæpɪt(ə)l ˈɡeɪn/ *noun* an amount of money made by selling a fixed asset

capital gains tax /ˈkæpɪt(ə)l ˈɡeɪnz tæks/ *noun* a tax paid on capital gains. Abbr **CGT**

capital goods /ˈkæpɪt(ə)l ɡʊdz/ *plural noun* machinery, buildings and raw materials which are used to make other goods

capital-intensive industry /ˈkæpɪt(ə)l ɪnˈtensɪv ˌɪndəstri/ *noun* an industry which needs a large amount of capital investment in plant to make it work

capitalise on /ˈkæpɪt(ə)laɪz ɒn/ *verb* to make a profit from ○ *We are seeking to capitalize on our market position.*

capitalism /ˈkæpɪt(ə)lɪz(ə)m/ *noun* the economic system in which each person has the right to invest money, to work in business, and to buy and sell, with no restriction from the state

capitalist /ˈkæpɪt(ə)lɪst/ *adjective* working according to the principles of capitalism ○ *the capitalist system* ○ *the*

capitalist countries or *world* ■ *noun* a person who invests capital in business enterprises

capitalist economy /ˌkæpɪt(ə)lɪst ɪˈkɒnəmi/ *noun* a system where each person has the right to invest money, to work in business, and to buy and sell, with no restrictions from the state

capital levy /ˌkæpɪt(ə)l ˈlevi/ *noun* a tax on the value of a person's property and possessions

capital loss /ˌkæpɪt(ə)l ˈlɒs/ *noun* a loss made by selling assets (NOTE: The opposite is capital gain.)

capital transfer tax /ˌkæpɪt(ə)l ˈtrænsfɜː ˌtæks/ *noun* formerly, a tax on gifts or bequests of money or property

captain /ˈkæptɪn/ *noun* same as **channel captain**

caption /ˈkæpʃən/ *noun* a short description at the bottom of an illustration or photograph ○ *Having no caption at the bottom of the illustration created more reader interest in the product.* ○ *It took the copywriter days to think of a suitable caption for the photograph.*

captive audience /ˌkæptɪv ˈɔːdiəns/ *noun* the people who cannot avoid being exposed to an advertisement ○ *Advertisers like to have their posters in underground stations where there is a large captive audience.*

captive market /ˌkæptɪv ˈmɑːkɪt/ *noun* a market where one supplier has a monopoly and the buyer has no choice over the product which they must purchase

capture /ˈkæptʃə/ *verb* to take or get control of something □ **to capture 10% of the market** to sell hard, and so take a 10% market share □ **to capture 20% of a company's shares** to buy shares in a company rapidly and so own 20% of it

car assembly plant /ˌkɑːr əˈsembli ˌplɑːnt/ *noun* a factory where cars are put together from parts made in other factories

car boot sale /ˈkɑː ˈbʊt ˌseɪl/ *noun* a type of jumble sale, organised in a large car park or sports field, where people

sell unwanted items from the back of their cars

car card /ˈkɑː kɑːd/ *noun* an advertisement display card which is placed in a vehicle such as a bus, taxi or train

card /kɑːd/ *noun* **1.** a small piece of cardboard or plastic, usually with information printed on it ○ *He showed his staff card to get a discount in the store.* **2.** a printed piece of cardboard with information on it

'…ever since October, when the banks' base rate climbed to 15 per cent, the main credit card issuers have faced the prospect of having to push interest rates above 30 per cent APR. Though store cards have charged interest at much higher rates than this for some years, 30 per cent APR is something the banks fight shy of' [*Financial Times Review*]

card deck /ˈkɑːd dek/ *noun* a series of small cards, advertising different products or services, which are mailed as a pack in a plastic envelope to prospective customers

cardholder /ˈkɑːdˌhəʊldə/ *noun* an individual or company that has an account with a credit card company and whose name usually appears on the card

card-issuing bank /ˈkɑːd ɪsjuːɪŋ ˌbæŋk/ *noun* same as **issuer**

card-not-present merchant account /ˌkɑːd nɒt prez(ə)nt ˈmɜːtʃənt əˌkaʊnt/ *noun* an account that enables businesses operating on the web to receive payments by credit card without the buyer or card being physically present when the transaction is made

card rate /ˈkɑːd reɪt/ *noun* an advertising charge which is based on the charges listed in a rate card, i.e. without any discounts. ♦ **escalator card, showcard**

careline /ˈkeəlaɪn/ *noun* a telephone number which links people to services which can help them such as social services departments, hospitals, or a similar service offered by shops to their customers

cargo /ˈkɑːgəʊ/ *noun* a load of goods which are sent in a ship or plane, etc. □ **the ship was taking on cargo** it was being loaded with goods □ **to load cargo** to put cargo on a ship

cargo liner /ˈkɑːgəʊ ˌlaɪnə/ *noun* a cargo ship with a regular schedule ○ *If the cargo liner's schedule doesn't suit us, we'll have to charter a ship.* ○ *The cargo liner makes regular trips between Southampton and Lisbon.*

cargo ship /ˈkɑːgəʊ ʃɪp/ *noun* a ship which carries cargo, not passengers

car mart /ˈkɑː mɑːt/ *noun* US a secondhand car salesroom

carnet /ˈkɑːneɪ/ *noun* an international document which allows dutiable goods to cross several European countries by road without paying duty until the goods reach their final destination

carriage /ˈkærɪdʒ/ *noun* **1.** the transporting of goods from one place to another ○ *to pay for carriage* **2.** the cost of transport of goods ○ *to allow 10% for carriage* ○ *Carriage is 15% of the total cost.* □ **carriage free** a deal where the customer does not pay for the shipping □ **carriage paid** a deal where the seller has paid for the shipping □ **carriage prepaid** a note showing that the transport costs have been paid in advance

carrier /ˈkærɪə/ *noun* **1.** a company which transports goods ○ *We only use reputable carriers.* **2.** a vehicle or ship which transports goods

carrier bag /ˈkærɪə bæg/ *noun* a shopping bag made of strong paper

carrier's risk /ˌkærɪəz ˈrɪsk/ *noun* the responsibility of a carrier to pay for damage or loss of goods being shipped

carry /ˈkæri/ *verb* **1.** to take from one place to another ○ *a tanker carrying oil from the Gulf* ○ *The truck was carrying goods to the supermarket.* ○ *The train was carrying a consignment of cars for export.* **2.** to keep in stock ○ *to carry a line of goods* ○ *We do not carry pens.* (NOTE: **carries- carrying- carried**)

carrying /ˈkæriɪŋ/ *noun* transporting from one place to another ○ *carrying charges* ○ *carrying cost*

carry over /ˌkæri ˈəʊvə/ *verb* □ **to carry over a balance** to take a balance from the end of one page or period to the beginning of the next

carry-over effect /ˌkæri ˈəʊvər ɪˌfekt/ *noun* the effect of something af-

ter it has happened ○ *The carry-over effect of the currency devaluation was a good few years of lucrative exporting.* ○ *The political unrest in our key export markets had disastrous carry-over effects on our international marketing.*

cart /kɑːt/ *noun* a flat open goods vehicle pulled by a horse

cartage /ˈkɑːtɪdʒ/ *noun* carrying goods by road

cartel /kɑːˈtel/ *noun* a group of companies which try to fix the price or to regulate the supply of a product so that they can make more profit

carter /ˈkɑːtə/ *noun* a person who transports goods by road

carton /ˈkɑːt(ə)n/ *noun* a box made of cardboard ○ *a carton of milk*

case /keɪs/ *noun* a cardboard or wooden box for packing and carrying goods □ **six cases of wine** six boxes, each containing twelve bottles

case study /ˈkeɪs ˌstʌdi/ *noun* a true or invented business situation used in business training to practise decision-making ○ *The marketing case study consisted of a long history of the company, the present situation and a choice of strategic plans.* ○ *The case study was about territory-planning in a city in which there were a number of accounts of varying importance.*

cash /kæʃ/ *noun* **1.** money in coins or notes **2.** using money in coins or notes □ **to pay cash down** to pay in cash immediately ■ *verb* □ **to cash a cheque** to exchange a cheque for cash

cashable /ˈkæʃəb(ə)l/ *adjective* which can be cashed ○ *A crossed cheque is not cashable at any bank.*

cash account /ˈkæʃ əˌkaʊnt/ *noun* an account which records the money which is received and spent

cash advance /kæʃ ədˈvɑːns/ *noun* a loan in cash against a future payment

cash against documents /ˌkæʃ əgenst ˈdɒkjʊmənts/ *noun* a system whereby a buyer receives documents for the goods on payment of a bill of exchange

cash and carry /ˌkæʃ ən ˈkæri/ *noun* a large store selling goods at low

prices, where the customer pays cash and takes the goods away immediately ○ *We get our supplies every morning from the cash and carry.*

'...the small independent retailer who stocks up using cash and carries could be hit hard by the loss of footfall associated with any increase in smuggled goods' [*The Grocer*]

cashback /'kæʃbæk/ *noun* a discount system where a purchaser receives a cash discount on the completion of the purchase

cash balance /'kæʃ ˌbæləns/ *noun* a balance in cash, as opposed to amounts owed

cash book /'kæʃ bʊk/ *noun* a book which records cash received and paid out

cash budget /'kæʃ ˌbʌdʒɪt/ *noun* a plan of cash income and expenditure

cash card /'kæʃ kɑːd/ *noun* a plastic card used to obtain money from a cash dispenser

cash cow /'kæʃ kaʊ/ *noun* a product or subsidiary company that consistently generates good profits but does not provide growth

cash deal /'kæʃ diːl/ *noun* a sale done for cash

cash desk /'kæʃ desk/ *noun* the place in a store where you pay for the goods bought

cash discount /kæʃ 'dɪskaʊnt/ *noun* a discount given for payment in cash

cash dispenser /'kæʃ dɪˌspensə/ *noun* a machine which gives out money when a special card is inserted and instructions given

cash float /'kæʃ fləʊt/ *noun* cash put into the cash box at the beginning of the day or week to allow change to be given to customers

cash flow /'kæʃ fləʊ/ *noun* cash which comes into a company from sales (cash inflow) or the money which goes out in purchases or overhead expenditure (cash outflow) □ **the company is suffering from cash flow problems** cash income is not coming in fast enough to pay the expenditure going out

cash flow forecast /'kæʃ fləʊ ˌfɔːkɑːst/ *noun* a forecast of when cash will be received or paid out

cash flow statement /'kæʃ fləʊ ˌsteɪtmənt/ *noun* a report which shows cash sales and purchases

cashier /kæˈʃɪə/ *noun* **1.** a person who takes money from customers in a shop or who deals with the money that has been paid **2.** a person who deals with customers in a bank and takes or gives cash at the counter

cash in hand /ˌkæʃ ɪn 'hænd/ *noun* money and notes, kept to pay small amounts but not deposited in the bank

cash items /'kæʃ ˌaɪtəmz/ *plural noun* goods sold for cash

cash offer /'kæʃ ˌɒfə/ *noun* an offer to pay in cash, especially an offer to pay cash when buying shares in a takeover bid

cash on delivery /ˌkæʃ ɒn dɪˈlɪv(ə)ri/ *noun* payment in cash when goods are delivered. Abbr **COD**

cash payment /'kæʃ ˌpeɪmənt/ *noun* payment in cash

cash purchase /'kæʃ ˌpɜːtʃəs/ *noun* a purchase made in cash

cash register /'kæʃ ˌredʒɪstə/ *noun* a machine which shows and adds the prices of items bought, with a drawer for keeping the cash received

cash sale /'kæʃ seɪl/ *noun* a transaction paid for in cash

cash terms /'kæʃ tɜːmz/ *plural noun* lower terms which apply if the customer pays cash

cash till /'kæʃ tɪl/ *noun* same as **cash register**

cash transaction /'kæʃ trænˌzækʃən/ *noun* a transaction paid for in cash

cash up /ˌkæʃ 'ʌp/ *verb* to add up the cash in a shop at the end of the day

cash voucher /'kæʃ ˌvaʊtʃə/ *noun* a piece of paper which can be exchanged for cash ○ *With every £20 of purchases, the customer gets a cash voucher to the value of £2.*

catalogue /'kæt(ə)lɒg/ *noun* a publication which lists items for sale, usually

showing their prices ○ *an office equipment catalogue* ○ *They sent us a catalogue of their new range of products.* (NOTE: American English is usually **catalog**) ■ *verb* to put an item into a catalogue (NOTE: American English is usually **catalog**)

catalogue house /ˈkæt(ə)lɒɡ haʊs/ *noun* a company which mainly or solely sells by catalogue

catalogue price /ˈkæt(ə)lɒɡ praɪs/ *noun* a price as marked in a catalogue or list

catalogue store /ˈkæt(ə)lɒɡ stɔː/, **catalogue showroom** /ˈkæt(ə)lɒɡ ˌʃəʊruːm/ *noun* a shop where customers can examine a catalogue and choose goods from it

catchment area /ˈkætʃmənt ˌeəriə/ *noun* the area around a shop or shopping centre, where the customers live

catchpenny /ˈkætʃpeni/ *noun* an article which has only superficial appeal, but which attracts buyers ○ *A closer look at the doll showed it to be just a shoddily made catchpenny.*

category extension /ˈkætɪɡ(ə)ri ɪkˌstenʃən/ *noun* the applying of an existing brand name to a new product category

category management /ˈkætɪɡ(ə)ri ˌmænɪdʒmənt/ *noun* a system where managers have responsibility for the marketing of a particular category or line of products

caterer /ˈkeɪtərə/ *noun* a person or company that supplies food and drink, especially for parties

cater for /ˈkeɪtə fɔː/ *verb* to deal with or provide for ○ *The store caters mainly for overseas customers.*

catering /ˈkeɪtərɪŋ/ *noun* supplying food and drink for a party etc. ■ *adjective* □ **catering for** which provides for ○ *a store catering for overseas visitors*

catering trade /ˈkeɪtərɪŋ treɪd/ *noun* the food trade, especially businesses supplying food that is ready to eat

caveat emptor /ˌkæviæt ˈemptɔː/ phrase meaning that the buyer is responsible for checking that what he or she buys is in good order. same as **let the buyer beware**

'…the idea that buyers at a car boot sale should have any rights at all is laughable. Even those who do not understand Latin know that caveat emptor is the rule' [*Times*]

CCTV *abbr* closed circuit television

Ceefax /ˈsiːfæks/ *noun* teletext services broadcast by the BBC

ceiling /ˈsiːlɪŋ/ *noun* the highest point that something can reach, e.g. the highest rate of interest or the largest amount of money which a depositor may deposit ○ *to fix a ceiling for a budget* ○ *There is a ceiling of $100,000 on deposits.* ○ *Output reached its ceiling in June and has since fallen back.*

census /ˈsensəs/ *noun* an official count of a country's population, including such data as the age, sex, and occupation of individuals ○ *The market research department made a careful study of the census in different areas of the country to see where demand would be highest.* ◊ **distribution census**

central /ˈsentrəl/ *adjective* organised by one main point

'…central bankers in Europe and Japan are reassessing their intervention policy' [*Duns Business Month*]

centralise /ˈsentrəlaɪz/, **centralize** *verb* to organise from a central point ○ *All purchasing has been centralised in our main office.* ○ *The group benefits from a highly centralised organisational structure.* ○ *The company has become very centralised, and far more staff work at headquarters.*

centralised distribution /ˌsentrəlaɪzd dɪstrɪˈbjuːʃ(ə)n/ *noun* a system of distribution of goods to retail stores in a chain, from a central or local warehouse, so avoiding direct distribution from the manufacturer, and making stock control easier

centralised organisational structure /ˌsentrəlaɪzd ɔːɡənaɪˌzeɪʃ(ə)n(ə)l ˈstrʌktʃə/ *noun* a method of organising international advertising and promotion where all decisions are made in a company's central office

centralised system /ˌsentrəlaɪzd ˈsɪstəm/ *noun* a system where advertising and other marketing activities are

run from one central marketing department

central office /ˌsentrəl 'ɒfɪs/ *noun* the main office which controls all smaller offices

Central Office of Information /ˌsentrəl ˌɒfɪs əv ɪnfəˈmeɪʃ(ə)n/ a British government organisation which provides a publicity service and advice on international trade for British companies wishing to export. Abbr **COI**

central purchasing /ˌsentrəl 'pɜːtʃɪsɪŋ/ *noun* purchasing organised by a central office for all branches of a company

centre spread /ˌsentə 'spred/ *noun* two facing pages in the centre of a newspaper or magazine used by an advertiser for one advertisement ○ *The whole centre spread for three days cost the advertiser £150,000.* ○ *The centre spread was taken up with a large advertisement for a new model of car.*

certificate of approval /səˌtɪfɪkət əv əˈpruːv(ə)l/ *noun* a document showing that an item has been approved officially

certificate of origin /səˌtɪfɪkət əv 'ɒrɪdʒɪn/ *noun* a document showing where imported goods come from or were made

certified public accountant /ˌsɜːtɪfaɪd ˌpʌblɪk əˈkauntənt/ *noun* US an accountant who has passed professional examinations

CGT *abbr* capital gains tax

chain /tʃeɪn/ *noun* a series of stores or other businesses belonging to the same company ○ *a chain of hotels* or *a hotel chain* ○ *the chairman of a large do-it-yourself chain* ○ *He runs a chain of shoe shops.* ○ *She bought several garden centres and gradually built up a chain.*

'...the giant US group is better known for its chain of cinemas and hotels rather than its involvement in shipping' [*Lloyd's List*]

chairman and managing director /ˌtʃeəmən ən ˌmænɪdʒɪŋ daɪˈrektə/ *noun* a managing director who is also chairman of the board of directors

challenger /'tʃælɪndʒə/ *noun* a company which challenges other companies which are already established in the marketplace

channel /'tʃænl/ *noun* a means by which information or goods pass from one place to another □ **to go through the official channels** to deal with government officials, especially when making a request □ **to open up new channels of communication** to find new ways of communicating with someone □ **channels of influence** the ways in which a company can influence consumers to buy their products, i.e. personal influence channels such as salesmen, or non-personal channels such as press advertising ○ *Owing to lack of capital there were not many channels of influence open to the company.* ○ *It was decided that personal selling was the most effective channel of influence for such a specialised product.*

channel captain /'tʃæn(ə)l ˌkæptɪn/ *noun* a business which controls or has the most influence in a distribution channel ○ *The production company became a channel captain by acquiring a number of important retail outlets.* ○ *Only businesses with enough financial resources to acquire other companies can become channel captains.*

channel communications /'tʃæn(ə)l kəmjuːnɪˌkeɪʃ(ə)ŋz/ *plural noun* communications to a marketing channel such as the company's sales force or to selected retailers

channel management /'tʃæn(ə)l ˌmænɪdʒmənt/ *noun* the managing of a marketing channel and the business partners which form part of it

channel members /'tʃæn(ə)l ˌmembəz/ *plural noun* the various companies which form a distribution channel

channel power /'tʃæn(ə)l pauə/ *noun* the influence which one company in a trading channel has over the other companies in the channel

channel strip /'tʃæn(ə)l strɪp/ *noun* the front edge of a shelf on which details

of the products displayed can be put such as price, weight, code numbers

channel support /'tʃæn(ə)l sə,pɔːt/ *noun* support given to a marketing channel, that is to the people or companies that help to sell the product

character /'kærɪktə/ *noun* a letter, number or sign used in typesetting, e.g. a letter of the alphabet, a number or a punctuation mark

charge /tʃɑːdʒ/ *noun* **1.** money which must be paid, or price of a service ○ *to make no charge for delivery* ○ *to make a small charge for rental* ○ *There is no charge for this service* or *No charge is made for this service.* □ **charges forward** charges which will be paid by the customer **2.** a debit on an account ○ *It appears as a charge on the accounts.* ■ *verb* **1.** to ask someone to pay for services later □ **to charge the packing to the customer** *or* **to charge the customer with the packing** the customer has to pay for packing **2.** to ask for money to be paid ○ *to charge £5 for delivery* ○ *How much does he charge?*

'…traveller's cheques cost 1% of their face value – some banks charge more for small amounts' [*Sunday Times*]

chargeable /'tʃɑːdʒəb(ə)l/ *adjective* which can be charged ○ *repairs chargeable to the occupier*

charge account /'tʃɑːdʒ ə,kaʊnt/ *noun* an arrangement which a customer has with a store to buy goods and to pay for them at a later date, usually when the invoice is sent at the end of the month (NOTE: The customer will make regular monthly payments into the account and is allowed credit of a multiple of those payments.)

charity /'tʃærɪti/ *noun* an organisation which offers free help or services to those in need ○ *Because the organisation is a charity it does not have to pay taxes.* ○ *The charity owes its success to clever marketing strategies in its fund-raising.*

charity shop /'tʃærɪti ʃɒp/ *noun* a shop organised by a charity, usually paying low rent and manned by volunteer staff, selling second-hand or specially bought products

chart /tʃɑːt/ *noun* a diagram displaying information as a series of lines, blocks, etc.

charter /'tʃɑːtə/ *noun* hiring transport for a special purpose □ **boat on charter to Mr Smith** a boat which Mr Smith has hired for a voyage ■ *verb* to hire for a special purpose ○ *to charter a plane* or *a boat* or *a bus*

chartered /'tʃɑːtəd/ *adjective* □ **a chartered ship, bus, plane** a ship, bus or plane which has been hired for a special purpose

charterer /'tʃɑːtərə/ *noun* a person who hires a ship etc. for a special purpose

charter flight /'tʃɑːtə flaɪt/ *noun* a flight in an aircraft which has been hired for that purpose

chartering /'tʃɑːtərɪŋ/ *noun* the act of hiring for a special purpose

charter party /'tʃɑːtə ,pɑːti/ *noun* a contract between the owner and the charterer of a ship

charter plane /'tʃɑːtə pleɪn/ *noun* a plane which has been chartered

cheap money /tʃiːp 'mʌni/ *noun* money which can be borrowed at a low rate of interest

checkbook /'tʃekbʊk/ *noun* US spelling of **cheque book**

checklist /'tʃeklɪst/ *noun* a list of points which have to be checked before something can be regarded as finished, or as part of a procedure for evaluating something

checkout /'tʃekaʊt/ *noun* the place where goods are paid for in a shop or supermarket ○ *We have opened two more checkouts to cope with the Saturday rush.*

checkout staff /'tʃekaʊt stɑːf/ *noun* the people who work at checkouts

check sample /'tʃek ,sɑːmp(ə)l/ *noun* a sample to be used to see if a consignment is acceptable

cheque /tʃek/ *noun* a note to a bank asking them to pay money from your account to the account of the person whose name is written on the note ○ *a cheque for £10* or *a £10 cheque* (NOTE: American English is usually **check**) □

cheque to the bearer a cheque with no name written on it, so that the person who holds it can cash it □ **to endorse a cheque** to sign a cheque on the back to show that you accept it □ **to pay a cheque into your account** to deposit a cheque □ **the bank referred the cheque to the drawer** it returned the cheque to the person who wrote it because there was not enough money in the account to pay it □ **to sign a cheque** to sign on the front of a cheque to show that you authorise the bank to pay the money from your account □ **to stop a cheque** to ask a bank not to pay a cheque which has been signed and sent

cheque account /'tʃek ə,kaʊnt/ *noun* a bank account which allows the customer to write cheques

cheque book /'tʃek bʊk/ *noun* a booklet with new blank cheques (NOTE: American English is usually **checkbook**)

cheque (guarantee) card /'tʃek gærən'tiː 'kɑːd/ *noun* a plastic card from a bank which guarantees payment of a cheque up to a specific amount, even if there is no money in the account

cherry-picking /'tʃeri ,pɪkɪŋ/ *noun* **1.** going from shop to shop or from supplier to supplier, looking for special bargains ○ *Cherry-picking has become so widespread that prices may be forced down.* **2.** choosing only the best or most valuable items from among a group

churn /tʃɜːn/ *verb* **1.** to persuade an investor to change the shares in his or her portfolio frequently because the broker is paid every time the investor buys a new share **2.** to be in a situation where many employees stay for only a short time and then leave and have to be replaced **3.** to buy many different products or services one after the other without showing loyalty to any of them (NOTE: Churning often happens when companies have competitive marketing strategies and continually undercut their rivals' prices. This encourages customers to switch brands constantly in order to take advantage of cheaper or more attractive offers.)

churn rate /'tʃɜːn reɪt/ *noun* **1.** a measurement of how often new customers try a product or service and then stop using it **2.** a measurement of how many stocks and bonds are traded in a brokerage account and how often they are traded

c.i.f. *abbr* cost, insurance and freight

cinema advertising /'sɪnɪmə ,ædvətaɪzɪŋ/ *noun* advertising by short films or still messages on cinema screens

circular /'sɜːkjʊlə/ *adjective* sent to many people ■ *noun* a leaflet or letter sent to many people ○ *They sent out a circular offering a 10% discount.*

circularise /'sɜːkjʊləraɪz/, **circularize** *verb* to send a circular to ○ *The committee has agreed to circularise the members of the society.* ○ *They circularised all their customers with a new list of prices.*

circular letter /,sɜːkjʊlə 'letə/ *noun* a letter sent to many people

circular letter of credit /,sɜːkjʊlə ,letər əv 'kredɪt/ *noun* a letter of credit sent to all branches of the bank which issues it

circulate /'sɜːkjʊleɪt/ *verb* **1.** □ **to circulate freely** (*of money*) to move about without restriction by the government **2.** to send information to ○ *They circulated a new list of prices to all their customers.* ○ *They circulated information about job vacancies to all colleges in the area.*

circulation /,sɜːkjʊ'leɪʃ(ə)n/ *noun* the number of readers of a newspaper or magazine. It is audited and is not the same as 'readership'.

'…the level of currency in circulation increased to N4.9 billion in the month of August' [*Business Times (Lagos)*]

circulation battle /,sɜːkjʊ'leɪʃ(ə)n ,bæt(ə)l/ *noun* a competition between two papers to try to sell more copies in the same market

city /'sɪti/ *noun* a large town ○ *The largest cities in Europe are linked by hourly flights.*

city centre /,sɪti 'sentə/ *noun* the centre of a large town, usually where the main shops and offices are situated

CKD *abbr* Completely Knocked Down products

claim form /'kleɪm fɔːm/ *noun* a form which has to be filled in when making an insurance claim

class /klɑːs/ *noun* a category or group into which things are classified

classification /ˌklæsɪfɪ'keɪʃ(ə)n/ *noun* arrangement into classes or categories according to specific characteristics ○ *the classification of employees by ages or skills* ○ *Jobs in this organisation fall into several classifications.*

classified advertisements /ˌklæsɪfaɪd əd'vɜːtɪsmənts/ *plural noun* advertisements listed in a newspaper under special headings such as 'property for sale' or 'jobs wanted'

classified catalogue /ˌklæsɪfaɪd 'kæt(ə)lɒg/ *noun* a catalogue which groups articles into categories ○ *The classified catalogue is divided into two sections, electrical and non-electrical products.* ○ *The department store publishes a classified catalogue with a section for each department.* ○ *There is no entry for garden furniture in the classified catalogue.*

classified directory /ˌklæsɪfaɪd daɪ'rekt(ə)ri/ *noun* a list of businesses grouped under various headings such as computer shops or newsagents

classified display advertising /ˌklæsɪfaɪd dɪs'pleɪ ˌædvɜːtaɪzɪŋ/ *noun* advertising that, although it is classified, may also have individual features such as its own box border or the company logo

classify /'klæsɪfaɪ/ *verb* to put into classes or categories according to specific characteristics (NOTE: **classfies- classifying- classified**)

clause /klɔːz/ *noun* a section of a contract ○ *There are ten clauses in the contract of employment.* ○ *There is a clause in this contract concerning the employer's right to dismiss an employee.*

claused bill of lading /ˌklɔːzd bɪl əv 'leɪdɪŋ/ *noun* a bill of lading stating that goods did not arrive on board in good condition

clean /kliːn/ *adjective* straightforward or with no complications

clean acceptance /kliːn ək-'septəns/ *noun* an unconditional acceptance of a bill of lading ○ *A clean acceptance ensures a quick and uncomplicated transaction.*

clean bill of lading /ˌkliːn bɪl əv 'leɪdɪŋ/ *noun* a bill of lading with no note to say the shipment is faulty or damaged

clear /klɪə/ *verb* **1.** to sell cheaply in order to get rid of stock ○ *'Demonstration models to clear'* **2.** to obtain a slot for broadcasting an advertisement

clearance /'klɪərəns/ *noun* □ **to effect customs clearance** to clear goods through customs

clearance sale /'klɪərəns seɪl/ *noun* a sale of items at low prices to get rid of stock

clear profit /klɪə 'prɒfɪt/ *noun* profit after all expenses have been paid ○ *We made $6,000 clear profit on the deal.*

clerical error /ˌklerɪk(ə)l 'erə/ *noun* a mistake made by someone doing office work

click /klɪk/ *verb* to press a key or button on a keyboard or mouse

click rate /'klɪk reɪt/ *noun* same as **click-through rate**

clicks and bricks /ˌklɪks ən 'brɪks/ *noun* a way of doing business that combines e-commerce and traditional shops

clicks-and-mortar /ˌklɪks ən 'mɔːtə/ *adjective* conducting business both through e-commerce and also in the traditional way in buildings such as shops and warehouses (NOTE: Compare this term with bricks-and-mortar.)

'…there may be a silver lining for 'clicks-and-mortar' stores that have both an online and a high street presence. Many of these are accepting returns of goods purchased online at their traditional stores. This is a service that may make them more popular as consumers become more experienced online shoppers' [*Financial Times*]

clicks-and-mortar business /ˌklɪks ən 'mɔːtə ˌbɪznɪs/ *noun* a business that uses both e-commerce and buildings such as shops to market its products

click-through /'klɪk θruː/ *noun* an act of clicking on a banner or other on-screen advertising that takes the user through to the advertiser's website (NOTE: The number of times users click on an advertisement can be counted, and the total number of click-throughs is a way of measuring how successful the advertisement has been.)

click-through rate /'klɪk θruː reɪt/ *noun* a method of charging an advertiser for the display of a banner advertisement on a website. Each time a visitor clicks on a displayed advertisement which links to the advertiser's main site, the advertiser is charged a fee. A click-through rate of just a few percent is common and most advertisers have to pay per thousand impressions of their banner ad, sometimes written CTM (click-through per thousand). (NOTE: The click-through rate is expressed as a percentage of ad views and is used to measure how successful an advertisement has been.)

client /'klaɪənt/ *noun* a person with whom business is done or who pays for a service ○ *One of our major clients has defaulted on her payments.*

client base /'klaɪənt beɪs/ *noun* same as **client list**

clientele /ˌkliːɒn'tel/ *noun* all the clients of a business

client list /'klaɪənt lɪst/ *noun* a list of clients of an advertising agency

clip /klɪp/ *noun* a short extract from a film

clipping /'klɪpɪŋ/ *noun* a piece cut out from a publication which refers to an item of particular interest

clipping service /'klɪpɪŋ ˌsɜːvɪs/ *noun* the service of cutting out references to a client in newspapers or magazines and sending them to him

close /kləʊs/ *noun* the end of a sales negotiation ■ *verb* **1.** to bring to an end □ **to close a sale** to end a sales negotiation and persuade a buyer to make a purchase **2.** to stop doing business for the day ○ *The office closes at 5.30.* ○ *We close early on Saturdays.* **3.** □ **to close a market** to restrict a market to one agent or distributor, and refuse to allow others

to deal in the area **4.** to stop something being open

'Toronto stocks closed at an all-time high, posting their fifth straight day of advances in heavy trading' [*Financial Times*]

closed /kləʊzd/ *adjective* **1.** not open for business, or not doing business ○ *The office is closed on Mondays.* ○ *These warehouses are usually closed to the public.* **2.** restricted

closed circuit television /ˌkləʊzd sɜːkɪt teliˈvɪʒ(ə)n/ *noun* a system where TV is shown only to a small group of people within a limited area such as a building. Abbr **CCTV**

closed market /kləʊzd ˈmɑːkɪt/ *noun* a market where a supplier deals only with one agent or distributor and does not supply any others direct ○ *They signed a closed-market agreement with an Egyptian company.*

close down /ˌkləʊz ˈdaʊn/ *verb* to shut a shop, factory or service for a long period or for ever ○ *The company is closing down its London office.* ○ *The accident closed down the station for a period.*

'...the best thing would be to have a few more plants close down and bring supply more in line with current demand' [*Fortune*]

closing /'kləʊzɪŋ/ *adjective* **1.** final or coming at the end **2.** at the end of an accounting period ○ *At the end of the quarter the bookkeeper has to calculate the closing balance.* ■ *noun* □ **the closing of an account** the act of stopping supply to a customer on credit

closing bid /'kləʊzɪŋ bɪd/ *noun* the last bid at an auction, the bid which is successful

closing date /'kləʊzɪŋ deɪt/ *noun* the last date ○ *The closing date for tenders to be received is May 1st.*

closing-down sale /ˌkləʊzɪŋ ˈdaʊn ˌseɪl/ *noun* the sale of goods when a shop is closing for ever

closing price /'kləʊzɪŋ praɪs/ *noun* the price of a share at the end of a day's trading

closing sentence /'kləʊzɪŋ ˌsentəns/ *noun* the last sentence in a marketing email which pushes the customer to take action

closing stock /'kləʊzɪŋ stɒk/ *noun* the details of stock at the end of an accounting period ○ *At the end of the month the closing stock was 10% higher than at the end of the previous month.*

closing technique /'kləʊzɪŋ tek-ˌniːk/ *noun* a special technique of persuasion used by salespeople to close sales ○ *The training manager demonstrated some presentation and closing techniques.* ○ *Most of our sales force develop their own selling methods, including closing techniques.*

closing time /'kləʊzɪŋ taɪm/ *noun* the time when a shop or office stops work

closure /'kləʊʒə/ *noun* the act of closing

club /klʌb/ *noun* a group of people who have the same interest, or the place where these people meet ○ *If you want the managing director, you can phone him at his club.* ○ *She has applied to join the sports club.*

cluster /'klʌstə/ *noun* a group of things or people taken together

cluster analysis /'klʌstər əˌnæləsɪs/ *noun* a method whereby samples are classified into groups according to characteristics

cluster sampling /'klʌstə ˌsɑːmplɪŋ/ *noun* sampling on the basis of well-defined groups ○ *Cluster sampling was used in the survey since there were several very distinct groups in the population under study.*

clutter /'klʌtə/ *noun* masses of advertising units shown together, so that any single advertisement or commercial tends to get lost

code /kəʊd/ *noun* a system of signs, numbers, or letters which mean something

code of practice /ˌkəʊd əv 'præktɪs/ *noun* formally established ways in which members of a profession agree to work ○ *Advertisers have agreed to abide by the code of practice set out by the advertising council.*

coefficient of correlation /kəʊɪ-ˌfɪʃ(ə)nt əv kɒrə'leɪʃ(ə)n/ *noun* a measurement of correlation or relationship between two sets of data on a continuum from –1 to +1

cognitive dissonance /ˌkɒgnətɪv 'dɪsənəns/ *noun* the feeling of dissatisfaction experienced by a person who cannot reconcile apparently contradictory information, as when making buying decisions or comparing purchases with the claims made for them in advertising

cognitive processing /ˌkɒgnɪtɪv 'prəʊsesɪŋ/ *noun* the way in which a person changes external information into patterns of thought and how these are used to form judgments or choices

cognitive responses /ˌkɒgnɪtɪv rɪ-'spɒnsɪz/ *plural noun* thoughts that come to the mind of someone receiving a message when reading or viewing a message

COI *abbr* Central Office of Information

cold /kəʊld/ *adjective* without being prepared

'...the board is considering the introduction of a set of common provisions on unsolicited calls to investors. The board is aiming to permit the cold calling of customer agreements for the provision of services relating to listed securities. Cold calling would be allowed when the investor is not a private investor' [*Accountancy*]

cold call /kəʊld 'kɔːl/ *noun* a telephone call or sales visit where the salesperson has no appointment and the client is not an established customer

cold list /'kəʊld lɪst/ *noun* a list of names and addresses of people who have not been approached before by a seller

cold start /kəʊld 'stɑːt/ *noun* the act of beginning a new business or opening a new shop with no previous turnover to base it on

cold storage /kəʊld 'stɔːrɪdʒ/ *noun* the keeping of food in a cold store to prevent it or other goods from going bad

cold store /'kəʊld stɔː/ *noun* a warehouse or room where food can be kept cold

collateral /kə'læt(ə)rəl/ *adjective, noun* referring to security used to provide a guarantee for a loan

'...examiners have come to inspect the collateral that thrifts may use in borrowing from the Fed' [*Wall Street Journal*]

collateral services /kəˌlæt(ə)rəl ˌsɜːvɪsɪz/ *plural noun* agencies which provide specialised services such as package design, production of advertising material, or marketing research

collect /kə'lekt/ *verb* **1.** to make someone pay money which is owed □ **to collect a debt** to go and make someone pay a debt **2.** to take things away from a place ○ *We have to collect the stock from the warehouse.* ○ *Can you collect my letters from the typing pool?* □ **letters are collected twice a day** the post office workers take them from the letter box to the post office for dispatch ■ *adverb, adjective* referring to a phone call which the person receiving the call agrees to pay for

collectibles /kə'lektɪb(ə)lz/ *plural noun* items which people collect, e.g. stamps, playing cards, matchboxes

collecting agency /kə'lektɪŋ ˌeɪdʒənsɪ/ *noun* an agency which collects money owed to other companies for a commission

colour supplement /'kʌlə ˌsʌplɪmənt/ *noun* a magazine which accompanies a newspaper, usually with the weekend issue, printed in colour on art paper, and containing a lot of advertising ○ *The spring colour supplements were mostly devoted to holiday advertising.* ○ *The clothing company bought advertising space on three pages of the colour supplement.*

colour swatch /'kʌlə swɒtʃ/ *noun* a small sample of colour which the finished product must look like

colour theory /'kʌlə ˌθɪəri/ *noun* knowledge about colours and their psychological effect on prospective customers

column /'kɒləm/ *noun* a section of printed words in a newspaper or magazine

column-centimetre /ˌkɒləm 'sentɪmiːtə/ *noun* the space in centimetres in a newspaper column, used for calculating charges for advertising

combination commercial /ˌkɒmbɪ'neɪʃ(ə)n kə,mɜːʃ(ə)l/ *noun* a television advertisement which combines still pictures with action shots

combination rate /ˌkɒmbɪ'neɪʃ(ə)n reɪt/ *noun* a special rate or discount for advertising in two or more magazines

comeback /'kʌmbæk/ *noun* a means of getting compensation for a complaint or claim ○ *If you throw away the till receipt you will have no comeback if the goods turn out to be faulty.*

comfortable belongers /ˌkʌmf(ə)təb(ə)l bɪ'lɒŋəz/ *plural noun* a large group of consumers who are conservative in outlook and happy with their existence

commando selling /kə'mɑːndəʊ ˌselɪŋ/ *noun* hard intensive selling ○ *Commando selling campaigns were started in all the new markets where the company's products were virtually unknown.* ○ *Commando selling is needed to obtain a reasonable market share in a market dominated by a powerful competitor.*

commerce /'kɒmɜːs/ *noun* the buying and selling of goods and services

commerce service provider /ˌkɒmɜːs 'sɜːvɪs prəˌvaɪdə/ *noun* an organisation that provides a service that helps companies with some aspect of e-commerce, e.g., by acting as an Internet payment gateway

commercial /kə'mɜːʃ(ə)l/ *adjective* **1.** referring to business □ **'sample only – of no commercial value'** not worth anything if sold **2.** profitable □ **not a commercial proposition** not likely to make a profit ■ *noun* an advertisement on television

'…commercial radio has never had it so good – more stations, more listeners, and soaring advertising revenue' [*Marketing Week*]

commercial agent /kəˌmɜːʃ(ə)l 'eɪdʒənt/ *noun* a person or business selling a company's products or services for a commission ○ *The commercial agent earned a 30% commission on sales he made.* ○ *As a commercial agent, she represents several companies.*

commercial aircraft /kəˌmɜːʃ(ə)l 'eəkrɑːft/ *noun* an aircraft used to carry cargo or passengers for payment

commercial artist /kə,mɜːʃ(ə)l ˈɑːtɪst/ *noun* an artist who designs advertisements, posters, etc. for payment

commercial break /kə,mɜːʃ(ə)l ˈbreɪk/ *noun* the time set aside for commercials on television ○ *The advertiser wished to specify exactly when in the commercial break the advertisements were to appear.* ○ *The advertising manager placed one advertisement in each commercial break of the day on the radio channel.*

commercial college /kə'mɜːʃ(ə)l ,kɒlɪdʒ/ *noun* a college which teaches business studies

commercial counsellor /kə-,mɜːʃ(ə)l ˈkaʊns(ə)lə/ *noun* a person who advises on commercial matters in an embassy ○ *The commercial counsellor gave us sound advice on marketing in the country he represented.*

commercial course /kə'mɜːʃ(ə)l kɔːs/ *noun* a course where business skills are studied ○ *He took a commercial course by correspondence.*

commercial district /kə'mɜːʃ(ə)l ,dɪstrɪkt/ *noun* the part of a town where offices and shops are located

commercialisation /kəmɜːʃəlaɪ-ˈzeɪʃn/, **commercialization** *noun* the act of making something into a business proposition ○ *the commercialization of museums*

commercialise /kə'mɜːʃəlaɪz/, **commercialize** *verb* to make something into a business ○ *The holiday town has become unpleasantly commercialised.*

commercial law /kə,mɜːʃ(ə)l ˈlɔː/ *noun* the laws regarding business

commercial load /kə'mɜːʃ(ə)l ləʊd/ *noun* the amount of goods or number of passengers which a bus, train, or plane has to carry to make a profit

commercially /kə'mɜːʃ(ə)li/ *adverb* in a business way □ **not commercially viable** not likely to make a profit

commercial port /kə'mɜːʃ(ə)l pɔːt/ *noun* a port which has only goods traffic and no passengers

commercial protection /kə-,mɜːʃ(ə)l prə'tekʃən/ *noun* the guarantee that rival products will not be advertised directly before or after a particular advertisement

commercial radio /kə,mɜːʃ(ə)l ˈreɪdiəʊ/, **commercial TV** /kə-,mɜːʃ(ə)l tiː'viː/ *noun* a radio or TV station which broadcasts advertisements, which help to pay for its programming costs

commercial services /kə,mɜːʃ(ə)l ˈsɜːvɪsɪz/ *plural noun* services which support trade, e.g. banking and advertising ○ *The recession has affected commercial services and the industries they support and supply.*

commercial time /kə'mɜːʃ(ə)l taɪm/ *noun* the time that a television or radio station devotes to advertising ○ *The TV station is extending its commercial time in order to increase revenue.*

commercial traveller /kə,mɜːʃ(ə)l ˈtræv(ə)lə/ *noun* a salesperson who travels round an area visiting customers on behalf of his or her company (NOTE: the modern term for a commercial traveller is **sales representative**)

commercial value /kə,mɜːʃ(ə)l ˈvæljuː/ *noun* how much something is worth if it is sold

commission /kə'mɪʃ(ə)n/ *noun* money paid to a salesperson or agent, usually a percentage of the sales made ○ *She gets 10% commission on everything she sells.* □ **he charges 10% commission** he asks for 10% of sales as his payment

commission agent /kə'mɪʃ(ə)n ,eɪdʒənt/ *noun* an agent who is paid a percentage of sales

commission rebating /kə'mɪʃ(ə)n ,riːbeɪtɪŋ/ *noun* an advertising agency's discounting of invoices for media costs sent to clients, in effect taking them out of its own commission or profit margin

commission rep /kə'mɪʃ(ə)n rep/ *noun* a representative who is not paid a salary but receives a commission on sales

commitment /kə'mɪtmənt/ *noun* **1.** something which you have agreed to do ○ *The company has a commitment to provide a cheap service.* **2.** money which you have agreed to spend

commodity /kə'mɒdɪtɪ/ *noun* something sold in very large quantities, especially a raw material such as a metal and food such as wheat

commodity exchange /kə'mɒdɪti ɪks,tʃeɪndʒ/ *noun* a place where commodities are bought and sold

commodity futures /kə,mɒdɪti 'fjuːtʃəz/ *plural noun* trading in commodities for delivery at a later date ○ *Silver rose 5% on the commodity futures market yesterday.*

commodity trader /kə'mɒdɪti ,treɪdə/ *noun* a person whose business is buying and selling commodities

common /'kɒmən/ *adjective* **1.** which happens frequently ○ *Unrealistic salary expectations in younger staff was a common problem they had to deal with.* **2.** belonging to several different people or to everyone

common carrier /,kɒmən 'kæriə/ *noun* a firm which carries goods or passengers, and which anyone can use

Common Market /'kɒmən 'mɑːkɪt/ *noun* an association of nations who join together in order to remove or reduce the barriers to trade between them

common ownership /,kɒmən 'əʊnəʃɪp/ *noun* a situation where a business is owned by the people who work in it

common pricing /,kɒmən 'praɪsɪŋ/ *noun* the illegal fixing of prices by several businesses so that they all charge the same price

common stock /,kɒmən 'stɒk/ *noun* US ordinary shares in a company, giving shareholders a right to vote at meetings and to receive dividends

communication /kə,mjuːnɪ'keɪʃ(ə)n/ *noun* the passing on of views or information ○ *A house journal was started to improve communication between management and staff.* ○ *Customers complained about the lack of communication about the unexpected delay.* □ **to enter into communication with someone** to start discussing something with someone, usually in writing ○ *We have entered into communication with the relevant government department.*

communication objectives /kə,mjuːnɪ'keɪʃ(ə)n əb,dʒektɪvz/ *plural noun* objectives that a company tries to achieve through its advertising, e.g. creating awareness, knowledge, images, attitudes, preferences, or purchase intentions

communications /kə,mjuːnɪ'keɪʃ(ə)nz/ *plural noun* **1.** being able to contact people or to pass messages ○ *After the flood all communications with the outside world were broken.* **2.** systems or technologies used for sending and receiving messages, e.g. postal and telephone networks **3.** messages sent from one individual or organisation to another

communications channel /kə,mjuːnɪ'keɪʃ(ə)nz ,tʃæn(ə)l/ *noun* a means of passing messages from one individual or organisation to another (NOTE: Communications channels include the spoken, written, and printed word, and media such as radio and television, telephones, video-conferencing and electronic mail.)

communication skills /kə,mjuːnɪ'keɪʃ(ə)n skɪlz/ *plural noun* the ability to pass information to others easily and intelligibly

communications management /kə,mjuːnɪ'keɪʃ(ə)nz ,mænɪdʒmənt/ *noun* the managing of communications, so that advertising messages are sent efficiently to people who need to receive them

communications strategy /kə,mjuːnɪ'keɪʃ(ə)nz ,strætədʒi/ *noun* planning the best way of communicating with potential customers

communication task /kə,mjuːnɪ'keɪʃ(ə)n tɑːsk/ *noun* things that can be attributed to advertising, e.g. awareness, comprehension, conviction, and action, following the DAGMAR approach to setting advertising goals and objectives

communisuasion /kə,mjuːnɪ'sweɪʒ(ə)n/ *noun* US communication that is intended to persuade ○ *The sales reps are being trained in the subtleties of communisuasion.*

community /kə'mju:nɪti/ *noun* a group of people living or working in the same place

community initiative /kə,mju:nɪti ɪ'nɪʃətɪv/ *noun* a particular scheme set up by a business organisation with the aim of making a positive contribution to the life of the community by helping local people take practical action to solve their problems

community involvement /kə-,mju:nɪti ɪn'vɒlvmənt/ *noun* the contribution that business organisations make to the life of their local community in the form of community initiatives (NOTE: Community involvement developed as a result of the growing emphasis on the social responsibility of business in the 1960s and 1970s and often involves companies not only giving money to finance local projects but also sending trained staff to help set them up.)

Community legislation /kə-,mju:nɪti 'ledʒɪsleɪʃ(ə)n/ *noun* directives issued by the EU commission

Community ministers /kə-,mju:nɪti 'mɪnɪstəz/ *plural noun* the ministers of member states of the EU

company report /,kʌmp(ə)ni rɪ-'pɔːt/ *noun* a document that sets out in detail what a company has done and how well it has performed (NOTE: Companies are legally required to write annual reports and financial reports and to submit them to the authorities in the country where they are registered, but they may also produce other reports on specific subjects, for example, on the environmental or social impact of a project they are undertaking.)

comparative /kəm'pærətɪv/ *adjective* which can be compared with something else

comparative advertising /kəm-,pærətɪv 'ædvətaɪzɪŋ/ *noun* advertising which compares a company's product with competing brands to its own advantage ○ *Disparaging remarks in comparative advertising were strongly discouraged in the industry.* ○ *The company uses comparative advertising to highlight the advantages of its products.*

comparative analysis /kəm-,pærətɪv ə'næləsɪs/ *noun* an analysis of different media and vehicle options by an advertiser ○ *A tight advertising budget made a thorough comparative analysis essential.* ○ *Comparative analysis is difficult when the various media offer such different advantages.*

comparative pricing /kəm,pærətɪv 'praɪsɪŋ/ *noun* the indication of a price by comparing it with another, e.g. '15% reduction'

comparison /kəm'pærɪs(ə)n/ *noun* the act of comparing one thing with another ○ *Sales are down in comparison with last year.*

comparison-shop /kəm'pærɪs(ə)n ʃɒp/ *verb* to compare prices and features of items for sale in different shops to find the best deal

compete /kəm'piːt/ *verb* □ **to compete with someone** *or* **with a company** to try to do better than another person or another company ○ *We have to compete with cheap imports from the Far East.* ○ *They were competing unsuccessfully with local companies on their home territory.* □ **the two companies are competing for a market share** *or* **for a contract** each company is trying to win a larger part of the market, trying to win the contract

competing /kəm'piːtɪŋ/ *adjective* which competes □ **competing firms** firms which compete with each other □ **competing products** products from different companies which have the same use and are sold in the same markets at similar prices

competition /,kɒmpə'tɪʃ(ə)n/ *noun* **1.** the action of companies or individuals who are trying to do better than others, to win a larger share of the market, to control the use of resources, etc. □ **keen competition** strong competition ○ *We are facing keen competition from European manufacturers.* **2.** □ **the competition** companies which are trying to compete with your product ○ *We have lowered our prices to beat the competition.* ○ *The competition have brought out a new range of products.*

'…profit margins in the industries most exposed to foreign competition are worse than usual' [*Sunday Times*]

'…competition is steadily increasing and could affect profit margins as the company tries to retain its market share' [*Citizen (Ottawa)*]

competition-oriented pricing /kɒmpə,tɪʃ(ə)n ,ɔːrientɪd 'praɪsɪŋ/ *noun* putting low prices on goods so as to compete with other competing products

competitions /,kɒmpə'tɪʃ(ə)nz/ *plural noun* a sales promotion which enables consumers who can show that they have bought a minimum number of purchases to compete in a game ○ *The company uses competitions to sell off an excess supply of tinned food.* ○ *Competitions involve prizes ranging from washing-machines to holidays abroad.* ○ *Competitions and free gifts make up a large part of the company's sales promotions.*

competitive /kəm'petɪtɪv/ *adjective* which competes fairly □ **a competitive price** a low price aimed to compete with a rival product □ **competitive products** products made to compete with existing products

'…the company blamed fiercely competitive market conditions in Europe for a £14m operating loss last year' [*Financial Times*]

competitive advantage /kəm,petɪtɪv əd'vɑːntɪdʒ/ *noun* a factor that gives a special advantage to a nation, company, group, or individual when it is competing with others

competitive analysis /kəm,petɪtɪv ə'næləsɪs/ *noun* analysis for marketing purposes that can include industry, customer, and competitor analysis and aims to discover how competitive an organisation, project, or product is, especially by evaluating the capabilities of key competitors

competitive check /kəm,petɪtɪv 'tʃek/ *noun* analysing rival advertising levels and patterns, often conducted on the basis of data supplied by monitoring organisations

competitive demand /kəm,petɪtɪv dɪ'mɑːnd/ *noun* demand for products that are competing for sales

competitive edge /kəm,petɪtɪv 'edʒ/, **competitive advantage** /kəm,petɪtɪv əd'vɑːntɪdʒ/ *noun* an advantage that one company or product has over its rivals in the market ○ *Any competitive edge we have in this market is due to our good after-sales service.* ○ *Why does this product have the competitive edge over its rivals?*

competitive forces /kəm,petɪtɪv 'fɔːsɪz/ *plural noun* economic and business factors that force an organisation to become more competitive if wants to survive and succeed

competitive intelligence /kəm,petɪtɪv ɪn'telɪdʒəns/ *noun* information, especially information concerning the plans, activities, and products of its competitors, that an organisation gathers and analyses in order to make itself more competitive (NOTE: Competitive intelligence may sometimes be gained through industrial espionage.)

competitively /kəm'petɪtɪvli/ *adverb* □ **competitively priced** sold at a low price which competes with the price of similar products from other companies

competitiveness /kəm'petɪtɪvnəs/ *noun* being competitive

'…farmers are increasingly worried by the growing lack of competitiveness for their products on world markets' [*Australian Financial Review*]

competitiveness index /kəm-'petɪtɪvnəs ,ɪndeks/ *noun* a list of countries ranked in order of their competitive performance

competitive parity /kəm,petɪtɪv 'pærɪti/ *noun* a method of budgeting marketing or promotional expenses according to the amounts being spent by competitors

competitive pricing /kəm,petɪtɪv 'praɪsɪŋ/ *noun* putting low prices on goods so as to compete with other products

competitive separation /kəm,petɪtɪv sepə'reɪʃ(ə)n/ *noun* a guarantee that rival products will not be advertised directly before or after a particular advertisement ○ *If our advertising campaign is to be really effective, we must insist on competitive separation.*

competitor /kəm'petɪtə/ *noun* a person or company which competes ○ *Two German firms are our main competitors.*

'…sterling labour costs continue to rise between 3% and 5% a year faster than in most of our competitor countries' [*Sunday Times*]

competitor analysis /kəm,petɪtə ə'næləsɪs/ *noun* the process of analysing information about competitors and their products in order to build up a picture of where their strengths and weaknesses lie

competitor profiling /kəm,petɪtə 'prəʊfaɪlɪŋ/ *noun* same as **competitor analysis**

complaint /kəm'pleɪnt/ *noun* a statement that you feel something is wrong ○ *complaints from the workforce about conditions in the factory* ○ *When making a complaint, always quote the reference number.* ○ *She sent her letter of complaint to the managing director.*

complaints department /kəm-'pleɪnts dɪ,pɑːtmənt/ *noun* a department in a company or store to which customers can send or bring complaints about its products or service

complaints management /kəm-'pleɪnts ,mænɪdʒmənt/ *noun* the management of complaints from customers

complementary /,kɒmplɪ-'ment(ə)ri/ *adjective* which adds to or completes something else

complementary demand /,kɒmplɪment(ə)ri dɪ'mɑːnd/ *noun* demand for two or more products that are needed together ○ *The demand for cars and petrol was an example of complementary demand.*

complementary product /,kɒmplɪment(ə)ri 'prɒdʌkt/ *noun* a product for which demand is dependent on the demand for another product ○ *When demand for our product fell, producers of complementary products also suffered.*

complementary supply /,kɒmplɪment(ə)ri sə'plaɪ/ *noun* the supply of two or more products from the same production process

complementor /'kɒmplɪmentə/ *noun* a company that makes something that your product needs in or-

der to function successfully (NOTE: Software companies, for example, are complementors to computer companies.)

Completely Knocked Down products /kəm,pliːtli nɒkt daʊn 'praɪsɪz/ *plural noun* products which are sold in pieces, which the purchaser has to assemble, and are therefore sold at reasonably low prices ○ *Many low-income buyers buy CKD products.* ○ *CKD products are popular with DIY enthusiasts.* Abbr **CKD products**

compliance documentation /kəm'plaɪəns dɒkjumen'teɪʃ(ə)n/ *noun* documents that a company has to publish when it issues shares in order to comply with the regulations governing share issues

compliance officer /kəm'plaɪəns ,ɒfɪsə/ *noun* an employee of a financial organisation whose job is to make sure that the organisation complies with the regulations governing its business

complimentary /,kɒmplɪ'ment(ə)ri/ *adjective* free

complimentary ticket /,kɒmplɪment(ə)ri 'tɪkɪt/ *noun* a free ticket, given as a present

compliments slip /'kɒmplɪmənts slɪp/ *noun* a piece of paper with the name of the company printed on it, sent with documents or gifts etc. instead of a letter

component /kəm'pəʊnənt/ *noun* a piece of machinery or a part which will be put into a final product ○ *The assembly line stopped because the supply of a vital component was delayed.*

components factory /kəm-'pəʊnənts ,fækt(ə)ri/ *noun* a factory which makes parts which are used in other factories to make finished products

composite demand /'kɒmpəzɪt dɪ-,mɑːnd/ *noun* the total demand for a product that has many uses ○ *Composite demand for the construction equipment came from construction companies and DIY enthusiasts.*

computer /kəm'pjuːtə/ *noun* an electronic machine which calculates or

stores information and processes it automatically

computer bureau /kəm'pjuːtə ˌbjʊərəʊ/ *noun* an office which offers to do work on its computers for companies which do not own their own computers

computer department /kəm'pjuːtə dɪˌpɑːtmənt/ *noun* a department in a company which manages the company's computers

computer error /kəmˌpjuːtər 'erə/ *noun* a mistake made by a computer

computer file /kəm'pjuːtə faɪl/ *noun* a section of information on a computer, e.g. the payroll, list of addresses, or customer accounts

computer hardware /kəmˌpjuːtə 'hɑːdweə/ *noun* machines used in data processing, including the computers and printers, but not the programs

computerise /kəm'pjuːtəraɪz/, **computerize** *verb* to change from a manual system to one using computers ○ *We have computerised all our records.* ○ *Stock control is now completely computerised.*

computerised /kəm'pjuːtəraɪzd/, **computerized** *adjective* worked by computers ○ *a computerised invoicing system* ○ *a computerised filing system*

computer language /kəm'pjuːtə ˌlæŋgwɪdʒ/ *noun* a system of signs, letters and words used to instruct a computer

computer listing /kəmˌpjuːtə 'lɪstɪŋ/ *noun* a printout of a list of items taken from data stored in a computer

computer magazine /kəm'pjuːtə mægəˌziːn/ *noun* a magazine with articles on computers and programs

computer manager /kəm'pjuːtə ˌmænɪdʒə/ *noun* a person in charge of a computer department

computer network /kəmˌpjuːtə 'netwɜːk/ *noun* a computer system where several PCs are linked so that they all draw on the same database

computer-readable /kəmˌpjuːtə 'riːdəb(ə)l/ *adjective* which can be read and understood by a computer ○ *computer-readable codes*

computer run /kəm'pjuːtə rʌn/ *noun* a period of work done by a computer

computer services /kəm'pjuːtə ˌsɜːvɪsɪz/ *plural noun* work using a computer, done by a computer bureau

computer system /kəm'pjuːtə ˌsɪstəm/ *noun* a set of programs, commands, etc. which run a computer

computer telephony integration /kəmˌpjuːtə təˈlefəni ˌɪntɪ'greɪʃ(ə)n/ *noun* a technology that links computers and telephones and enables computers to dial telephone numbers and send and receive messages (NOTE: One product of computer telephony integration is calling line identification, which identifies the telephone number a customer is calling from, searches the customer database to identify the caller, and displays his or her account on a computer screen.)

computer time /kəm'pjuːtə taɪm/ *noun* the time when a computer is being used, paid for at an hourly rate

computing /kəm'pjuːtɪŋ/ *noun* the operating of computers

computing speed /kəm'pjuːtɪŋ spiːd/ *noun* the speed at which a computer calculates

concentrated marketing /ˌkɒnsəntreɪtɪd 'mɑːkətɪŋ/, **concentrated segmentation** /ˌkɒnsəntreɪtɪd ˌsegmən'teɪʃ(ə)n/ *noun* niche marketing, the promotion of a product aimed at one particular area of the market ○ *When it became obvious that the general public were interested in our product, we switched from concentrated marketing to a much broader approach.* ♦ differentiated marketing strategy, undifferentiated product

concentration /ˌkɒnsən'treɪʃ(ə)n/ *noun* the degree to which a small number of businesses control a large section of the market ○ *Too much concentration created resentment among small businesses trying to enter the market.* ○ *Concentration has meant too little competition and therefore higher prices to the consumer.*

concept /'kɒnsept/ *noun* an idea

concept testing /'kɒnsept ˌtestɪŋ/ *noun* the evaluation of a new product idea, usually by consulting representatives from all the main departments in a company, and/or by interviewing a sample of consumers ○ *The new product idea did not survive concept testing because it didn't answer an existing demand.* ○ *After thorough concept testing the idea of a disposable pen was rejected as the company's production capacity was too limited.*

concession /kən'seʃ(ə)n/ *noun* **1.** the right to use someone else's property for business purposes **2.** the right to be the only seller of a product in a place ○ *She runs a jewellery concession in a department store.* **3.** allowing something to be done, which is not normally done ○ *The union obtained some important concessions from management during negotiations.*

concessionaire /kən,seʃə'neə/ *noun* a person or business that has the right to be the only seller of a product in a place

concession close /kən'seʃ(ə)n kləʊz/ *noun* the act of offering a concession to a potential buyer in order to close a sale ○ *The trainee sales reps were told to resort to concession closes only when meeting with strong sales resistance.* ○ *A full morning's bargaining finally ended with a concession close.*

condition /kən'dɪʃ(ə)n/ *noun* something which has to be carried out as part of a contract or which has to be agreed before a contract becomes valid □ **on condition that** provided that ○ *They were granted the lease on condition that they paid the legal costs.*

conditional /kən'dɪʃ(ə)n(ə)l/ *adjective* provided that specific conditions are taken into account □ **to give a conditional acceptance** to accept, provided that specific things happen or that specific terms apply □ **the offer is conditional on the board's acceptance** the offer is only valid provided the board accepts

conditional offer /kən,dɪʃ(ə)nəl 'ɒfə/ *noun* an offer to buy, provided that specific terms apply

conditions of sale /kən,dɪʃ(ə)nz əv 'seɪl/ *plural noun* agreed ways in which a sale takes place, e.g. discounts or credit terms

conference /'kɒnf(ə)rəns/ *noun* a meeting of people to discuss problems ○ *Many useful tips can be picked up at a sales conference.* ○ *The conference of HR managers included talks on payment and recruitment policies.* □ **to be in conference** to be in a meeting

conference call /'kɒnf(ə)rəns kɔːl/ *noun* a telephone call that connects three or more lines so that people in different places can talk to one another (NOTE: Conference calls reduce the cost of meetings by making it unnecessary for the participants to spend time and money on getting together in one place.)

confidence /'kɒnfɪd(ə)ns/ *noun* the state of feeling sure or being certain ○ *The sales teams do not have much confidence in their manager.* ○ *The board has total confidence in the managing director.*

confidence level /'kɒnfɪd(ə)ns ˌlev(ə)l/ *noun* a measurement, shown as a percentage, of how reliable or accurate the results of a survey can be expected to be

confidentiality agreement /ˌkɒnfɪdenʃi'æliti əˌɡriːmənt/ *noun* an agreement in which an organisation that has important information about the plans and activities of another organisation promises not to pass that information on to outsiders (NOTE: Confidentiality agreements are often used when someone is planning to buy a company and is given access to confidential information and in partnerships and benchmarking programmes.)

confirm /kən'fɜːm/ *verb* to say that something is certain ○ *to confirm a hotel reservation* or *a ticket* or *an agreement* or *a booking* □ **to confirm someone in a job** to say that someone is now permanently in the job

confirmation /ˌkɒnfə'meɪʃ(ə)n/ *noun* **1.** the act of making certain □ **confirmation of a booking** the act of

checking that a booking is certain **2.** a document which confirms something ○ *She received confirmation from the bank that the deeds had been deposited.*

confirmed credit /kən,fɜːmd 'kredɪt/ *noun* credit that is official and binding

confirming house /kənˈfɜːmɪŋ haʊs/ *noun* an organisation that confirms a buyer's order with a supplier and makes transport arrangements ○ *A reputable confirming house acted for the buyers of the machinery.* ○ *We will need a confirming house to arrange for a new supply of office furniture to be delivered to our shop by December.*

conflict of interest /,kɒnflɪkt əv 'ɪntrəst/ *noun* a situation where a person or firm may profit personally from decisions taken in an official capacity

conglomerate /kənˈglɒmərət/ *noun* a group of subsidiary companies linked together and forming a group, each making very different types of products

conjoint analysis /kən,dʒɔɪnt əˈnæləsɪs/ *noun* a research method aimed at discovering the best combination of features for a product or service, e.g. price and size

connectivity /,kɒnekˈtɪvɪti/ *noun* the ability of an electronic product to connect with other similar products, or the extent to which individuals, companies and countries can connect with one another electronically

consign /kənˈsaɪn/ *verb* □ **to consign goods to someone** to send goods to someone for them to use or to sell for you

consignation /,kɒnsaɪˈneɪʃ(ə)n/ *noun* the act of consigning

consignee /,kɒnsaɪˈniː/ *noun* a person who receives goods from someone for their own use or to sell for the sender

consignment /kənˈsaɪnmənt/ *noun* the sending of goods to someone who will sell them for you □ **goods on consignment** goods kept for another company to be sold on their behalf for a commission

'…some of the most prominent stores are gradually moving away from the traditional consignment system, under which

manufacturers agree to repurchase any unsold goods, and in return dictate prices and sales strategies and even dispatch staff to sell the products' [*Nikkei Weekly*]

consignment note /kənˈsaɪnmənt nəʊt/ *noun* a note saying that goods have been sent

consignor /kənˈsaɪnə/ *noun* a person who consigns goods to someone

consolidate /kənˈsɒlɪdeɪt/ *verb* **1.** to include the accounts of several subsidiary companies as well as the holding company in a single set of accounts **2.** to group goods together for shipping

consolidated profit and loss account /kən,sɒlɪdeɪtɪd ,prɒfɪt ən 'lɒs ə,kaʊnt/ *noun* profit and loss accounts of the holding company and its subsidiary companies, grouped together into a single profit and loss account (NOTE: American English is **profit and loss statement** or **income statement**)

consolidated shipment /kən-,sɒlɪdeɪtɪd 'ʃɪpmənt/ *noun* goods from different companies grouped together into a single shipment

consolidation /kən,sɒlɪˈdeɪʃ(ə)n/ *noun* the grouping together of goods for shipping

consolidator /kənˈsɒlɪdeɪtə/ *noun* a firm which groups together orders from different companies into one shipment

consortium /kənˈsɔːtiəm/ *noun* a group of companies which work together ○ *A consortium of Canadian companies* or *a Canadian consortium has tendered for the job.* (NOTE: plural is **consortia**)

'…the consortium was one of only four bidders for the £2 billion contract to run the lines, seen as potentially the most difficult contract because of the need for huge investment' [*Times*]

conspicuous consumption /kən-,spɪkjuəs kənˈsʌmpʃən/ *noun* the consumption of goods for show or to get approval, rather than because they are useful. ◊ **consumption**

consult /kənˈsʌlt/ *verb* to ask an expert for advice ○ *We consulted our accountant about our tax.*

consultancy /kənˈsʌltənsi/ *noun* the act of giving specialist advice ○ *a consultancy firm* ○ *he offers a consultancy service*

consultant /kən'sʌltənt/ *noun* a specialist who gives advice ○ *an engineering consultant* ○ *a management consultant* ○ *a tax consultant*

consulting /kən'sʌltɪŋ/ *adjective* giving specialist advice ○ *a consulting engineer*

consumable goods/ kən-ˌsjuːməb(ə)l 'gʊdz/, **consumables** /kən'sjuːməb(ə)lz/ *plural noun* goods which are bought by members of the public and not by companies

consumer /kən'sjuːmə/ *noun* a person or company which buys and uses goods and services ○ *Gas consumers are protesting at the increase in prices.* ○ *The factory is a heavy consumer of water.*

'...forecasting consumer response is one problem which will never be finally solved' [*Marketing Week*]

'...consumer tastes in the UK are becoming much more varied' [*Marketing*]

'...the marketing director's brief will be to develop the holiday villages as a consumer brand, aimed at the upper end of the tourist market' [*Marketing Week*]

consumer advertising /kən-'sjuːmə ˌædvɜːtaɪzɪŋ/ *noun* advertising direct to individual consumers, as opposed to businesses

consumer cooperative /kən-ˌsjuːmə kəʊ'ɒp(ə)rətɪv/ *noun* a retailing business owned by consumers who share in its profits

consumer council /kən,sjuːmə 'kaʊns(ə)l/ *noun* a group representing the interests of consumers

consumer credit /kən,sjuːmə 'kredɪt/ *noun* the credit given by shops, banks and other financial institutions to consumers so that they can buy goods (NOTE: Lenders have to be licensed under the Consumer Credit Act, 1974.)

Consumer Credit Act, 1974 /kən-ˌsjuːmə 'kredɪt ækt/ *noun* an Act of Parliament which licenses lenders, and requires them to state clearly the full terms of loans which they make, including the APR

consumer durables /kən,sjuːmə 'djʊərəb(ə)lz/ *plural noun* items which are bought and used by the public, e.g. washing machines, refrigerators, or cookers

consumerism /kən'sjuːmərɪzm/ *noun* the activities concerned with protecting the rights and interests of consumers

consumer list /kən'sjuːmə lɪst/ *noun* a list of individuals who can be mailed with details of a product or service, e.g. from the electoral register

consumer magazine /kən'sjuːmə mægəˌziːn/ *noun* a magazine published for consumers, giving details of product tests, special legal problems regarding services offered, etc.

consumer mailing list /kən-ˌsjuːmə 'meɪlɪŋ lɪst/ *noun* same as **consumer list**

consumer market /kən'sjuːmə ˌmɑːkɪt/ *noun* the customers who buy consumer goods ○ *There is a growing consumer market for construction materials owing to the increased popularity of DIY.* ○ *Both consumer markets and industrial markets have been affected by the recession.*

consumer panel /kən'sjuːmə ˌpæn(ə)l/ *noun* a group of consumers who report on products they have used so that the manufacturers can improve them or use what the panel says about them in advertising

Consumer Price Index /kən-ˌsjuːmə 'praɪs ˌɪndeks/ *noun* an American index showing how prices of consumer goods have risen over a period of time, used as a way of measuring inflation and the cost of living (NOTE: The British equivalent is the Retail Prices Index or RPI.)

'...analysis of the consumer price index for the first half of the year shows that the rate of inflation went down by about 12.9 per cent' [*Business Times (Lagos)*]

consumer profile /kən,sjuːmə 'prəʊfaɪl/ *noun* a description of the relevant details of the average customer for a product or service

Consumer Protection Act, 1987 /kən,sjuːmə prə'tekʃən ækt/ *noun* an Act of Parliament which bans the use of misleading information given to potential purchasers to encourage them to buy

consumer research /kən,sjuːmə rɪˈsɜːtʃ/ *noun* research into why consumers buy goods and what goods they may want to buy

consumer resistance /kən,sjuːmə rɪˈzɪstəns/ *noun* a lack of interest by consumers in buying a new product ○ *The new product met no consumer resistance even though the price was high.*

Consumers Association /kənˈsjuːməz əsəʊsi,eiʃ(ə)n/ *noun* an independent organisation which protects consumers and represents their interests, and reports on the quality of products and services in its regular magazine. Abbr **CA**

consumer society /kən,sjuːmə səˈsaɪəti/ *noun* a type of society where consumers are encouraged to buy goods

consumer sovereignty /kən,sjuːmə ˈsɒvrɪnti/ *noun* the power of consumers to influence trends in production and marketing

consumer spending /kən,sjuːmə ˈspendɪŋ/ *noun* spending by private households on goods and services

'...companies selling in the UK market are worried about reduced consumer spending as a consequence of higher interest rates and inflation' [*Business*]

consumer's surplus /kən,sjuːməz ˈsɜːpləs/ *noun* the difference between what a consumer is willing to pay for something and what he or she actually does pay for it ○ *When the brand manager realised how big the consumer's surplus was she decided to raise the price of the product.*

consumer survey /kən,sjuːmə ˈsɜːveɪ/ *noun* a survey of existing and potential demand for a product

consumer-to-consumer commerce /kən,sjuːmə tə kənˈsjuːmə ˌkɒmɜːs/ *noun* business, especially e-business, done by one individual with another and not involving any business organisation

consumption /kənˈsʌmpʃən/ *noun* the act of buying or using goods or services ○ *a car with low petrol consumption* ○ *The factory has a heavy consumption of coal.*

contain /kənˈteɪn/ *verb* to hold something inside ○ *a barrel contains 250 litres* ○ *Each crate contains two computers and their peripherals.* ○ *We have lost a file containing important documents.*

container /kənˈteɪnə/ *noun* **1.** a box, bottle, can, etc. which can hold goods ○ *The gas is shipped in strong metal containers.* ○ *The container burst during shipping.* **2.** a very large metal case of a standard size for loading and transporting goods on trucks, trains, and ships ○ *to ship goods in containers* □ **a container-load of spare parts** a shipment of spare parts sent in a container

containerisation /kən,teɪnəraɪˈzeɪʃ(ə)n/, **containerization** *noun* the act of shipping goods in containers

containerise /kənˈteɪnəraɪz/, **containerize** *verb* to put or ship goods in containers

content /ˈkɒntent/ *noun* the text, illustrations and graphics of a piece of publicity

content management /ˈkɒntent ˌmænɪdʒmənt/ *noun* the management of the textual and graphical material contained on a website (NOTE: Owners of large sites with thousands of pages often invest in a content management application system to help with the creation and organisation of the content of these sites.)

contest /ˈkɒntest/ *noun* a type of promotion where prizes are given to people who give the right answers to a series of questions

contested takeover /kən,testɪd ˈteɪkəʊvə/ *noun* a takeover bid where the board of the target company does not recommend it to the shareholders and tries to fight it (NOTE: also called a **hostile bid**)

contingency plan /kənˈtɪndʒənsi plæn/ *noun* a plan which will be put into action if something happens which no one expects to happen

contingent liability /kən,tɪndʒənt laɪəˈbɪlɪti/ *noun* a liability which may or may not occur, but for which provision is made in a company's accounts, as opposed to 'provisions', where

money is set aside for an anticipated expenditure

continuity /ˌkɒntɪˈnjuːɪti/ noun the act of maintaining a continuous stable level of advertising activity ○ *Continuity must be the watchword of this promotional campaign to keep the product firmly in the minds of the target audience.* ○ *Shall we aim for a sudden short blast of advertising or should continuity be the essence of our strategy?*

continuity programme /ˌkɒntɪˈnjuːɪti ˌprəʊɡræm/ noun a marketing programme which offers a series of products which are sent to customers at regular intervals

continuous /kənˈtɪnjuəs/ adjective with no end or with no breaks ○ *a continuous production line*

continuous process production /kənˌtɪnjuəs ˈprəʊses prəˌdʌkʃən/ noun automated production of many identical products

continuous research /kənˌtɪnjuəs rɪˈsɜːtʃ/ noun regular ongoing market research ○ *Continuous research will tell us if sales are dropping off.*

contra /ˈkɒntrə/ verb □ **to contra an entry** to enter a similar amount in the opposite side of an account

contra account /ˈkɒntrə əˌkaʊnt/ noun an account which offsets another account, e.g. where a company's supplier is not only a creditor in that company's books but also a debtor because it has purchased goods on credit

contraband /ˈkɒntrəbænd/ noun goods brought into a country illegally, without paying customs duty

contract noun /ˈkɒntrækt/ **1.** a legal agreement between two parties ○ *to draw up a contract* ○ *to draft a contract* ○ *to sign a contract* □ **the contract is binding on both parties** both parties signing the contract must do what is agreed □ **under contract** bound by the terms of a contract ○ *The firm is under contract to deliver the goods by November.* □ **to void a contract** to make a contract invalid **2.** □ **by private contract** by private legal agreement **3.** an agreement for the supply of a service or goods ○ *a contract for the supply of*

spare parts ○ *to enter into a contract to supply spare parts* ○ *to sign a contract for £10,000 worth of spare parts* □ **to put work out to contract** to decide that work should be done by another company on a contract, rather than by employing members of staff to do it □ **to award a contract to a company** *or* **to place a contract with a company** to decide that a company shall have the contract to do work for you □ **to tender for a contract** to put forward an estimate of cost for work under contract ■ verb /kənˈtrækt/ to agree to do some work on the basis of a legally binding contract ○ *to contract to supply spare parts* or *to contract for the supply of spare parts* □ **the supply of spare parts was contracted out to Smith Ltd** Smith Ltd was given the contract for supplying spare parts □ **to contract out of an agreement** to withdraw from an agreement with the written permission of the other party

contract carrier /ˈkɒntrækt ˌkæriə/ noun a carrier or transportation company which has special contracts with businesses ○ *a contract carrier which ships coffee beans from Brazil to coffee wholesalers in Britain*

contract hire /ˈkɒntrækt haɪə/ noun a system that allows organisations to hire equipment that they need to use for a long period, e.g. cars or office machines, from other organisations instead of buying it, on condition that they sign a contract for the hire with owners (NOTE: Contract hire agreements often include arrangements for maintenance and replacement.)

contracting company /kənˌtræktɪŋ ˈkʌmp(ə)ni/ noun an independent broadcasting company that sells advertising time ○ *With two new contracting companies being set up this year, advertisers will have more choice.*

contracting party /kənˌtræktɪŋ ˈpɑːti/ noun a person or company that signs a contract

contract manufacturing /ˌkɒntrækt mænjʊˈfæktʃərɪŋ/ noun an agreement which allows an overseas manufacturer to manufacture or assemble your products in that country for sale

there ○ *Under a contract manufacturing agreement a local company is making our cars in France.*

contract note /'kɒntrækt nəʊt/ *noun* a note showing that shares have been bought or sold but not yet paid for, also including the commission

contractor /kən'træktə/ *noun* a person or company that does work according to a written agreement

contractual /kən'træktʃuəl/ *adjective* according to a contract □ **to fulfil your contractual obligations** to do what you have agreed to do in a contract

contractual liability /kən-ˌtræktʃuəl ˌlaɪə'bɪlɪti/ *noun* a legal responsibility for something as stated in a contract

contractually /kən'træktjuəli/ *adverb* according to a contract ○ *The company is contractually bound to pay our expenses.*

contractual obligation /kən-ˌtræktʃuəl ɒblɪ'geɪʃ(ə)n/ *noun* he has signed no agreement to buy

contract work /'kɒntrækt wɜːk/ *noun* work done according to a written agreement

contra deal /'kɒntrə ˌdiːl/ *noun* a deal between two businesses to exchange goods and services

contra entry /'kɒntrə ˌentri/ *noun* an entry made in the opposite side of an account to make an earlier entry worthless, i.e. a debit against a credit

contribute /kən'trɪbjuːt/ *verb* to give money or add to money ○ *We agreed to contribute 10% of the profits.* ○ *They had contributed to the pension fund for 10 years.*

contribution /ˌkɒntrɪ'bjuːʃ(ə)n/ *noun* something that is contributed

contribution analysis /ˌkɒntrɪ-'bjuːʃ(ə)n əˌnæləsɪs/ *noun* analysis of how much each of a company's products contributes to fixed costs, based on its profit margin and sales ○ *Contribution analysis helps to streamline production and marketing.* ○ *Thorough contribution analysis led to six products being dropped from the product range.*

contribution margin /ˌkɒntrɪ-'bjuːʃ(ə)n ˌmɑːdʒɪn/ *noun* the difference between the revenue generated by a product and its total variable costs

contribution of capital /kɒntrɪ-ˌbjuːʃ(ə)n əv 'kæpɪt(ə)l/ *noun* money paid to a company as additional capital

contribution pricing /ˌkɒntrɪ-'bjuːʃ(ə)n ˌpraɪsɪŋ/ *noun* a pricing method based on maximising the contribution of each product to fixed costs

contributor /kən'trɪbjʊtə/ *noun* a person who gives money □ **contributor of capital** person who contributes capital

control /kən'trəʊl/ *noun* **1.** the power or ability to direct something ○ *The company is under the control of three shareholders.* □ **to lose control of a business** to find that you have less than 50% of the shares in a company, and so are not longer able to direct it ○ *The family lost control of its business.* **2.** restricting or checking something or making sure that something is kept in check □ **under control** kept in check ○ *Expenses are kept under tight control.* ○ *The company is trying to bring its overheads back under control.* □ **out of control** not kept in check ○ *Costs have got out of control.* ■ *verb* **1.** □ **to control a business** to direct a business ○ *The business is controlled by a company based in Luxembourg.* ○ *The company is controlled by the majority shareholder.* **2.** to make sure that something is kept in check or is not allowed to develop ○ *The government is fighting to control inflation* or *to control the rise in the cost of living.* (NOTE: **controlling – controlled**)

control group /kən'trəʊl gruːp/ *noun* a small group which is used to check a sample group

controllable /kən'trəʊləb(ə)l/ *adjective* which can be controlled

controllable variables /kən-ˌtrəʊləb(ə)l 'veəriəb(ə)lz/ *plural noun* factors that can be controlled, e.g. a company's marketing mix ○ *Because there were so few controllable variables the outcome of the marketing plan was very uncertain.*

controlled /kən'trəʊld/ *adjective* ruled or kept in check

controlled circulation /kən,trəʊld sɜːkjʊ'leɪʃ(ə)n/ *noun* distribution of a publication to a specialist readership who are members of a particular organisation or profession (often a free controlled circulation, where the magazine is distributed free to key executives, and is paid for by the advertisers) ○ *The professional institute publishes a quarterly magazine with a controlled circulation.* ○ *The newspaper has a controlled circulation and is suitable for advertisements for highly specialised products.*

controlled circulation magazine /kən,trəʊld sɜːkjʊ,leɪʃ(ə)n mægə-'ziːn/ *noun* a magazine which is sent free to a limited number of readers, and is paid for by the advertising it contains

controlled economy /kən,trəʊld ɪ'kɒnəmi/ *noun* an economy where most business activity is directed by orders from the government

control question /kən'trəʊl ,kwestʃən/ *noun* a question in a questionnaire designed to check that answers are consistent ○ *A control question was included to check that respondents were not lying about their age.* ○ *If control questions show that answers are not honest, the interview is ended.*

control systems /kən'trəʊl ,sɪstəmz/ *plural noun* the systems used to check that a computer system is working correctly

convenience /kən'viːniəns/ *noun* □ **at your earliest convenience** as soon as you find it possible

convenience food /kən'viːniəns fuːd/ *noun* food which is prepared by the shop before it is sold, so that it needs only heating to be made ready to eat

convenience goods /kən'viːniəns gʊdz/ *plural noun* ordinary everyday products that people have to buy but which command little or no brand loyalty ○ *Price competition is very fierce in the convenience goods market.*

convenience store /kən'viːniəns stɔː/ *noun* a small store selling food or household goods, open until late at night, or even 24 hours per day

'…the nation's largest convenience store chain has expanded the range of bills it takes payments for to include gas and telephone services' [*Nikkei Weekly*]

convenient /kən'viːniənt/ *adjective* suitable or handy ○ *A bank draft is a convenient way of sending money abroad.* ○ *Is 9.30 a convenient time for the meeting?*

conversion /kən'vɜːʃ(ə)n/ *noun* the action of converting a prospective customer into an actual purchaser

conversion rate /kən'vɜːʃ(ə)n reɪt/ *noun* the proportion of contacts, by mailing, advertising or email marketing, who actually end up purchasing the product or service

convertible currency /kən-,vɜːtəb(ə)l 'kʌrənsi/ *noun* a currency which can easily be exchanged for another

cooling-off laws /,kuːlɪŋ 'ɒf lɔːz/ *plural noun* US state laws allowing cancellation of an order within a specific period after signing an agreement ○ *Cooling-off laws are making buyers less hesitant about placing large orders.*

cooling-off period /,kuːlɪŋ ,ɒf ,piːriəd/ *noun* **1.** during an industrial dispute, a period when negotiations have to be carried on and no action can be taken by either side **2.** a period when a person is allowed to think about something which they have agreed to buy on hire purchase and possibly change their mind ○ *New York has a three day cooling-off period for telephone sales.* **3.** a period of ten days during which a person who has signed a life assurance policy may cancel it

co-op /'kəʊ ɒp/ *noun* same as **cooperative**

co-operate /kəʊ'ɒpəreɪt/ *verb* to work together ○ *The regional governments are co-operating in the fight against piracy.* ○ *The two firms have co-operated on the computer project.*

co-operation /kəʊ,ɒpə'reɪʃ(ə)n/ *noun* the act of working together ○ *The project was completed ahead of schedule with the co-operation of the workforce.*

cooperative /kəʊˈɒp(ə)rətɪv/ *adjective* willing to work together ○ *The workforce has not been cooperative over the management's productivity plan.* ■ *noun* **1.** a business run by a group of employees who are also the owners and who share the profits ○ *The product is marketed by an agricultural cooperative.* ○ *They set up a workers' cooperative to run the factory.* **2.** a business which organises cooperative mailing or advertising for different companies

cooperative advertising /kəʊ-ˌɒp(ə)rətɪv ˈædvəˌtaɪzɪŋ/ *noun* **1.** the sharing by two companies, often a producer and a distributor, of advertising costs ○ *A cooperative advertising agreement means that two companies can enjoy quantity discounts offered by the media.* **2.** mailing advertising material from different companies in the same mailing pack

cooperative marketing /kəʊ-ˌɒp(ə)rətɪv ˈmɑːkɪtɪŋ/ *noun* an arrangement whereby various producers cooperate in the marketing of their products or services ○ *Cooperative marketing proved an economic method of selling for companies with few financial resources.*

cooperative movement /kəʊ-ˈɒp(ə)rətɪv ˌmuːvmənt/ *noun* a movement that encourages the setting-up of cooperative businesses that are jointly owned by their members who share the profits and benefits they gain from trading amongst themselves (NOTE: The movement was founded in Rochdale, Lancashire in 1844 by 28 weavers and, in Britain, has launched not only a chain of shops, but also manufacturing and wholesale businesses as well as insurance and financial services.)

co-opetition /kəʊˌɒpəˈtɪʃ(ə)n/ *noun* cooperation between competing companies

copier /ˈkɒpɪə/ *noun* a machine which makes copies of documents (NOTE: also called **copying machine, photocopier**)

copy /ˈkɒpɪ/ *verb* to make a second document which is like the first ○ *He*

copied the company report and took it home. (NOTE: **copies- copying- copied**)

copy brief /ˈkɒpɪ briːf/ *noun* the instructions from an advertiser to a copywriter explaining the objectives of an advertising campaign ○ *The copy brief made it clear that the advertisements were to be aimed at young people.* ○ *The advertisers blamed the agency for not paying enough attention to the copy brief.*

copy clearance /ˈkɒpɪ ˌklɪərəns/ *noun* the passing of an advertiser's copy as neither misleading nor offensive ○ *It is doubtful the advertisement will get copy clearance since it directly disparages the competition.* ○ *The advertisement has received copy clearance because all its claims can be substantiated.* ○ *You will not get copy clearance for this ad because the caption is sure to offend a lot of women readers.*

copy date /ˈkɒpɪ deɪt/ *noun* the date by which an advertisement must be delivered to the media concerned ○ *The creative teams are working flat out because the copy date is only one week away.* ○ *Let's work on the advertisements with the earliest copy dates.*

copy fitting /ˈkɒpɪ ˌfɪtɪŋ/ *noun* the arrangement of advertising text so it fits the space allowed for it

copying machine /ˈkɒpɪɪŋ məˌʃiːn/ *noun* a machine which makes copies of documents

copy platform /ˈkɒpɪ ˌplætfɔːm/ *noun* the main theme of an advertisement's copy ○ *There is no point in discussing details until we decide on a copy platform.*

copyright /ˈkɒpɪraɪt/ *noun* **1.** an author's legal right to publish his or her own work and not to have it copied, lasting seventy years after the author's death **2.** a similar right protecting logos, brand names, etc. ■ *adjective* covered by the laws of copyright ○ *It is illegal to photocopy a copyright work.*

copy testing /ˈkɒpɪ ˌtestɪŋ/ *noun* the act of testing the effectiveness of an advertisement's copy ○ *Copy testing led to the copywriter having to rethink the*

wording of the message. ○ *Copy testing will tell us whether or not the advertisements are offensive to the public in general.*

copywriter /ˈkɒpiraɪtə/ *noun* a person who writes advertisements

core /kɔː/ *noun* the central or main part

core activity /ˈkɔːr ækˌtɪvɪti/ *noun* the central activity of a company, which is its basic product or service

core business /ˈkɔː ˌbɪznɪs/ *noun* the most important work that an organisation does, that it is most expert at, that makes it different from other organisations, that contributes most to its success and, usually, that it was originally set up to do (NOTE: The concept of core business became prominent in the 1980s when attempts at diversification by large companies proved less successful than expected.)

core capability /kɔːr keɪpəˈbɪlɪti/ *noun* same as **core competence**

core competence /kɔːr ˈkɒmpɪt(ə)ns/ *noun* a skill or an area of expertise possessed by an organisation that makes it particularly good at doing some things and makes an important contribution to its success by giving it competitive advantage over other organisations

core product /kɔː ˈprɒdʌkt/ *noun* **1.** the main product which a company makes or sells **2.** a basic product, without added benefits such as credit terms, installation service, etc.

core values /kɔː ˈvæljuːz/ *plural noun* **1.** the main commercial and moral principles that influence the way an organisation is run and the way it conducts its business, and that are supposed to be shared by everyone in the organisation from senior management to ordinary employees (NOTE: Core values are often reflected in an organisation's mission statement.) **2.** a set of concepts and ideals that guide a person's life and help him or her to make important decisions

corner /ˈkɔːnə/ *verb* □ **to corner the market** to own most or all of the supply of a commodity and so control the price ○ *The syndicate tried to corner the market in silver.*

corner shop /ˈkɔːnə ʃɒp/ *noun* a small privately owned general store

corporate /ˈkɔːp(ə)rət/ *adjective* referring to a whole company

'...the prime rate is the rate at which banks lend to their top corporate borrowers' [*Wall Street Journal*]

'...if corporate forecasts are met, sales will exceed $50 million next year' [*Citizen (Ottawa)*]

corporate advertising /ˌkɔːp(ə)rət ˈædvətaɪzɪŋ/ *noun* the advertising of an organisation rather than a product ○ *Our corporate advertising is designed to present us as a caring organisation.* ○ *No amount of corporate advertising will ever persuade the consumer that the company stands for quality.*

corporate brand /ˌkɔːp(ə)rət ˈbrænd/ *noun* the overall image that a company presents to the outside world, or the image of it that exists in the minds of its customers, its employees and the public, that encapsulates what it does and what it stands for

corporate communication /ˌkɔːp(ə)rət kəmjuːnɪˈkeɪʃ(ə)n/ *noun* the activities undertaken by an organisation to pass on information both to its own employees and to its existing and prospective customers and the general public

corporate culture /ˌkɔːp(ə)rət ˈkʌltʃə/ *noun* the often unspoken beliefs and values that determine the way an organisation does things, the atmosphere that exists within it and the way people who work for it behave (NOTE: The culture of an organisation is often summed up as 'the way we do things around here'.)

corporate discount /ˌkɔːp(ə)rət ˈdɪskaʊnt/ *noun* a reduction in advertising charges calculated on the basis of the total advertising revenue from all the brands of a company

corporate hospitality /ˌkɔːp(ə)rət hɒspɪˈtælɪti/ *noun* entertainment provided by an organisation, originally intended to help salespeople build relationships with customers, but now increasingly used as an incentive for staff and in team-building and training exercises for employees

corporate identity /ˌkɔːp(ə)rət aɪ-ˈdentɪti/ *noun* the way in which a corporation is distinguished from others

corporate image /ˌkɔːp(ə)rət ˈɪmɪdʒ/ *noun* an idea which a company would like the public to have of it

corporate name /ˌkɔːp(ə)rət ˈneɪm/ *noun* the name of a large corporation

corporate plan /ˌkɔːp(ə)rət ˈplæn/ *noun* a plan for the future work of a whole company

corporate planning /ˌkɔːp(ə)rət ˈplænɪŋ/ *noun* planning the future work of a whole company

corporate portal /ˌkɔːp(ə)rət ˈpɔːt(ə)l/ *noun* a main website that allows access to all the information and software applications held by an organisation and provides links to information from outside it (NOTE: A corporate portal is a development of intranet technology and, ideally, should allow users to access groupware, email, and desktop applications, and to customise the way information is presented and the way it is used.)

corporate profits /ˌkɔːp(ə)rət ˈprɒfɪts/ *plural noun* the profits of a corporation

'...corporate profits for the first quarter showed a 4 per cent drop from last year' [*Financial Times*]

corporate strategy /ˌkɔːp(ə)rət ˈstrætədʒi/ *noun* the plans for future action by a corporation

corporate vision /ˌkɔːp(ə)rət ˈvɪʒ(ə)n/ *noun* the overall aim or purpose of an organisation that all its business activities are designed to help it achieve (NOTE: An organisation's corporate vision is usually summed up in its vision statement.)

corporation /ˌkɔːpəˈreɪʃ(ə)n/ *noun* **1.** a large company **2.** *US* a company which is incorporated in the United States

corporation income tax /ˌkɔːpəreɪʃ(ə)n ˈɪnkʌm tæks/ *noun* a tax on profits made by incorporated companies

corporation tax /ˌkɔːpəˈreɪʃ(ə)n tæks/ *noun* a tax on profits and capital gains made by companies, calculated before dividends are paid. Abbr **CT**

correlation /ˌkɒrəˈleɪʃ(ə)n/ *noun* the degree to which there is a relationship between two sets of data ○ *Is there any correlation between people's incomes and the amount they spend on clothing?* ♦ **coefficient of correlation, multiple correlation**

cosmetic /kɒzˈmetɪk/ *adjective* referring to the appearance of people or things ○ *We've made some cosmetic changes to our product line.* ○ *Packaging has both practical as well as cosmetic importance.*

cost /kɒst/ *noun* the amount of money which has to be paid for something ○ *What is the cost of a first class ticket to New York?* ○ *Computer costs are falling each year.* ○ *We cannot afford the cost of two cars.* □ **to cover costs** to produce enough money in sales to pay for the costs of production ○ *The sales revenue barely covers the costs of advertising* or *the advertising costs.* □ **to sell at cost** to sell at a price which is the same as the cost of manufacture or the wholesale cost ■ *verb* **1.** to have a price ○ *How much does the machine cost?* ○ *This cloth costs £10 a metre.* **2.** □ **to cost a product** to calculate how much money will be needed to make a product, and so work out its selling price

cost, insurance, and freight /ˌkɒst ɪnˌʃʊərəns ən ˈfreɪt/ *noun* the estimate of a price, which includes the cost of the goods, the insurance, and the transport charges. Abbr **CIF**

cost accountant /ˈkɒst əˌkaʊntənt/ *noun* an accountant who gives managers information about their business costs

cost accounting /ˈkɒst əˌkaʊntɪŋ/ *noun* preparing special accounts of manufacturing and sales costs

cost analysis /ˈkɒst əˌnæləsɪs/ *noun* calculating in advance what a new product will cost

cost-benefit analysis /ˌkɒst ˈbenɪfɪt əˌnæləsɪs/ *noun* comparing the costs and benefits of different possible ways of using available resources

cost centre /ˈkɒst ˌsentə/ *noun* **1.** a person or group whose costs can be

itemised and to which costs can be allocated in accounts **2.** a unit, a process, or an individual that provides a service needed by another part of an organisation and whose cost is therefore accepted as an overhead of the business

cost-cutting /'kɒst ˌkʌtɪŋ/ *noun* reducing costs ○ *We have made three secretaries redundant as part of our cost-cutting programme.* ○ *We have taken out the second telephone line as a cost-cutting exercise.*

cost driver /'kɒst ˌdraɪvə/ *noun* a factor that determines how much it costs to carry out a particular task or project, e.g. the amount of resources needed for it, or the activities involved in completing it

cost-effective /ˌkɒstɪ 'fektɪv/ *adjective* which gives good value when compared with the original cost ○ *We find advertising in the Sunday newspapers very cost-effective.*

cost-effectiveness /ˌkɒst ɪ'fektɪvnəs/, **cost efficiency** /ˌkɒst 'fɪʃ(ə)nsi/ *noun* being cost-effective ○ *Can we calculate the cost-effectiveness of air freight against shipping by sea?*

cost factor /'kɒst ˌfæktə/ *noun* the problem of cost

costing /'kɒstɪŋ/ *noun* a calculation of the manufacturing costs, and so the selling price of a product ○ *The costings give us a retail price of $2.95.* ○ *We cannot do the costing until we have details of all the production expenditure.*

costly /'kɒstli/ *adjective* costing a lot of money, or costing too much money ○ *Defending the court case was a costly process.* ○ *The mistakes were time-consuming and costly.*

cost of entry /ˌkɒst əv 'entri/ *noun* the cost of going into a market for the first time

cost-of-living increase /ˌkɒst əv 'lɪvɪŋ ˌɪnkriːs/ *noun* an increase in salary to allow it to keep up with the increased cost of living

cost-of-living index /ˌkɒst əv 'lɪvɪŋ ˌɪndeks/ *noun* the way of measuring the cost of living which is shown as a percentage increase on the figure for the previous year. It is similar to the consumer price index, but includes other items such as the interest on mortgages.

cost of sales /ˌkɒst əv 'seɪlz/ *noun* all the costs of a product sold, including manufacturing costs and the staff costs of the production department, before general overheads are calculated

cost per acquisition /ˌkɒst pər ækwɪ'zɪʃ(ə)n/ *noun* the average cost for each acquisition of a new customer in response to an advertisement. Abbr **CPA**

cost per click-through /ˌkɒst pə 'klɪk θruː/ *noun* a method of pricing online advertising, based on the principle that the seller gets paid whenever a visitor clicks on an advertisement

cost per customer /ˌkɒst pə 'kʌstəmə/ *noun* a measure of cost-effectiveness based on the cost per sale generated

cost per inquiry /ˌkɒst pər ɪn'kwaɪəri/ *noun* the average cost for each inquiry in response to an advertisement

cost per order /ˌkɒst pər 'ɔːdə/ *noun* a measure used to determine the number of orders generated compared to the cost of running the advertisement. Abbr **CPO**

cost per thousand /ˌkɒst pə 'θaʊz(ə)nd/, **cost per mille** /ˌkɒst pə 'mɪl/ *noun* the cost of an advertisement, calculated as the cost for every thousand people reached or the cost of a thousand impressions for a website ○ *This newspaper has the highest cost per thousand but a very high proportion of its readers fall within our target audience.* Abbr **CPT, CPM**

cost plus /kɒst 'plʌs/ *noun* a system of calculating a price, by taking the cost of production of goods or services and adding a percentage to cover the supplier's overheads and margin ○ *We are charging for the work on a cost plus basis.*

cost-plus pricing /kɒst 'plʌs ˌpraɪsɪŋ/ *noun* a pricing method that involves basing the price on the production costs and adding a percentage for margin

cost price /'kɒst praɪs/ *noun* a selling price which is the same as the price, either the manufacturing price or the wholesale price, which the seller paid for the item

costs /kɒsts/ *plural noun* the expenses involved in a court case ○ *The judge awarded costs to the defendant.* ○ *Costs of the case will be borne by the prosecution.*

cottage industry /ˌkɒtɪdʒ 'ɪndəstri/ *noun* the production of goods or some other type of work, carried out by people working in their own homes

counter /'kaʊntə/ *noun* a long flat surface in a shop for displaying and selling goods □ **glove counter** the section of a shop where gloves are sold □ **goods sold over the counter** retail sales of goods in shops ○ *Some drugs are sold over the counter, but others need to be recommended by a doctor.* □ **under the counter** illegally

counter- /kaʊntə/ *prefix* against

counteradvertising /ˌkaʊntər-'ædvətaɪzɪŋ/ *noun* advertising aimed as a reply to a competitor's advertisements

counter-argument /'kaʊntər ˌɑːɡjʊmənt/ *noun* a response that is opposed to the position advocated in an advertising message

counterbid /'kaʊntəbɪd/ *noun* a higher bid in reply to a previous bid ○ *When I bid £20 they put in a counterbid of £25.*

counter-jumper /'kaʊntə ˌdʒʌmpə/ *noun* a person who sells goods over the counter (*informal*) ○ *He was a counter-jumper for many years before he became a manager.* ○ *Five years as a counter-jumper gave her plenty of experience of customer relations.*

countermand /ˌkaʊntə'mɑːnd/ *verb* to cancel an order

counter-offer /'kaʊntər ˌɒfə/ *noun* a higher or lower offer made in reply to another offer ○ *Smith Ltd made an offer of £1m for the property, and Blacks replied with a counter-offer of £1.4m.*

'…the company set about paring costs and improving the design of its product. It came up with a price cut of 14%, but its counter-offer –

for an order that was to have provided 8% of its workload next year – was too late and too expensive' [*Wall Street Journal*]

counterpack /'kaʊntəpæk/ *noun* a box for the display of goods for sale, placed on the counter or on another flat surface in a shop

counter-programming /'kaʊntə ˌprəʊɡræmɪŋ/ *noun* the presenting of TV programmes that are designed to appeal to the audience of competing programmes run during at the same time

countersign /'kaʊntəsaɪn/ *verb* to sign a document which has already been signed by someone else ○ *All our cheques have to be countersigned by the finance director.* ○ *The sales director countersigns all my orders.*

counter staff /'kaʊntə stɑːf/ *noun* sales staff who serve behind counters

country of origin /ˌkʌntri əv 'ɒrɪdʒɪn/ *noun* a country where a product is manufactured or where a food product comes from ○ *All produce must be labelled to show the country of origin.*

coupon /'kuːpɒn/ *noun* **1.** a piece of paper used in place of money **2.** a piece of paper which replaces an order form

coupon ad /'kuːpɒn æd/ *noun* an advertisement with a form attached, which you cut out and return to the advertiser with your name and address for further information

couponed /'kuːpɒnd/ *adjective* with a coupon attached ○ *The agency is using couponed direct response advertising.*

couponing /'kuːpɒnɪŋ/ *noun* a selling method using coupons delivered to homes, giving special discounts on some items

'…it employs selective mailings and package inserts such as the couponed offers sent out with credit card statements' [*PR Week*]

course /kɔːs/ *noun* a series of lessons or programme of instruction ○ *She has finished her secretarial course.* ○ *Tthe company has paid for her to attend a course for trainee sales managers.* ○ *Management trainees all took a six-month course in business studies.* ○ *The training officer was constantly on the lookout for new courses in manage-*

ment studies. ○ *The company sent her on a management course.*

courtesy /'kɜːtəsi/ *adjective* supplied free of charge ○ *A courtesy sample is sent with the sales literature.*

courtesy car /'kɜːtəsi kɑː/ *noun* the use of a car offered free to a customer

cover /'kʌvə/ *noun* **1.** coverage, the proportion of a target audience reached by advertising **2.** one of the outside pages of a publication. The four cover pages are front cover, inside front cover, inside back cover and back cover. ○ *We could never afford to advertise on the cover of this magazine.*

coverage /'kʌv(ə)rɪdʒ/ *noun* the proportion of a target market that is reached by an advertisement ○ *The advertisement itself was effective but it had very poor coverage.* ○ *We must consider both the cost of the advertisement and its coverage before committing ourselves any further.*

    '...from a PR point of view it is easier to get press coverage when you are selling an industry and not a brand' [*PR Week*]

cover charge /'kʌvə tʃɑːdʒ/ *noun* (*in restaurants*) a charge for a place at the table in addition to the charge for food

covered market /ˌkʌvəd 'mɑːkɪt/ *noun* a market which is held in a special building

covering letter /ˌkʌvərɪŋ 'letə/, **covering note** /ˌkʌvərɪŋ 'nəʊt/ *noun* a letter sent with documents to say why they are being sent

cover note /'kʌvə 'nəʊt/ *noun* a letter from an insurance company giving details of an insurance policy and confirming that the policy exists

cover page /'kʌvə peɪdʒ/ *noun* the front or back cover of a publication

cover price /'kʌvə praɪs/ *noun* the price of a newspaper or magazine which is printed on the cover and paid by the final purchaser

CPA *abbr* cost per acquisition

CPM *abbr* cost per mille

CPO *abbr* cost per order

CPT *abbr* cost per thousand

crash-test /'kræʃ test/ *verb* to establish the safety and reliability of something by testing it in different ways

creaming /'kriːmɪŋ/ *noun* the act of fixing a high price for a product in order to achieve high short-term profits

create /kri'eɪt/ *verb* to make something new ○ *By acquiring small unprofitable companies he soon created a large manufacturing group.* ○ *The government scheme aims at creating new jobs for young people.*

    '...he insisted that the tax advantages he directed towards small businesses will help create jobs and reduce the unemployment rate' [*Toronto Star*]

creative *adjective* /kri'eɪtɪv/ relating to the conceptual or artistic side of advertising ○ *There are three copywriters and four illustrators in the agency's creative department.* ○ *He has had good experience working on both the creative and the administrative sides of advertising.* ■ *noun* someone who works in the conceptual or artistic side of a business

    '...agencies are being called on to produce great creative work and at the same time deliver value for money' [*Marketing Week*]

creative director /kri,eɪtɪv daɪ-'rektə/ *noun* an employee of an advertising agency who is in overall charge of finding the right words and images to promote the product during an advertising campaign

creative selling /kri,eɪtɪv 'selɪŋ/ *noun* a sales technique where the main emphasis is on generating new business

creative shop /kri,eɪtɪv 'ʃɒp/, **creative boutique** /kri,eɪtɪv buː-'tiːk/ *noun* a highly specialised business offering creative customer advertising services ○ *A group of copywriters and designers have left the agency to set their own creative shop.* ○ *The creative shop made short advertising films and designed some press ads for us.*

creative strategy /kri'eɪtɪv ˌstrætədʒi/ *noun* a strategy to determine what message an advertisement will communicate

creative thinking /kri,eɪtɪv 'θɪŋkɪŋ/ *noun* same as **creativity**

creativity /ˌkriːeɪ'tɪvɪti/ *noun* the ability to generate new ideas, especially

by taking a fresh and imaginative approach to old problems or existing procedures (NOTE: Creativity is considered important not just in the development of new products and services, but also in organisational decision-making and problem-solving, and many organisations try to encourage it through their corporate culture and by using techniques such as brainstorming and lateral thinking.)

credere /'kreɪdəri/ *noun* ◊ **del credere agent**

credibility /ˌkredɪ'bɪlɪti/ *noun* the state of being trusted

credibility gap /ˌkredɪ'bɪlɪti ɡæp/ *noun* a discrepancy between claims for a product made by the manufacturer and acceptance of these claims by the target audience ○ *The credibility gap that we face is partly due to our product's bad performance record.* ♦ **source credibility**

credit /'kredɪt/ *noun* **1.** the period of time allowed before a customer has to pay a debt incurred for goods or services ○ *to give someone six months' credit* ○ *to sell on good credit terms* □ **to open a line of credit** *or* **a credit line** to make credit available to someone □ **on credit** without paying immediately ○ *to live on credit* ○ *We buy everything on sixty days credit.* ○ *The company exists on credit from its suppliers.* **2.** an amount entered in accounts to show a decrease in assets or expenses or an increase in liabilities, revenue or capital. In accounts, credits are entered in the right-hand column. ○ *to enter £100 to someone's credit* ○ *to pay in £100 to the credit of Mr Smith* Compare **debit** □ **account in credit** an account where the credits are higher than the debits **3.** money set against a client's account because an advertisement was not run at the correct time

credit account /'kredɪt əˌkaʊnt/ *noun* an account which a customer has with a shop which allows them to buy goods and pay for them later

credit agency /'kredɪt ˌeɪdʒənsi/ *noun* a company which reports on the creditworthiness of customers to show whether they should be allowed credit

credit bank /'kredɪt bæŋk/ *noun* a bank which lends money

credit card /'kredɪt kɑːd/ *noun* a plastic card which allows you to borrow money and to buy goods without paying for them immediately (you pay the credit card company at a later date)

credit card sale /'kredɪt kɑːd ˌseɪl/ *noun* the act of selling something for credit, using a credit card

credit column /'kredɪt ˌkɒləm/ *noun* the right-hand column in accounts showing money received

credit control /'kredɪt kənˌtrəʊl/ *noun* a check that customers pay on time and do not owe more than their credit limit

credit entry /'kredɪt ˌentri/ *noun* an entry on the credit side of an account

credit facilities /'kredɪt fəˌsɪlɪtiz/ *plural noun* an arrangement with a bank or supplier to have credit so as to buy goods

credit freeze /'kredɪt friːz/ *noun* a period when lending by banks is restricted by the government

credit history /'kredɪt ˌhɪst(ə)ri/ *noun* a record of how a potential borrower has repaid his or her previous debts

credit limit /'kredɪt ˌlɪmɪt/ *noun* the largest amount of money which a customer can borrow

credit memorandum /'kredɪt ˌmemərændəm/, **credit memo** /-'kredɪt ˌmeməʊ/ *noun US* a note showing that money is owed to a customer ○ *When the buyer paid too much money for the goods he was immediately sent a credit memorandum.* ○ *I hope we receive a credit memo from the suppliers for the money they owe us.*

credit note /'kredɪt nəʊt/ *noun* a note showing that money is owed to a customer ○ *The company sent the wrong order and so had to issue a credit note.* Abbr **C/N**

creditor /'kredɪtə/ *noun* a person or company that is owed money, i.e. a company's creditors are its liabilities

creditors' meeting /ˈkredɪtəz ˌmiːtɪŋ/ *noun* a meeting of all the people to whom an insolvent company owes money, to decide how to obtain the money owed

credit rating agency /ˈkredɪt reɪtɪŋ ˌeɪdʒənsi/ *noun US* a company used by businesses and banks to assess the creditworthiness of people

credit-reference agency /ˈkredɪt ˌref(ə)rens ˌeɪdʒənsi/ *noun* a company used by businesses and banks to assess the creditworthiness of people

credits /ˈkredɪts/ *plural noun* a list of the names of people who have worked on a film, TV programme, etc.

credit sale /ˈkredɪt seɪl/ *noun* a sale where the purchaser will pay for the goods bought at a later date

credit scoring /ˈkredɪt ˌskɔːrɪŋ/ *noun* a calculation made when assessing the creditworthiness of someone or something

credit side /ˈkredɪt saɪd/ *noun* the right-hand column of accounts showing money received

credit system /ˈkredɪt ˌsɪstəm/ *noun* the system that governs the way that loans are made to people and organisations, especially the regulations that relate to loans and to organisations that provide loans

credit union /ˈkredɪt ˌjuːnjən/ *noun* a group of people who pay in regular deposits or subscriptions which earn interest and are used to make loans to other members of the group

creditworthiness /ˈkredɪtˌwɜːðɪnəs/ *noun* the ability of a customer to pay for goods bought on credit

creditworthy /ˈkredɪtwɜːði/ *adjective* having enough money to be able to buy goods on credit ○ *We will do some checks on her to see if she is creditworthy.*

crisis /ˈkraɪsɪs/ *noun* a serious situation where decisions have to be taken rapidly

crisis management /ˈkraɪsɪs ˌmænɪdʒmənt/ *noun* management of a business or a country's economy during a period of crisis

critical mass /ˌkrɪtɪk(ə)l ˈmæs/ *noun* the point at which an organisation or a project is generating enough income or has gained a large enough market share to be able to survive on its own or to be worth investing more money or resources in

critical path analysis /ˌkrɪtɪk(ə)l ˈpɑːθ əˌnæləsɪs/ *noun* **1.** analysis of the way a project is organised in terms of the minimum time it will take to complete, calculating which parts can be delayed without holding up the rest of the project **2.** same as **critical-path method**

critical-path method /ˌkrɪtɪk(ə)l ˈpɑːθ ˌmeθəd/ *noun* a technique used in project management to identify the activities within a project that are critical to its success, usually by showing on a diagram or flow chart the order in which activities must be carried out so that the project can be completed in the shortest time and at the least cost

CRM *abbr* customer relations management *or* customer relationship management

cross /krɒs/ *verb* **1.** to go across ○ *Concorde only takes three hours to cross the Atlantic.* ○ *To get to the bank, you turn left and cross the street at the post office.* **2.** □ **to cross a cheque** to write two lines across a cheque to show that it has to be paid into a bank

crossed cheque /ˌkrɒst ˈtʃek/ *noun* a cheque with two lines across it showing that it can only be deposited at a bank and not exchanged for cash

cross elasticity of demand /ˌkrɒs ɪlæˌstɪsɪti əv dɪˈmɑːnd/ *noun* changes in demand for an item depending on the selling price of a competing product

cross-media advertising /ˌkrɒs miːdiə ˈædvətaɪzɪŋ/ *noun* advertising the same product or service in several different types of media which are offered by a single-company media provider

cross-selling /krɒs ˈselɪŋ/ *noun* **1.** selling two products which go with each other, by placing them side by side in a store **2.** selling a new product which

goes with another product a customer has already bought

cross-tracks /'krɒs træks/ *noun* a poster site next to a railway track

CTM *noun* ◊ **click-through rate**

CTR *abbr* click through rate

cume /kjuːm/ *noun* same as **cumulative audience** (*informal*)

cumulative /'kjuːmjʊlətɪv/ *adjective* added to regularly over a period of time

cumulative audience /-ˌkjuːmjʊlətɪv 'ɔːdiəns/, **cumulative reach** /ˌkjuːmjʊlətɪv 'riːtʃ/ *noun* the number of people reached by an advertisement at least once over a period of time

cumulative interest /ˌkjuːmjʊlətɪv 'ɪntrəst/ *noun* the interest which is added to the capital each year

cumulative quantity discount /ˌkjuːmjʊlətɪv ˌkwɒntəti 'dɪskaʊnt/ *noun* a discount based on a quantity bought or the value of purchases over a period of time ○ *We have purchased only from these suppliers over the last few months in order to enjoy a cumulative quantity discount.*

cumulative reach /ˌkjuːmjʊlətɪv 'riːtʃ/ *noun* same as **cumulative audience**

currency /'kʌrənsɪ/ *noun* money in coins and notes which is used in a particular country

'…today's wide daily variations in exchange rates show the instability of a system based on a single currency, namely the dollar' [*Economist*]

'…the level of currency in circulation increased to N4.9 billion in the month of August' [*Business Times (Lagos)*]

currency backing /'kʌrənsi ˌbækɪŋ/ *noun* gold or government securities which maintain the strength of a currency

currency note /'kʌrənsi nəʊt/ *noun* a bank note (NOTE: **currency** has no plural when it refers to the money of one country: **he was arrested trying to take currency out of the country**)

current /'kʌrənt/ *adjective* referring to the present time ○ *the current round of wage negotiations*

'…crude oil output plunged during the past month and is likely to remain at its current level for the near future' [*Wall Street Journal*]

current account /'kʌrənt əˌkaʊnt/ *noun* **1.** an account in an bank from which the customer can withdraw money when they want. Current accounts do not always pay interest. ○ *to pay money into a current account* (NOTE: American English is **checking account**) **2.** an account of the balance of payments of a country relating to the sale or purchase of raw materials, goods and invisibles

'…customers' current deposit and current accounts also rose to $655.31 million at the end of December' [*Hongkong Standard*]

'…a surplus in the current account is of such vital importance to economists and currency traders because the more Japanese goods that are exported, the more dollars overseas customers have to pay for these products. That pushes up the value of the yen' [*Nikkei Weekly*]

current assets /ˌkʌrənt 'æsets/ *plural noun* the assets used by a company in its ordinary work, e.g. materials, finished goods, cash, monies due, and which are held for a short time only

current cost accounting /ˌkʌrənt 'kɒst əˌkaʊntɪŋ/ *noun* a method of accounting which notes the cost of replacing assets at current prices, rather than valuing assets at their original cost. Abbr **CCA**

current liabilities /ˌkʌrənt laɪə'bɪlɪtiz/ *plural noun* the debts which a company has to pay within the next accounting period. In a company's annual accounts, these would be debts which must be paid within the year and are usually payments for goods or services received.

current price /ˌkʌrənt 'praɪs/ *noun* today's price

current rate of exchange /ˌkʌrənt reɪt əv ɪks'tʃeɪndʒ/ *noun* today's rate of exchange

current yield /ˌkʌrənt 'jiːld/ *noun* a dividend calculated as a percentage of the current price of a share on the stock market

curriculum vitae /kəˌrɪkjʊləm 'viːtaɪ/ *noun* a summary of a person's work experience and qualifications sent to a prospective employer by someone

applying for a job ○ *Candidates should send a letter of application with a curriculum vitae to the HR manager.* ○ *The curriculum vitae listed all the candidate's previous jobs and her reasons for leaving them.* Abbr **CV** (NOTE: the plural is **curriculums** or **curricula vitae.** American English is **résumé**)

curve /kɜːv/ *noun* a line which is not straight, e.g. a line on a graph ○ *The graph shows an upward curve.*

custom /ˈkʌstəm/ *noun* **1.** the use of a shop by regular shoppers □ **to lose someone's custom** to do something which makes a regular customer go to another shop **2.** □ **the customs of the trade** the general way of working in a trade ○ *It is the custom of the book trade to allow unlimited returns for credit.*

custom-built /ˌkʌstəm ˈbɪlt/ *adjective* made specially for one customer ○ *He drives a custom-built Rolls Royce.*

customer /ˈkʌstəmə/ *noun* a person or company that buys goods ○ *The shop was full of customers.* ○ *Can you serve this customer first please?* ○ *She's a regular customer of ours.* (NOTE: The customer may not be the consumer or end user of the product.)

'…unless advertising and promotion is done in the context of an overall customer orientation, it cannot seriously be thought of as marketing' [*Quarterly Review of Marketing*]

customer appeal /ˈkʌstəmər əˌpiːl/ *noun* what attracts customers to a product

customer capital /ˌkʌstəmə ˈkæpɪt(ə)l/ *noun* an organisation's relationships with its customers considered as a business asset

customer care /ˌkʌstəmə ˈkeə/ *noun* looking after customers, so that they do not become dissatisfied

customer-centric model /ˌkʌstəmə ˈsentrɪk ˌmɒd(ə)l/ *noun* a business model that is based on an assessment of what the customer needs

customer complaint /ˌkʌstəmə kəmˈpleɪnt/ *noun* same as **complaint**

customer expectation /ˌkʌstəmər ekspekˈteɪʃ(ə)n/ *noun* the ideas and feelings that a customer has about a product or service, based on what he or she needs from it and expects it to do (NOTE: Customer expectation can be created by previous experience, advertising, what other people say about it, awareness of competitors' products, and brand image. If customer expectations are met, then customer satisfaction results.)

customer flow /ˈkʌstəmə fləʊ/ *noun* the number of customers in a store and the pattern of their movements round the store

customer focus /ˌkʌstəmə ˈfəʊkəs/ *noun* the aiming of all marketing operations towards the customer

customer loyalty /ˌkʌstəmə ˈlɔɪəlti/ *noun* the feeling of customers who always shop at the same shop

'…a difficult market to get into, China nevertheless offers a high degree of customer loyalty once successfully entered' [*Economist*]

customer profile /ˌkʌstəmə ˈprəʊfaɪl/ *noun* a description of an average customer for a product or service ○ *The customer profile shows our average buyer to be male, aged 25–30, and employed in the service industries.*

customer profitability /ˌkʌstəmə ˌprɒfɪtəˈbɪliti/ *noun* the amount of profit generated by each individual customer. Usually a small percentage of customers generate the most profit.

customer relations /ˌkʌstəmə rɪˈleɪʃ(ə)nz/ *plural noun* relations between a company and its customers

customer relations management /ˌkʌstəmə rɪˈleɪʃ(ə)nz ˌmænɪdʒmənt/, **customer relationship management** /ˌkʌstəmə rɪˈleɪʃ(ə)nʃɪp ˌmænɪdʒmənt/ *noun* the management of relations between a company and its customers, keeping them informed of new products or services and dealing sympathetically with their complaints or inquiries. Abbr **CRM**

customer retention /ˌkʌstəmə rɪˈtenʃən/ *noun* same as **retention**

customer satisfaction /ˌkʌstəmə ˌsætɪsˈfækʃən/ *noun* the act of making customers pleased with what they have bought

customer service /ˌkʌstəmə ˈsɜːvɪs/ *noun* a service given to custom-

ers once they have made their decision to buy, including delivery, after-sales service, installation, training, etc.

customer service department /ˌkʌstəmə ˈsɜːvɪs dɪˌpɑːtmənt/ *noun* a department which deals with customers and their complaints and orders

customisation /ˌkʌstəmaɪˈzeɪʃ(ə)n/, **customization** *noun* the process of making changes to products or services that enable them to satisfy the particular needs of individual customers

customise /ˈkʌstəmaɪz/, **customize** *verb* to change something to fit the special needs of a customer ○ *We use customized computer terminals.*

customised service /ˌkʌstəmaɪzd ˈsɜːvɪs/ *noun* a service that is specifically designed to satisfy the particular needs of an individual customer

custom publisher /ˈkʌstəm ˌpʌblɪʃə/ *noun* a company which creates a magazine for a company to use as publicity

customs /ˈkʌstəmz/ *plural noun* the government department which organises the collection of taxes on imports, or an office of this department at a port or airport ○ *He was stopped by customs.* ○ *Her car was searched by customs.* □ **to go through customs** to pass through the area of a port or airport where customs officials examine goods □ **to take something through customs** to carry something illegal through a customs area without declaring it □ **the crates had to go through a customs examination** the crates had to be examined by customs officials

customs broker /ˈkʌstəmz ˌbrəʊkə/ *noun* a person or company that takes goods through customs for a shipping company

customs clearance /ˈkʌstəmz ˌklɪərəns/ *noun* **1.** the act of passing goods through customs so that they can enter or leave the country **2.** a document given by customs to a shipper to show that customs duty has been paid and the goods can be shipped ○ *to wait for customs clearance*

customs declaration /ˈkʌstəmz dekləˌreɪʃ(ə)n/ *noun* a statement showing goods being imported on which duty will have to be paid ○ *to fill in a customs declaration form*

customs entry point /ˌkʌstəmz ˈentri pɔɪnt/ *noun* a place at a border between two countries where goods are declared to customs

customs invoice /ˈkʌstəmz ˌɪnvɔɪs/ *noun* a customs form containing a list of goods with their values in both the exporter's and importer's countries

customs seal /ˈkʌstəmz siːl/ *noun* a seal attached by a customs officer to a box, to show that the contents have not passed through customs

customs tariff /ˈkʌstəmz ˌtærɪf/ *noun* a list of taxes to be paid on imported goods

customs warehouse /ˈkʌstəmz ˌweəhaʊs/ *noun* a government-run warehouse where goods are stored until duty is paid ○ *The goods will remain in the customs warehouse until the buyer claims them.*

cut-off /ˈkʌt ɒf/ *noun* the time after which a spot cannot be broadcast, usually late at night

cut-price /ˌkʌt ˈpraɪs/ *adjective* cheaper than usual

cut-price store /ˌkʌt praɪs ˈstɔː/ *noun* a store selling cut-price goods

cut-throat competition /ˌkʌt θrəʊt kɒmpəˈtɪʃ(ə)n/ *noun* sharp competition which cuts prices and offers high discounts

cutting /ˈkʌtɪŋ/ *noun* a piece cut out of a publication which refers to an item of particular interest

cutting-edge /ˌkʌtɪŋ ˈedʒ/ *adjective* using or involving the latest and most advanced techniques and technologies

CV *abbr* curriculum vitae ○ *Please apply in writing, enclosing a current CV.*

cyber mall /ˈsaɪbəmɔːl/ *noun* a website that provides information and links for a number of online businesses

cybermarketing /ˈsaɪbəˌmɑːkɪtɪŋ/ *noun* marketing that uses any kind of Internet-based promotion, e.g. targeted

emails, bulletin boards, websites, or sites from which the customer can download files

cycle /'saɪk(ə)l/ *noun* a set of events which happen in a regularly repeated sequence

cycle models /'saɪk(ə)l ˌmʌd(ə)lz/ *plural noun* models which are used to explain cyclical change ○ *Cycle models*

were used in the case study to show recent developments in retailing.

cyclical /'sɪklɪk(ə)l/ *adjective* which happens in cycles

'…general retailers should in theory suffer from rising interest rates. And food retailers in particular have cyclical exposure without price power' [*Investors Chronicle*]

cyclical factors /ˌsɪklɪk(ə)l 'fæktəz/ *plural noun* the way in which a trade cycle affects businesses

D

DAGMAR /'dægmɑː/ *noun* a model showing stages in the effect of advertising on a consumer, e.g. awareness, comprehension, conviction and action. Full form **defining advertising goals for measured advertising results**

DAR *abbr* day after recall test

data /'deɪtə/ *noun* information available on computer, e.g. letters or figures ○ *All important data on employees was fed into the computer.* ○ *To calculate the weekly wages, you need data on hours worked and rates of pay.* □ **data bank** *or* **bank of data** a store of information in a computer

data acquisition /'deɪtə ækwɪ-ˌzɪʃ(ə)n/ *noun* gathering information about a subject

database /'deɪtəbeɪs/ *noun* a set of data stored in an organised way in a computer system ○ *We can extract the lists of potential customers from our database.*

database cleaning /'deɪtəbeɪs ˌkliːnɪŋ/, **database cleansing** /'deɪtəbeɪs ˌklenzɪŋ/ *noun* checking the details of a database to make sure they are correct

database management system /ˌdeɪtəbeɪs 'mænɪdʒmənt ˌsɪstəm/ *noun* a computer program that is specially designed to organise and process the information contained in a database

database marketing /'deɪtəbeɪs ˌmɑːkɪtɪŋ/ *noun* using a database to market a product or service by building up a relationship with customers

database modelling /'deɪtəbeɪs ˌmɒd(ə)lɪŋ/ *noun* using the information from a database to create a website or to forecast trends in a market

database publishing /'deɪtəbeɪs ˌpʌblɪʃɪŋ/ *noun* the publishing of information selected from a database, either on-line where the user pays for it on a per-page inspection basis or as a CD-ROM

data capture /'deɪtə ˌkæptʃə/, **data entry** /'deɪtə 'entri/ *noun* the act of putting information onto a computer by keyboarding or by scanning

data cleansing /'deɪtə ˌklenzɪŋ/, **data cleaning** /'deɪtə ˌkliːnɪŋ/ *noun* checking data to make sure it is correct

data mining /'deɪtə ˌmaɪnɪŋ/ *noun* the use of advanced software to search online databases and identify statistical patterns or relationships in the data that may be commercially useful

data protection /'deɪtə prəˌtekʃən/ *noun* making sure that computerised information about people is not misused

data sheet /'deɪtə ʃiːt/ *noun* a leaflet with data *or* information about a product

data warehouse /'deɪtə ˌweəhaʊs/ *noun* a large collection data that is collected over a period of time from different sources and stored on a computer in a standard format so that is easy to retrieve. It can be used, e.g., to support managerial decision-making. (NOTE: Organisations often use data warehouses for marketing purposes, for example, in order to store and analyse customer information.)

date /deɪt/ *noun* the number of day, month and year ○ *I have received your letter of yesterday's date.* □ **date of receipt** the date when something is received

date coding /'deɪt ˌkəʊdɪŋ/ *noun* the act of showing the date by which a product should be consumed

date-in-charge /ˌdeɪt ɪn ˈtʃɑːdʒ/ *noun* the date from which a poster site is charged ○ *We will have three weeks of exposure from the date-in-charge.*

day /deɪ/ *noun* a period of 24 hours ○ *There are thirty days in June.* ○ *The first day of the month is a public holiday.* □ **days of grace** the days allowed for payment after it becomes due ○ *Let's send the cheque at once since we have only five days of grace left.* ○ *Because the shopowner has so little cash available, we will have to allow him additional days of grace.*

day after recall test /ˌdeɪ ɑːftə ˈriːkɔːl test/ *noun* an advertising research test to see how much someone can remember of an advertisement, the day after it appeared or was broadcast. Abbr **DAR**

daypart /ˈdeɪpɑːt/ *noun* a section of a day, used for measuring audience ratings on TV

DBS *abbr* direct broadcast by satellite

dead /ded/ *adjective* not working □ **the line went dead** the telephone line suddenly stopped working

dead account /ded əˈkaʊnt/ *noun* an account which is no longer used

dead freight /ded ˈfreɪt/ *noun* payment by a charterer for unfilled space in a ship or plane ○ *Too much dead freight is making it impossible for the company to continue to charter ships.*

deadline /ˈdedlaɪn/ *noun* the date by which something has to be done □ **to meet a deadline** to finish something in time □ **to miss a deadline** to finish something later than it was planned ○ *We've missed our October 1st deadline.*

dead loss /ded ˈlɒs/ *noun* a total loss ○ *The car was written off as a dead loss.*

dead season /ˈded ˌsiːz(ə)n/ *noun* the time of year when there are few tourists about

deadweight /ˈdedweɪt/ *noun* heavy goods, e.g. coal, iron or sand

deadweight cargo /ˌdedweɪt ˈkɑːgəʊ/ *noun* a heavy cargo which is charged by weight, not by volume

deal /diːl/ *noun* a business agreement, affair or contract ○ *to sign a deal* ○ *The sales director set up a deal with a Russian bank.* ○ *The deal will be signed tomorrow.* ○ *They did a deal with an American airline.* □ **to call off a deal** to stop an agreement ○ *When the chairman heard about the deal he called it off.* ■ *verb* **1.** □ **to deal with** something to organise something ○ *Leave it to the filing clerk – he'll deal with it.* □ **to deal with an order** to work to supply an order **2.** to buy and sell □ **to deal with someone** to do business with someone □ **to deal in leather or options** to buy and sell leather or options □ **he deals on the Stock Exchange** his work involves buying and selling shares on the Stock Exchange for clients

dealer /ˈdiːlə/ *noun* a person who buys and sells ○ *a used-car dealer*

dealer aids /ˈdiːlə eɪdz/ *plural noun* types of advertising material used by shops to stimulate sales

dealer's brand /ˈdiːləz brænd/ *noun* a brand owned by a distributor rather by a producer ○ *I bought the dealer's brand of soap since the store is well known for its high quality goods.*

dealership /ˈdiːləʃɪp/ *noun* **1.** the authority to sell some products or services **2.** a business run by an authorised dealer

dealer tie-in /ˌdiːlə ˈtaɪ ɪn/ *noun* advertising which includes the names of local dealers that stock the product being advertised

deal in /ˈdiːl ɪn/ *noun* sales promotion to the trade

deal out /ˈdiːl aʊt/ *noun* sales promotion to consumers

dear money /ˈdɪə ˌmʌni/ *noun* money which has to be borrowed at a high interest rate, and so restricts expenditure by companies

death duty /ˈdeθ ˌdjuːti/**, death tax** /ˈdeθ tæks/ *noun* US a tax paid on the property left by a dead person (NOTE: the British equivalent is **inheritance tax**)

deaveraging /diːˈæv(ə)rɪdʒɪŋ/ *noun* the act of treating customers in different ways according to the amount they buy, by rewarding the best and penalising the worst

debit /'debɪt/ *noun* an amount entered in accounts which shows an increase in assets or expenses or a decrease in liabilities, revenue or capital. In accounts, debits are entered in the left-hand column. Compare **credit** ■ *verb* □ **to debit an account** to charge an account with a cost ○ *His account was debited with the sum of £25.*

debitable /'debɪtəb(ə)l/ *adjective* which can be debited

debit card /'debɪt kɑːd/ *noun* a plastic card, similar to a credit card, but which debits the holder's account immediately through an EPOS system

debit column /'debɪt ˌkɒləm/ *noun* the left-hand column in accounts showing the money paid or owed to others

debit entry /'debɪt ˌentri/ *noun* an entry on the debit side of an account

debit note /'debɪt nəʊt/ *noun* a note showing that a customer owes money ○ *We undercharged Mr Smith and had to send him a debit note for the extra amount.*

debits and credits /ˌdebɪts ən 'kredɪts/ *plural noun* money which a company owes and money it receives, figures which are entered in the accounts to record increases or decreases in assets, expenses, liabilities, revenue or capital

debt /det/ *noun* money owed for goods or services ○ *The company stopped trading with debts of over £1 million.* □ **to be in debt** to owe money □ **he is in debt to the tune of £250,000** he owes £250,000 □ **to get into debt** to start to borrow more money than you can pay back □ **the company is out of debt** the company does not owe money any more □ **to pay back a debt** to pay all the money owed □ **to pay off a debt** to finish paying money owed □ **to service a debt** to pay interest on a debt ○ *The company is having problems in servicing its debts.* □ **debts due** money owed which is due for repayment

debt collection /'det kəˌlekʃ(ə)n/ *noun* collecting money which is owed

debt collector /'det kəˌlektə/ *noun* a person who collects debts

debtor /'detə/ *noun* a person who owes money

'…the United States is now a debtor nation for the first time since 1914, owing more to foreigners than it is owed itself' [*Economist*]

debtor side /'detə saɪd/ *noun* the debit side of an account

decentralise /diː'sentrəlaɪz/, **decentralize** *verb* to move power or authority or action from a central point to local areas

decentralised system /diːˌsentrəlaɪzd 'sɪstəm/*noun* a system where responsibility for marketing, advertising, and promotion lies with a product manager rather than a centralised department

deception /dɪ'sepʃən/ *noun* telling a lie in order to mislead a customer

decide /dɪ'saɪd/ *verb* to make up your mind to do something ○ *to decide on a course of action* ○ *to decide to appoint a new managing director*

decider /dɪ'saɪdə/ *noun* a person who makes decisions, especially the person who makes the decision to buy

deciding factor /dɪˌsaɪdɪŋ 'fæktə/ *noun* the most important factor which influences a decision ○ *A deciding factor in marketing our range of sports goods in the country was the rising standard of living there.*

decimal system /'desɪm(ə)l ˌsɪstəm/ *noun* a system of mathematics based on the number 10

decision /dɪ'sɪʒ(ə)n/ *noun* a choice made after thinking about what to do ○ *It took the committee some time to come to a decision* or *to reach a decision.*

decision-maker /dɪ'sɪʒ(ə)n ˌmeɪkə/ *noun* a person who takes decisions. ♦ **marketmaker**

decision-making /dɪ'sɪʒ(ə)n ˌmeɪkɪŋ/ *noun* the act of coming to a decision

decision-making unit /dɪ'sɪʒ(ə)n meɪkɪŋ ˌjuːnɪt/ *noun* a group of people who decide on the purchase of a product. For the purchase of a new piece of equipment, they would be the manager, the financial controller and the operator who will use the equipment. Abbr **DMU**

decision theory /dɪˈsɪʒ(ə)n ˌθɪəri/ *noun* the mathematical methods for weighing the various factors in making decisions ○ *In practice it is difficult to apply decision theory to our planning.* ○ *Students study decision theory to help them suggest strategies in case-studies.*

decision tree /dɪˈsɪʒ(ə)n triː/ *noun* a model for decision-making, showing the possible outcomes of different decisions ○ *This computer programme incorporates a decision tree.*

deck /dek/ *noun* a flat floor in a ship

deck cargo /ˈdek ˌkɑːgəʊ/ *noun* the cargo carried on the open top deck of a ship

decline /dɪˈklaɪn/ *noun* **1.** a gradual fall ○ *the decline in the value of the dollar* ○ *a decline in buying power* ○ *The last year has seen a decline in real wages.* **2.** the final stage in the life cycle of a product when the sales and profitability are falling off and the product is no longer worth investing in ■ *verb* to fall slowly or decrease ○ *Shares declined in a weak market.* ○ *New job applications have declined over the last year.* ○ *The economy declined during the last government.*

'Saudi oil production has declined by three quarters to around 2.5m barrels a day' [*Economist*]

'…this gives an average monthly decline of 2.15 per cent during the period' [*Business Times (Lagos)*]

'…share prices disclosed a weak tendency right from the onset of business and declined further, showing losses over a broad front' [*The Hindu*]

decode /diːˈkəʊd/ *verb* to translate and interpret a coded message

deduplication /diːˌdjuːplɪˈkeɪʃ(ə)n/ *noun* removing duplicate entries from a database

deep-rooted demand /ˌdiːp ruːtɪd dɪˈmɑːnd/ *noun* brand loyalty which survives even if the product no longer offers value for money ○ *There is deep-rooted demand for this product which is a household name.*

de facto standard /deɪ ˌfæktəʊ ˈstændəd/ *noun* a standard set in a particular market by a highly successful product or service

defensive spending /dɪˌfensɪv ˈspendɪŋ/ *noun* a budget strategy that promotes areas where sales are currently strong rather than potential areas where sales could be made

defer /dɪˈfɜː/ *verb* to put back to a later date, or to postpone ○ *We will have to defer payment until January.* ○ *The decision has been deferred until the next meeting.* (NOTE: **deferring – deferred**)

deferment /dɪˈfɜːmənt/ *noun* the act of leaving until a later date ○ *deferment of payment* ○ *deferment of a decision*

deferred /dɪˈfɜːd/ *adjective* put back to a later date

deferred creditor /dɪˌfɜːd ˈkredɪtə/ *noun* a person who is owed money by a bankrupt but who is paid only after all other creditors

deferred payment /dɪˌfɜːd ˈpeɪmənt/ *noun* **1.** money paid later than the agreed date **2.** payment for goods by instalments over a long period

deferred rebate /dɪˌfɜːd ˈriːbeɪt/ *noun* a discount given to a customer who buys up to a specified quantity over a specified period

deferred stock /dɪˌfɜːd ˈstɒk/ *noun* shares which receive a dividend after all other dividends have been paid

deficit /ˈdefɪsɪt/ *noun* the amount by which spending is higher than income □ **the accounts show a deficit** the accounts show a loss □ **to make good a deficit** to put money into an account to balance it

deficit financing /ˈdefɪsɪt ˌfaɪnænsɪŋ/ *noun* planning by a government to cover the shortfall between tax income and expenditure by borrowing money

deflate /diːˈfleɪt/ *verb* □ **to deflate the economy** to reduce activity in the economy by cutting the supply of money

deflation /diːˈfleɪʃ(ə)n/ *noun* a general reduction in economic activity as a result of a reduced supply of money and credit, leading to lower prices ○ *The oil crisis resulted in worldwide deflation.*

'…the reluctance of people to spend is one of the main reasons behind 26 consecutive months of price deflation, a key economic ill that has led to price wars, depressed the profit margins of

state enterprises and hit incomes among the rural population' [*Financial Times*]

deflationary /diː'fleɪʃ(ə)n(ə)ri/ *adjective* which can cause deflation ○ *The government has introduced some deflationary measures in the budget.*

'...the strong dollar's deflationary impact on European economies as national governments push up interest rates' [*Duns Business Month*]

delay /dɪ'leɪ/ *noun* the time when someone or something is later than planned ○ *There was a delay of thirty minutes before the AGM started* or *the AGM started after a thirty-minute delay.* ○ *We are sorry for the delay in supplying your order* or *in replying to your letter.* ■ *verb* to be late, or to make someone late ○ *The company has delayed payment of all invoices.* ○ *She was delayed because her taxi was involved in an accident.*

delayed response /dɪ,leɪd rɪ-'spɒns/ *noun* a slower than expected response by consumers to a company's promotion ○ *If there is a delayed response we will only reap the benefits next year.* ○ *A delayed response is not usual in such a new product.*

del credere agent /del 'kreɪdəri ,eɪdʒənt/ *noun* an agent who receives a high commission because they guarantee payment by customers

delegation /,delɪ'geɪʃ(ə)n/ *noun* **1.** a group of delegates ○ *A Chinese trade delegation is visiting the UK.* ○ *The management met a union delegation.* **2.** an act of passing authority or responsibility to someone else

delete /dɪ'liːt/ *verb* to remove a product from a company's product range ○ *We have decided to delete three old products as the new ones are coming on stream.*

deletion /dɪ'liːʃ(ə)n/ *noun* the act of removing an old product from the market ○ *The product has lost market share and is a candidate for deletion.*

delight factor /dɪ'laɪt ,fæktə/ *noun* the customer's pleasure at making a purchase

deliver /dɪ'lɪvə/ *verb* to transport goods to a customer □ **goods delivered free** *or* **free delivered goods** goods transported to the customer's address at a price which includes transport costs □ **goods delivered on board** goods transported free to the ship or plane but not to the customer's warehouse

delivered price /dɪ'lɪvəd praɪs/ *noun* a price which includes packing and transport

delivery /dɪ'lɪv(ə)ri/ *noun* **1.** the transporting of goods to a customer ○ *allow 28 days for delivery* ○ *delivery is not allowed for* or *is not included* ○ *parcels awaiting delivery* ○ *free delivery* or *delivery free* ○ *a delivery date* ○ *delivery within 28 days* ○ *We have a pallet of parcels awaiting delivery.* □ **to take delivery of goods** to accept goods when they are delivered ○ *We took delivery of the stock into our warehouse on the 25th.* **2.** goods being delivered ○ *We take in three deliveries a day.* ○ *There were four items missing in the last delivery.* **3.** the transfer of a bill of exchange

delivery note /dɪ'lɪv(ə)ri nəʊt/ *noun* a list of goods being delivered, given to the customer with the goods

delivery of goods /dɪ,lɪv(ə)ri əv 'gʊdz/ *noun* the transport of goods to a customer's address

delivery order /dɪ'lɪv(ə)ri ,ɔːdə/ *noun* the instructions given by the customer to the person holding her goods, to tell her where and when to deliver them

delivery receipt /dɪ'lɪv(ə)ri rɪ,siːt/ *noun* a delivery note when it has been signed by the person receiving the goods

delivery service /dɪ'lɪv(ə)ri ,sɜːvɪs/ *noun* the store will deliver goods to all parts of the town

delivery time /dɪ'lɪv(ə)ri taɪm/ *noun* the number of days before something will be delivered

delivery van /dɪ'lɪv(ə)ri væn/ *noun* a van for delivering goods to customers

delphi method /'delfaɪ ,meθəd/ *noun* a method of forming strategies by soliciting individual estimates on the time-scale of projected developments and then inviting further estimates on the basis of all those already made until a consensus is reached

demand /dɪˈmɑːnd/ *noun* **1.** asking for payment □ **payable on demand** which must be paid when payment is asked for **2.** the requirement by a prospective purchaser for a commodity ○ *There was an active demand for oil shares on the stock market.* □ **there is not much demand for this item** not many people want to buy it □ **this book is in great demand** *or* **there is a great demand for this book** many people want to buy it □ **to meet/fill a demand** to supply what is needed ○ *The factory had to increase production to meet the extra demand.* ○ *The factory had to cut production when demand slackened.* ○ *The office cleaning company cannot keep up with the demand for its services.* ■ *verb* to ask for something and expect to get it ○ *She demanded a refund.* ○ *The suppliers are demanding immediate payment of their outstanding invoices.* ○ *The shop stewards demanded an urgent meeting with the managing director.*

'…spot prices are now relatively stable in the run-up to the winter's peak demand' [*Economist*]

'…the demand for the company's products remained strong throughout the first six months of the year with production and sales showing significant increases' [*Business Times (Lagos)*]

'…growth in demand is still coming from the private rather than the public sector' [*Lloyd's List*]

demand bill /dɪˈmɑːnd bɪl/ *noun* a bill of exchange which must be paid when payment is asked for

demand deposit /dɪˈmɑːnd dɪˌpɒzɪt/ *noun US* money in a deposit account which can be taken out when you want it by writing a cheque

demand forecasting /dɪˈmɑːnd ˌfɔːkɑːstɪŋ/ *noun* estimating what demand would exist at various prices, used as a method of calculating prices

demand-led inflation /dɪˌmɑːnd led ɪnˈfleɪʃ(ə)n/ *noun* inflation caused by rising demand which cannot be met

demand price /dɪˈmɑːnd praɪs/ *noun* the price at which a quantity of goods will be bought

demand schedule /dɪˈmɑːnd ˌʃedʒuːl/ *noun* a table showing demand for a product or service at different prices

demand theory /dɪˈmɑːnd ˌθɪəri/ *noun* a branch of economics concerned with consumer buying habits and factors which determine demand

demarketing /diːˈmɑːkɪtɪŋ/ *noun* the act of attempting to reduce the demand for a product ○ *Demarketing was the keynote in the industry when rationing was introduced.*

demographic /ˌdeməˈɡræfɪk/ *adjective* referring to demography ○ *A full demographic study of the country must be done before we decide how to export there.*

demographic edition /ˌdeməˈɡræfɪk ɪˌdɪʃ(ə)n/ *noun* a special edition of a magazine targeted at a specific demographic group

demographics /ˌdeməˈɡræfɪks/ *plural noun* the details of the population of a country, in particular its age and gender, which affect marketing

demographic segmentation /ˌdeməˌɡræfɪk seɡmenˈteɪʃ(ə)n/ *noun* the act of dividing a market up into segments according to the age, sex, income levels, etc. of the potential customers

demography /dɪˈmɒɡrəfi/ *noun* a study of populations and population statistics such as age, sex, income and education

demonstrate /ˈdemənstreɪt/ *verb* to show how something works ○ *He was demonstrating a new tractor when he was killed.* ○ *The managers saw the new stock-control system being demonstrated.*

demonstration /ˌdemənˈstreɪʃ(ə)n/ *noun* an act of showing or explaining how something works ○ *We went to a demonstration of new laser equipment.*

demonstration effect /ˌdemənˈstreɪʃ(ə)n ɪˌfekt/ *noun* the theory stating that people buy products to impress or keep up with their neighbours ○ *The promotion of luxury goods is intended to exploit the demonstration effect.*

demonstration model /ˌdemənˈstreɪʃ(ə)n ˌmɒd(ə)l/ *noun* a piece of equipment used in demonstrations and later sold off cheaply

demonstrator /'demənstreɪtə/ *noun* **1.** a person who demonstrates pieces of equipment **2.** same as **demonstration model**

demurrage /dɪ'mʌrɪdʒ/ *noun* money paid to a customer when a shipment is delayed at a port or by customs

department /dɪ'pɑːtmənt/ *noun* **1.** a specialised section of a large organisation ○ *Trainee managers work for a while in each department to get an idea of the organisation as a whole.* **2.** a section of a large store selling one type of product ○ *You will find beds in the furniture department.*

departmental   **manager** /ˌdiːpɑːtment(ə)l 'mænɪdʒə/ *noun* the manager of a department

departmental system *noun* a way of organising an advertising agency into departments such as creative, media, administration, etc.

depend /dɪ'pend/ *verb* **1.** □ **to depend on** to need someone or something to exist ○ *The company depends on efficient service from its suppliers.* ○ *We depend on government grants to pay the salary bill.* **2.** to happen because of something ○ *The success of the launch will depend on the publicity campaign.* □ **depending on** which varies according to something ○ *Depending on the advertising budget, the new product will be launched on radio or on TV.*

dependent /dɪ'pendənt/ *adjective* supported financially by someone else ○ *employees may be granted leave to care for dependent relatives*

dependent variable /dɪˌpendənt 'veəriəb(ə)l/ *noun* a variable or factor which changes as a result of a change in another (the 'independent variable') ○ *We are trying to understand the effects of several independent variables on one dependent variable, in this case, sales.*

deposit /dɪ'pɒzɪt/ *noun* money given in advance so that the thing which you want to buy will not be sold to someone else ○ *to pay a deposit on a watch* ○ *to leave £10 as deposit*

depot /'depəʊ/ *noun* a central warehouse or storage area for goods, or a place for keeping vehicles used for transport ○ *a goods depot* ○ *an oil storage depot* ○ *a freight depot* ○ *a bus depot*

depreciate /dɪ'priːʃieɪt/ *verb* **1.** to reduce the value of assets in accounts ○ *We depreciate our company cars over three years.* **2.** to lose value ○ *a share which has depreciated by 10% over the year* ○ *The pound has depreciated by 5% against the dollar.*

'...this involved reinvesting funds on items which could be depreciated against income for three years' [*Australian Financial Review*]

'...buildings are depreciated at two per cent per annum on the estimated cost of construction' [*Hongkong Standard*]

'...the euro's downward drift sparked alarmed reactions from the European Central Bank which has seen the new currency depreciate by almost 15% since its launch' [*Times*]

COMMENT: Various methods of depreciating assets are used, such as the 'straight line method', where the asset is depreciated at a constant percentage of its cost each year and the 'reducing balance method', where the asset is depreciated at a constant percentage which is applied to the cost of the asset after each of the previous years' depreciation has been deducted.

depreciation /dɪˌpriːʃi'eɪʃ(ə)n/ *noun* **1.** a reduction in value of an asset **2.** a loss of value ○ *a share which has shown a depreciation of 10% over the year* ○ *the depreciation of the pound against the dollar*

depreciation rate /dɪˌpriːʃi'eɪʃ(ə)n reɪt/ *noun* the rate at which an asset is depreciated each year in the company accounts

depress /dɪ'pres/ *verb* to reduce ○ *Reducing the money supply has the effect of depressing demand for consumer goods.*

depressed /dɪ'prest/ *adjective* feeling miserable and worried ○ *She was depressed when she was not promoted.*

depressed area /dɪˌprest 'eəriə/ *noun* a part of a country suffering from depression

depressed market /dɪˌprest 'mɑːkɪt/ *noun* a market where there are more goods than customers

depression /dɪ'preʃ(ə)n/ *noun* a period of economic crisis with high unem-

ployment and loss of trade ○ *an economic depression* ○ *The country entered a period of economic depression.*

depth /depθ/ *noun* the variety in a product line

depth interview /'depθ ˌɪntəvjuː/ *noun* an interview with no preset questions and following no fixed pattern, but which can last a long time and allows the respondent time to express personal views and tastes ○ *Depth interviews elicited some very original points of view.*

deregulation /diːˌreɡjʊ'leɪʃ(ə)n/ *noun* the reduction of government control over an industry ○ *the deregulation of the airlines*

'…after the slump in receipts last year that followed liner shipping deregulation in the US, carriers are probably still losing money on their transatlantic services. But with a possible contraction in capacity and healthy trade growth, this year has begun in a much more promising fashion than last' [*Lloyd's List*]

derived demand /dɪˌraɪvd dɪ-'mɑːnd/ *noun* demand for a product because it is needed to produce another product which is in demand

describe /dɪ'skraɪb/ *verb* to say what someone or something is like ○ *The leaflet describes the services the company can offer.* ○ *The managing director described the difficulties the company was having with cash flow.*

description /dɪ'skrɪpʃən/ *noun* a detailed account of what something is like □ **false description of contents** the act of wrongly stating the contents of a packet to trick customers into buying it

design /dɪ'zaɪn/ *noun* **1.** the planning or drawing of a product before it is built or manufactured **2.** the planning of the visual aspect of an advertisement ■ *verb* to plan or to draw something before it is built or manufactured ○ *He designed a new car factory.* ○ *She designs garden furniture.*

designate /'dezɪɡneɪt/ *verb* to identify something or someone in a particular way

designated market area /ˌdezɪɡneɪt 'mɑːkɪt ˌeəriə/ *noun* geographical areas used in measuring the size of an audience. Abbr **DMA**

design audit /dɪ'zaɪn ˌɔːdɪt/ *noun* the checking and evaluating of design, especially in advertising materials or on a website

design consultancy /dɪ'zaɪn kən-ˌsʌltənsi/ *noun* a firm which gives specialist advice on design

design department /dɪ'zaɪn dɪ-ˌpɑːtmənt/ *noun* the department in a large company which designs the company's products or its advertising

designer /dɪ'zaɪnə/ *noun* a person who designs ○ *She is the designer of the new computer.* ■ *adjective* expensive and fashionable ○ *designer jeans*

designer product /dɪˌzaɪnə 'prɒdʌkt/ *noun* a fashionable product created by a well-known designer ○ *Recent wealth in the cities has increased the demand for designer products.* ○ *Jeans and sportswear are only some of our designer products.*

design factor /dɪ'zaɪn ˌfæktə/ *noun* the ratio of sampling error of a complex sample or sample design to that of a completely random sample

design for manufacturability /dɪ-ˌzaɪn fə ˌmænjʊfæktʃərə'bɪlɪti/ *noun* the process of adapting the design of a product so that it fits as well as possible into the manufacturing system of an organisation, thus reducing the problems of bringing the product to market (NOTE: The manufacturing issues that need to be taken into account in design for manufacturability include selecting appropriate materials, making the product easy to assemble and minimising the number of machine set-ups required.)

design protection /dɪ'zaɪn prə-ˌtekʃən/ *noun* making sure that a design is not copied by an unauthorised user

design studio /dɪ'zaɪn ˌstjuːdiəʊ/ *noun* an independent firm which specialises in creating designs

desire /dɪ'zaɪə/ *noun* the wish to do something

desire to purchase /dɪˌzaɪə tə 'pɜːtʃɪs/ *noun* the feeling of a customer that he or she needs to purchase a product. ♦ **AIDA**

desk /desk/ *noun* a writing table in an office, usually with drawers for stationery ○ *a desk diary* ○ *a desk drawer* ○ *a desk light*

desk research /ˈdesk rɪˌsɜːtʃ/ *noun* looking for information which is in printed sources such as directories

desk researcher /ˈdesk rɪˌsɜːtʃə/ *noun* a person who carries out desk research

devaluation /ˌdiːvæljuˈeɪʃ(ə)n/ *noun* a reduction in value of a currency against other currencies ○ *the devaluation of the rand*

devalue /diːˈvæljuː/ *verb* to reduce the value of a currency against other currencies ○ *The pound has been devalued by 7%.*

develop /dɪˈveləp/ *verb* **1.** to plan and produce ○ *to develop a new product* **2.** to plan and build an area ○ *to develop an industrial estate*

developed country /dɪˌveləpt ˈkʌntri/ *noun* a country which has an advanced manufacturing system

'…developed countries would gain $135 billion a year and developing countries, such as the former centrally planned economies of Eastern Europe, would gain $85 billion a year. The study also notes that the poorest countries would lose an annual $7 billion' [*Times*]

developing country /dɪˌveləpɪŋ ˈkʌntri/, **developing nation** /dɪˌveləpɪŋ ˈneɪʃ(ə)n/ *noun* a country which is not fully industrialised

development /dɪˈveləpmənt/ *noun* the planning of the production of a new product and constructing the first prototypes ○ *We spend a great deal on research and development.*

development cycle /dɪˈveləpmənt ˌsaɪk(ə)l/ *noun* the various stages which are involved in the development of a product from the initial concept to its manufacture and marketing

deviation /ˌdiːviˈeɪʃ(ə)n/ *noun* a change of route or strategy ○ *Advertising in the tabloids will mean a deviation from our normal marketing strategy.*

diadic test /daɪˌædɪk ˈtest/ *noun* a product test in which respondents compare two products

diagram /ˈdaɪəgræm/ *noun* a drawing which presents information visually ○ *a diagram showing sales locations* ○ *a diagram of the company's organisational structure* ○ *The first diagram shows how our decision-making processes work.*

diagrammatic /ˌdaɪəgrəˈmætɪk/ *adjective* □ **in diagrammatic form** in the form of a diagram ○ *The chart showed the sales pattern in diagrammatic form.*

diagrammatically /ˌdaɪəgrəˈmætɪkli/ *adverb* using a diagram ○ *The chart shows the sales pattern diagrammatically.*

dial /ˈdaɪəl/ *verb* to call a telephone number on a telephone ○ *to dial a number* ○ *to dial the operator*

dial-and-smile /ˌdaɪəl ən ˈsmaɪl/ *verb* to try to appear pleasant when cold-calling potential customers

diarise /ˈdaɪəraɪz/, **diarize** *verb* to enter a date you have to remember in a diary

diary /ˈdaɪəri/ *noun* a book in which you can write notes or appointments for each day of the week ○ *She checked her engagements in her desk diary.*

diary method /ˈdaɪəri ˌmeθəd/ *noun* a market research method whereby respondents keep a regular written account of advertising noticed or purchases made or products used

diary panel /ˈdaɪəri ˌpæn(ə)l/ *noun* a group of people who are asked to keep notes of their purchases on a daily basis

dice /daɪs/ *verb* to cut food into small cubes

dichotomous question /daɪˌkɒtəməs ˈkwestʃən/ *noun* a question in a questionnaire that can only be answered by 'yes' or 'no'

differential /ˌdɪfəˈrenʃəl/ *adjective* which shows a difference ■ *noun* □ **to erode wage differentials** to reduce differences in salary gradually

differential advantage /ˌdɪfərenʃəl ədˈvɑːntɪdʒ/ *noun* an advantage that one product has over rival products in the market ○ *We are confident that our toothpaste has a differential advantage.*

differential pricing /ˌdɪfərenʃəl 'praɪsɪŋ/ *noun* giving different products in a range different prices so as to distinguish them from each other

differential tariffs /ˌdɪfərenʃəl 'tærɪfs/ *plural noun* different tariffs for different classes of goods as, e.g., when imports from certain countries are taxed more heavily than similar imports from other countries

differentiated marketing strategy /dɪfəˌrenʃieɪtɪd 'mɑːkɪtɪŋ ˌstrætɪdʒɪ/ *noun* a method of marketing where the product is modified to suit each potential market. ♦ **concentrated marketing, undifferentiated product**

differentiation /ˌdɪfərenʃiˈeɪʃ(ə)n/ *noun* ensuring that a product has some unique features that distinguish it from competing products ○ *We are adding some extra features to our watches in the interest of product differentiation.* ○ *The aim of differentiation should be to catch the customer's eye.*

diffusion /dɪˈfjuːʒ(ə)n/ *noun* the process by which a product is gradually adopted by consumers

diffusion curve /dɪˈfjuːʒ(ə)n kɜːv/ *noun* the geographical representation of how many consumers adopt a product at different times. ♦ **exponential diffusion**

digital /ˈdɪdʒɪt(ə)l/ *adjective* converted into a form that can be processed by computers and accurately reproduced

digital cash /ˈdɪdʒɪt(ə)l kæʃ/ *noun* a form of digital money that can be used like physical cash to make online purchases and is anonymous because there is no way of obtaining information about the buyer when it is used

digital colour proof /ˌdɪdʒɪt(ə)l 'kʌlə pruːf/ *noun* a colour proof taken from digital files prior to film output at high or low resolution

digital economy /ˌdɪdʒɪt(ə)l ɪˈkɒnəmi/ *noun* an economy that is based on electronic commerce, e.g., trade on the Internet

digital goods /ˌdɪdʒɪt(ə)l 'gʊdz/ *plural noun* goods that are sold and delivered electronically, usually over the Internet

digital money /ˈdɪdʒɪt(ə)l ˌmʌni/ *noun* a series of numbers that has a value equivalent to a sum of money in a physical currency

digital nervous system /ˌdɪdʒɪt(ə)l 'nɜːvəs ˌsɪstəm/ *noun* a digital information system containing accumulated knowledge that will enable an organisation to respond speedily and effectively to external events

digital TV /ˌdɪdʒɪt(ə)l tiːˈviː/ *noun* TV where the picture has been changed into a form which a computer can process

digital wallet /ˌdɪdʒɪt(ə)l 'wɒlɪt/ *noun* a piece of personalised software on the hard drive of a user's computer that contains, in coded form, such items as credit card information, digital cash, a digital identity certificate, and standardised shipping information, and can be used when paying for a transaction electronically

Dinkies /ˈdɪŋkiz/ *plural noun* couples who are both wage-earners and have no children (NOTE: short for **Double Income No Kids**)

direct /daɪˈrekt/ *verb* to manage or organise ○ *He directs our South-East Asian operations.* ○ *She was directing the development unit until last year.* ■ *adjective* straight or without interference ■ *adverb* with no third party involved ○ *We pay income tax direct to the government.* □ **to dial direct** to contact a phone number yourself without asking the operator to do it for you ○ *You can dial New York direct from London if you want.*

direct-action advertising /daɪˌrekt ˌækʃən 'ædvətaɪzɪŋ/ *noun* advertising which aims to get a quick response ○ *We'll need some direct-action advertising if we're not to fall behind our competitors this spring.* ○ *Direct-action advertising will only help us in the short term.*

direct-action marketing /daɪˌrekt ˌækʃən 'mɑːkɪtɪŋ/ *noun* same as **direct response advertising**

direct broadcast by satellite /daɪˌrekt ˌbrɔːdkɑːst baɪ 'sætəlaɪt/ *noun* TV and radio signals broadcast over a

wide area from an earth station via a satellite, received with a dish aerial. Abbr **DBS**

direct channel /daɪˌrekt ˈtʃæn(ə)l/ *noun* a marketing channel where a producer and consumer deal directly with one another

direct close /daɪˌrekt ˈkləʊz/ *noun* the act of ending a sale by asking the customer if they want to buy

direct demand /daɪˌrekt dɪˈmɑːnd/ *noun* demand for a product or service for its own sake, and not for what can be derived from it

direct export /daɪˌrekt ˈekspɔːt/ *noun* selling a product direct to the overseas customer without going through a middleman ○ *Direct export is the only way to keep down the retail price.* ○ *Our overseas marketing consists mainly of direct export to German department stores.*

direct headline /daɪˌrekt ˈhedlaɪn/ *noun* an eye-catching headline that presents its message directly to its target audience

direction /daɪˈrekʃən/ *noun* **1.** the process of organising or managing ○ *He took over the direction of a multinational group.* **2.** □ **directions for use** instructions showing how to use something

directional /daɪˈrekʃən(ə)l/ *adjective* pointing in a specific direction

directional medium /daɪˌrekʃ(ə)l ˈmiːdiəm/ *noun* an advertising medium that tells potential customers where to find products or services, e.g. a directory

directive interview /daɪˈrektɪv ˈɪntəvjuː/ *noun* an interview using preset questions and following a fixed pattern

direct labour /daɪˌrekt ˈleɪbə/ *noun* the cost of the workers employed which can be allocated to a product, not including materials or overheads

directly /daɪˈrektlɪ/ *adverb* with no third party involved ○ *We deal directly with the manufacturer, without using a wholesaler.*

direct mail /daɪˌrekt ˈmeɪl/ *noun* the practice of selling a product by sending publicity material to possible buyers through the post ○ *These calculators are only sold by direct mail.* ○ *The company runs a successful direct-mail operation.*

'…all of those who had used direct marketing techniques had used direct mail, 79% had used some kind of telephone technique and 63% had tried off-the-page selling' [*Precision marketing*]

direct-mail advertising /daɪˌrekt meɪl ˈædvətaɪzɪŋ/ *noun* advertising by sending leaflets to people through the post

direct mailing /daɪˌrekt ˈmeɪlɪŋ/ *noun* the sending of publicity material by post to possible buyers

direct mail preference scheme /daɪˌrekt meɪl ˈpref(ə)rəns skiːm/ *noun* a scheme where an addressee can have his or her name removed from a mailing list

direct marketing /daɪˌrekt ˈmɑːkɪtɪŋ/ *noun* same as **direct response advertising**

'…after five years of explosive growth, fuelled by the boom in financial services, the direct marketing world is becoming a lot more competitive' [*Marketing Workshop*]

'…direct marketing is all about targeting the audience, individualising the message and getting a response' [*PR Week*]

direct-marketing media /daɪˌrekt ˈmɑːkɪtɪŋ ˌmiːdiə/ *plural noun* media that are used for direct marketing, e.g. direct mail, telemarketing, and TV

director /daɪˈrektə/ *noun* **1.** the person appointed by the shareholders to help run a company **2.** the person who is in charge of a project, an official institute or other organisation ○ *the director of the government research institute* ○ *She was appointed director of the trade association.*

'…the research director will manage and direct a team of business analysts reporting on the latest developments in retail distribution throughout the UK' [*Times*]

directorate /daɪˈrekt(ə)rət/ *noun* a group of directors

directorship /daɪˈrektəʃɪp/ *noun* the post of director ○ *She was offered a directorship with Smith Ltd.*

'…what benefits does the executive derive from his directorship? In the first place compensation has increased sharply in recent years' [*Duns Business Month*]

directors' report /daɪˌrektəz rɪ-ˈpɔːt/ *noun* the annual report from the board of directors to the shareholders

directory /daɪˈrekt(ə)rɪ/ *noun* a reference book containing information on companies and their products

direct response advertising /daɪˌrekt rɪˈspɒns ˌædvətaɪzɪŋ/ *noun* advertising in such a way as to get customers to send in inquiries or orders directly by mail

direct response agency /daɪˌrekt rɪˈspɒns ˌeɪdʒənsi/ *noun* a company which provides direct marketing services to its clients such as database management, direct mail, and response collecting

direct response marketing /daɪˌrekt rɪˈspɒns ˌmɑːkɪtɪŋ/ *noun* same as **direct response advertising**

direct selling /daɪˌrekt ˈselɪŋ/ *noun* selling a product direct to the customer without going through a shop

direct services /daɪˌrekt ˈsɜːvɪsɪz/ *plural noun* personal services to the public, e.g. catering, dentistry or hairdressing ○ *There is little manufacturing industry in the area, and direct services account for most of the wealth.*

dirty /ˈdɜːti/ *adjective* not clean

dirty bill of lading /ˌdɜːti bɪl əv ˈleɪdɪŋ/, **foul bill of lading** /ˌfaʊl bɪl əv ˈleɪdɪŋ/ *noun* a bill of lading stating that the goods did not arrive on board in good condition

disclosure of information /dɪsˌkləʊʒər əv ɪnfəˈmeɪʃ(ə)n/ *noun* the passing on of information that was intended to be kept secret or private to someone else

discount *noun* /ˈdɪskaʊnt/ the percentage by which the seller reduces the full price for the buyer ○ *to give a discount on bulk purchases* □ **to sell goods at a discount** *or* **at a discount price** to sell goods below the normal price □ **10% discount for cash** *or* **10% cash discount** you pay 10% less if you pay in cash ■ *verb* □ **to discount bills of ex-**

change to buy or sell bills of exchange for less than the value written on them in order to cash them later

'…banks refrained from quoting forward US/Hongkong dollar exchange rates as premiums of 100 points replaced the previous day's discounts of up to 50 points' [*South China Morning Post*]

discountable /ˈdɪskaʊntəb(ə)l/ *adjective* which can be discounted ○ *These bills are not discountable.*

discounted cash flow /ˌdɪskaʊntɪd ˈkæʃ fləʊ/ *noun* the calculation of the forecast return on capital investment by discounting future cash flows from the investment, usually at a rate equivalent to the company's minimum required rate of return. Abbr **DCF**

discounted value /ˌdɪskaʊntɪd ˈvæljuː/ *noun* the difference between the face value of a share and its lower market price

discounter /ˈdɪskaʊntə/ *noun* a person or company that discounts bills or invoices, or sells goods at a discount

'…invoice discounting is an instant finance raiser. Cash is advanced by a factor or discounter against the value of invoices sent out by the client company. Debt collection is still in the hands of the client company, which also continues to run its own bought ledger' [*Times*]

'…a 100,000 square-foot warehouse generates ten times the volume of a discount retailer; it can turn its inventory over 18 times a year, more than triple a big discounter's turnover' [*Duns Business Month*]

discount house /ˈdɪskaʊnt haʊs/ *noun* **1.** a financial company which specialises in discounting bills **2.** a shop which specialises in selling cheap goods bought at a high discount

discount price /ˈdɪskaʊnt praɪs/ *noun* the full price less a discount

discount rate /ˈdɪskaʊnt reɪt/ *noun* the percentage taken when a bank buys bills

'…pressure on the Federal Reserve Board to ease monetary policy and possibly cut its discount rate mounted yesterday' [*Financial Times*]

discount store /ˈdɪskaʊnt stɔː/ *noun* a shop which specialises in cheap goods bought at a high discount

discrepancy /dɪˈskrepənsi/ *noun* a lack of agreement between figures in invoices or accounts

discretion /dɪˈskreʃ(ə)n/ *noun* being able to decide correctly what should be done □ **I leave it to your discretion** I leave it for you to decide what to do □ **at the discretion of someone** according to what someone decides ○ *Membership is at the discretion of the committee.*

discretionary /dɪˈskreʃ(ə)n(ə)ri/ *adjective* which can be done if someone wants □ **the minister's discretionary powers** powers which the minister could use if they thought it necessary

discretionary income /dɪˌskreʃ(ə)n(ə)ri ˈɪnkʌm/ *noun* income left after fixed payments have been made and whose spending is therefore subject to advertising influence ○ *Discretionary incomes generally increase in a recession.*

discrimination /dɪˌskrɪmɪˈneɪʃ(ə)n/ *noun* treating people in different ways because of class, religion, race, language, colour or sex

discrimination test /dɪˌskrɪmɪˈneɪʃ(ə)n test/ *noun* a product test designed to show how one product differs from another ○ *The discrimination test showed our product to be superior to that of our closest competitor.*

discussion board /dɪˈskʌʃ(ə)n bɔːd/, **discussion group** /dɪˈskʌʃ(ə)n gruːp/ *noun* a group of people who discuss something by sending emails to the group and where each member can respond and see the responses of other members

discussion list /dɪˈskʌʃ(ə)n lɪst/ *noun* a list of addresses of members of a discussion board

diseconomies of scale /dɪsɪˌkɒnənmiz əv ˈskeɪl/ *plural noun* a situation where increased production leads to a higher production cost per unit or average production cost

disequilibrium /ˌdɪsiːkwɪˈlɪbriəm/ *noun* an imbalance in the economy when supply does not equal demand

dishoarding /dɪsˈhɔːdɪŋ/ *noun* putting goods back onto the market when they have been hoarded or stored for some time

dishonour /dɪsˈɒnə/ *verb* (NOTE: the American spelling is **dishonor**) □ **to dishonour a bill** not to pay a bill

dishonoured cheque /dɪsˌɒnəd ˈtʃek/ *noun* a cheque which the bank will not pay because there is not enough money in the account to pay it

disintegration /dɪsˌɪntɪˈgreɪʃ(ə)n/ *noun* the decision to stop producing some goods or supplies and to buy them in instead ○ *Disintegration has meant we now have to buy all of our plastic parts.* ○ *Part of the company's disintegration policy involved selling off the factories.*

disintermediation /dɪsˌɪntəmiːdiˈeɪʃ(ə)n/ *noun* the removal of any intermediaries from a process so that, e.g., manufacturers sell direct to consumers instead of selling their products through wholesalers and retailers

disparage /dɪˈspærɪdʒ/ *verb* to criticise

disparaging copy /dɪsˌpærədʒɪŋ ˈkɒpi/, **knocking copy** /ˈnɒkɪŋ ˌkɒpi/ *noun* advertising copy which is critical of another company's products ○ *Their disparaging copy has given them a bad name in the industry.*

dispatch /dɪˈspætʃ/ *noun* **1.** the sending of goods to a customer ○ *Production difficulties held up dispatch for several weeks.* **2.** goods which have been sent ○ *The weekly dispatch went off yesterday.* ■ *verb* to send goods to customers ○ *The goods were dispatched last Friday.*

dispatch department /dɪˈspætʃ dɪˌpɑːtmənt/ *noun* the department which deals with the packing and sending of goods to customers

dispatcher /dɪˈspætʃə/ *noun* a person who sends goods to customers

dispatch note /dɪˈspætʃ nəʊt/ *noun* a note saying that goods have been sent

dispatch rider /dɪˈspætʃ ˌraɪdə/ *noun* a motorcyclist who delivers messages or parcels in a town

dispenser /dɪˈspensə/ *noun* a machine which automatically provides something such as an object, a drink, or an item of food, often when money is

put in ○ *an automatic dispenser* ○ *a towel dispenser*

dispersion /dɪˈspɜːʃ(ə)n/ *noun* the attempt by a distributor to distribute a product to a market

display /dɪˈspleɪ/ *noun* the showing of goods for sale ○ *an attractive display of kitchen equipment* ○ *The shop has several car models on display.* ■ *verb* to show ○ *The company was displaying three new car models at the show.*

display advertisement /dɪˈspleɪ əd.vɜːtɪsmənt/, **display ad** /dɪˈspleɪ æd/ *noun* an advertisement which is well designed or printed in bold type to attract attention

display advertising /dɪˈspleɪ ˌædvətaɪzɪŋ/ *noun* advertising that has individual features such as photographs, its own box border or the company logo in addition to text

display material /dɪˈspleɪ mə.tɪəriəl/ *noun* material used to attract attention to goods which are for sale, e.g. posters and photographs

display outer /dɪˈspleɪ ˌaʊtə/ *noun* a container for protecting goods in transit which can also be used as an attractive display container for the goods in a shop

display panel /dɪˈspleɪ ˌpæn(ə)l/ *noun* a flat area for displaying goods in a shop window

disposable /dɪˈspəʊzəb(ə)l/ *adjective* which can be used and then thrown away ○ *The machine serves soup in disposable paper cups.*

disposable income /dɪˌspəʊzəb(ə)l ˈɪnkʌm/, **disposable personal income** /dɪˌspəʊzəb(ə)l ˌpɜːs(ə)nəl ˈɪnkʌm/ *noun* the income left after tax and national insurance have been deducted

disposal /dɪˈspəʊz(ə)l/ *noun* a sale ○ *disposal of securities* or *of property* ○ *The company has started a systematic disposal of its property portfolio.* □ **lease for disposal** or **business for disposal** a lease or business for sale

dispose /dɪˈspəʊz/ *verb* □ **to dispose of** to get rid of or to sell cheaply ○ *to dispose of excess stock* ○ *He is planning*

to dispose of his business in the new year.

disrewarding /ˌdɪsrɪˈwɔːdɪŋ/ *noun* the penalising of bad customers to allow the company to give special terms to the best customers

dissonance/attribution model /ˌdɪsənəns ˌætrɪˌbjuːʃ(ə)n ˌmɒd(ə)l/ *noun* a response model which follows the opposite sequence from normal: consumers first act in a specific way, then develop feelings as a result of their behaviour, and then look for information that supports their attitude and behaviour

dissonance reduction /ˈdɪsənəns rɪˌdʌkʃən/ *noun* a reduction in worries experienced by the purchaser after a product has been purchased, by increasing their awareness of the positive features of the product and reducing their fears about its negative features. ♦ **cognitive dissonance**

distance freight /ˈdɪstəns freɪt/ *noun* freight charges based on the distance over which the goods are transported

distinctive competence /dɪˌstɪŋktɪv ˈkɒmpɪt(ə)ns/ *noun* an advantage that one company or producer has over competitors in the market ○ *Our distinctive competence is a highly professional sales force.* ○ *The company could not survive with high costs and no distinctive competence.*

distress merchandise /dɪˈstres ˌmɜːtʃəndaɪs/ *noun US* goods sold cheaply to pay a company's debts

distress sale /dɪˈstres seɪl/ *noun* a sale of goods at low prices to pay a company's debts

distress selling /dɪˈstres ˌselɪŋ/ *noun* the sale of goods cheaply in order to pay off debts ○ *Difficult circumstances forced the producers to resort to distress selling.*

distribute /dɪˈstrɪbjuːt/ *verb* **1.** to share out dividends ○ *Profits were distributed among the shareholders.* **2.** to send out goods from a manufacturer's warehouse to retail shops ○ *Smith Ltd distributes for several smaller compa-*

nies. ○ *All orders are distributed from our warehouse near Oxford.*

distribution /ˌdɪstrɪˈbjuːʃ(ə)n/ *noun* the act of sending goods from the manufacturer to the wholesaler and then to retailers ○ *Stock is held in a distribution centre which deals with all order processing.* ○ *Distribution costs have risen sharply over the last 18 months.* ○ *She has several years' experience as distribution manager.*

'British distribution companies are poised to capture a major share of the European market' [*Management News*]

distribution census /ˌdɪstrɪˈbjuːʃ(ə)n ˌsensəs/ *noun* official statistics regarding the number of distributors and their businesses ○ *Using the distribution census, we drew up a list of wholesalers who were worth approaching.*

distribution centre /ˌdɪstrɪˈbjuːʃ(ə)n ˌsentə/ *noun* a place where goods are collected and stored temporarily but whose main function is to send them on to wholesalers, retailers, or consumers

distribution channel /ˌdɪstrɪˈbjuːʃ(ə)n ˌtʃæn(ə)l/ *noun* the route by which a product or service reaches a customer after it leaves the producer or supplier (NOTE: A distribution channel usually consists of a chain of intermediaries, for example wholesalers and retailers, that is designed to move goods from the point of production to the point of consumption in the most efficient way.)

'…there is evidence that distribution channels are supply driven' [*Quarterly Review of Marketing*]

distribution management /ˌdɪstrɪˈbjuːʃ(ə)n ˌmænɪdʒmənt/ *noun* the management of the efficient transfer of goods from the place where they are manufactured to the place where they are sold or used (NOTE: Distribution management involves such activities as warehousing, materials handling, packaging, stock control, order processing, and transport.)

distribution network /ˌdɪstrɪˈbjuːʃ(ə)n ˌnetwɜːk/ *noun* a series of

points or small warehouses from which goods are sent all over a country

distribution resource planning /ˌdɪstrɪˌbjuːʃ(ə)n rɪˈsɔːs ˌplænɪŋ/ *noun* planning, especially using a computerised system, that is intended to ensure the most efficient use of the resources used in distributing goods (NOTE: Effective distribution resource planning integrates distribution with manufacturing and synchronises supply and demand by identifying requirements for finished goods and by producing schedules for the movement of goods along the distribution chain so that they reach the customer as soon as possible.)

distributive /dɪˈstrɪbjʊtɪv/ *adjective* referring to distribution

distributive trades /dɪˈstrɪbjʊtɪv ˌtreɪdz/ *plural noun* all business involved in the distribution of goods

distributor /dɪˈstrɪbjʊtə/ *noun* a company which sells goods for another company which makes them □ **a network of distributors** a series of distributors spread all over a country

distributor's brand /dɪˈstrɪbjʊtəz ˌbrænd/ *noun* goods specially packed for a store with the store's name printed on them ○ *I bought the distributor's brand of soap because it was the cheapest.*

distributorship /dɪˈstrɪbjʊtəʃɪp/ *noun* the position of being a distributor for a company

distributor support /dɪˌstrɪbjʊtə səˈpɔːt/ *noun* the action of a supplier of a product or service in providing help to distributors, by offering training, promotional material, etc.

divergent marketing /daɪˌvɜːdʒənt ˈmɑːkɪtɪŋ/ *noun* a separate marketing treatment for each of a company's products ○ *Divergent marketing is giving way to a more coordinated and integrated marketing effort.*

diversification /daɪˌvɜːsɪfɪˈkeɪʃ(ə)n/ *noun* the process of adding another quite different type of business to a firm's existing trade

diversify /daɪˈvɜːsɪfaɪ/ *verb* **1.** to add new types of business to existing ones ○ *The company is planning to diversify*

into new products. **2.** to invest in different types of shares or savings so as to spread the risk of loss

divert /daɪˈvɜːt/ *verb* **1.** to send to another place or in another direction **2.** to buy stock in a special offer and then sell it on to customers living outside the special-offer area

divestment /daɪˈvestmənt/ *noun* the dropping or sale of a whole product line, to allow the company to concentrate on other products

division /dɪˈvɪʒ(ə)n/ *noun* **1.** the main section of a large company ○ *the marketing division* ○ *the production division* ○ *the retail division* ○ *the hotel division of the leisure group* **2.** a company which is part of a large group ○ *Smith's is now a division of the Brown group of companies.*

divisional /dɪˈvɪʒ(ə)n(ə)l/ *adjective* referring to a division ○ *a divisional director* ○ *the divisional headquarters*

DM *abbr* direct marketing

DMA *abbr* designated market area

DMU *abbr* decision-making unit

document /ˈdɒkjʊmənt/ *noun* a paper, especially an official paper, with written information on it ○ *He left a file of documents in the taxi.* ○ *She asked to see the documents relating to the case.*

documentary /ˌdɒkjʊˈment(ə)ri/ *adjective* in the form of documents ○ *documentary evidence* ○ *documentary proof* ■ *noun* a film concerning actual facts or real events

documentation /ˌdɒkjʊmenˈteɪʃ(ə)n/ *noun* all documents referring to something ○ *Please send me the complete documentation concerning the sale.*

document of title /ˌdɒkjʊmənt əv ˈtaɪt(ə)l/ *noun* a document allowing the holder to handle goods as if they own them

documents against acceptance /ˌdɒkjʊmənts əgenst əkˈseptəns/ *noun* an arrangement whereby a buyer receives documents for the goods on their acceptance of a bill of exchange

documents against cash /ˌdɒkjʊmənts əgenst ˈkæʃ/, **docu-**

ments against presentation /ˌdɒkjʊmənts əgenst prez(ə)nˈteɪʃ(ə)n/ *noun* an arrangement whereby a buyer receives documents for the goods on payment of a bill of exchange

dog /dɒg/ *noun* a product that has a low market share and a low growth rate, and so is likely to be dropped from the company's product line

dog-eat-dog /ˌdɒg iːt ˈdɒg/ *noun* marketing activity where everyone fights for their own product and attacks competitors mercilessly (*informal*)

do-it-yourself /ˌduː ɪt jəˈself/ *adjective* done by an ordinary person, not by a skilled worker. Abbr **DIY**

do-it-yourself conveyancing /ˌduː ɪt jəself kənˈveɪənsɪŋ/ *noun* the drawing up of a legal conveyance by the person selling a property, without the help of a lawyer

do-it-yourself magazine /ˌduː ɪt jəself mægəˈziːn/ *noun* a magazine with articles on work which the average person can do to repair or paint his or her house

do-it-yourself store /ˌduː ɪt jəself ˈstɔː/ *noun* a large store specialising in selling materials for the repair and improvement of houses, for gardening and for light car maintenance

domestic /dəˈmestɪk/ *adjective* **1.** referring to the home market or the market of the country where the business is situated ○ *Domestic sales have increased over the last six months.* **2.** for use in the home ○ *Glue which is intended for both domestic and industrial use.*

domestic appliances /dəˌmestɪk əˈplaɪənsɪz/ *plural noun* electrical machines which are used in the home, e.g. washing machines

domestic consumption /dəˌmestɪk kənˈsʌmpʃən/ *noun* use in the home country ○ *Domestic consumption of oil has fallen sharply.*

domestic market /dəˌmestɪk ˈmɑːkɪt/ *noun* the market in the country where a company is based ○ *They produce goods for the domestic market.*

domestic production /də,mestɪk prə'dʌkʃən/ *noun* the production of goods for use in the home country

door /dɔː/ *noun* the piece of wood, metal, or other material which closes the entrance to a building or room ○ *The finance director knocked on the chairman's door and walked in.* □ **the store opened its doors on June 1st** the store started doing business on June 1st

door drop /'dɔː drɒp/ *noun* a delivery of promotional literature by hand to all the houses in an area

door-to-door /,dɔː tə 'dɔː/ *adjective* going from one house to the next, asking the occupiers to buy something or to vote for someone ○ *door-to-door canvassing* ○ *We have 200 door-to-door salesmen.* ○ *Door-to-door selling is banned in this part of the village.*

door-to-door salesman /,dɔː tə dɔː 'seɪlzmən/ *noun* a man who goes from one house to the next, asking people to buy something

door-to-door service /,dɔː tə dɔː 'sɜːvɪs/ *noun* a transportation service that takes goods directly to the buyer's address

dormant /'dɔːmənt/ *adjective* no longer active or no longer operating

dormant account /,dɔːmənt ə'kaʊnt/ *noun* a past customer who is no longer buying ○ *Let's re-establish contact with some of our dormant accounts.* ○ *All the old reports on dormant accounts have been filed away.*

'...the agency has been responsible for the dormant account since its last campaign was run three years ago' [*Marketing Week*]

double /'dʌb(ə)l/ *adjective* twice as large or two times the size ○ *Their turnover is double ours.* □ **to be on double time** to earn twice the usual wages for working on Sundays or other holidays □ **in double figures** with two figures, from 10 to 99 ○ *Inflation is in double figures.* ○ *We have had double-figure inflation for some years.* ■ *verb* to become twice as big, or make something twice as big ○ *We have doubled our profits this year* or *our profits have doubled this year.* ○ *The company's borrowings have doubled.*

double column /,dʌb(ə)l 'kɒləm/ *noun* two columns spanned by an advertisement

double crown /,dʌb(ə)l 'kraʊn/ *noun* a basic poster size, 30 inches deep by 20 inches wide

double-decker /,dʌb(ə)l 'dekə/ *noun* two advertising panels, one on top of the other

double-page spread /,dʌb(ə)l peɪdʒ 'spred/ *noun* two facing pages in a magazine or newspaper, used by an advertiser

double-pricing /,dʌb(ə)l 'praɪsɪŋ/ *noun* the practice of showing two prices on a product, to make buyers think there has been a price reduction

double-spotting /,dʌb(ə)l 'spɒtɪŋ/ *noun* running an advertising spot twice

down /daʊn/ *adverb, preposition* in a lower position or to a lower position ○ *The inflation rate is gradually coming down.* ○ *Shares are slightly down on the day.* ○ *The price of petrol has gone down.* □ **to pay money down** to pay a deposit ○ *They paid £50 down and the rest in monthly instalments.*

downmarket /'daʊnmɑːkɪt/ *adverb, adjective* cheaper or appealing to a less wealthy section of the population ○ *The company has adopted a downmarket image.* □ **the company has decided to go downmarket** the company has decided to make products which appeal to a wider section of the public

downside /'daʊnsaɪd/ *noun* □ **the sales force have been asked to give downside forecasts** they have been asked for pessimistic forecasts

downside factor /'daʊnsaɪd ,fæktə/ *noun* the possibility of making a loss in an investment

down tools /,daʊn 'tuːlz/ *verb* to stop working ○ *The entire workforce downed tools in protest.*

downturn /'daʊntɜːn/ *noun* the movement towards lower prices, sales or profits ○ *a downturn in the market price* ○ *The last quarter saw a downturn in the economy.*

draft /drɑːft/ *noun* an order for money to be paid by a bank ○ *We asked for*

payment by banker's draft. □ **to make a draft on a bank** to ask a bank to pay money for you

draw /drɔː/ *verb* **1.** to take money away ○ *to draw money out of an account* □ **to draw a salary** to have a salary paid by the company ○ *The chairman does not draw a salary.* **2.** to write a cheque ○ *He paid the invoice with a cheque drawn on an Egyptian bank.* (NOTE: **drawing – drew – has drawn**)

drawback /'drɔːbæk/ *noun* **1.** something which is not convenient or which is likely to cause problems ○ *One of the main drawbacks of the scheme is that it will take six years to complete.* **2.** a rebate on customs duty for imported goods when these are then used in producing exports

drawee /drɔː'iː/ *noun* the person or bank asked to make a payment by a drawer

drawer /'drɔːə/ *noun* the person who writes a cheque or a bill asking a drawee to pay money to a payee □ **the bank returned the cheque to drawer** the bank would not pay the cheque because the person who wrote it did not have enough money in the account to pay it

drawing account /'drɔːɪŋ ə,kaʊnt/ *noun* a current account from which the customer may take money when he or she wants

drilling down /,drɪlɪŋ 'daʊn/ *noun* the action of sorting data into hierarchies, each of which is more detailed than the previous one

drip /drɪp/, **drip campaign** /'drɪp kæm,peɪn/, **drip method** /'drɪp ,meθəd/ *noun* the placing of advertisements for a product at fairly long intervals, making a long-drawn-out advertising campaign

drive /draɪv/ *noun* an energetic way of doing things □ **he has a lot of drive** he is very energetic in business

driver /'draɪvə/ *noun* something or someone that provides an impetus for something to happen

drive time /'draɪv taɪm/ *noun* the time when people are most likely to be listening to the radio in their cars, hence

a good time for broadcasting commercials

driving licence /'draɪvɪŋ ,laɪs(ə)ns/ *noun* the official document which shows someone is legally allowed to drive a car, a truck or other vehicle ○ *Applicants for the job should hold a valid driving licence.* (NOTE: the American English is **driver's license**)

drop /drɒp/ *noun* a fall ○ *a drop in sales* ○ *Sales show a drop of 10%.* ○ *The drop in prices resulted in no significant increase in sales.* ■ *verb* **1.** to fall ○ *Sales have dropped by 10%* or *have dropped 10%.* ○ *The pound dropped three points against the dollar.* **2.** not to keep in a product range ○ *We have dropped these items from the catalogue because they've been losing sales steadily for some time.* (NOTE: **dropping – dropped**)

'…while unemployment dropped by 1.6 per cent in the rural areas, it rose by 1.9 per cent in urban areas during the period under review' [*Business Times (Lagos)*]

'…corporate profits for the first quarter showed a 4 per cent drop from last year's final three months' [*Financial Times*]

'…since last summer American interest rates have dropped by between three and four percentage points' [*Sunday Times*]

drop ship /,drɒp 'ʃɪp/ *verb* to deliver a large order direct to a customer

drop shipment /'drɒp ,ʃɪpmənt/ *noun* the delivery of a large order from the manufacturer direct to a customer's shop or warehouse without going through an agent or wholesaler

dud /dʌd/ *adjective, noun* (of a coin or banknote) false or not good (*informal*) ○ *The £50 note was a dud.*

dud cheque /,dʌd 'tʃek/ *noun* a cheque which cannot be cashed because the person writing it has not enough money in the account to pay it

due /djuː/ *adjective* **1.** owed ○ *a sum due from a debtor* □ **to fall/become due** to be ready for payment □ **bill due on May 1st** a bill which has to be paid on May 1st □ **balance due to us** amount owed to us which should be paid **2.** expected to arrive ○ *The plane is due to arrive at 10.30* or *is due at 10.30.* **3.** □ **in due form** written in the correct legal form ○ *a receipt in due form* ○ *a con-*

tract drawn up in due form □ **after due consideration of the problem** after thinking seriously about the problem □ **due to** caused by ○ *Supplies have been delayed due to a problem at the manufacturers.* ○ *The company pays the wages of staff who are absent due to illness.*

'…many expect the US economic indicators for April, due out this Thursday, to show faster economic growth' [*Australian Financial Review*]

dues /djuːz/ *plural noun* orders taken but not supplied until new stock arrives □ **to release dues** to send off orders which had been piling up while a product was out of stock ○ *We have recorded thousands of dues for that item and our supplier cannot supply it.*

dummy /ˈdʌmi/ *noun* an imitation product to test the reaction of potential customers to its design

dummy pack /ˈdʌmi pæk/ *noun* an empty pack for display in a shop

dump /dʌmp/ *verb* □ **to dump goods on a market** to get rid of large quantities of excess goods cheaply in an overseas market

'…a serious threat lies in the 400,000 tonnes of subsidized beef in European cold stores. If dumped, this meat will have disastrous effects in Pacific Basin markets' [*Australian Financial Review*]

dump bin /ˈdʌmp bɪn/ *noun* display container like a large box which is filled with goods for sale

dump display /ˈdʌmp dɪˌspleɪ/ *noun* goods on special display in a container for purchasers to select themselves in a shop ○ *We will use dump displays with price reductions clearly marked.* ○ *There are several dump displays near the counters in the supermarket.*

dumping /ˈdʌmpɪŋ/ *noun* the act of getting rid of excess goods cheaply in an overseas market ○ *The government has passed anti-dumping legislation.* ○ *Dumping of goods on the European market is banned.* □ **panic dumping of sterling** a rush to sell sterling at any price because of possible devaluation

duopoly /djuːˈɒpəli/ *noun* the existence of only two producers or suppliers in a market ○ *The duopoly meant that*

the two businesses collaborated to keep prices at very high levels. ○ *When they took over their only competitor in the market, the duopoly became a monopoly.* Compare **monopoly**

duplication /ˌdjuːplɪˈkeɪʃ(ə)n/ *noun* running an advertisement twice to the same audience

durable /ˈdjʊərəb(ə)l/ *adjective* □ **durable effects** effects which will be felt for a long time ○ *These demographic changes will have durable effects on the economy.*

durable goods /ˈdjʊərəb(ə)l ɡʊdz/ *plural noun* goods which will be used for a long time, e.g. washing machines or refrigerators

dustbin check /ˈdʌstbɪn tʃek/ *noun* a consumer audit for which a panel of householders keep the empty containers of products bought so that these can be regularly checked for product type, size and brand

Dutch auction /ˌdʌtʃ ˈɔːkʃən/ *noun* an auction where the auctioneer offers an item for sale at a high price and then gradually reduces the price until someone makes a bid

duty /ˈdjuːti/ *noun* a tax which has to be paid ○ *Traders are asking the government to take the duty off alcohol* or *to put a duty on cigarettes.* □ **goods which are liable to duty** goods on which customs or excise tax has to be paid

'Canadian and European negotiators agreed to a deal under which Canada could lower its import duties on $150 million worth of European goods' [*Globe and Mail (Toronto)*]

'…the Department of Customs and Excise collected a total of N79m under the new advance duty payment scheme' [*Business Times (Lagos)*]

duty-free /ˌdjuːti ˈfriː/ *adjective, adverb* sold with no duty to be paid ○ *He bought a duty-free watch at the airport.* ○ *He bought the watch duty-free.*

duty-free shop /ˌdjuːti ˈfriː ʃɒp/ *noun* a shop at an airport or on a ship where goods can be bought without paying duty

duty-paid goods /ˌdjuːti ˈpeɪd ɡʊdz/ *plural noun* goods where the duty has been paid

dyadic communication /daɪˌædɪk kəˌmjuːnɪˈkeɪʃ(ə)n/ *noun* direct conversation between two people such as a salesperson and a customer

dynamic obsolescence /daɪˌnæmɪk ˌɒbsəˈles(ə)ns/ *noun* the redesigning of a company's product in order to make previous models and other products on the market obsolete

dynamic pricing /daɪˌnæmɪk ˈpraɪsɪŋ/ *noun* pricing that changes when the demand for something increases or decreases

E

e-alliance /'iː ə,laɪəns/ *noun* a partnership between organisations that do business over the web

e. & o.e. *abbr* errors and omissions excepted

ear /ɪə/ *noun* a space at the top left or right corner of the front page of a newspaper, set aside for advertising

early /'ɜːlɪ/ *adjective, adverb* before the usual time ○ *The mail arrived early.* ○ *We retired early and bought a house in Cornwall.* □ **at an early date** very soon

early adopters /,ɜːlɪ ə'dɒptəz/ *plural noun* the category of buyers of a product who use it or buy it later than innovators, but earlier than the late majority

early closing day /,ɜːlɪ 'kləʊzɪŋ deɪ/ *noun* a weekday, usually Wednesday or Thursday, when some shops close in the afternoon

early majority /,ɜːlɪ mə'dʒɒrɪti/ *noun* a category of buyers of a product who buy it later than the early adopters

earned rate /,ɜːnd 'reɪt/ *noun* the actual rate for a printed advertising space after taking discounts into account

earnest /'ɜːnɪst/ *noun* money paid as an initial payment by a buyer to a seller, to show commitment to the contract of sale

earning potential /'ɜːnɪŋ pə,tenʃəl/ *noun* **1.** the amount of money which someone should be able to earn **2.** the amount of dividend which a share is capable of earning

easy terms /,iːzi 'tɜːmz/ *plural noun* financial terms which are not difficult to accept ○ *The shop is let on very easy terms.*

e-business /'iː ,bɪznəs/ *noun* **1.** business activities, e.g. buying and selling, servicing customers and communicating with business partners, that are carried out electronically, especially on the Internet **2.** a company that does its business using the Internet

'…the enormous potential of e-business is that it can automate the link between suppliers and customers' [*Investors Chronicle*]

ecoconsumer /'iːkəʊkən,sjuːmə/ *noun* a customer who will buy goods that have been produced in a way that does not harm the environment

ecolabel /'iːkəʊleɪb(ə)l/ *noun* a label used to mark products that are produced and can be used and disposed of in a way that does not harm the environment

e-commerce /'iː ,kɒmɜːs/ *noun* the exchange of goods, information, products or services via an electronic medium such as the Internet (NOTE: Although e-commerce was originally limited to buying and selling, it has now evolved and includes such things as customer service, marketing, and advertising.)

'…the problem is that if e-commerce takes just a 3 per cent slice of the market that would be enough to reduce margins to ribbons' [*Investors Chronicle*]

'…the new economy requires new company structures. He believes that other blue-chip organizations are going to find that new set-ups would be needed to attract and retain the best talent for e-commerce' [*Times*]

e-commerce mall /'iː kɒmɜːs mɔːl/ *noun* same as **cyber mall**

e-company /'iː ,kʌmp(ə)ni/ *noun* a company that does all its business using the Internet

econometrics /ɪ,kɒnə'metrɪks/ *plural noun* the study of the statistics of economics, using computers to analyse these statistics and make forecasts using

mathematical models (NOTE: takes a singular verb)

economic /ˌiːkəˈnɒmɪk/ *adjective* **1.** which provides enough money to make a profit ○ *The flat is let at an economic rent.* ○ *It is hardly economic for the company to run its own warehouse.* **2.** referring to the financial state of a country ○ *economic planning* ○ *economic trends* ○ *Economic planners are expecting a comsumer-led boom.* ○ *The government's economic policy is in ruins after the devaluation.* ○ *The economic situation is getting worse.* ○ *The country's economic system needs more regulation.*

'...each of the major issues on the agenda at this week's meeting is important to the government's success in overall economic management' [*Australian Financial Review*]

economical /ˌiːkəˈnɒmɪk(ə)l/ *adjective* which saves money or materials or which is cheap □ **economical car** a car which does not use much petrol □ **an economical use of resources** using resources as carefully as possible

economic development /ˌiːkənɒmɪk dɪˈveləpmənt/ *noun* the expansion of the commercial and financial situation ○ *The economic development of the region has totally changed since oil was discovered there.* ○ *The government has offered tax incentives to speed up the economic development of the region.* ○ *Economic development has been relatively slow in the north, compared with the rest of the country.*

economic growth /ˌiːkənɒmɪk ˈɡrəʊθ/ *noun* the rate at which a country's national income grows

economic indicators /ˌiːkənɒmɪk ˈɪndɪkeɪtəz/ *plural noun* a set of statistics which shows how the economy is going to perform in the short or long term, e.g. the unemployment rate or overseas trade

economic infrastructure /ˌiːkənɒmɪk ˈɪnfrəstrʌktʃə/ *noun* the road and rail systems of a country

economic model /ˌiːkənɒmɪk ˈmɒd(ə)l/ *noun* a computerised plan of a country's economic system, used for forecasting economic trends

economic order quantity /ˌiːkənɒmɪk ˈɔːdə ˌkwɒntɪti/ *noun* the quantity of stocks which a company should hold, calculated on the basis of the costs of warehousing, of lower unit costs because of higher quantities purchased, the rate at which stocks are used and the time it takes for suppliers to deliver new orders. Abbr **EOQ**

economic planning /ˌiːkənɒmɪk ˈplænɪŋ/ *noun* the process of planning the future financial state of the country for the government

economics /ˌiːkəˈnɒmɪks/ *noun* the study of the production, distribution, selling and use of goods and services (NOTE: takes a singular verb) ■ *plural noun* the study of financial structures to show how a product or service is costed and what returns it produces ○ *I do not understand the economics of the coal industry.* (NOTE: takes a plural verb)

'...believers in free-market economics often find it hard to sort out their views on the issue' [*Economist*]

economic stagnation /ˌiːkənɒmɪk stæɡˈneɪʃ(ə)n/ *noun* a lack of expansion in the economy

economic trend /ˌiːkənɒmɪk ˈtrend/ *noun* the way in which a country's economy is moving

economies of scale /ɪˌkɒnəmiz əv ˈskeɪl/ *plural noun* a situation in which a product is made more profitable by manufacturing it in larger quantities so that each unit costs less to make. Compare **diseconomies of scale**

economist /ɪˈkɒnəmɪst/ *noun* a person who specialises in the study of economics ○ *Government economists are forecasting a growth rate of 3% next year.* ○ *An agricultural economist studies the economics of the agriculture industry.*

economy /ɪˈkɒnəmi/ *noun* **1.** being careful not to waste money or materials □ **to introduce economies** *or* **economy measures into the system** to start using methods to save money or materials **2.** the financial state of a country, or the way in which a country makes and uses its money ○ *The country's economy is in ruins.*

'...the European economies are being held back by rigid labor markets and wage structures, huge expenditures on social welfare programs and restrictions on the free movement of goods' [*Duns Business Month*]

economy car /ɪˈkɒnəmi kɑː/ *noun* a car which does not use much petrol

economy drive /ɪˈkɒnəmi draɪv/ *noun* vigorous effort to save money or materials

economy measure /ɪˈkɒnəmi ˌmeʒə/ *noun* an action to save money or materials

economy size /ɪˈkɒnəmi saɪz/ *noun* a large size or large packet which is cheaper than normal

editing /ˈedɪtɪŋ/ *noun* **1.** the process of checking the results of a survey to confirm that data has been collected correctly **2.** the process of modifying or correcting a text or film ○ *This sales literature needs editing to make it less long-winded.*

edition /ɪˈdɪʃ(ə)n/ *noun* an issue of a publication such as a newspaper, trade magazine or book ○ *We are too late to advertise in this month's edition.* ○ *There will be too many competing advertisements in that edition.*

editorial /ˌedɪˈtɔːriəl/ *adjective* referring to editors or to editing ■ *noun* the main article in a newspaper, written by the editor

editorial advertisement /edɪˌtɔːriəl ədˈvɜːtɪsmənt/ *noun* an advertisement in the form of text material in a magazine

editorial board /edɪˈtɔːriəl bɔːd/ *noun* a group of editors on a newspaper or other publication

editorial environment /edɪˌtɔːriəl ɪnˈvaɪərənmənt/ *noun* the general editorial tone and philosophy of a medium

editorial matter /edɪˈtɔːriəl ˌmætə/ *noun* the text of a magazine which is written by journalists, and not part of an advertisement

editorial publicity /edɪˌtɔːriəl pʌbˈlɪsɪti/ *noun* free publicity which is given to a product by a newspaper or magazine in an editorial or article, rather than in an advertisement which must be paid for

EDMA *abbr* European Direct Marketing Association

educational advertising /edjʊˌkeɪʃ(ə)nəl ˈædvətaɪzɪŋ/ *noun* advertising that informs consumers about a product, particularly important when the product has only recently been introduced ○ *Educational advertising has made the public aware that our product is just as safe as more traditional devices on the market.*

e-economy /ˈiː ɪˌkɒnəmi/ *noun* an economy in which the use of the Internet and information technology plays a major role

effect /ɪˈfekt/ *noun* **1.** a result ○ *The effect of the pay increase was to raise productivity levels.* **2.** □ **terms of a contract which take effect** *or* **come into effect from January 1st** terms which start to operate on January 1st □ **prices are increased 10% with effect from January 1st** new prices will apply from January 1st □ **to remain in effect** to continue to be applied **3.** meaning □ **a clause to the effect that** a clause which means that □ **we have made provision to this effect** we have put into the contract terms which will make this work ■ *verb* to carry out □ **to effect a payment** to make a payment □ **to effect customs clearance** to clear something through customs □ **to effect a settlement between two parties** to bring two parties together and make them agree to a settlement

effective /ɪˈfektɪv/ *adjective* **1.** actual, as opposed to theoretical **2.** □ **a clause effective as from January 1st** a clause which starts to be applied on January 1st **3.** which works or produces results ○ *Advertising in the Sunday papers is the most effective way of selling.* ○ *She is an effective marketing manager.* ♦ **cost-effective**

effective cover /ɪˌfektɪv ˈkʌvə/ *noun* a situation where consumers in the target audience will have seen the advertisement at least four times on average

effective date /ɪˌfektɪv ˈdeɪt/ *noun* the date on which a rule or contract

starts to be applied, or on which a transaction takes place

effective demand /ɪˌfektɪv dɪ-ˈmɑːnd/ *noun* the actual demand for a product which can be paid for

effectiveness /ɪˈfektɪvnəs/ *noun* the quality of working or producing results ○ *I doubt the effectiveness of television advertising.* ♦ **cost-effectiveness**

effective reach /ɪˌfektɪv ˈriːtʃ/ *noun* the actual number of people who will see an advertisement once

effective sample size /ɪˌfektɪv ˈsɑːmpəl saɪz/ *noun* the size of a sample after all irrelevant factors have been removed

effectual /ɪˈfektʃuəl/ *adjective* which produces a correct result

ego /ˈiːɡəʊ, ˈeɡəʊ/ *noun* the psychological term for a person's consciousness of himself or herself ○ *We are designing clothes to boost men's egos.* ○ *Glamorous advertising appeals to the customer's ego.*

eighty/twenty rule /ˌeɪti ˈtwenti ruːl/ *noun* the rule that a small percentage of customers may account for a large percentage of sales. ♦ **Pareto's Law**

elastic /ɪˈlæstɪk/ *adjective* which can expand or contract easily because of small changes in price

elastic demand /ɪˌlæstɪk dɪˈmɑːnd/ *noun* demand which experiences a comparatively large percentage change in response to a change in price

elasticity /ˌɪlæˈstɪsəti/ *noun* the ability to change easily in response to a change in circumstances □ **elasticity of supply and demand** changes in supply and demand of an item depending on its market price

elastic supply /ɪˌlæstɪk səˈplaɪ/ *noun* supply which experiences a comparatively large percentage change in response to a change in price

electronic /ˌelɪkˈtrɒnɪk/ *adjective* referring to computers and electronics

electronic cash /ˌelɪktrɒnɪk ˈkæʃ/ *noun* same as **digital cash**

electronic catalogue /ˌelɪktrɒnɪk ˈkæt(ə)lɒɡ/ *noun* a catalogue of the goods that a supplier has for sale, which can be viewed in an electronic format, e.g., on a website

electronic commerce /ˌelɪktrɒnɪk ˈkɒmɜːs/ *noun* same as **e-commerce**

electronic data capture /ˌelɪktrɒnɪk ˈdeɪtə ˌkæptʃə/ *noun* the use of data-processing equipment to collect data, especially the use of electronic point-of-sale equipment to collect, validate and submit data when credit or debit cards are used in transactions

electronic data interchange /ˌelɪktrɒnɪk ˈdeɪtə ˌɪntətʃeɪndʒ/ *noun* a standard format used when business documents such as invoices and purchase orders are exchanged over electronic networks such as the Internet

electronic data processing /ˌelɪktrɒnɪk ˈdeɪtə ˌprəʊsesɪŋ/ *noun* the process of selecting and examining data stored in a computer to produce information. Abbr **EDP**

electronic funds transfer at point of sale /ˌelɪktrɒnɪk fʌndz ˈtrænsfɜː ət ˌpɔɪnt əv ˈseɪl/ *noun* a system for transferring money directly from the purchaser's account to the seller's, when a sale is made using a plastic card. Abbr **EFTPOS**

electronic mail /ˌelɪktrɒnɪk ˈmeɪl/ *noun* same as **email 1**

electronic media /ˌelɪktrɒnɪk ˈmiːdiə/ *plural noun* electronic-based media, e.g. television and radio ○ *Advertising in the electronic media would certainly increase sales, but we can only afford to advertise in the press.*

electronic payment system /ˌelɪktrɒnɪk ˈpeɪmənt ˌsɪstəm/ *noun* a means of making payments over an electronic network such as the Internet

electronic point of sale /ˌelɪktrɒnɪk pɔɪnt əv ˈseɪl/ *noun* a system where sales are charged automatically to a customer's credit card and stock is controlled by the shop's computer. Abbr **EPOS**

electronic shopping /ˌelɪktrɒnɪk ˈʃɒpɪŋ/ *noun* shopping for goods or services which takes place over an electronic network such as the Internet

eliminate /ɪˈlɪmɪneɪt/ *verb* to remove ○ *to eliminate defects in the system* ○ *Using a computer should eliminate all possibility of error.* ○ *We have decided to eliminate this series of old products from our range.* ○ *Most of the candidates were eliminated after the first batch of tests.*

elimination /ɪˌlɪmɪˈneɪʃ(ə)n/ *noun* the act of removing something

email /ˈiːmeɪl/ *noun* **1.** a system of sending messages from one computer terminal to another, using a modem and telephone lines ○ *You can contact me by phone or email if you want.* **2.** a message sent electronically ○ *I had six emails from him today.* ■ *verb* to send a message from one computer to another, using a modem and telephone lines ○ *She emailed her order to the warehouse.* ○ *I emailed him about the meeting.*

email campaign /ˈiːmeɪl kæmˌpeɪn/ *noun* a series of emails which deliver marketing messages to individuals

email mailing list /ˌiː meɪl ˈmeɪlɪŋ lɪst/ *noun* a marketing technique that involves contacting a group of people from anywhere in the world and inviting them to discuss a particular topic and share information and experience by email (NOTE: An email mailing list is run by a moderator who compiles a list of email addresses for possible members, mails them with the theme for discussion, collects their contributions, and publishes them by email so that other members of the group can respond to them.)

e-marketplace /iː ˈmɑːkɪtpleɪs/ *noun* a network of connections that brings business-to-business buyers and sellers together on the Internet and enables them to trade more efficiently online

embargo /ɪmˈbɑːɡəʊ/ *noun* **1.** a government order which stops a type of trade □ **to lay** *or* **put an embargo on trade with a country** to say that trade with a country must not take place ○ *The government has put an embargo on the export of computer equipment.* □ **to lift an embargo** to allow trade to start again ○ *The government has lifted the* *embargo on the export of computers.* □ **to be under an embargo** to be forbidden **2.** a period of time during which specific information in a press release must not be published (NOTE: plural is **embargoes**) ■ *verb* **1.** to stop trade or not to allow trade ○ *The government has embargoed trade with the Eastern countries.* **2.** not to allow publication of information for a period of time ○ *The news of the merger has been embargoed until next Wednesday.*

'…the Commerce Department is planning to loosen export controls for products that have been embargoed but are readily available elsewhere in the West' [*Duns Business Month*]

e-money /ˈiː ˌmʌni/ *noun* same as **digital money**

emotional appeal /ɪˌməʊʃ(ə)n(ə)l əˈpiːl/ *noun* an attempt by advertising to persuade through an emotional rather than a rational message ○ *The charity used the emotional appeal of starving children to raise funds.* ○ *Emotional appeal was an obvious feature in all the political parties' campaign films.*

empirical data /ɪmˌpɪrɪk(ə)l ˈdeɪtə/ *noun* data or information which comes from actual observation or which can be proved ○ *We have no empirical data concerning our competitors' sales last year.*

employers' liability insurance /ɪmˌplɔɪəz ˌlaɪəˈbɪlɪti ɪnˌʃʊərəns/ *noun* insurance to cover accidents which may happen at work, and for which the company may be responsible

employers' organization /ɪmˈplɔɪəz ɔːɡənaɪˌzeɪʃ(ə)n/, **employers' association** /ɪmˈplɔɪəz əsəʊsiˌeɪʃ(ə)n/ *noun* a group of employers with similar interests

employment agency /ɪmˈplɔɪmənt ˌeɪdʒənsi/ *noun* an office which finds jobs for staff

emporium /ɪmˈpɔːriəm/ *noun* a large shop (NOTE: plural is **emporia**)

emptor /ˈemptə/ *noun* ◊ **caveat emptor**

empty nesters /ˌempti ˈnestəz/ *plural noun* couples whose children have grown up and left the home

enc, encl *abbr* enclosure

enclose /ɪnˈkləʊz/ *verb* to put something inside an envelope with a letter ○ *to enclose an invoice with a letter* ○ *I am enclosing a copy of the contract.* ○ *Please find the cheque enclosed herewith.* ○ *Please enclose a recent photograph with your CV.*

enclosure /ɪnˈkləʊʒə/ *noun* a document enclosed with a letter or package ○ *The enclosure turned out to be a free sample of perfume.* ○ *Sales material on other products was sent out as an enclosure.*

encode /ɪnˈkəʊd/ *verb* to write something in a code so that it cannot be read or used by other people

end /end/ *noun* the final point or last part ○ *at the end of the contract period*

end consumer /end kənˈsjuːmə/ *noun* a person who uses a product ○ *The survey was designed to assess the attitudes of end consumers to the product.*

end of season sale /ˌend əv ˈsiːz(ə)n seɪl/ *noun* a sale of goods at a lower price when the season in which they would be used is over such as summer clothes sold cheaply in the autumn

endorse /ɪnˈdɔːs/ *verb* to say that a product is good □ **to endorse a bill** *or* **a cheque** to sign a bill or cheque on the back to show that you accept it

endorsee /endɔːˈsiː/ *noun* a person whose name is written on a bill or cheque as having the right to cash it

endorsement /ɪnˈdɔːsmənt/ *noun* **1.** the act of endorsing **2.** signature on a document which endorses it

endorsement advertising /ɪnˈdɔːsmənt ˌædvətaɪzɪŋ/ *noun* same as **product endorsement**

endorser /ɪnˈdɔːsə/ *noun* a person who endorses a bill which is then paid to him or her

end user /end ˈjuːzə/ *noun* a person who actually uses a product

enhancement /ɪnˈhɑːnsmənt/ *noun* increase or improvement in quality of service, value for money, etc.

ent /ent/ *noun* a test of number sequences for large quantities of data

enterprise /ˈentəpraɪz/ *noun* **1.** a system of carrying on a business **2.** a business

enterprise zone /ˈentəpraɪz zəʊn/ *noun* an area of the country where businesses are encouraged to develop by offering special conditions such as easy planning permission for buildings or a reduction in the business rate

entrant /ˈentrənt/ *noun* a company which goes into a market for the first time

entrepot port /ˈɒntrəpəʊ pɔːt/ *noun* a town with a large international commercial port dealing in re-exports

entrepot trade /ˈɒntrəpəʊ treɪd/ *noun* the exporting of imported goods

entrepreneur /ˌɒntrəprəˈnɜː/ *noun* a person who directs a company and takes commercial risks

entrepreneurial /ˌɒntrəprəˈnɜːriəl/ *adjective* taking commercial risks ○ *an entrepreneurial decision*

entry barrier /ˈentri ˌbæriə/ *noun* same as **barrier to entry**

E number /ˈiː ˌnʌmbə/ *noun* a classification of additives to food according to the European Union

COMMENT: Additives are classified as follows: colouring substances: E100 – E180; preservatives: E200 – E297; antioxidants: E300 – E321; emulsifiers and stabilizers: E322 – E495; acids and bases: E500 – E529; anti-caking additives: E530 – E578; flavour enhancers and sweeteners: E620 – E637.

envelope stuffer /ˈenvələʊp ˌstʌfə/ *noun* advertising material which is mailed in an envelope

environment /ɪnˈvaɪrənmənt/ *noun* the area in which an organisation works

environmental analysis /ɪnˌvaɪrənˌment(ə)l əˈnæləsɪs/ *noun* analysis of factors outside an organisation such as demography or politics, in order to make strategic planning more effective ○ *Our environmental analysis must cover all the countries we sell in.* ○ *Environmental analysis made clear that some markets were too unstable to enter.*

environmental management /ɪnvaɪrən‚ment(ə)l 'mænɪdʒmənt/ *noun* a planned approach to minimising an organisation's impact on the environment

epos /'iːpɒs/, **EPOS, EPoS** *abbr* electronic point of sale

equilibrium /‚iːkwɪ'lɪbriəm/ *noun* the state of balance in the economy where supply equals demand

equity capital /'ekwɪti ‚kæpɪt(ə)l/ *noun* the nominal value of the shares owned by the ordinary shareholders of a company (NOTE: Preference shares are not equity capital. If the company were wound up, none of the equity capital would be distributed to preference shareholders.)

e-retailer /'iː ‚riːteɪlə/ *noun* a business that uses an electronic network such as the Internet to sell its goods or services

erode /ɪ'rəʊd/ *verb* to wear away gradually □ **to erode wage differentials** to reduce gradually differences in salary between different grades

error /'erə/ *noun* a mistake ○ *He made an error in calculating the total.* ○ *The secretary must have made a typing error.*

error rate /'erə reɪt/ *noun* the number of mistakes per thousand entries or per page

escalate /'eskəleɪt/ *verb* to increase steadily

escalation /‚eskə'leɪʃ(ə)n/ *noun* a steady increase ○ *an escalation of wage demands* ○ *The union has threatened an escalation in strike action.* □ **escalation of prices** a steady increase in prices

escalation clause /‚eskə'leɪʃ(ə)n klɔːz/ *noun* same as **escalator clause**

escalator /'eskəleɪtə/ *noun* a moving staircase

escalator card /'eskəleɪtə kɑːd/ *noun* an advertisement on either side of an escalator in underground stations ○ *The media buyer compared the cost of posters and escalator cards.*

escalator clause /'eskəleɪtə klɔːz/ *noun* a clause in a contract allowing for regular price increases because of increased costs, or regular wage increases because of the increased cost of living

escrow /'eskrəʊ/ *noun* □ **in escrow** held in safe keeping by a third party □ **document held in escrow** a document given to a third party to keep and to pass on to someone when money has been paid

escrow account /'eskrəʊ ə‚kaʊnt/ *noun US* an account where money is held in escrow until a contract is signed or until goods are delivered

essential /ɪ'senʃəl/ *adjective* very important ○ *It is essential that an agreement be reached before the end of the month.* ○ *The factory is lacking essential spare parts.*

essential goods /ɪ‚senʃəl 'gʊdz/, **essential products** /ɪ‚senʃəl 'prɒdʌktz/ *plural noun* basic goods or products necessary for everyday life

estate duty /ɪ'steɪt ‚djuːti/ *noun* a tax paid on the property left by a dead person

estimate *noun* /'estɪmət/ **1.** a calculation of probable cost, size or time of something □ **these figures are only an estimate** these are not the final accurate figures ○ *Can you give me an estimate of how much time was spent on the job?* **2.** a calculation by a contractor or seller of a service of how much something is likely to cost, given to a client in advance of an order ○ *You should ask for an estimate before committing yourselves.* ○ *Before we can give the grant we must have an estimate of the total costs involved.* ○ *Unfortunately the final bill was quite different from the estimate.* □ **to put in an estimate** to give someone a written calculation of the probable costs of carrying out a job ○ *Three firms put in estimates for the job.* ■ *verb* /'estɪmeɪt/ **1.** to calculate the probable cost, size or time of something ○ *to estimate that it will cost £1m* or *to estimate costs at £1m* ○ *We estimate current sales at only 60% of last year.* **2.** □ **to estimate for a job** to state in writing the future costs of carrying out a piece of work so that a client can make an order ○ *Three firms estimated for the refitting of the offices.*

estimated /'estɪmeɪtɪd/ *adjective* calculated approximately ○ *estimated sales* ○ *Costs were slightly more than the estimated figure.*

estimation /ˌestɪ'meɪʃ(ə)n/ *noun* an approximate calculation

estimator /'estɪmeɪtə/ *noun* a person whose job is to calculate estimates for carrying out work

e-tailer /'iː teɪlə/ *noun* same as **e-retailer**

e-tailing /'iː teɪlɪŋ/ *noun* **1.** the selling of goods and services using an electronic network such as the Internet **2.** same as **e-commerce**

ethics /'eθɪks/ *noun* the moral aspects of decision-making ○ *Whether or not we use such aggressive sales tactics is a matter of ethics.* (NOTE: takes a singular verb)

ethnic /'eθnɪk/ *adjective* relating to people who share the same race, culture and traditions

ethnic media /ˌeθnɪk 'miːdiə/ *plural noun* magazines or TV stations which appeal to ethnic audiences

ethnocentric stage /ˌeθnəʊ 'sentrɪk steɪdʒ/ *noun US* an early stage in a company's marketing when goods are sent overseas with no concessions to local needs or tastes

EU /'iː'juː/ *abbr* European Union ○ *EU ministers met today in Brussels.* ○ *The USA is increasing its trade with the EU.*

European Community /ˌjʊərə-ˌpiːən kə'mjuːnɪti/ *noun* formerly, the name of the European Union

European Direct Marketing Association /ˌjʊərəpiːən daɪˌrekt 'maːkɪtɪŋ əˌsəʊsieɪʃ(ə)n/ an organisation based in Switzerland which monitors new techniques in direct marketing and represents the interests of its members. Abbr **EDMA**

European Union /jʊərə'piːən 'jʊnɪən/ (formerly, the European Economic Community (EEC), the Common Market) a group of European countries linked together by the Treaty of Rome in such a way that trade is more free, people can move from one country to another more freely and people can

work more freely in other countries of the group

evaluate /ɪ'væljueɪt/ *verb* to examine something to see how good it is

evaluation /ɪˌvæljʊ'eɪʃ(ə)n/ *noun* the examination of a product to see how good it is

evaluative /ɪ'væljuətɪv/ *adjective* referring to the calculation of value

evaluative criteria /ɪˌvæljuətɪv kraɪ'tɪəriə/ *plural noun* the criteria used to compare different products or services

even number /ˌiːv(ə)n 'nʌmbə/ *noun* a number which can be divided by two, e.g. 24 or 80

event /ɪ'vent/ *noun* a thing which happens, e.g. a sports competition, a flower show

event marketing /ɪ'vent ˌmaːkɪtɪŋ/ *noun* promotional activity to advertise an event

event sponsorship /ɪ'vent ˌspɒnsəʃɪp/ *noun* a promotional deal by which a company sponsors a particular event such as a concert, sporting event, or other activity, on a regular basis

evoke /ɪ'vəʊk/ *verb* to call up an image

evoked set /ɪˌvəʊkt 'set/ *noun* the various brands which are identified by a consumer as possible purchases and which he or she considers during the alternative evaluation process

ex /eks/ *preposition* **1.** out of or from □ **price ex warehouse** a price for a product which is to be collected from the manufacturer's or agent's warehouse and so does not include delivery □ **price ex works** *or* **ex factory** a price not including transport from the maker's factory **2.** without

ex- /eks/ *prefix* former ○ *an ex-director of the company*

excess /ɪk'ses, 'ekses/ *noun* an amount which is more than what is allowed ○ *an excess of expenditure over revenue*

'…most airlines give business class the same baggage allowance as first class, which can save large sums in excess baggage' [*Business Traveller*]

'...control of materials provides manufacturers with an opportunity to reduce the amount of money tied up in excess materials' [*Duns Business Month*]

excess baggage /ˌekses ˈbægɪdʒ/ *noun* an extra payment at an airport for taking baggage which is heavier than the normal passenger's allowance

excess capacity /ˌekses kəˈpæsɪti/ *noun* spare capacity which is not being used

excess demand /ˌekses dɪˈmɑːnd/ *noun* more demand at the present price than sellers can satisfy ○ *Much more machinery and labour must be acquired to meet excess demand.*

excess profit /ˌekses ˈprɒfɪt/ *noun* profit which is higher than what is thought to be normal

excess supply /ˌekses səˈplaɪ/ *noun* more supply at the present price than buyers want to buy

exchange /ɪksˈtʃeɪndʒ/ *noun* the act of giving one thing for another □ **exchange of contracts** the point in the sale of property when the buyer and the seller both sign the contract of sale which then becomes binding ■ *verb* **1.** □ **to exchange something (for something else)** to give one thing in place of something else ○ *He exchanged his motorcycle for a car.* ○ *If the trousers are too small you can take them back and exchange them for a larger pair.* ○ *Goods can be exchanged only on production of the sales slip.* **2.** to change money of one country for money of another ○ *to exchange euros for pounds*

'...under the barter agreements, Nigeria will export crude oil in exchange for trucks, food, planes and chemicals' [*Wall Street Journal*]

exchangeable /ɪksˈtʃeɪndʒəb(ə)l/ *adjective* which can be exchanged

exchange control /ɪksˈtʃeɪndʒ kənˌtrəʊl/ *noun* the control by a government of the way in which its currency may be exchanged for foreign currencies ○ *The government had to impose exchange controls to stop the rush to buy dollars.*

exchange controls /ɪksˈtʃeɪndʒ kənˌtrəʊlz/ *plural noun* government restrictions on changing the local currency into foreign currency ○ *The government*

has imposed exchange controls. ○ *They say the government is going to lift exchange controls.*

exchange dealer /ɪksˈtʃeɪndʒ ˌdiːlə/ *noun* a person who buys and sells foreign currency

exchange dealings /ɪksˈtʃeɪndʒ ˌdiːlɪŋz/ *plural noun* the buying and selling of foreign currency

exchange economy /ɪksˈtʃeɪndʒ ɪˌkɒnəmi/ *noun* an economy based on the exchange of goods and services

exchange premium /ɪksˈtʃeɪndʒ ˌpriːmiəm/ *noun* an extra cost above the normal rate for buying a foreign currency

exchanger /ɪksˈtʃeɪndʒə/ *noun* a person who buys and sells foreign currency

exchange rate /ɪksˈtʃeɪndʒ reɪt/ *noun* a figure that expresses how much a unit of one country's currency is worth in terms of the currency of another country

'...can free trade be reconciled with a strong dollar resulting from floating exchange rates' [*Duns Business Month*]

'...a draft report on changes in the international monetary system casts doubt on any return to fixed exchange-rate parities' [*Wall Street Journal*]

exchange transaction /ɪksˈtʃeɪndʒ trænˌzækʃən/ *noun* a purchase or sale of foreign currency

excise duty /ˈeksaɪz ˌdjuːti/ *noun* a tax on goods such as alcohol and petrol which are produced in the country

exclusion clause /ɪkˈskluːʒ(ə)n klɔːz/ *noun* a clause in an insurance policy or warranty which says which items or events are not covered

exclusive *adjective* /ɪkˈskluːsɪv/ **1.** limited to one person or group □ **to have exclusive right to market a product** to be the only person who has the right to market a product **2.** □ **exclusive of** not including ○ *All payments are exclusive of tax.* ○ *The invoice is exclusive of VAT.* ■ *noun* the exclusive rights to a news story or the story itself

exclusive agreement /ɪkˌskluːsɪv əˈgriːmənt/ *noun* an agreement where a

person is made sole agent for a product in a market

exclusivity /ˌeksklu:'sɪvɪtɪ/ *noun* the exclusive right to market a product

ex dividend /eks 'dɪvɪdend/ *adjective* referring to a share price not including the right to receive the next dividend ○ *The shares went ex dividend yesterday.*

exempt /ɪg'zempt/ *adjective* not covered by a law, or not forced to obey a law ○ *Anyone over 65 is exempt from charges* □ **exempt from tax** not required to pay tax ○ *As a non-profit-making organisation we are exempt from tax.* ■ *verb* **1.** to free something from having tax paid on it ○ *Non-profit-making organisations are exempted from tax.* **2.** to free someone from having to pay tax ○ *Food is exempted from sales tax.*

'Companies with sales under $500,000 a year will be exempt from the minimum-wage requirements' [*Nation's Business*]

exempt rating /ɪg'zempt ˌreɪtɪŋ/ *noun* the legal right of a business not to add VAT to the prices of some products or services

exempt supplies /ɪgˌzempt sə'plaɪz/ *plural noun* products or services on which the supplier does not have to charge VAT

ex gratia /eks 'greɪʃə/ *adjective* done as a favour

ex gratia payment /eks ˌgreɪʃə 'peɪmənt/ *noun* a payment made as a gift, with no other obligations

exhibit /ɪg'zɪbɪt/ *noun* **1.** a thing which is shown ○ *The buyers admired the exhibits on our stand.* **2.** a single section of an exhibition ○ *the British Trade Exhibit at the International Computer Fair* ■ *verb* □ **to exhibit at the Motor Show** to display new models of cars at the Motor Show

exhibition /ˌeksɪ'bɪʃ(ə)n/ *noun* an occasion for the display of goods so that buyers can look at them and decide what to buy ○ *The government has sponsored an exhibition of good design.* ○ *We have a stand at the Ideal Home Exhibition.* ○ *The agricultural exhibition grounds were crowded with visitors.*

exhibition stand /ˌeksɪ'bɪʃ(ə)n stænd/ *noun* a separate section of an exhibition where a company exhibits its products or services

exhibitor /ɪg'zɪbɪtə/ *noun* a person or company that shows products at an exhibition

exorbitant /ɪg'zɔ:bɪtənt/ *adjective* unreasonably high in price ○ *$10,000 a minute, that's exorbitant and quite unjustified.* ○ *Their fees may seem exorbitant, but their costs are very high.*

expand /ɪk'spænd/ *verb* to get bigger, or make something bigger ○ *an expanding economy* ○ *The company is expanding fast.* ○ *We have had to expand our sales force.*

expansion /ɪk'spænʃən/ *noun* an increase in size ○ *The expansion of the domestic market.* ○ *The company had difficulty in financing its current expansion programme.*

'...inflation-adjusted GNP moved up at a 1.3% annual rate, its worst performance since the economic expansion began' [*Fortune*]

'...the businesses we back range from start-up ventures to established businesses in need of further capital for expansion' [*Times*]

'...the group is undergoing a period of rapid expansion and this has created an exciting opportunity for a qualified accountant' [*Financial Times*]

expect /ɪk'spekt/ *verb* to hope that something is going to happen ○ *We are expecting him to arrive at 10.45.* ○ *They are expecting a cheque from their agent next week.* ○ *The house was sold for more than the expected price.*

'...he observed that he expected exports to grow faster than imports in the coming year' [*Sydney Morning Herald*]

'American business as a whole has seen profits well above the levels normally expected at this stage of the cycle' [*Sunday Times*]

expectation /ˌekspek'teɪʃ(ə)n/ *noun* **1.** what someone believes will happen, especially concerning their future prosperity **2.** what someone believes about an item or service to be purchased, which is one of the reasons for making the purchase

expected price /ek'spektɪd praɪs/ *noun* the price of a product which consumers consider corresponds to its true value

expense /ɪk'spens/ *noun* money spent ○ *It is not worth the expense.* ○ *The expense is too much for my bank balance.* ○ *The likely profits do not justify the expense of setting up the project.* ○ *It was well worth the expense to get really high-quality equipment.*

expense account /ɪk'spens ə,kaʊnt/ *noun* an allowance of money which a business pays for an employee to spend on travelling and entertaining clients in connection with that business ○ *I can put this lunch on my expense account*

expenses /ɪk'spensɪz/ *plural noun* money paid to cover the costs incurred by someone when doing something ○ *The salary offered is £10,000 plus expenses.* □ **all expenses paid** with all costs paid by the company ○ *The company sent him to San Francisco all expenses paid.* □ **to cut down on expenses** to reduce spending

expensive /ɪk'spensɪv/ *adjective* which costs a lot of money ○ *First-class air travel is becoming more and more expensive.*

experience /ɪk'spɪərɪəns/ *noun* knowledge or skill that comes from having had to deal with many different situations ○ *She has a lot of experience of dealing with German companies.* ○ *I gained most of my experience abroad.* ○ *Considerable experience is required for this job.* ○ *The applicant was pleasant, but did not have any relevant experience.* ■ *verb* to live through a situation ○ *The company experienced a period of falling sales.*

experience curve /ɪk'spɪərɪəns kɜːv/ *noun* a graph showing the relationship between the cumulative amount of products produced and the production cost per unit ○ *The experience curve shows how increasing efficiency has brought down our costs.*

experienced /ɪk'spɪərɪənst/ *adjective* referring to a person who has lived through many situations and has learnt from them ○ *You are the most experienced negotiator I know.* ○ *We have appointed a very experienced candidate as sales director.* ○ *Our more experienced* staff will have dealt with a crisis like this before.

experience effect /ɪk'spɪərɪəns ɪ,fekt/ *noun* the role of experience in improving business efficiency ○ *The experience effect is evident in the rise in our profits as our workforce becomes more skilled.*

experiencer /ek'spɪərɪənsə/ *noun* in the VALS lifestyle classification system, a young person who likes new and unusual things and spends a lot of money on hobbies and socialising

experiential advertising /ek-,spɪərienʃəl 'ædvətaɪzɪŋ/ *noun* advertising which conveys to the customer the real sensation of using the product

experimental method /eksperɪ-'ment(ə)l ,meθəd/ *noun* the use of controlled experiments to discover the influence of various variables in marketing such as types of promotion and sales training

expert /'ekspɜːt/ *noun* a person who knows a lot about something ○ *an expert in the field of electronics* or *an electronics expert* ○ *The company asked a financial expert for advice* or *asked for expert financial advice.* □ **expert's report** a report written by an expert

expertise /,ekspə'tiːz/ *noun* specialist knowledge or skill in a particular field ○ *With years of experience in the industry, we have plenty of expertise to draw on.* ○ *Lack of marketing expertise led to low sales figures.* ○ *We hired Mr Smith because of his financial expertise* or *because of his expertise in finance.*

expert system /'ekspɜːt 'sɪstəm/ *noun* a computer program that is designed to imitate the way a human expert in a particular field thinks and makes decisions (NOTE: Expert systems, which are an application of artificial intelligence, are used for a wide variety of tasks including medical diagnostics and financial decision-making and can be used by non-experts to solve well-defined problems when human experts are unavailable.)

exploit /ɪk'splɔɪt/ *verb* to use something to make a profit ○ *The company is exploiting its contacts in the Ministry of*

Trade. ○ *We hope to exploit the oil resources in the China Sea.*

exponential diffusion /ˌekspə-ˌnenʃ(ə)l dɪˈfjuːʒ(ə)n/, **exponential growth** /ekspəˌnenʃ(ə)l ˈgrəʊθ/ *noun* a typical growth pattern of new products that involves a slow start, followed by acceleration and finally a slowing down

exponential smoothing /ekspə-ˌnenʃ(ə)l ˈsmuːðɪŋ/*noun* a technique for working out averages while allowing for recent changes in values by moving forward the period under consideration at regular intervals

export *noun* /ˈekspɔːt/ the practice or business of sending goods to foreign countries to be sold ○ *50% of the company's profits come from the export trade* or *the export market.* ■ *verb* /ɪkˈspɔːt/ to send goods to foreign countries for sale ○ *50% of our production is exported.* ○ *The company imports raw materials and exports the finished products.*

'…in the past, export documentation was a major stumbling block for some companies' [*Marketing & Sales Management*]

'Europe's gross exports of white goods climbed to 2.4 billion, about a quarter of total production' [*Economist*]

'…the New Zealand producers are now aiming to export more fresh meat as opposed to frozen which has formed the majority of its UK imports in the past' [*Marketing*]

export agent /ˈekspɔːt ˌeɪdʒənt/ *noun* a person who sells overseas on behalf of a company and earns a commission ○ *An export agent is developing our business in West Africa.* ○ *She is working in London as an export agent for a French company.*

exportation /ˌekspɔːˈteɪʃ(ə)n/ *noun* the act of sending goods to foreign countries for sale

export bounty /ˈekspɔːt ˌbaʊnti/ *noun* a government payment to businesses to encourage specific types of export

Export Credit Guarantee Department /ˌekspɔːt ˌkredɪt gærənˈtiː dɪ-ˌpɑːtmənt/ *noun* a British government department which insures sellers of exports sold on credit against the possibility of non-payment by the purchasers. Abbr **ECGD**

export department /ˈekspɔːt dɪ-ˌpɑːtmənt/ *noun* the section of a company which deals in sales to foreign countries

export duty /ˈekspɔːt ˌdjuːti/ *noun* a tax paid on goods sent out of a country for sale

exporter /ɪkˈspɔːtə/ *noun* a person, company or country that sells goods in foreign countries ○ *a major furniture exporter* ○ *Canada is an important exporter of oil* or *an important oil exporter.*

export house /ˈekspɔːt haʊs/ *noun* a company which specialises in the export of goods manufactured by other companies

exporting /ekˈspɔːtɪŋ/ *adjective* which exports □ **oil-exporting countries** countries which produce oil and sell it to other countries

export licence /ˈekspɔːt ˌlaɪs(ə)ns/ *noun* a government permit allowing something to be exported ○ *The government has refused an export licence for computer parts.*

export manager /ˈekspɔːt ˌmænɪdʒə/ *noun* the person in charge of an export department in a company ○ *The export manager planned to set up a sales force in Southern Europe.* ○ *Sales managers from all export markets report to our export manager.*

exports /ˈekspɔːts/ *plural noun* goods sent to a foreign country to be sold ○ *Exports to Africa have increased by 25%.* (NOTE: usually used in the plural, but the singular form is used before a noun)

exposition /ˌekspəˈzɪʃ(ə)n/ *noun US* same as **exhibition**

exposure /ɪkˈspəʊʒə/ *noun* publicity given to an organisation or product ○ *Our company has achieved more exposure since we decided to advertise nationally.*

'…it attributed the poor result to the bank's high exposure to residential mortgages, which showed a significant slowdown in the past few months' [*South China Morning Post*]

express /ɪkˈspres/ *adjective* rapid or very fast ○ *an express letter* ■ *verb* to send something very fast ○ *We ex-*

pressed the order to the customer's warehouse.

expressage /ɪkˈspresɪdʒ/ *noun US* a very fast transport service

express delivery /ɪkˌspres dɪˈlɪv(ə)ri/ *noun* very fast delivery

extend /ɪkˈstend/ *verb* **1.** to offer ○ *to extend credit to a customer* **2.** to make longer ○ *Her contract of employment was extended for two years.* ○ *We have extended the deadline for making the appointment by two weeks.*

extended credit /ɪkˌstendɪd ˈkredɪt/ *noun* credit allowing the borrower a very long time to pay ○ *We sell to Australia on extended credit.*

extended guarantee /ɪkˌstendɪd ɡærənˈtiː/ *noun* a guarantee, offered by a dealer on consumer durables such as dishwashers, which goes beyond the time specified in the manufacturer's guarantee

extension /ɪkˈstenʃən/ *noun* allowing a longer time for something than was originally agreed □ **to get an extension of credit** to get more time to pay back □ **extension of a contract** the continuing of a contract for a further period

'…the White House refusal to ask for an extension of the auto import quotas' [*Duns Business Month*]

extension strategy /ɪkˈstenʃən ˌstrætədʒi/ *noun* a marketing strategy aimed at extending the life of a product either by making small changes in it, finding new uses for it or finding new markets ○ *An extension strategy is needed to ensure demand for another few years.* ○ *The extension strategy consisted in providing a greater choice of colours and upholstery for the range of cars.*

extensive /ɪkˈstensɪv/ *adjective* very large or covering a wide area ○ *an extensive network of sales outlets*

extensive marketing /ɪkˌstensɪv ˈmɑːkɪtɪŋ/ *noun* the practice of using a wide network of distributors and a great variety of promotional activities to gain as large a section of the market as possible ○ *Only a company with vast resources could embark on this type of extensive marketing.*

extensive problem-solving /ɪkˌstensɪv ˈprɒbləm ˌsɒlvɪŋ/ *noun* detailed research and decision-making by a buyer who needs to examine carefully all options open to him or her

external /ɪkˈstɜːn(ə)l/ *adjective* **1.** outside a country **2.** outside a company

external account /ɪkˌstɜːn(ə)l əˈkaʊnt/ *noun* an account in a British bank of someone who is living in another country

external analysis /ɪkˌstɜːn(ə)l əˈnæləsɪs/ *noun* the analysis of an organisation's customers, market segments, competitors, and marketing environment

external audience /ɪkˌstɜːn(ə)l ˈɔːdiəns/ *noun* people, such as the general public, who do not belong to an organisation

external audit /ɪkˈstɜːn(ə)l ˈɔːdɪt/ *noun* an evaluation of the effectiveness of a company's public relations carried out by an outside agency

external communication /ɪkˌstɜːn(ə)l kəmjuːnɪˈkeɪʃ(ə)n/ *noun* the exchange of information and messages between an organisation and other organisations, groups, or individuals that are not part of it (NOTE: External communication includes the fields of public relations, media relations, advertising, and marketing management.)

external desk research /ɪkˌstɜːn(ə)l ˈdesk rɪˌsɜːtʃ/ *noun* research based on material outside the company's own records, e.g. in libraries or government departments

external search /ɪkˌstɜːn(ə)l ˈsɜːtʃ/ *noun* a method of finding information from external sources such as advertising, or from the web using a search engine

external search engine /ɪkˌstɜːn(ə)l ˈsɜːtʃ ˌendʒɪn/ *noun* a search engine that allows the user to search millions of Internet pages rapidly

external trade /ɪkˌstɜːn(ə)l ˈtreɪd/ *noun* trade with foreign countries (NOTE: the opposite is **internal trade**)

extra /ˈekstrə/ *adjective* which is added or which is more than usual ○ *to*

charge 10% extra for postage ○ *service is extra* ○ *There is no extra charge for heating.* ○ *We get £25 extra pay for working on Sunday.*

extranet /'ekstrənet/ *noun* a closed network of websites and email systems that is accessible to the people who belong to an organisation and to some others who do not, and that allows the outsiders access to the organisation's internal applications or information—usually subject to some kind of signed agreement (NOTE: Like intranets, extranets provide all the benefits of Internet technology (browsers, web servers, HTML, etc.) with the added benefit of security, since the network cannot be used by the general public.)

extraordinary items /ɪk-'strɔːd(ə)n(ə)ri ˌaɪtəmz/ *plural noun* large items of income or expenditure which do not arise from normal trading and which do not occur every year. They are shown separately on the profit and loss account after taxation, as opposed to exceptional items, which are calculated before the pre-tax profit.

extrapolation /ɪkˌstræpə'leɪʃ(ə)n/ *noun* a forecasting technique which involves projecting past trends into the future ○ *We are using extrapolation to forecast demand for a new product based on the demand for a similar product over the last five years.*

extras /'ekstrəz/ *plural noun* items which are not included in a price ○ *Packing and postage are extras.*

eyeballing /'aɪbɔːlɪŋ/ *noun* simply looking at statistical data to make a quick and informal assessment of the results (*informal*)

eyeballs /'aɪbɔːlz/ *plural noun* a measure of the number of visits made to a website (*slang*)

eye candy /'aɪ ˌkændi/ *noun* visually attractive material (*slang*)

eye-movement test /'aɪ ˌmuːvmənt ˌtest/, **eye tracking** /'aɪ ˌtrækɪŋ/ *noun* an advertising research test which involves recording the movement of a person's eyes as they look at an advertisement to see which parts are of special interest ○ *The eye-movement test will tell us what to highlight in future advertisements.*

e-zine /'iː ziːn/ *noun* a publication on a particular topic that is distributed regularly in electronic form, mainly via the web but also by email

F

face-lift /'feɪslɪft/ *noun* an improvement to the design of products and packaging or of an organisation's image ○ *These products need a face-lift if they are going to retain their appeal.*

face out /'feɪs aʊt/ *adverb* used to refer to the displaying of books on bookshop shelves, showing the front cover

face-to-face selling /ˌfeɪs tə feɪs 'selɪŋ/ *noun* person-to-person or direct selling, involving a meeting between seller and buyer ○ *Six months of face-to-face selling will give trainees direct experience of the market.* ○ *We need confident outgoing people to do our face-to-face selling.*

face value /feɪs 'væljuː/ *noun* the value written on a coin, banknote or share certificate

'…travellers cheques cost 1% of their face value – some banks charge more for small amounts' [*Sunday Times*]

facia /'feɪʃə/ *noun* another spelling of **fascia**

facilities /fə'sɪlɪtiz/ *plural noun* services, equipment or buildings which make it possible to do something ○ *There are no facilities for unloading* or *there are no unloading facilities.* ○ *Our storage facilities are the best in the region.* ○ *Transport facilities in the area are not satisfactory.* ○ *There are no facilities for disabled visitors.*

facility /fə'sɪlɪti/ *noun* **1.** the total amount of credit which a lender will allow a borrower **2.** US a single large building ○ *We have opened our new warehouse facility.*

facing /'feɪsɪŋ/ *adjective* opposite

facing matter /'feɪsɪŋ ˌmætə/, **facing text matter** /ˌfeɪsɪŋ 'tekst ˌmætə/ *noun* an advertisement on a page opposite to one containing editorial matter

facing page /'feɪsɪŋ peɪdʒ/ *noun* the page opposite

facsimile /fæk'sɪmɪli/ *noun* an exact copy of a text or illustration

fact /fækt/ *noun* a piece of information ○ *The chairman asked to see all the facts on the income tax claim.* ○ *The sales director can give you the facts and figures about the African operation.*

fact book /'fækt bʊk/ *noun* data put together about a product on the market that can be used for reference by the producers or by an advertising agency

fact-finding mission /'fækt faɪndɪŋ ˌmɪʃ(ə)n/ *noun* a visit by a person or group of people, usually to another country, to obtain information about a specific issue ○ *The minister went on a fact-finding tour of the region.*

factor /'fæktə/ *noun* **1.** something which is important or which is taken into account when making a decision ○ *The drop in sales is an important factor in the company's lower profits.* ○ *Motivation was an important factor in drawing up the new pay scheme.* **2.** a person who sells for a business or another person and earns a commission ■ *verb* to buy debts from a company at a discount

'…factors 'buy' invoices from a company, which then gets an immediate cash advance representing most of their value. The balance is paid when the debt is met. The client company is charged a fee as well as interest on the cash advanced' [*Times*]

factorage /'fæktərɪdʒ/ *noun* a commission earned by a factor ○ *What percentage is the factorage?*

factor analysis /'fæktə əˌnæləsɪs/ *noun* a process of identifying key factors that influence the results in an attitude research programme

factoring /ˈfæktərɪŋ/ *noun* the business of buying debts at a discount

factoring agent /ˈfæktərɪŋ ˌeɪdʒənt/ *noun* a person who sells for a business or another person and earns a commission

factoring charges /ˈfæktərɪŋ ˌtʃɑːdʒɪz/ *plural noun* the cost of selling debts to a factor for a commission

factory /ˈfækt(ə)ri/ *noun* a building where products are manufactured ○ *a car factory* ○ *a shoe factory* ○ *The company is proposing to close three of its factories with the loss of 200 jobs.*

factory gate price /ˌfækt(ə)ri ˈɡeɪt praɪs/ *noun* the actual cost of manufacturing goods before any mark-up is added to give profit (NOTE: The factory gate price includes direct costs such as labour, raw materials, and energy, and indirect costs such as interest on loans, plant maintenance or rent.)

factory outlet /ˈfækt(ə)ri ˌaʊtlet/ *noun* a shop where merchandise is sold direct to the public from the factory, usually at wholesale prices

factory unit /ˈfækt(ə)ri ˈjuːnɪt/ *noun* a single building on an industrial estate

fact sheet /ˈfækt ʃiːt/ *noun* a sheet of paper giving information about a product or service which can be used for publicity purposes

fad /fæd/ *noun* a short-lived fashion or craze

failure /ˈfeɪljə/ *noun* not doing something which you promised to do

failure fee /ˈfeɪljə fiː/ *noun* a fee charged by a distributor to the manufacturer of a product whose sales are less than those agreed in advance

fair /feə/ *noun* same as **trade fair** ○ *The computer fair runs from April 1st to 6th.* ■ *adjective* honest or correct

fair deal /feə ˈdiːl/ *noun* an arrangement where both parties are treated equally ○ *The workers feel they did not get a fair deal from the management.*

fair price /feə ˈpraɪs/ *noun* a good price for both buyer and seller

fair trade /feə ˈtreɪd/ *noun* an international business system where countries agree not to charge import duties on some items imported from their trading partners

fall /fɔːl/ *noun* a sudden drop or loss of value ○ *a fall in the exchange rate* ○ *a fall in the price of gold* ○ *a fall on the Stock Exchange* ○ *Profits showed a 10% fall.* ■ *verb* **1.** to drop suddenly to a lower price ○ *Shares fell on the market today.* ○ *Gold shares fell 10% or fell 45 cents on the Stock Exchange.* ○ *The price of gold fell for the second day running.* ○ *The pound fell against the euro.* **2.** to happen or to take place ○ *The public holiday falls on a Tuesday.* □ **payments which fall due** payments which are now due to be made

'…market analysts described the falls in the second half of last week as a technical correction to the market' [*AustralianFinancial Review*]

'…for the first time since mortgage rates began falling in March a financial institution has raised charges on homeowner loans' [*Globe and Mail (Toronto)*]

'…interest rates were still falling as late as June, and underlying inflation remains below the government's target of 2.5 per cent' [*Financial Times*]

fall away /ˌfɔːl əˈweɪ/ *verb* to become less ○ *Hotel bookings have fallen away since the tourist season ended.*

fall back /ˌfɔːl ˈbæk/ *verb* to become lower or cheaper after rising in price ○ *Shares fell back in light trading.*

fall back on /ˌfɔːl ˈbæk ɒn/ *verb* to have to use something kept for emergencies ○ *to fall back on cash reserves* ○ *The management fell back on the usual old excuses.*

fall-back price /ˈfɔːl bæk ˌpraɪs/ *noun* the lowest price which a seller will accept ○ *The buyer tries to guess the seller's fall-back price.* ○ *The fall-back price must not be any lower or there won't be any profit in the deal.*

fall behind /ˌfɔːl bɪˈhaɪnd/ *verb* to be late in doing something ○ *They fell behind with their mortgage repayments.*

falling /ˈfɔːlɪŋ/ *adjective* which is becoming smaller or dropping in price

'…falling profitability means falling share prices' [*Investors Chronicle*]

falling market /ˌfɔːlɪŋ ˈmɑːkɪt/ *noun* a market where prices are coming down

falling pound /ˌfɔːlɪŋ ˈpaʊnd/ *noun* the pound when it is losing its value against other currencies

fall off /ˌfɔːl ˈɒf/ *verb* to become lower, cheaper or less ○ *Sales have fallen off since the tourist season ended.*

fall out /ˌfɔːl ˈaʊt/ *verb* □ **the bottom has fallen out of the market** sales have fallen below what previously seemed to be their lowest point

fall through /ˌfɔːl ˈθruː/ *verb* not to happen or not to take place ○ *The plan fell through at the last moment.*

false /fɔːls/ *adjective* not true or not correct ○ *to make a false claim for a product*

false claim /fɔːls ˈkleɪm/ *noun* an untrue or exaggerated claim made in the advertising of a product ○ *A voluntary control body was set up to discourage false claims in the advertising business.*

false weight /fɔːls ˈweɪt/ *noun* weight on a shop scales which is wrong and so cheats customers

falsification /ˌfɔːlsɪfɪˈkeɪʃ(ə)n/ *noun* the act of making false entries in accounts

falsify /ˈfɔːlsɪfaɪ/ *verb* to change something to make it wrong ○ *They were accused of falsifying the accounts.*

family /ˈfæm(ə)li/ *noun* **1.** a group of products which are linked by a brand name or by their packaging **2.** a group of people, formed of parents and children

family branding /ˌfæm(ə)li ˈbrændɪŋ/ *noun* the practice of selling a variety of different products under the same brand name

family life cycle /ˌfæm(ə)li ˈlaɪf ˌsaɪk(ə)l/ *noun* the stages through which consumers pass in their lives, as they have families, e.g. 'young singles', 'young marrieds', 'young couples with small children', 'couples with adolescent children still at home' and 'retired couples', which correspond to different types of buying behaviour

family packaging /ˌfæm(ə)li ˈpækɪdʒɪŋ/ *noun* the practice of selling a whole range of products in similar packaging ○ *We hope that family pack-*

aging will make for a clear company image.

fancy goods /ˈfænsi ɡʊdz/ *plural noun* small attractive items

fascia /ˈfeɪʃə/, **facia** *noun* **1.** a board over a shop on which the name of the shop is written **2.** a board above an exhibition stand on which the name of the company represented is written

fast /fɑːst/ *adjective, adverb* quick or quickly ○ *The train is the fastest way of getting to our supplier's factory.* ○ *Home computers sell fast in the pre-Christmas period.*

fast food /fɑːst ˈfʊd/ *noun* food that can be cooked and sold quickly to customers, often using franchises, e.g. hamburgers and pizzas

fastmarketing /ˈfɑːstˌmɑːkɪtɪŋ/ *noun* the concept of concentrating all promotions into a short space of time, so that customers cannot avoid being affected

'…fastmarketing tactics mark a radical departure from more traditional marketing. Instead of dotting commercials over a 4 or 5 week campaign, fastmarketers try to squeeze them into just a few days' [*Times*]

fast-moving consumer goods /ˌfɑːst muːvɪŋ kənˈsjuːmə ɡʊdz/ *plural noun* essential low-price goods which get repeat orders ○ *He couldn't work in FMCGs because his only experience was in industrial selling.* Abbr **FMCGs**

fast-selling item /ˌfɑːst selɪŋ ˈaɪtəmz/ *noun* an item which sells quickly

favourable /ˈfeɪv(ə)rəb(ə)l/ *adjective* which gives an advantage (NOTE: the American spelling is **favorable**) □ **on favourable terms** on specially good terms ○ *The shop is let on very favourable terms.*

favourable balance of trade /ˌfeɪv(ə)rəb(ə)l ˌbæləns əv ˈtreɪd/ *noun* a situation where a country's exports are larger than its imports

fax /fæks/ *noun* **1.** a system for sending the exact copy of a document via telephone lines ○ *Can you confirm the booking by fax?* **2.** a document sent by this method ○ *We received a fax of the*

order this morning. ■ *verb* to send a message by fax ○ *The details of the offer were faxed to the brokers this morning.* ○ *I've faxed the documents to our New York office.*

faxback /ˈfæksbæk/ *noun* a system of responding by fax, e.g. by downloading pages from a website direct to a fax machine, or where customers dial a fax number and get a fax back on their fax machine

fear /fɪə/ *noun* the feeling of being afraid

fear appeal /ˈfɪə əˌpiːl/ *noun* an advertising message that makes the reader anxious about something, especially about not doing something

feasibility report /ˌfiːzəˈbɪlɪti rɪˌpɔːt/ *noun* a document which says if it is worth undertaking something

feasibility study /ˌfiːzəˈbɪlɪti ˌstʌdi/ *noun* the careful investigation of a project to see whether it is worth undertaking ○ *We will carry out a feasibility study to decide whether it is worth setting up an agency in North America.*

feasibility test /ˌfiːzəˈbɪlɪti test/ *noun* a test to see if something is possible

feature /ˈfiːtʃə/ *noun* an article in a newspaper or magazine that deals with one subject in depth ○ *There is a feature in the next issue describing the history of our company.*

features /ˈfiːtʃəz/ *plural noun* the particular important aspects of a product or service which are advertised as an attraction to the purchaser, as opposed to 'benefits' which show how the product or service will improve the quality of life of the purchaser

Federal Trade Commission /ˌfed(ə)rəl ˈtreɪd kəˌmɪʃ(ə)n/ *noun* a federal agency established to keep business competition free and fair

feed /fiːd/ *verb* to give information or tips to another salesperson regarding promising customers or areas for sales ○ *I can feed you some interesting sales leads.* (NOTE: **feeding- fed**)

feedback /ˈfiːdbæk/ *noun* information, especially about the result of an ac-

tivity which allows adjustments to be made to the way it is done in future ○ *We are getting positive feedback about our after-sales service.* ○ *It would be useful to have some feedback from people who had a test drive but didn't buy the car.* ○ *Are we getting any feedback on customer reaction to our new product?*

'…the service is particularly useful when we are working in a crisis management area and we need fast feedback from consumers' [*PR Week*]

field /fiːld/ *noun* □ **in the field** outside the office, among the customers ○ *We have sixteen reps in the field.* □ **first in the field** being the first company to bring out a product or to start a service ○ *Smith Ltd has a great advantage in being first in the field with a reliable electric car.*

field of experience /ˌfiːld əv ɪkˈspɪərəns/ *noun* the general experience that a sender and receiver of a message use in considering the message

field research /ˈfiːld rɪˌsɜːtʃ/, **field work** /ˈfiːld wɜːk/ *noun* looking for information that is not yet published and must be obtained in surveys ○ *They had to do a lot of fieldwork before they found the right market for the product.* ○ *Field research is carried out to gauge potential demand.*

field sales force /fiːld ˈseɪlz fɔːs/ *noun* salespeople working outside the company's offices, in the field ○ *After working for a year in the field sales force, she became field sales manager.* ○ *The field sales force operates in three main areas.*

field sales manager /fiːld ˈseɪlz ˌmænɪdʒə/ *noun* the manager in charge of a group of salespeople

field trials /ˈfiːld traɪəlz/, **field tests** /ˈfiːld tests/ *plural noun* a test of a new product or of something such as an advertisement on real customers

field work /ˈfiːld wɜːk/ *noun* **1.** an examination of the situation among possible customers ○ *They had to do a lot of field work to find the right market for the product.* **2.** same as **field research**

filing system /ˈfaɪlɪŋ ˌsɪstəm/ *noun* a way of putting documents in order for easy reference

filler /ˈfɪlə/ *noun* something which fills a space

filter question /ˈfɪltə ˌkwestʃən/ *noun* a question in a questionnaire designed to separate respondents who are worth questioning further from those who are not

finance /ˈfaɪnæns/ *noun* money used by a company, provided by the shareholders or by loans ○ *Where will they get the necessary finance for the project?* ■ *verb* to provide money to pay for something ○ *They plan to finance the operation with short-term loans.*

'...an official said that the company began to experience a sharp increase in demand for longer-term mortgages at a time when the flow of money used to finance these loans diminished' [*Globe and Mail*]

Finance Act /ˈfaɪnæns ækt/ *noun* GB an annual Act of Parliament which gives the government the power to obtain money from taxes as proposed in the Budget

finance department /ˈfaɪnæns dɪˌpɑːtmənt/, **finance committee** /ˈfaɪnæns kəˈmɪti/ *noun* the department or committee which manages the money used in an organisation

finance market /ˈfaɪnæns ˌmɑːkɪt/ *noun* a place where large sums of money can be lent or borrowed

finances /ˈfaɪnænsɪz/ *plural noun* money or cash which is available ○ *the bad state of the company's finances*

financial /faɪˈnænʃəl/ *adjective* concerning money

financial advertising /faɪˌnænʃəl ˈædvətaɪzɪŋ/ *noun* advertising by companies in the field of financial investment

financial audit /faɪˌnænʃəl ˈɔːdɪt/ *noun* an examination of the books and accounts of an advertising agency

financial correspondent /faɪˌnænʃəl kɒrɪsˈpɒndənt/ *noun* a journalist who writes articles on money matters for a newspaper

financial institution /faɪˌnænʃəl ɪnstɪˈtjuːʃ(ə)n/ *noun* a bank, investment trust or insurance company whose work involves lending or investing large sums of money

financially /faɪˈnænʃəli/ *adverb* regarding money □ **a company which is financially sound** a company which is profitable and has strong assets

financial position /faɪˌnænʃəl pəˈzɪʃ(ə)n/ *noun* the state of a person's or company's bank balance in terms of assets and debts ○ *She must think of her financial position.*

financial resources /faɪˌnænʃəl rɪˈzɔːsɪz/ *plural noun* supply of money for something ○ *a company with strong financial resources*

financial risk /faɪˌnænʃəl ˈrɪsk/ *noun* the possibility of losing money ○ *The company is taking a considerable financial risk in manufacturing 25 million units without doing any market research.* ○ *There is always some financial risk in selling on credit.*

financial statement /faɪˌnænʃəl ˈsteɪtmənt/ *noun* a document which shows the financial situation of a company ○ *The accounts department has prepared a financial statement for the shareholders.*

Financial Times Index /faɪˌnænʃəl ˈtaɪmz ɪnˌdeks/ *noun* an index which shows percentage rises or falls in share prices on the London Stock Exchange based on a small group of major companies

financier /faɪˈnænsɪə/ *noun* a person who lends large amounts of money to companies or who buys shares in companies as an investment

financing /ˈfaɪnænsɪŋ/ *noun* the act of providing money for a project ○ *The financing of the project was done by two international banks.*

find time /ˈfaɪnd taɪm/ *noun* the time taken by a customer to find what he or she wants in a store

fine /faɪn/ *adverb* very thin or very small □ **we are cutting our margins very fine** we are reducing our margins to the smallest possible amount

finished goods /'fɪnɪʃt gʊdz/ *noun* manufactured goods which are ready to be sold

fire-fight /'faɪə faɪt/ *verb* to fight bad publicity for a client ○ *The agency has done fire-fighting work for the egg producers.*

fire sale /'faɪə seɪl/ *noun* 1. a sale of fire-damaged goods 2. a sale of anything at a very low price

firm /fɜːm/ *noun* a company, business or partnership ○ *a manufacturing firm* ○ *an important publishing firm* ○ *She is a partner in a law firm.* ■ *adjective* 1. which cannot be changed ○ *to make a firm offer for something* ○ *to place a firm order for two aircraft* 2. not dropping in price and possibly going to rise ○ *Sterling was firmer on the foreign exchange markets.* ○ *Shares remained firm.* ■ *verb* to remain at a price and seem likely to rise ○ *The shares firmed at £1.50.*

'...some profit-taking was noted, but underlying sentiment remained firm' [*Financial Times*]

firm price /fɜːm 'praɪs/ *noun* a price which will not change ○ *They are quoting a firm price of $1.23 a unit.*

firm up /'fɜːm ʌp/ *verb* to agree on final details ○ *We expect to firm up the deal at the next trade fair.*

first choice /fɜːst 'tʃɔɪs/ *noun* a prospective customer who chooses the first option available, as opposed to a 'tyrekicker' who wants to examine every option before coming to a decision

first-hand /ˌfɜːst 'hænd/ *adjective* 1. coming directly from the original source 2. new or unused ○ *I actually bought the TV first-hand, but at a second-hand price.*

first-hand information /ˌfɜːst hænd ɪnfə'meɪʃ(ə)n/ *noun* information from an original source ○ *We had a first-hand account of what happened at the sales meeting from one of the salesreps who was there.*

first-line management /ˌfɜːst laɪn 'mænɪdʒmənt/ *noun* the managers who have immediate contact with the workforce

first mover /fɜːst 'muːvə/ *noun* a person or company that is the first to launch a product in a market

first mover advantage /fɜːst 'muːvə əd,vɑːntɪdʒ/ *noun* the advantage a company gets in being the first to enter a market

first-run syndication /ˌfɜːst rʌn sɪndɪ'keɪʃ(ə)n/ *noun* material produced specifically for the syndication market

fishy-back freight /'fɪʃi bæk ˌfreɪt/ *noun* US the transportation of trucks or freight-train cars on ferries or barges (NOTE: compare **piggy-back freight**)

fix /fɪks/ *verb* 1. to arrange or to agree ○ *to fix a budget* ○ *to fix a meeting for 3 p.m.* ○ *The date has still to be fixed.* ○ *The price of gold was fixed at $300.* ○ *The mortgage rate has been fixed at 5%.* 2. to mend ○ *The technicians are coming to fix the phone system.* ○ *Can you fix the photocopier?*

'...coupons are fixed by reference to interest rates at the time a gilt is first issued' [*Investors Chronicle*]

fixed /fɪkst/ *adjective* unable to be changed or removed

fixed assets /fɪkst 'æsets/ *plural noun* property or machinery which a company owns and uses, but which the company does not buy or sell as part of its regular trade, including the company's investments in shares of other companies

fixed break /fɪkst 'breɪk/ *noun* the placing of a television or radio advertisement in a specific commercial break on a specific day, at the advertiser's insistence

fixed costs /fɪkst 'kɒsts/ *plural noun* business costs which do not change with the quantity of the product made

fixed expenses /fɪkst ɪk'spensɪz/ *plural noun* expenses which do not vary with different levels of production, e.g. rent, secretaries' salaries, insurance

fixed-fee arrangement /fɪkst 'fiː ə,reɪndʒmənt/ *noun* a way of agreeing the fees for an agency before the agency starts work on a project

fixed position /fɪkst pə'zɪʃ(ə)n/ *noun* the placing of an advertisement in a specific location in a publication, or

running a commercial at a fixed time of day, at the advertiser's insistence

fixed-price agreement /fɪkst 'praɪs ə,griːmənt/ *noun* an agreement where a company provides a service or a product at a price which stays the same for the whole period of the agreement

fixed rate /fɪkst 'reɪt/ *noun* a rate, e.g. an exchange rate, which does not change

'…you must offer shippers and importers fixed rates over a reasonable period of time' [*Lloyd's List*]

fixed scale of charges /,fɪkst skeɪl əv 'tʃɑːdʒɪz/ *noun* a rate of charging which does not change

fixed spot /fɪkst 'spɒt/ *noun* the placing of a TV or radio commercial in a specific position, at the advertiser's insistence

fixing /'fɪksɪŋ/ *noun* arranging ○ *the fixing of charges* ○ *the fixing of a mortgage rate*

flagship /'flægʃɪp/ *noun* the key product in a range, on which the reputation of the producer most depends

flagship store /'flægʃɪp stɔː/, **flagship hotel** /'flægʃɪp həʊ,tel/ *noun* the main store or hotel in a chain

flash pack /'flæʃ pæk/ *noun* a pack or package which shows a price reduction very clearly in order to attract customers ○ *Flash packs are displayed at eye-level on the supermarket shelves to attract the attention of passing customers.*

flat rate /flæt 'reɪt/ *noun* a charge which always stays the same ○ *a flat-rate increase of 10%* ○ *We pay a flat rate for electricity each quarter.* ○ *He is paid a flat rate of £2 per thousand.*

flier /'flaɪə/ *noun* a promotional leaflet

flight /flaɪt/ *verb* to arrange a scheduling pattern for something

flighting by number /,flaɪtɪŋ baɪ 'nʌmbə/ *noun* scheduling things in a series of groups, with the same number in each group

floating population /,fləʊtɪŋ pɒpjʊ'leɪʃ(ə)n/ *noun* people who move from place to place

flood /flʌd/ *noun* a large quantity ○ *We received a flood of orders.* ○ *Floods of tourists filled the hotels.* ■ *verb* to fill with a large quantity of something ○ *The market was flooded with cheap imitations.* ○ *The sales department is flooded with orders* or *with complaints.*

floor /flɔː/ *noun* **1.** the part of the room which you walk on **2.** all rooms on one level in a building ○ *The shoe department is on the first floor.* ○ *Her office is on the 26th floor.* (NOTE: In Britain the floor at street level is the **ground floor**, but in the USA it is the **first floor**. Each floor in the USA is one number higher than the same floor in Britain.)

floor manager /'flɔː ,mænɪdʒə/ *noun US* a person in charge of the sales staff in a department store

floor space /'flɔː speɪs/ *noun* an area of floor in an office or warehouse ○ *We have 3,500 square metres of floor space to let.*

floor stand /'flɔː stænd/ *noun* a display stand which stands on the floor, as opposed to one which stands on a table or counter

floorwalker /'flɔːwɔːkə/ *noun* an employee of a department store who advises customers, and supervises the shop assistants in a department

flop /flɒp/ *noun* a failure or something which has not been successful ○ *The new model was a flop.* ■ *verb* to fail or not be a success ○ *The launch of the new shampoo flopped badly.* (NOTE: **flopping – flopped**)

flowchart /'fləʊtʃɑːt/, **flow diagram** /'fləʊ ,daɪəgræm/ *noun* a chart which shows the arrangement of work processes in a series □ **fluff it and fly it** (*informal*) give a product an attractive appearance and then sell it

fluidity /flu'ɪdɪti/ *noun* ease of movement or change

fluidity of labour /flu,ɪdɪti əv 'leɪbə/ *noun* the extent to which employees move from one place to another to work or from one occupation to another

fly poster /'flaɪ ,pəʊstə/ *noun* a poster which is pasted to a site without permission and without being paid for

fly-posting /ˈflaɪ ˌpəʊstɪŋ/ *noun* the practice of sticking posters up illegally, without permission of the site owner and without making any payment

FMCGs *abbr* fast-moving consumer goods

focus group /ˈfəʊkəs gruːp/ *noun* a group of people who are brought together to discuss informally a market-research question

fold-out /ˈfəʊld aʊt/ *noun* a folded page in a publication, which opens out to show a much larger advertisement

follow /ˈfɒləʊ/ *verb* to come behind or to come afterwards ○ *The samples will follow by surface mail.* ○ *We will pay £10,000 down, with the balance to follow in six months' time.*

follower /ˈfɒləʊə/ *noun* a company which follows others into a market

following reading matter /ˌfɒləʊɪŋ ˈriːdɪŋ ˌmætə/ *noun* a good position for an advertisement, which follows an interesting article in a newspaper or magazine

follow up /ˈfɒləʊ ʌp/ *verb* to examine something further ○ *I'll follow up your idea of targeting our address list with a special mailing.* □ **to follow up an initiative** to take action once someone else has decided to do something

font /fɒnt/ *noun* a set of characters all of the same size and face

foot /fʊt/ *verb* □ **to foot the bill** to pay the costs

footfall /ˈfʊtfɔːl/ *noun* the number of customers who come into and walk round a shop

'…the small independent retailer who stocks up using cash and carries could be hit hard by the loss of footfall associated with any increase in smuggled goods' [*The Grocer*]

force /fɔːs/ *noun* **1.** strength □ **to be in force** to be operating or working ○ *The rules have been in force since 1986.* □ **to come into force** to start to operate or work ○ *The new regulations will come into force on January 1st.* **2.** a group of people ■ *verb* to make someone do something ○ *Competition has forced the company to lower its prices.* ○ *After the takeover several of the managers were forced to take early retirement.*

forced consumption /fɔːst kənˈsʌmpʃən/ *noun* the attempt to impose a rate or type of consumption on consumers

force down /ˌfɔːs ˈdaʊn/ *verb* to make something such as prices become lower □ **to force prices down** to make prices come down ○ *Competition has forced prices down.*

forced sale /fɔːst ˈseɪl/ *noun* a sale which takes place because a court orders it or because it is the only way to avoid a financial crisis

force majeure /ˌfɔːs mæˈʒɜː/ *noun* something which happens which is out of the control of the parties who have signed a contract, e.g. a strike, war or storm

force up /ˌfɔːs ˈʌp/ *verb* to make something become higher □ **to force prices up** to make prices go up ○ *The war forced up the price of oil.*

forecast /ˈfɔːkɑːst/ *noun* a description or calculation of what will probably happen in the future ○ *The chairman did not believe the sales director's forecast of higher turnover.* ■ *verb* to calculate or to say what will probably happen in the future ○ *We are forecasting sales of £2m.* ○ *Economists have forecast a fall in the exchange rate.* (NOTE: **forecasting – forecast**)

forecasting /ˈfɔːkɑːstɪŋ/ *noun* calculating what will probably happen in the future ○ *Manpower planning will depend on forecasting the future levels of production.*

foreign /ˈfɒrɪn/ *adjective* not belonging to your own country ○ *Foreign cars have flooded our market.* ○ *We are increasing our trade with foreign countries.*

'…a sharp setback in foreign trade accounted for most of the winter slowdown' [*Fortune*]

'…the dollar recovered a little lost ground on the foreign exchanges yesterday' [*Financial Times*]

foreign currency /ˌfɒrɪn ˈkʌrənsi/ *noun* money of another country

foreign currency account /ˌfɒrɪn ˈkʌrənsi əˌkaʊnt/ *noun* a bank account in the currency of another country, e.g. a dollar account in a British bank

foreign currency reserves /ˌfɒrɪn
ˈkʌrənsi rɪˌzɜːvz/ *plural noun* a country's reserves held in currencies of other countries

'…the treasury says it needs the cash to rebuild its foreign reserves which have fallen from $19 billion when the government took office to $7 billion in August' [*Economist*]

foreigner /ˈfɒrɪnə/ *noun* a person from another country

'…a sharp setback in foreign trade accounted for most of the winter slowdown' [*Fortune*]

foreign exchange market₁ /ˌfɒrɪn
ɪksˈtʃeɪndʒ ˌmɑːkɪt/ *noun* dealings in foreign currencies ○ *She trades on the foreign exchange market.* ○ *Foreign exchange markets were very active after the dollar devalued.*

foreign exchange market₂ *noun* market where people buy and sell foreign currencies

foreign exchange reserves /-
ˌfɒrɪn ɪksˈtʃeɪndʒ rɪˌzɜːvz/ *plural noun* foreign money held by a government to support its own currency and pay its debts

foreign exchange transfer /ˌfɒrɪn
ɪksˈtʃeɪndʒ ˌtrænsfɜː/ *noun* the sending of money from one country to another

foreign goods /ˈfɒrɪn ɡʊdz/ *plural noun* goods manufactured in other countries

foreign investments /ˌfɒrɪn ɪnˈvestmənts/ *plural noun* money invested in other countries

forfeit /ˈfɔːfɪt/ *noun* the taking away of something as a punishment □ **the goods were declared forfeit** the court said that the goods had to be taken away from the person who was holding them ■ *verb* to have something taken away as a punishment □ **to forfeit a deposit** to lose a deposit which was left for an item because you have decided not to buy that item

forfeit clause /ˈfɔːfɪt klɔːz/ *noun* a clause in a contract which says that goods or a deposit will be taken away if the contract is not obeyed

forfeiture /ˈfɔːfɪtʃə/ *noun* the act of forfeiting a property

form /fɔːm/ *noun* **1.** □ **form of words** words correctly laid out for a legal document □ **receipt in due form** a correctly written receipt **2.** official printed paper with blank spaces which have to be filled in with information ○ *You have to fill in form A20.* ○ *Each passenger was given a customs declaration form.* ○ *The reps carry pads of order forms.*

forma /ˈfɔːmə/ *noun* ◊ **pro forma**

format /ˈfɔːmæt/ *noun* **1.** the general page design or size of a publication **2.** the general style of an email or electronic marketing piece

form utility /ˈfɔːm juːˌtɪlɪti/ *noun* a use for a product created by the introduction of the product

forty-eight sheet /ˌfɔːti ˈeɪt ˈʃiːt/ *noun* a large poster-sized sheet of paper

forum /ˈfɔːrəm/ *noun* an online area where Internet users can read, post, and respond to messages

forward /ˈfɔːwəd/ *adjective* in advance or to be paid at a later date ■ *adverb* □ **to date a cheque forward** to put a later date than the present one on a cheque ■ *verb* □ **to forward something to someone** to send something to someone ○ *to forward a consignment to Nigeria* □ **'please forward'** *or* **'to be forwarded'** words written on an envelope, asking the person receiving it to send it on to the person whose name is written on it

forward contract /ˌfɔːwəd
ˈkɒntrækt/ *noun* a one-off agreement to buy foreign currency or shares or commodities for delivery at a later date at a specific price

forwarding /ˈfɔːwədɪŋ/ *noun* the act of arranging shipping and customs documents

forwarding address /ˈfɔːwədɪŋ
əˌdres/ *noun* the address to which a person's mail can be sent on

forwarding agent /ˈfɔːwədɪŋ
ˌeɪdʒənt/ *noun* a person or company which arranges shipping and customs documents

forward integration /ˌfɔːwəd ɪntəˈɡreɪʃ(ə)n/ *noun* a process of expansion in which a company becomes its own

distributor or takes over a company in the same line of business as itself ○ *Forward integration will give the company greater control over its selling.* ○ *Forward integration has brought the company closer to its consumers and has made it aware of their buying habits.* Compare **backward integration**

forward market /ˌfɔːwəd ˈmɑːkɪt/ *noun* a market for purchasing foreign currency, oil or commodities for delivery at a later date. These are one-off deals, as opposed to futures contracts which are continuous.

forward price /ˈfɔːwəd praɪs/ *noun* a price of goods which are to be delivered in the future

forward (exchange) rate /ˌfɔːwəd ɪksˈtʃeɪndʒ reɪt/ *noun* a rate for purchase of foreign currency at a fixed price for delivery at a later date ○ *What are the forward rates for the pound?*

forward sales /ˈfɔːwəd seɪlz/ *plural noun* the sales of shares, commodities or foreign exchange for delivery at a later date

foul bill of lading /ˌfaʊl bɪl əv ˈleɪdɪŋ/ *noun* a bill of lading which says that the goods were in bad condition when received by the shipper

four-colour process /ˌfɔː kʌlə ˈprəʊses/ *noun* a printing process where the three primary colours and black are used to create a wide range of shades

four Cs /fɔː ˈsiːz/ *plural noun* a simple way of referring to the four important points regarding customers: value to the Customer, Cost, Convenience for the customer and Communication between seller and buyer

four O's /fɔː ˈəʊz/ *plural noun* a simple way of summarizing the essentials of a marketing operation, which are Objects, Objectives, Organisation and Operations

four-plus cover /fɔː ˈplʌs ˌkʌvə/ *noun* a situation where consumers in the target audience will have seen an advertisement at least four times on average

four P's /fɔː ˈpiːz/ *plural noun* a simple way of summarising the essentials of the marketing mix, which are Product, Price, Promotion and Place

fraction /ˈfrækʃən/ *noun* a part of a whole

fragile /ˈfrædʒaɪl/ *adjective* which can be easily broken ○ *There is an extra premium for insuring fragile goods in shipment.*

fragment /frægˈment/ *verb* to split into sections

'…the consumer market is fragmenting, which means that brand advertising to the whole market is no longer enough' [*Financial Times*]

fragmentation /ˌfrægmənˈteɪʃ(ə)n/ *noun* the use of a variety of media for a publicity campaign

fragmented market /frægˌmentɪd ˈmɑːkɪt/ *noun* a market which is split into many small segments, which are more difficult to sell into

frame /freɪm/ *noun* same as **sampling frame**

franchise /ˈfræntʃaɪz/ *noun* a licence to trade using a brand name and paying a royalty for it ○ *He's bought a printing franchise* or *a pizza franchise.* ■ *verb* to sell licences for people to trade using a brand name and paying a royalty ○ *His sandwich bar was so successful that he decided to franchise it.*

'…many new types of franchised businesses will join the ranks of the giant chains of fast-food restaurants, hotels and motels and rental car agencies' [*Franchising Opportunities*]

'…a quarter of a million Britons are seeking to become their own bosses by purchasing franchises' [*Marketing Week*]

'…feelings are already running high over the question of how to allocate the next TV franchises' [*Marketing*]

franchise agreement /ˈfræntʃaɪz əˌgriːmənt/, **franchise contract** /ˈfræntʃaɪz ˌkɒntrækt/ *noun* a legal contract to trade using a brand name and paying a royalty for it

franchise-building promotion /ˈfræntʃaɪz ˌbɪldɪŋ prəˌməʊʃ(ə)n/ *noun* a sales promotion aimed at building up long-term repeat sales and customer loyalty

franchise chain /ˈfræntʃaɪz tʃeɪn/ *noun* a series of retail stores or fast-food outlets which are operated as franchises from the main operator

franchisee /ˌfræntʃaɪˈziː/ *noun* a person who runs a franchise

franchiser /ˈfræntʃaɪzə/ *noun* a person who licenses a franchise

franchising /ˈfræntʃaɪzɪŋ/ *noun* the act of selling a licence to trade as a franchise ○ *He runs his sandwich chain as a franchising operation.*

franchisor /ˈfræntʃaɪzə/ *noun* another spelling of **franchiser**

franco /ˈfræŋkəʊ/ *adverb* free

fraudulent misrepresentation /ˌfrɔːdjʊlənt mɪsˌreprɪzenˈteɪʃ(ə)n/ *noun* the act of making a false statement with the intention of tricking a customer

free /friː/ *adjective, adverb* **1.** not costing any money ○ *I have been given a free ticket to the exhibition.* ○ *The price includes free delivery.* ○ *All goods in the store are delivered free.* ○ *A catalogue will be sent free on request.* □ **free alongside ship** referring to a price that includes all costs up to delivery of goods next to the ship on the quay □ **free docks** referring to a price that includes all costs up to delivery of goods to the docks □ **free of charge** with no payment to be made □ **free on quay** referring to a price that includes all costs up to delivery of goods next to the ship on the quay □ **free overboard** *or* **free overside** referring to a price that includes all costs up to arrival of the ship at a port **2.** with no restrictions □ **free of tax** with no tax having to be paid ○ *interest is paid free of tax* □ **free of duty** with no duty to be paid ○ *to import wine free of duty* **3.** not busy or not occupied ○ *Are there any free tables in the restaurant?* ○ *I shall be free in a few minutes.* ○ *The chairman always keeps Friday afternoon free for a game of bridge.* ■ *verb* to make something available or easy ○ *The government's decision has freed millions of pounds for investment.*

'American business as a whole is increasingly free from heavy dependence on manufacturing' [*Sunday Times*]

free advertisement /friː ədˈvɜːtɪsmənt/ *noun* an advertisement shown without any charge to the advertiser ○ *The newspaper agreed to place a* free advertisement for the charity on the back page.

freebie /ˈfriːbi/ *noun* a product or service supplied free of charge, especially a gift to an agent or journalist (*informal*)

free collective bargaining /ˌfriː kəˌlektɪv ˈbɑːɡɪnɪŋ/ *noun* negotiations between management and trade unions about wage increases and working conditions

free competition /ˌfriː kɒmpəˈtɪʃ(ə)n/ *noun* being free to compete without government interference

free currency /friː ˈkʌrənsi/ *noun* a currency which is allowed by the government to be bought and sold without restriction

free delivery area /friː dɪˈlɪv(ə)ri ˌeəriə/ *noun* an area within which a seller will deliver purchases free ○ *The total price will be low as the goods are being delivered in a free delivery area.*

free enterprise /ˌfriː ˈentəpraɪz/ *noun* a system of business free from government interference

free gift /friː ˈɡɪft/ *noun* a present given by a shop to a customer who buys a specific amount of goods ○ *There is a free gift worth £25 to any customer buying a washing machine.*

free market /friː ˈmɑːkɪt/ *noun* a market in which there is no government control of supply and demand, and the rights of individuals and organisations to physical and intellectual property are upheld

free market economy /friː ˌmɑːkɪt ɪˈkɒnəmi/ *noun* a system where the government does not interfere in business activity in any way

free on board /ˌfriː ɒn ˈbɔːd/ **1.** including in the price all the seller's costs until the goods are on the ship for transportation. Abbr **f.o.b. 2.** including in the price all the seller's costs until the goods are delivered to a place

free paper /friː ˈpeɪpə/ *noun* a newspaper which is given away free, and which relies for its income on its advertising

freephone /ˈfriːfəʊn/, **freefone** *noun* a system where you can telephone to re-

ply to an advertisement, to place an order or to ask for information and the seller pays for the call

free port /'fri: pɔːt/ *noun* a port where there are no customs duties to be paid

freepost /'fri:pəʊst/ *noun* a system where someone can write to an advertiser to place an order or to ask for information to be sent, without paying for a stamp. The company paying for the postage on receipt of the envelope.

free sample /fri: 'sɑːmpəl/ *noun* a sample given free to advertise a product

free-standing insert /,fri: stændɪŋ 'ɪnsɜːt/ *noun* advertising material on one or more pages which is inserted into a newspaper. Abbr **FSI**

free trade /fri: 'treɪd/ *noun* a system where goods can go from one country to another without any restrictions

'…can free trade be reconciled with a strong dollar resulting from floating exchange rates?' [*Duns Business Month*]

free trader /fri: 'treɪdə/ *noun* a person who is in favour of free trade

'…free traders hold that the strong dollar is the primary cause of the nation's trade problems' [*Duns Business Month*]

free trade zone /fri: 'treɪd ,zəʊn/ *noun* an area where there are no customs duties

free trial /fri: 'traɪəl/ *noun* an opportunity to test a machine or product with no payment involved

freeware /'fri:weə/ *noun* free software programs

freeze /fri:z/ *verb* to keep something such as money or costs at their present level and not allow them to rise ○ *to freeze wages and prices* ○ *to freeze credits* ○ *to freeze company dividends* ○ *We have frozen expenditure at last year's level.* (NOTE: **freezing – froze – has frozen**)

freeze out /,fri:z 'aʊt/ *verb* □ **to freeze out the competition** to trade successfully and cheaply and so prevent competitors from operating

freight /freɪt/ *noun* **1.** the cost of transporting goods by air, sea or land ○ *At an auction, the buyer pays the freight.* **2.** goods which are transported □ **to take on freight** to load goods onto a ship, train or truck ■ *verb* □ **to freight goods** to send goods ○ *We freight goods to all parts of the USA.*

freightage /'freɪtɪdʒ/ *noun* the cost of transporting goods

freight collect /freɪt kə'lekt/ *noun* US an arrangement whereby the customer pays for transporting the goods

freight costs /'freɪt kɒsts/ *plural noun* money paid to transport goods

freight depot /'freɪt ,depəʊ/ *noun* a central point where goods are collected before being shipped

freight elevator /'freɪt ,eləveɪtə/ *noun* a strong lift for carrying goods up and down inside a building

freighter /'freɪtə/ *noun* **1.** an aircraft or ship which carries goods **2.** a person or company that organiess the transport of goods

freight forward /freɪt 'fɔːwəd/ *noun* a deal where the customer pays for transporting the goods

freight forwarder /'freɪt ,fɔːwədə/ *noun* a person or company that arranges shipping and customs documents for several shipments from different companies, putting them together to form one large shipment

'…the airline will allow freight forwarder customers to track and trace consignments on the airline's website' [*Lloyd's List*]

freight plane /'freɪt pleɪn/ *noun* an aircraft which carries goods, not passengers

frequency /'fri:kwənsɪ/ *noun* **1.** the number of times something happens **2.** the number of times an advertisement appears in a specific period ○ *The plan is to have larger advertisements but less frequency.* **3.** the number of times a person sees an advertisement during a campaign ○ *We feel that a frequency of two showings per night is enough for the first week of the campaign.*

frequency analysis /'fri:kwənsɪ ə-,næləsɪs/ *noun* analysis of frequency distribution statistics

frequency discount /'fri:kwənsɪ ,dɪskaʊnt/ *noun* reduced rates offered for frequent use of a advertising medium

frequency distribution /ˈfriːkwənsi dɪstrɪˌbjuːʃ(ə)n/ *noun* statistics, usually in the form of a graph, showing how often a sample group responded in a certain way to a questionnaire

frequent /ˈfriːkwənt/ *adjective* which comes, goes or takes place often ○ *There is a frequent ferry service to France.* ○ *We send frequent faxes to New York.* ○ *How frequent are the planes to Birmingham?*

frequently /ˈfriːkwəntli/ *adverb* often ○ *The photocopier is frequently out of use.* ○ *We email our New York office frequently – at least four times a day.*

fringe account /ˈfrɪndʒ əˌkaʊnt/ *noun* accounts or customers that are not very profitable for the supplier ○ *The salespeople are not giving priority to these fringe accounts.* ○ *It is hoped that some of these fringe accounts will soon start buying in larger quantities.*

fringe benefit /frɪndʒ ˈbenɪfɪt/ *noun* an extra item given by a company to employees in addition to their salaries, e.g. a company car, private health insurance

fringe benefits /frɪndʒ ˈbenɪfɪts/ *plural noun* extra items given by a company to workers in addition to a salary, e.g. company cars or private health insurance ○ *The fringe benefits make up for the poor pay.* ○ *Use of the company recreation facilities is one of the fringe benefits of the job.*

fringe time /ˈfrɪndʒ taɪm/ *noun* TV time around primetime where there is usually more availability

front /frʌnt/ *noun* a part of something which faces away from the back ○ *The front of the office building is on the High Street.* ○ *Our ad appeared on the front page of the newspaper.* ○ *There is a photograph of the managing director on the front page of the company report.*

frontage /ˈfrʌntɪdʒ/ *noun* the width of a shop which faces onto the street

front cover /frʌnt ˈkʌvə/ *noun* the front outside page of a publication, as opposed to the back cover

front end /ˈfrʌnt end/ *noun* the part of an organisation that meets and deals with customers face-to-face

front-line management /ˌfrʌnt laɪn ˈmænɪdʒmənt/ *noun* managers who have immediate contact with the workers

frontload /ˈfrʌntləʊd/ *verb* to plan a publicity campaign where most costs are incurred in the early stages. Compare **backload**

front man /ˈfrʌnt mæn/ *noun* a person who seems honest but is hiding an illegal trade

front of book /ˌfrʌnt əv ˈbʊk/ *noun* the first few pages of a magazine

FSI *abbr* free-standing insert

fudge /fʌdʒ/ *noun* a mistake made in an advertisement

fulfil /fʊlˈfɪl/ *verb* to complete something in a satisfactory way ○ *The clause regarding payments has not been fulfilled.* (NOTE: the American spelling is **fulfill**) □ **to fulfil an order** to supply the items which have been ordered ○ *We are so understaffed that we cannot fulfil any more orders before Christmas.*

fulfilment /fʊlˈfɪlmənt/ *noun* carrying something out in a satisfactory way (NOTE: the American spelling is **fulfillment**)

fulfilment house /fʊlˈfɪlmənt haʊs/ *noun* a company which supplies orders on behalf of a mail-order company

full /fʊl/ *adjective* **1.** complete, including everything □ **we are working at full capacity** we are doing as much work as possible **2.** □ **in full** completely ○ *Give your full name and address* or *your name and address in full.* ○ *He accepted all our conditions in full.* ○ *Full refund* or *refund paid in full.*

full cost pricing /ˌfʊl kɒst ˈpraɪsɪŋ/ *noun* a pricing method based on assessing the full production cost of each product unit and adding a profit margin

full costs /fʊl ˈkɒsts/ *plural noun* all the costs of manufacturing a product, including both fixed and variable costs

full cover /fʊl ˈkʌvə/ *noun* insurance cover against all risks

full employment /ˌfʊl ɪmˈplɔɪmənt/ *noun* a situation where all the people who can work have jobs

full-function wholesaler /ˌfʊl fʌŋkʃ(ə)n ˈhəʊlseɪlə/ *noun* a distributor performing all the normal functions of a wholesaler such as storage and transport ○ *There is room for only one full-function wholesaler dealing with this product in the Southampton area.*

full-line forcing /ˌfʊl laɪn ˈfɔːsɪŋ/ *noun* a situation where a supplier pressures a customer to buy from that supplier only ○ *If the supplier succeeds in full-line forcing, he will probably raise prices.*

full nester /fʊl ˈnestə/ *noun* an older customer who has their own home and who is interested in a good quality of life, eats in restaurants, buys new gadgets, and is not influenced by advertising. ◗ **empty nesters**

full page /ˈfʊl peɪdʒ/ *noun* a size of advertisement taking up one complete page

full price /ˈfʊl praɪs/ *noun* a price with no discount ○ *She bought a full-price ticket.*

full rate /fʊl ˈreɪt/ *noun* the full charge, with no reductions

full repairing lease /fʊl rɪˈpeərɪŋ liːs/ *noun* a lease where the tenant has to pay for all repairs to the property

full-scale /ˈfʊl skeɪl/ *adjective* complete or very thorough ○ *The MD ordered a full-scale review of credit terms.*

'…the administration launched a full-scale investigation into maintenance procedures' [*Fortune*]

full-service advertising agency /ˌfʊl sɜːvɪs ˈædvətaɪzɪŋ ˌeɪdʒ(ə)nsi/, **full-service agency** /fʊl ˌsɜːvɪs ˈeɪdʒənsi/ *noun* an advertising agency offering a full range of services such as sales promotion, design of house style, advice on public relations and market research and creating stands for exhibitions ○ *We have so little marketing expertise, we'll need a full-service advertising agency.*

full-time /ˈfʊl taɪm/ *adjective, adverb* working all the normal working time, i.e. about eight hours a day, five days a

week ○ *She's in full-time work* or *She works full-time* or *She's in full-time employment.* ○ *He is one of our full-time staff.*

full-timer /fʊl ˈtaɪmə/ *noun* a person who works full-time

function /ˈfʌŋkʃən/ *noun* a duty or job ■ *verb* to work ○ *The advertising campaign is functioning smoothly.* ○ *The new management structure does not seem to be functioning very well.*

functional /ˈfʌŋkʃən(ə)l/ *adjective* which can function properly

functional consequences /ˌfʌŋkʃən(ə)l ˈkɒnsɪkwensɪz/ *plural noun* the tangible effects of a product or service which a customer experiences directly

functional discount /ˌfʌŋkʃən(ə)l ˈdɪskaʊnt/ *noun* a discount offered on goods sold to distributors

functional product differentiation /ˌfʌŋkʃən(ə)l ˈprɒdʌkt dɪfərenʃɪˌeɪʃ(ə)n/ *noun* the process of ensuring that a product has some functional features that distinguish it from competing ones

functional title /ˈfʌŋkʃən(ə)l ˌtaɪt(ə)l/ *noun* a job title, the description of a person's job which is used as part of his or her address, e.g.'marketing manager' or 'head buyer'

fund /fʌnd/ *noun* money set aside for a special purpose

'…small innovative companies have been hampered for lack of funds' [*Sunday Times*]

'…the company was set up with funds totalling NorKr 145m' [*Lloyd's List*]

funded debt /ˌfʌndɪd ˈdet/ *noun* the part of the British National Debt which pays interest, but with no date for repayment of the principal

future /ˈfjuːtʃə/ *adjective* referring to time to come or to something which has not yet happened ■ *noun* the time which has not yet happened ○ *Try to be more careful in future.* ○ *In future all reports must be sent to Australia by air.*

future delivery /ˌfjuːtʃə dɪˈlɪv(ə)ri/ *noun* a delivery at a later date

futurology /ˌfjuːtʃəˈrɒlədʒi/ *noun* the prediction and study of future trends

G

gable end /ˈɡeɪb(ə)l end/ *noun* the end of a building which is used as a poster site

gain /ɡeɪn/ *noun* **1.** an increase or becoming larger □ **gain in experience** the act of getting more experience □ **gain in profitability** the act of becoming more profitable **2.** an increase in profit, price or value ○ *Oil shares showed gains on the Stock Exchange.* ○ *Property shares put on gains of 10%-15%.* ■ *verb* **1.** to get or to obtain ○ *He gained some useful experience working in a bank.* □ **to gain control of a business** to buy more than 50% of the shares so that you can direct the business **2.** to rise in value ○ *The dollar gained six points on the foreign exchange markets.*

galleria /ˌɡæləˈriːə/ *noun* a large shopping complex with many different stores under one roof, usually built round a large open space, with fountains, plants, etc.

galley /ˈɡæli/, **galley proof** /ˈɡæli/ *noun* the first proof of typesetting, before the text is made up into pages

galloping inflation /ˌɡæləpɪŋ ɪnˈfleɪʃ(ə)n/ *noun* very rapid inflation which is almost impossible to reduce

game /ɡeɪm/ *noun* a form of promotional material where people have a chance of winning a prize

game theory /ˈɡeɪm ˌθɪəri/ *noun* the principles, developed from business games, which relate to making the best choice from a number of possible strategies in various hypothetical situations where conflicting interests are involved

gap /ɡæp/ *noun* an empty space □ **gap in the market** an opportunity to make a product or provide a service which is needed but which no one has sold before

○ *to look for* or *to find a gap in the market* ○ *This laptop has filled a real gap in the market.*

'…these savings are still not great enough to overcome the price gap between American products and those of other nations' [*Duns Business Month*]

gap analysis /ˈɡæp əˌnæləsɪs/ *noun* analysis of a market to try to find a particular area that is not at present being satisfied ○ *Gap analysis showed that there was a whole area of the market we were not exploiting.* ○ *The computer performed a gap analysis and came up with suggestions for a medium-priced machine suitable for the small business market.*

gatefold /ˈɡeɪtfəʊld/ *noun* a double-page spread in which both pages are folded over, and which open out like a gate to give a spread of almost four pages

general cargo /ˌdʒen(ə)rəl ˈkɑːɡəʊ/ *noun* a cargo made up of various types of goods ○ *The ship left the port with a general cargo bound for various destinations.*

General Delivery /ˌdʒen(ə)rəl dɪˈlɪv(ə)ri/ *noun US* a system where letters can be addressed to someone at a post office, where they can be collected ○ *They received the mail-order items via General Delivery.* (NOTE: British English is **poste restante**)

general preplanning input /ˌdʒen(ə)rəl priːˈplænɪŋ ˌɪnpʊt/ *noun* market research which can be used to prepare the initial stages of an advertising campaign

general store /ˈdʒen(ə)rəl stɔː/ *noun* a small country shop which sells a large range of goods

general trading /ˌdʒen(ə)rəl ˈtreɪdɪŋ/ *noun* dealing in all types of goods

general wholesaler /ˌdʒen(ə)rəl ˈhəʊlseɪlə/ *noun* a wholesaler selling a variety of goods

generation /ˌdʒenəˈreɪʃ(ə)n/ *noun* a stage in the development of a product. Each new generation is a new version of the product with certain technical improvements on the preceding version.

Generation X /ˌdʒenəreɪʃ(ə)n ˈeks/ *noun* the generation of people who were born between 1963 and 1981 and began their working lives from the 1980s onwards (NOTE: The people who belong to Generation X are said to have challenged traditional corporate expectations by not being solely motivated by money. Instead they want to establish a balance between their professional and personal lives, being in favour of flexible working practices and valuing opportunities for learning and self-advancement.)

generic /dʒəˈnerɪk/ *adjective* which is shared by a group, and does not refer to one individual ■ *noun* **1.** a product sold without a brand name ○ *Generics are cheap since they have no name to advertise.* **2.** a brand name which is now given to a product rather than to a particular brand, e.g. hoover, kleenex or thermos

generic product /dʒə,nerɪk ˈprɒdʌkt/ *noun* same as **generic** ○ *Next to the brightly packaged branded goods the generic products on display were easily overlooked.*

gentleman's agreement /ˌdʒent(ə)lmənz əˈgriːmənt/ *noun* a verbal agreement between two parties who trust each other

geocentric stage /ˌdʒiːəʊˈsentrɪk steɪdʒ/ *noun US* an advanced stage in a company's international marketing when there is great co-ordination of overseas marketing activities

geographical /ˌdʒiːəˈgræfɪk(ə)l/ *adjective* referring to an area

geographical concentration /dʒiːə,græfɪk(ə)l ,kɒnsənˈtreɪʃ(ə)n/ *noun* the degree to which consumers in

a market are concentrated dispersed in a country or area ○ *The number of salespersonnel needed will depend on the geographical concentration of the market.*

geographical information system /dʒiːə,græfɪk(ə)l ɪnfəˈmeɪʃ(ə)n ,sɪstəm/ *noun* a type of database which is sorted on geographical data, such as a census, or one which provides maps on-screen. Abbr **GIS**

geographical segmentation /dʒiːə,græfɪk(ə)l ,segmənˈteɪʃ(ə)n/ *noun* the division of a market according to areas or regions

geographical weighting /dʒiːə-,græfɪk(ə)l ˈweɪtɪŋ/ *noun* a statistical process which gives more importance to some geographic areas than others in the process of reaching a final figure or result

gestation period /dʒeˈsteɪʃ(ə)n ,pɪəriəd/ *noun* the period of time between the initial inquiry about a product and the placing of an order ○ *The long gestation period is due to inefficient decision-making procedures in the buying company.*

GHI *abbr* guaranteed homes impressions

ghosting /ˈgəʊstɪŋ/ *noun* the practice of showing a little of the product itself by removing a small part of the packaging

GHR *abbr* guaranteed homes ratings

giant retailer /ˌdʒaɪənt ˈriːteɪlə/ *noun* a very large retailing group, e.g. a department store or chain store

GIF /gɪf/ *noun* a common file format for web graphics and banners. Full form **graphic interchange format**

GIF89 /ˌgɪf eɪti ˈnaɪn/ *noun* a commonly used version of GIF

gift coupon /ˈgɪft ,kuːpɒn/, **gift token** /ˈgɪft ,təʊkən/, **gift voucher** /ˈgɪft ,vaʊtʃə/ *noun* a card that can be used to buy specified goods up to the value printed on it, often issued by chain stores. The person receiving the voucher is able to redeem it in any store in the chain. ○ *We gave her a gift token for her birthday.*

gift-wrap /'gɪft ræp/ *verb* to wrap a present in attractive paper ○ *Do you want this book gift-wrapped?* (NOTE: **gift-wrapping- gift-wrapped**)

gimmick /'gɪmɪk/ *noun* a clever idea or trick ○ *a publicity gimmick*

give away /ˌgɪv ə'weɪ/ *verb* to give something as a free present ○ *We are giving away a pocket calculator with each £10 of purchases.*

giveaway /'gɪvəweɪ/ *adjective* □ **to sell at giveaway prices** to sell at very cheap prices ■ *noun* something which is given as a free gift when another item is bought

giveaway paper /'gɪvəweɪ ˌpeɪpə/ *noun* a newspaper which is given away free, and which relies for its income on its advertising

global /'gləʊb(ə)l/ *adjective* referring to the whole world ○ *We offer a 24-hour global delivery service.*

global advertising /ˌ'gləʊb(ə)l 'ædvətaɪzɪŋ/ *noun* using the same advertising message to advertise the same product internationally

global brand /ˌgləʊb(ə)l 'brænd/ *noun* a famous brand name which is recognised and sold all over the world

globalisation /ˌgləʊbəlaɪ'zeɪʃ(ə)n/, **globalization** *noun* the process of making something international or worldwide, especially the process of expanding business interests, operations and strategies to countries all over the world (NOTE: Globalisation is due to technological developments that make global communications possible, political developments such as the fall of communism and developments in transportation that make travelling faster and more frequent. It can benefit companies by opening up new markets, giving access to new raw materials and investment opportunities and enabling them to take advantage of lower operating costs in other countries.)

global marketing /ˌgləʊb(ə)l 'mɑːkɪtɪŋ/ *noun* using a common marketing plan to sell the same product or services everywhere in the world

global product /ˌgləʊb(ə)l 'prɒdʌkt/ *noun* a product with a famous brand name which is recognised and sold all over the world

global retailer /ˌgləʊb(ə)l 'riːteɪlə/ *noun* a company which sells its products all over the world

glue /gluː/ *noun* something such as information that unifies organisations, supply chains and other commercial groups

glut /glʌt/ *noun* □ **a glut of produce** too much produce, which is then difficult to sell ○ *a coffee glut* or *a glut of coffee* □ **a glut of money** a situation where there is too much money available to borrowers ■ *verb* to fill the market with something which is then difficult to sell ○ *The market is glutted with cheap cameras.* (NOTE: **glutting – glutted**)

goal /gəʊl/ *noun* something which you try to achieve ○ *Our goal is to break even within twelve months.* ○ *The company achieved all its goals.*

going rate /ˌgəʊɪŋ 'reɪt/ *noun* the usual or current rate of payment ○ *We pay the going rate for typists.* ○ *The going rate for offices is £10 per square metre.*

gondola /'gɒndələ/ *noun* a free-standing display in a supermarket which shoppers can walk round

gone aways /'gɒn əˌweɪz/ *plural noun* people who have moved away from the address they have in a mailing list

good industrial relations /gʊd ɪnˌdʌstrɪəl rɪ'leɪʃ(ə)nz/ *plural noun* a situation where management and employees understand each others' problems and work together for the good of the company

goods /gʊdz/ *plural noun* **1.** □ **goods and chattels** moveable personal possessions □ **goods in progress** the value of goods being manufactured which are not complete at the end of an accounting period ○ *Our current assets are made up of stock, goods in progress, and cash.* □ **goods sold loose** goods sold by weight, not prepacked in bags **2.** items which can be moved and are for sale

'…profit margins are lower in the industries most exposed to foreign competition – machinery, transportation equipment and electrical goods' [*Sunday Times*]

'…the minister wants people buying goods ranging from washing machines to houses to demand facts on energy costs' [*Times*]

goods depot /ˈgʊdz ˌdepəʊ/ *noun* a central warehouse where goods can be stored until they are moved

goods train /ˈgʊdz treɪn/ *noun* a train for carrying freight

goodwill /gʊdˈwɪl/ *noun* good feeling towards someone ○ *to show goodwill, the management increased the terms of the offer*

GOTS *abbr* gross opportunity to see

government contractor /ˌgʌv(ə)nmənt kənˈtræktə/ *noun* a company which supplies the government with goods by contract

government-controlled /ˌgʌvnmənt kənˈtrəʊld/ *adjective* under the direct control of the government ○ *Advertisements cannot be placed in the government-controlled newspapers.*

government economic indicators /ˌgʌv(ə)nmənt iːkəˌnɒmɪk ˈɪndɪkeɪtəz/ *plural noun* statistics which show how the country's economy is going to perform in the short or long term

government organisation /ˌgʌv(ə)nmənt ˌɔːgənaɪˈzeɪʃ(ə)n/ *noun* an official body, run by the government

grade /greɪd/ *noun* a level or rank ○ *to reach the top grade in the civil service* ■ *verb* **1.** to sort something into different levels of quality ○ *to grade coal* **2.** to make something rise in steps according to quantity □ **graded advertising rates** rates which become cheaper as you take more advertising space

graded hotel /ˌgreɪdɪd həʊˈtel/ *noun* a good-quality hotel

graded tax /ˌgreɪdɪd ˈtæks/ *noun US* **1.** a tax which rises according to income **2.** a tax on property which is higher if the property has not been kept in a good state by the owner

grade level /ˈgreɪd ˌlev(ə)l/ *noun* the classification of a product's quality

written on a label attached to the product ○ *Many consumers do not properly understand the grade levels.*

grand /grænd/ *adjective* important □ **grand plan** *or* **grand strategy** a major plan ○ *They explained their grand plan for redeveloping the factory site.* ■ *noun* one thousand pounds or dollars (*informal*) ○ *They offered him fifty grand for the information.*

grand total /grænd ˈtəʊt(ə)l/ *noun* the final total made by adding several subtotals

grapevine /ˈgreɪpvaɪn/ *noun* an informal and unofficial communications network within an organisation that passes on information by word of mouth (NOTE: A grapevine may distort information or spread gossip and rumour, but it can also back up the official communications network, provide feedback and strengthen social relationships within the organisation.)

graph /grɑːf/ *noun* a diagram which shows the relationship between two sets of quantities or values, each of which is represented on an axis ○ *A graph was used to show salary increases in relation to increases in output.* ○ *According to the graph, as average salaries have risen so has absenteeism.* ○ *We need to set out the results of the questionnaire in a graph.*

graphics /ˈgræfɪks/ *plural noun* designs and illustrations in printed work, especially designs which are created by computers ○ *In this series of advertisements the graphics do not do justice to the copy.*

graph paper /ˈgrɑːf ˌpeɪpə/ *noun* a special type of paper with many little squares, used for drawing graphs

gratis /ˈgrætɪs/ *adverb* free or not costing anything ○ *We got into the exhibition gratis.*

green issues /ˈgriːn ˌɪsjuːz/ *plural noun* same as **environmental management**

green marketing /ˈgriːn ˌmɑːkɪtɪŋ/ *noun* marketing products and services on the basis of their environmental acceptability

grey market /'greɪ ˌmɑːkɪt/ *noun* **1.** the unofficial legal buying and selling of scarce, highly priced goods ○ *If the government puts a ceiling on prices for these products the grey market will become a black market.* **2.** a market formed of people over 60 years of age. ♦ **silver market**

grid /grɪd/ *noun* a graph with lines crossing at right angles and items written in the boxes, used for comparison

gross /grəʊs/ *adverb* with no deductions ○ *My salary is paid gross.* ■ *verb* to make a gross profit ○ *The group grossed £25m in 1999.*

gross audience /grəʊs 'ɔːdiəns/ *noun* the total number of people who have seen an advertisement, multiplied by the number of times it has been run

gross circulation /grəʊs ˌsɜːkjʊ-'leɪʃ(ə)n/ *noun* the total sales of a publication before adjusting for error or discounting unsold copies

gross cover /grəʊs 'kʌvə/ *noun* the number of times a television or radio spot has been seen based on television ratings

gross domestic product /grəʊs dəˌmestɪk 'prɒdʌkt/ *noun* the annual value of goods sold and services paid for inside a country. Abbr **GDP**

gross earnings /grəʊs 'ɜːnɪŋz/ *plural noun* total earnings before tax and other deductions

gross impressions /grəʊs ɪm-'preʃ(ə)nz/ *plural noun* the total number of people who have seen an advertisement, multiplied by the number of times it has been run. ♦ **guaranteed homes impressions**

gross margin /grəʊs 'mɑːdʒɪn/ *noun* the percentage difference between the received price and the unit manufacturing cost or purchase price of goods for resale

gross national product /grəʊs ˌnæʃ(ə)n(ə)l 'prɒdʌkt/ *noun* the annual value of goods and services in a country including income from other countries. Abbr **GNP**

'...news that gross national product increased only 1.3% in the first quarter of the year sent the dollar down on foreign exchange markets' [*Fortune*]

gross opportunity to see *noun* the number of opportunities that an average member of the target audience will have to see the advertisements in an advertising campaign. Abbr **GOTS**

gross profit /grəʊs 'prɒfɪt/ *noun* profit calculated as sales income less the cost of the goods sold, i.e. without deducting any other expenses

gross rating point /grəʊs 'reɪtɪŋ pɔɪnt/ *noun US* a way of calculating the effectiveness of outdoor advertising, where each point represents one per cent of the population in a specific market. Abbr **GRP**

gross reach /grəʊs 'riːtʃ/ *noun* the total number of opportunities for people to see a company's advertisements in a campaign, i.e. the total number of publications sold multiplied by the number of advertisements appearing in each one

gross receipts /grəʊs rɪ'siːts/ *plural noun* the total amount of money received before expenses are deducted

gross sales /grəʊs 'seɪlz/ *plural noun* money received from sales before deductions for goods returned, special discounts, etc. ○ *Gross sales are impressive since many buyers seem to be ordering more than they will eventually need.*

gross weight /grəʊs 'weɪt/ *noun* the weight of both the container and its contents

ground transportation /'graʊnd trænspɔːˌteɪʃ(ə)n/ *noun* the means of transport available to take passengers from an airport to the town, e.g. buses, taxis, or trains

group /gruːp/ *noun* **1.** several things or people together ○ *A group of managers has sent a memo to the chairman complaining about noise in the office.* ○ *The respondents were interviewed in groups of three or four, and then singly.* **2.** several companies linked together in the same organisation ○ *the group chairman* or *the chairman of the group* ○ *group turnover* or *turnover for the group* ○ *the Granada Group* ■ *verb* □ **to group together** to put several items

together ○ *Sales from six different agencies are grouped together under the heading 'European sales'.*

group discussion /gruːp dɪ-ˈskʌʃ(ə)n/ *noun* a survey method in which a focus group is brought together to discuss informally a market-research question ○ *The group discussion was taken over by one or two strong personalities.* ○ *A sample of young people took part in a group discussion on the new shampoo.*

group interview /gruːp ˈɪntəvjuː/ *noun* an interview with a group of respondents such as a family in order to discover the views of the group as a whole ○ *There were group interviews with all the classes in the school in order to gauge reactions to the new educational programme.*

group results /gruːp rɪˈzʌlts/ *plural noun* the results of a group of companies taken together

group system /ˈgruːp ˌsɪstəm/ *noun* a system of organising an advertising agency in groups, each group having specialists in creative, media, marketing services, and other areas, and each group dealing with particular accounts

groupware /ˈgruːpweə/ *noun* software that enables a group of people who are based in different locations to work together and share information (NOTE: Groupware usually provides communal diaries, address books, work planners, bulletin boards and newsletters in electronic format on a closed network.)

grow /grəʊ/ *verb* to cause something such as a business to develop or expand

'…the thrift had grown from $4.7 million in assets to $1.5 billion' [*Barrons*]

growth /grəʊθ/ *noun* **1.** an increase in size **2.** the second stage in a product life cycle, following the launch, when demand for the product increases rapidly □ **the company is aiming for growth** the company is aiming to expand rapidly

'…a general price freeze succeeded in slowing the growth in consumer prices' [*Financial Times*]

'…growth in demand is still coming from the private rather than the public sector' [*Lloyd's List*]

'…population growth in the south-west is again reflected by the level of rental values' [*Lloyd's List*]

growth area /ˈgrəʊθ ˌeəriə/ *noun* an area where sales are increasing rapidly

growth index /ˈgrəʊθ ˌɪndeks/ *noun* an index showing how something has grown

growth industry /ˈgrəʊθ ˌɪndəstri/ *noun* an industry that is expanding or has the potential to expand faster than other industries

growth market /ˈgrəʊθ ˌmɑːkɪt/ *noun* a market where sales are increasing rapidly ○ *We plan to build a factory in the Far East, which is a growth market for our products.*

growth rate /ˈgrəʊθ reɪt/ *noun* the speed at which something grows

growth share matrix /ˈgrəʊθ ʃeə ˌmeɪtrɪks/ *noun* a model for a marketing strategy with various categories of product based on present performance and growth rate ○ *The growth share matrix helped to decide what products needed extra marketing efforts.*

growth vector matrix /ˈgrəʊθ ˌvektə ˌmeɪtrɪks/ *noun* a model for a marketing strategy with various choices and combinations of strategy based on product and market development

GRP *abbr* gross rating point

guarantee /ˌɡærənˈtiː/ *noun* **1.** a legal document in which the producer agrees to compensate the buyer if the product is faulty or becomes faulty before a specific date after purchase ○ *a certificate of guarantee* or *a guarantee certificate* ○ *The guarantee lasts for two years.* ○ *It is sold with a twelve-month guarantee.* □ **the car is still under guarantee** the car is still covered by the maker's guarantee **2.** a promise that someone will pay another person's debts □ **to go guarantee for someone** to act as security for someone's debts **3.** something given as a security ○ *to leave share certificates as a guarantee* ■ *verb* **1.** to give a promise that something will happen □ **to guarantee a debt** to promise that you will pay a debt made by someone else □ **to guarantee an associate company** to promise that an associ-

ate company will pay its debts □ **to guarantee a bill of exchange** to promise that the bill will be paid **2.** □ **the product is guaranteed for twelve months** the manufacturer says that the product will work well for twelve months, and will mend it free of charge if it breaks down

guaranteed circulation /ˌgærəntiːd ˌsɜːkjʊˈleɪʃ(ə)n/ *noun* the audited circulation of a magazine which is used as a basis for calculating advertising rates

guaranteed homes impressions /ˌgærəntiːd ˈhəʊmz ɪmˌpreʃ(ə)nz/, **guaranteed homes ratings** /ˌgærəntiːd ˈhəʊmz ˌreɪtɪŋz/ *plural noun* an advertising package offered by television companies which guarantees the advertisers that their advertising will reach a specified number of people, but leaves it to the TV company to choose the number and timing of the spots. Abbr **GHI, GHR**

guaranteed prices /ˌgærəntiːd ˈpraɪsɪz/ *plural noun* minimum prices guaranteed to an industry by the government, with the payment of a subsidy to make up for market prices that fall below this level ○ *Guaranteed prices help bring some security to a notoriously unstable industry.*

guaranteed wage /ˌgærəntiːd ˈweɪdʒ/ *noun* a wage which a company promises will not fall below a specific figure

guarantor /ˌgærənˈtɔː/ *noun* a person who promises to pay someone's debts ○ *She stood guarantor for her brother.*

guard book /ˈgɑːd bʊk/ *noun* a hardcover album which allows pages to be inserted into it, e.g. for showing samples or advertising material

guerrilla marketing /gəˈrɪlə ˌmɑːkɪtɪŋ/ *noun* a form of unconventional flexible marketing, adapted to the products or services sold, or to the type of customer targeted

guesstimate /ˈgestɪmət/ *noun* a rough calculation (*informal*)

gutter /ˈgʌtə/ *noun* the area where the two pages meet in a book or magazine. It can be left blank as a centre margin, or can be printed across to form a double-page spread.

H

habit /ˈhæbɪt/ *noun* the practice of doing something regularly ○ *Most consumers continue to buy the same brands from force of habit.*

habit buying /ˈhæbɪt ˌbaɪɪŋ/ *noun* the practice of buying a particular product again and again out of habit, without making any conscious decision to buy

haggle /ˈhæg(ə)l/ *verb* to discuss prices and terms and try to reduce them ○ *to haggle about* or *over the details of a contract* ○ *After two days' haggling the contract was signed.*

half-price sale /ˌhɑːf praɪs ˈseɪl/ *noun* a sale of items at half the usual price

hallmark /ˈhɔːlmɑːk/ *noun* a mark put on gold or silver items to show that the metal is of the correct quality ■ *verb* to put a hallmark on a piece of gold or silver ○ *a hallmarked spoon*

hallmark of excellence /ˌhɔːlmɑːk əv ˈeksələns/ *noun* the reputation that a brand name has for high quality

hall test /ˈhɔːl test/ *noun* a market-research test where respondents are asked to go into a public building or central place to answer questions or to test new products ○ *The hall test was conducted in the town's main school.*

halo effect /ˈheɪləʊ ɪˌfekt/ *noun* a series of positive impressions of a product which consumers retain and which can be revealed by a respondent when questioned in a survey

hand /hænd/ *noun* **1.** the part of the body at the end of each arm □ **to shake hands** to hold someone's hand when meeting to show you are pleased to meet them, or to show that an agreement has been reached ○ *The two negotiating teams shook hands and sat down at the* conference table. □ **to shake hands on a deal** to shake hands to show that a deal has been agreed **2.** □ **in hand** kept in reserve ○ *we have £10,000 in hand* □ **balance in hand** or **cash in hand** cash held to pay small debts and running costs □ **work in hand** work which is in progress but not finished

handbill /ˈhændbɪl/ *noun* a sheet of printed paper handed out to members of the public as an advertisement

handbook /ˈhændbʊk/ *noun* a book which gives instructions on how to use something ○ *The handbook does not say how you open the photocopier.*

handed-overs /ˈhændɪd ˌəʊvəz/ *plural noun* sales leads which have been passed on to the client to pursue

handle /ˈhænd(ə)l/ *verb* **1.** to deal with something or to organise something ○ *The accounts department handles all the cash.* ○ *We can handle orders for up to 15,000 units.* ○ *They handle all our overseas orders.* **2.** to sell or to trade in a type of product ○ *We do not handle foreign cars.* ○ *They will not handle goods produced by other firms.*

handling /ˈhændlɪŋ/ *noun* the process of receiving, storing and sending off goods

'…shipping companies continue to bear the extra financial burden of cargo handling operations at the ports' [*Business Times (Lagos)*]

handling charge /ˈhændlɪŋ tʃɑːdʒ/ *noun* money to be paid for packing, invoicing and dealing with goods which are being shipped

handout /ˈhændaʊt/ *noun* a free gift, especially of money ○ *The company exists on handouts from the government.*

hard /hɑːd/ *adjective* □ **to drive a hard bargain** to be a difficult negotia-

tor □ **to strike a hard bargain** to agree a deal where the terms are favourable to you

hard cash /hɑːd 'kæʃ/ *noun* money in notes and coins, as opposed to cheques or credit cards

'...few of the paper millionaires sold out and transformed themselves into hard cash millionaires' [*Investors Chronicle*]

hard currency /hɑːd 'kʌrənsi/ *noun* the currency of a country which has a strong economy, and which can be changed into other currencies easily ○ *to pay for imports in hard currency* ○ *to sell raw materials to earn hard currency*

hardening /'hɑːdnɪŋ/ *noun* □ **a hardening of prices** prices which are becoming settled at a higher level

hardness /'hɑːdnəs/ *noun* □ **hardness of the market** the state of the market as being strong and not being likely to fall

hard sell /hɑːd 'sel/ *noun* □ **to give a product the hard sell** to make great efforts to persuade people to buy a product □ **he tried to give me the hard sell** he put a lot of effort into trying to make me buy

hard selling /hɑːd 'selɪŋ/ *noun* the act of selling by using great efforts ○ *A lot of hard selling went into that deal.*

hardware /'hɑːdweə/ *noun* **1.** machines used in data processing, including the computers and printers, but not the programs **2.** solid goods for use in the house, e.g. frying pans or hammers ○ *a hardware shop*

harvesting /'hɑːvɪstɪŋ/ *noun* the practice of cutting marketing investment on a particular product prior to withdrawing it from the market

haulage /'hɔːlɪdʒ/ *noun* the cost of transporting goods by road ○ *Haulage is increasing by 5% per annum.*

haulage contractor /'hɔːlɪdʒ kən-ˌtræktə/ *noun* a company which transports goods by contract

hawk /hɔːk/ *verb* to sell goods from door to door or in the street □ **to hawk something round** to take a product, an idea or a project to various companies to see if one will accept it ○ *He hawked his*

idea for a plastic car body round all the major car constructors.

hawker /'hɔːkə/ *noun* a person who sells goods from door to door or in the street

head buyer /hed 'baɪə/ *noun* the most important buyer in a store ○ *She is the shoe buyer for a London department store.* ○ *He is the paper buyer for a large magazine chain.*

headhunt /'hedhʌnt/ *verb* to look for managers and offer them jobs in other companies □ **she was headhunted** she was approached by a headhunter and offered a new job

headhunter /'hedhʌntə/ *noun* a person or company whose job is to find suitable top managers to fill jobs in companies

headline /'hedlaɪn/ *noun* the heading of an article or advertisement, which is set in much larger type than the rest

head-on position /ˌhed ɒn pə-ˌzɪʃ(ə)n/ *noun* a poster site directly facing traffic ○ *Let's try to obtain a head-on position in the central part of town.*

heads of agreement /ˌhedz əv ə'griːmənt/ *noun* the most important parts of a commercial agreement

heat sealing /'hiːt ˌsiːlɪŋ/ *noun* a method of closing plastic food containers

COMMENT: Air is removed from a plastic bag with the food inside. The bag is then pressed by a hot plate which melts the plastic and seals the contents in the vacuum.

heavy /'hevi/ *adjective* large or in large quantities ○ *a programme of heavy investment overseas* ○ *He suffered heavy losses on the Stock Exchange.* ○ *The government imposed a heavy tax on luxury goods.* □ **heavy costs** *or* **heavy expenditure** spending large sums of money

'...heavy selling sent many blue chips tumbling in Tokyo yesterday' [*Financial Times*]

heavy half /ˌhevi 'hɑːf/ *noun* a situation where a small number of customers make up more than half of the total demand for a product

heavy industry /ˌhevi ˈɪndəstri/ noun an industry which deals in heavy raw materials such as coal or makes large products such as ships or engines

heavy user /ˌhevi ˈjuːzə/ noun a consumer who buys more of a product than average ○ *Heavy users will be particularly affected by the price rise.*

heavy viewer /ˌhevi ˈvjuːə/ noun a person who watches a lot of television, and is part of the target audience for commercials ○ *Heavy viewers gave us the most interesting comments on our advertising.*

helicopter view /ˈhelɪkɒptə vjuː/ noun a general or broad view of a problem as a whole, which does not go into details (*slang*)

helpline /ˈhelplaɪn/ noun a telephone number which links people to services that can give them specialist advice, or a similar service offered by shops to their customers

heterogeneous /ˌhetərəʊˈdʒiːniəs/ adjective varied

heterogeneous shopping goods /ˌhetərəʊdʒiːniəs ˈʃɒpɪŋ ɡʊdz/ plural noun goods which vary in quality and style from brand to brand and which consumers spend time in choosing. Compare **homogeneous shopping goods**

heuristics /hjʊəˈrɪstɪks/ noun simple decision rules used by ordinary customers when choosing what to buy, e.g. buying whatever is cheapest

hierarchy /ˈhaɪərɑːki/ noun a series of items ranged in order of importance □ **hierarchy of needs** the theory that needs of individuals are arranged in an order based on their importance, such as safety, social needs, esteem, etc.

hierarchy of effects /ˌhaɪərɑːki əv ɪˈfekts/ noun a model showing the stages in the effect of advertising on a consumer such as awareness, knowledge, liking, preference, conviction and purchase

high /haɪ/ adjective **1.** tall ○ *The shelves are 30 cm high. ○ The door is not high enough to let us get the machines into the building. ○ They are planning a 30-storey-high office block.*

2. large, not low ○ *High overhead costs increase the unit price. ○ High prices put customers off. ○ They are budgeting for a high level of expenditure. ○ High interest rates are crippling small businesses.* □ **high sales** a large amount of revenue produced by sales □ **high taxation** taxation which imposes large taxes on incomes or profits □ **highest tax bracket** the group which pays the most tax □ **high volume (of sales)** a large number of items sold **3.** □ **the highest bidder** the person who offers the most money at an auction ○ *The tender will be awarded to the highest bidder. ○ The property was sold to the highest bidder.* ■ adverb □ **prices are running high** prices are above their usual level ■ noun a point where prices or sales are very large ○ *the highs and lows on the Stock Exchange ○ Prices have dropped by 10% since the high of January 2nd. ○ Prices have dropped by 10% since the January 2nd high.* □ **sales volume has reached an all-time high** the sales volume has reached the highest point it has ever been at

'American interest rates remain exceptionally high in relation to likely inflation rates' [*Sunday Times*]

'…faster economic growth would tend to push US interest rates, and therefore the dollar, higher' [*Australian Financial Review*]

'…in a leveraged buyout the acquirer raises money by selling high-yielding debentures to private investors' [*Fortune*]

high-end /ˈhaɪ end/ adjective more expensive, more advanced or more powerful than the other items in a range of things, e.g., computers

high finance /haɪ ˈfaɪnæns/ noun the lending, investing and borrowing of very large sums of money organised by financiers

high-grade /ˈhaɪɡreɪd/ adjective of very good quality ○ *high-grade petrol* □ **high-grade trade delegation** a delegation made up of very important people

'…the accepted wisdom built upon for well over 100 years that government and high-grade corporate bonds were almost riskless' [*Forbes Magazine*]

high-involvement product /ˌhaɪ ɪnˈvɒlvmənt ˌprɒdʌkt/ noun a high-priced or high-tech product that is

carefully considered by a consumer before being bought

high pressure /haɪ ˈpreʃə/ *noun* a strong insistence that somebody should do something □ **working under high pressure** working with a manager telling you what to do and to do it quickly or with customers asking for supplies urgently

high-pressure salesman /ˌhaɪ ˌpreʃə ˈseɪlzmən/, **high-pressure saleswoman** *noun* a salesman or saleswoman who forces a customer to buy something he or she does not really want

high-pressure sales technique /ˌhaɪ ˌpreʃə ˈseɪlz tekˌniːk/ *noun* forcing a customer to buy something he or she does not really want

high-quality /ˌhaɪ ˈkwɒlɪti/ *adjective* of very good quality ○ *high-quality goods* ○ *a high-quality product*

high season /haɪ ˈsiːz(ə)n/ *noun* the period when there are most travellers and tourists

high street /ˈhaɪ striːt/ *noun* **1.** the main shopping street in a British town ○ *the high street shops* ○ *a high street bookshop* **2.** a main street considered as an important retail area

High Street banks /ˌhaɪ striːt ˈbæŋks/ *plural noun* main British banks which accept deposits from individual customers

hire purchase /haɪə ˈpɜːtʃɪs/ *noun* a system of buying something by paying a sum regularly each month ○ *to buy a refrigerator on hire purchase* Abbr **HP** (NOTE: American English is **installment plan** or **installment sale**) □ **to sign a hire-purchase agreement** to sign a contract to pay for something by instalments

hire-purchase company /haɪə ˈpɜːtʃɪs ˌkʌmp(ə)ni/ *noun* a company which provides money for hire purchase

histogram /ˈhɪstəɡræm/ *noun* a chart or diagram with bars set on a base-line, the length of each bar expressing the quantity of an item or unit

historic /hɪˈstɒrɪk/, **historical** /hɪˈstɒrɪk(ə)l/ *adjective* which goes back over a period of time

'…the Federal Reserve Board has eased interest rates in the past year, but they are still at historically high levels' [*Sunday Times*]

'…the historic p/e for the FTSE all-share index is 28.3 and the dividend yield is barely 2 per cent. Both indicators suggest that the stock markets are very highly priced' [*Times*]

historical figures /hɪˌstɒrɪk(ə)l ˈfɪɡəz/ *plural noun* figures which were current in the past

historical trend /hɪˌstɒrɪk(ə)l ˈtrend/ *noun* a trend detected in the past on the basis of historical data ○ *Historical trends may help us to predict how the economy will develop in the future.* ○ *It is difficult to detect any clear historical trends in consumer reaction to our past product launches.*

historic(al) cost /hɪˌstɒrɪk(ə)l ˈkɒst/ *noun* the actual cost of purchasing something which was bought some time ago

hit /hɪt/ *noun* **1.** a response to a request sent from an Internet browser (NOTE: When a browser conducts a search, the number of hits it gets is the number of websites, files or images it finds that fit the criteria set for the search.) **2.** a successful match or search of a database

hit rate /ˈhɪt reɪt/ *noun* the rate at which a target is reached such as the number of mail shots needed before a customer makes an order for a product advertised on them, or the number of customers who reply to a mail shot compared to the total number of customers mailed

hive off /ˌhaɪv ˈɒf/ *verb* to split off part of a large company to form a smaller subsidiary ○ *The new managing director hived off the retail sections of the company.*

hoard /hɔːd/ *verb* **1.** to buy and store goods in case of need **2.** to keep cash instead of investing it

hoarder /ˈhɔːdə/ *noun* a person who buys and stores goods in case of need

hoarding /ˈhɔːdɪŋ/ *noun* **1.** □ **hoarding of supplies** the buying of large quantities of money or goods to keep in

case of need **2.** a large wooden board for posters

'...as a result of hoarding, rice has become scarce with prices shooting up' [*Business Times (Lagos)*]

home audit /həʊm ˈɔːdɪt/ *noun* a survey method whereby a panel of householders keeps records of purchases so that these can be regularly checked for quantity and brand ○ *The home audit showed that although wholesalers were buying the product in large quantities, consumers were not.* ○ *The home audit suggested that there is little brand loyalty for this type of product.*

home country /həʊm ˈkʌntri/ *noun* a country where a company is based

homegrown /ˈhəʊmɡrəʊn/ *adjective* which has been developed in a local area or in a country where the company is based ○ *a homegrown computer industry* ○ *India's homegrown car industry*

home industry /həʊm ˈɪndəstri/ *noun* productive work carried out by people at home ○ *In third world countries there are still many home industries.* ○ *Home industries are disappearing as mass production takes over.*

home market /həʊm ˈmɑːkɪt/ *noun* the market in the country where the selling company is based ○ *Sales in the home market rose by 22%.*

homepage /ˈhəʊmpeɪdʒ/ *noun* the first page that is displayed when you visit a site on the Internet

home-produced product /ˌhəʊm prəˌdjuːst ˈprɒdʌkts/ *noun* a product manufactured in the country where the company is based

home shopping /həʊm ˈʃɒpɪŋ/ *noun* buying items direct from the customer's house, using a computer linked to the telephone which is linked to the store's ordering department

home trade /ˈhəʊm treɪd/ *noun* trade in the country where a company is based

homeward /ˈhəʊmwəd/ *adjective* going towards the home country ○ *The ship is carrying homeward freight.* ○ *The liner left Buenos Aires on her homeward journey.*

homewards /ˈhəʊmwədz/ *adverb* towards the home country ○ *cargo homewards*

homogeneous /ˌhəʊməʊˈdʒiːniəs/ *adjective* uniform or unvaried

homogeneous shopping goods /ˌhəʊməʊdʒiːniəs ˈʃɒpɪŋ ɡʊdz/ *plural noun* goods which vary little in style and quality from brand to brand and which consumers spend little time choosing. Compare **heterogeneous shopping goods**

horizontal /ˌhɒrɪˈzɒnt(ə)l/ *adjective* at the same level or with the same status ○ *Her new job is a horizontal move into a different branch of the business.*

horizontal communication /ˌhɒrɪzɒnt(ə)l kəˌmjuːnɪˈkeɪʃ(ə)n/ *noun* communication between employees at the same level

horizontal cooperative advertising /ˌhɒrɪzɒnt(ə)l kəʊˌɒp(ə)rətɪv ˈædvətaɪzɪŋ/ *noun* cooperative advertising where the advertising is sponsored by a group of retailers

horizontal industrial market /æ(noun), ˌhɒrɪzɒnt(ə)l ɪnˌdʌstriəl ˈmɑːkɪt/ *noun* a market in which a product is used by many industries

horizontal integration /hɒrɪˌzɒnt(ə)l ɪntəˈɡreɪʃ(ə)n/ *noun* the process of joining similar companies or taking over a company in the same line of business as yourself

horizontal marketing system /ˌhɒrɪzɒnt(ə)l ˈmɑːkɪtɪŋ ˌsɪstəm/ *noun* cooperation between or merger of two or more companies whose assets are complementary and who therefore all gain from coming together

horizontal publication /ˌhɒrɪzɒnt(ə)l ˌpʌblɪˈkeɪʃ(ə)n/ *noun* a publication which is aimed at people in similar levels of occupation in different industries

horizontal rotation /ˌhɒrɪzɒnt(ə)l rəʊˈteɪʃ(ə)n/ *noun* distributing broadcast spots on different days of the week at the same time of day

horse trading /ˈhɔːs ˌtreɪdɪŋ/ *noun* hard bargaining which ends with some-

one giving something in return for a concession from the other side

hostess party selling /ˌhəʊstes ˈpɑːti ˌseliŋ/ *noun* a method of selling certain items such as household goods directly by the manufacturer's agent at a party to which potential customers are invited

host service /ˈhəʊst ˌsɜːvɪs/, **hosting service provider** /ˌhəʊstɪŋ ˈsɜːvɪs/ *noun* a company that provides connections to the Internet and storage space on its computers, which can store the files for a user's website

hot button /ˈhɒt ˌbʌt(ə)n/ *noun* the immediate interest a customer has in a product or service offered for sale

hotline /ˈhɒtlaɪn/ *noun* a special telephone ordering service set up for a special period ○ *a Christmas hotline*

hot money /hɒt ˈmʌni/ *noun* money which is moved from country to country to get the best returns

house /haʊs/ *noun* **1.** the building in which someone lives **2.** a company ○ *the largest London finance house* ○ *He works for a broking house* or *a publishing house.*

house advertisment /ˈhaʊs ədˈvɜːtɪsmənt/, **house ad** /ˈhaʊs æd/ *noun* an advertisement in a publication which is placed by the publication itself, e.g. one offering a readers' advice service or selling back numbers of the publication

house agency /ˈhaʊz ˌeɪdʒənsi/ *noun* an advertising agency owned and used by a large company, and which other companies may also use

house agent /ˈhaʊs ˌeɪdʒənt/ *noun* an estate agent who deals in buying or selling houses or flats

house brand /ˈhaʊs brænd/ *noun* a brand owned by a retailer rather than by the producer

household /ˈhaʊshəʊld/ *noun* a unit formed of all the people living together in a single house or flat, whether it is a single person living alone, a married couple or a large family

'…the extent of single women households has implications for marketing' [*Precision Marketing*]

household appliances /ˌhaʊshəʊld əˈplaɪənsɪz/ *plural noun* appliances which are used in carrying out day-to-day work in the house, e.g. dishwashers and refrigerators

household goods /ˌhaʊshəʊld ˈɡʊdz/ *plural noun* items which are used in the home

household name /ˌhaʊshəʊld neɪm/ *noun* a brand name which is recognised by a large number of consumers

households using television /ˌhaʊshəʊldz ˌjuːzɪŋ teliˈvɪʒ(ə)n/ *noun* the percentage of homes watching television during a specific time period and within a specific area. Abbr **HUT**

house journal /æ(noun), ˈhaʊs ˌdʒɜːn(ə)l/, **house magazine** /ˈhaʊs mægəˌziːn/ *noun* a magazine produced for the employees or shareholders in a company to give them news about the company

house property /ˈhaʊs ˌprɒpəti/ *noun* private houses or flats, not shops, offices or factories

house style /ˈhaʊs staɪl/ *noun* a company's own design which is used in all its products, including packaging and stationery

house-to-house /ˌhaʊs tə ˈhaʊs/ *adjective* going from one house to the next, asking people to buy something or to vote for someone ○ *house-to-house canvassing* ○ *He trained as a house-to-house salesman.* ○ *House-to-house selling is banned in this area.*

housing market /ˈhaʊzɪŋ ˌmɑːkɪt/, **property market** /ˈprɒpəti ˌmɑːkɪt/ *noun* the sale of houses

HTML *noun* the standard computer code used to build and develop webpages

human resources /ˌhjuːmən rɪˈsɔːsɪz/ *plural noun* the employees which an organisation has available ○ *Our human resources must be looked after and developed if we are to raise productivity successfully.*

'…effective use and management of human resources hold the key to future business development and success' [*Management Today*]

hunch marketing /'hʌntʃ ˌmɑːkɪtɪŋ/ *noun* the process of making marketing decisions following a hunch, rather than relying on market research

HUT *abbr* households using television

hype /haɪp/ *noun* excessive claims made in advertising ○ *all the hype surrounding the launch of the new soap* ○ *Many consumers were actually put off by all the media hype surrounding the launch of the new magazine.* ■ *verb* to make excessive claims in advertising

hyperlink /'haɪpəlɪŋk/ *noun* **1.** an image or a piece of text that a user clicks on in order to move directly from one webpage to another (NOTE: Hyperlinks can be added to webpages by using simple HTML commands; they can also be used in email messages, for example, to include the address of a company's website.) **2.** a series of commands attached to a button or word on one webpage that link it to another page, so that if a user clicks on the button or word, the hyperlink will move the user to another position or display another page

hypermarket /'haɪpəmɑːkɪt/ *noun* a very large supermarket, usually outside a large town, with car-parking facilities

hypertext /'haɪpətekst/ *noun* a system of organising information in which certain words in a document link to other documents and display the text when the word is selected

hypertext link /'haɪpətekst lɪŋk/ *noun* same as **hyperlink**

hypertext markup language /ˌhaɪpətekst 'mɑːkʌp ˌlæŋgwɪdʒ/ *noun* full form of **HTML**

hypoing /'haɪpəʊɪŋ/ *noun* using special promotions to increase the audience of a TV station during the sweep periods and so affect the ratings

hypothesis /haɪ'pɒθəsɪs/ *noun* an assumption or theory which must be tested to be confirmed or proved correct ○ *Let us assume, as a working hypothesis, that we can win a 5% market share within two years of the launch.* ○ *Surveys proved that our original hypothesis about likely consumer behaviour was by and large correct.* (NOTE: plural is **hypotheses**)

I

iceberg principle /ˈaɪsbɜːg ˌprɪnsɪp(ə)l/ *noun* the principle that strong needs and desires lie deep in the human personality and that advertising must work at this level if it is to be effective

ident /ˈaɪdent/ *noun* a short TV image which identifies a channel

image /ˈɪmɪdʒ/ *noun* the general idea that the public has of a product, brand or company ○ *They are spending a lot of advertising money to improve the company's image.* ○ *The company has adopted a down-market image.* □ **to promote the corporate image** to publicise a company so that its reputation is improved

    '...charities are also ready to buy air time to promote their corporate image' [*Marketing Week*]

image advertising /ˈɪmɪdʒ ˌædvətaɪzɪŋ/ *noun* advertising with the aim of making a brand or company name easily remembered

image-maker /ˈɪmɪdʒ ˌmeɪkə/ *noun* someone who is employed to create a favourable public image for an organisation, product or public figure

image manipulation /ˈɪmɪdʒ mənɪpjʊˌleɪʃ(ə)n/ *noun* alteration of digital images using special computer software

image setter /ˈɪmɪdʒ ˌsetə/ *noun* a typesetting device that can process a PostScript page and produce a high-resolution output

image transfer /ˈɪmɪdʒ ˌtrænsfɜː/ *noun* the technique of transferring images from one medium to another, e.g. from a photograph to a computer disk

imitate /ˈɪmɪteɪt/ *verb* to do what someone else does ○ *They imitate all our sales gimmicks.*

imitation /ˌɪmɪˈteɪʃ(ə)n/ *noun* something which is a copy of an original □ **beware of imitations** be careful not to buy low-quality goods which are made to look like other more expensive items

immediate /ɪˈmiːdiət/ *adjective* happening at once ○ *We wrote an immediate letter of complaint.* ○ *Your order will receive immediate attention.*

immediate environment /ɪˌmiːdiət ɪnˈvaɪrənmənt/ *noun* elements or factors outside a business organisation which directly affect its work, such as the supply of raw materials and demand for its products ○ *The unreliability of our suppliers is one of the worst features of our immediate environment.*

impact /ɪmˈpækt/ *noun* a shock or strong effect ○ *the impact of new technology on the cotton trade* ○ *The new design has made little impact on the buying public.*

    '...the strong dollar's deflationary impact on European economies as governments push up interest rates to support their sinking currencies' [*Duns Business Month*]

impactaplan /ɪmˈpæktəplæn/ *noun* an extensive poster advertising campaign

impact scheduling /ˈɪmpækt ˌʃedjuːlɪŋ/ *noun* the practice of running advertisements for the same product close together so as to make a strong impression on the target audience ○ *Impact scheduling can achieve rapid brand awareness.*

imperfect /ɪmˈpɜːfɪkt/ *adjective* having defects ○ *They are holding a sale of imperfect items.* ○ *Check the batch for imperfect products.*

imperfect competition /ɪmˌpɜːfɪkt ˌkɒmpəˈtɪʃ(ə)n/ *noun* the degree of competition in a market which is some-

imperfection /ˌɪmpə'fekʃən/ *noun* a defect in something ○ *to check a batch for imperfections*

where between a monopoly at one extreme and perfect competition at the other

implied close /ɪmˌplaɪd 'kləʊz/ *noun* an act of ending a sale by assuming that the customer will make the purchase

import /ɪm'pɔːt/ *verb* to bring goods from abroad into a country for sale ○ *The company imports television sets from Japan.* ○ *This car was imported from France.*

'European manufacturers rely heavily on imported raw materials which are mostly priced in dollars' [*Duns Business Month*]

importation /ˌɪmpɔː'teɪʃ(ə)n/ *noun* the act of importing ○ *The importation of arms is forbidden.* ○ *The importation of livestock is subject to very strict controls.*

import ban /'ɪmpɔːt bæn/ *noun* an order forbidding imports ○ *The government has imposed an import ban on arms.*

import duty /'ɪmpɔːt ˌdjuːti/ *noun* a tax on goods imported into a country

importer /ɪm'pɔːtə/ *noun* a person or company that imports goods ○ *a cigar importer* ○ *The company is a big importer of foreign cars.*

import-export /ˌɪmpɔːt 'ekspɔːt/ *noun, adjective* referring to a business which deals with both bringing foreign goods into a country and sending locally made goods abroad ○ *Rotterdam is an important centre for the import-export trade.* ○ *He works in import-export.*

importing /ɪm'pɔːtɪŋ/ *adjective* which imports ○ *oil-importing countries* ○ *an importing company* ■ *noun* the act of bringing foreign goods into a country for sale ○ *The importing of arms into the country is illegal.* ○ *The level of importing is bound to affect domestic industries.*

import levy /'ɪmpɔːt ˌlevi/ *noun* a tax on imports, especially in the EU a tax on imports of farm produce from outside the EU

import licence /'ɪmpɔːt ˌlaɪs(ə)ns/, **import permit** /'ɪmpɔːt ˌpɜːmɪt/ *noun* official documents which allow goods to be exported or imported

import quota /'ɪmpɔːt ˌkwəʊtə/ *noun* a fixed quantity of a particular type of goods which the government allows to be imported ○ *The government has imposed a quota on the importation of cars.* ○ *The quota on imported cars has been lifted.*

imports /'ɪmpɔːts/ *plural noun* goods brought into a country from abroad for sale ○ *Imports from Poland have risen to $1m a year.*

import surcharge /ˌɪmpɔːt 'sɜːtʃɑːdʒ/ *noun* the extra duty charged on imported goods, to try to stop them from being imported and to encourage local manufacture

impression /ɪm'preʃ(ə)n/ *noun* **1.** one person's single exposure to an advertisement ○ *One impression can be enough to induce a consumer to buy.* ○ *Too many impressions can put consumers off.* **2.** the number of times an ad banner is displayed

impression cover /ɪm'preʃ(ə)n ˌkʌvə/ *noun* the amount of advertising necessary to ensure the required number of impressions

impulse /'ɪmpʌls/ *noun* a sudden decision □ **to do something on impulse** to do something because you have just thought of it, not because it was planned

impulse buyer /'ɪmpʌls ˌbaɪə/ *noun* a person who buys something on impulse, not because he or she intended to buy it

impulse buying /'ɪmpʌls ˌbaɪɪŋ/ *noun* the practice of buying items which you have just seen, not because you had planned to buy them

impulse purchase /'ɪmpʌls ˌpɜːtʃɪs/ *noun* something bought as soon as it is seen

incentive /ɪn'sentɪv/ *noun* something which encourages a customer to buy or staff to work better

'…some further profit-taking was seen yesterday as investors continued to lack fresh incentives to renew buying activity' [*Financial Times*]

'…a well-designed plan can help companies retain talented employees and offer enticing performance incentives – all at an affordable cost' [*Fortune*]

incentive-based system /ɪn-ˈsentɪv beɪst ˌsɪstəm/ *noun* a payment system by which an advertising agency's commission depends on how well it performs

incentive marketing /ɪnˈsentɪv ˌmɑːkɪtɪŋ/ *noun* any additional incentives to buy apart from advertising, e.g. free gifts ○ *We will have to use incentive marketing to break down sales resistance.*

incentive programme /ɪnˈsentɪv ˌprəʊɡræm/ *noun* a programme to encourage something by offering incentives

incentive scheme /ɪnˈsentɪv skiːm/ *noun* a plan to encourage better work by paying higher commission or bonuses ○ *Incentive schemes are boosting production.*

inch rate /ˈɪnʃ reɪt/ *noun* an advertising rate for periodicals, calculated on a normal column width, one inch in depth

inclusive charge /ɪnˌkluːsɪv ˈtʃɑːdʒ/ *noun* a charge which includes all items

income /ˈɪnkʌm/ *noun* money which a person receives as salary or dividends □ **lower income bracket** *or* **upper income bracket** groups of people who earn low or high salaries considered for tax purposes □ **he comes into the higher income bracket** he is in a group of people earning high incomes and therefore paying more tax

'…there is no risk-free way of taking regular income from your money much higher than the rate of inflation' [*Guardian*]

income distribution /ˈɪnkʌm dɪstrɪˌbjuːʃ(ə)n/ *noun* the way in which the national income is distributed among the various classes and occupations in a country

income effect /ˈɪnkʌm ɪˌfekt/ *noun* the effect that a change in a person's income has on his or her spending

incomes policy /ˈɪnkʌmz ˌpɒlɪsi/ *noun* the government's ideas on how incomes should be controlled

income statement /ˈɪnkʌm ˌsteɪtmənt/ *noun US* a statement of company expenditure and sales which shows whether the company has made a profit or loss (NOTE: the British equivalent is **profit and loss account**)

incorrectly labelled parcel /ˌɪnkərektli ˌleɪb(ə)ld ˈpɑːs(ə)l/ *noun* a parcel with the wrong information on the label

indemnity /ɪnˈdemnɪti/ *noun* a guarantee of payment after a loss ○ *She had to pay an indemnity of £100.*

indent *noun* /ˈɪndent/ **1.** an order placed by an importer for goods from overseas ○ *They put in an indent for a new stock of soap.* **2.** a line of typing which starts several spaces from the left-hand margin ■ *verb* /ɪnˈdent/ **1.** □ **to indent for something** to put in an order for something ○ *The department has indented for a new computer.* **2.** to start a line of typing several spaces from the left-hand margin ○ *Indent the first line three spaces.*

independent /ˌɪndɪˈpendənt/ *adjective* not under the control or authority of anyone else

independent company /ˌɪndɪpendənt ˈkʌmp(ə)ni/ *noun* a company which is not controlled by another company

independents /ˌɪndɪˈpendənts/ *plural noun* shops or companies which are owned by private individuals or families

'…many independents took advantage of the bank holiday period when the big multiples were closed' [*The Grocer*]

independent television /ˌɪndɪpendənt ˈtelɪvɪʒ(ə)n/ *noun* British commercial television

Independent Television Commission /ˌɪndɪpendənt ˈtelɪvɪʒ(ə)n kəˌmɪʃ(ə)n/ the British statutory body which operates transmitting stations and oversees commercial television and radio. Abbr **ITC**

independent trader /ˌɪndɪpendənt ˈtreɪdə/, **independent shop** /ˌɪndɪpendənt ˈʃɒp/ *noun* a shop which is owned by an individual proprietor, not by a chain

independent variable /ˌɪndɪpendənt 'veəriəb(ə)l/ *noun* a factor whose value, when it changes, influences one or more other variables called 'dependent variables' ○ *In this model personal income is the independent variable and expenditure the dependent variable.*

index /'ɪndeks/ *noun* a regular statistical report which shows rises and falls in prices, values or levels

'…the index of industrial production sank 0.2 per cent for the latest month after rising 0.3 per cent in March' [*Financial Times*]

'…an analysis of the consumer price index for the first half of the year shows that the rate of inflation went down by 12.9 per cent' [*Business Times (Lagos)*]

indexation /ˌɪndek'seɪʃ(ə)n/ *noun* the linking of something to an index

indexation of wage increases /ˌɪndekseɪʃ(ə)n əv 'weɪdʒ ˌɪnkriːsɪz/ *noun* the linking of wage increases to the percentage rise in the cost of living

indexing /'ɪndeksɪŋ/ *noun* a method of showing changes in a value over time by starting with a simple base point such as 100, which then serves as a reference point for future years ○ *Indexing is used to show the rise in the cost of living over a ten-year period.*

index-linked /ˌɪndeks 'lɪŋkt/ *adjective* which rises automatically by the percentage increase in the cost of living ○ *index-linked government bonds* ○ *Inflation did not affect her as she has an index-linked pension.*

'…two-year index-linked savings certificates now pay 3 per cent a year tax free, in addition to index-linking' [*Financial Times*]

indicate /'ɪndɪkeɪt/ *verb* to show ○ *The latest figures indicate a fall in the inflation rate.* ○ *Our sales for last year indicate a move from the home market to exports.*

indicator /'ɪndɪkeɪtə/ *noun* something which indicates

'…it reduces this month's growth in the key M3 indicator from about 19% to 12%' [*Sunday Times*]

'…we may expect the US leading economic indicators for April to show faster economic growth' [*Australian Financial Review*]

'…other indicators, such as high real interest rates, suggest that monetary conditions are extremely tight' [*Economist*]

indicia /ɪn'dɪsiə/ *noun US* a stamp printed on an envelope to show that postage has been paid by the sender

indifference curve /ɪn'dɪf(ə)rəns kɜːv/ *noun* a line on a graph that joins various points, each point representing a combination of two commodities, each combination giving the customer equal satisfaction

indigenous /ɪn'dɪdʒɪnəs/ *adjective* belonging to a particular country or area ○ *Cocoa is not indigenous to the area, but has been grown there for some years.*

indirect /ˌɪndaɪ'rekt/ *adjective* not direct

indirect channel /ˌɪndaɪrekt 'tʃæn(ə)l/ *noun* a marketing channel where intermediaries such as wholesalers and retailers are used to sell a product, as opposed to using a direct sales force

indirect exporting /ˌɪndaɪrekt ek'spɔːtɪŋ/ *noun* selling products to a customer overseas through a middleman in your own country ○ *There is no need for indirect exporting as we can sell directly to the major department stores in Spain.* ○ *Indirect exporting saved the company from having to worry about export documentation and transportation.*

indirect headline /ˌɪndaɪrekt 'hedlaɪn/ *noun* a headline which does not directly try to sell a product or service but rather tries to attract the customer's attention or plays on his or her emotions

indirect labour costs /ˌɪndaɪrekt 'leɪbə kɒsts/ *plural noun* the cost of paying employees not directly involved in making a product such as cleaners or canteen staff. Such costs cannot be allocated to a cost centre.

individual /ˌɪndɪ'vɪdʒuəl/ *noun* one single person ○ *a savings plan tailored to the requirements of the private individual* ■ *adjective* single or belonging to one person ○ *a pension plan designed to meet each person's individual requirements* ○ *We sell individual portions of ice cream.*

individual demand /ˌɪndɪvɪdʒuəl dɪˈmɑːnd/ *noun* demand from one single consumer

industrial /ɪnˈdʌstriəl/ *adjective* referring to manufacturing work □ **to take industrial action** to go on strike or go-slow

'ACAS has a legal obligation to try and solve industrial grievances before they reach industrial tribunals' [*Personnel Today*]

'Britain's industrial relations climate is changing' [*Personnel Today*]

'…indications of renewed weakness in the US economy were contained in figures on industrial production for April' [*Financial Times*]

industrial advertising /ɪnˌdʌstriəl ˈædvətaɪzɪŋ/ *noun* advertising to businesses, not to private individuals

industrial capacity /ɪnˌdʌstriəl kəˈpæsɪti/ *noun* the amount of work which can be done in a factory or several factories

industrial centre /ɪnˈdʌstriəl ˌsentə/ *noun* a large town with many industries

industrial consumer /ɪnˌdʌstriəl kənˈsjuːmə/ *noun* a business which buys industrial goods

industrial design /ɪnˌdʌstriəl dɪˈzaɪn/ *noun* the design of products made by machines such as cars and refrigerators

industrial development /ɪnˌdʌstriəl dɪˈveləpmənt/ *noun* the planning and building of new industries in special areas

industrial espionage /ɪnˌdʌstriəl ˈespiənɑːʒ/ *noun* trying to find out the secrets of a competitor's work or products, usually by illegal means

industrial expansion /ɪnˌdʌstriəl ɪkˈspænʃən/ *noun* the growth of industries in a country or a region

industrial goods /ɪnˈdʌstriəl ɡʊdz/, **industrial products** /ɪnˌdʌstriəl ˈprɒdʌkts/ *plural noun* **1.** goods or products bought by producers to be used in production processes ○ *Our industrial products are advertised in the specialised press.* ○ *He is an engineer by profession and sells industrial goods to factories.* **2.** goods produced for use by industry, which include pro-cessed or raw materials and goods such as machinery and equipment that are used to produce other goods

industrial injury /ɪnˌdʌstriəl ˈɪndʒəri/ *noun* an injury to an employee that occurs in the workplace

industrialisation /ɪnˌdʌstriəlaɪˈzeɪʃ(ə)n/, **industrialization** *noun* the process of change by which an economy becomes based on industrial production rather than on agriculture

industrialise /ɪnˈdʌstriəlaɪz/, **industrialize** *verb* to set up industries in a country which had none before

'…central bank and finance ministry officials of the industrialized countries will continue work on the report' [*Wall Street Journal*]

industrialised society /ɪnˌdʌstriəˌlaɪzd səˈsaɪəti/ *noun* a country which has many industries

industrialist /ɪnˈdʌstriəlɪst/ *noun* an owner or director of a factory

industrial market /ɪnˈdʌstriəl ˌmɑːkɪt/ *noun* customers who buy goods to be used in production

industrial marketing /ɪnˌdʌstriəl ˈmɑːkɪtɪŋ/ *noun* the marketing of industrial products ○ *After doing a course in industrial marketing, I got a job selling machinery to aircraft manufacturers.*

industrial market research /ɪnˌdʌstriəl mɑːkɪt rɪˈsɜːtʃ/ *noun* market research into selling to businesses as opposed to private individuals

industrial services marketing /ɪnˌdʌstriəl ˈsɜːvɪsɪz ˌmɑːkɪtɪŋ/ *noun* the marketing to business customers of such services as debt collection, office cleaning, etc.

industrial user /ɪnˌdʌstriəl ˈjuːzə/ *noun* a customer who buys industrial products to use in production

industry /ˈɪndəstri/ *noun* **1.** all factories, companies or processes involved in the manufacturing of products ○ *All sectors of industry have shown rises in output.* **2.** a group of companies making the same type of product or offering the same type of service ○ *the aircraft industry* ○ *the food-processing industry* ○ *the petroleum industry* ○ *the advertising industry*

'…with the present overcapacity in the airline industry, discounting of tickets is widespread' [*Business Traveller*]

inelastic demand /ˌɪnɪˌlæstɪk dɪ-ˈmɑːnd/ *noun* demand which experiences a comparatively small percentage change in response to a percentage change in price ○ *Where a product is a household necessity, you almost always find an inelastic demand.*

inelastic supply /ˌɪnɪˌlæstɪk səˈplaɪ/ *noun* supply which experiences a comparatively small percentage change in response to a percentage change in price

inertia selling /ɪˈnɜːʃə ˌselɪŋ/ *noun* a method of selling items by sending them when they have not been ordered and assuming that if the items are not returned, the person who has received them is willing to buy them

inferior /ɪnˈfɪəriə/ *adjective* not as good as others ○ *products of inferior quality*

inferior product /ɪnˌfɪəriə ˈprɒdʌkt/ *noun* a product which consumers buy less of as their incomes rise ○ *Margarine was clearly an inferior product before it came to be considered healthier than butter.* ○ *As the recession hit, sales of inferior products soared.*

inflation /ɪnˈfleɪʃ(ə)n/ *noun* a greater increase in the supply of money or credit than in the production of goods and services, resulting in higher prices and a fall in the purchasing power of money □ **we have 3% inflation** *or* **inflation is running at 3%** prices are 3% higher than at the same time last year ○ *to take measures to reduce inflation* ○ *High interest rates tend to increase inflation.*

'…the decision by the government to tighten monetary policy will push the annual inflation rate above the year's previous high' [*Financial Times*]

'…when you invest to get a return, you want a 'real' return – above the inflation rate' [*Investors Chronicle*]

'…the retail prices index rose 0.4 per cent in the month, taking the annual headline inflation rate to 1.7 per cent. The underlying inflation rate, which excludes mortgage interest payments, increased to an annual rate of 3.1 per cent' [*Times*]

inflationary /ɪnˈfleɪʃ(ə)n(ə)ri/ *adjective* which tends to increase inflation ○

inflationary trends in the economy □ **the economy is in an inflationary spiral** the economy is in a situation where price rises encourage higher wage demands which in turn make prices rise

'…inflationary expectations fell somewhat this month, but remained a long way above the actual inflation rate, according to figures released yesterday. The annual rate of inflation measured by the consumer price index has been below 2 per cent for over 18 months' [*Australian Financial Review*]

inflight advertising /ˌɪnflaɪt ˈædvətaɪzɪŋ/ *noun* advertising on TV screens inside a plane

inflight audience /ˌɪnflaɪt ˈɔːdiəns/ *noun* travellers, especially business executives, seen as a market for advertisers

influencer /ˈɪnfluənsə/ *noun* an expert in the decision-making unit who advises on technical aspects of the product or service under consideration

infomercial /ˌɪnfəʊˈmɜːʃ(ə)l/ *noun* a TV commercial that is longer than the normal 30 seconds, and contains information about the product or service being sold

inform /ɪnˈfɔːm/ *verb* to tell someone officially ○ *I regret to inform you that your tender was not acceptable.* ○ *We are pleased to inform you that you have been selected for interview.* ○ *We have been informed by the Department that new regulations are coming into force.*

informant /ɪnˈfɔːmənt/ *noun* a person who answers questions in a survey ○ *So far only two informants have said that they never buy the product.*

information /ˌɪnfəˈmeɪʃ(ə)n/ *noun* details which explain something ○ *to disclose a piece of information* ○ *to answer a request for information* ○ *Please send me information on* or *about holidays in the USA.* ○ *Have you any information on* or *about deposit accounts?* ○ *I enclose this leaflet for your information.* ○ *For further information, please write to Department 27.* □ **disclosure of confidential information** the act of telling someone information which should be secret

informational appeal /ɪnfə-ˌmeɪʃ(ə)n(ə)l əˈpiːl/ *noun* same as **rational appeal**

information and communications technologies /ɪnfəˌmeɪʃ(ə)n ən kəˌmjuːnɪˈkeɪʃ(ə)nz tekˌnɒlədʒiz/ *plural noun* computer and telecommunications technologies considered together and as a whole (NOTE: It is the coming together of information and communications technology that has possible made such things as the Internet, videoconferencing, groupware, intranets, and third-generation mobile phones.)

information management /ɪnfəˈmeɪʃ(ə)n ˌmænɪdʒmənt/ *noun* the task of controlling information and the flow of information within an organisation, that involves acquiring, recording, organising, storing, distributing, and retrieving it (NOTE: Good information management has been described as getting the right information to the right person in the right format at the right time.)

information officer /ɪnfəˈmeɪʃ(ə)n ˌɒfɪsə/ *noun* **1.** a person whose job is to give information about a company, an organisation or a government department to the public **2.** a person whose job is to give information to other departments in the same organisation

information processing model /ɪnfəˌmeɪʃ(ə)n ˈprəʊsesɪŋ ˌmɒd(ə)l/ *noun* a way of evaluating the effect of advertising by seeing the receiver of the message as someone who processes information and deals with problems

information retrieval /ɪnfə-ˌmeɪʃ(ə)n rɪˈtriːv(ə)l/ *noun* the finding of stored data in a computer

infotainment /æ(noun), ˌɪnfəʊ-ˈteɪnmənt/ *noun* entertainment that is informative, especially television programmes that deal with serious issues or current affairs in an entertaining way

ingredient /ɪnˈɡriːdiənt/ *noun* material or a substance which goes to make something

ingredient sponsored cooperative advertising /ɪnˌɡriːdiənt spɒnsəd kəʊˌɒp(ə)rətɪv ˈædvətaɪzɪŋ/ *noun* advertising sponsored by the producers of raw materials which aims to encourage the production of products that use these raw materials

inherent drama /ɪnˌhɪərənt ˈdrɑːmə/ *noun* advertising that emphasizes the benefits of purchasing a product or service and the vital interest which the user has in the product such as the speed of a car, the nutrition value of cereals, etc.

inherent vice /ɪnˌhɪərənt ˈvaɪs/ *noun* the tendency of some goods to spoil during transportation ○ *Inherent vice discouraged us from importing tropical fruit.*

in-home selling /ˌɪn həʊm ˈselɪŋ/, **in-home retailing** /ˌɪn həʊm ˈriːteɪlɪŋ/ *noun* selling to a customer in his or her home, either by direct contact or by telephone ○ *In-home selling is the national strategy for our products.* ○ *In-home selling is useful when housewives are the target market.*

in-house /ɪn ˈhaʊs/ *adverb, adjective* done by somebody employed by a company on their premises, not by an outside contractor ○ *the in-house staff* ○ *We do all our data processing in-house.*

in-house agency /ˌɪn haʊs ˈeɪdʒənsi/ *noun* an advertising agency which is owned and operated by an company and is responsible for the company's advertising programme

in-house newsletter /ˌɪn haʊs ˈnjuːzletə/ *noun* same as **newsletter**

initial /ɪˈnɪʃ(ə)l/ *adjective* first or starting ○ *The initial response to the TV advertising has been very good.*

'...the founding group has subscribed NKr 14.5m of the initial NKr 30m share capital' [*Financial Times*]

'...career prospects are excellent for someone with potential, and initial salary is negotiable around $45,000 per annum' [*Australian Financial Review*]

initial capital /ɪˌnɪʃ(ə)l ˈkæpɪt(ə)l/ *noun* capital which is used to start a business

initial sales /ɪˌnɪʃ(ə)l ˈseɪlz/ *plural noun* the first sales of a new product

ink-jet printing /ˈɪŋk dʒet ˌprɪntɪŋ/, **ink-jet imaging** /ˈɪŋk dʒet ˌɪmɪdʒɪŋ/

noun a printing process where text is reproduced by projecting dots of electronically charged ink onto the paper

inland port /ˌɪnlənd ˈpɔːt/ *noun* a port on a river or canal

innovate /ˈɪnəʊveɪt/ *verb* to bring in new ideas or new methods

innovation /ˌɪnəˈveɪʃ(ə)n/ *noun* the development of new products or new ways of selling

'…if innovation equates with daring, then 'who dares wins' will be a marketing commandment' [*Marketing Workshop*]

innovation-adoption model /ɪnə-ˌveɪʃ(ə)n əˈdɒpʃ(ə)n ˌmɒd(ə)l/ *noun* a model that shows the stages in the adoption process for a new product by a consumer, which are: awareness, interest, evaluation, trial, and adoption

innovative /ˈɪnəveɪtɪv/ *adjective* referring to a person or thing which is new and makes changes

'…small innovative companies in IT have been hampered for lack of funds' [*Sunday Times*]

innovator /ˈɪnəveɪtə/ *noun* **1.** a person or company that brings in new ideas and methods **2.** a person who buys a new product first **3.** in the VALS lifestyle classification, a successful person, often a leader in their profession, who buys a lot of new and expensive products

in-pack /ˈɪn pæk/ *noun* something placed inside the packaging with the product ○ *In-pack promotion may include information on other products in the same line.*

input tax /ˈɪnpʊt tæks/ *noun* VAT which is paid by a company on goods or services bought

inquiry /ɪŋˈkwaɪəri/ *noun* a request for information about a product

inquiry test /ɪŋˈkwaɪəri test/ *noun* a measuring of the effectiveness of advertising based on responses following the advertisement such as requests for information, phone calls, or the number of coupons redeemed

insert *noun* /ˈɪnsɜːt/ a form or leaflet which is put inside something, usually a magazine or newspaper □ **an insert in a magazine mailing** *or* **a magazine insert** an advertising sheet put into a mag-

azine when it is mailed ■ *verb* /ɪnˈsɜːt/ to put something in ○ *to insert a clause into a contract* ○ *to insert a publicity piece into a magazine mailing*

insertion /ɪnˈsɜːʃ(ə)n/ *noun* the act of putting an advertisement into a magazine or newspaper

insertion rate /ɪnˈsɜːʃ(ə)n reɪt/ *noun* the rate charged for a single insertion of an advertisement

inset /ˈɪnset/ *noun* same as **insert**

inside back cover /ˌɪnsaɪd bæk ˈkʌvə/ the page on the inside of the back cover used for advertising ○ *We have advertised on the inside back cover of every issue this year.* ○ *The survey is trying to establish how much notice readers take of the inside back cover.*

inside front cover /ˌɪnsaɪd ˌfrʌnt ˈkʌvə/ *noun* the page on the inside of the front cover of a magazine, used for advertisements

instability /ˌɪnstəˈbɪlɪti/ *noun* the state of being unstable or moving up and down □ **a period of instability in the money markets** a period when currencies fluctuate rapidly

install /ɪnˈstɔːl/ *verb* **1.** to put a machine into an office or into a factory ○ *We are planning to install the new machinery over the weekend.* ○ *They must install a new data processing system because the old one cannot cope with the mass of work involved.* **2.** to set up a new computer system so that it fits the user's requirements **3.** to configure a new computer program to the existing system requirements

installation /ˌɪnstəˈleɪʃ(ə)n/ *noun* **1.** machines, equipment and buildings ○ *Harbour installations were picketed by striking dockers.* ○ *The fire seriously damaged the oil installations.* **2.** putting new machines into an office or a factory ○ *to supervise the installation of new equipment* **3.** setting up a new computer system

installment /ɪnˈstɔːlmənt/ *noun* US spelling of **instalment**

installment plan /ɪnˈstɔːlmənt plæn/, **installment sales** /ɪnˈstɔːlmənt seɪlz/, **installment buying** /ɪnˈstɔːlmənt ˌbaɪɪŋ/ *noun US* a sys-

tem of buying something by paying a sum regularly each month ○ *to buy a car on the installment plan* (NOTE: the British equivalent is **hire purchase**)

instalment /ɪnˈstɔːlmənt/ *noun* a part of a payment which is paid regularly until the total amount is paid ○ *The first instalment is payable on signature of the agreement.* (NOTE: the American spelling is **installment**) □ **the final instalment is now due** the last of a series of payments should be paid now □ **to pay £25 down and monthly instalments of £20** to pay a first payment of £25 and the rest in payments of £20 each month □ **to miss an instalment** not to pay an instalment at the right time

instalment credit /ɪnˈstɔːlmənt ˌkredɪt/ *noun* an arrangement by which a purchaser pays for goods bought in instalments over a period of time

institution /ˌɪnstɪˈtjuːʃ(ə)n/ *noun* an organisation or society set up for a particular purpose

institutional /ˌɪnstɪˈtjuːʃ(ə)n(ə)l/ *adjective* referring to a financial institution

'…during the 1970s commercial property was regarded by big institutional investors as an alternative to equities' [*Investors Chronicle*]

institutional advertising /ˌɪnstɪtjuːʃ(ə)n(ə)l ˈædvətaɪzɪŋ/ *noun* advertising an organisation rather than a product

institutional investor /ˌɪnstɪtjuːʃ(ə)n(ə)l ɪnˈvestə/ *noun* a financial institution which invests money in securities

in-store /ˈɪn stɔː/ *adjective* inside a store

'…dissatisfied with traditional media advertising, manufacturers in the USA are shifting their money into in-store promotion. The reason why marketers in the US put more effort into in-store marketing is the greater penetration of EPOS' [*Marketing Week*]

in-store bakery /ˌɪn stɔː ˈbeɪkəri/ *noun* a bakery in a large supermarket, where bread is baked fresh for the customers

in-store demonstration /ˌɪn stɔː ˌdemənˈstreɪʃ(ə)n/ *noun* a demonstration of a product such as a piece of kitchen equipment inside a store

in-store media /ˌɪn stɔː ˈmiːdiə/ *noun* promotional material used inside a store, e.g. POS material, display banners, and advertisements on trolleys

in-store promotion /ˌɪn stɔː prəˈməʊʃ(ə)n/ *noun* a promotion of a product inside a shop, e.g. by demonstrations or special gift counters

instrument /ˈɪnstrʊmənt/ *noun* a legal document

instrumental conditioning /ˌɪnstrʊmənt(ə)l kənˈdɪʃ(ə)nɪŋ/ *noun* same as **operant conditioning**

insurance rates /ɪnˈʃʊərəns reɪts/ *plural noun* the amount of premium which has to be paid per £1000 of insurance

intangible assets /ɪnˌtændʒɪb(ə)l ˈæsets/ *plural noun* assets which have a value, but which cannot be seen, e.g. goodwill, or a patent or a trademark

integrate /ˈɪntɪgreɪt/ *verb* to link things together to form one whole group

integrated information response model /ˌɪntɪgreɪtɪd ɪnfəˈmeɪʃ(ə)n rɪˌspɒns ˌmɒd(ə)l/ *noun* a model showing the response process to an advertising message which suggests that advertising leads to a low acceptance rate of information, but that after trials of the product the acceptance rate increases and this in turn leads to brand loyalty

integrated marketing /ˌɪntɪgreɪtɪd ˈmɑːkɪtɪŋ/ *noun* co-ordination of all of a company's marketing activities in establishing marketing strategies such as packaging, media promotion, POS material or after-sales service ○ *The separation of departments makes integrated marketing difficult to achieve.*

integrated marketing communications concept /ˌɪntɪgreɪtɪd kəmjuːnɪˈkeɪʃ(ə)nz ˌkɒnsept/ *noun* US the concept or principle that a company should link all its promotions, either of its own image or of the products and services it sells, in a consistent way on several different levels

integrated marketing communications objectives /ˌɪntɪgreɪtɪd ˌmɑːkɪtɪŋ kəmjuːnɪˈkeɪʃ(ə)nz əbˌdʒektɪvz/ *plural noun* listing the ob-

jectives of an integrated marketing communications programme such as communication tasks, anticipated sales, and increased market share

integrated processes /ˌɪntɪɡreɪtɪd ˈprəʊsesɪz/ *plural noun* the processes by which knowledge of products, and beliefs about their excellence combine to help the purchaser evaluate alternative products

integration /ˌɪntɪˈɡreɪʃ(ə)n/ *noun* bringing several businesses together under a central control

intellectual property /ˌɪntɪˈlektjʊəl ˈprɒpəti/ *noun* ideas, designs and inventions, including copyrights, patents and trademarks, that were created by and legally belong to an individual or an organisation (NOTE: Intellectual property is protected by law in most countries, and the World Intellectual Property Organisation is responsible for harmonising the law in different countries and promoting the protection of intellectual property rights.)

intensive distribution /ɪnˌtensɪv ˌdɪstrɪˈbjuːʃ(ə)n/ *noun* the use by a producer of as wide a network of distributors as possible to sell products ○ *Without intensive distribution we cannot hope to achieve these ambitious sales targets.* ○ *Intensive distribution makes us rely on too many retailers and wholesalers.*

intention to buy /ɪnˌtenʃ(ə)n tə ˈbaɪ/ *noun* a statement by a respondent that he or she intends to buy a product or service, which may or may not be true

interactive /ˌɪntərˈæktɪv/ *adjective* allowing the customer and seller to influence the presentation of information or the development of strategies

interactive marketing /ˌɪntəræktɪv ˈmɑːkɪtɪŋ/ *noun* marketing strategies which are developed as a result of decisions taken by both salespeople and customers

interactive media /ˌɪntəræktɪv ˈmiːdiə/ *plural noun* media that allow the customer to interact with the source of the message, receiving information and replying to questions, etc.

interactive voice response /ˌɪntəræktɪv ˈvɔɪs rɪˌspɒns/ *noun* a telephone or Internet system which is activated by the voice of the caller and responds to the caller's queries. Abbr **IVR**

intercompany comparison /ˌɪntəkʌmpəni kəmˈpærɪs(ə)n/, **interfirm comparison** /ˌɪntəfɜːm kəmˈpærɪs(ə)n/ *noun* a comparison of different companies to see how much they spend on promotion, what their return on investment is, etc.

interconnect /ˌɪntəkəˈnekt/ *noun* two or more cable systems joined together for advertising purposes so as to give a wider geographical spread

interest /ˈɪntrəst/ *noun* **1.** special attention ○ *The buyers showed a lot of interest in our new product range.* **2.** payment made by a borrower for the use of money, calculated as a percentage of the capital borrowed ■ *verb* to attract someone's attention ○ *She tried to interest several companies in her new invention.* ○ *The company is trying to interest a wide range of customers in its products.*

'…since last summer American interest rates have dropped by between three and four percentage points' [*Sunday Times*]

'…a lot of money is said to be tied up in sterling because of the interest-rate differential between US and British rates' [*Australian Financial Review*]

interest charges /ˈɪntrəst ˌtʃɑːdʒɪz/ *plural noun* money paid as interest on a loan

intermedia comparison /ˌɪntəmiːdiə kəmˈpærɪs(ə)n/ *noun* a comparison of different media to decide how suitable they are for advertising ○ *We will carry out intermedia comparisons before deciding on our promotional strategy.* Compare **intramedia comparison**

intermediate goods /ɪntəˈmiːdiət ɡʊdz/ *plural noun* goods bought for use in the production of other goods

internal /ɪnˈtɜːn(ə)l/ *adjective* **1.** inside a company □ **we decided to make an internal appointment** we decided to appoint an existing member of staff to

the post, and not bring someone in from outside the company **2.** inside a country

internal analysis /ɪn,tɜːn(ə)l əˈnæləsɪs/ *noun* detailed examination and reports on the product or service offered and the company itself

internal communication /ɪn,tɜːn(ə)l kə,mjuːnɪˈkeɪʃ(ə)n/ *noun* communication between employees or departments of the same organisation (NOTE: Internal communication can take various forms such as team briefings, interviewing, employee or works councils, meetings, memos, an intranet, newsletters, suggestion schemes, the grapevine, and reports.)

internal desk research /ɪn,tɜːn(ə)l desk rɪ,sɜːtʃ/ *noun* research based on information in a company's own records such as customer accounts and sales reports

internal flight /ɪn,tɜːn(ə)l ˈflaɪt/ *noun* a flight to a town inside the same country

internalisation /ɪn,tɜːnəlaɪˈzeɪʃ(ə)n/, **internalization** *noun* a process by which individuals identify information which is relevant to them personally and so acquire values and norms which allow them to make decisions

internally /ɪnˈtɜːn(ə)li/ *adverb* inside a company ○ *The job was advertised internally.*

internal marketing /ɪn,tɜːn(ə)l ˈmɑːkɪtɪŋ/ *noun* marketing conducted inside a large organisation, where independent departments sell goods or services to each other

Internal Revenue Service /ɪn,tɜːn(ə)l ˈrevənjuː ,sɜːvɪs/ *noun US* a government department which deals with tax. Abbr **IRS**

internal search /ɪn,tɜːn(ə)l ˈsɜːtʃ/ *noun* the process by which a consumer acquires information from past experience or something he or she has remembered

internal telephone /ɪn,tɜːn(ə)l ˈtelɪfəʊn/ *noun* a telephone which is linked to other telephones in an office

internal trade /ɪn,tɜːn(ə)l ˈtreɪd/ *noun* trade between various parts of a country (NOTE: the opposite is **external trade**)

international /,ɪntəˈnæʃ(ə)nəl/ *adjective* working between countries

international marketing /,ɪntənæʃ(ə)nəl ˈmɑːkɪtɪŋ/ *noun* the marketing of a company's products abroad ○ *Our international marketing so far consists of exporting to three countries.* ○ *The next stage in the company's international marketing was the setting up of factories overseas.*

international media /,ɪntənæʃ(ə)nəl ˈmiːdiə/ *plural noun* advertising media that cover several countries and can be used to reach audiences in them

International Monetary Fund /,ɪntənæʃ(ə)nəl ˈmʌnɪt(ə)ri ,fʌnd/ a type of bank which is part of the United Nations and helps member states in financial difficulties, gives financial advice to members and encourages world trade. Abbr **IMF**

international monetary system /,ɪntənæʃ(ə)nəl ˈmʌnɪt(ə)ri ,sɪstəm/ *noun* methods of controlling and exchanging currencies between countries

international postal reply coupon /,ɪntənæʃ(ə)nəl ,pəʊst(ə)l rɪˈplaɪ kuː,pɒn/ *noun* a coupon which can be used in another country to pay the postage of replying to a letter ○ *Shee enclosed an international reply coupon with her letter.*

international trade /,ɪntənæʃ(ə)nəl ˈtreɪd/ *noun* trade between different countries

Internet /ˈɪntənet/ *noun* the global, public network of computers and telephone links that houses websites, allows email to be sent and is accessed with the aid of a modem (NOTE: The Internet uses the Internet Protocol (IP) as a communication standard.)

'…they predict a tenfold increase in sales via internet or TV between 1999 and 2004' [*Investors Chronicle*]

'…in two significant decisions, the Securities and Exchange Board of India today allowed trading of shares through the Internet and set a

deadline for companies to conform to norms for good corporate governance' [*The Hindu*]

Internet commerce /ˈɪntənet ˌkɒmɜːs/ *noun* the part of e-commerce that consists of commercial business transactions conducted over the Internet

Internet marketing /ˈɪntənet ˌmɑːkɪtɪŋ/ *noun* the marketing of products or services over the Internet

Internet merchant /ˈɪntənet ˌmɜːtʃənt/ *noun* a businessman or businesswoman who sells a product or service over the Internet

Internet payment system /ˌɪntənet ˈpeɪmənt ˌsɪstəm/ *noun* any mechanism that enables funds to be transferred from a customer to seller or from one business to another via the Internet

Internet security /ˌɪntənet sɪ-ˈkjʊərɪti/ *noun* the means used to protect websites and other electronic files against attacks by hackers and viruses

interpolation /ɪnˌtɜːpəˈleɪʃ(ə)n/ *noun* a method of estimating a value between two established values

interstate commerce /ˌɪntəsteɪt ˈkɒmɜːs/ *noun US* commerce between different states which is therefore subject to federal government control

interstitial /ˌɪntəˈstɪʃ(ə)l/ *noun* a page of advertising which is inserted into a website

interview /ˈɪntəvjuː/ *noun* talking to a person who is applying for a job to find out whether they are suitable for it ○ *We called six people for interview.* ○ *During my appraisal interview my boss and I agreed some targets for the next few months.* ○ *I have an interview next week or I am going for an interview next week.* ■ *verb* to talk to a person applying for a job to see if they are suitable ○ *We interviewed ten candidates, but found no one suitable.*

interviewee /ˌɪntəvjuːˈiː/ *noun* the person who is being interviewed ○ *The interviewer did everything to put the interviewee at ease.* ○ *The interviewees were all nervous as they waited to be called into the interview room.*

interviewer /ˈɪntəvjuːə/ *noun* the person who is conducting an interview

intramedia comparison /ˌɪntrəmiːdiə kəmˈpærɪs(ə)n/ *noun* a comparison of different advertising options within the same medium ○ *After extensive intramedia comparison we now know all the possibilities of TV advertising.* Compare **intermedia comparison**

intranet /ˈɪntrənet/ *noun* a network of computers and telephone links that uses Internet technology but is accessible only to the employees of a particular organisation (NOTE: An intranet that is extended beyond the employees of an organisation to include, for example, suppliers, customers or distributors, it is called an extranet.)

intransient /ɪnˈtrænziənt/ *adjective* referring to an advertisement which the target audience can keep and look at again, e.g. in a newspaper or magazine, as opposed to a transient advertisement on TV or radio

intrinsic value /ɪnˌtrɪnsɪk ˈvæljuː/ *noun* the material value of something ○ *These objects have sentimental value, but no intrinsic value at all.* ○ *The intrinsic value of jewellery makes it a good investment.*

introduce /ˌɪntrəˈdjuːs/ *verb* to make someone get to know somebody or something □ **to introduce a client** to bring in a new client and make them known to someone □ **to introduce a new product on the market** to produce a new product and launch it on the market

introductory offer /ˌɪntrədʌkt(ə)ri ˈɒfə/ *noun* a special price offered on a new product to attract customers

inventory /ˈɪnvənt(ə)ri/ *noun* 1. *(especially US)* all the stock or goods in a warehouse or shop ○ *to carry a high inventory* ○ *to aim to reduce inventory* 2. a list of the contents of a building such as a house for sale or an office for rent ○ *to draw up an inventory of fixtures and fittings* □ **to agree the inventory** to agree that the inventory is correct 3. advertising time or space which is not used and is available ■ *verb* to make a list of stock or contents

'...a warehouse needs to tie up less capital in inventory and with its huge volume spreads out costs over bigger sales' [*Duns Business Month*]

inventory control /'ɪnvənt(ə)ri kən,trəʊl/ *noun* a system of checking that there is not too much stock in a warehouse, but just enough to meet requirements

investment /ɪn'vestmənt/ *noun* the placing of money so that it will produce interest and increase in value ○ *They called for more government investment in new industries.* ○ *She was advised to make investments in oil companies.*

'...investment trusts, like unit trusts, consist of portfolios of shares and therefore provide a spread of investments' [*Investors Chronicle*]

'...investment companies took the view that prices had reached rock bottom and could only go up' [*Lloyd's List*]

investment advertising /ɪn-'vestmənt ,ædvətaɪzɪŋ/ *noun* large expenditure on advertising to achieve long-term objectives

investment spending /ɪn-'vestmənt ,spendɪŋ/ *noun* spending more than normal on advertising with the expectation of increased sales and profits

investor relations research /ɪn-,vestə rɪ'leɪʃ(ə)nz rɪ,sɜːtʃ/ *noun* research that allows a company to see how financial institutions such as merchant banks view the company

invisible assets /ɪn,vɪzɪb(ə)l 'æsets/ *plural noun* assets which have a value but which cannot be seen, e.g. goodwill or patents

invisibles /ɪn'vɪzɪb(ə)lz/ *plural noun* invisible imports and exports

invitation to tender /,ɪnvɪteɪʃ(ə)n tə 'tendə/ *noun* a formal request, sent to a small number of suppliers, asking them to submit a detailed proposal for completing a particular piece of work

invoice /'ɪnvɔɪs/ *noun* a note asking for payment for goods or services supplied ○ *your invoice dated November 10th* ○ *to make out an invoice for £250* ○ *to settle* or *to pay an invoice* ○ *They sent in their invoice six weeks late.* □ **the total is payable within thirty days of invoice** the total sum has to be paid within thirty days of the date on the in-

voice ■ *verb* to send an invoice to someone ○ *to invoice a customer* □ **we invoiced you on November 10th** we sent you the invoice on November 10th

invoice clerk /'ɪnvɔɪs klɑːk/ *noun* an office worker who deals with invoices

invoice price /'ɪnvɔɪs praɪs/ *noun* the price as given on an invoice, including any discount and VAT

invoicing /'ɪnvɔɪsɪŋ/ *noun* the sending of invoices ○ *All our invoicing is done by computer.* □ **invoicing in triplicate** the preparation of three copies of invoices

invoicing department /'ɪnvɔɪsɪŋ dɪ,pɑːtmənt/ *noun* the department in a company which deals with preparing and sending invoices

inward /'ɪnwəd/ *adjective* towards the home country

inward bill /'ɪnwəd bɪl/ *noun* a bill of lading for goods arriving in a country

inward mission /,ɪnwəd 'mɪʃ(ə)n/ *noun* a visit to your home country by a group of foreign businesspeople

IP address /aɪ 'piː ə,dres/ *noun* a unique 32-bit number that defines the precise location of a computer connected to a network or the Internet

irrevocable /ɪ'revəkəb(ə)l/ *adjective* which cannot be changed

irrevocable acceptance /ɪ-,revəkəb(ə)l ək'septəns/ *noun* acceptance which cannot be withdrawn

island display /'aɪlənd dɪs,pleɪ/ *noun* same as **island site**

island position /,aɪlənd pə'zɪʃ(ə)n/ *noun* advertising space separated from other advertising space in a newspaper or magazine ○ *An island position is expensive but will attract great attention.*

island site /'aɪlənd saɪt/, **island display** /'aɪlənd dɪs,pleɪ/ *noun* an exhibition stand separated from others ○ *There are only two island sites at the exhibition and we have one of them.* ○ *An island site means that visitors can approach the stand from several directions.*

issue /'ɪʃuː/ *noun* the number of a newspaper or magazine ○ *We have an ad in the January issue of the magazine.*

■ *verb* to put out or to give out ○ *to issue a letter of credit* ○ *to issue shares in a new company* ○ *to issue a writ against someone* ○ *The government issued a report on London's traffic.*

issue life /'ɪʃuː laɪf/ *noun* the time between one issue of a publication and another ○ *The reason the magazine's advertising rates are so expensive is because it has an issue life of three months.*

issuer /'ɪʃuə/ *noun* a financial institution that issues credit and debit cards and maintains the systems for billing and payment

ITC *abbr* Independent Television Commission

item /'aɪtəm/ *noun* **1.** something for sale □ **we are holding orders for out-of-stock items** we are holding orders for goods which are not in stock ○ *Please find enclosed an order for the following items from your catalogue.* **2.** a piece of information ○ *items on a balance sheet* □ **item of expenditure** goods or services which have been paid for and appear in the accounts **3.** a point on a list □ **we will now take item four on the agenda** we will now discuss the fourth point on the agenda

itemise /'aɪtəmaɪz/, **itemize** *verb* to make a detailed list of things ○ *Itemizing the sales figures will take about two days.*

itemised account /ˌaɪtəmaɪzd ə-'kaʊnt/ *noun* a detailed record of money paid or owed

itemised invoice /ˌaɪtəmaɪzd 'ɪnvɔɪs/ *noun* an invoice which lists each item separately

itinerary /aɪ'tɪnərəri/ *noun* a list of places to be visited on one journey ○ *a salesrep's itinerary*

IVR *abbr* interactive voice response

J K

jargon /'dʒɑːgən/ *noun* a special sort of language used by a trade or profession or particular group of people

job /dʒɒb/ *noun* **1.** a piece of work **2.** an order being worked on ○ *We are working on six jobs at the moment.* ○ *The shipyard has a big job starting in August.*

jobber /'dʒɒbə/ *noun US* a wholesaler

'…warehouse clubs buy directly from manufacturers, eliminating jobbers and wholesale middlemen' [*Duns Business Month*]

jobbing /'dʒɒbɪŋ/ *noun* the practice of doing small pieces of work

jobbing printer /'dʒɒbɪŋ ˌprɪntə/ *noun* a person who does small printing jobs

jobbing production /ˌdʒɒbɪŋ prə-'dʌkʃən/ *noun* the production of several different articles, each to individual requirements

job classification /'dʒɒb klæsɪfɪ-ˌkeɪʃ(ə)n/ *noun* describing jobs listed in various groups

job description /'dʒɒb dɪˌskrɪpʃən/ *noun* a description of what a job consists of and what skills are needed for it ○ *The letter enclosed an application form and a job description.*

job lot /dʒɒb 'lɒt/ *noun* a group of miscellaneous items sold together ○ *They sold the household furniture as a job lot.*

job opening /'dʒɒb ˌəʊp(ə)nɪŋ/ *noun* jobs which are empty and need filling ○ *We have job openings for office staff.*

job satisfaction /'dʒɒb sætɪs-ˌfækʃən/ *noun* an employee's feeling that he or she is happy at work and pleased with the work he or she does

job specification /'dʒɒb spesɪfɪ-'keɪʃ(ə)n/ *noun* a very detailed description of what is involved in a job

joined-up /'dʒɔɪnd ʌp/ *adjective* involving two or more individuals or organisations who share information and co-ordinate their activities in order to achieve their aims more effectively

joint account /dʒɔɪnt ə'kaʊnt/ *noun* a bank or building society account shared by two people ○ *Many married couples have joint accounts so that they can pay for household expenses.*

Joint Photographics Experts Group *noun* full form of **JPEG**

journal /'dʒɜːn(ə)l/ *noun* **1.** a book with the account of sales and purchases made each day **2.** a magazine

journalist /'dʒɜːn(ə)lɪst/ *noun* a person who writes for a newspaper

journey /'dʒɜːni/ *noun* a long trip, especially a trip made by a salesperson ○ *She planned her journey so that she could visit all her accounts in two days.*

journey mapping /'dʒɜːni ˌmæpɪŋ/ *noun* a method of calculating how many people pass a poster site ○ *Journey mapping allows us to pinpoint the ten key sites we will be renting for the next three months.*

journey order /'dʒɜːni ˌɔːdə/ *noun* an order given by a shopkeeper to a salesperson when they call

journey planning /'dʒɜːni ˌplænɪŋ/ *noun* the act of planning what calls a salesperson will make and how they will be reached most efficiently, giving priority to the more profitable accounts ○ *The sales manager will stress how good journey planning will save precious time.* ○ *Inefficient journey planning*

means miles of unnecessary travelling for the sales force every day.

JPEG /'dʒeɪ peg/ *noun* a file format used to compress and store photographic images for transfer over the Internet

judgement /'dʒʌdʒmənt/, **judgment** *noun* an assessment or evaluation of the quality of someone or something

judgement forecasting /'dʒʌdʒmənt ˌfɔːkɑːstɪŋ/ *noun* forecasting based on judgement rather than on any scientific techniques ○ *We need more precise information so that we can extrapolate rather than use judgement forecasting.* ○ *Market research departments find judgement forecasting too subjective and unreliable.*

judgement sampling /'dʒʌdʒmənt ˌsɑːmplɪŋ/ *noun* the choosing of a sample for a survey based on judgement of what criteria would be especially significant rather than applying any scientific techniques ○ *Judgement sampling can produce an insufficiently representative sample.*

jumbo /'dʒʌmbəʊ/ *adjective* very large ○ *jumbo-sized pack* or *jumbo pack*

junk mail /'dʒʌŋk meɪl/ *noun* unsolicited advertising material sent through the post and usually thrown away immediately by the people who receive it

jury of executive opinion /ˌdʒʊəri əv ɪgˌzekjʊtɪv ə'pɪnjən/ *noun* a panel of executives used to contribute to forecasting

just-in-time /'dʒʌstɪn'taɪm/ *noun* abbr **JIT**

just-in-time production /ˌdʒʌst ɪn ˌtaɪm prə'dʌkʃən/ *noun* making goods to order just before they are needed, so as to avoid having too many goods in stock. Abbr **JIT**

just-in-time purchasing /ˌdʒʌst ɪn ˌtaɪm 'pɜːtʃɪsɪŋ/ *noun* a purchasing system where goods are purchased immediately before they are needed, so as to avoid carrying high levels of stock. Abbr **JIT**

KAM *abbr* key account management

keen /kiːn/ *adjective* **1.** eager or active □ **keen competition** strong competition

○ *We are facing some keen competition from European manufacturers.* □ **keen demand** wide demand ○ *There is a keen demand for home computers.* **2.** □ **keen prices** prices which are kept low so as to be competitive ○ *Our prices are the keenest on the market.*

kerbside conference /ˌkɜːbsaɪd 'kɒnf(ə)rəns/ *noun* a discussion of selling techniques between a trainee salesperson and the person training them after making a sales call ○ *In the kerbside conference, the sales trainer described a number of different approaches that might have been made to a particular customer.*

key /kiː/ *adjective* important ○ *a key factor* ○ *key industries* ○ *key personnel* ○ *a key member of our management team* ○ *She has a key post in the organisation.* ○ *We don't want to lose any key staff in the reorganisation.*

'…he gave up the finance job in September to devote more time to his global responsibilities as chairman and to work more closely with key clients' [*Times*]

key account /'kiː əˌkaʊnt/ *noun* an important account or client, e.g. of an advertising agency

key account management /'kiː əˌkaʊnt ˌmænɪdʒmənt/ *noun* the management of the small number of key accounts which represent the bulk of a company's business. Abbr **KAM**

keyboard /'kiːbɔːrd/ *noun* the part of a computer or other device with keys which are pressed to make letters or figures ■ *verb* to press the keys on a keyboard to type something ○ *She is keyboarding our address list.*

keyboarder /'kiːbɔːdə/ *noun* a person who types information into a computer

keyboarding /'kiːbɔːdɪŋ/ *noun* the act of typing on a keyboard ○ *Keyboarding costs have risen sharply.*

key code /'kiː kəʊd/ *noun* a letter and number code printed on mailshots so that the respondents can be identified

keyed advertisement /ˌkiːd əd'vɜːtɪsmənt/ *noun* an advertisement which asks people to write to a specially coded address which will indicate where

they saw it, thus helping the advertisers to evaluate the effectiveness of advertising in that particular newspaper or magazine

key number /'ki: ˌnʌmbə/ *noun* the number used in a keyed advertisement

keypad /'ki:pæd/ *noun* a set of keys on a computer

key prospects /ki: 'prɒspekts/ *plural noun* potential customers ○ *In this sales campaign we will be concentrating on key prospects.* ○ *This is bad journey planning since it does not allow sufficient time to visit all the key prospects.*

keyword /'ki:wɜːd/ *noun* a word used by a search engine to help it locate a particular type of website (NOTE: Companies need to think very carefully about the keywords they place in their webpages in order to attract relevant search-engine traffic.)

keyword search /'ki:wɜːd sɜːtʃ/ *noun* a search for documents containing one or more words that are specified by a search-engine user

kickback /'kɪkbæk/ *noun* an illegal commission paid to someone, especially a government official, who helps in a business deal

Kimball tag /'kɪmb(ə)l tæg/ *noun* a paper tag attached to an item for sale, which is removed when the item has been sold and kept by the store so that it can be used for stock control

king-size /'kɪŋ saɪz/ *adjective* **1.** referring to an extra large container of a product, usually comparatively economical to buy **2.** referring to a very large size of poster

kiosk /'ki:ɒsk/ *noun* a small wooden shelter, for selling goods out of doors ○

She had a newspaper kiosk near the station for 20 years.

KISS /kɪs/ *noun* the need to make sure your advertising is clear and concise so as to improve its chances of getting a response. Full form **keep it simple, stupid**

Kitemark /'kaɪt mɑːk/ *trademark GB* a mark on goods to show that they meet official standards

knock /nɒk/ *verb* □ **to knock the competition** to hit competing firms hard by vigorous selling

knock down /ˌnɒk 'daʊn/ *verb* □ **to knock something down to a bidder** to sell something to somebody at an auction ○ *The furniture was knocked down to him for £100.*

knockdown /'nɒkdaʊn/ *noun* □ **knockdown (KD) goods** goods sold in parts, which must be assembled by the buyer

knocking copy /'nɒkɪŋ ˌkɒpi/ *noun* advertising material which criticises competing products

knock off /ˌnɒk 'ɒf/ *verb* to reduce a price by a particular amount ○ *She knocked £10 off the price for cash.*

know-how /'nəʊ haʊ/ *noun* knowledge or skill in a particular field ○ *to acquire computer know-how*

knowledge capital /'nɒlɪdʒ ˌkæpɪt(ə)l/ *noun* knowledge, especially specialist knowledge, that a company and its employees possess and that can be put to profitable use

knowledge management /'nɒlɪdʒ ˌmænɪdʒmənt/ *noun* **1.** the task of co-ordinating the specialist knowledge possessed by employees so that it can be exploited to create benefits and competitive advantage for the organisation **2.** same as **information management**

L

label /ˈleɪb(ə)l/ *noun* a piece of paper or card attached to something to show its price or an address or instructions for use ■ *verb* to attach a label to something

labelling /ˈleɪb(ə)lɪŋ/ *noun* the act of putting a label on something (NOTE: **labelling- labelled**. The American spelling is **labeling- labeled**.)

labelling department /ˈleɪb(ə)lɪŋ dɪˌpɑːtmənt/ *noun* a section of a factory where labels are attached to the product

laboratory test /ləˈbɒrət(ə)ri test/ *noun* a test carried out under controlled conditions, e.g. of the reactions of consumers to advertising

labour-intensive industry /ˌleɪbər ɪnˌtensɪv ˈɪndəstri/ *noun* an industry which needs large numbers of workers, where labour costs are high in relation to turnover

labour market /ˈleɪbə ˌmɑːkɪt/ *noun* the number of wokers who are available for work ○ *25,000 school-leavers have just come on to the labour market.*

lading /ˈleɪdɪŋ/ *noun* the putting of goods on a ship

laggards /ˈlægədz/ *plural noun* a category of buyers of a product who are the last to buy it or use it

laissez-faire economy /ˌleseɪ ˈfeər ɪˌkɒnəmi/ *noun* an economy where the government does not interfere because it believes it is right to let the economy run itself

land /lænd/ *verb* to put goods or passengers onto land after a voyage by sea or by air ○ *The ship landed some goods at Mombasa.* ○ *The plane stopped for thirty minutes at the local airport to land passengers and mail.*

landed costs /ˌlændɪd ˈkɒsts/ *plural noun* the costs of goods which have been delivered to a port, unloaded and passed through customs

landing card /ˈlændɪŋ kɑːd/ *noun* a card given to passengers who have passed through customs and can land from a ship or an aircraft

landing charges /ˈlændɪŋ ˌtʃɑːdʒɪz/ *plural noun* payment for putting goods on land and paying customs duties

landing order /ˈlændɪŋ ˌɔːdə/ *noun* a permit which allows goods to be unloaded into a bonded warehouse without paying customs duty

landing page /ˈlændɪŋ peɪdʒ/ *noun* the page on a website where the user arrives, in particular the page you arrive on when directed by a hyperlink

landscape /ˈlændskeɪp/ *noun* an illustration page or book whose width is greater than its height. Compare **portrait**

laser printer /ˈleɪzə ˌprɪntə/ *noun* computer printer which uses a laser source to print high-quality dot matrix characters on paper

laser printing /ˈleɪzə ˌprɪntɪŋ/ *noun* printing using a laser printer

late /leɪt/ *adjective* **1.** after the time stated or agreed ○ *We apologise for the late arrival of the plane from Amsterdam.* □ **there is a penalty for late delivery** if delivery is later than the agreed date, the supplier has to pay a fine **2.** at the end of a period of time □ **latest date for signature of the contract** the last acceptable date for signing the contract ■ *adverb* after the time stated or agreed ○ *The shipment was landed late.* ○ *The plane was two hours late.*

late majority /ˌleɪt məˈdʒɒrɪti/ *noun* a category of buyers of a product who buy it later than the early majority but before the laggards

latent /ˈleɪt(ə)nt/ *adjective* present but not yet developed □ **latent market** a potential market which has not so far been touched

latent demand /ˌleɪt(ə)nt dɪˈmɑːnd/ *noun* a situation where there is demand for a product but potential customers are unable to pay for it ○ *We will have to wait for the economy to improve in countries where there is latent demand.* ○ *Situation analysis has shown that there is only latent demand.*

lateral /ˈlæt(ə)rəl/ *adjective* at the same level or with the same status ○ *Her transfer to Marketing was something of a lateral move.*

lateral diversification /ˌlæt(ə)rəl daɪˌvɜːsɪfɪˈkeɪʃ(ə)n/ *noun* the act of diversifying into quite a different type of business

lateral integration /ˌlæt(ə)rəl ɪntəˈɡreɪʃ(ə)n/ *noun* the act of joining similar companies or taking over a company in the same line of business as yourself ○ *Lateral integration will allow a pooling of resources.* ○ *Lateral integration in the form of a merger will improve the efficiency of both businesses involved.*

lateral thinking /ˌlæt(ə)rəl ˈθɪŋkɪŋ/ *noun* an imaginative approach to problem-solving which involves changing established patterns of thinking to help make a breakthrough ○ *Lateral thinking resulted in finding a completely new use for an existing product.* ○ *Brainstorming sessions encourage lateral thinking and originality.*

latest /ˈleɪtɪst/ *adjective* most recent ○ *He always drives the latest model of car.* ○ *Here are the latest sales figures.*

launch /lɔːntʃ/ *verb* to put a new product on the market, usually spending money on advertising it ○ *They launched their new car model at the motor show.* ○ *The company is spending thousands of pounds on launching a new brand of soap.* ■ *noun* the act of putting a new product on the market ○ *The launch of the new model has been*

put back three months. ○ *The management has decided on a September launch date.* ○ *The company is geared up for the launch of its first microcomputer.*

launching /ˈlɔːntʃɪŋ/ *noun* the act of putting a new product on the market

launching costs /ˈlɔːntʃɪŋ kɒsts/ *plural noun* the costs of publicity for a new product

launching date /ˈlɔːntʃɪŋ deɪt/ *noun* the date when a new product is officially shown to the public for the first time

launching party /ˈlɔːntʃɪŋ ˌpɑːti/ *noun* a party held to advertise the launching of a new product

law /lɔː/ *noun* a general rule

law of diminishing returns /ˌlɔːr əv dɪˌmɪnɪʃɪŋ rɪˈtɜːnz/ *noun* a general rule that as more factors of production such as land, labour and capital are added to the existing factors, so the amount they produce is proportionately smaller

law of inertia of large numbers /ˌlɔːr əv ɪˌnɜːʃər əv ˌlɑːdʒ ˈnʌmbəz/ *noun* a general rule that larger samples are more likely to be representative of the population than small ones

law of statistical regularity /ˌlɔːr əv stəˌtɪstɪk(ə)l reɡjʊˈlærɪti/ *noun* a general rule that a group of people or objects taken from a larger group of people or objects will tend to resemble the larger group

law of supply and demand /ˌlɔːr əv səˌplaɪ ən dɪˈmɑːnd/ *noun* a general rule that the amount of a product which is available is related to the needs of potential customers

layout /ˈleɪaʊt/ *noun* **1.** the arrangement of the inside space of a building or its contents ○ *They have altered the layout of the offices.* **2.** the arrangement of words and pictures on a printed page, in an advertisement, on an email advertising message, etc., including the headline, illustrations, text, and trademarks ○ *I like the illustration and the copy but not the layout.* ○ *The layout needs to be changed so that other features are highlighted.*

lead /liːd/ *verb* to be the main person in a group ○ *She will lead the trade mission to Nigeria.* ○ *The tour of American factories will be led by the minister.* (NOTE: **leading – led**) ◼ *noun* **1.** information which may lead to a sale ○ *It has been difficult starting selling in this territory with no leads to follow up.* ○ *I was given some useful leads by the sales rep who used to cover this territory.* **2.** a prospective purchaser who is the main decision-maker when buying a product or service

leader /ˈliːdə/ *noun* **1.** a person who manages or directs others ○ *the leader of the construction workers' union* or *the construction workers' leader* ○ *She is the leader of the trade mission to Nigeria.* ○ *The minister was the leader of the party of industrialists on a tour of American factories.* ○ *The leader of the trade delegation was invited to meet the President.* **2.** a product which sells best

'...market leaders may benefit from scale economies or other cost advantages; they may enjoy a reputation for quality simply by being at the top, or they may actually produce a superior product that gives them both a large market share and high profits' [*Accountancy*]

leader pricing /ˈliːdə ˌpraɪsɪŋ/ *noun* the practice of cutting prices on some goods in the hope that they attract customers to the shop where more profitable sales can be made

lead generation /ˈliːd dʒenəˌreɪʃ(ə)n/ *noun* the process of finding prospective purchasers

leading question /ˌliːdɪŋ ˈkweʃtʃən/ *noun* a question in a questionnaire which, by its phrasing, suggests a certain answer ○ *Interviewers were trained to avoid bias and leading questions.* ○ *The leading question pressurized the respondent into answering untruthfully.*

lead partner /ˈliːd ˌpɑːtnə/ *noun* the organisation that takes the leading role in an alliance

lead sourcing /ˈliːd ˌsɔːsɪŋ/ *noun* searching through online databases to find the addresses of potential customers

leaflet /ˈliːflət/ *noun* a sheet of paper giving information, used to advertise something ○ *to mail leaflets advertising a new hairdressing salon* ○ *They are handing out leaflets describing the financial services they offer.* ○ *We made a leaflet mailing to 20,000 addresses.*

leakage /ˈliːkɪdʒ/ *noun* an amount of goods lost in storage, e.g. by going bad or by being stolen or by leaking from the container

learning curve /ˈlɜːnɪŋ kɜːv/ *noun* a gradual process of learning, as shown on an imaginary scale

learning organisation /ˈlɜːnɪŋ ɔːɡənaɪˌzeɪʃ(ə)n/ *noun* an organisation whose employees are willing and eager to share information with each other, to learn from each other, and to work as a team to achieve their goals

lease /liːs/ *noun* a written contract for letting or renting a building, a piece of land or a piece of equipment for a period against payment of a fee ○ *to rent office space on a twenty-year lease* □ **the lease expires next year** *or* **the lease runs out next year** the lease comes to an end next year

leave leaflet /ˈliːv ˌliːflət/ *noun* a promotional leaflet left by a salesperson with a prospective customer

ledger /ˈledʒə/ *noun* a book in which accounts are written

legal /ˈliːɡ(ə)l/ *adjective* **1.** according to the law or allowed by the law ○ *The company's action was completely legal.* **2.** referring to the law □ **to take legal action** to sue someone or to take someone to court □ **to take legal advice** to ask a lawyer to advise about a legal problem

legal adviser /ˌliːɡ(ə)l ədˈvaɪzə/ *noun* a person who advises clients about the law

legal currency /ˌliːɡ(ə)l ˈkʌrənsi/ *noun* money which is legally used in a country

legalisation /ˌliːɡəlaɪˈzeɪʃ(ə)n/, **legalization** *noun* the act of making something legal ○ *the campaign for the legalisation of cannabis*

legalise /ˈliːɡəlaɪz/, **legalize** *verb* to make something legal

legality /lɪ'gælətɪ/ *noun* the fact of being allowed by law ○ *There is doubt about the legality of the company's action in dismissing him.*

legally /'liːgəli/ *adverb* according to the law □ **the contract is legally binding** according to the law, the contract has to be obeyed □ **the directors are legally responsible** the law says that the directors are responsible

legend /'ledʒənd/ *noun* a short note printed underneath an illustration to explain it

legislation /ˌledʒɪ'sleɪʃ(ə)n/ *noun* laws

legs /legz/ *plural noun* the ability of an advertising campaign, a film, a book, or other usually short-lived product to interest people for a much longer time than normal (*informal*)

leisure market /'leʒə ˌmɑːkɪt/ *noun* people who have plenty of leisure time and are willing to buy products or services to occupy their time

lemon /'lemən/ *noun* **1.** a product, especially a car, that is defective in some way **2.** an investment that is performing poorly

lending limit /'lendɪŋ ˌlɪmɪt/ *noun* a restriction on the amount of money a bank can lend

letter /'letə/ *noun* a piece of writing sent from one person or company to another to ask for or to give information

letterhead /'letəhed/ *noun* the name and address of a company printed at the top of a piece of notepaper

letter of acknowledgement /ˌletər əv ək'nɒlɪdʒmənt/ *noun* a letter which says that something has been received

letter of advice /ˌletər əv əd'vaɪs/ *noun* a letter to a customer giving details of goods ordered and shipped but not yet delivered ○ *The letter of advice stated that the goods would be at Southampton on the morning of the 6th.* ○ *The letter of advice reminded the customer of the agreed payment terms.*

letter of agreement /ˌletər əv ə'griːmənt/ *noun* a document that sets out what has been agreed between two people or organisations and acts as a simple form of contract

letter of complaint /ˌletər əv kəm'pleɪnt/ *noun* a letter in which someone complains

letter of credit /ˌletər əv 'kredɪt/ *noun* a document issued by a bank on behalf of a customer authorising payment to a supplier when the conditions specified in the document are met (this is a common method of guaranteeing payment by overseas customers). Abbr **L/C**

letter of indemnity /ˌletər əv ɪn'demnɪti/ *noun* a letter promising payment as compensation for a loss

letter of inquiry /ˌletər əv ɪn'kwaɪəri/ *noun* a letter from a prospective buyer to a supplier inquiring about products and their prices ○ *The letter of inquiry requested us to send our catalogues and price lists.* ○ *We received a letter of inquiry concerning possible trade discounts.*

lettershop /'letəʃɒp/ *noun* a company that puts together the various elements of a direct mailing shot, and sorts the envelopes by addresses

letters of administration /ˌletəz əv ədmɪnɪ'streɪʃ(ə)n/ *plural noun* a letter given by a court to allow someone to deal with the estate of a person who has died

letters patent /ˌletəz 'peɪt(ə)nt/ *plural noun* the official term for a patent

level /'lev(ə)l/ *noun* the position of something compared to others ○ *low levels of productivity* or *low productivity levels* ○ *to raise the level of employee benefits* ○ *to lower the level of borrowings*

'…figures from the Fed on industrial production for April show a decline to levels last seen in June 1984' [*Sunday Times*]

'…applications for mortgages are running at a high level' [*Times*]

'…employers having got their staff back up to a reasonable level are waiting until the scope for overtime working is exhausted before hiring' [*Sydney Morning Herald*]

level playing field /ˌlev(ə)l 'pleɪɪŋ fiːld/ *noun* a situation in which the same rules apply for all competitors and none

of them has any special advantage over the others

levy /ˈlevi/ *noun* money which is demanded and collected by the government □ **levies on luxury items** taxes on luxury items

liabilities /ˌlaɪəˈbɪlɪtiz/ *plural noun* the debts of a business, including dividends owed to shareholders ○ *The balance sheet shows the company's assets and liabilities.* □ **he was not able to meet his liabilities** he could not pay his debts □ **to discharge your liabilities in full** to pay everything which you owe

liability /ˌlaɪəˈbɪlɪti/ *noun* a legal responsibility for damage or loss, etc. ○ *The brand name has become a liability to the company.* □ **to accept liability for something** to agree that you are responsible for something □ **to refuse liability for something** to refuse to agree that you are responsible for something

liable /ˈlaɪəb(ə)l/ *adjective* □ **liable for** legally responsible for ○ *The customer is liable for breakages.* ○ *The chairman was personally liable for the company's debts.*

licence /ˈlaɪs(ə)ns/ *noun* **1.** an official document which allows someone to do something (NOTE: the American spelling is **license**) **2.** □ **goods manufactured under licence** goods made with the permission of the owner of the copyright or patent

licence agreement /ˈlaɪs(ə)ns əˌgriːmənt/ *noun* a legal document which comes with a software product and defines how you can use the software and how many people are allowed to use it

license /ˈlaɪs(ə)ns/ *noun* US spelling of **licence** ■ *verb* to give someone official permission to do something for a fee, as when a company allows another company to manufacture its products abroad ○ *licensed to sell beers, wines and spirits* ○ *to license a company to manufacture spare parts* ○ *She is licensed to run an employment agency.*

licensee /ˌlaɪs(ə)nˈsiː/ *noun* a person who has a licence, especially a licence to sell alcohol or to manufacture something

licensing /ˈlaɪs(ə)nsɪŋ/ *adjective* referring to licences ○ *a licensing agreement* ○ *licensing laws*

licensing agreement /ˈlaɪs(ə)nsɪŋ əˌgriːmənt/ *noun* an agreement where a person or company is granted a licence to manufacture something or to use something, but not an outright sale

licensing hours /ˈlaɪs(ə)nsɪŋ ˌaʊəz/ *plural noun* the hours of the day when alcohol can be sold

licensing laws /ˈlaɪs(ə)nsɪŋ ˌlɔːz/ *plural noun* the laws which control when and where alcohol can be sold

licensor /ˈlaɪsensə/ *noun* a person who licenses someone

lien /liːn/ *noun* the legal right to hold someone's goods and keep them until a debt has been paid

life /laɪf/ *noun* the period of time for which something or someone exists

life cycle /ˈlaɪf ˌsaɪk(ə)l/ *noun* a concept used for charting the different stages in the life of people, animals or products

life expectancy /laɪf ɪkˈspektənsi/ *noun* the number of years a person is likely to live

lifestyle /ˈlaɪf staɪl/ *noun* a way of living of a particular section of society ○ *These upmarket products appeal to people with an extravagant lifestyle.* ○ *The magazine ran a series of articles on the lifestyles of some successful businessmen.*

lifestyle segmentation /ˈlaɪf staɪl segmenˌteɪʃ(ə)n/ *noun* the dividing of a market into segments according to the way in which customers live. ♦ **VALS**

lifetime /ˈlaɪftaɪm/ *noun* the time when you are alive

lifetime customer value /ˌlaɪftaɪm ˈkʌstəmə ˌvæljuː/, **lifetime value** /ˈlaɪftaɪm ˌvæljuː/ *noun* the value of a customer to a firm during the customer's lifetime, which can be charted using technology and market research

light /laɪt/ *adjective* not heavy

light industry /ˌlaɪt ˈɪndəstri/ *noun* an industry making small products such as clothes, books, or calculators

light pen /'laɪt pen/ *noun* a type of electronic pen which directs a beam of light which, when passed over a bar code, can read it and send information back to a computer

light viewer /laɪt 'vjuːə/ *noun* a person who watches little television ○ *If too many of the target audience are light viewers, the impact of the commercials will be wasted.*

limit /'lɪmɪt/ *noun* the point at which something ends or the point where you can go no further □ **to set limits to imports** *or* **to impose import limits** to allow only a specific amount of imports ■ *verb* to stop something from going beyond a specific point □ **the banks have limited their credit** the banks have allowed their customers only a specific amount of credit □ **each agent is limited to twenty-five units** each agent is allowed only twenty-five units to sell

'…the biggest surprise of 1999 was the rebound in the price of oil. In the early months of the year commentators were talking about a fall to $5 a barrel but for the first time in two decades, the oil exporting countries got their act together, limited production and succeeded in pushing prices up' [*Financial Times*]

limitation /ˌlɪmɪ'teɪʃ(ə)n/ *noun* the act of allowing only a specific quantity of something ○ *The contract imposes limitations on the number of cars which can be imported.* □ **limitation of liability** the fact of making someone liable for only a part of the damage or loss

limited /'lɪmɪtɪd/ *adjective* restricted

limited company /ˌlɪmɪtɪd 'kʌmp(ə)ni/, **limited liability company** /ˌlɪmɪtɪd laɪə'bɪlɪti ˌkʌmp(ə)ni/ *noun* a company where each shareholder is responsible for repaying the company's debts only to the face value of the shares they own (NOTE: shortened to **Ltd**)

limited function wholesaler /ˌlɪmɪtɪd 'fʌŋkʃən ˌhəʊlseɪlə/ *noun* a distributor performing only some of the functions of a wholesaler ○ *As a limited function wholesaler the dealer did not provide a delivery service to retailers.*

limited liability /ˌlɪmɪtɪd laɪə'bɪlɪti/ *noun* a situation where someone's liability for debt is limited by law

limited market /ˌlɪmɪtɪd 'mɑːkɪt/ *noun* a market which can take only a specific quantity of goods

limiting /'lɪmɪtɪŋ/ *adjective* which limits ○ *a limiting clause in a contract* ○ *The short holiday season is a limiting factor on the hotel trade.*

line /laɪn/ *noun* **1.** a long mark printed or written on paper ○ *paper with thin blue lines* ○ *I prefer notepaper without any lines.* ○ *She drew a thick line before the column of figures.* **2.** same as **product line 3.** a row of letters or figures on a page □ **to open a line of credit** *or* a **credit line** to make credit available to someone

'…cash paid for overstocked lines, factory seconds, slow sellers, etc.' [*Australian Financial Review*]

lineage /'laɪnɪdʒ/ *noun* a method of measuring a classified advertisement by counting the lines, used for charging purposes

linear /'lɪniə/ *adjective* calculated by length

linear measurement /ˌlɪniə 'meʒəmənt/, **linear footage** /ˌlɪniə 'fʊtɪdʒ/ *noun* a measurement of how long something is such as the length of shelving available for a display

line block /'laɪn blɒk/ *noun* a printing block for line drawings

line chart /'laɪn tʃɑːt/ *noun* a chart or graph using lines to indicate values

line divestment /'laɪn daɪˌvestmənt/ *noun* the dropping or selling of an entire product line so as to concentrate on other products

line drawing /'laɪn ˌdrɔːɪŋ/, **line illustration** /'laɪn ɪləˌstreɪʃ(ə)n/ *noun* a drawing or illustration consisting only of lines and no tones. Shades are shown by lines drawn close together.

line extension /'laɪn ɪkˌstenʃən/ *noun* the adding of another product to a product line

line filling /'laɪn ˌfɪlɪŋ/ *noun* the filling of gaps in a product line

line management /'laɪn ˌmænɪdʒmənt/, **line organization** /'laɪn ɔːɡənaɪˌzeɪʃ(ə)n/ *noun* the organisation of a business where each

manager is responsible for doing what his superior tells him to do

line rate /ˈlaɪn reɪt/ *noun* the rate charged for advertising space, based on the line space used in a newspaper or magazine

line simplification /ˈlaɪn ˌsɪmplɪfɪ-ˌkeɪʃ(ə)n/ *noun* the removal of some products from a product line to make the whole line more easily manageable

link /lɪŋk/ *noun* graphics or an image which moves the user to another page or online location when the user clicks on it. ♦ **hyperlink**

liquid assets /ˌlɪkwɪd ˈæsets/ *plural noun* cash, or investments which can be quickly converted into cash

liquor licence /ˈlɪkə ˌlaɪs(ə)ns/ *noun* a government document allowing someone to sell alcohol

list /lɪst/ *noun* **1.** several items written one after the other ○ *They have an attractive list of products* or *product list.* ○ *I can't find that item on our stock list.* ○ *Please add this item to the list.* ○ *She crossed the item off her list.* **2.** a catalogue ■ *verb* to write a series of items one after the other ○ *to list products by category* ○ *to list representatives by area* ○ *to list products in a catalogue* ○ *The catalogue lists ten models of fax machine.*

list broker /ˈlɪst ˌbrəʊkə/ *noun* a person who arranges to sell mailing lists to users, but who does not own the lists

list building /ˈlɪst ˌbɪldɪŋ/ *noun* finding names and addresses and entering them into a database for direct marketing purposes

list cleaning /ˈlɪst ˌkliːnɪŋ/ *noun* checking the details of a mailing list to make sure they are correct

listen /ˈlɪs(ə)n/ *verb* to pay attention to someone who is talking or to something which you can hear

listening area /ˈlɪs(ə)nɪŋ ˌeəriə/ *noun* the area covered by a radio station's signal

listening share /ˈlɪs(ə)nɪŋ ʃeə/ *noun* the share of the total audience enjoyed by a radio station

list host /ˈlɪst həʊst/ *noun* a company that provides connections to the Internet and storage space on its computers which can store the files for a user's website (NOTE: also called a 'host service *or* hosting service provider')

list maintenance /ˈlɪst ˌmeɪntənəns/ *noun* the process of keeping a mailing list up to date

list manager /ˈlɪst ˌmænɪdʒə/ *noun* a person who promotes a mailing list to potential users

list price /ˈlɪst praɪs/ *noun* the price for something as given in a catalogue

list rental /ˈlɪst ˌrent(ə)l/ *noun* the action of renting a mailing list

list renting /ˈlɪst ˌrentɪŋ/ *noun* an arrangement in which a company that owns a direct mail list lets another company use it for a fee

literature /ˈlɪt(ə)rətʃə/ *noun* written information about something ○ *Please send me literature about your new product range.*

lithography /lɪˈθɒɡrəfi/ *noun* a printing process by which a design is applied to a smooth flat surface with greasy ink or a crayon. The surface is wetted and ink will adhere to the greasy parts, but not to the wet parts.

livery /ˈlɪvəri/ *noun* a company's own special design and colours, used e.g. on uniforms, office decoration and vehicles

living /ˈlɪvɪŋ/ *noun* □ **he does not earn a living wage** he does not earn enough to pay for essentials such as food, heat and rent

load /ləʊd/ *noun* goods which are transported □ **the load of a lorry/of a container** the goods carried by a lorry or in a container □ **maximum load** the largest weight of goods which a lorry or plane can carry ■ *verb* **1.** □ **to load a lorry** *or* **a ship** to put goods into a lorry or a ship for transporting ○ *to load cargo onto a ship* ○ *a truck loaded with boxes* ○ *a ship loaded with iron* □ **a fully loaded ship** a ship which is full of cargo **2.** (*of a ship*) to take on cargo ○ *The ship is loading a cargo of wood.* **3.** to put a program into a computer ○ *Load the word-processing program be-*

fore you start keyboarding. **4.** to add extra charges to a price

load-carrying capacity /ˈləʊd ˌkæriɪŋ kəˌpæsɪti/ *noun* the amount of goods which a lorry is capable of carrying

loaded price /ˌləʊdɪd ˈpraɪs/ *noun* a price which includes an unusually large extra payment for some service ○ *That company is notorious for loading its prices.*

loading /ˈləʊdɪŋ/ *noun* assigning work to workers or machines ○ *The production manager has to ensure that careful loading makes the best use of human resources.*

loading dock /ˈləʊdɪŋ dɒk/ *noun* the part of a harbour where ships can load or unload

load time /ˈləʊd taɪm/ *noun* in computing, the time it takes for a page of data to open completely in a window

lobby /ˈlɒbi/ *noun* a pressure group that tries to persuade a government or law-makers to support a particular cause or interest

local /ˈləʊk(ə)l/ *adjective* located in or providing a service for a restricted area

'...each cheque can be made out for the local equivalent of £100 rounded up to a convenient figure' [*Sunday Times*]

'...the business agent for Local 414 of the Store Union said his committee will recommend that the membership ratify the agreement' [*Toronto Star*]

'EC regulations insist that customers can buy cars anywhere in the EC at the local pre-tax price' [*Financial Times*]

local advertising /ˌləʊk(ə)l ˈædvətaɪzɪŋ/ *noun* advertising in the area where a company is based

localised /ˈləʊkəlaɪzd/, **localized** *adjective* which occurs in one area only

localised advertising strategy /ˌləʊkəlaɪzd ˈædvətaɪzɪŋ ˌstrætədʒi/ *noun* planning an advertising campaign for a particular country or area of a market rather than a global campaign

local media /ˌləʊk(ə)l ˈmiːdiə/ *plural noun* newspapers and radio and TV stations in a small area of the country

local newspaper /ˌləʊk(ə)l ˈnjuːzpeɪpə/ *noun* a newspaper which

is sold only in a restricted area, and mainly carries news about that area

local press /ˌləʊk(ə)l ˈpres/ *noun* newspapers which are sold in a small area of the country ○ *The product was only advertised in the local press as it was only being distributed in that area of the country.*

local radio station /ˌləʊk(ə)l ˈreɪdiəʊ ˌsteɪʃ(ə)n/ *noun* a radio station which broadcasts over a small area of the country

location /ləʊˈkeɪʃ(ə)n/ *noun* **1.** a place where something is **2.** a place, especially a site where still photographs or films are made ○ *We still have to decide on locations for the advertisements.*

logical models /ˌlɒdʒɪk(ə)l ˈmɒd(ə)lz/ *plural noun* models of buyer decision-making which assume that purchasing is the result of a set of rational decisions made by the purchaser ○ *Logical models do not allow for the unpredictable side of buying behaviour.*

logistics /ləˈdʒɪstɪks/ *noun* the task or science of managing the movement, storage, and processing of materials and information in a supply chain (NOTE: Logistics includes the acquisition of raw materials and components, manufacturing or processing, and the distribution of finished products to the end user.)

logistics management /ləˈdʒɪstɪks ˌmænɪdʒmənt/ *noun* the management of the distribution of products to the market

logo /ˈləʊgəʊ/ *noun* a symbol, design or group of letters used by a company as a mark on its products and in advertising

London gold fixing /ˌlʌndən ˈgəʊld ˌfɪksɪŋ/ *noun* system where the world price for gold is set each day in London

long lease /lɒŋ ˈliːs/ *noun* a lease which runs for fifty years or more ○ *to take an office building on a long lease*

long-range /ˌlɒŋ ˈreɪndʒ/ *adjective* for a long period of time in the future □ **long-range economic forecast** a forecast which covers a period of several years

long-standing /ˌlɒŋ ˈstændɪŋ/ *adjective* which has been arranged for a long time ○ *a long-standing agreement* □ **long-standing customer** *or* **customer of long standing** a person who has been a customer for many years

long-term /ˌlɒŋ ˈtɜːm/ *adjective* □ **on a long-term basis** for a long period of time □ **long-term debts** debts which will be repaid many years later □ **long-term forecast** a forecast for a period of over three years □ **long-term loan** a loan to be repaid many years later □ **long-term objectives** aims which will take years to achieve

'…land held under long-term leases is not amortized' [*Hongkong Standard*]

'…the company began to experience a demand for longer-term mortgages when the flow of money used to finance these loans diminished' [*Globe and Mail (Toronto)*]

look and feel /ˌlʊk ən ˈfiːl/ *noun* the appeal of the design, layout and ease of use of a website to potential customers and the way the site fits the image the company is trying to put across

loose /luːs/ *adjective* not attached

loose insert /luːs ˈɪnsɜːt/ *noun* a sheet of advertising material slipped between the pages of a publication

lorry-load /ˈlɒri ləʊd/ *noun* the amount of goods carried on a lorry or in a container ○ *They delivered six lorry-loads of coal.*

lose /luːz/ *verb* not to have something any more □ **to lose an order** not to get an order which you were hoping to get ○ *During the strike, the company lost six orders to American competitors.* □ **to lose customers** to have fewer customers ○ *Their service is so slow that they have been losing customers.* □ **the company is losing sales** *or* **is losing market share** the company has fewer sales or a smaller share of the market than before

lose out /ˌluːz ˈaʊt/ *verb* to suffer as a result of something ○ *The company has lost out in the rush to make cheap computers.* ○ *We lost out to a Japanese company who put in a lower tender for the job.*

loss /lɒs/ *noun* **1.** not having something any more □ **loss of customers** not keeping customers because of bad service, high prices, etc. □ **loss of an order** not getting an order which was expected □ **the company suffered a loss of market penetration** the company found it had a smaller share of the market **2.** the state of having less money than before or not making a profit □ **the company suffered a loss** the company did not make a profit □ **to report a loss** not to show a profit in the accounts at the end of the year ○ *The company reported a loss of £1m on the first year's trading.* □ **the car was written off as a dead loss/a total loss** the car was so badly damaged that the insurers said it had no value □ **at a loss** making a loss, not making any profit ○ *The company is trading at a loss.* ○ *We sold the shop at a loss.* □ **to cut your losses** to stop doing something which is losing money **3.** the state of being worth less or having a lower value ○ *Shares showed losses of up to 5% on the Stock Exchange.* **4.** the state of weighing less □ **loss in weight** goods which weigh less than when they were packed □ **loss in transport** the amount of weight which is lost while goods are being transported

'…against losses of FFr 7.7m two years ago, the company made a net profit of FFr 300,000 last year' [*Financial Times*]

low-grade /ˈləʊ ɡreɪd/ *adjective* **1.** not very important ○ *a low-grade official from the Ministry of Commerce* **2.** not of very good quality ○ *The car runs best on low-grade petrol.*

low-hanging fruit /ˌləʊ hæŋɪŋ ˈfruːt/ *noun* an easy short-term sales or market opportunity which provides a quick profit without too much effort (*informal*)

low-involvement hierarchy /ˌləʊ ɪnˈvɒlvmənt ˌhaɪrɑːki/ *noun* a hierarchy of response to advertising where the customer is relatively indifferent to the product or service and only responds to repeated marketing

low-involvement product /ˌləʊ ɪnˈvɒlvmənt ˌprɒdʌkt/ *noun* a low-priced product for everyday use that is bought by consumers without giving much thought to brands

low-pressure /ˌləʊ ˈpreʃə/ *adjective* □ **low-pressure sales** sales where the

salesperson does not force someone to buy, but only encourages them to do so

low-quality /ˌləʊ ˈkwɒlɪti/ *adjective* not of good quality ○ *They tried to sell us some low-quality steel.*

low season /ləʊ ˈsiːz(ə)n/ *noun* a period when there are few travellers ○ *Air fares are cheaper in the low season.*

loyal /ˈlɔɪəl/ *adjective* always buying the same brand or using the same shop ○ *The aim of the advertising is to keep the customers loyal.* (NOTE: you are loyal **to** someone *or* something)

loyalty card /ˈlɔɪəlti kɑːd/ *noun* a special plastic card which gives customers discounts over a period of time to encourage them to remain as customers

loyalty scheme /ˈlɔɪəlti skiːm/ *noun* a scheme to keep the business of existing customers, e.g. by special discounts for loyalty card holders

lull /lʌl/ *noun* a quiet period ○ *After last week's hectic trading this week's lull was welcome.*

lump sum /lʌmp ˈsʌm/ *noun* money paid in one single amount, not in several small sums ○ *When he retired he was given a lump-sum bonus.* ○ *She sold her house and invested the money as a lump sum.*

luxury /ˈlʌkʃəri/ *noun, adjective* referring to an expensive thing which is not necessary but which is good to have ○ *Luxury items are taxed very heavily.*

luxury goods /ˈlʌkʃəri ɡʊdz/ *plural noun* expensive items which are not basic necessities

luxury product /ˈlʌkʃəri ˌprɒdʌkt/ *noun* a product which people buy more of as their incomes rise ○ *The company has gone upmarket and is now selling luxury products.*

M

Ma and Pa shop /ˌmɑː ən ˈpɑː ʃɒp/ noun a small family-run business

macro- /mækrəʊ/ prefix very large, covering a wide area

macroeconomics /ˌmækrəʊiːkə-ˈnɒmɪks/ noun a study of the economics of a whole area, a whole industry, a whole group of the population or a whole country, in order to help in economic planning. Compare **microeconomics** (NOTE: **macroeconomics** takes a singular verb) □ **macroeconomic conditions** factors that influence the state of the overall economy, e.g. changes in gross national product, interest rates, inflation, recession, and employment levels

macroenvironment /ˈmækrəʊ ɪn-ˌvaɪrənmənt/ noun **1.** the general environmental factors that affect an organisation, such as legislation or the country's economy ○ We must develop a flexible planning system to allow for major changes in the macroenvironment. **2.** factors outside the area of marketing which cannot be influenced by the marketing effort, including demographics, the natural environment, etc.

macromarketing /ˈmækrəʊ ˌmɑːkɪtɪŋ/ noun the study of trading activity within a whole economic system such as a country, with its political, economic and social implications

made-to-measure /ˌmeɪd tə ˈmeʒə/ adjective made to fit the requirements of the customer ○ made-to-measure kitchen cabinets ○ a made-to-measure suit

magazine /mægəˈziːn/ noun **1.** a paper, usually with pictures and printed on glossy paper, which comes out regularly, every month or every week **2.** a special colour supplement published with a newspaper □ **magazine insert** an advertising sheet put into a magazine when it is mailed or sold □ **to insert a leaflet in a specialist magazine** to put an advertising leaflet into a magazine before it is mailed or sold

magazine mailing /mægəˈziːn ˌmeɪlɪŋ/ noun the sending of copies of a magazine by post to subscribers

magazine network /mægəˈziːn ˌnetwɜːk/ noun a group of magazines owned by one publisher and offering advertisers the possibility of buying space in several publications as a packaged deal

mail /meɪl/ noun **1.** a system of sending letters and parcels from one place to another ○ The cheque was lost in the mail. ○ The invoice was put in the mail yesterday. ○ Mail to some of the islands in the Pacific can take six weeks. □ **by mail** using the postal services, not sending something by hand or by messenger □ **to send a package by surface mail** to send a package by land or sea, not by air □ **by sea mail** sent by post abroad, using a ship □ **by air mail** sent by post abroad, using a plane □ **we sent the order by first-class mail** we sent the order by the most expensive mail service, designed to be faster **2.** letters sent or received ○ Has the mail arrived yet? ○ The first thing I do is open the mail. ○ The receipt was in this morning's mail. **3.** same as **email** ■ verb **1.** to send something by post ○ to mail a letter ○ We mailed our order last Wednesday. ○ They mailed their catalogue to three thousand customers in Europe. **2.** same as **email**

mail drop /'meɪl drɒp/ *noun* the mailing of promotional material to a large number of addresses

mailer /'meɪlə/ *noun* packaging made of folded cardboard, used to mail items which need protection ○ *a diskette mailer*

mailing /'meɪlɪŋ/ *noun* the sending of something by post ○ *the mailing of publicity material* □ **to buy a mailing list** to pay a society or other organisation money to buy the list of members so that you can use it to mail publicity material

mailing house /'meɪlɪŋ haʊs/ *noun* a company which specialises in carrying out mailings for other companies

mailing list /'meɪlɪŋ lɪst/ *noun* a list of names and addresses of people who might be interested in a product, list of names and addresses of members of a society ○ *to build up a mailing list* ○ *Your name is on our mailing list.*

mailing tube /'meɪlɪŋ tjuːb/ *noun* a stiff cardboard or plastic tube, used for mailing large pieces of paper such as posters

mail interview /'meɪl ˌɪntəvjuː/, **mail survey** /'meɪl ˌsɜːveɪ/ *noun US* the sending of a questionnaire to respondents by post for a survey ○ *Not enough consumers responded to the mail interview.* ○ *To encourage people to cooperate in the mail survey we'll include a free sample with the questionnaire.*

mail merge /'meɪl mɜːdʒ/ *noun* a word-processing program that allows a standard form letter to be printed out to a series of different names and addresses

mail order /ˌmeɪl 'ɔːdə/ *noun* a system of buying and selling from a catalogue, placing orders and sending goods by mail ○ *We bought our kitchen units by mail order.*

mail-order catalogue /'meɪl ɔːdə ˌkæt(ə)lɒg/ *noun* a catalogue from which a customer can order items to be sent by mail

mail-order selling /'meɪl ɔːdə ˌselɪŋ/ *noun* selling by taking orders and supplying a product by post

mail out /ˌmeɪl 'aʊt/ *verb* to send promotional material by mail

mailout /'meɪl aʊt/ *noun* a piece of promotional material sent by direct mail, usually accompanied by a letter which may be personalised

mailsort /'meɪlsɔːt/ *noun* computer software used by mailing companies to sort mailings before they are sent to the post office, usually by using special labels with barcodes

Main Street /'meɪn striːt/ *noun US* the most important street in a town, where the shops and banks are

majority /mə'dʒɒrɪti/ *noun* more than half of a group

major selling idea /ˌmeɪdʒə 'selɪŋ aɪˌdɪə/ *adjective* the central theme in an advertising campaign

make /meɪk/ *noun* a brand or type of product manufactured ○ *Japanese makes of cars* ○ *a standard make of equipment* ○ *What make is the new computer system* or *What's the make of the new computer system?* ■ *verb* **1.** to produce or to manufacture ○ *The workmen spent ten weeks making the table.* ○ *The factory makes three hundred cars a day.* **2.** □ **to make a profit** to have more money after a deal

makegood /'meɪkgʊd/ *noun* an advertisement placed again in a magazine or newspaper free of charge, because a mistake was made in it when it was previously published

make out /meɪk 'aʊt/ *verb* to write ○ *to make out an invoice* ○ *The bill is made out to Smith & Co.* □ **to make out a cheque to someone** to write someone's name on a cheque

maker /'meɪkə/ *noun* in the VALS lifestyle classification, a practical, independent person who is interested in products that are good value but not necessarily fashionable

make-to-order /ˌmeɪk tʊ 'ɔːdə/ *noun* the making of goods or components to fulfil an existing order (NOTE: Make-to-order products are made to the customer's specification, and are often processed in small batches.)

manage /'mænɪdʒ/ *verb* **1.** to direct or to be in charge of ○ *to manage a department* ○ *to manage a branch office* **2.** □ **to manage property** to look after rented property for the owner

'…the research director will manage and direct a team of graduate business analysts reporting on consumer behaviour throughout the UK' [*Times*]

manageable /'mænɪdʒəb(ə)l/ *adjective* which can be dealt with easily ○ *The problems which the company faces are too large to be manageable by one person.*

managed economy /,mænɪdʒd ɪ'kɒnəmi/ *noun* an economy that is controlled by a government

management /'mænɪdʒmənt/ *noun* **1.** directing or running a business ○ *She studied management at university.* ○ *Good management* or *efficient management is essential in a large organisation.* ○ *Bad management* or *inefficient management can ruin a business.* ○ *a management graduate* or *a graduate in management* **2.** a group of managers or directors ○ *The management has decided to give everyone a pay increase.*

'…the management says that the rate of loss-making has come down and it expects further improvement in the next few years' [*Financial Times*]

management accountant /'mænɪdʒmənt ə,kaʊntənt/ *noun* an accountant who prepares financial information for managers so that they can take decisions

management accounting /'mænɪdʒmənt ə,kaʊntɪŋ/ *noun* the preparation and use of financial information to support management decisions

management accounts /'mænɪdʒmənt ə,kaʊnts/ *plural noun* financial information prepared for a manager so that decisions can be made, including monthly or quarterly financial statements, often in great detail, with analysis of actual performance against the budget

management buyout /,mænɪdʒmənt 'baɪaʊt/ *noun* the take-over of a company by a group of em-ployees, usually senior managers and directors. Abbr **MBO**

management by exception /,mænɪdʒmənt baɪ ɪk'sepʃən/ *noun* a management system whereby deviations from plans are located and corrected

management by objectives /,mænɪdʒmənt baɪ əb'dʒektɪvz/ *noun* a way of managing a business by planning work for the managers to do and testing if it is completed correctly and on time

management consultant /'mænɪdʒmənt kən,sʌltənt/ *noun* a person who gives advice on how to manage a business

management course /'mænɪdʒmənt kɔːs/ *noun* a training course for managers

management development /'mænɪdʒmənt dɪ,veləpmənt/ *noun* the selection and training of potential managers

management team /'mænɪdʒmənt tiːm/ *noun* a group of all the managers working in the same company

management technique /'mænɪdʒmənt tek,niːks/ *noun* a way of managing a business

manager /'mænɪdʒə/ *noun* **1.** the head of a department in a company ○ *She's a department manager in an engineering company.* ○ *Go and see the human resources manager if you have a problem.* ○ *The production manager has been with the company for only two weeks.* ○ *Our sales manager started as a rep in London.* **2.** the person in charge of a branch or shop ○ *Mr Smith is the manager of our local Lloyds Bank.* ○ *The manager of our Lagos branch is in London for a series of meetings.*

'…the No. 1 managerial productivity problem in America is managers who are out of touch with their people and out of touch with their customers' [*Fortune*]

managerial /,mænə'dʒɪəriəl/ *adjective* referring to managers ○ *All the managerial staff are sent for training every year.* □ **to be appointed to a managerial position** to be appointed a manager □ **decisions taken at managerial level** decisions taken by managers

managership /'mænɪdʒəʃɪp/ *noun* the job of being a manager ○ *After six years, she was offered the managership of a branch in Scotland.*

managing director /ˌmænədʒɪŋ daɪ'rektə/ *noun* the director who is in charge of a whole company. Abbr **MD**

mandatory /'mændət(ə)ri/ *adjective* required by law or stipulated in a contract

'…the wage talks are focusing on employment issues such as sharing of work among employees and extension of employment beyond the mandatory retirement age of 60 years' [*Nikkei Weekly*]

mandatory blurb /ˌmændət(ə)ri 'blɜːb/, **mandatory copy** /ˌmændət(ə)ri 'kɒpi/ *noun* certain words which are required by law to be included in an advertisement, e.g. a health warning on cigarette advertisements

manifest /'mænɪfest/ *noun* a list of goods in a shipment

mannequin /'mænɪkɪn/ *noun* a model of a person, used to display clothes in a shop window or inside a store

manpower /'mænpaʊə/ *noun* the number of employees in an organisation, industry or country

manpower forecasting /'mænpaʊə ˌfɔːkɑːstɪŋ/ *noun* calculating how many employees will be needed in the future, and how many will actually be available

manpower planning /'mænpaʊə ˌplænɪŋ/ *noun* the process of planning to obtain the right number of employees in each job

manpower requirements /'mænpaʊə rɪˌkwaɪəmənts/, **manpower needs** /'mænpaʊə niːdz/ *plural noun* the number of employees needed

manufacture /ˌmænjʊ'fæktʃə/ *verb* to make a product for sale, using machines ○ *manufactured goods* ○ *The company manufactures spare parts for cars.* ■ *noun* the making of a product for sale, using machines □ **products of foreign manufacture** products made in foreign countries

manufactured goods /ˌmænjʊ-'fæktʃəd gʊdz/ *plural noun* items which are made by machine

manufacturer /ˌmænjʊ'fæktʃərə/ *noun* a person or company that produces machine-made products ○ *a big Indian cotton manufacturer* ○ *Foreign manufacturers have set up factories here.*

manufacturer's agent /mænjʊ-ˌfæktʃərəz 'eɪdʒənt/ *noun* a person who sells on behalf of a manufacturer and earns a commission

manufacturer's brand /mænjʊ-ˌfæktʃərəz 'brænd/ *noun* a brand which belongs to the manufacturer and has the same name

manufacturer's recommended price /mænjʊˌfæktʃərəz ˌrekəmendɪd 'praɪs/ *noun* a price at which the manufacturer suggests the product should be sold on the retail market, which is often reduced by the retailer ○ *'All china – 20% off the manufacturer's recommended price'* Abbr **MRP**

manufacturing /ˌmænjʊ'fæktʃərɪŋ/ *noun* the production of machine-made products for sale ○ *We must try to reduce the manufacturing overheads.* ○ *Manufacturing processes are continually being updated.*

manufacturing capacity /ˌmænjʊ-'fæktʃərɪŋ kəˌpæsɪti/ *noun* the amount of a product which a factory is capable of making

manufacturing industries /ˌmænjʊ'fæktʃərɪŋ ˌɪndəstriz/ *plural noun* industries which take raw materials and make them into finished products

map /mæp/ *noun* a chart which shows a geographical area

mapping /'mæpɪŋ/ *noun* the drawing up of a map of an area

margin /'mɑːdʒɪn/ *noun* **1.** the difference between the money received when selling a product and the money paid for it □ **we are cutting our margins very fine** we are reducing our margins to the smallest possible in order to be competitive □ **our margins have been squeezed** profits have been reduced because our margins have to be smaller to

stay competitive **2.** extra space or time allowed

'…profit margins in the industries most exposed to foreign competition – machinery, transportation equipment and electrical goods – are significantly worse than usual' [*Australian Financial Review*]

marginal /'mɑːdʒɪn(ə)l/ *adjective* **1.** hardly worth the money paid **2.** not very profitable ○ *a marginal return on investment* **3.** hardly worth the money paid

'…pensioner groups claim that pensioners have the highest marginal rates of tax. Income earned by pensioners above $30 a week is taxed at 62.5 per cent, more than the highest marginal rate' [*Australian Financial Review*]

marginal cost /,mɑːdʒɪn(ə)l 'kɒst/ *noun* the cost of making a single extra unit above the number already planned

marginal cost pricing /,mɑːdʒɪn(ə)l 'kɒst ,praɪsɪŋ/ *noun* a pricing method that involves fixing a price per unit that covers marginal costs and makes an acceptable contribution to fixed costs

marginal land /'mɑːdʒɪn(ə)l lænd/ *noun* land which is almost not worth farming

marginal pricing /,mɑːdʒɪn(ə)l 'praɪsɪŋ/ *noun* the practice of basing the selling price of a product on its variable costs of production plus a margin, but excluding fixed costs

marginal productivity /,mɑːdʒɪn(ə)l prɒdʌk'tɪvɪti/ *noun* extra productivity achieved by the use of one more factor of production

marginal purchase /,mɑːdʒɪn(ə)l 'pɜːtʃɪs/ *noun* something which a buyer feels is only just worth buying

marginal revenue /,mɑːdʒɪn(ə)l 'revenjuː/ *noun* the income from selling a single extra unit above the number already sold

marginal utility /,mɑːdʒɪn(ə)l juː'tɪlɪti/ *noun* satisfaction gained from using one more unit of a product

margin of error /,mɑːdʒɪn əv 'erə/ *noun* the number of mistakes which can be accepted in a document or in a calculation

marine /mə'riːn/ *adjective* referring to the sea

marine insurance /mə,riːn ɪn'ʃʊərəns/ *noun* the insurance of ships and their cargoes

marine underwriter /mə,riːn 'ʌndəraɪtə/ *noun* a person or company that insures ships and their cargoes

maritime /æ(adjective), 'mærɪtaɪm/ *adjective* referring to the sea

maritime lawyer /,mærɪtaɪm 'lɔːjə/ *noun* a lawyer who specialises in legal matters concerning ships and cargoes

maritime trade /,mærɪtaɪm 'treɪd/ *noun* the transporting of commercial goods by sea

mark /mɑːk/ *noun* **1.** a sign put on an item to show something **2.** money formerly used in Germany ○ *The price was twenty-five marks.* ○ *The mark rose against the dollar.* (NOTE: usually written **DM** after a figure: **25DM**. Also called **Deutschmark, D-Mark**) ■ *verb* to put a sign on something ○ *to mark a product 'for export only'* ○ *an article marked at £1.50* ○ *She used a black pen to mark the price on the book.*

mark down /,mɑːk 'daʊn/ *verb* to make the price of something lower

mark-down /'mɑːkdaʊn/ *noun* **1.** a reduction of the price of something to less than its usual price **2.** the percentage amount by which a price has been lowered ○ *There has been a 30% mark-down on all goods in the sale.*

marked price /mɑːkt 'praɪs/ *noun* the price which is marked on or attached to an article for sale

market /'mɑːkɪt/ *noun* **1.** a place, often in the open air where farm produce and household goods are sold ○ *The fish market is held every Thursday.* ○ *The open-air market is held in the central square.* ○ *Here are this week's market prices for sheep.* **2.** an area where a product might be sold or the group of people who might buy a product **3.** the possible sales of a specific product or demand for a specific product ○ *The market for home computers has fallen sharply.* ○ *We have 20% of the British car market.* ○ *There's no market for electric typewriters.* **4.** □ **to pay black market prices** to pay high prices to get items which are not easily available ■

verb to sell a product ○ *This product is being marketed in all European countries.*

'...market analysts described the falls in the second half of last week as a technical correction to a market which had been pushed by demand to over the 900 index level' [*Australian Financial Review*]

marketable /ˈmɑːkɪtəb(ə)l/ *adjective* which can be sold easily

market analysis /ˌmɑːkɪt əˈnæləsɪs/ *noun* the detailed examination and report of a market

market area /ˈmɑːkɪt ˌeəriə/ *noun* a geographical area which represents a particular market, e.g. a TV viewing area or a representative's territory

market build-up method /ˌmɑːkɪt ˈbɪld ʌp ˌmeθəd/ *noun* a method of assessing the sales potential of a product by adding up the number of potential buyers in each market segment

market challenger strategy /ˌmɑːkɪt ˈtʃælɪndʒə ˌstrætədʒi/ *noun* a strategy adopted by a company which is challenging the market leaders through pricing, promotion or product design ○ *It's a new aggressive company adopting a market challenger strategy.*

market coverage /ˌmɑːkɪt ˈkʌv(ə)rɪdʒ/ *noun* a market share or measurement of what proportion of the sales of an article is accounted for by a particular brand ○ *The marketing director's brief was to increase market coverage by at least ten per cent.*

market day /ˈmɑːkɪt deɪ/ *noun* the day when a market is regularly held ○ *Tuesday is market day, so the streets are closed to traffic.*

market demand /ˌmɑːkɪt dɪˈmɑːnd/ *noun* the total demand for a product in the market ○ *Market demand for this product is falling, as fashions have changed.*

market development /ˌmɑːkɪt dɪˈveləpmənt/ *noun* a strategy involving the search for and exploitation of new markets for a product ○ *Market development for our tractors is part of the company's growth strategy.*

market-driven /ˈmɑːkɪt ˌdrɪv(ə)n/ *adjective* which is driven by market forces

market dues /ˈmɑːkɪt djuːz/ *plural noun* the rent to be paid for a stall in a market

market economist /ˌmɑːkɪt ɪˈkɒnəmɪst/ *noun* a person who specialises in the study of financial structures and the return on investments in the stock market

market economy /ˌmɑːkɪt ɪˈkɒnəmi/ *noun* an economy in which there is a free market in goods and services

marketeer /ˌmɑːkɪˈtɪə/ *noun* same as **marketer**

marketer /ˈmɑːkɪtə/ *noun* a person or company that carries out marketing activities ○ *The company has been in manufacturing for ten years, and is now becoming a marketer of its own products as well. ○ Most direct marketers support the Post Office, which is almost the sole channel for their services.*

marketface /ˈmɑːkɪtfeɪs/ *noun* the point of contact between suppliers and their customers

market-facing enterprise /ˈmɑːkɪt feɪsɪŋ ˌentəpraɪz/ *noun* an organisation that is sensitive to the needs of its markets and customers and arranges its activities with them in mind

market factor analysis /ˌmɑːkɪt ˌfæktə əˈnæləsɪs/ *noun* a forecasting method which concentrates on key market factors that are believed to affect demand

market follower strategy /ˌmɑːkɪt ˈfɒləʊə ˌstrætədʒi/ *noun* a strategy of a company which does not directly challenge the market leaders, but attempts to benefit from their innovations and gain a profitable corner of the market ○ *Adopting a market follower strategy greatly reduces expenditure on research and development.*

market forces /ˌmɑːkɪt ˈfɔːsɪz/ *plural noun* the influences on the sales of a product which bring about a change in prices

market forecast /ˌmɑːkɪt ˈfɔːkɑːst/ *noun* a forecast of prices on the stock market

market fragmentation /ˌmɑːkɪt ˌfrægmənˈteɪʃ(ə)n/ *noun* the splitting of a market into many small segments, which are more difficult to sell into

market gap /ˌmɑːkɪt ˈgæp/ *noun* an opportunity to sell a product or service which is needed but which no one has sold before. ♦ **gap**

market hall /ˈmɑːkɪt hɔːl/ *noun* the building in which a market is held regularly

marketing /ˈmɑːkɪtɪŋ/ *noun* the process of identifying needs and satisfying these needs with suitable goods or services, through product design, distribution and promotion, either as a business or as a non-profit-making organisation

'…reporting to the marketing director, the successful applicant will be responsible for the development of a training programme for the new sales force' [*Times*]

marketing agreement /ˈmɑːkɪtɪŋ əˌgriːmənt/ *noun* a contract by which one company will market another company's products

marketing audit /ˈmɑːkɪtɪŋ ˌɔːdɪt/ *noun* an examination of the effectiveness of a company's marketing plans

marketing board /ˈmɑːkɪtɪŋ bɔːd/ *noun* an organisation set up by the government or by a group of producers to help producers to market a certain type of product

marketing budget /ˈmɑːkɪtɪŋ ˌbʌdʒɪt/ *noun* money set aside by an organisation for its marketing activities

marketing channels /ˈmɑːkɪtɪŋ ˌtʃæn(ə)lz/ *plural noun* the means of communicating a message involved in the process of marketing

marketing communications /ˈmɑːkɪtɪŋ kəmjuːnɪˈkeɪʃ(ə)nz/ *plural noun* all methods of communicating used in marketing, e.g. television, radio and sales literature

marketing concept /ˈmɑːkɪtɪŋ ˌkɒnsept/ *noun* a business idea or philosophy based on the importance of profit, consumer satisfaction and the welfare of the general public

marketing consultancy /ˈmɑːkɪtɪŋ kənˌsʌltənsi/ *noun* a firm which gives specialist advice on marketing

marketing department /ˈmɑːkɪtɪŋ dɪˌpɑːtmənt/ *noun* the section of a company dealing with marketing and sales

marketing director /ˈmɑːkɪtɪŋ daɪˌrektə/ *noun* a director who is responsible for an organisation's marketing activities

marketing information system /ˌmɑːkɪtɪŋ ɪnfəˈmeɪʃ(ə)n ˌsɪstəm/ *noun* computer software which analyses marketing information and produces material on which marketers can make decisions

marketing intelligence /ˈmɑːkɪtɪŋ ɪnˌtelɪdʒəns/ *noun* information about a market that can help a marketing effort

marketing management /ˈmɑːkɪtɪŋ ˌmænɪdʒmənt/ *noun* the organising of a company's marketing

marketing manager /ˈmɑːkɪtɪŋ ˌmænɪdʒə/ *noun* a person in charge of a marketing department ○ *The marketing manager has decided to start a new advertising campaign.*

marketing mix /ˈmɑːkɪtɪŋ mɪks/ *noun* the combination of all the elements that make up marketing such as price, distribution and advertising ○ *Personal selling is a vital part of the company's marketing mix.* Compare **the four P's**

marketing model /ˈmɑːkɪtɪŋ ˌmɒd(ə)l/ *noun* an overview of the entire marketing process which can be shown graphically, often using a computer, and used to solve problems

marketing myopia /ˌmɑːkɪtɪŋ maɪˈəʊpiə/ *noun* a problem which occurs when a business is 'short-sighted' and only views the world from its own perspective, and fails to see the point of view of the customer

marketing objectives /ˈmɑːkɪtɪŋ əbˌdʒektɪvz/ *plural noun* aims set for an organisation's marketing programme, including sales, market share, and profitability

marketing plan /'mɑːkɪtɪŋ plæn/ *noun* a plan, usually annual, for a company's marketing activities, specifying expenditure and expected revenue and profits ○ *Has this year's marketing plan been drawn up yet?* ○ *The marketing plan is flexible enough to allow for an increase in advertising costs.*

marketing planning /'mɑːkɪtɪŋ ˌplænɪŋ/ *noun* making a plan for a company's marketing activities, specifying expenditure and expected revenue and profits

marketing policy /'mɑːkɪtɪŋ ˌpɒlɪsi/ *noun* the basic attitudes underlying a company's marketing activities

marketing research /ˌmɑːkɪtɪŋ rɪ-'sɜːtʃ/ *noun* all research carried out in the interests of successful marketing, including market research, media research and product research

marketing services /'mɑːkɪtɪŋ ˌsɜːvɪsɪz/ *plural noun* marketing functions other than selling, e.g. market research and advertising ○ *Our sales drive is supported by well-developed and effective marketing services.*

marketing strategy /'mɑːkɪtɪŋ ˌstrætədʒi/ *noun* a strategy or plan for marketing activities ○ *What marketing strategy should be adopted to reach these long-term objectives?* ○ *The marketing strategy was one of expansion through diversification and market development.*

market intelligence /'mɑːkɪt ɪn-ˌtelɪdʒəns/ *noun* information about a market that can help a marketing effort

market leader /ˌmɑːkɪt 'liːdə/ *noun* the company with the largest market share ○ *We are the market leader in home computers.*

    '…market leaders may benefit from scale economies or other cost advantages; they may enjoy a reputation for quality simply by being at the top, or they may actually produce a superior product that gives them both a large market share and high profits' [*Accountancy*]

market leader strategy /ˌmɑːkɪt 'liːdə ˌstrætədʒi/ *noun* a strategy of a company which is a market leader and wants to maintain a dominant market share or to keep its reputation as an innovator

marketmaker /'mɑːkɪtmeɪkə/ *noun* a person who buys or sells shares on the stock market and offers to do so in a certain list of securities (a marketmaker operates a book, listing the securities he or she is willing to buy or sell, and makes his or her money by charging a commission on each transaction)

market map /'mɑːkɪt mæp/ *noun* a graph showing the structure of a market in terms of the number and type of consumers and the activity of competitors ○ *One look at the market map shows we are aiming at the wrong target market.*

market niche /'mɑːkɪt niːʃ/ *noun* a particular segment or specialised area of a market ○ *In producing this unusual product, the company has found itself a market niche.*

market opening /'mɑːkɪt ˌəʊp(ə)nɪŋ/ *noun* the possibility of starting to do business in a new market

market opportunity /ˌmɑːkɪt ɒpə-'tjuːnɪti/ *noun* the possibility of going into a market for the first time

market penetration /ˌmɑːkɪt ˌpenɪ'treɪʃ(ə)n/ *noun* the percentage of a total market which the sales of a company cover

market penetration pricing /ˌmɑːkɪt penɪ'treɪʃ(ə)n ˌpraɪsɪŋ/ *noun* pricing a product low enough to achieve market penetration

marketplace /'mɑːkɪtpleɪs/ *noun* **1.** the open space in the middle of a town where a market is held ○ *You can park in the marketplace when there is no market.* **2.** the situation and environment in which goods are sold ○ *Our salespeople find life difficult in the marketplace.* ○ *What's the reaction to the new car in the marketplace?* ○ *What's the marketplace reaction to the new car?*

    '…most discounted fares are sold by bucket shops but in today's competitive marketplace any agent can supply them' [*Business Traveller*]

market position /ˌmɑːkɪt pə-'zɪʃ(ə)n/ *noun* the place a company holds in a market

market potential /ˌmɑːkɪt pə-'tenʃəl/ *noun* the sales of a product that should be achieved with the right kind of marketing effort ○ *The product is*

promising but has not yet achieved its full market potential.

market power /'mɑːkɪt ˌpaʊə/ *noun* the power of a business within a market, usually based on the firm's market position

market price /'mɑːkɪt praɪs/ *noun* the price at which a product can be sold

market profile /ˌmɑːkɪt 'prəʊfaɪl/ *noun* the basic characteristics of a particular market

market rate /'mɑːkɪt reɪt/ *noun* the normal price in the market ○ *We pay the market rate for secretaries* or *We pay secretaries the market rate*

'...after the prime rate cut yesterday, there was a further fall in short-term market rates' [*Financial Times*]

market research /ˌmɑːkɪt rɪ'sɜːtʃ/ *noun* the process of examining the possible sales of a product and the possible customers for it before it is put on the market

market sector /ˌmɑːkɪt 'sektə/ *noun* a particular section of a market, especially an area into which a firm sells

market segment /ˌmɑːkɪt 'segmənt/ *noun* a group of consumers in a market who are definable by their particular needs

market segmentation /ˌmɑːkɪt segmen'teɪʃ(ə)n/ *noun* the division of the market or consumers into categories according to their buying habits ○ *Our strategy is based on satisfying the demands of many different types of buyer and therefore requires thorough market segmentation.*

market share /ˌmɑːkɪt 'ʃeə/ *noun* the percentage of a total market which the sales of a company's product cover ○ *We hope our new product range will increase our market share.*

market specialist /ˌmɑːkɪt 'speʃəlɪst/ *noun* a person who concentrates on a few markets, and has an expertise in the media industry in these markets

market stall /'mɑːkɪt stɔːl/ *noun* a light wooden stand where a trader sells goods in a market

market structure /ˌmɑːkɪt 'strʌktʃə/ *noun* the way in which a market is organised, including the concentration of suppliers or consumers, the ease of entry or barriers to entry, and the competitiveness of players in the market

market survey /ˌmɑːkɪt 'sɜːveɪ/ *noun* a survey or general report on market conditions ○ *The market survey suggests that there is no longer much demand for this type of product.*

market targeting /ˌmɑːkɪt 'tɑːgɪtɪŋ/ *noun* planning how to sell a product or service into a particular market

market test /ˌmɑːkɪt 'test/ *noun* an examination to see if a sample of a product will sell in a market

market trends /ˌmɑːkɪt 'trendz/ *plural noun* gradual changes taking place in a market

market value /ˌmɑːkɪt 'vælju:/ *noun* value of an asset, a share, a product or a company if sold today

mark up /ˌmɑːk 'ʌp/ *verb* to increase the price of something

mark-up /'mɑːk ʌp/ *noun* **1.** an increase in price ○ *We put into effect a 10% mark-up of all prices in June.* ○ *Since I was last in the store they have put at least a 10% mark-up on the whole range of items.* **2.** the difference between the cost of a product or service and its selling price (NOTE: Mark-up is often calculated as a percentage of the production and overhead costs, and represents the profit made on the product or service.) □ **we work to a 3.5 times mark-up** *or* **to a 350% mark-up** we take the unit cost and multiply by 3.5 to give the selling price

mark-up percentage /'mɑːk ʌp pə-ˌsentɪdʒ/ *noun* the mark-up expressed as a percentage either of the cost price or of the selling price ○ *What's the mark-up percentage on these items?*

marque /mɑːk/ *noun* a famous brand name for a car, e.g. Jaguar, MG, or Ferrari

mart /mɑːt/ *noun* a place where things are sold

mass /mæs/ *noun* **1.** a large group of people **2.** a large number ○ *We have a mass of letters* or *masses of letters to*

write. ○ *They received a mass of orders* or *masses of orders after the TV commercials.*

mass customisation /ˌmæs kʌstəmaɪˈzeɪʃ(ə)n/ *noun* a process that allows a standard, mass-produced item, e.g., a bicycle, to be altered to fit the specific requirements of individual customers

mass market /mæs ˈmɑːkɪt/ *noun* the whole market, consisting of a very large number of customers

mass marketing /mæs ˈmɑːkɪtɪŋ/ *noun* marketing which aims at reaching large numbers of people

'…in the good old days of mass marketing, the things marketers did to attract new customers tended to be the same as the things they did to keep existing customers – competitive prices, high quality and good service' [*Marketing Week*]

mass media /mæs ˈmiːdiə/ *noun* the means of communication by which large numbers of people are reached, e.g. radio, television or newspapers

mass-produce /ˌmæs prəˈdjuːs/ *verb* to manufacture identical products in large quantities ○ *to mass-produce cars*

master /ˈmɑːstə/ *adjective* main or original □ **master budget** a budget prepared by amalgamating budgets from various profit and cost centres such as sales, production, marketing or administration in order to provide a main budget for the whole company □ **the master copy of a file** the main copy of a computer file, kept for security purposes

master franchise /ˈmɑːstə ˌfræntʃaɪz/ *noun* a franchise given to a single entrepreneur who then sells subsidiary franchises to others

Master of Business Administration (MBA) *noun* full form of **MBA**

master sample /ˈmɑːstə ˌsɑːmpəl/ *noun* a collection of basic sampling units (such as parliamentary constituencies) compiled by research organisations to help a company's market research

masthead /ˈmɑːsthed/ *noun* the area at the top of a webpage, which usually contains the logo of the organisation that owns the page, and often a search

box and a set of links to important areas of the website

matched sample /ˌmætʃd ˈsɑːmpəl/ *noun* the use of two samples of people with the same characteristics to compare reactions to different products in tests

material /məˈtɪəriəl/ *noun* a substance which can be used to make a finished product □ **materials control** a system to check that a company has enough materials in stock to do its work □ **materials handling** the moving of materials from one part of a factory to another in an efficient way

matrix /ˈmeɪtrɪks/ *noun* an arrangement of data in horizontal and vertical columns (NOTE: plural is **matrices**)

matrix management /ˈmeɪtrɪks ˌmænɪdʒmənt/ *noun* management that operates both through the hierarchical chain of command within the organisation, and through relationships at the same level with other managers working in other locations or on different products or projects

mature /məˈtʃʊə/ *adjective* □ **mature economy** a fully developed economy ■ *verb* to become due □ **bills which mature in three weeks' time** bills which will be due for payment in three weeks

mature market /məˌtʃʊə ˈmɑːkɪt/ *noun* a well-established market, with little potential for increased sales

maturity /məˈtʃʊərɪti/ *noun* the third stage in a product life cycle when a product is well established in the market though no longer enjoying increasing sales, after which sooner or later it will start to decline

maximal awareness /ˌmæksɪməl əˈweənəs/ *noun* the point at which a consumer is convinced enough by a product's advertising to buy the product ○ *The marketing director considered the advertisement's message too weak to achieve maximal awareness.*

maximisation /ˌmæksɪmaɪˈzeɪʃ(ə)n/, **maximization** *noun* the process of making something as large as possible ○ *profit maximisation* or *maximiatison of profit*

maximise /'mæksɪmaɪz/, **maximize** *verb* to make as large as possible ○ *Our aim is to maximie sprofits.* ○ *The cooperation of the workforce will be needed if we are to maximise production.* ○ *He is paid on results, and so has to work flat out to maximise his earnings.*

maximum /'mæksɪməm/ *noun* the largest possible number, price or quantity ○ *It is the maximum the insurance company will pay.* □ **up to a maximum of £10** no more than £10 □ **to increase exports to the maximum** to increase exports as much as possible ■ *adjective* largest possible ○ *40% is the maximum income tax rate* or *the maximum rate of tax.* ○ *The maximum load for the truck is one ton.* ○ *Maximum production levels were reached last week.* □ **to increase production to the maximum level** to increase it as much as possible

maximum price /ˌmæksɪməm 'praɪs/ *noun* the highest legal price for a product ○ *The government insists on such a low maximum price that we'll never break even.* ○ *Demand for the product is so low that no company is charging the maximum price.*

MBA /ˌem biː 'eɪ/ *noun* a degree awarded to graduates who have completed a further course in business studies. Full form **Master of Business Administration**

m-commerce /'em ˌkɒmɜːs/ *noun* marketing functions other than selling, e.g. market research and advertising

mean /miːn/ *adjective* average ○ *The mean annual increase in sales is 3.20%.* ■ *noun* the average or number calculated by adding several quantities together and dividing by the number of quantities added ○ *Unit sales are over the mean for the first quarter* or *above the first-quarter mean.*

means /miːnz/ *noun* a way of doing something ○ *Air freight is the fastest means of getting stock to South America.* ○ *Do we have any means of copying all these documents quickly?* ○ *Bank transfer is the easiest means of payment.* (NOTE: plural is same) ■ *plural noun* money or resources ○ *The company has the means to launch the new product.* ○

Such a level of investment is beyond the means of a small private company.

means test /'miːnz test/ *noun* an inquiry into how much money someone earns to see if they are eligible for state benefits

mechanical /mɪ'kænɪk(ə)l/ *adjective* worked by a machine ○ *a mechanical pump*

mechanical data /mɪˌkænɪk(ə)l 'deɪtə/ *noun* information regarding the printing of newspapers or magazines, e.g. format or column width

media /'miːdiə/ *noun* the means of communicating a message about a product or service to the public (NOTE: **media** is followed by a singular or plural verb)

'…both advertisers and agencies agree that the media owners do their bit to keep advertisers well informed' [*Marketing Workshop*]

'…media costs represent a major expense for advertisers' [*Marketing*]

media broker /'miːdiə ˌbrəʊkə/ *noun* a business which offers organisations a media-buying service and possibly additional services such as media planning

media buyer /'miːdiə ˌbaɪə/ *noun* a person in an advertising agency who places advertisements in the media on behalf of clients

media buying /'miːdiə ˌbaɪɪŋ/ *noun* the placing of advertisements in the media on behalf of an organisation ○ *Efficient media buying is impossible without a good knowledge of comparative media costs.*

media class /'miːdiə klɑːs/ *noun* a basic type of medium, e.g. TV, radio or the press

media coverage /'miːdiə ˌkʌv(ə)rɪdʒ/ *noun* reports about something in the media ○ *We got good media coverage for the launch of the new model.*

media data form /ˌmiːdiə 'deɪtə fɔːm/ *noun* a document giving basic data or information about a publication such as circulation, readership and geographical distribution

media event /ˌmiːdiə ɪ'vent/ *noun* a happening which is staged by or organ-

ised so as to attract the attention of the mass media

media independent /ˌmiːdiə ɪndɪ-ˈpendənt/, **media shop** /ˈmiːdiə ʃɒp/ *noun* a business which offers organisations a media-buying service, but without the creative services usually offered by advertising agencies

median /ˈmiːdiən/ *noun* the middle number in a list of numbers

media objectives /ˌmiːdiə əb-ˈdʒektɪvz/ *plural noun* aims which an advertiser has in advertising through the media

media option /ˈmiːdiə ˌɒpʃən/ *noun* a single unit of advertising space or time

media organizations /ˈmiːdiə ɔːɡənaɪˌzeɪʃ(ə)nz/ *plural noun* organisations whose aim is to provide information or entertainment to their subscribers, viewers, or readers while at the same offering marketers a way of reaching audiences with print and broadcast messages

media owner /ˈmiːdiə ˌəʊnə/ *noun* a person or company that owns a magazine or newspaper or radio or TV station

media plan /ˈmiːdiə plæn/ *noun* a plan showing what type of media will be used and how much advertising will be done and when

media planner /ˈmiːdiə ˌplænə/ *noun* a person who deals with media planning

media planning /ˈmiːdiə ˌplænɪŋ/ *noun* a strategy concerned with what type of media should be used and how much advertising should be done and when ○ *The marketing manager and media buyer are having a media planning session.* ○ *Proper media planning avoids overexpenditure on promotion.*

media research /ˈmiːdiə rɪˌsɜːtʃ/ *noun* the study or evaluation of a target audience in order to improve an organisation's promotional activities

media schedule /ˈmiːdiə ˌʃedʒuːl/ *noun* all the details of advertising to be used in a promotional campaign, e.g. the timing and positioning of advertisements

media selection /ˈmiːdiə sɪˌlekʃən/ *noun* the process of choosing the right type of media for a promotional campaign ○ *The agency will give us guidance on media selection.*

media service /ˈmiːdiə ˌsɜːvɪs/ *noun* an organisation which provides the full range of media functions to its clients

media shop /ˈmiːdiə ʃɒp/ *noun* same as **media independent**

media strategy /ˈmiːdiə ˌstrætədʒi/ *noun* action plans for achieving media objectives

media vehicle /ˈmiːdiə ˌviːɪk(ə)l/ *noun* the specific programme or publication used to carry an advertising message

medium /ˈmiːdiəm/ *noun* one particular means of communicating information to the public (NOTE: plural is **media**)

medium-term /ˈmiːdiəm tɜːm/ *adjective* referring to a point between short term and long term □ **medium-term forecast** a forecast for two or three years

megastore /ˈmegəstɔː/ *noun* a very large store

mercantile /ˈmɜːkəntaɪl/ *adjective* commercial □ **mercantile country** a country which earns income from trade □ **mercantile law** laws relating to business

mercantile agent /ˈmɜːkəntaɪl ˌeɪdʒənt/ *noun* a person who sells on behalf of a business or another person and earns a commission

mercantile marine /ˌmɜːkəntaɪl məˈriːn/ *noun* all the commercial ships of a country

mercantile paper /ˈmɜːkəntaɪl ˌpeɪpə/ *noun* a negotiable document used in commerce

merchandise *noun* /ˈmɜːtʃəndaɪz/ goods which are for sale or which have been sold ○ *The merchandise is shipped through two ports.* ■ *verb* to sell goods by a wide variety of means, such as display, advertising or sending samples ○ *to merchandise a product*

'...fill huge warehouses with large quantities but limited assortments of top-brand, first-quality merchandise and sell the goods at rock-bottom prices' [*Duns Business Month*]

merchandise₂ /'mɜːtʃəndaɪz/, **merchandize** *verb* to sell goods by a wide variety of means, such as display, advertising or sending samples ○ *to merchandise a product*

merchandising /'mɜːtʃəndaɪzɪŋ/, **merchandizing** *noun* the process of organising the display and promotion of goods in retail outlets ○ *the merchandising of a product* ○ *the merchandising department*

merchandiser /'mɜːtʃəndaɪzə/ *noun* a person or company that organises the display and promotion of goods

merchant /'mɜːtʃənt/ *noun* a businessperson who buys and sells, especially one who buys imported goods in bulk for retail sale ○ *a coal merchant* ○ *a wine merchant*

merchantable /'mɜːtʃəntəb(ə)l/ *adjective* of good enough quality for sale and use

merchant account /'mɜːtʃənt əˌkaʊnt/ *noun* an account opened by an e-merchant at a financial institution to receive the proceeds of credit-card transactions

merchant bank /'mɜːtʃənt bæŋk/ *noun* a bank which arranges loans to companies, deals in international finance, buys and sells shares, launches new companies on the Stock Exchange, but does not provide normal banking services to the general public

merchanting /'mɜːtʃəntɪŋ/ *noun* the action of buying and selling

merchantman /'mɜːtʃəntmən/ *noun* a commercial ship

merchant marine /ˌmɜːtʃənt məˈriːn/ *noun* all the commercial ships of a country

merge /mɜːdʒ/ *verb* to join together ○ *The two companies have merged.* ○ *The firm merged with its main competitor.*

merge-purge /'mɜːdʒ pɜːdʒ/ *noun* combining two mailing lists and checking to remove duplicate addresses

merger /'mɜːdʒə/ *noun* the joining together of two or more companies ○ *As a result of the merger, the company is now the largest in the field.*

message /'mesɪdʒ/ *noun* **1.** a piece of news which is sent to someone ○ *He says he never received the message.* ○ *I'll leave a message with her secretary.* **2.** an idea that is communicated by promotion ○ *The agency was given clear instructions as to what message the advertisement should convey.* ○ *Few people interviewed in the survey knew what the advertisement's message was supposed to be.* ○ *The message on the poster was conveyed in only three words.*

message effect /'mesɪdʒ ɪˌfekt/ *noun* the effect of an advertisement's message on the target audience ○ *The message effect was lost because so many people didn't understand the joke used in the advertisement.* ○ *After the campaign we'll try to assess what the message effect has been.*

metamarketing /'metəmɑːkɪtɪŋ/ *noun* US marketing applied to all kinds of organisations, such as hospitals, churches and religions, as well as to profit-making concerns

me-too product /miː 'tuː ˌprɒdʌkt/ *noun* a product which is a very similar to an existing market leader

metro area /'metrəʊ ˌeəriə/ *noun* the central part of a large city

micro- /maɪkrəʊ/ *prefix* very small

microeconomics /'maɪkrəʊ iːkəˌnɒmɪks/ *noun* the study of the economics of people or single companies. Compare **macroeconomics** □ **microeconomic trends** trends in a country's economy, e.g. consumer income and patterns of spending, wages, savings, or debt

microenvironment /'maɪkrəʊ ɪnˌvaɪrənmənt/ *noun* the elements or factors outside a business organisation which directly affect it, such as supply of raw materials, demand for its products and rival companies ○ *Unreliability of suppliers is one the greatest problems in our microenvironment.*

micromarketing /'maɪkrəʊ ,mɑːkɪtɪŋ/ *prefix* the study of the marketing strategy of an individual business

middleman /'mɪd(ə)l,mæn/ *noun* a businessperson who buys from the manufacturer and sells to retailers or to the public ○ *We sell direct from the factory to the customer and cut out the middleman.* (NOTE: plural is **middlemen**)

military hardware /,mɪlɪt(ə)ri 'hɑːdweə/ *noun* military equipment, e.g. guns, rockets and tanks

milk /mɪlk/ *verb* to make as much profit for as long as possible from a particular product or service ○ *We intend to milk the product hard for the next two years, before it becomes obsolete.*

mindset /'maɪndset/ *noun* a way of thinking or general attitude to things

mindshare /'maɪndʃeə/ *noun* the density of the interconnects found by a search engine, that is the number of pages that have links to a website

minicontainer /'mɪnɪkən,teɪnə/ *noun* a small container

minimarket /'mɪni,mɑːkɪt/ *noun* a very small self-service store

minimum frequency /,mɪnɪməm 'friːkwənsi/ *noun* the minimum number of exposures for an advertisement to be effective

mining concession /'maɪnɪŋ kən ,seʃ(ə)n/ *noun* the right to dig a mine on a piece of land

miscellaneous /,mɪsə'leɪniəs/ *adjective* various, mixed, or not all of the same sort ○ *miscellaneous items on the agenda* ○ *a box of miscellaneous pieces of equipment* ○ *Miscellaneous expenditure is not itemized in the accounts.*

misrepresentation /mɪs,reprɪzen 'teɪʃ(ə)n/ *noun* the act of making a wrong statement in order to persuade someone to enter into a contract such as one for buying a product or service

mission /'mɪʃ(ə)n/ *noun* a group of people going on a journey for a special purpose

missionary sales /'mɪʃ(ə)n(ə)ri seɪlz/ *plural noun* a sales pitch where a salesperson emphasises support services rather than taking orders

missionary salesperson /'mɪʃ(ə)n(ə)ri ,seɪlzpɜːs(ə)n/ *noun* a salesperson who approaches a new market with a product

missionary selling /'mɪʃ(ə)n(ə)ri ,selɪŋ/ *noun* the act of approaching new customers with a product ○ *We have never sold there before, so be prepared for missionary selling.* ○ *Some sales reps are not aggressive enough for missionary selling.*

mission statement /'mɪʃ(ə)n ,steɪtmənt/ *noun* a short statement of the reasons for the existence of an organisation

mix /mɪks/ *noun* an arrangement of different things together

mixed /mɪkst/ *adjective* made up of different sorts or of different types of things together

mixed economy /mɪkst ɪ'kɒnəmi/ *noun* a system which contains both nationalised industries and private enterprise

mixed media /,mɪkst 'miːdiə/ *plural noun* various types of media used together in a promotional campaign

mnemonic /nɪ'mɒnɪks/ *noun* a word, sentence or little poem which helps you remember something

mobile /'məʊbaɪl/ *adjective* which can move about

mock-up /'mɒk ʌp/ *noun* the model of a new product for testing or to show to possible buyers ○ *The sales team were shown a mock-up of the new car.*

mode /məʊd/ *noun* a way of doing something □ **mode of payment** the way in which payment is made, e.g. cash or cheque

model /'mɒd(ə)l/ *noun* **1.** a small copy of something made to show what it will look like when finished ○ *They showed us a model of the new office building.* **2.** a style or type of product ○ *this is the latest model* ○ *The model on display is last year's.* ○ *I drive a 2001 model Range Rover.* **3.** a person whose job is to wear new clothes to show them to possible buyers **4.** description in the form of mathematical data ■ *adjective* which is a perfect example to be copied

○ *a model agreement* ■ *verb* to wear new clothes to show them to possible buyers ○ *She has decided on a career in modelling.* (NOTE: **modelling – modelled**. The American spelling is **modeling – modeled**)

modem /'məʊdem/ *noun* the device which links a computer to a telephone line, allowing data to be sent from one computer to another

modification /ˌmɒdɪfɪ'keɪʃ(ə)n/ *noun* a change ○ *The board wanted to make or to carry out modifications to the plan.* ○ *The new model has had several important modifications.* ○ *The client pressed for modifications to the contract.*

modified rebuy /ˌmɒdɪfaɪd 'riːbaɪ/ *noun* a buying decision where either the product or the supplier has changed from the time of the previous purchase

modify /'mɒdɪfaɪ/ *verb* to change or to make something fit a different use ○ *The car will have to be modified to pass the government tests.* ○ *The refrigerator was considerably modified before it went into production.*

modular /'mɒdjʊlə/ *adjective* made of various sections

mom-and-pop operation /ˌmɒm ən 'pɒp ɒpəˌreɪʃ(ə)n/ *noun US* a small business owned and run by a couple

monadic test /mɒ'nædɪk test/ *noun* a product test involving only one product

monetary /'mʌnɪt(ə)ri/ *adjective* referring to money or currency

'…a draft report on changes in the international monetary system' [*Wall Street Journal*]

monetary policy /ˌmʌnɪt(ə)ri 'pɒlɪsi/ *noun* the government's policy relating to finance, e.g. bank interest rates, taxes, government expenditure and borrowing

'…the decision by the government to tighten monetary policy will push the annual inflation rate above the year's previous high' [*Financial Times*]

monetary standard /ˌmʌnɪt(ə)ri 'stændəd/ *noun* the fixing of a fixed exchange rate for a currency

money /'mʌni/ *noun* coins and notes used for buying and selling □ **to earn**

money to have a wage or salary □ **to earn good money** to have a large wage or salary □ **to lose money** to make a loss, not to make a profit □ **the company has been losing money for months** the company has been working at a loss for months □ **to get your money back** to make enough profit to cover your original investment □ **to make money** to make a profit □ **to put money into the bank** to deposit money into a bank account □ **to put money into a business** to invest money in a business ○ *She put all her redundancy money into a shop.* □ **to put money down** to pay cash, especially as a deposit ○ *We put £25 down and paid the rest in instalments.* □ **money up front** payment in advance ○ *They are asking for £10,000 up front before they will consider the deal.* ○ *He had to put money up front before he could clinch the deal.*

money-back guarantee /ˌmʌni 'bæk ɡærənˌtiː/, **money-back offer** /ˌmʌni 'bæk ˌɒfə/ *noun* a guarantee that money will be paid back to customers who are not satisfied with their purchases

money-making /'mʌni ˌmeɪkɪŋ/ *adjective* which makes money ○ *a money-making plan*

money-off coupon /ˌmʌni 'ɒf ˌkuːpɒn/ *noun* a coupon in a newspaper or on a package which can be cut off and used to claim a discount on the next purchase

money order /'mʌni ˌɔːdə/ *noun* a document which can be bought for sending money through the post

money rates /'mʌni reɪts/ rates of interest for borrowers or lenders

money-spinner /'mʌni ˌspɪnə/ *noun* an item which sells very well or which is very profitable ○ *The home-delivery service has proved to be a real money-spinner.*

money supply /'mʌni səˌplaɪ/ *noun* the amount of money which exists in a country

monies /'mʌniz/ *plural noun* sums of money ○ *monies owing to the company* ○ *to collect monies due*

monopolisation /məˌnɒpəlaɪ-'zeɪʃ(ə)n/, **monopolization** *noun* the process of making a monopoly

monopolise /mə'nɒpəlaɪz/, **monopolize** *verb* to create a monopoly or to get control of all the supply of a product

monopolist /mə'nɒpəlɪst/ *noun* a business which is the sole seller in a market

monopolistic competition /mənɒpəˌlɪstɪk kɒmpə'tɪʃ(ə)n/ *noun* a situation where there are only a few producers who therefore control the market between them ○ *With only three suppliers of cotton in the country it was a clear case of monopolistic competition.*

monopoly /mə'nɒpəli/ *noun* a situation where one person or company is the only supplier of a particular product or service ○ *to be in a monopoly situation* ○ *The company has the monopoly of imports of French wine.*

monopoly profit /mə'nɒpəli ˌprɒfɪt/ *noun* profit earned by a business through having a monopoly

monopsonist /mə'nɒpsənɪst/ *noun* a sole buyer of a particular product or service

monopsony /mə'nɒpsəni/ *noun* a situation where there is only one buyer for a particular product or service ○ *Monopsony gives the buyer leverage in demanding a low price.*

monthly /'mʌnθli/ *noun* a magazine which is published each month ○ *The holidays were advertised in all the monthlies.* (NOTE: plural is **monthlies**)

monthly sales report /ˌmʌnθli 'seɪlz rɪˌpɔːt/ *noun* a report made every month showing the number of items sold or the amount of money a company has received for selling stock ○ *In the sales reports all the European countries are bracketed together.* ○ *Detailed sales reports help the sales manager work out an effective sales strategy.*

morphological analysis /mɔːfə-ˌlɒdʒɪk(ə)l ə'næləsɪs/ *noun* a method of identifying the most profitable market segments by exploring various dimensions such as countries and market types

most favoured nation /məʊst ˌfeɪvəd 'neɪʃ(ə)n/ *noun* a country which has the best trade terms

motivate /'məʊtɪveɪt/ *verb* to encourage someone to do something, especially to work or to sell □ **highly motivated sales staff** sales staff who are very eager to sell

'...creative people aren't necessarily motivated by money or titles, they may not want a larger office or more work, they don't often want more responsibility. They want to see their ideas implemented' [*Nation's Business*]

motivation /ˌməʊtɪ'veɪʃ(ə)n/ *noun* **1.** an encouragement to staff **2.** eagerness to work well or sell large quantities of a product □ **the sales staff lack motivation** the sales staff are not eager enough to sell

motivation research /məʊtɪ-'veɪʃən rɪˌsɜːtʃ/, **motivational research** /məʊtɪˌveɪʃən(ə)l rɪ'sɜːtʃ/ *noun* research designed to find out the consumer's motives for purchasing a product or service

motive /'məʊtɪv/ *noun* something that forces someone to take a particular action

move /muːv/ *verb* to be sold, or to sell ○ *Over Christmas the stock hardly moved at all but noe it is finally starting to sell.* ○ *The sales staff will have to work hard if they want to move all that stock by the end of the month.*

moving averages /ˌmuːvɪŋ 'æv(ə)rɪdʒɪz/ *plural noun* a method for working out averages while allowing for seasonal variations, in which the period under consideration is moved forward at regular intervals

multi- /'mʌlti/ *prefix* referring to many things

multi-channel /ˌmʌlti 'tʃæn(ə)l/ *adjective* using both online and offline methods of communication to do business

multi-channel system /'mʌlti ˌtʃæn(ə)l ˌsɪstəm/ *noun* a distribution system used by a producer which makes use of more than one distribution channel

multi-dimensional scaling /ˌmʌlti daɪˌmenʃ(ə)nəl 'skeɪlɪŋ/ *noun* a

method of carrying out market research, in which the respondents are given a scale (usually 1 to 5) on which they base their replies

multilateral /ˌmʌltiˈlæt(ə)rəl/ *adjective* between several parties ○ *a multilateral agreement* □ **multilateral trade** trade between several countries

multilevel marketing /mʌlti ˈlev(ə)l ˌmɑːkɪtɪŋ/ *noun* same as **network marketing**

multimagazine deal /ˌmʌltimægə-ˈziːn diːl/ *plural noun* a deal where different publishers offer advertisers the opportunity to buy space in their magazines at the same time

multimedia /ˌmʌltiˈmiːdiə/ *adjective* referring to several media used in a project ○ *We are going for an all-out multimedia advertising campaign.*

multimedia document /ˌmʌlti-ˈmiːdiə ˌdɒkjʊmənt/ *noun* an electronic document that contains interactive material from a range of different media such as text, video, sound, graphics, and animation

multinational /ˌmʌltiˈnæʃ(ə)nəl/ *noun* a company which has branches or subsidiary companies in several countries ○ *The company has been bought by one of the big multinationals.*

multi-pack offer /ˈmʌlti pæk ˌɒfə/ *noun* a special promotional offer in which an extra pack is offered free, or at a reduced price, for each pack bought at full price

multiple /ˈmʌltɪp(ə)l/ *adjective* many ■ *noun* a company with stores in several different towns

'…many independents took advantage of the bank holiday period when the big multiples were closed' [*The Grocer*]

'…the multiple brought the price down to £2.49 in some stores. We had not agreed to this deal and they sold out very rapidly. When they reordered we would not give it to them. This kind of activity is bad for the brand and we cannot afford it' [*The Grocer*]

multiple choice question /ˌmʌltɪp(ə)l ˈtʃɔɪs ˌkwetʃən/ *noun* a type of question used in a survey which allows the respondent to choose a single answer from several possible ones ○ *The questionnaire had eight multiple choice questions, two dichotomous questions and one open question.*

multiple correlation /ˌmʌltɪp(ə)l kɒrəˈleɪʃ(ə)n/ *noun* a method for measuring the effect of several independent variables on one dependent variable

multiple discriminant analysis /ˌmʌltɪp(ə)l dɪˈskrɪmɪnənt əˌnæləsɪs/ *noun* a method for assessing products by separating out their various attributes, and estimating the relative values of these attributes to different market segments. The whole process produces an assessment of the general potential of a product.

multiple pricing /ˌmʌltɪp(ə)l ˈpraɪsɪŋ/ *noun* the practice of fixing the same price for several different products

multiple regression analysis /ˌmʌltɪp(ə)l rɪˈgreʃ(ə)n əˌnæləsɪs/ *noun* a method for discovering the relationship between several independent variables and one dependent variable

multiple store /ˈmʌltɪp(ə)l stɔː/ *noun* one store in a chain of stores

multiplexing /ˈmʌltɪpleksɪŋ/ *noun* an arrangement where several TV channels are transmitted by one cable network, or where several messages are combined in the same transmission medium

multi-stage sample /mʌltɪ ˌsteɪdʒ ˈsɑːmpəl/ *noun* a sample selected by ensuring equal proportions of various categories existing in the population and then using random sampling to select respondents within these categories

multitasking /ˈmʌltitɑːskɪŋ/ *noun* performing several different tasks at the same time

mystery /ˈmɪst(ə)ri/ *noun* something which cannot be explained

mystery shopper /ˈmɪst(ə)ri ˌʃɒpə/ *noun* a person employed by a market-research company to visit shops anonymously to test the quality of service

mystery shopping /ˈmɪst(ə)ri ˌʃɒpɪŋ/ *noun* shopping done by anonymous employees of a market-research company to test staff reactions, etc.

N

naira /ˈnaɪrə/ *noun* currency used in Nigeria (NOTE: no plural; naira is usually written **N** before figures: **N2,000** say 'two thousand naira')

name /neɪm/ *noun* the word used for referring to a person, animal or thing ○ *I cannot remember the name of the managing director of Smith's Ltd.* ○ *His first name is John, but I am not sure of his other names.* □ **under the name of** using a particular name □ **trading under the name of 'Best Foods'** using the name 'Best Foods' as a commercial name, and not the name of the company

named /neɪmd/ *adjective* □ **the person named in the policy** the person whose name is given on an insurance policy as the person insured

narrowcasting /ˈnærəʊkɑːstɪŋ/ *noun* the act of reaching only a small special audience through an electronic medium such as cable television

nation /ˈneɪʃ(ə)n/ *noun* a country and the people living in it

national /ˈnæʃ(ə)nəl/ *adjective* referring to the whole of a particular country □ **national advertising** advertising in every part of a country, not just in the capital ○ *We took national advertising to promote our new 24-hour delivery service.* □ **national campaign** a sales or publicity campaign in every part of a country

national account /ˌnæʃ(ə)nəl əˈkaʊnt/ *noun* a customer with branches or offices all over the country

national advertiser /ˌnæʃ(ə)nəl ˈædvətaɪzə/ *noun* a company that advertises in every part of a country, not just in the capital city

national brand /ˈnæʃ(ə)nəl brænd/ *noun* a brand which is recognised throughout a whole country, not just in a local area

National Debt /ˌnæʃ(ə)nəl ˈdet/ *noun* money borrowed by a government

national income /ˌnæʃ(ə)nəl ˈɪnkʌm/ *noun* the value of income from the sales of goods and services in a country

nationalisation /ˌnæʃ(ə)nəlaɪˈzeɪʃ(ə)n/, **nationalization** *noun* the taking over of private industry by the state

national launch /ˌnæʃ(ə)nəl ˈlɔːntʃ/ *noun* a launch of a product over the whole country at the same time, as opposed to launching it in some areas only

national newspaper /ˌnæʃ(ə)nəl ˈnjuːzpeɪpə/ *noun* a newspaper which is sold throughout a whole country and carries national and international news

national press /ˌnæʃ(ə)nəl ˈpres/ *noun* newspapers which sell in all parts of the country ○ *The new car has been advertised in the national press.*

national retailer /ˌnæʃ(ə)nəl ˈriːteɪlə/ *noun* a retailing company which has branches throughout a country

nationwide /ˈneɪʃənwaɪd/ *adjective* all over a country ○ *We offer a nationwide delivery service.* ○ *The new car is being launched with a nationwide sales campaign.*

natural /ˈnætʃ(ə)rəl/ *adjective* **1.** found in the earth ○ *The offices are heated by natural gas.* **2.** not made by people ○ *They use only natural fibres for their best cloths.* **3.** normal ○ *It was only natural that the shopkeeper should feel annoyed when the hypermarket was built close to his shop.* ○ *It was natural for the workers to feel aggrieved when*

the management decided to change production methods without consultation.

natural break /ˌnætʃ(ə)rəl 'breɪk/ *noun* a convenient or reasonable point in a TV programme for a commercial break

natural resources /ˌnætʃ(ə)rəl rɪ-'zɔːsɪz/ *plural noun* raw materials which are found in the earth, e.g. coal, gas or iron

navigation /ˌnævɪ'geɪʃ(ə)n/ *noun* the action of guiding and steering, in particular the graphics which lead users to different websites

necessity /nə'sesɪti/ *noun* something which is vitally important, without which nothing can be done or no one can survive ○ *Being unemployed makes it difficult to afford even the basic necessities.* (NOTE: plural is **necessities**)

necessity product /nə'sesɪti ˌprɒdʌkt/ *noun* an ordinary everyday product which consumers tend not to buy much more of as their incomes rise ○ *Consumers find shopping for necessity products boring.* ○ *Fancy packaging will not increase sales of necessity products.*

negative /'negətɪv/ *adjective* meaning 'No' □ **the answer was in the negative** the answer was 'no'

negative cash flow /ˌnegətɪv 'kæʃ fləʊ/ *noun* a situation where more money is going out of a company than is coming in

negative demand /ˌnegətɪv dɪ-'mɑːnd/ *noun* firm decisions by consumers not to buy a particular product ○ *Negative demand was due to offensive advertising.*

negative variance /ˌnegətɪv 'veəriəns/ *noun* a difference between a financial plan and its outcome that means a less favourable profit than expected ○ *The unexpected increase in raw material prices meant a negative variance of $5000.* ○ *A sudden fall in revenue resulted in a negative variance for the year as a whole.*

negotiable /nɪ'gəʊʃiəb(ə)l/ *adjective* which can be transferred from one person to another or exchanged for cash □ **not negotiable** which cannot be ex-

changed for cash □ **'not negotiable'** words written on a cheque to show that it can be paid only to a specific person □ **negotiable cheque** a cheque made payable to bearer, i.e. to anyone who holds it

negotiable instrument /nɪ-ˌgəʊʃiəb(ə)l 'ɪnstrʊmənt/ *noun* a document which can be exchanged for cash, e.g. a bill of exchange or a cheque

negotiable paper /nɪˌgəʊʃiəb(ə)l 'peɪpə/ *noun* a document which can be transferred from one owner to another for cash

negotiate /nɪ'gəʊʃieɪt/ *verb* □ **to negotiate with someone** to discuss a problem formally with someone, so as to reach an agreement ○ *The management refused to negotiate with the union.* □ **to negotiate terms and conditions** *or* **to negotiate a contract** to discuss and agree the terms of a contract □ **he negotiated a £250,000 loan with the bank** he came to an agreement with the bank for a loan of £250,000

'…many of the large travel agency chains are able to negotiate even greater discounts' [*Duns Business Month*]

negotiated commission /nɪ-ˌgəʊʃieɪtɪd kə'mɪʃ(ə)n/ *noun* commission agreed with an advertising agency before work starts, and which may be different from standard commissions

negotiation /nɪˌgəʊʃi'eɪʃ(ə)n/ *noun* the discussion of terms and conditions in order to reach an agreement □ **contract under negotiation** a contract which is being discussed □ **a matter for negotiation** something which must be discussed before a decision is reached □ **to enter into negotiations** *or* **to start negotiations** to start discussing a problem □ **to resume negotiations** to start discussing a problem again, after talks have stopped for a time □ **to break off negotiations** to stop discussing a problem □ **to conduct negotiations** to negotiate □ **negotiations broke down after six hours** discussions stopped because no agreement was possible

'…after three days of tough negotiations, the company reached agreement with its 1,200 unionized workers' [*Toronto Star*]

negotiator /nɪ'gəʊʃieɪtə/ *noun* **1.** a person who discusses a problem with the aim of achieving agreement between different people or groups of people **2.** a person who works in an estate agency

nester /'nestə/ *noun* a person who has left the family home and is buying his or her own home

net /net/ *adjective* referring to a price, weight, pay, etc., after all deductions have been made ■ *verb* to make a true profit ○ *to net a profit of £10,000* (NOTE: **netting – netted**)

'...out of its earnings a company will pay a dividend. When shareholders receive this it will be net, that is it will have had tax deducted at 30 per cent' [*Investors Chronicle*]

net cash flow /net 'kæʃ fləʊ/ *noun* the difference between the money coming in and the money going out

net circulation /ˌnet ˌsɜːkjʊ-'leɪʃ(ə)n/ *noun* the total sales figure of a publication after adjusting for error and discounting unsold copies

net cover /net 'kʌvə/ *noun* the proportion of a target audience exposed to an advertisement at least once

net loss /net 'lɒs/ *noun* an actual loss, after deducting overheads

net margin /net 'mɑːdʒɪn/ *noun* the percentage difference between received price and all costs, including overheads

net names /net 'neɪmz/ *plural noun* the names left in a mailing list after a merge-purge has removed the duplicate entries

net national product /net ˌnæʃ(ə)nəl 'prɒdʌkt/ *noun* the gross national product less investment on capital goods and depreciation

net price /net 'praɪs/ *noun* the price of goods or services which cannot be reduced by a discount

net profit /net 'prɒfɪt/ *noun* the amount by which income from sales is larger than all expenditure

net reach /net 'riːtʃ/ *noun* the total number of people who have seen an advertisement at least once

net receipts /net rɪ'siːts/ *plural noun* receipts after deducting commission, tax, discounts, etc.

net sales /net 'seɪlz/ *plural noun* sales less damaged or returned items, discounts to retailers, etc.

net weight /net 'weɪt/ *noun* the weight of goods after deducting the packing material and container

network /'netwɜːk/ *noun* a system which links different points together ■ *verb* to link together in a network □ **to network a television programme** to send out the same television programme through several TV stations

network analysis /'netwɜːk əˌnæləsɪs/ *noun* an analysis of a project that charts the individual activities involved, each with the time needed for its completion, so that the timing of the whole can be planned and controlled

networked system /ˌnetwɜːkt 'sɪstəm/ *noun* a computer system where several PCs are linked together so that they all draw on the same database or use the same server

networking /'netwɜːkɪŋ/ *noun* keeping in contact with former colleagues, school friends, etc., so that all the members of the group can help each other in their careers

network marketing /'netwɜːk ˌmɑːkɪtɪŋ/ *noun* a marketing campaign carried out through a complete magazine network

network programming /'netwɜːk ˌprəʊgræmɪŋ/ *noun* the practice of scheduling TV programmes over the whole network

network society /'netwɜːk sə-ˌsaɪəti/ *noun* a society that regularly uses global networks for the purposes of work, communication, and government

net worth /net 'wɜːθ/ *adjective* the value of all the property of a person or company after taking away what the person or company owes ○ *The upmarket product is targeted at individuals of high net worth.*

net yield /net 'jiːld/ *noun* profit from investments after deduction of tax

neural network /ˌnjʊərəl 'netwɜːk/ *noun* a computer system designed to imitate the nerve patterns of the human brain

never-never /ˌnevə 'nevə/ *noun* buying on credit (*informal*) ○ *She bought her car on the never-never.*

new /njuː/ *adjective* recent or not old

new buy /njuː 'baɪ/ *noun* a type of organisational buying in which a completely new product is bought

new entrant /njuː 'entrənt/ *noun* a company which is going into a market for the first time

new issues department /njuː 'ɪʃuːz dɪˌpɑːtmənt/ *noun* the section of a bank which deals with issues of new shares

new product committee /njuː 'prɒdʌkt kəˌmɪti/ *noun* a group of people from different departments in a company who work together on a new product development project ○ *The new product committee met regularly to monitor the progress in the product's development.*

new product development /njuː 'prɒdʌkt dɪˌveləpmənt/ *noun* the process of developing completely new products or improving existing ones ○ *The company fell behind because it failed to invest enough in new product development.* Abbr **NPD**

news /njuːz/ *noun* information about things which have happened ○ *She always reads the business news or financial news first in the paper.* ○ *Financial markets were shocked by the news of the devaluation.*

news agency /'njuːz ˌeɪdʒənsi/ *noun* an office which distributes news to newspapers and television stations

new season /njuː 'siːz(ə)n/ *noun* the start of the TV 'year', usually taken to be the autumn and winter programming season

newsletter /'njuːzletə/ *noun* □ **company newsletter** a printed sheet or small newspaper giving news about a company

newspaper /'njuːzpeɪpə/ *noun* a regular publication, usually daily or weekly, which gives items of general news, sold to the general public

news release /'njuːz rɪˌliːs/ *noun* a sheet giving information about a new event which is sent to newspapers and TV and radio stations so that they can use it ○ *The company sent out a news release about the new product launch.*

news stand /'njuːz stænd/ *noun* a small wooden shop on a pavement, for selling newspapers

new technology /njuː tek'nɒlədʒi/ *noun* electronic devices which have recently been invented

next matter /nekst 'mætə/, **next-to-reading matter** /ˌnekst tə 'riːdɪŋ ˌmætə/ *noun* advertising material placed next to editorial matter in a publication

niche /niːʃ/ *noun* a special place in a market, occupied by one company (a 'niche company') ○ *They seem to have discovered a niche in the market.*

niche market /niːʃ 'mɑːkɪt/ *noun* small speciality market, where there is little competition

niche marketing /niːʃ 'mɑːkɪtɪŋ/ *noun* the promotion of a product aimed at one particular area of the market. ♦ **concentrated marketing**

Nielsen Index /'niːlsən ˌɪndeks/ an American publication belonging to A.C. Nielsen, with a number of different retail and wholesale audit services referring to various types of outlet and different areas of the country

night rate /'naɪt reɪt/ *noun* cheap rate for telephone calls at night

nixies /'nɪksiz/ *plural noun US* (*informal*) **1.** records that do not match a file correctly **2.** mail returned as unable to be delivered

no-change discount /nəʊ 'tʃeɪndʒ ˌdɪskaʊnt/ *noun* a reduction in the price of an advertisement which uses the same artwork as a previous one

noise /nɔɪz/ *noun* a random signal present in addition to any wanted signal, caused by static, temperature, power supply, magnetic or electric fields and also from stars and the sun

noise level /'nɔɪz ˌlev(ə)l/ *noun* the amount of unwanted information found when searching the Internet

nominal ledger /ˌnɒmɪn(ə)l 'ledʒə/ *noun* a book which records a company's

transactions in the various accounts (normally, all accounts except those relating to debtors, creditors and cash, which are kept in separate ledgers)

non- /nɒn/ *prefix* not

non-acceptance /ˌnɒn əkˈseptəns/ *noun* a situation in which the person who is to pay a bill of exchange does not accept it

non-business organisation /nɒn ˌbɪznɪs ˌɔːɡənaɪˈzeɪʃ(ə)n/ *noun US* an organisation (such as a club) which is not allowed by law to make a profit ○ *Though only a non-business organisation, the charity used highly sophisticated marketing techniques.* ○ *He became a fundraiser for a non-business organisation.*

non-delivery /nɒn dɪˈlɪv(ə)rɪ/ *noun* the failure to deliver goods that have been ordered

non-directive interview /nɒn daɪˈrektɪv ˌɪntəvjuː/, **non-directed interview** /nɒn daɪˈrektɪd ˌɪntəvjuː/ *noun* an interview in which the questions are not set in advance and no fixed pattern is followed ○ *Non-directed interviews give candidates a good chance to show their creative potential.*

non-durables /nɒn ˈdjʊərəb(ə)lz/, **non-durable goods** /nɒn ˈdjʊərəb(ə)l ɡʊdz/ *plural noun* goods which are used up soon after they have been bought, e.g. food or newspapers

non-franchise-building promotion /nɒn ˌfræntʃaɪz bɪldɪŋ prəˈməʊʃ(ə)nz/ *noun* sales promotion aimed at increasing sales in the short term, without increasing customer loyalty or repeat sales

non-negotiable instrument /nɒn nɪˌɡəʊʃəb(ə)l ˈɪnstrʊmənt/ *noun* a document which cannot be exchanged for cash, e.g. a crossed cheque

non-payment /nɒn ˈpeɪmənt/ *noun* □ **non-payment of a debt** the act of not paying a debt that is due

non-personal /nɒn ˈpɜːs(ə)n(ə)l/ *adjective* which does not apply to an individual person

non-personal channels /nɒn ˌpɜːs(ə)n(ə)l ˈtʃæn(ə)lz/ *plural noun*

channels that carry a message without involving any contact between the advertiser and an individual customer

non-price competition /nɒn ˈpraɪs kɒmpəˌtɪʃ(ə)n/ *noun* an attempt to compete in a market through other means than price such as quality of product and promotion

non-profit-making organisation /ˈnɒnˌprɒfɪtˈmeɪkɪŋ ɔːɡənaɪˈzeɪʃən/, **non-profit organisation** /nɒn ˈprɒfɪt ɔːɡənaɪˌzeɪʃ(ə)n/ *noun* an organisation (such as a club) which is not allowed by law to make a profit ○ *Non-profit-making organisations are exempted from tax.* (NOTE: Non-profit organisations include charities, professional associations, trade unions, and religious, arts, community, research, and campaigning bodies. The American English is **non-profit corporation**.)

non-refundable /nɒn rɪˈfʌndəb(ə)l/ *adjective* which will not be refunded ○ *You will be asked to make a non-refundable deposit.*

non-returnable /nɒn rɪˈtɜːnəb(ə)l/ *adjective* which cannot be returned

non-returnable packing /nɒn rɪˌtɜːnəb(ə)l ˈpækɪŋ/ *noun* packing which is to be thrown away when it has been used and not returned to the sender

non-statistical error /nɒn stəˌtɪstɪk(ə)l ˈerə/ *noun* a distortion of the results of a survey owing to bias and mistakes made in conducting the survey

non-store retailing /ˌnɒn stɔːˈriːteɪlɪŋ/ *noun* the selling of goods and services electronically without setting up a physical shop

non-traditional media /ˌnɒn trəˌdɪʃ(ə)n(ə)l ˈmiːdiə/ *noun* ◊ **support media**

non-verbal communication /nɒn ˌvɜːb(ə)l kəˌmjuːnɪˈkeɪʃ(ə)n/ *noun* any form of communication that is not expressed in words (NOTE: Non-verbal communication, which includes, for example, body language, silence, failure or slowness to respond to a message and lateness in arriving for a meeting, is estimated to make up 65–90% of all communication.)

no returns policy /nəʊ rɪ'tɜːnz ˌpɒlɪsi/ *noun* a trading policy where the supplier will not take back unsold merchandise in exchange for credit, and in return allows the retailer an extra discount

normal /'nɔːm(ə)l/ *adjective* usual or which happens regularly ○ *Normal deliveries are made on Tuesdays and Fridays.* ○ *Now that supply difficulties have been resolved we hope to resume normal service as soon as possible.* □ **under normal conditions** if things work in the usual way ○ *Under normal conditions a package takes two days to get to Copenhagen.*

normal distribution /ˌnɔːm(ə)l dɪstrɪ'bjuːʃ(ə)n/ *noun* a term used in sampling theory, referring to the results of a sample and meaning a symmetrical distribution of values around a mean or average, so that you can be confident that the sample is properly representative of the people being surveyed in a study

normal price /ˌnɔːm(ə)l 'praɪs/ *noun* the price that can be expected for a product under normal market conditions

normal product /ˌnɔːm(ə)l 'prɒdʌkt/ *noun* a product which people buy more of as their incomes rise and less of as their incomes fall

normal profit /ˌnɔːm(ə)l 'prɒfɪt/ *noun* a minimum profit that can motivate a business to carry on a type of production or selling

note /nəʊt/ *noun* a short letter or short piece of information ○ *to send someone a note* ○ *I left a note on her desk.* ■ *verb* to notice an advertisement in a publication but not necessarily read or understand it

notice /'nəʊtɪs/ *noun* **1.** an official warning that a contract is going to end or that terms are going to be changed □ **until further notice** until different instructions are given ○ *You must pay*

£200 *on the 30th of each month until further notice.* **2.** the time allowed before something takes place □ **at short notice** with very little warning ○ *The bank manager will not see anyone at short notice.* □ **you must give seven days' notice of withdrawal** you must ask to take money out of the account seven days before you want it

noticeboard /'nəʊtɪsbɔːd/ *noun* a board fixed to a wall where notices can be put up ○ *Did you see the new list of prices on the noticeboard?*

noting /'nəʊtɪŋ/ *noun* the act of noticing, though not necessarily reading and understanding, an advertisement in a publication

noting score /'nəʊtɪŋ skɔː/ *noun* the percentage of total readers who note an advertisement ○ *The amount of advertising we will need to do depends on the anticipated noting score.*

novelty /'nɒv(ə)lti/ *noun* an original amusing article which is often bought as a gift ○ *A novelty shop provided paper hats for parties.*

NPD *abbr* new product development

null /nʌl/ *adjective* **1.** with no meaning **2.** which cannot be enforced □ **the contract was declared null and void** the contract was said to be not valid □ **to render a decision null** to make a decision useless or to cancel it

nullification /ˌnʌlɪfɪ'keɪʃ(ə)n/ *noun* an act of making something invalid

nullify /'nʌlɪfaɪ/ *verb* to make something invalid or to cancel something (NOTE: **nullifying- nullified**)

numeric /njuː'merɪk/, **numerical** /njuː'merɪk(ə)l/ *adjective* referring to numbers □ **in numerical order** in the order of figures, e.g. 1 before 2, 33 before 34 ○ *File these invoices in numerical order.*

numeric data /njuːˌmerɪk 'deɪtə/ *noun* data in the form of figures

O

O & M *abbr* organisation and methods

objective /əb'dʒektɪv/ *noun* something which you hope to achieve ○ *The company has achieved its objectives.* ○ *We set the sales forces specific objectives.* ■ *adjective* considered from a general point of view rather than from that of the person involved ○ *You must be objective in assessing the performance of the staff.* ○ *They have been asked to carry out an objective survey of the market.*

objective and task method /əb,dʒektɪv 'meθəd/ *noun* a method of calculating an advertising appropriation by setting objectives, deciding what tasks are needed to achieve them and then calculating the actual costs involved

obligation /ˌɒblɪ'ɡeɪʃ(ə)n/ *noun* **1.** a duty to do something ○ *There is no obligation to buy.* □ **two weeks' free trial without obligation** the customer can try the item at home for two weeks without having to buy it at the end of the test □ **to be under an obligation to do something** to feel it is your duty to do something □ **he is under no contractual obligation to buy** he has signed no contract which forces him to buy **2.** a debt □ **to meet your obligations** to pay your debts

observation method /ɒbzə'veɪʃən ˌmeθəd/, **observational research** /ˌɒbzə,veɪʃən(ə)l rɪ'sɜːtʃ/ *noun* a market research method that obtains information through personal observation, rather than interviews ○ *The observation method does not tell you anything about the consumers' attitudes to the product.*

obsolescence /ˌɒbsə'les(ə)ns/ *noun* the process of a product going out of date because of progress in design or technology, and therefore becoming less useful or valuable

obsolescent /ˌɒbsə'les(ə)nt/ *adjective* becoming out of date

obsolete /'ɒbsəliːt/ *adjective* no longer used ○ *Computer technology changes so fast that hardware soon becomes obsolete.*

odd /ɒd/ *adjective* one of a group □ **we have a few odd boxes left** we have a few boxes left out of the total shipment □ **to do odd jobs** to do various pieces of work

odd-even pricing /ɒd 'iːv(ə)n ˌpraɪsɪŋ/ *noun* the practice of using odd numbers such as 0.95 or 0.99 or even numbers such as 1.00 or 2.50 when pricing, because this seems to be most effective psychologically in persuading customers to buy ○ *Students can study the psychological bases of odd-even pricing.*

odd lot /ɒd 'lɒt/ *noun* a group of miscellaneous items for sale at an auction

oddments /'ɒdmənts/ *plural noun* **1.** items left over **2.** pieces of large items sold separately

odd number /ɒd 'nʌmbəz/ *noun* numbers which cannot be divided by two, e.g. 17 or 33 ○ *Buildings with odd numbers are on the south side of the street*

odd size /ɒd 'saɪz/ *noun* a size which is not usual

off /ɒf/ *adverb* **1.** not working or not in operation ○ *The agreement is off.* ○ *They called the strike off.* **2.** lower than a previous price ○ *The shares closed 2% off.* ○ *We give 5% off for quick settlement.* ■ *preposition* subtracted from ○

/'ɒpəreɪt/ *verb* **1.** to be in ... *The new terms of service will ... from January 1st.* ○ *The rules ... on inland postal services only.* ... something work or function ... **rate a machine** to make a ma- ... ork ○ *He is learning to operate ... telephone switchboard.*

... company gets valuable restaurant ... which will be converted to the ... yle restaurant chain that it operates and ... s throughout most parts of the US' ...]

...ing /'ɒpəreɪtɪŋ/ *noun* the gen- ...nning of a business or of a ...

... company blamed over-capacity and ...tive market conditions in Europe for a ...erating loss last year' [*Financial Times*]

...ing budget /'ɒpəreɪtɪŋ / *noun* a forecast of income and ...ture over a period of time

...ing manual /'ɒpəreɪtɪŋ ...əl/ *noun* a book which shows ... work a machine

...ting statement /'ɒpəreɪtɪŋ ...ənt/ *noun* a financial statement ...shows a company's expenditure ...ome and consequently its final ...r loss ○ *The operating statement ... unexpected electricity costs.* ○ ...ook at the operating statement to ...t month's expenditure.

...ting supplies /'ɒpəreɪtɪŋ sə- ...*plural noun* low-priced industrial ...ts that are normally bought by ...ers ○ *Production came to a ...ill for lack of operating supplies. ...are now ordering operating sup- ...r next month's production.*

...ating system /'ɒpəreɪtɪŋ ...m/ *noun* the main program which ...es a computer

...ation /ˌɒpəˈreɪʃ(ə)n/ *noun* busi- ...rganisation and work ○ *the com- ...s operations in West Africa* ○ *He ...up the operations in Northern ...e.*

... leading manufacturer of business, ...trial and commercial products requires a ...h manager to head up its mid-western ...da operations based in Winnipeg' ...e and Mail (Toronto)]

operational /ˌɒpəˈreɪʃ(ə)nəl/ *adjective* **1.** referring to how something works **2.** working or in operation

operational budget /ˌɒpəreɪʃ(ə)nəl 'bʌdʒɪt/ *noun* a forecast of expenditure on running a business

operational costs /ˌɒpəreɪʃ(ə)nəl 'kɒsts/ *plural noun* the costs of running a business

operational planning /ˌɒpəreɪʃ(ə)nəl 'plænɪŋ/ *noun* the planning of how a business is to be run

operational research /ˌɒpəreɪʃ(ə)nəl rɪ'sɜːtʃ/ *noun* a study of a company's way of working to see if it can be made more efficient and profitable

operations review /ˌɒpəreɪʃ(ə)z rɪ'vjuː/ *noun* examining the way in which a company or department works to see how it can be made more efficient and profitable

opinion-former /ə'pɪnjən ˌfɔːmə/, **opinion-leader** /ə'pɪnjən ˌliːdə/ *noun* someone well known whose opinions influence others in society ○ *A pop-star is the ideal opinion-leader if we are aiming at the teenage market.* ○ *The celebrity used in the sales promotion campaign was not respected enough to be a true opinion-former.*

opinion-leader research /ə'pɪnjən liːdə rɪ'sɜːtʃ/ *noun* research into the attitudes of opinion-leaders

opinion poll /ə'pɪnjən 'pəʊl/ *noun* asking a sample group of people what their opinion is, so as to guess the opinion of the whole population ○ *Opinion polls showed that the public preferred butter to margarine.* ○ *Before starting the new service, the company carried out nationwide opinion polls.*

opinion shopping /ə'pɪnjən ˌʃɒpɪŋ/ *noun* the practice of trying to find an auditor who interprets the law in the same way that the company does, is likely to view the company's actions sympathetically and will approve the company's financial statements, even if the company has been involved in dealings that other auditors might consider questionable

to take £25 off the price ○ *We give 10% off our normal prices.*

'...its stock closed Monday at $21.875 a share in NYSE composite trading, off 56% from its high last July' [*Wall Street Journal*]

off-card rate /ɒf 'kɑːd reɪt/ *noun* a specially arranged price, lower than that on the rate card, for advertising space or time ○ *The newspaper offered us an off-card rate for space which was still empty the day before publication.*

offensive spending /ə,fensɪv 'spendɪŋ/ *noun* spending on advertising which aims to attract users of a rival brand or to attack the competition

offer /'ɒfə/ *noun* **1.** a statement that you are willing to pay a specific amount of money to buy something ○ *to make an offer for a company* ○ *We made an offer of £10 a share.* ○ *We made a written offer for the house.* ○ *£1,000 is the best offer I can make.* ○ *We accepted an offer of £1,000 for the car.* □ **the house is under offer** someone has made an offer to buy the house and the offer has been accepted provisionally □ **we are open to offers** we are ready to discuss the price which we are asking □ **or near offer** *or* **or best offer** *US* or an offer of a price which is slightly less than the price asked ○ *The car is for sale at £2,000 or near offer.* **2.** a statement that you are willing to sell something □ **offer for sale** a situation where a company advertises new shares for sale to the public as a way of launching the company on the Stock Exchange. The other ways of launching a company are a 'tender' or a 'placing'. **3.** □ **She received six offers of jobs/six job offers** six companies told her she could have a job with them ■ *verb* **1.** to say that you are willing to pay a specific amount of money for something ○ *to offer someone £100,000 for their house* ○ *She offered £10 a share.* **2.** to say that you are willing to sell something ○ *We offered the house for sale.* ○ *They are offering special prices on winter holidays in the USA.*

Office of Fair Trading /ˌɒfɪs əv feə 'treɪdɪŋ/ *noun* a government department which protects consumers against unfair or illegal business. Abbr **OFT**

official receiver /əˌfɪʃ(ə)l rɪ'siːvə/ *noun* a government official who is appointed to run a company which is in financial difficulties, to pay off its debts as far as possible, and to close it down ○ *The court appointed a receiver for the company.* ○ *The company is in the hands of the receiver.*

off-licence /'ɒf ˌlaɪs(ə)ns/ *noun* **1.** a shop which sells alcohol for drinking at home **2.** a licence to sell alcohol for drinking away from the place where you buy it

offload /ɒf'ləʊd/ *verb* to pass something which you do not want to someone else □ **to offload excess stock** to try to sell excess stock □ **to offload costs onto a subsidiary company** to try to get a subsidiary company to pay some charges so as to reduce tax

off-peak /ɒf 'piːk/ *adjective* not during the most busy time

off-peak period /ɒf 'piːk ˌpɪəriəd/ *noun* the time when business is less busy

off-price label /ɒf 'praɪs ˌleɪb(ə)l/ *noun* a label on a product which shows a reduced price

off-season *noun* /'ɒf ˌsiːz(ə)n/ the less busy season for travel, usually during the winter ○ *Air fares are cheaper in the off-season.*

offset /'ɒfset/ *noun* a method of printing from a plate to a rubber surface and then to paper

offset lithography /ˌɒfset lɪ'θɒgrəfi/ *noun* a printing process used for printing books, where the ink sticks to image areas on the plate and is transferred to an offset cylinder from which it is printed on to the paper

off-the-page buying /ˌɒf ðə 'peɪdʒ ˌbaɪɪŋ/ *noun* the buying of items which have been advertised in magazines or newspapers

off-the-peg /ɒf ðə 'peg/ *adjective*, *adverb* ready made in standard sizes, and not fitted specially ○ *She buys all her clothes off-the-peg.*

off-the-peg research /ɒf ðə peg rɪ'sɜːtʃ/ *noun* the practice of taking research which has already been carried

out in another context, and using it as the basis for taking particular decisions

oil-exporting country /'ɔɪl ɪk-ˌspɔːtɪŋ ˌkʌntri/ *noun* country which produces oil and sells it to others

oligopoly /ɒlɪ'gɒpəli/ *noun* a situation where only a few sellers control the market ○ *An oligopoly means that prices can be kept high.*

oligopsony /ɒlɪ'gɒpsəni/ *noun* a situation where only a few buyers control the market

omnibus advertisement /'ɒmnɪbəs ədˌvɜːtɪsmənt/ *noun* an advertisement which covers several different products

omnibus agreement /'ɒmnɪbəs əˌgriːmənt/ *noun* an agreement which covers many different items

omnibus research /'ɒmnɪbəs rɪ-ˌsɜːtʃ/, **omnibus survey** /'ɒmnɪbəs ˌsɜːveɪ/ *noun* a survey to which several companies subscribe, each adding specific questions of its own

oncosts /'ɒnkɒsts/ *plural noun* money spent in producing a product which does not rise with the quantity of the product made (NOTE: also called **fixed costs**)

one-sided /wʌn 'saɪdɪd/ *adjective* which favours one side and not the other in a negotiation ○ *a one-sided agreement*

one-sided message /wʌn ˌsaɪdɪd 'mesɪdʒ/ *noun* a message which only gives the benefits of a product or service

one-step approach /ˌwʌn step ə'prəʊtʃ/ *noun* a form of direct marketing where advertisements are used to obtain orders directly

one-stop /ˌwʌn stɒp 'ʃɒpɪŋ/ *adjective* offering a wide range of services to a customer, not necessarily services which are related to the product or services which the company normally sells

one-stop shopping centre /ˌwʌn stɒp 'ʃɒpɪŋ ˌsentə/ *noun* a shopping centre with a comprehensive choice of shops and supermarkets, designed to cover all of a customer's shopping needs

one-time order /ˌwʌn taɪm 'ɔːdə/ *noun* an order for an advertising spot for a particular time which is not scheduled to be repeated

one-time rate /wʌn 'taɪm reɪt/ *noun* a special rate for an advertisement that is only placed once

one-to-one /ˌwʌn tə 'wʌn/ *adjective* where one person has to deal with one other person only

one-to-one marketing /ˌwʌn tə wʌn 'mɑːkɪtɪŋ/ *noun* marketing through a website which aims to establish a personal relationship with a customer, selling to each customer as an individual and trying to differentiate between customers

on-hold advertising /ɒn 'həʊld ˌædvətaɪzɪŋ/ *noun* advertising to telephone callers while they are waiting to be connected to the person they want to speak to, usually involving voice messages about the firm and its products

online /ɒn'laɪn/ *adverb* linked directly to a mainframe computer ○ *The sales office is online to the warehouse.* ○ *We get our data online from the stock control department.*

'...there may be a silver lining for 'clicks-and-mortar' stores that have both an online and a high street presence. Many of these are accepting returns of goods purchased online at their traditional stores. This is a service that may make them more popular as consumers become more experienced online shoppers' [*Financial Times*]

online shopping /ˌɒnlaɪn 'ʃɒpɪŋ/ *noun* same as **electronic shopping**

online shopping mall /ˌɒnlaɪn 'ʃɒpɪŋ mɔːl/ *noun* same as **cyber mall**

on-pack promotion /ɒn 'pæk prə-ˌməʊʃ(ə)n/ *noun* advertising material on the outside of packaged goods ○ *We use on-pack promotion to stimulate buying at the point-of-sale.* ○ *Our on-pack promotion is designed to complement the TV advertising campaign.*

op-ed /ɒp 'ed/ *noun* in a newspaper, a page that has signed articles expressing personal opinions, usually found opposite the editorial page

open /'əʊpən/ *adjective* ready to accept something □ **the job is open to all applicants** anyone can apply for the job

□ **open to offers** ready to accept a reasonable offer □ **the company is open to offers for the empty factory** the company is ready to discuss an offer which is lower than the suggested price ■ *verb* to start a new business ○ *She has opened a shop in the High Street.* ○ *We have opened a branch in London.*

open account /ˌəʊpən ə'kaʊnt/ *noun* an account where the supplier offers the purchaser credit without security

open-air market /ˌəʊpən eə 'mɑːkɪt/ *noun* a market which is held on stalls in the open air

open communication /ˌəʊpən kəmjuːnɪ'keɪʃ(ə)n/ *noun* a policy intended to ensure that employees are able to find out everything they want to know about their organisation

open credit /ˌəʊpən 'kredɪt/ *noun* credit given to good customers without security

open dating /ˌəʊpən 'deɪtɪŋ/ *noun* the practice of putting the sell-by date on a packet in an uncoded form which can be understood by the consumers ○ *Open dating is considered by many to be an important feature of consumer protection in food products.*

open-door policy /ˌəʊpən 'dɔː ˌpɒlɪsi/ *noun* policy in which a country accepts imports from all other countries on equal terms

open-ended /ˌəʊpən 'endɪd/ *adjective* with no fixed limit or with some items not specified ○ *They signed an open-ended agreement.* ○ *The candidate was offered an open-ended contract with a good career plan.* (NOTE: American English is **open-end**)

open-ended question /ˌəʊpən endɪd 'kwestʃən/ *noun* a question in a questionnaire which allows respondents to answer in some detail as they like without having simply to say 'yes' or 'no' ○ *Open-ended questions elicit answers that are original but hard to evaluate.* ○ *An open-ended question is needed here, since the question involves the respondent's personal feelings.*

open general licence /ˌəʊpən ˌdʒen(ə)rəl 'laɪs(ə)ns/ *noun* an import

licence for a
to special im

opening /'ə
of starting a n
of a new bran
market or *of a*
2. opportunity
tive being at t
of several

opening
ˌbæləns/ *nour*
ning of an acco

opening bid
the first bid at a

opening ent
noun the first e

opening hou
plural noun hou
ness is open

opening se
'sentəns/ *noun*
email

opening sto
noun the stock
of an accounting

open market /
a market where a

open pricing /
the attempt by
some cooperatio
pricing ○ *Repres*
jor companies in
ing to establish an

open rate /'əʊp
vertising rate whe
able for frequent o

open standard
noun a standard f
lated products th
equipment from di
to operate with eac

open up /ˌəʊpən
up new markets t
ness in markets whe
not been done befor

operant condit
kənˌdɪʃ(ə)nɪŋ/ *nou*
stating that behavio
by stimuli and also b
which follow on f
itself

operat
force ○
operate
operate
2. to m
□ **to op**
chine w
the new

'...the
locatio
family
franch
[*Fortu*

opera
eral r
machi

'...the
compe
£14m

opera
ˌbʌdʒ
expen

oper
ˌmæn
how t

oper
ˌsteɪt
which
and i
profit
shows
Let's
find l

oper
ˌplaɪ
prod
prod
stanc
○ *W*
plies

ope
ˌsɪst
oper

ope
ness
pany
head
Euro

'..
ind
bra
Ca
[G

opportunities to see /ˌɒpəˌtjuːnɪtiz tə ˈsiː/ *plural noun* the number of opportunities an average member of the target audience will have to see an advertisement. Abbr **OTS**

opportunity /ˌɒpəˈtjuːnɪti/ *noun* the chance to do something successfully

'…the group is currently undergoing a period of rapid expansion and this has created an exciting opportunity for a qualified accountant' [*Financial Times*]

opportunity and threat analysis /ˌɒpəˌtjuːnɪti ən ˈθret əˌnæləsɪs/ *noun* a company's analysis of both the advantages and disadvantages in its situation, done in order to ensure sound strategic planning

opportunity cost /ˌɒpəˈtjuːnɪti kɒst/ *noun* the cost of a business initiative in terms of profits that could have been gained through an alternative plan ○ *It's a good investment plan and we will not be deterred by the opportunity cost.*

optimal /ˈɒptɪm(ə)l/ *adjective* best

optimal balance /ˌɒptɪm(ə)l ˈbæləns/ *noun* the best combination of elements or activities that can be achieved in a marketing mix ○ *If it achieves optimal balance the company will soon be a market leader.*

opt-in /ˈɒpt ɪn/ *noun* a process that requires people who want to receive information or services for a website to do something that shows they have actively chosen to do so, before the website owner can send them email

opt-in mailing list /ˌɒpt ɪn ˈmeɪlɪŋ lɪst/ *noun* a list of email addresses in which each recipient has specifically asked to receive advertising email messages, normally so that they can keep up to date with a topic or industry

option /ˈɒpʃən/ *noun* the opportunity to buy or sell something within a fixed period of time at a fixed price □ **to have first option on something** to have the right to be the first to have the possibility of deciding something □ **to grant someone a six-month option on a product** to allow someone six months to decide if they want to be the agent or if they want to manufacture the product, etc. □ **to take up an option** *or* **to exer-**

cise an option to accept the option which has been offered and to put it into action ○ *They exercised their option* or *they took up their option to acquire sole marketing rights to the product.* □ **I want to leave my options open** I want to be able to decide what to do when the time is right

optional /ˈɒpʃən(ə)l/ *adjective* which can be added if the customer wants ○ *The insurance cover is optional.*

optional extra /ˌɒpʃən(ə)l ˈekstrə/ *noun* an item that is not essential but can be added if wanted

opt out /ˈɒpt ˈaʊt/ *noun* the action of asking not to receive advertising email messages and being removed from an email list

OR *abbr* operational research

Oracle /ˈɒrək(ə)l/ a UK teletext service broadcast by the IBA

orange goods /ˈɒrɪndʒ ɡʊdz/ *plural noun* goods which are not bought as often as fast-moving items but are replaced from time to time, e.g. clothing. Compare **red goods, yellow goods**

orbit /ˈɔːbɪt/ *noun* the practice of rotating advertisements among different programmes on a TV station

order /ˈɔːdə/ *noun* **1.** an official request for goods to be supplied ○ *to give someone an order* or *to place an order with someone for twenty filing cabinets* □ **to fill an order** *or* **to fulfil an order** to supply items which have been ordered ○ *We are so understaffed we cannot fulfil any more orders before Christmas.* □ **items available to order only** items which will be manufactured only if someone orders them □ **on order** ordered but not delivered ○ *This item is out of stock, but is on order.* **2.** an item which has been ordered ○ *The order is to be delivered to our warehouse.* **3.** an instruction **4.** a document which allows money to be paid to someone ○ *She sent us an order on the Chartered Bank.* **5.** □ **pay to Mr Smith or order** pay money to Mr Smith or as he orders □ **pay to the order of Mr Smith** pay money directly to Mr Smith or to his account ■ *verb* **1.** to ask for goods to be supplied ○ *They ordered a new Rolls Royce for the man-*

aging director. **2.** to instruct ○ *to order twenty filing cabinets to be delivered to the warehouse*

order book /ˈɔːdə bʊk/ *noun* a book which records orders received

order confirmation /ˈɔːdə kɒnfˌmeɪʃ(ə)n/ *noun* an email message informing a purchaser that an order has been received

order form /ˈɔːdə fɔːm/ *noun* a pad of blank forms for orders to be written on

order fulfilment /ˈɔːdə fʊlˌfɪlmənt/ *noun* supplying items which have been ordered

order number /ˈɔːdə ˌnʌmbə/ *noun* the reference number printed on an order

order picking /ˈɔːdə ˌpɪkɪŋ/ *noun* the process of collecting various items in a warehouse in order to make up an order to be sent to a customer

order taking /ˈɔːdə ˌteɪkɪŋ/ *noun* the action of taking an order, the main responsibility of the salesperson

organisation /ˌɔːɡənaɪˈzeɪʃ(ə)n/, **organization** *noun* **1.** a way of arranging something so that it works efficiently ○ *the organisation of the head office into departments* ○ *The chairman handles the organisation of the AGM.* ○ *The organisation of the group is too centralised to be efficient.* **2.** a group or institution which is arranged for efficient work

'...working with a client base which includes many major commercial organizations and nationalized industries' [*Times*]

organisational buying /ˌɔːɡənaɪˈzeɪʃ(ə)nəl ˌbaɪɪŋ/ *noun* buying by a large organisation, such as a company or government department, as opposed to purchases by individual consumers

organisation chart /ˌɔːɡənaɪˈzeɪʃ(ə)n tʃɑːt/ *noun* a diagram showing how a company or an office is organised

organise /ˈɔːɡənaɪz/, **organize** *verb* to set up a system for doing something ○ *the company is organised into six profit centres* ○ *the group is organised by sales areas*

'...we organize a rate with importers who have large orders and guarantee them space at a fixed rate so that they can plan their costs' [*Lloyd's List*]

'...governments are coming under increasing pressure from politicians, organized labour and business to stimulate economic growth' [*Duns Business Month*]

organised market /ˌɔːɡənaɪzd ˈmɑːkɪt/ *noun* a market controlled by regulations set down by government or an official organisation ○ *The government feels that an organised market is not conducive to business initiative.*

organisation and methods /ˌɔːɡənaɪˌzeɪʃ(ə)n ən ˈmeθədz/ *noun* a process of examining how an office works, and suggesting how it can be made more efficient. Abbr **O & M**

orientation /ˌɔːriənˈteɪʃ(ə)n/ *noun* the main interest or type of activity ○ *The company's orientation is towards production and it has little marketing experience.*

oriented /ˈɔːrientɪd/, **orientated** /ˈɔːriənˌteɪtɪd/ *adjective* interested in or involved with ○ *Our strategy is oriented towards achieving further growth in the export market.* ○ *The promotion is entirely product-oriented.*

origin /ˈɒrɪdʒɪn/ *noun* the place where something or someone originally comes from ○ *spare parts of European origin*

original /əˈrɪdʒən(ə)l/ *adjective* which was used or made first ○ *They sent a copy of the original invoice.* ○ *He kept the original receipt for reference.* ■ *noun* the first copy made ○ *Send the original and file two copies.*

originally /əˈrɪdʒən(ə)li/ *adverb* first or at the beginning

original purchase /əˌrɪdʒən(ə)l ˈpɜːtʃɪs/ *noun* a copy of a magazine or newspaper which is actually bought by the reader, rather than simply read by them

OS *abbr* outsize

O/S *abbr* out of stock

OTO *abbr* one time only

OTS *abbr* opportunities to see

outbid /aʊtˈbɪd/ *verb* to offer a better price than someone else ○ *We offered £100,000 for the warehouse, but an-*

other company outbid us. (NOTE: **out-bidding – outbid**)

outdoor /aʊtˈdɔː/ *adjective* in the open air

outdoor advertising /ˌaʊtdɔːr ˈædvətaɪzɪŋ/ *noun* **1.** advertising on the outside of a building or in the open air, using posters on hoardings or neon signs **2.** advertising in the open air, including advertising in public transport, on roadsides, at bus stops, skywriting, etc.

outer /ˈaʊtə/ *noun* a piece of packaging which covers items which already are in packages

outer pack /ˈaʊtə pæk/ *noun* a container which holds a number of smaller packaged items ○ *The goods are sold in outer packs, each containing twenty packets.*

outlet /ˈaʊtlet/ *noun* a place where something can be sold

out-of-date /ˌaʊt əv ˈdeɪt/ *adjective, adverb* old-fashioned or no longer modern ○ *Their computer system is years out of date.* ○ *They're still using out-of-date equipment.*

out-of-home advertising /ˌaʊt əv həʊm ˈædvətaɪzɪŋ/ *noun* outdoor advertising including transport, skywriting, etc.

out of stock /aʊt əv ˈstɒk/ *adjective, adverb* with no stock left ○ *Those books are temporarily out of stock.* ○ *Several out-of-stock items have been on order for weeks.* Abbr **O/S**

output /ˈaʊtpʊt/ *noun* the amount which a company, person or machine produces ○ *Output has increased by 10%.* ○ *25% of our output is exported.*

'…crude oil output plunged during the last month and is likely to remain near its present level for the near future' [*Wall Street Journal*]

output bonus /ˈaʊtpʊt ˌbəʊnəs/, **output-based bonus** /ˌaʊtpʊt beɪst ˈbəʊnəs/ *noun* an extra payment for increased production

output per hour /ˌaʊtpʊt pər ˈaʊə/ *noun* the amount of something produced in one hour

output tax /ˈaʊtpʊt tæks/ *noun* VAT charged by a company on goods or services sold, and which the company pays to the government

outsell /aʊtˈsel/ *verb* to sell more than someone ○ *The company is easily outselling its competitors.* (NOTE: **outselling – outsold**)

outside broadcast /ˌaʊtsaɪd ˈbrɔːdkɑːst/ *noun* a programme not transmitted from a studio

outside director /ˌaʊtsaɪd daɪˈrektə/ *noun* a director who is not employed by the company, a non-executive director

outside poster /ˌaʊtsaɪd ˈpəʊstəz/ *noun* a poster on public transport such as buses, taxis, trains and the underground

outsize /ˈaʊtsaɪz/ *noun* a size which is larger than usual. Abbr **OS** □ **outsize order** a very large order

outsource /ˈaʊtˌsɔːs/ *verb* to use a source outside a company or business to do the work that is needed

outsourcing /ˈaʊtsɔːsɪŋ/ *noun* the transfer of work previously done by employees of an organisation to another organisation, usually one that specialises in that type of work (NOTE: Things that have usually been outsourced in the past include legal services, transport, catering, and security, but nowadays IT services, training, and public relations are often added to the list.)

'…organizations in the public and private sectors are increasingly buying in specialist services – or outsourcing – allowing them to cut costs and concentrate on their core business activities' [*Financial Times*]

outstanding /aʊtˈstændɪŋ/ *adjective* not yet paid or completed □ **outstanding debts** debts which are waiting to be paid □ **outstanding orders** orders received but not yet supplied □ **what is the amount outstanding?** how much money is still owed? □ **matters outstanding from the previous meeting** questions which were not settled at previous meeting

outward mission /ˌaʊtwəd ˈmɪʃ(ə)n/ *noun* a visit by a group of businesspeople to a foreign country

over- /əʊvə/ *prefix* more than □ **shop which caters to the over-60s** a shop which has goods which appeal to people who are more than sixty years old

overall /ˌəʊvərˈɔːl/ *adjective* covering or including everything □ **the company reported an overall fall in profits** the company reported a general fall in profits □ **overall plan** a plan which covers everything

overcharge *noun* /ˈəʊvətʃɑːdʒ/ a charge which is higher than it should be ○ *to pay back an overcharge* ■ *verb* /ˌəʊvəˈtʃɑːdʒ/ to ask too much money ○ *They overcharged us for our meals.* ○ *We asked for a refund because we'd been overcharged.*

overhead budget /ˌəʊvəhed ˈbʌdʒɪt/ *noun* a plan of probable overhead costs

overhead costs /ˌəʊvəhed ˈkɒsts/, **overhead expenses** /ˌəʊvəhed ɪkˈspensɪz/ *plural noun* money spent on the day-to-day cost of a business

overheads /ˈəʊvəhedz/ *plural noun* the costs of the day-to-day running of a business ○ *The sales revenue covers the manufacturing costs but not the overheads.* (NOTE: American English is usually **overhead**.)

'…it ties up less capital in inventory and with its huge volume spreads out costs over bigger sales; add in low overhead (i.e. minimum staff, no deliveries, no credit cards) and a warehouse club can offer bargain prices' [*Duns Business Month*]

overkill /ˈəʊvəkɪl/ *noun* a very intensive and expensive marketing campaign which has the effect of putting potential customers off

overlay /ˌəʊvəˈleɪ/ *noun* a transparent plastic sheet placed over artwork with instructions for changing it, or showing the artwork is to be printed

overmatter /ˈəʊvəmætə/, **oversetting** /ˈəʊvəsetɪŋ/ *noun* text which, when it is typeset, is too long for the space available

overpayment /ˌəʊvəˈpeɪmənt/ *noun* an act of paying too much

overprice /ˌəʊvəˈpraɪs/ *verb* to give a higher price to something than seems reasonable

overpricing /ˌəʊvəˈpraɪsɪŋ/ *noun* the charging of a higher price than is justified by demand ○ *Overpricing led to the producer being priced out of the market.*

overprint /ˌəʊvəˈprɪnt/ *verb* to print text on paper which already contains printed matter ○ *The retailer's name and address is overprinted on the catalogue.* ○ *We will overprint the catalogue with the retailer's name and address.*

overproduce /ˌəʊvəprəˈdjuːs/ *verb* to produce too much of a product

overproduction /ˌəʊvəprəˈdʌkʃən/ *noun* the manufacturing of too much of a product

overrider /ˈəʊvəraɪdə/, **overriding commission** /ˈəʊvəraɪdɪŋ kəˈmɪʃ(ə)n/ *noun* a special extra commission which is above all other commissions

overseas *adjective* /ˈəʊvəsiːz/ across the sea or to foreign countries ○ *Management trainees knew that they would be sent overseas to learn about the export markets.* ○ *Some workers are going overseas to find new jobs.* □ **overseas markets** markets in foreign countries □ **overseas trade** trade with foreign countries ■ *noun* foreign countries ○ *The profits from overseas are far higher than those of the home division.*

overseas call /ˌəʊvəsiːz ˈkɔːl/ *noun* a call to another country

overseas division /ˌəʊvəsiːz dɪˈvɪʒ(ə)n/ *noun* the section of a company dealing with trade with other countries

oversell /ˌəʊvəˈsel/ *verb* to sell more than you can produce □ **he is oversold** he has agreed to sell more product than he can produce □ **the market is oversold** stock-market prices are too low, because there have been too many sellers

overspend /ˌəʊvəˈspend/ *verb* to spend too much

overstock /ˌəʊvəˈstɒk/ *verb* to have more stock than is needed □ **to be overstocked with spare parts** to have too many spare parts in stock

overstocks /ˈəʊvəstɒks/ *plural noun* US more stock than is needed to supply orders ○ *We will have to sell off the overstocks to make room in the warehouse.*

over-the-counter sales /ˌəʊvə ðə ˈkaʊntə ˌseɪlz/ *plural noun* the legal

selling of shares which are not listed in the official Stock Exchange list, usually carried out by telephone

overweight /ˌəʊvəˈweɪt/ *adjective* □ **the package is sixty grams overweight** the package weighs sixty grams too much

'Cash paid for your stock: any quantity, any products, overstocked lines, factory seconds' [*Australian Financial Review*]

own brand /ˈəʊn brænd/ *noun* the name of a store which is used on products which are specially packed for that store

own-brand goods /ˌəʊn brænd ˈɡʊdz/ *plural noun* products specially packed for a store with the store's name on them

owner /ˈəʊnə/ *noun* a person who owns something □ **goods sent at owner's risk** a situation where the owner has to insure the goods while they are being transported

own label /əʊn ˈleɪb(ə)l/ *noun* goods specially produced for a store with the store's name on them

own-label goods /ˌəʊn ˌleɪb(ə)l ˈɡʊdz/ *plural noun* goods specially produced for a store with the store's name on them

'…the company is hunting for a marketing director as part of an effort to expand its non-food division and introduce own-label. It will also review its entire own-label ranges and look at the possibility of rolling out the non-food division own-label brands' [*Marketing Week*]

'…its survey of brand development indicates that whereas branded goods appeal to over-45 year olds, supermarket own-label goods are favoured by consumers under the age of 34' [*Marketing Week*]

P

P2P /ˌpiː tə 'piː/ *adjective* referring to direct communications or dealings between one computer to another without a central server being involved (NOTE: P2P stands for peer-to-peer.)

pack /pæk/ *noun* items put together in a container or shrink-wrapped for selling □ **items sold in packs of 200** items sold in boxes containing 200 items □ **blister pack** *or* **bubble pack** a type of packing where the item for sale is covered with a stiff plastic cover sealed to a card backing ■ *verb* to put things into a container for selling or sending ○ *to pack goods into cartons* ○ *Your order has been packed and is ready for shipping.* ○ *The biscuits are packed in plastic wrappers.*

package /'pækɪdʒ/ *noun* **1.** goods packed and wrapped for sending by mail ○ *The Post Office does not accept bulky packages.* ○ *The goods are to be sent in airtight packages.* **2.** a group of different items joined together in one deal **3.** a group of TV or radio programmes or commercial spots offered with a discount by a station ■ *verb* □ **to package goods** to wrap and pack goods in an attractive way

'…airlines offer special stopover rates and hotel packages to attract customers to certain routes' [*Business Traveller*]

'…the remuneration package will include an attractive salary, profit sharing and a company car' [*Times*]

'…airlines will book not only tickets but also hotels and car hire to provide a complete package' [*Business Traveller*]

packaged /'pækɪdʒd/ *adjective* put into a package ○ *packaged goods*

'…in today's fast-growing packaged goods area many companies are discovering that a well-recognized brand name can be a priceless asset' [*Duns Business Month*]

package deal /'pækɪdʒ diːl/ *noun* an agreement where several different items are agreed at the same time ○ *They agreed a package deal which involves the construction of the factory, training of staff and purchase of the product.*

package holiday /'pækɪdʒ ˌhɒlɪdeɪ/, **packaged holiday** /'pækɪdʒd ˌhɒlɪdeɪ/ *noun* a holiday whose price includes transport and accomodation, and sometimes also meals ○ *The travel company is arranging a package trip to the international trade fair.*

packaging /'pækɪdʒɪŋ/ *noun* **1.** the act of putting things into packages **2.** material used to protect goods which are being packed ○ *bubble wrap and other packaging material* ○ *The fruit is sold in airtight packaging.* **3.** attractive material used to wrap goods for display

'…the consumer wants to be challenged by more individual products and more innovative packaging' [*Marketing*]

'…promotional packaging can mean rethinking more than just the pack graphics' [*Marketing*]

packer /'pækə/ *noun* a person who packs goods

packet /'pækɪt/ *noun* a small box of goods for selling ○ *Can you get me a packet of cigarettes?* ○ *She bought a packet of biscuits.* ○ *We need two packets of filing cards.* □ **item sold in packets of 20** items are sold in boxes containing 20 items each

packing /'pækɪŋ/ *noun* **1.** the act of putting goods into boxes and wrapping them for shipping ○ *What is the cost of the packing?* ○ *Packing is included in the price.* **2.** material used to protect goods ○ *The fruit is packed in airtight packing.*

packing case /'pækɪŋ keɪs/ *noun* a large wooden box for carrying items which can be easily broken

packing charges /'pækɪŋ ˌtʃɑːdʒɪz/ *plural noun* money charged for putting goods into boxes

packing station /'pækɪŋ ˌsteɪʃ(ə)n/ *noun* a place where goods are packed for transport ○ *From the production line the goods are taken directly to the packing station.* ○ *The company has three packing stations, each one dealing with goods for a particular part of the world.*

page /peɪdʒ/ *noun* one side of a sheet of printed paper in a book, newspaper or magazine

page impressions /'peɪdʒ ɪmˌpreʃ(ə)nz/ *plural noun* the number of customers who land on a webpage, e.g. in an ad view

page make-up /peɪdʒ 'meɪk ʌp/ *noun* the arranging of material into pages in a publication

page proof /'peɪdʒ pruːf/ *noun* a proof after the text has been made up into pages, ready for checking before printing

page rate /'peɪdʒ reɪt/ *noun* the cost of a whole page of advertising space ○ *What's the page rate in that paper?* ○ *The page rate is lower in August when circulation is at its lowest.*

page traffic /'peɪdʒ ˌtræfɪk/ *noun* the proportion of readers of a publication who read a particular page ○ *Let's find out the page traffic before we decide to advertise on page two.*

page view /'peɪdʒ vjuː/ *noun* the number of times a page containing an advertisement is seen or how many times a page is displayed

paid circulation /ˌpeɪd ˌsɜːkjʊ'leɪʃ(ə)n/ *noun* the number of copies of a newspaper or magazine which have been bought. ♦ **controlled circulation, subscribed circulation**

paired comparisons /ˌpeəd kəm'pærɪs(ə)nz/ *plural noun* a test in which respondents compare two brands on the basis of attributes which are common to both

pallet /'pælət/ *noun* a flat wooden base on which goods can be stacked for easy handling by a fork-lift truck, and on which they remain for the whole of their transportation (NOTE: American English is **skid**)

palletise /'pælətaɪz/, **palletize** *verb* to put goods on pallets ○ *palletised cartons*

pamphlet /'pæmflət/ *noun* a small booklet of advertising material or of information

panel /'pæn(ə)l/ *noun* **1.** a flat surface standing upright **2.** a group of people who give advice on a problem ○ *a panel of experts*

panel study /'pæn(ə)l ˌstʌdi/ *noun* a study that collects and analyses the opinions of a selected group of people over a period of time

panic buying /'pænɪk ˌbaɪɪŋ/ *noun* a rush to buy something at any price because stocks may run out

pantry check /'pæntri tʃek/, **pantry audit** /'pæntri ˌɔːdɪt/ *noun* a survey method where a panel or sample of householders keep records of purchases so that these can be regularly checked for quantity and brand ○ *The pantry check suggests that there is little brand loyalty for that type of product.*

paper /'peɪpə/ *noun* **1.** a newspaper **2.** documents which can represent money, e.g. bills of exchange or promissory notes

'...the profits were tax-free and the interest on the loans they incurred qualified for income tax relief; the paper gains were rarely changed into spending money' [*Investors Chronicle*]

paper loss /'peɪpə lɒs/ *noun* a loss made when an asset has fallen in value but has not been sold

paper profit /'peɪpə ˌprɒfɪt/ *noun* a profit on an asset which has increased in price but has not been sold ○ *He is showing a paper profit of £25,000 on his investment.*

parallel billboard /ˌpærəlel 'bɪlbɔːd/ *noun* a billboard which is parallel to a main road

parcel /'pɑːs(ə)l/ *noun* goods wrapped up in paper or plastic to be sent by post ○ *to do up goods into parcels* □ **to tie up**

a parcel to fasten a parcel with string □ **parcel rates** the charges for sending parcels by post ■ *verb* to wrap and tie up in a parcel ○ *to parcel up a consignment of books* (NOTE: **parcelling – parcelled**. The American spelling is **parceling – parceled**)

parcel delivery service /ˌpɑːs(ə)l dɪˈlɪv(ə)ri ˌsɜːvɪs/ *noun* a private company which delivers parcels within a specific area

parcel post /ˈpɑːs(ə)l pəʊst/ *noun* a mail service for sending parcels ○ *Send the order by parcel post.*

parcels office /ˈpɑːs(ə)lz ˌɒfɪs/ *noun* an office where parcels can be handed in for sending by mail

Pareto's Law /pəˌriːtəʊz ˈlɔː/, **Pareto Effect** /pəˈriːtəʊ ɪˌfekt/ *noun* the theory that a small percentage of a total is responsible for a large proportion of value or resources

part exchange /ˌpɑːt ɪksˈtʃeɪndʒ/ *noun* the act of giving an old product as part of the payment for a new one ○ *to take a car in part exchange*

participation /pɑːˌtɪsɪˈpeɪʃ(ə)n/ *noun* taking part in something, e.g. when advertisers buy commercial time on TV

partnering /ˈpɑːtnərɪŋ/ *noun* same as **strategic partnering**

partnership /ˈpɑːtnəʃɪp/ *noun* a business set up by two or more people who make a contract with each other agreeing to share the profits and losses (NOTE: A partnership is not an incorporated company and the individual partners are responsible for decisions and debts.)

part payment /ˌpɑːt ˈpeɪmənt/ *noun* the paying of part of a whole payment ○ *I gave him £250 as part payment for the car.*

party /ˈpɑːti/ *noun* **1.** an organisation or person involved in a legal dispute or legal agreement ○ *How many parties are there to the contract?* ○ *The company is not a party to the agreement.* **2.** a group of people who meet to celebrate something or to enjoy themselves

party-plan selling /ˈpɑːti plæn ˌselɪŋ/ *noun* selling by salespeople who present their products at parties organised in their homes ○ *Party-plan selling provides a relaxed atmosphere in which people are more inclined to buy the products being shown.*

par value /pɑː ˈvæljuː/ *noun* the value written on a share certificate

passenger manifest /ˌpæsɪndʒə ˈmænɪfest/ *noun* a list of passengers on a ship or plane

passing trade /ˌpɑːsɪŋ ˈtreɪd/ *noun* selling to people who go past the shop without intending to buy

pass off /ˌpɑːs ˈɒf/ *verb* □ **to pass something off as something else** to pretend that something is another thing in order to cheat a customer ○ *She tried to pass off the wine as French, when in fact it came from outside the EU.*

pass-on readership /ˈpɑːs ɒn ˌriːdəʃɪp/ *noun* the number of people who read a publication who have not bought it, but have borrowed it from a purchaser ○ *We know the magazine's circulation, but will have to estimate the level of pass-on readership.* (NOTE: American English is **pass-along readership**)

patent /ˈpeɪtənt, ˈpætənt/ *noun* an official document showing that a person has the exclusive right to make and sell an invention ○ *to take out a patent for a new type of light bulb* ○ *to apply for a patent for a new invention* □ **'patent applied for'** *or* **'patent pending'** words on a product showing that the inventor has applied for a patent for it □ **to forfeit a patent** to lose a patent because payments have not been made □ **to infringe a patent** to make and sell a product which works in the same way as a patented product and not pay a royalty for it □ **to file a patent application** to apply for a patent ■ *verb* □ **to patent an invention** to register an invention with the patent office to prevent other people from copying it

patent agent /ˈpeɪt(ə)nt ˌeɪdʒənt/ *noun* a person who advises on patents and applies for patents on behalf of clients

patented /'peɪtəntɪd, 'pætəntɪd/ *adjective* which is protected by a patent

patentee /ˌpɔɪtənˈtiː/ *noun* a person or business that has acquired a patent ○ *We shall have to obtain the patentee's permission to manufacture the product.*

patent medicine /ˌpeɪt(ə)nt 'med(ə)s(ə)n/ *noun* a medicine which is registered as a patent

patent office /'pæt(ə)nt ˌɒfɪs/ *noun* a government office which grants patents and supervises them

patent rights /'peɪt(ə)nt raɪts/ *plural noun* the rights which an inventor holds because of a patent

patron /'peɪtrən/ *noun* **1.** a regular customer, e.g. of a hotel, restaurant, etc. ○ *The car park is for the use of hotel patrons only.* **2.** a person who gives an organisation or charity financial support ○ *She is a patron of several leading charities.*

patronage /'pætrənɪdʒ/ *noun* the state of being a regular customer

patronise /'pætrənaɪz/, **patronize** *verb* to be a regular customer ○ *I stopped patronising that restaurant when their prices went up.*

pattern /'pæt(ə)n/ *noun* the general way in which something usually happens ○ *the pattern of sales* or *The sales pattern is quite different this year.*

pattern advertising /'pæt(ə)n ˌædvətaɪzɪŋ/ *noun* an advertising campaign that follows a general global approach

pattern book /'pæt(ə)n bʊk/ *noun* a book showing examples of design

patterned interview /ˌpæt(ə)nd 'ɪntəvjuː/ *noun* an interview using questions set in advance and following a fixed pattern

pay /peɪ/ *verb* **1.** to give money to buy an item or a service ○ *to pay £1,000 for a car* ○ *How much did you pay to have the office cleaned?* □ **'pay cash'** words written on a crossed cheque to show that it can be paid in cash if necessary □ **to pay in advance** to pay before you receive the item bought or before the service has been completed ○ *We had to pay in advance to have the new tele-*phone system installed. □ **to pay in instalments** to pay for an item by giving small amounts regularly ○ *We are buying the van by paying instalments of £500 a month.* □ **to pay cash** to pay the complete sum in cash □ **to pay by cheque** to pay by giving a cheque, not by using cash or credit card □ **to pay by credit card** to pay using a credit card, not a cheque or cash **2.** to give money which is owed or which has to be paid ○ *He was late paying the bill.* ○ *We phoned to ask when they were going to pay the invoice.* ○ *You will have to pay duty on these imports.* ○ *She pays tax at the highest rate.* (NOTE: **paying- paid**) □ **to pay on demand** to pay money when it is asked for, not after a period of credit □ **please pay the sum of £10** please give £10 in cash or by cheque

'…recession encourages communication not because it makes redundancies easier, but because it makes low or zero pay increases easier to accept' [*Economist*]

'…the yield figure means that if you buy the shares at their current price you will be getting 5% before tax on your money if the company pays the same dividend as in its last financial year' [*Investors Chronicle*]

payable /'peɪəb(ə)l/ *adjective* which is due to be paid □ **payable in advance** which has to be paid before the goods are delivered □ **payable on delivery** which has to be paid when the goods are delivered □ **payable on demand** which must be paid when payment is asked for □ **payable at sixty days** which has to be paid by sixty days after the date on the invoice □ **cheque made payable to bearer** a cheque which will be paid to the person who has it, not to any particular name written on it □ **shares payable on application** shares which must be paid for when you apply to buy them

payback period /'peɪbæk ˌpɪəriəd/ *noun* the length of time it will take to earn back the money invested in a project

pay-cheque /'peɪ tʃek/ *noun* a monthly cheque by which an employee is paid (NOTE: the American spelling is **paycheck**)

pay down /peɪ 'daʊn/ *verb* □ **to pay money down** to make a deposit ○ *They*

paid £50 down and the rest in monthly instalments.

payee /peɪˈiː/ *noun* a person who receives money from someone, or the person whose name is on a cheque

payer /ˈpeɪə/ *noun* a person who gives money to someone

payload /ˈpeɪləʊd/ *noun* the cargo or passengers carried by a ship, train or plane for which payment is made

payment /ˈpeɪmənt/ *noun* **1.** the money exchanged for goods or a service ○ *We always ask for payment in cash or cash payment and not payment by cheque.* ○ *The payment of interest or the interest payment should be made on the 22nd of each month.* □ **payment after delivery** paying for goods at an agreed date after delivery ○ *There is a 10% discount for payment on delivery, but none for payment after delivery.* □ **payment on account** paying part of the money owed □ **payment on delivery** paying for goods when they are delivered ○ *Some customers won't agree to payment on delivery and want more time to settle up.* □ **payment on invoice** paying money as soon as an invoice is received □ **payment in kind** paying by giving goods or food, but not money □ **payment by results** money given which increases with the amount of work done or goods produced □ **payment supra protest** payment of a bill of exchange by a third party to protect the debtor's honour **2.** money paid □ **repayable in easy payments** repayable with small sums regularly

payment gateway /ˈpeɪmənt ˌɡeɪtweɪ/ *noun* software that processes online credit-card payments. It gets authorisation for the payment from the credit-card company and transfers money into the retailer's bank account.

payment terms /ˈpeɪmənt tɜːmz/ *plural noun* the conditions laid down by a business regarding when it should be paid for goods or services that it supplies, e.g. cash with order, payment on delivery or payment within a particular number of days of the invoice date

pay package /ˈpeɪ ˌpækɪdʒ/ *noun* the salary and other benefits offered

with a job ○ *The job carries an attractive salary package.*

pay-per-click /ˌpeɪ pə ˈklɪk/ *noun* same as **pay-per-view**

pay-per-play /ˌpeɪ pə ˈpleɪ/ *noun* a website where the user has to pay to play an interactive game over the Internet

pay-per-view /peɪ pə/ *noun* a website where the user has to pay to see digital information, e.g., an e-book or e-magazine

pay television /ˈpeɪ telɪˌvɪʒ(ə)n/, **pay TV** /ˈpeɪ tiː viː/ *noun* a television service that is paid for by regular subscriptions

PC *abbr* personal computer

PD *abbr* physical distribution

peak /piːk/ *noun* the highest point ○ *The shares reached their peak in January.* ○ *The share index has fallen 10% since the peak in January.* ○ *Withdrawals from bank accounts reached a peak in the week before Christmas.* ○ *He has reached the peak of his career.* ■ *verb* to reach the highest point ○ *Productivity peaked in January.* ○ *Shares have peaked and are beginning to slip back.* ○ *He peaked early and never achieved his ambition of becoming managing director.* ○ *Demand peaks in August, after which sales usually decline.*

peak output /ˌpiːk ˈaʊtpʊt/ *noun* the highest output

peak period /ˈpiːk ˌpɪəriəd/ *noun* the time of the day when something is at its highest point, e.g. when most commuters are travelling or when most electricity is being used

peak time /ˈpiːk taɪm/ *noun* the time during the day when the greatest number of people are watching television ○ *For the price of a 30-second spot at peak time we can get two minutes in mid-morning.*

peak year /ˈpiːk jɪə/ *noun* year when the largest quantity of products was produced or when sales were highest

pedestrian precinct /pəˌdestriən ˈpriːsɪŋkt/ *noun* the part of a town which is closed to traffic so that people can walk about and shop

peer group /ˈpɪə ˌgruːp/ *noun* the class of people that a person can respect or identify with, because they belong to the same age group, social class or have the same opinions ○ *Consumers are found to be especially influenced by the tastes and opinions of those in their peer groups.*

peer-to-peer *adjective* full form of **P2P**

peg /peg/ *verb* to maintain prices at a specific level (NOTE: **pegging-pegged**) ■ *noun* a hook to hang clothes on

pen /pen/ *noun* an instrument for writing with, using ink

penalty clause /ˈpen(ə)lti klɔːz/ *noun* a clause which lists the penalties which will be imposed if the terms of the contract are not fulfilled ○ *The contract contains a penalty clause which fines the company 1% for every week the completion date is late.*

penetrate /ˈpenɪtreɪt/ *verb* □ **to penetrate a market** to get into a market and capture a share of it

penetrated market /ˌpenɪtreɪtɪd ˈmɑːkɪt/ *noun* a market where more of a company's products are sold, shown as a percentage of the total market, using aggressive pricing and advertising

penetration /penɪˈtreɪʃ(ə)n/ *noun* **1.** the percentage of a target market that accepts a product **2.** the percentage of a target audience reached by an advertisement

penetration pricing /penɪˈtreɪʃ(ə)n ˌpraɪsɪŋ/ *noun* the practice of pricing a product low enough to achieve market penetration ○ *Penetration pricing is helping us acquire a bigger market share at the expense of short term profits.*

penetration strategy /penɪˈtreɪʃ(ə)n ˌstrætədʒi/ *noun* selling more of a company's products into a market segment, shown as a percentage of the total market, by aggressive pricing and advertising. ♦ **market penetration**

per annum /pər ˈænəm/ *adverb* in a year ○ *What is their turnover per annum?* ○ *What is his total income per an-num?* ○ *She earns over £100,000 per annum.*

per capita /pə ˈkæpɪtə/ *adjective, adverb* for each person

per-capita expenditure /pə ˌkæpɪtə ɪkˈspendɪʃə/ *noun* the total money spent divided by the number of people involved

per capita income /pɜː ˌkæpɪtə ˈɪnkʌm/ *noun* the average income of each member of a particular group of people, e.g., the citizens of a country

percentage bounced back /pə-ˌsentɪdʒ baʊnst ˈbæk/ *noun* the number of email messages returned as undeliverable, shown as a percentage of the total sent

percentile /pəˈsentaɪl/ *noun* one of a series of ninety-nine figures below which a percentage of the total falls

perception /pəˈsepʃən/ *noun* the way in which something is viewed and assessed by a person

perceptual map /pəˌseptʃuəl ˈmæp/ *noun* a map or diagram which represents how consumers view various comparative products on the basis of specific factors or attributes ○ *Thorough analysis of perceptual maps was followed by decisions on changes in product design and marketing strategy.*

perfect *adjective* /ˈpɜːfɪkt/ completely correct with no mistakes ○ *We check each batch to make sure it is perfect.* ○ *She did a perfect keyboarding test.* ■ *verb* /pəˈfekt/ to develop or improve something until it is as good as it can be ○ *They perfected the process for making high-grade steel.*

perfect competition /ˌpɜːfɪkt kɒmpəˈtɪʃ(ə)n/ *noun* (*in economic theory*) the ideal market, where all products are equal in price and all customers are provided with all information about the products

perfect market /ˌpɜːfɪkt ˈmɑːkɪt/ *noun* an imaginary market where there is perfect competition

periodical /ˌpɪəriˈɒdɪk(ə)l/ *noun* a magazine which comes out regularly, usually once a month or once a week

perishable /ˈperɪʃəb(ə)l/ *adjective* which can go bad or become rotten easily ○ *perishable goods* ○ *perishable items* ○ *a perishable cargo*

perishables /ˈperɪʃəb(ə)lz/ *plural noun* goods which can go bad easily

'...the survey, which covered 7,376 supermarkets run by 119 companies, found that sales of food at the stores dropped by 2.9%. That decline, also the largest on record, was due to increasing price awareness among customers and the lower price of perishables' [*Nikkei Weekly*]

permanent /ˈpɜːmənənt/ *adjective* which will last for a long time or for ever ○ *He has found a permanent job.* ○ *the permanent staff and part-timers* ○ *She is in permanent employment.*

permanent income hypothesis /ˌpɜːmənənt ˈɪnkʌm haɪˌpɒθəsɪs/ *noun* the theory that people spend according to the average income they expect to receive in their lifetime

permission marketing /pəˈmɪʃ(ə)n ˌmɑːkɪtɪŋ/ *noun* any form of online direct marketing that requires the seller to get permission from each recipient before sending him or her any promotional material

permit *noun* /ˈpɜːmɪt/ an official document which allows someone to do something ■ *verb* /pəˈmɪt/ to allow someone to do something ○ *This document permits you to export twenty-five computer systems.* ○ *The ticket permits three people to go into the exhibition.* ○ *Will we be permitted to use her name in the advertising copy?* ○ *Smoking is not permitted in the design studio.* (NOTE: **permitting- permitted**)

persistent demand /pəˌsɪstənt dɪˈmɑːnd/ *noun* a continuous or stable demand for a product ○ *Persistent demand for the product means that there is very little pressure to adapt it.* ○ *The product is so useful that it is not surprising there is a persistent demand for it.*

personal /ˈpɜːs(ə)n(ə)l/ *adjective* referring to one person

personal call /ˈpɜːs(ə)n(ə)l kɔːl/ *noun* 1. a telephone call where you ask the operator to connect you with a particular person 2. a telephone call not related to business ○ *Staff are not allowed to make personal calls during office hours.*

personal computer /ˌpɜːs(ə)n(ə)l kəmˈpjuːtə/ *noun* a small computer which can be used by one person in the home or office. Abbr **PC**

Personal Identification Number /ˌpɜːs(ə)n(ə)l aɪdentɪfɪˈkeɪʃ(ə)n ˌnʌmbə/ *noun* a unique number allocated to the holder of a cash card or credit card, by which he or she can enter an automatic banking system, as, e.g., to withdraw cash from a cash machine or to pay in a store

personal interview /ˌpɜːs(ə)n(ə)l ˈɪntəvjuː/ *noun* an act of questioning respondents in a survey directly, by meeting them ○ *The advantage of a personal interview is that we have the chance to explain the questions.* ○ *It's possible that interviewers' bias may influence results in a personal interview.*

personalisation /ˌpɜːs(ə)nəlaɪˈzeɪʃ(ə)n/, **personalization** *noun* **1.** the process by which a website presents customers with selected information that is designed to meet their individual needs **2.** using personal information such as the addressee's first name in a mailing campaign

personalised /ˈpɜːs(ə)nəlaɪzd/, **personalized** *adjective* with the name or initials of a person printed on it ○ *She has a personalised briefcase.*

personalised   mailing /ˌpɜːs(ə)nəlaɪzd ˈmeɪlɪŋ/ *noun* a mailing of letters addressed to particular people by name

personality /ˌpɜːsəˈnælɪtɪ/ *noun* **1.** a famous person, usually connected with television or sport **2.** the character, especially the tone of an advertising email, e.g. serious, cheerful, etc.

personality advertising /ˌpɜːsəˈnælɪtɪ ˌædvətaɪzɪŋ/, **personality promotion** /ˌpɜːsəˈnælɪtɪ prəˌməʊʃ(ə)n/ *noun* a promotion which makes use of a famous person to endorse a product ○ *Personality promotion is a tried and tested method of promoting beauty products.* ○ *A famous pop star was chosen for the personality*

promotion because of her widespread popularity among the target audience.

personal selling /ˈpɜːs(ə)n(ə)l ˌselɪŋ/ noun selling to a customer by personal contact, either face to face or by telephone ○ *Personal selling allows any doubts the prospective customer may have to be cleared up by the salesman.*

persuade /pəˈsweɪd/ verb to talk to someone and get them to do what you want ○ *We could not persuade the French company to sign the contract.*

persuasibility /pəˌsweɪzɪˈbɪlɪti/ noun US the degree to which a target audience can be persuaded through advertising that a product has good qualities ○ *Persuasibility will depend on consumer's experience with products similar to the ones we are promoting.*

persuasion /pəˈsweɪʒ(ə)n/ noun the act of persuading

persuasion matrix /pəˈsweɪʒ(ə)n ˌmeɪtrɪks/ noun a planning model which shows how responses are affected by the communications they receive

PESTLE /ˈpes(ə)l/ noun analysis of the various outside influences on a firm, shown as Political, Environmental, Social, Technological, Legislative and Economic

photoengraving /ˌfəʊtəʊɪnˈgreɪvɪŋ/ noun a process of producing a metal plate for printing, by photographing an image onto the plate which is then etched in such a way that prints can be taken from it

photogravure /ˌfəʊtəʊgrəˈvjʊə/ noun a type of photoengraving where the design is etched into the metal rather than in relief

photo opportunity /ˈfəʊtəʊ ɒpəˈtjuːnɪti/ noun an arranged situation where a famous person can be filmed or photographed by journalists

phototypesetting /ˌfəʊtəʊˈtaɪpsetɪŋ/ noun typesetting by photographic means rather than by using metal type

physical distribution /ˌfɪzɪk(ə)l dɪstrɪˈbjuːʃ(ə)n/ noun the process of moving goods from the producer to the wholesaler, then to the retailer and so to the end user ○ *Physical distribution is always a problem because of high transportation costs.* Abbr **PD**

physical inventory /ˌfɪzɪk(ə)l ˈɪnvənt(ə)ri/ noun an act of counting actual items of stock

physical retail shopping /ˌfɪzɪk(ə)l ˈriːteɪl ˌʃɒpɪŋ/ noun shopping that involves visiting actual shops rather than buying online

physical stock /ˌfɪzɪk(ə)l ˈstɒk/ noun the actual items of stock held in a warehouse

picking /ˈpɪkɪŋ/ noun selecting a product according to its packaging or place on the shelf, rather than by making a conscious decision to buy

picking list /ˈpɪkɪŋ lɪst/ noun a list of items in an order, listed according to where they can be found in the warehouse

pickup /ˈpɪk ˌʌp/ noun a type of small van for transporting goods

pickup and delivery service /ˌpɪkʌp ən dɪˈlɪv(ə)ri ˌsɜːvɪs/ noun **1.** a service which takes goods from the warehouse and delivers them to the customer **2.** a service which takes something away for cleaning or servicing and returns it to the owner when finished

picture messaging /ˈpɪktʃə ˌmesɪdʒɪŋ/ noun the transmission of images and photographs from one mobile phone to another

piggy-back advertising /ˈpɪgi bæk ˌædvətaɪzɪŋ/, **piggy-back promotion** /ˈpɪgi bæk prəˌməʊʃ(ə)n/ noun sales promotion for one product which accompanies promotion for another product made by the same company

piggy-back freight /ˌpɪgi bæk ˈfreɪt ˌsɜːvɪs/ noun US the transport of loaded trucks on freight trains. Compare **fishy-back freight**

pilferage /ˈpɪlfərɪdʒ/, **pilfering** /ˈpɪlfərɪŋ/ noun the stealing of small amounts of money or small items from an office or shop

pilot /ˈpaɪlət/ adjective used as a test, which if successful will then be ex-

panded into a full operation ○ *The company set up a pilot project to see if the proposed manufacturing system was efficient.* ○ *The pilot factory has been built to test the new production processes.* ○ *She is directing a pilot scheme for training unemployed young people.* ■ *verb* to test a project on a small number of people, to see if it will work in practice ■ *noun* **1.** a trial episode of a proposed TV series **2.** a pilot project

pilot survey /'paɪlət ˌsɜːveɪ/ *noun* a preliminary survey carried out to see if a full survey would be worth while

PIN *abbr* Personal Identification Number

pink advertising /ˌpɪŋk 'ædvətaɪzɪŋ/ *noun* advertising aimed specifically at the gay and lesbian market

pink dollar /ˌpɪŋk 'dɒlə/ *noun US* money spent by gay and lesbian customers

pink market /'pɪŋk ˌmɑːkɪt/ *noun* the market that consists of gay and lesbian people

pink pound /ˌpɪŋk 'paʊnd/ *noun* money spent by gay and lesbian customers

pioneer /ˌpaɪə'nɪə/ *verb* to be the first to do something ○ *The company pioneered developments in the field of electronics.*

pioneer selling /paɪə'nɪə ˌselɪŋ/ *noun* hard intensive selling in new markets ○ *A campaign of pioneer selling was organised to educate the public in the use of the new product.* ○ *There was a lot of consumer resistance to pioneer selling, since few customers had heard of the product or thought they needed it.*

pipeline /'paɪplaɪn/ *noun* a distribution channel from the manufacturer through wholesalers and retailers to the customer ○ *How many different businesses are involved in the product's pipeline?*

piracy /'paɪrəsi/ *noun* the copying of patented inventions or copyright works

pirate /'paɪrət/ *noun* a person who copies a patented invention or a copyright work and sells it ■ *verb* to copy a

copyright work ○ *a pirated book* ○ *The designs for the new dress collection were pirated in the Far East.* ■ *adjective* copied without permission ○ *a pirate copy of a book*

pitch /pɪtʃ/ *noun* presentation by an advertising agency to a potential customer

'...the head of marketing says the company is reviewing its advertising agency arrangements, but does not have a pitch list at this stage' [*Marketing Week*]

pix /pɪks/ *plural noun* pictures used in advertising or design (*informal*)

pixel /'pɪksəl/ *noun* the smallest single unit or point on a display or on a printer whose colour or brightness can be controlled. A monitor normally has a resolution of 72 pixels per inch, whereas a laser printer has a resolution of 300–600 pixels (also called dots) per inch.

placard /'plækɑːd/ *noun* **1.** a poster of double crown size (i.e. 30 inches deep by 20 inches wide) **2.** a large advertisement on a stiff card

placement test /'pleɪsmənt test/ *noun* a test where different versions of a new product are tested in different places and with different types of consumer (as opposed to market tests, where the new product is actually sold through normal distribution channels in the test areas)

placement testing /'pleɪsmənt ˌtestɪŋ/ *noun* the practice of sending a product to different places for trial and then interviewing the users on its performance ○ *Placement testing revealed that the product was too easily breakable.*

place utility /'pleɪs juːˌtɪlɪti/ *noun* the usefulness to a customer of receiving a product at a particular place

plain cover /pleɪn 'kʌvə/ *noun* □ **to send something under plain cover** to send something in an ordinary envelope with no company name printed on it

plan /plæn/ *noun* a way of doing something which has been decided on and organised in advance ■ *verb* to decide on and organise something in advance (NOTE: **planning – planned**)

'...the benefits package is attractive and the compensation plan includes base, incentive and

car allowance totalling $50,000+'
[*Globe and Mail (Toronto)*]

planned obsolescence /ˌplænd ˌɒbsəˈles(ə)ns/ *adjective* built-in obsolescence ○ *Planned obsolescence was condemned by the consumer organisation as a cynical marketing ploy.*

planning /ˈplænɪŋ/ *noun* the process of organising how something should be done in the future ○ *Setting up a new incentive scheme with insufficient planning could be a disaster.* ○ *The long-term planning* or *short-term planning of the project has been completed.*

'…buildings are closely regulated by planning restrictions' [*Investors Chronicle*]

plans board /ˈplænz bɔːd/ *noun* a group of senior managers that meets to discuss campaign strategy ○ *The plans board will meet on Monday to discuss the latest sales figures.* ○ *The plans board has decided to concentrate the campaign in those areas where there are most sales representatives.*

plastic /ˈplæstɪk/ *noun* a plastic card, especially a credit or debit card, for use as a means of payment

plateau /ˈplætəʊ/ *noun* a level point, e.g. when sales or costs stop increasing

plateau pricing /ˈplætəʊ ˌpraɪsɪŋ/ *noun* the setting of a medium price for a product where the raw materials used in making it are likely to change a lot in price

platform /ˈplætfɔːm/ *noun* a high pavement in a station, so that passengers can get on or off trains ○ *The train for Birmingham leaves from Platform 12.*

Plc *abbr* Public Limited Company

PLC *abbr* product life cycle

ploy /plɔɪ/ *noun* a trick or gimmick, used to attract customers

plug /plʌg/ *noun* □ **to give a plug to a new product** to publicise a new product ■ *verb* to publicise or advertise ○ *They ran six commercials plugging holidays in Spain.* (NOTE: **plugging- plugged**)

point /pɔɪnt/ *noun* a place or position

'…sterling M3, the most closely watched measure, rose by 13% in the year to August – seven percentage points faster than the rate of inflation' [*Economist*]

'…banks refrained from quoting forward US/Hongkong dollar exchange rates as premiums of 100 points replaced discounts of up to 50 points' [*South China Morning Post*]

point of action /ˌpɔɪnt əv ˈækʃən/ *noun* a place in a presentation that encourages the prospective purchaser to take action. Abbr **POA**

point of purchase /ˌpɔɪnt əv ˈpɜːtʃɪs/ *noun* **1.** a place where a product is bought, which is usually the same as point of sale, though not always, as in the case of mail-order purchases. Abbr **POP 2.** same as **point of sale**

point-of-purchase advertising /ˌpɔɪnt əv ˌpɜːtʃɪs ˈædvətaɪzɪŋ/ *noun* advertising at the place where the products are bought, e.g. posters or dump bins. Abbr **POPA**

point-of-purchase display /ˌpɔɪnt əv ˌpɜːtʃɪs dɪsˈpleɪ/ *noun* an arrangement of products and marketing material at the place where an item is bought, which is designed to encourage sales

point of sale /ˌpɔɪnt əv ˈseɪl/ *noun* **1.** a place where a product is sold, e.g. a shop. Abbr **POS 2.** the place where a product is bought by the customer (NOTE: The point of sale can be a particular shop, or a display case or even a particular shelf inside a shop.)

point-of-sale material /ˌpɔɪnt əv ˈseɪl məˌtɪəriəl/ *noun* display material to advertise a product where it is being sold, e.g. posters or dump bins

policy /ˈpɒlɪsi/ *noun* decisions on the general way of doing something ○ *a company's trading policy* ○ *The country's economic policy seems to lack any direction.* ○ *Our policy is to submit all contracts to the legal department.* □ **company policy** the company's agreed plan of action or the company's way of doing things ○ *What is the company policy on credit?* ○ *It is against company policy to give more than thirty days' credit.*

poll /pəʊl/ *noun* same as **opinion poll** ■ *verb* □ **to poll a sample of the population** to ask a sample group of people what they feel about something

poly bag /ˌpɒli ˈbæg/ *noun US* a plastic bag used in packaging

polycentric stage /ˌpɒliˈsentrɪk steɪdʒ/ *noun US* the stage in a company's international marketing when there is a separate marketing planning unit for each country ○ *It's an expanding multinational in its polycentric stage.*

POP *abbr* point of purchase

POPA *abbr* point-of-purchase advertising

popular /ˈpɒpjʊlə/ *adjective* liked by many people ○ *This is our most popular model.* ○ *The South Coast is the most popular area for holidays.*

popular price /ˌpɒpjʊlə ˈpraɪsɪz/ *noun* a price which is low and therefore liked

popular pricing /ˌpɒpjʊlə ˈpraɪsɪŋ/ *noun* a pricing method which tries to fix prices that will be popular with customers ○ *Our competitor's popular pricing strategy is a serious threat to our sales.*

population /ˌpɒpjʊˈleɪʃ(ə)n/ *noun* **1.** the number of people who live in a country or in a town ○ *Paris has a population of over three million.* ○ *Population statistics show a rise in the 18–25 age group.* ○ *Population trends have to be taken into account when drawing up economic plans.* ○ *The working population of the country is getting older.* **2.** the group of items or people in a survey or study

population forecast /ˌpɒpjʊˈleɪʃ(ə)n ˌfɔːkɑːst/ *noun* a calculation of how many people will be living in a country or in a town at some point in the future

pop-under ad /ˈpɒp ʌndər ˌæd/ *noun* a web advertisement that appears in a separate browser window from the rest of a website

port /pɔːt/ *noun* a harbour where ships come to load or unload ○ *the port of Rotterdam* □ **to call at a port** to stop at a port to load or unload cargo

portal /ˈpɔːt(ə)l/ *noun* a website that provides access and links to other sites and pages on the web (NOTE: Search engines and directories are the most common portal sites.)

port authority /pɔːt ɔːˈθɒrɪti/ *noun* an organisation which runs a port

portfolio /pɔːtˈfəʊliəʊ/ *noun* a folder containing a selection of samples ○ *The student brought a portfolio of designs to show the design department manager.*

port installations /ˌpɔːt ɪnstəˈleɪʃ(ə)nz/ *plural noun* the buildings and equipment of a port

port of call /ˌpɔːt əv ˈkɔːl/ *noun* a port at which a ship often stops

portrait /ˈpɔːtrɪt/ *noun* an illustration, page or book whose height is greater than its width. Compare **landscape**

position /pəˈzɪʃ(ə)n/ *noun* a situation or state of affairs □ **what is the cash position?** what is the state of the company's current account?

positioning /pəˈzɪʃ(ə)nɪŋ/ *noun* **1.** the creation of an image for a product in the minds of consumers **2.** the placing of an advertisement in a specific place on a specific page of a magazine **3.** the promotion of a product in a particular area of a market

positive /ˈpɒzɪtɪv/ *adjective* meaning 'yes' ○ *The board gave a positive reply.*

'…as the group's shares are already widely held, the listing will be via an introduction. It will also be accompanied by a deeply-discounted £25m rights issue, leaving the company cash positive' [*Sunday Times*]

positive appeal /ˌpɒzɪtɪv əˈpiːl/ *noun* advertising which shows why a product is attractive

positive cash flow /ˌpɒzɪtɪv ˈkæʃ fləʊ/ *noun* a situation where more money is coming into a company than is going out

positive variance /ˌpɒzɪtɪv ˈveəriəns/ *noun* a difference between a financial plan and its outcome, that means a more favourable profit than expected ○ *The managing director is pleased because costs this year show a £60,000 positive variance.*

possession utility /pəˈzeʃ(ə)n juːˌtɪlɪti/ *noun* same as **marginal utility**

post /pəʊst/ *noun* **1.** a system of sending letters and parcels from one place to another ○ *to send an invoice by post* ○ *He put the letter in the post.* ○ *The cheque was lost in the post.* □ **to send a**

reply by return of post to reply to a letter immediately □ **post free** without having to pay any postage ○ *The game is obtainable post free from the manufacturer.* **2.** letters sent or received ○ *Has the post arrived yet?* ○ *The first thing I do is open the post.* ○ *The receipt was in this morning's post.* ○ *The letter didn't arrive by the first post this morning.* (NOTE: British English uses both **mail** and **post** but American English only uses **mail**) ■ *verb* to send something by post ○ *to post a letter* or *to post a parcel*

post- /pəʊst/ *prefix* meaning after

postage /'pəʊstɪdʒ/ *noun* payment for sending a letter or parcel by post ○ *What is the postage for this airmail packet to China?* □ **'postage paid'** words printed on an envelope to show that the sender has paid the postage even though there is no stamp on it

postal /'pəʊst(ə)l/ *adjective* referring to the post

postal interview /,pəʊst(ə)l 'ɪntəvjuː/ *noun* same as **postal survey**

postal order /'pəʊst(ə)l ,ɔːdə/ *noun* a document bought at a post office, used as a method of paying small amounts of money by post

postal packet /'pəʊst(ə)l ,pækɪt/ *noun* a small container of goods sent by post

postal sales /'pəʊst(ə)l seɪlz/ *plural noun* sales of products by post, through advertisements in the press ○ *The company carried out postal sales from a big warehouse in the north.*

postal survey /,pəʊst(ə)l 'sɜːveɪ/ *noun* a survey in which questionnaires are sent by post for respondents to fill in and send back ○ *Not enough consumers responded to the postal survey.*

postcode /'pəʊstkəʊd/ *noun* a series of numbers and letters which forms part of an address, indicating the street and the town in a way which can be read by a scanner (NOTE: the American equivalent is **ZIP code**)

poster /'pəʊstə/ *noun* a large eye-catching notice or advertisement which is stuck up outdoors or placed prominently inside a store

poster site /'pəʊstə saɪt/ *noun* a hoarding, wall or other surface, where posters are put up ○ *We want a poster site in a busy street.* ○ *I wish we could afford a prime poster site for our fund-raising campaign.* ♦ **bill poster, fly poster**

postpaid /pəʊst'peɪd/ *adjective* with the postage already paid ○ *The price is £5.95 postpaid.*

post-purchase /,pəʊst 'pɜːtʃɪs/ *adjective* after a purchase has been made

post-purchase advertising /,pəʊst pɜːtʃɪs 'ædvətaɪzɪŋ/ *noun* advertising designed to minimise post-purchase anxiety

post-purchase anxiety /,pəʊst pɜːtʃɪs æŋ'zaɪəti/ *noun* feelings of doubt about a purchase after it has been made

post-purchase assessment /,pəʊst pɜːtʃɪs ə'sesmənt/ *noun* the assessment of a product by the purchaser after it has been bought and used

post room /'pəʊst ruːm/ *noun* a room in a building where the post is sorted and sent to each department or collected from each department for sending

post-test /'pəʊst test/ *noun* an evaluation of an advertising campaign after it has taken place, or of a product after it has been launched ○ *The post-test showed that an unnecessary amount of money had been spent.*

post-testing /'pəʊst ,testɪŋ/ *noun* the evaluation of an advertising campaign after it has been run, or of a product after it has been launched

potential /pə'tenʃəl/ *adjective* possible □ **potential customers** people who could be customers □ **potential market** a market which could be exploited □ **the product has potential sales of 100,000 units** the product will possibly sell 100,000 units □ **she is a potential managing director** she is the sort of person who could become managing director ■ *noun* the possibility of becoming something □ **a product with considerable sales potential** a product which is likely to have very large sales □ **to analyse the**

market potential to examine the market to see how large it possibly is

'…career prospects are excellent for someone with growth potential' [*Australian Financial Review*]

'…for sale: established general cleaning business; has potential to be increased to over 1 million dollar turnover' [*Australian Financial Review*]

potential demand /pə‚tenʃəl dɪ-'mɑːnd/ *noun* a situation where there is no demand as yet for a product but there is money to buy it ○ *Though there is no interest in our product in Saudi Arabia as yet, there is considerable potential demand.*

power /'paʊə/ *noun* the ability to control people or events

power brand /'paʊə brænd/ *noun* a very powerful brand which covers several best-selling products and is known worldwide

PR /‚piː'ɑː/ *abbr* public relations ○ *he is working in PR* ○ *A PR firm is handling all our publicity.* ○ *The PR people gave away 100,000 balloons.*

preapproach /'priːə‚praʊtʃ/ *noun* the stage in a salesperson's preparation for a sale devoted to planning actual meetings with customers ○ *Preapproach sessions cover techniques in assessing customers and their needs.*

precinct /'priːsɪŋkt/ *noun* a separate area

pre-coding /priː 'kəʊdɪŋ/ *noun* the process of assigning codes to items on questionnaires in order to facilitate reference and evaluation ○ *Much time was lost in the survey through a confusing pre-coding system.* ○ *Freelance interviewers should be given a complete explanation of the pre-coding of questionnaires.*

predatory /'predət(ə)ri/ *adjective* which tries to attack □ **a predatory pricing policy** a policy of reducing prices as low as possible to try to get market share from weaker competitors

pre-empt /priː'empt/ *verb* to get an advantage by doing something quickly before anyone else ○ *They staged a management buyout to pre-empt a takeover bid.*

pre-emption /priː'empʃən/ *noun* getting an advantage by doing something quickly before anyone else

pre-empt selling /priː 'empt ‚selɪŋ/ *noun* the practice of selling television advertising time at a lower rate with the proviso that another advertiser can take it over if the full rate is offered ○ *As we're on a tight advertising budget we'll have to go for pre-empt selling.*

preferred position /prɪ‚fɜːd pə-'zɪʃ(ə)n/ *noun* the place in a publication where an advertiser asks for the advertisement to be put

preferred position rate /prɪ‚fɜːd pə'zɪʃ(ə)n reɪt/ *noun* a higher rate charged for placing an advertisement in the position requested

prelaunch /'priːlɔːntʃ/ *adjective* before a launch

prelaunch period /'priːlɔːntʃ ‚pɪəriəd/ *noun* the period before the launch of a new product

premium /'priːmiəm/ *noun* **1.** the amount added to a normal price or rate for a product or service **2.** free gift offered to a prospective purchaser as an inducement to make a purchase

'…greenmail, the practice of buying back stock at a premium from an acquirer who threatens a takeover' [*Duns Business Month*]

'…responsibilities include the production of premium quality business reports' [*Times*]

premium offer /'priːmiəm ‚ɒfə/ *noun* a free gift offered to attract more customers

premium pricing /'priːmiəm ‚praɪsɪŋ/ *noun* giving products or services high prices either to give the impression that the product is worth more than it really is, or as a means of offering customers an extra service

prepack /priː'pæk/, **prepackage** /priː'pækɪdʒ/ *verb* to pack something before putting it on sale ○ *The fruit are prepacked in plastic trays.* ○ *The watches are prepacked in attractive display boxes.*

prepaid /priː'peɪd/ *adjective* paid in advance

prepaid reply card /‚priːpeɪd rɪ-'plaɪ kɑːd/ *noun* a stamped addressed card which is sent to someone so that

they can reply without paying the postage

preparatory set /prɪˈpærət(ə)ri set/ *noun* the principle that people have pre-conceived ideas about brands which influence their buying decisions

prepay /priːˈpeɪ/ *verb* to pay in advance (NOTE: **prepaying – prepaid**)

prepayment /priːˈpeɪmənt/ *noun* a payment in advance □ **to ask for prepayment of a fee** to ask for the fee to be paid before the work is done

pre-press /priː ˈpres/ *adjective* before going to press

pre-press work /priː ˈpres wɜːk/ *noun* the work needed to change original copy and artwork into the form required for printing

prequalification /ˌpriːkwɒlɪfɪˈkeɪʃ(ə)n/ *noun* researching the value of a potential customer, especially one who wants to take out a loan or a contractor for a project

presence /ˈprez(ə)ns/ *noun* a measurement of an advertisement's real audience as opposed to its potential audience ○ *With an impressive presence our advertisement should have considerable effect.*

present /prɪˈzent/ *verb* to give a talk about or demonstration of something ○ *I've been asked to present at the sales conference.* ○ *The HR director will present the new staff structure to the Board.*

presentation /ˌprez(ə)nˈteɪʃ(ə)n/ *noun* **1.** the showing of a document □ **cheque payable on presentation** a cheque which will be paid when it is presented □ **free admission on presentation of this card** you do not pay to go in if you show this card **2.** a demonstration or exhibition of a proposed plan ○ *The distribution company gave a presentation of the services they could offer.* ○ *We have asked two PR firms to make presentations of proposed publicity campaigns.*

press /pres/ *noun* newspapers and magazines ○ *We plan to give the product a lot of press publicity.* ○ *There was no mention of the new product in the press.*

press advertising /ˈpres ˌædvətaɪzɪŋ/ *noun* advertising in newspapers and magazines

press clipping /ˈpres ˌklɪpɪŋ/ *noun* US a copy of a news item kept by a company because it contains important business information or is a record of news published about the company

press communications /ˈpres kəmjuːnɪˌkeɪʃ(ə)nz/ *plural noun* communications which increase the awareness of journalists of a product or firm, e.g. press releases or news flashes

press conference /ˈpres ˌkɒnf(ə)rəns/ *noun* a meeting where newspaper and TV reporters are invited to hear news of something such as a new product a takeover bid

press cutting /ˈpres ˌkʌtɪŋ/ *noun* a piece cut out of a newspaper or magazine which refers to an item which you find interesting such as a client or product ○ *We have kept a file of press cuttings about the new car.*

press cutting agency /ˈpres ˌkʌtɪŋ ˌeɪdʒənsi/ *noun* a company which cuts out references to clients from newspapers and magazines and sends them on to them

press date /ˈpres deɪt/ *noun* the date on which a publication is printed

press relations /pres rɪˈleɪʃ(ə)nz/ *plural noun* part of the public relations activity of an organisation, aimed at building up good relations with the press ○ *If the company image is to improve we must first improve our press relations.*

press release /ˈpres rɪˌliːs/ *noun* a sheet giving news about something which is sent to newspapers and TV and radio stations so that they can use the information ○ *The company sent out a press release about the launch of the new car.*

pressure /ˈpreʃə/ *noun* something which forces you to do something

pressure group /ˈpreʃə gruːp/ *noun* a group of people who try to influence the government, the local town council or some other organisation

prestige /pre'stiːʒ/ *noun* **1.** importance because of factors such as high quality or high value □ **prestige product** an expensive luxury product □ **prestige offices** expensive offices in a good area of the town **2.** status achieved because of being successful, wealthy or powerful

prestige advertising /pre'stiːʒ ˌædvətaɪzɪŋ/ *noun* advertising in high-quality magazines to increase a company's reputation

prestige pricing /pre'stiːʒ ˌpraɪsɪŋ/ *noun* same as **premium pricing**

pretax profit /ˌpriːtæks 'prɒfɪt/ *noun* the amount of profit a company makes before taxes are deducted

pretest /'priːtest/ *noun* evaluation of an advertising campaign before it is run

pre-testing /'priː testɪŋ/ *noun* the testing or evaluation of a product or advertising campaign before it is launched or run ○ *Pre-testing has shown that the product would do well in the country as a whole.* ○ *The area chosen for pre-testing may not be representative enough of the whole country.*

preview /'priːvjuː/ *noun* a showing of a film, a television commercial or an exhibition to a specially invited audience before the general public sees it

price /praɪs/ *noun* **1.** money which has to be paid to buy something □ **competitive price** a low price aimed to compete with a rival product □ **to sell goods off at half price** to sell goods at half the price at which they were being sold before □ **cars in the £18–19,000 price range** cars of different makes, selling for between £18,000 and £19,000 □ **price ex ship** the price that includes all costs up to the arrival of the ship at port □ **price ex warehouse** the price for a product which is to be collected from the manufacturer's or agent's warehouse and so does not include delivery **2.** □ **to increase in price** to become more expensive ○ *Petrol has increased in price* or *the price of petrol has increased.* □ **to increase prices** or **to raise prices** to make items more expensive □ **we will try to meet your price** we will try to offer a price which is acceptable to you □

to cut prices to reduce prices suddenly □ **to lower prices** or **to reduce prices** to make items cheaper ■ *verb* to give a price to a product ○ *We have two used cars for sale, both priced at £5,000.* □ **competitively priced** sold at a low price which competes with that of similar goods from other companies □ **the company has priced itself out of the market** the company has raised its prices so high that its products do not sell

'…the average price per kilogram for this season has been 300c' [*Australian Financial Review*]

'European manufacturers rely heavily on imported raw materials which are mostly priced in dollars' [*Duns Business Month*]

'…after years of relying on low wages for their competitive edge, Spanish companies are finding that rising costs and the strength of the peseta are pricing them out of the market' [*Wall Street Journal*]

price band /'praɪs bænd/ *noun* a method of grouping articles within a narrow range of prices

price ceiling /'praɪs ˌsiːlɪŋ/ *noun* the highest price which can be reached

price competition /'praɪs kɒmpəˌtɪʃ(ə)n/ *noun* the attempt to compete in a market through skilful pricing

price controls /'praɪs kənˌtrəʊlz/ *plural noun* legal measures to prevent prices rising too fast

price cutting /'praɪs ˌkʌtɪŋ/ *noun* a sudden lowering of prices

'…in today's circumstances, price-cutting is inevitable in an attempt to build up market share' [*Marketing Week*]

price differential /'praɪs dɪfəˌrenʃəl/ *noun* the difference in price between products in a range

price differentiation /'praɪs dɪfərenʃiˌeɪʃ(ə)n/ *noun* a pricing strategy in which a company sells the same product at different prices in different markets

price discrimination /'praɪs dɪskrɪmɪˌneɪʃ(ə)n/ *noun* the practice of charging different prices in different markets or to different types of customer ○ *Price discrimination has caused some ill-feeling among customers.*

price effect /'praɪs ɪˌfekt/ *noun* the result of a change in price on a person's

buying habits ○ *Before fixing the price, we'll have to carry out a survey to determine the price effect.*

price elasticity /'praɪs iːlæˌstɪsɪti/ *noun* a situation where a change in price has the effect of causing a big change in demand

price escalation clause /ˌpraɪs eskəˈleɪʃ(ə)n klɔːz/ *noun* a clause in a contract that permits the seller to raise prices if its costs increase

price fixing /'praɪs ˌfɪksɪŋ/ *noun* an illegal agreement between companies to charge the same price for competing products

price-insensitive /ˌpraɪs ɪnˈsensətɪv/ *adjective* describing essential goods or services for which sales remain constant regardless of price

price leadership /'praɪs ˌliːdəʃɪp/ *noun* a situation where the producers model their prices on those of one leading producer

price level /'praɪs ˌlev(ə)l/ *noun* the average price of a particular product in a country at a particular time

price list /'praɪs lɪst/ *noun* a sheet giving prices of goods for sale

price maintenance /'praɪs ˌmeɪntənəns/ *noun* an agreement between producers or distributors on a minimum price for a product

price-off label /praɪs 'ɒf ˌleɪb(ə)l/ *noun* a label on a product showing a reduced price

price pegging /'praɪs ˌpegɪŋ/ *noun* the practice of maintaining prices at a specific level

price point /'praɪs pɔɪnt/ *noun* the exact price for a range of different products which is psychologically important for the customer, since if an article is given a higher price it will discourage sales ○ *We must have a meeting to determine price points for our products.*

price range /'praɪs reɪndʒ/ *noun* a series of prices for similar products from different suppliers

price ring /'praɪs rɪŋ/ *noun* a group of producers or distributors who agree to control prices and market conditions in their industry

price-sensitive /ˌpraɪs ˌsensɪtɪv 'prɒdʌkt/ *adjective* referring to a product for which demand will change significantly if its price is increased or decreased. Products show an increased demand if the price falls and reduced demand if the price rises.

price tag /'praɪs tæg/ *noun* **1.** a label attached to an item being sold that shows its price **2.** the value of a person or thing

price ticket /'praɪs ˌtɪkɪt/ *noun* a piece of paper showing a price

price war /'praɪs wɔː/ *noun* a competition between companies to get a larger market share by cutting prices

pricing /'praɪsɪŋ/ *noun* the giving of a price to a product

pricing policy /'praɪsɪŋ ˌpɒlisi/ *noun* a company's policy in giving prices to its products ○ *Our pricing policy aims at producing a 35% gross margin.*

primacy /'praɪməsi/ *noun* the fact of being in first place or being the most important

primacy effect theory /'praɪməsi ɪfekt ˌθɪəri/ *noun* the theory that the first information in a message is most likely to be remembered

primary /'praɪməri/ *adjective* basic

'…farmers are convinced that primary industry no longer has the capacity to meet new capital taxes or charges on farm inputs' [*Australian Financial Review*]

primary brand /'praɪməri brænd/ *noun* a brand owned by a distributor rather than by a producer. Compare **private brand**

primary commodities /ˌpraɪməri kəˈmɒdɪtiz/ *plural noun* raw materials or food

primary data /ˌpraɪməri 'deɪtə/, **primary information** /ˌpraɪməri ɪnfəˈmeɪʃ(ə)n/ *noun* data or information which has not yet been published and must therefore be found by field research ○ *The company's market research proved very expensive since it needed so much primary data.*

primary demand /ˌpraɪməri dɪˈmɑːnd/ *noun* demand for a product in general, as opposed to demand for a par-

ticular brand ○ *The main producer companies are cooperating to create primary demand since this type of product is quite new to the public.*

primary industry /ˌpraɪməri ˈɪndəstri/ *noun* an industry dealing with basic raw materials such as coal, wood or farm produce

primary products /ˈpraɪməri ˈprɒdʌktz/ *plural noun* products which are basic raw materials, e.g. wood, milk or fish

prime /praɪm/ *adjective* most important

prime cost /ˌpraɪm ˈkɒst/ *noun* the cost involved in producing a product, excluding overheads

prime rate /ˈpraɪm reɪt/ *noun* the best rate of interest at which a bank lends to its customers

prime time /ˈpraɪm taɪm/ *noun* the most expensive advertising time for TV commercials ○ *We are putting out a series of prime-time commercials.*

principal /ˈprɪnsɪp(ə)l/ *noun* a person or company that is represented by an agent ○ *The agent has come to London to see his principals.* ■ *adjective* most important ○ *The principal shareholders asked for a meeting.* ○ *The country's principal products are paper and wood.* ○ *The company's principal asset is its design staff.*

'...the company was set up with funds totalling NorKr 145m with the principal aim of making capital gains on the secondhand market' [*Lloyd's List*]

print /prɪnt/ *noun* the action of marking letters or pictures on paper by a machine, and so producing a book, leaflet, newspaper, etc.

printed matter /ˈprɪntɪd ˌmætə/ *noun* printed items, e.g. books, newspapers and publicity sheets

print farming /ˈprɪnt ˌfɑːmɪŋ/ *noun* organising the printing by outside printers of printed material required by an organisation, such as advertising leaflets, catalogues, letterheads, etc.

print media /ˌprɪntɪd ˈmiːdiə/ *plural noun* advertising media, e.g. magazines and newspapers

print run /ˈprɪnt rʌn/ *noun* the number of copies of a publication or piece of advertising material which are printed ○ *The company has ordered a print run of 100,000 for their new catalogue.*

privacy /ˈprɪvəsi/ *noun* a situation of not being disturbed by other people, especially the knowledge that communications are private and cannot be accessed by others

private /ˈpraɪvət/ *adjective* belonging to a single person, not to a company or the state □ **a letter marked 'private and confidential'** a letter which must not be opened by anyone other than the person it is addressed to

'...management had offered to take the company private through a leveraged buyout for $825 million' [*Fortune*]

private brand /ˈpraɪvət brænd/ *noun* a brand owned by a distributor rather than by a producer. Compare **primary brand**

private enterprise /ˌpraɪvət ˈentəpraɪz/ *noun* businesses which are owned privately, not nationalised ○ *The project is completely funded by private enterprise.*

private label /ˈpraɪvət ˌleɪb(ə)l/ *noun* a brand name which is owned by a store, rather than the producer

private label goods /ˈpraɪvət ˌleɪb(ə)l ɡʊdz/ *plural noun* goods with a brand name which is owned by the store, rather than the producer

private limited company /ˌpraɪvət ˌlɪmɪtɪd ˈkʌmp(ə)ni/ *noun* **1.** a company with a small number of shareholders, whose shares are not traded on the Stock Exchange (NOTE: shortened to **Ltd**) **2.** a subsidiary company whose shares are not listed on the Stock Exchange, while those of its parent company are

privately /ˈpraɪvətli/ *adverb* away from other people ○ *The deal was negotiated privately.*

private means /ˌpraɪvət ˈmiːnz/ *plural noun* income from dividends, interest or rent which is not part of someone's salary

private property /ˌpraɪvət ˈprɒpəti/ noun property which belongs to a private person, not to the public

private sector /ˈpraɪvət ˌsektə/ noun all companies which are owned by private shareholders, not by the state ○ The expansion is completely funded by the private sector. ○ Salaries in the private sector have increased faster than in the public sector.

'…in the private sector the total number of new house starts was 3 per cent higher than in the corresponding period last year, while public sector starts were 23 per cent lower' [Financial Times]

privatisation /ˌpraɪvətaɪˈzeɪʃ(ə)n/, **privatization** noun the process of selling a nationalised industry to private owners

'…even without privatization, water charges would probably have to rise to pay for meeting EC water-quality rules' [Economist]

privatise /ˈpraɪvətaɪz/, **privatize** verb to sell a nationalised industry to private owners

probability /ˌprɒbəˈbɪlɪti/ noun the likelihood that something will happen, expressed mathematically

probability sampling /ˌprɒbəˈbɪlɪti ˌsɑːmplɪŋ/ noun the choosing of samples for testing without any special selection method

probable /ˈprɒbəb(ə)l/ adjective likely to happen ○ They are trying to prevent the probable collapse of the company. ○ It is probable that the company will collapse if a rescue package is not organised before the end of the month.

probing /ˈprəʊbɪŋ/ noun an attempt by an interviewer to get the interviewee to develop an answer ○ No amount of probing would induce the housewife to say why she did not like the new washing powder.

problem children /ˈprɒbləm ˌtʃɪldr(ə)n/ plural noun in the Boston matrix, products which are not very profitable, and have a low market share and a high growth rate ○ The problem children in our range make very little contribution to the company profits. (NOTE: also called **question marks**

and **wild cats**; the singular is **problem child**)

procurement /prəˈkjuːəmənt/ noun the act of buying equipment or raw materials for a company ○ Procurement of raw materials is becoming very complicated with the entry of so many new suppliers into the market.

produce noun /ˈprɒdjuːs/ foodstuffs grown on the land ○ home produce ○ agricultural produce ○ farm produce ■ verb /prəˈdjuːs/ to make or manufacture ○ the factory produces cars or engines

producer /prəˈdjuːsə/ noun a person, company or country that manufactures ○ a country which is a producer of high-quality watches ○ The company is a major car producer.

producer market /prəˈdjuːsə ˌmɑːkɪt/ noun customers who buy goods to be used in production

producer's surplus /prəˌdjuːsəz ˈsɜːpləs/ noun the amount by which the actual price of a product is more than the minimum which the producer would accept for it ○ There is a considerable producer's surplus because the product is in short supply. ○ If our customer knew the producer's surplus she would have offered much less than the asking price.

product /ˈprɒdʌkt/ noun **1.** something which is made or manufactured **2.** a manufactured item for sale

'…today new marketing is about new products based on consumer understanding and technology' [Marketing Week]

'…consistency of product is probably essential for successful branding' [Marketing Workshop]

'…any expansion or change in market share is most likely to come from the development and improvement of existing products' [Marketing]

product abandonment /ˌprɒdʌkt əˈbændənmənt/ noun the stopping of production and selling of a product

product acceptance /ˌprɒdʌkt əkˈseptəns/ noun the degree to which a product is accepted by the market and so sells well ○ We do not know what product acceptance will be in such an unknown market.

product advertising /ˈprɒdʌkt ˌædvətaɪzɪŋ/ noun the advertising of a

particular named product, not the company which makes it

product analysis /ˌprɒdʌkt əˈnæləsɪs/ *noun* an examination of each separate product in a company's range to find out why it sells, who buys it, etc.

product assortment /ˌprɒdʌkt əˈsɔːtmənt/ *noun* a collection of different products for sale

product churning /ˈprɒdʌkt ˌtʃɜːnɪŋ/ *noun* the practice of putting many new products onto the market in the hope that one of them will become successful (NOTE: Product churning is especially prevalent in Japan.)

product deletion /ˌprɒdʌkt dɪˈliːʃ(ə)n/ *noun* the removal of old products from the market as new ones are added to the company's range ○ *Product deletion was caused by poor sales.* ○ *If production costs continue to rise then product deletion will be the only answer.*

product design /ˈprɒdʌkt dɪˌzaɪn/ *noun* the design of consumer products

product development /ˌprɒdʌkt dɪˈveləpmənt/ *noun* the process of improving an existing product line to meet the needs of the market. ♦ **new product development**

product development cycle /ˌprɒdʌkt dɪˈveləpmənt ˌsaɪk(ə)l/ *noun* the stages in the development of a new product

product differentiation /ˌprɒdʌkt dɪfəˌrenʃiˈeɪʃ(ə)n/ *noun* the process of ensuring that a product has some unique features that distinguish it from competing ones ○ *We are adding some extra features to our watches in the interest of product differentiation.*

product endorsement /ˈprɒdʌkt ɪnˌdɔːsmənt/, **endorsement advertising** /ɪnˈdɔːsmənt ˌædvətaɪzɪŋ/ *noun* advertising which makes use of famous or qualified people to endorse a product ○ *Which celebrities have agreed to contribute to our endorsement advertising?* ○ *Product endorsement will, we hope, help our fund-raising campaign.*

product family /ˈprɒdʌkt ˌfæm(ə)li/ *noun* a group of interrelated products made by the same manufacturer

product idea /ˈprɒdʌkt aɪˌdɪə/ *noun* an idea for a totally new product or an adaptation of an existing one

product idea testing /ˌprɒdʌkt aɪˈdɪə ˌtestɪŋ/ *noun* the evaluation of a new product idea, usually by consulting representatives from all main departments in a company and interviewing a sample of consumers

product image /ˈprɒdʌkt ˌɪmɪdʒ/ *noun* the general idea which the public has of a product ○ *We need a huge promotional campaign to create the desired product image.*

production /prəˈdʌkʃən/ *noun* the making or manufacturing of goods for sale ○ *Production will probably be held up by industrial action.* ○ *We are hoping to speed up production by installing new machinery.*

production cost /prəˈdʌkʃən kɒst/ *noun* the cost of making a product

production department /prəˈdʌkʃən dɪˌpɑːtmənt/ *noun* the section of a company which deals with the making of the company's products

production line /prəˈdʌkʃən laɪn/ *noun* a system of making a product, where each item such as a car moves slowly through the factory with new sections added to it as it goes along ○ *He works on the production line.* ○ *She is a production-line worker.*

production manager /prəˈdʌkʃən ˌmænɪdʒə/ *noun* the person in charge of the production department

production standards /prəˈdʌkʃən ˌstændədz/ *plural noun* the quality of production

production target /prəˈdʌkʃən ˌtɑːgɪt/ *noun* the amount of units a factory is expected to produce

production unit /prəˈdʌkʃən ˌjuːnɪt/ *noun* a separate small group of workers producing a product

productive /prəˈdʌktɪv/ *adjective* which produces □ **productive discussions** useful discussions which lead to an agreement or decision

productive capital /prəˌdʌktɪv ˈkæpɪt(ə)l/ *noun* capital which is invested to give interest

productivity /ˌprɒdʌk'tɪvɪti/ *noun* the rate of output per employee or per machine in a factory ○ *Bonus payments are linked to productivity.* ○ *The company is aiming to increase productivity.* ○ *Productivity has fallen ⊘ risen since the company was taken over.*

'...though there has been productivity growth, the absolute productivity gap between many British firms and their foreign rivals remains' [*Sunday Times*]

productivity agreement /ˌprɒdʌk-'tɪvɪti əˌɡriːmənt/ *noun* an agreement to pay a productivity bonus

productivity bonus /ˌprɒdʌk'tɪvɪti ˌbəʊnəs/ *noun* an extra payment made to employees because of increased production per employee

productivity drive /ˌprɒdʌk'tɪvɪti draɪv/ *noun* an extra effort to increase productivity

product launch /'prɒdʌkt lɔːntʃ/ *noun* the act of putting a new product on the market

product leader /ˌprɒdʌkt 'liːdə/ *noun* the person who is responsible for managing a product line

product liability /ˌprɒdʌkt laɪə-'bɪlɪti/ *noun* the liability of the maker of a product for negligence in the design or production of the product

product life cycle /ˌprɒdʌkt 'laɪf ˌsaɪk(ə)l/ *noun* stages in the life of a product in terms of sales and profitability, from its launch to its decline ○ *Growth is the first stage in the product life cycle.* ○ *The machine has reached a point in its product life cycle where we should be thinking about a replacement for it.* ♦ **family**

product line /'prɒdʌkt laɪn/ *noun* a series of different products which form a group, all made by the same company ○ *We do not stock that line.* ○ *Computers are not one of our best-selling lines.* ○ *They produce an interesting line in garden tools.*

product management /ˌprɒdʌkt 'mænɪdʒmənt/ *noun* the process of directing the making and selling of a product as an independent item

product manager /ˌprɒdʌkt 'mænɪdʒə/ *noun* the manager or executive responsible for the marketing of a particular product ○ *To co-ordinate the selling of our entire range we need more consultation between product managers.*

product market /ˌprɒdʌkt 'mɑːkɪt/ *noun* a group of consumers for a product which is different from other groups to which the product is also sold

product-market strategies *plural noun* basic marketing strategies consisting of either market penetration, market development, product development or diversification

product mix /'prɒdʌkt mɪks/ *noun* a range of different products which a company has for sale

product placement /'prɒdʌkt ˌpleɪsmənt/ *noun* placing products as props on TV shows or in films as a form of advertising

product-plus /'prɒdʌkt plʌs/ *noun* features of a product which make it particularly attractive

product portfolio /ˌprɒdʌkt pɔːt-'fəʊliəʊ/ *noun* a collection of products made by the same company

product portfolio analysis /ˌprɒdʌkt pɔːt'fəʊliəʊ əˌnæləsɪs/ *noun* a model for a marketing strategy with various categories of product based on present performance and growth rate, which can help a business to plan its product development and strategy ○ *Product portfolio analysis showed that some products were neither performing well nor showing any signs of increasing their market share.*

product positioning /'prɒdʌkt pəˌzɪʃ(ə)nɪŋ/ *noun* the placing of a product in the market so that it is recognisable to the public

product range /'prɒdʌkt reɪndʒ/ *noun* **1.** a series of products from which the customer can choose **2.** a series of different products made by the same company which form a group

product recall /ˌprɒdʌkt 'riːkɔːl/ *noun* the removal from sale of products that may constitute a risk to consumers because of contamination, sabotage or faults

product research /ˌprɒdʌkt rɪ-
'sɜːtʃ/ *noun* research carried out to examine various competing products in a
market and the potential market for such
products

product strategy /'prɒdʌkt
ˌstrætədʒi/ *noun* the various elements
which a company has to take into account when developing a product, e.g.
price, design and availability

product testing /'prɒdʌkt ˌtestɪŋ/
noun the testing of a product by allowing a sample of consumers to use it
without knowing which brand it is ○
*Product testing showed that unfortu-
nately consumers preferred two other
brands to this one.*

profile /'prəʊfaɪl/ *noun* a brief description of the characteristics of something or someone ○ *They asked for a
profile of the possible partners in the
joint venture.* ○ *Her CV provided a profile of her education and career to date.*
'…the audience profile does vary greatly by
period: 41.6% of the adult audience is aged 16 to
34 during the morning period, but this figure
drops to 24% during peak viewing time'
[*Marketing Week*]

profit /'prɒfɪt/ *noun* money gained
from a sale which is more than the
money spent on making the item sold or
on providing the service offered □
profit after tax profit after tax being
paid □ **to take your profit** to sell shares
at a higher price than was paid for them,
and so realise the profit, rather than to
keep them as an investment □ **to show a
profit** to make a profit and state it in the
company accounts ○ *We are showing a
small profit for the first quarter.* □ **to
make a profit** to have more money as a
result of a deal □ **to move into profit** to
start to make a profit ○ *The company is
breaking even now, and expects to move
into profit within the next two months.* □
to sell at a profit to sell at a price which
gives you a profit □ **healthy profit** quite
a large profit
'…because capital gains are not taxed and
money taken out in profits and dividends is
taxed, owners of businesses will be using
accountants and tax experts to find loopholes in
the law' [*Toronto Star*]
'…the bank transferred $5 million to general
reserve compared with $10 million the previous
year which made the consolidated profit and

loss account look healthier' [*Hongkong
Standard*]

profitability /ˌprɒfɪtə'bɪlɪti/ *noun* **1.**
the ability to make a profit ○ *We doubt
the profitability of the project.* **2.** the
amount of profit made as a percentage
of costs

profitable /'prɒfɪtəb(ə)l/ *adjective*
which makes a profit ○ *She runs a very
profitable employment agency.*

**profit and loss account (P&L ac-
count)** /ˌprɒfɪt ən 'lɒs əˌkaʊnt/ *noun*
the accounts for a company showing expenditure and income over a period of
time, usually one calendar year, balanced to show a final profit or loss

profit centre /'prɒfɪt ˌsentə/ *noun* **1.**
a person or department that is considered separately for the purposes of calculating a profit ○ *We count the kitchen
equipment division as a single profit
centre.* **2.** a person, unit, or department
within an organisation that is considered
separately when calculating profit
(NOTE: Profit centres have a certain
amount of independence with regard
to marketing and pricing, and have responsibility for their own costs, revenues, and profits.)

profiteer /prɒfɪ'tɪə/ *noun* a person
who makes too much profit, especially
when goods are rationed or in short
supply

profiteering /prɒfɪ'tɪərɪŋ/ *noun* the
practice of making too much profit

profit-making /'prɒfɪt ˌmeɪkɪŋ/
adjective which makes a profit ○ *The
whole project was expected to be
profit-making by 2001 but it still hasn't
broken even.* ○ *It is hoped to make it
into a profit-making concern.*

profit margin /'prɒfɪt ˌmɑːdʒɪn/
noun the percentage difference between
sales income and the cost of sales

profit maximisation /'prɒfɪt
ˌmæksɪmaɪˌzeɪʃ(ə)n/ *noun* a business
strategy or policy based on achieving as
high a profit as possible ○ *The company
considers profit maximization a socially
irresponsible policy.*

pro forma /prəʊ 'fɔːmə/ *noun* a document issued before all relevant details

are known, usually followed by a final version

pro forma invoice /prəʊ ˌfɔːmə ˈɪnvɔɪs/, **pro forma** /prəʊ ˈfɔːmə/ *noun* an invoice sent to a buyer before the goods are sent, so that payment can be made or so that goods can be sent to a consignee who is not the buyer ○ *They sent us a pro forma invoice.* ○ *We only supply that account on pro forma.*

progress report /ˈprəʊgres rɪˌpɔːt/ *noun* a document which describes what progress has been made

project /ˈprɒdʒekt/ *noun* **1.** a plan ○ *He has drawn up a project for developing new markets in Europe.* **2.** a particular job of work which follows a plan ○ *We are just completing an engineering project in North Africa.* ○ *The company will start work on the project next month.*

project analysis /ˈprɒdʒekt əˌnæləsɪs/ *noun* the examination of all the costs or problems of a project before work on it is started

projected /prəˈdʒektɪd/ *adjective* planned or expected □ **projected sales** a forecast of sales ○ *Projected sales in Europe next year should be over £1m.*

projection /prəˈdʒekʃən/ *noun* a forecast of something which will happen in the future ○ *Projection of profits for the next three years.* ○ *The sales manager was asked to draw up sales projections for the next three years.*

project management /ˌprɒdʒekt ˈmænɪdʒmənt/ *noun* the coordination of the financial, material, and human resources needed to complete a project and the organisation of the work that the project involves

project manager /ˌprɒdʒekt ˈmænɪdʒə/ *noun* the manager in charge of a project

promissory note /ˈprɒmɪsəri ˌnəʊt/ *noun* a document stating that someone promises to pay an amount of money on a specific date

promote /prəˈməʊt/ *verb* to advertise □ **to promote a new product** to increase the sales of a new product by a sales campaign, by TV commercials or free gifts, or by giving discounts

promotion /prəˈməʊʃ(ə)n/ *noun* all means of conveying the message about a product or service to potential customers, e.g. publicity, a sales campaign, TV commercials or free gifts ○ *Our promotion budget has been doubled.* ○ *The promotion team has put forward plans for the launch.* ○ *We are offering free holidays in France as part of our special in-store promotion.*

'...finding the right promotion to appeal to children is no easy task' [*Marketing*]

'...you have to study the profiles and people involved very carefully and tailor the promotion to fill those needs' [*Marketing Week*]

promotional /prəˈməʊʃ(ə)n(ə)l/ *adjective* used in an advertising campaign ○ *The admen are using balloons as promotional material.*

'...the simplest way to boost sales at the expense of regional newspapers is by a heavyweight promotional campaign' [*Marketing Week*]

promotional allowance /prəˌməʊʃ(ə)n(ə)l əˈlaʊəns/ *noun* a discount which is offered to a buyer in return for some promotional activity in connection with the product sold

promotional budget /prəˌməʊʃ(ə)n(ə)l ˈbʌdʒɪt/ *noun* a forecast of the cost of promoting a new product

promotional discount /prəˌməʊʃ(ə)n(ə)l ˈdɪskaʊnt/ *noun* a special discount offered as part of the promotion for a product

promotional mix /prəˌməʊʃ(ə)n(ə)l ˈmɪks/ *noun* the combination of all the elements that make up a company's promotion ○ *Our promotional mix consists of an extended TV and radio advertising campaign.* ○ *The exact promotional mix will depend on the costs of the various media available.*

promotional price /prəˈməʊʃ(ə)n(ə)l praɪs/ *noun* a reduced price offered in order to maximise sales (often when a product is launched)

promotional products /prəˈməʊʃ(ə)n(ə)l ˌprɒdʌkts/ *plural noun* premium offers, gifts, prizes, etc.

promotional tools /prəˈməʊʃ(ə)n(ə)l tuːlz/ *plural noun* material used in promotion, e.g. display material and sales literature ○ *A draw*

for a free holiday on the exhibition stand is one of the best promotional tools I know. ○ *The salesreps are armed with a full range of promotional tools.*

promotools /ˈprəʊməʊtuːlz/ *plural noun* same as **promotional tools** (*informal*)

prompt /prɒmpt/ *adjective* rapid or done immediately ○ *We got very prompt service at the complaints desk.* ○ *Thank you for your prompt reply to my letter.* □ **prompt payment** payment made rapidly □ **prompt supplier** a supplier who delivers orders rapidly ■ *noun* information or an idea offered to people to help them answer a question in a survey ■ *verb* to give someone help in answering a question ○ *In order to avoid influencing the answers, the interviewer must prompt the respondent only when it is really necessary.*

'…they keep shipping costs low and can take advantage of quantity discounts and other allowances for prompt payment' [*Duns Business Month*]

prompted awareness test /ˌprɒmptɪd əˈweənəs test/ *noun* a test where the respondents are asked if they know the named product

prompted recall /ˌprɒmptɪd ˈriːkɔːl/ *noun* a test to see how well people can remember an advertisement in which the respondents are given some help such as a picture which they might associate with the advertisement ○ *After a prompted recall test, the company and its advertising agency decided to change the advertisement.*

proof /pruːf/ *noun* evidence which shows that something is true

proof of purchase /ˌpruːf əv ˈpɜːtʃɪs/ *noun* evidence, e.g. a sales slip, to show that an article has been purchased, used in order to claim some benefit such as a free gift, or in order to claim reimbursement

propaganda /ˌprɒpəˈɡændə/ *noun* an attempt to spread an idea through clever use of the media and other forms of communication ○ *The charity has been criticised for spreading political propaganda.*

propensity /prəˈpensɪti/ *noun* a tendency

propensity to consume /prəˌpensɪti tə kənˈsjuːm/ *noun* the ratio between consumers' needs and their expenditure on goods

propensity to import /prəˌpensɪti tə ɪmˈpɔːt/ *noun* the ratio between changes in the national income and changes in expenditure on imports

propensity to invest /prəˌpensɪti tə ɪnˈvest/ *noun* the tendency of producers to invest in capital goods

propensity to save /prəˌpensɪti tə ˈseɪv/ *noun* the tendency of consumers to save instead of spending on consumer goods

property developer /ˈprɒpəti dɪˌveləpə/ *noun* a person who buys old buildings or empty land and builds new buildings for sale or rent

proprietary goods /prəˈpraɪət(ə)ri ɡʊdz/ *plural noun* brands of a product such as medicines that are owned by the company which makes them

prospect /ˈprɒspekt/ *noun* **1.** □ **prospects for the market** *or* **market prospects are worse than those of last year** sales in the market are likely to be lower than they were last year **2.** a person who may become a customer ○ *The salesforce were looking out for prospects.*

prospecting /prəˈspektɪŋ/ *noun* the act of looking for new customers

prospective /prəˈspektɪv/ *adjective* which may happen in the future □ **a prospective buyer** someone who may buy in the future ○ *There is no shortage of prospective buyers for the computer.*

prospects /ˈprɒspekts/ *plural noun* the possibilities for the future

prospectus /prəˈspektəs/ *noun* a document which gives information to attract buyers or customers ○ *The restaurant has people handing out prospectuses in the street.*

'…when the prospectus emerges, existing shareholders and any prospective new investors can find out more by calling the free share information line; they will be sent a leaflet. Non-shareholders who register in this way will receive a prospectus when it is published; existing shareholders will be sent one automatically' [*Financial Times*]

protectionism /prəˈtekʃənɪz(ə)m/ noun the practice of protecting producers in the home country against foreign competitors by banning or taxing imports or by imposing import quotas

protest noun /ˈprəʊtest/ an official document which proves that a bill of exchange has not been paid ■ verb /prəˈtest/ □ **to protest a bill** to draw up a document to prove that a bill of exchange has not been paid

prototype /ˈprəʊtətaɪp/ noun the first model of a new product before it goes into production ○ a prototype car ○ a prototype plane ○ The company is showing the prototype of the new model at the exhibition.

provisional /prəˈvɪʒ(ə)n(ə)l/ adjective temporary or not final or permanent ○ The sales department has been asked to make a provisional forecast of sales. ○ The provisional budget has been drawn up for each department. ○ They faxed their provisional acceptance of the contract.

prune /pruːn/ verb to reduce a product range by deleting old products ○ The new marketing director insisted on pruning the product line to streamline the company's functions.

psychogalvanometer /ˌsaɪkəʊgælvəˈnɒmɪtə/ noun an instrument used to measure emotional reactions to advertising by checking the degree of sweating on the palms of the hands ○ The results of the psychogalvanometer test suggested that the ad was so dull it had no effect whatever on the public.

psychographics /ˌsaɪkəʊˈgræfɪks/ noun the study of the life style of different sectors of society for marketing purposes ○ Psychographics can help define the market segment we should be aiming for with our product. (NOTE: takes a singular verb)

psychographic segmentation /-ˌsaɪkəʊˌgræfɪk ˌsegmənˈteɪʃ(ə)n/ noun the division of a market into segments according to the lifestyles of the customers

public /ˈpʌblɪk/ adjective referring to all the people in general ■ noun □ **the public** or **the general public** the people

publication /ˌpʌblɪˈkeɪʃ(ə)n/ noun **1.** the act of making something public by publishing it ○ the publication of the latest trade figures **2.** a printed document which is to be sold or given to the public ○ We asked the library for a list of government publications.

public image /ˌpʌblɪk ˈɪmɪdʒ/ noun an idea which the people have of a company or a person ○ The minister is trying to improve her public image.

publicise /ˈpʌblɪsaɪz/, **publicize** verb to attract people's attention to a product for sale, a service or an entertainment ○ The campaign is intended to publicise the services of the tourist board. ○ We are trying to publicise our products by advertisements on buses.

publicity /pʌˈblɪsɪti/ noun the process of attracting the attention of the public to products or services by mentioning them in the media

publicity budget /pʌˈblɪsɪti ˌbʌdʒɪt/ noun money allowed for expenditure on publicity

publicity copy /pʌˈblɪsɪti ˌkɒpi/ noun the text of a proposed advertisement before it is printed ○ She writes publicity copy for a travel firm.

publicity department /pʌˈblɪsɪti dɪˌpɑːtmənt/ noun the section of a company which organises the company's publicity

publicity expenditure /pʌˈblɪsɪti ɪkˌspendɪtʃə/ noun money spent on publicity

publicity handout /pʌˈblɪsɪti ˌhændaʊt/ noun an information sheet which is given to members of the public

publicity manager /pʌˈblɪsɪti ˌmænɪdʒə/ noun the person in charge of a publicity department

publicity matter /pʌˈblɪsɪti ˌmætə/ noun sheets, posters or leaflets used for publicity

publicity slogan /pʌˈblɪsɪti ˌsləʊgən/ noun a group of words which can be easily remembered and which is used in publicity for a product ○ We are using the slogan 'Smiths can make it' on all our publicity.

public limited company /ˌpʌblɪk ˌlɪmɪtɪd ˈkʌmp(ə)ni/ *noun* a company whose shares can be bought on the Stock Exchange. Abbr **Plc**

public opinion /ˌpʌblɪk əˈpɪnjən/ *noun* what people think about something

public relations /ˌpʌblɪk rɪˈleɪʃ(ə)nz/ *plural noun* building up and keeping good relations between an organisation and the public, or an organisation and its employees, so that people know and think well of what the organisation is doing ○ *She works in public relations.* ○ *A public relations firm handles all our publicity.* Abbr **PR**

public relations consultancy /ˌpʌblɪk rɪˈleɪʃ(ə)nz kənˌsʌltənsi/ *noun* a firm which advises on public relations

public relations department /ˌpʌblɪk rɪˈleɪʃ(ə)nz dɪˌpɑːtmənt/ *noun* the section of a company which deals with relations with the public. Abbr **PR department**

public relations exercise /ˌpʌblɪk rɪˈleɪʃ(ə)nz ˌeksəsaɪz/ *noun* a campaign to improve public relations

public relations officer /ˌpʌblɪk rɪˈleɪʃ(ə)nz ˌɒfɪsə/ *noun* a person in an organisation who is responsible for public relations activities. Abbr **PRO**

publics /ˈpʌblɪks/ *plural noun* groups of people that are identified for marketing purposes ○ *What publics is this product likely to appeal to?* ○ *Different marketing messages need to be aimed at different publics.*

public sector /ˈpʌblɪk ˌsektə/ *noun* nationalised industries and services ○ *a report on wage rises in the public sector* or *on public-sector wage settlements*

public service advertising /ˌpʌblɪk ˈsɜːvɪs ˌædvətaɪzɪŋ/ *noun* the advertising of a public service or cause such as famine relief

public transport /ˌpʌblɪk ˈtrænspɔːt/ *noun* transport which is used by any member of the public, e.g. buses and trains

public transport system /ˌpʌblɪk ˈtrænspɔːt ˌsɪstəm/ *noun* a system of trains, buses, etc., used by the general public

public warehouse /ˌpʌblɪk ˈweəhaʊs/ *noun* a warehouse which stores goods which are awaiting shipment or which have just been landed

puff /pʌf/ *noun* a claim made for a product or an organisation in order to promote it ○ *The magazine article was supposed to be about telecommunications, but was just a puff for a new modem.*

puffery /ˈpʌfəri/ *noun* advertising which praises the product or service being sold in an exaggerated way, without any specific factual data

puff piece /ˈpʌf piːs/ *noun* a supposedly objective newspaper or magazine article about a product or service, which reads as if it were written by an in-house publicity department and may in fact be written by advertising people on behalf of a client

pull-push strategy /ˌpʊl ˈpʊʃ ˌstrætədʒi/ *noun* a combination of both pull and push strategies

pull strategy /ˈpʊl ˌstrætədʒi/ *noun* an attempt by a producer to use heavy advertising to persuade final users to buy a product, so 'pulling' the product through the distribution channel to the point of sale ○ *We must develop a better pull strategy to allow retailers to sell off their excess stocks.*

pump priming /ˈpʌmp ˌpraɪmɪŋ/ *noun* government investment in new projects which it hopes will benefit the economy

purchase /ˈpɜːtʃɪs/ *noun* a product or service which has been bought □ **to make a purchase** to buy something ■ *verb* to buy □ **to purchase something for cash** to pay cash for something

purchase book /ˈpɜːtʃɪs bʊk/ *noun* a book in which purchases are recorded

purchase history /ˈpɜːtʃɪs ˌhɪst(ə)ri/ *noun* a record of purchases which a customer has made in the past, or of sales made by a retail outlet, or of sales of a product over a specific period

purchase ledger /ˈpɜːtʃɪs ˌledʒə/ noun a book in which expenditure is noted

purchase order /ˈpɜːtʃɪs ˌɔːdə/ noun an official order made out by a purchasing department for goods which a company wants to buy ○ *We cannot supply you without a purchase order number.*

purchase price /ˈpɜːtʃɪs praɪs/ noun a price paid for something

purchaser /ˈpɜːtʃɪsə/ noun a person or company that purchases ○ *The company has found a purchaser for its warehouse.* □ **the company is looking for a purchaser** the company is trying to find someone who will buy it

purchase tax /ˈpɜːtʃɪs tæks/ noun a tax paid on things which are bought

purchasing /ˈpɜːtʃɪsɪŋ/ noun buying

purchasing department /ˈpɜːtʃɪsɪŋ dɪˌpɑːtmənt/ noun the section of a company which deals with the buying of stock, raw materials, equipment, etc.

purchasing manager /ˈpɜːtʃɪsɪŋ ˌmænɪdʒə/ noun the head of a purchasing department

purchasing officer /ˈpɜːtʃɪsɪŋ ˌɒfɪsə/ noun a person in a company or organisation who is responsible for buying stock, raw materials, equipment, etc.

purchasing opportunity /ˈpɜːtʃɪsɪŋ ɒpəˌtjuːnɪti/ noun a possibility for a customer to make a purchase

pure competition /ˌpjʊə ˌkɒmpɪˈtɪʃ(ə)n/ noun a hypothetical model of a market where all products of a particular type are identical, where there is complete information about market conditions available to buyers and sellers, and complete freedom for sellers to enter or leave the market

push /pʊʃ/ noun the action of making something move forward ◇ **push the envelope** /ˌpʊʃ ði ˈenvələʊp/ to go beyond normal limits and try to do something that is new and sometimes risky

push money /ˈpʊʃ ˌmʌni/ noun cash given to a sales force to encourage them to promote a product

push strategy /ˈpʊʃ ˌstrætədʒi/ noun **1.** an attempt by a manufacturer to push the product towards the customer **2.** an attempt by a producer to persuade distributors to take part in the marketing of a product, so 'pushing' it through the distribution channel

put down /ˌpʊt ˈdaʊn/ verb to make a deposit ○ *to put down money on a house* (NOTE: **putting- put**)

put in /ˌpʊt ˈɪn/ verb □ **to put an ad in a paper** to have an ad printed in a newspaper □ **to put in a bid for something** to offer to buy something, usually in writing □ **to put in an estimate for something** to give someone a written calculation of the probable costs of carrying out a job □ **to put in a claim for damage** to ask an insurance company to pay for damage

pyramid selling /ˈpɪrəmɪd ˌselɪŋ/ noun an illegal way of selling goods or investments to the public, where each selling agent pays for the franchise to sell the product or service, and sells that right on to other agents together with stock, so that in the end the person who makes most money is the original franchiser, and sub-agents or investors may lose all their investments

Q

quad crown /'kwɒd kraʊn/ *noun* a poster size corresponding to twice a double crown

qualified prospects /ˌkwɒlɪfaɪd 'prɒspekts/ *plural noun* prospective customers who can make buying decisions

qualitative /'kwɒlɪtətɪv/ *adjective* referring to quality

qualitative audit /ˌkwɒlɪtətɪv 'ɔːdɪt/ *noun* examining an advertising agency's work in planning and developing a client's advertising programme

qualitative data /ˌkwɒlɪtətɪv 'deɪtə/ *noun* data found in qualitative research

qualitative research /ˌkwɒlɪtətɪv rɪ'sɜːtʃ/ *noun* research based on finding the opinions and attitudes of respondents rather than any scientifically measurable data ○ *Qualitative research can be used to ascertain consumers' attitudes to a new advertising campaign.* ○ *Qualitative research will not give objective information.*

quality /'kwɒlɪti/ *noun* what something is like or how good or bad something is ○ *The poor quality of the service led to many complaints.* ○ *There is a market for good-quality secondhand computers.* □ **we sell only quality farm produce** we sell only farm produce of the best quality □ **high quality** *or* **top quality** of the very best quality ○ *The store specialises in high-quality imported items.*

quality control /'kwɒlɪti kən,trəʊl/ *noun* the process of making sure that the quality of a product is good

quality controller /'kwɒlɪti kən-,trəʊlə/ *noun* a person who checks the quality of a product

quality label /'kwɒlɪti ˌleɪb(ə)l/ *noun* a label which states the quality of something

quality press /'kwɒlɪti pres/ *noun* newspapers aiming at the upper end of the market ○ *We advertise in the quality press.*

quantitative /'kwɒntɪtətɪv/ *adjective* referring to quantity

'…the collection of consumer behaviour data in the book covers both qualitative and quantitative techniques' [*Quarterly Review of Marketing*]

quantitative data /ˌkwɒntɪtətɪv 'deɪtə/ *noun* data gathered in quantitative research

quantitative research /ˌkwɒntɪtətɪv rɪ'sɜːtʃ/ *noun* research based on measurable data gathered by sampling ○ *Quantitative research will provide a firm basis for strategy decisions.*

quantity /'kwɒntɪti/ *noun* **1.** the amount or number of items ○ *a small quantity of illegal drugs* ○ *She bought a large quantity of spare parts.* **2.** a large amount ○ *The company offers a discount for quantity purchase.*

quantity discount /ˌkwɒntɪti 'dɪskaʊnt/ *noun* a discount given to people who buy large quantities

quantity purchase /'kwɒntɪti ˌpɜːtʃɪs/ *noun* you pay 10% less if you buy a large quantity

quarterly /'kwɔːtəli/ *noun* a newspaper or magazine which appears four times a year ○ *We're advertising in a medical quarterly.*

quasi- /kweɪzaɪ/ *prefix* almost or which seems like ○ *a quasi-official body*

quasi-retailing /ˌkweɪzaɪ 'riːteɪlɪŋ/ *noun* retailing relating to the provision

of services, as in restaurants or hairdressers

quay /kiː/ *noun* the place in a port where ships can tie up □ **price ex quay** *or* **price ex dock** price of goods after they have been unloaded, not including transport from the harbour

question marks /ˈkwestʃən mɑːks/ *plural noun* same as **problem children**

questionnaire /ˌkwestʃəˈneə/ *noun* a printed list of questions aiming at collecting data in an unbiased way, especially used in market research ○ *We'll send out a questionnaire to test the opinions of users of the system.* ○ *We were asked to answer or to fill in a questionnaire about holidays abroad.*

quota /ˈkwəʊtə/ *noun* a limited amount of something which is allowed to be produced or imported, etc.

'Canada agreed to a new duty-free quota of 600,000 tonnes a year' [*Globe and Mail (Toronto)*]

quota sample /ˈkwəʊtə ˌsɑːmpəl/ *noun* a sample which is preselected on the basis of specific criteria so as best to represent the group of people sampled ○ *The quota sample was used to represent the various ethnic groupings in their correct proportions.*

quota system /ˈkwəʊtə ˌsɪstəm/ *noun* a system where imports or supplies are regulated by fixed maximum amounts

quotation /kwəʊˈteɪʃ(ə)n/ *noun* an estimate of how much something will cost ○ *They sent in their quotation for the job.* ○ *Our quotation was much lower than all the others.* ○ *We accepted the lowest quotation.*

quote /kwəʊt/ *verb* **1.** to repeat words or a reference number used by someone else ○ *He quoted figures from the annual report.* ○ *In reply please quote this number.* ○ *When making a complaint please quote the batch number printed on the box.* ○ *She replied, quoting the number of the account.* **2.** to estimate what costs are likely to be ○ *to quote a price for supplying stationery* ○ *He quoted me a price of £1,026.* ○ *Can you quote for supplying 20,000 envelopes?* ■ *noun* an estimate of how much something will cost (*informal*) ○ *to give someone a quote for supplying computers* ○ *We have asked for quotes for refitting the shop.* ○ *His quote was the lowest of three.* ○ *We accepted the lowest quote.*

'...banks operating on the foreign exchange market refrained from quoting forward US/Hongkong dollar exchange rates' [*South China Morning Post*]

R

rack /ræk/ *noun* a frame to hold items for display ○ *a magazine rack* ○ *Put the birthday-card display rack near the checkout.* ○ *We need a bigger display rack for these magazines.*

rack board /'ræk bɔːd/ *noun* a board on which items can be displayed, showing the names and prices of products

rack jobber /'ræk ˌdʒɒbə/ *noun* a wholesaler who sells goods by putting them on racks in retail shops

radio button /'reɪdiəʊ ˌbʌt(ə)n/ *noun* a device on a computer screen that can be used to select an option from a list

rail /reɪl/ *noun* a railway system ○ *Six million commuters travel to work by rail each day.* ○ *We ship all our goods by rail.* ○ *Rail travellers are complaining about rising fares.* ○ *Rail travel is cheaper than air travel.* □ **free on rail (FOR)** a price including all the seller's costs until the goods are delivered to the railway for shipment

railhead /'reɪlhed/ *noun* the end of a railway line ○ *The goods will be sent to the railhead by lorry.*

railway /'reɪlweɪ/ *noun* a system using trains to carry passengers and goods ○ *The local railway station has frequent trains to London.* ○ *They are planning to close the railway line as it isn't economic.* ○ *The country's railway network is being modernised.* (NOTE: American English is **railroad**)

rake-off /'reɪk ɒf/ *noun* a person's share of profits from a deal, especially if obtained illegally ○ *The group gets a rake-off on all the company's sales.* ○ *He got a £100,000 rake-off for introducing the new business.* (NOTE: plural is **rake-offs**)

R&D *abbr* research and development

random /'rændəm/ *adjective* done without making any special selection □ **at random** without special selection ○ *The chairman picked out two sales reports at random.*

random check /ˌrændəm 'tʃek/ *noun* a check on items taken from a group without any special selection

random error /ˌrændəm 'erə/ *noun* a computer error for which there is no special reason

random fluctuation /ˌrændəm flʌktʃu'eɪʃ(ə)n/ *noun* unforeseeable deviation from an expected trend

random observation method /ˌrændəm ɒbzə'veɪʃ(ə)n ˌmeθəd/ *noun* same as **activity sampling**

random sample /ˌrændəm 'saːmpəl/ *noun* a sample taken without any selection

random sampling /ˌrændəm 'saːmplɪŋ/ *noun* the choosing of samples for testing without any special selection

random walk /ˌrændəm 'wɔːk/ *noun* a sampling technique which allows for random selection within specific limits set up by a non-random technique

range /reɪndʒ/ *noun* **1.** a series of items from which the customer can choose ○ *Their range of products* or *product range is too narrow.* ○ *We offer a wide range of sizes* or *range of styles.* **2.** a spread of sizes or amounts within fixed limits ○ *We make shoes in a wide range of prices.* **3.** a set of activities or products of the same general type or variety ○ *This falls within the company's range of activities.* ■ *verb* to be within a group of sizes or amounts falling within fixed limits ○ *The company sells prod-*

ucts ranging from cheap downmarket pens to imported luxury items. ○ The company's salary scale ranges from £8,000 for a trainee to £150,000 for the managing director. ○ Our activities range from mining in the USA to computer services in Scotland.

'…the latest addition to the range features two hotplates, a storage cupboard, a refrigerator and a microwave oven' [*Sales & Marketing Management*]

'…the range has been extended to nine products' [*Marketing Week*]

rapport /ræˈpɔː/ noun good communication and understanding between two people ○ The interviewer managed to establish a good rapport with the interviewees. ○ Co-ordination is difficult owing to lack of rapport between the marketing manager and the managing director.

rate /reɪt/ noun **1.** money charged for time worked or work completed **2.** the value of one currency against another ○ What is today's rate or the current rate for the dollar? □ **to calculate costs on a fixed exchange rate** to calculate costs on an exchange rate which does not change **3.** an amount, number or speed compared with something else ○ the rate of increase in redundancies ○ The rate of absenteeism or the absenteeism rate always increases in fine weather.

'…state-owned banks cut their prime rate a percentage point to 11%' [*Wall Street Journal*]

'…the unions had argued that public sector pay rates had slipped behind rates applying in private sector employment' [*Australian Financial Review*]

'…royalties have been levied at a rate of 12.5% of full production' [*Lloyd's List*]

'…the minister is not happy that banks are paying low interest on current accounts of less than 10 per cent, but are charging rates of between 60 and 71 per cent on loans' [*Business in Africa*]

rate card /ˈreɪt kɑːd/ noun a list of charges for advertising issued by a newspaper or magazine

rate of exchange /reɪt əv/ noun same as **exchange rate**

rate of interest /ˌreɪt əv ˈɪntrəst/ noun the percentage of the basic sum involved that a borrower has to pay a lender for the use of his or her money or that is paid out to an investor

rate of return /ˌreɪt əv rɪˈtɜːn/ noun the amount of interest or dividend which comes from an investment, shown as a percentage of the money invested

rate of sales /ˌreɪt əv ˈseɪlz/ noun the speed at which units are sold

rate of turnover /ˌreɪt əv ˈtɜːnəʊvə/ noun the length of time taken from the purchase of an item of stock to its replacement after being sold ○ The rate of turnover is so low that some articles have been in the shop for more than a year.

rating /ˈreɪtɪŋ/ noun the act of giving something a value or the value given

ratings /ˈreɪtɪŋz/ plural noun the estimated number of people who watch TV programmes ○ The show is high in the ratings, which means it will attract good publicity.

ratings point /ˈreɪtɪŋz pɔɪnt/ noun one percentage point of a TV audience in a given area

ratio /ˈreɪʃiəʊ/ noun a proportion or quantity of something compared to something else ○ the ratio of successes to failures ○ Our product outsells theirs by a ratio of two to one.

rational /ˈræʃ(ə)n(ə)l/ adjective sensible, based on reason

rational appeal /ˌræʃ(ə)n(ə)l əˈpiːl/ noun advertising appeal to a prospective customer that uses logical arguments to show that the product satisfies the customer's practical needs (as opposed to an emotional appeal)

rationalisation /ˌræʃ(ə)nəlaɪˈzeɪʃ(ə)n/, **rationalization** noun the process of streamlining or making more efficient

rationalise /ˈræʃ(ə)nəlaɪz/, **rationalize** verb to streamline something or to make it more efficient ○ The rail company is trying to rationalize its freight services.

raw /rɔː/ adjective in the original state or not processed

'…it makes sense for them to produce goods for sale back home in the US from plants in Britain where raw materials are relatively cheap' [*Duns Business Month*]

raw data /rɔː ˈdeɪtə/ *noun* data as it is put into a computer, without being analysed

raw materials /rɔː məˈtɪəriəlz/ *plural noun* basic materials which have to be treated or processed in some way before they can be used, e.g. wood, iron ore or crude petroleum

reach /riːtʃ/ *verb* to get to an audience ■ *noun* the actual number of people who will see an advertisement once (as opposed to the frequency, which is the number of times one person sees an advertisement over a given period of time) ○ *The success of an advertisement depends on its reach.*

readability /ˌriːdəˈbɪlɪti/ *noun* the fact of being easy to read (either copy for an advertisement or the advertisement itself)

reader /ˈriːdə/ *noun* a person who reads a newspaper or magazine

reader advertisement /ˈriːdər ədˌvɜːtɪsmənt/ *noun* an advertisement in the form of editorial matter

reader loyalty /ˌriːdə ˈlɔɪəlti/ *noun* the inclination of a person to keep reading and buying the same publication

readership /ˈriːdəʃɪp/ *noun* all the people who read a particular publication ○ *Our readership has increased since we included more feature articles in the magazine.*

reader's inquiry card /ˌriːdəz ɪnˈkwaɪəri kɑːd/, **reader's service card** /ˌriːdəz ˈsɜːvɪs kɑːd/ *noun* a card bound into a magazine which contains a matrix of numbers and letters on which readers can mark codes for products they wish to have further information about. The card is returned to the publisher, who gets the advertiser to send the relevant information to the reader.

reading and noting /ˌriːdɪŋ ən ˈnəʊtɪŋ/ *noun* a research statistic showing the proportion of the readership of a publication who actually read a given advertisement

readvertise /riːˈædvətaɪz/ *verb* to advertise again □ **to readvertise a post** to put in a second advertisement for a vacant post ○ *All the candidates failed*

the test, so we will just have to readvertise.

readvertisement /ˌriːədˈvɜːtɪsmənt/ *noun* a second advertisement for a vacant post ○ *The readvertisement attracted only two new applicants.*

ready /ˈredi/ *adjective* **1.** fit to be used or to be sold ○ *The order will be ready for delivery next week.* ○ *The driver had to wait because the shipment was not ready.* **2.** quick □ **these items find a ready sale in the Middle East** these items sell rapidly or easily in the Middle East

ready cash /ˌredi ˈkæʃ/ *noun* money which is immediately available for payment

ready-made /ˌredi ˈmeɪd/, **ready-to-wear** /ˌredi təˈweə/ *adjective* referring to clothes which are mass-produced and not made for each customer personally ○ *The ready-to-wear trade has suffered from foreign competition.*

ready market /ˌredi ˈmɑːkɪt/ *noun* a market with a high turnover of goods ○ *Distribution has to be good in such a ready market.*

ready money /ˌredi ˈmʌni/ *noun* cash or money which is immediately available

ready sale /ˌredi ˈseɪl/ *noun* a sale that is easily achieved ○ *Lengthy negotiations are a trial for salespeople used to ready sales.*

real /rɪəl/ *adjective* **1.** genuine and not an imitation ○ *His case is made of real leather* or *he has a real leather case.* ○ *That car is a real bargain at £300.* **2.** (of prices) shown in terms of money adjusted for inflation □ **in real terms** actually or really ○ *Prices have gone up by 3% but with inflation running at 5% that is a fall in real terms.*

'…real wages have been held down dramatically: they have risen as an annual rate of only 1% in the last two years' [*Sunday Times*]

'…sterling M3 rose by 13.5% in the year to August – seven percentage points faster than the rate of inflation and the biggest increase in real terms for years' [*Economist*]

'Japan's gross national product for the April-June quarter dropped 0.4% in real terms from the previous quarter' [*Nikkei Weekly*]

real time credit card processing /ˌrɪəl taɪm ˈkredɪt kɑːd ˌprəʊsesɪŋ/ *noun* online checking of a credit card that either approves or rejects it for use during a transaction

real time transaction /ˌrɪəl taɪm trænˈzækʃən/ *noun* an Internet payment transaction that is either approved or rejected immediately when the customer completes the online order form

rebate /ˈriːbeɪt/ *noun* **1.** a reduction in the amount of money to be paid ○ *We are offering a 10% rebate on selected goods.* **2.** money returned to someone because they have paid too much ○ *She got a tax rebate at the end of the year.*

rebating /riːˈbeɪtɪŋ/ *noun* the offering of a rebate

rebound /rɪˈbaʊnd/ *verb* to go back up again quickly ○ *The market rebounded on the news of the government's decision.*

rebuy /ˈriːbaɪ/ *noun* the act of buying a product again

recall /rɪˈkɔːl/ *verb* (*of a manufacturer*) to ask for products to be returned because of possible faults ○ *They recalled 10,000 washing machines because of a faulty electrical connection.* ■ *noun* the ability to remember an advertisement

recall test /ˈriːkɔːl test/ *noun* in advertising, a research test that checks how well someone can remember an advertisement ○ *A disappointing number of respondents in the recall test failed to remember the advertisement.*

receipt /rɪˈsiːt/ *noun* a piece of paper showing that money has been paid or that something has been received ○ *He kept the customs receipt to show that he had paid duty on the goods.* ○ *She lost her taxi receipt.* ○ *Keep the receipt for items purchased in case you need to change them later.* ○ *Please produce your receipt if you want to exchange items.*

'…gross wool receipts for the selling season to end June appear likely to top $2 billion' [*Australian Financial Review*]

receipts /rɪˈsiːts/ *plural noun* money taken in sales ○ *to itemise receipts and expenditure* ○ *Receipts are down against the same period of last year.*

'…the public sector borrowing requirement is kept low by treating the receipts from selling public assets as a reduction in borrowing' [*Economist*]

recession /rɪˈseʃ(ə)n/ *noun* a fall in trade or in the economy ○ *The recession has reduced profits in many companies.* ○ *Several firms have closed factories because of the recession.*

recipient /rɪˈsɪpiənt/ *noun* a person who receives something ○ *She was the recipient of an allowance from the company.* ○ *He was the recipient of the award for salesperson of the year.* ○ *A registered letter must be signed for by the recipient.*

reciprocal /rɪˈsɪprək(ə)l/ *adjective* done by one person, company or country to another one, which does the same thing in return ○ *We signed a reciprocal agreement* or *a reciprocal contract with a Russian company.*

reciprocal holdings /rɪˌsɪprək(ə)l ˈhəʊldɪŋz/ *plural noun* a situation where two companies own shares in each other to prevent takeover bids

reciprocal trade /rɪˌsɪprək(ə)l ˈtreɪd/ *noun* trade between two countries

reciprocate /rɪˈsɪprəkeɪt/ *verb* to do the same thing for someone as that person has done to you ○ *They offered us an exclusive agency for their cars and we reciprocated with an offer of the agency for our buses.*

'…in 1934 Congress authorized President Roosevelt to seek lower tariffs with any country willing to reciprocate' [*Duns Business Month*]

recognise /ˈrekəgnaɪz/, **recognize** *verb* **1.** to know someone or something because you have seen or heard them before ○ *I recognised his voice before he said who he was.* ○ *Do you recognise the handwriting on the letter?* **2.** □ **to recognise a union** to accept that a union can act on behalf of staff ○ *Although more than half the staff had joined the union, the management refused to recognise it.*

recognised agent /ˌrekəgnaɪzd ˈeɪdʒənt/ *noun* an agent who is approved by the company for which they act

recognition /ˌrekəgˈnɪʃ(ə)n/ *noun* the act of recognising something or somebody

recognition test /ˌrekəgˈnɪʃ(ə)n test/ *noun* a research test in advertising that checks to see how well someone can remember an advertisement either with or without prompting or aided recall

recommended retail price /ˌrekəmendɪd ˈriːteɪl praɪs/ *noun* the price at which a manufacturer suggests a product should be sold on the retail market, though this may be reduced by the retailer. Abbr **RRP**

record /ˈrekɔːd, rɪˈkɔːd/ *noun* **1.** a description of what has happened in the past ○ *the salesperson's record of service* or *service record* ○ *the company's record in industrial relations* **2.** success which is better than anything before □ **we broke our record for June** we sold more than we have ever sold before in June ○ *Sales last year equalled the record set in 1997.* ■ *verb* /rɪˈkɔːd/ to note or to report ○ *The company has recorded another year of increased sales.* ○ *Your complaint has been recorded and will be investigated.*

record-breaking /ˈrekɔːd ˌbreɪkɪŋ/ *adjective* better or worse than anything which has happened before ○ *We are proud of our record-breaking profits in 2000.*

recorded delivery /rɪˌkɔːdɪd dɪˈlɪv(ə)ri/ *noun* a mail service where the letters are signed for by the person receiving them ○ *We sent the documents (by) recorded delivery.*

recording /rɪˈkɔːdɪŋ/ *noun* the making of a note ○ *the recording of an order* or *of a complaint*

records /ˈrekɔːdz/ *plural noun* documents which give information ○ *The names of customers are kept in the company's records.* ○ *We find from our records that our invoice number 1234 has not been paid.*

recruit /rɪˈkruːt/ *verb* □ **to recruit new staff** to look for new staff to join a company ○ *We are recruiting staff for our new store.*

recruitment /rɪˈkruːtmənt/, **recruiting** /rɪˈkruːtɪŋ/ *noun* □ **the recruitment of new staff** the process of looking for new staff to join a company

recruitment advertising /rɪˈkruːtmənt ˌædvətaɪzɪŋ/ *noun* the advertising of jobs ○ *A sudden need for labour has led to a huge demand for recruitment advertising.*

recycle /riːˈsaɪk(ə)l/ *verb* to take waste material and process it so that it can be used again

recycled paper /riːˌsaɪk(ə)ld ˈpeɪpə/ *noun* paper made from waste paper

redeem /rɪˈdiːm/ *verb* to exchange a voucher, coupon or stamp for a gift or a reduction in price

redemption /rɪˈdempʃən/ *noun* the exchanging of vouchers, coupons or stamps for a gift or a reduction in price

red goods /ˈred gʊdz/ *plural noun* fast-selling convenience goods, especially food items. Compare **orange goods, yellow goods**

reduced rate /rɪˌdjuːst ˈreɪt/ *noun* a specially cheap charge

reduction /rɪˈdʌkʃən/ *noun* making something smaller or less ○ *Reduction in demand has led to the cancellation of several new projects.* ○ *The company was forced to make job reductions.* ○ *The company was forced to make reductions in its advertising budget.* ○ *Price reductions have had no effect on our sales.* ○ *We expect the new government to introduce tax reductions.* ○ *The new MD has proposed a series of staff reductions.*

re-export *noun* /riːˈekspɔːt/ the exporting of goods which have been imported ○ *The port is a centre for the re-export trade.* ○ *We import wool for re-export.* ○ *The value of re-exports has increased.* ■ *verb* /ˌriːekˈspɔːt/ to export something which has been imported

re-exportation /ˌriːekspɔːˈteɪʃ(ə)n/ *noun* the exporting of goods which have been imported

refer /rɪˈfɜː/ *verb* □ **the bank referred the cheque to drawer** the bank returned the cheque to person who wrote it because there was not enough money in the account to pay it

reference group /ˈref(ə)rəns ˌgruːp/ *noun* a group of people who share some interest or aim and are used by consumers as a model to be imitated

reference site /ˈref(ə)rəns saɪt/ *noun* a customer site where a new technology is being used successfully

refund *noun* /ˈriːfʌnd/ money paid back ○ *The shoes don't fit – I'm going to ask for a refund.* ○ *She got a refund after complaining to the manager.* ■ *verb* /rɪˈfʌnd/ to pay back money ○ *to refund the cost of postage* ○ *All money will be refunded if the goods are not satisfactory.*

refundable /rɪˈfʌndəb(ə)l/ *adjective* which can be paid back ○ *We ask for a refundable deposit of £20.* ○ *The entrance fee is refundable if you purchase £5 worth of goods.*

refusal /rɪˈfjuːz(ə)l/ *noun* an act of saying no

regiocentre stage /ˈriːdʒiəʊsentə ˌsteɪdʒ/ *noun* *US* the stage in a company's international marketing when a region consisting of several countries is treated as one market

registered /ˈredʒɪstəd/ *adjective* which has been noted on an official list ○ *a registered share transaction*

registered design /ˌredʒɪstəd dɪˈzaɪn/ *noun* a design which is legally registered to protect the owner against unauthorised use of it by others

registered letter /ˌredʒɪstəd ˈletə/, **registered parcel** *noun* a letter or parcel which is noted by the post office before it is sent, so that the sender can claim compensation if it is lost

registered trademark /ˌredʒɪstəd ˈtreɪdmɑːk/ *noun* 1. a particular name, design, etc. which has been registered by the manufacturer and which cannot

be used by other manufacturers 2. same as **trademark**

registration /ˌredʒɪˈstreɪʃ(ə)n/ *noun* the act of having something noted on an official list ○ *the registration of a trademark* or *of a share transaction*

registration fee /ˌredʒɪˈstreɪʃ(ə)n fiː/ *noun* 1. money paid to have something registered 2. money paid to attend a conference

registration number /ˌredʒɪˈstreɪʃ(ə)n ˌnʌmbə/ *noun* an official number, e.g. the number of a car

regression analysis /rɪˈgreʃ(ə)n əˌnæləsɪs/ *noun* a method of discovering the ratio of one dependent variable and one or more independent variables, so as to give a value to the dependent variable

regular /ˈregjʊlə/ *adjective* ordinary or standard ○ *The regular price is $1.25, but we are offering them at 99 cents.*

regular customer /ˌregjʊlə ˈkʌstəmə/ *noun* a customer who always buys from the same shop

regular model /ˌregjʊlə ˈmɒd(ə)l/ *noun* the main product in a company's product range ○ *We estimate that 65% of the customers interested in our product range will buy the regular model.*

regular size /ˈregjʊlə saɪz/ *noun* the standard size (smaller than economy size or family size)

regular staff /ˈregjʊlə stɑːf/ *noun* the full-time staff

regulate /ˈregjʊleɪt/ *verb* 1. to adjust something so that it works well or is correct 2. to change or maintain something by law □ **prices are regulated by supply and demand** prices are increased or lowered according to supply and demand □ **government-regulated price** a price which is imposed by the government

regulation /ˌregjʊˈleɪʃ(ə)n/ *noun* the process of making sure that something will work well or correctly ○ *government regulation of trading practices*

'…fear of audit regulation, as much as financial pressures, is a major factor behind the increasing number of small accountancy firms deciding to

sell their practices or merge with another firm' [*Accountancy*]

regulations /ˌregjʊ'leɪʃ(ə)nz/ *plural noun* laws or rules ○ *the new government regulations on housing standards* ○ *Fire regulations* or *Safety regulations were not observed at the restaurant.* ○ *Regulations concerning imports and exports are set out in this leaflet.*

'EC regulations which came into effect in July insist that customers can buy cars anywhere in the EC at the local pre-tax price' [*Financial Times*]

'…a unit trust is established under the regulations of the Department of Trade, with a trustee, a management company and a stock of units' [*Investors Chronicle*]

regulator /'regjʊleɪtə/ *noun* a person whose job it is to see that regulations are followed

'…the regulators have sought to protect investors and other market participants from the impact of a firm collapsing' [*Banking Technology*]

reimport *noun* /riː'ɪmpɔːt/ the importing of goods which have been exported from the same country ■ *verb* /ˌriːɪm'pɔːt/ to import goods which have already been exported

reimportation /ˌriːɪmpɔː'teɪʃ(ə)n/ *noun* the importing of goods which have already been exported

reinforcement advertising /riːɪn'fɔːsmənt ˌædvətaɪzɪŋ/ *noun* advertising aimed at making the positive features of a product stronger in order to reassure people who have already purchased it

reject /'riːdʒekt/ *noun* something which has been thrown out because it is not of the usual standard ○ *sale of rejects* or *of reject items* ○ *to sell off reject stock*

reject shop /'riːdʒekt ʃɒp/ *noun* a shop which specialises in the sale of rejects

relation /rɪ'leɪʃ(ə)n/ *noun* □ **in relation to** referring to or connected with ○ *They asked to see all documents in relation to the agreement.*

relational database /rɪˌleɪʃ(ə)nl 'deɪtəbeɪs/ *noun* a computer database in which different types of data are linked for analysis

relationship /rɪ'leɪʃ(ə)nʃɪp/ *noun* a link or connection

relationship building /rɪ'leɪʃ(ə)nʃɪp ˌbɪldɪŋ/ *noun* taking actions to develop a long-term relationship with the customer

relationship management /rɪ'leɪʃ(ə)nʃɪp ˌmænɪdʒmənt/ *noun* the management of customers so as to build long-term relationships with them

relationship marketing /rɪ'leɪʃ(ə)nʃɪp ˌmɑːkɪtɪŋ/ *noun* a long-term marketing strategy to build relationships with individual customers

relative /'relətɪv/ *adjective* compared to something else

relative cost /ˌrelətɪv 'kɒst/ *noun* the relationship between the cost of advertising space and the size of the audience

relaunch *noun* /'riːlɔːntʃ/ the act of putting a product back on the market again, after adapting it to changing market conditions ○ *The relaunch is scheduled for August.* ■ *verb* /riː'lɔːntʃ/ to put a product on the market again ○ *The product will be relaunched with some minor modifications next autumn.*

release /rɪ'liːs/ *noun* **1.** the act of setting free ○ *release from a contract* ○ *the release of goods from customs* **2.** □ **new release** a new CD or a piece of software put on the market ■ *verb* to put on the market ○ *They released several new CDs this month.* □ **to release dues** to send off orders which had been piling up while a product was out of stock

'…pressure to ease monetary policy mounted yesterday with the release of a set of pessimistic economic statistics' [*Financial Times*]

'…the national accounts for the March quarter released by the Australian Bureau of Statistics showed a real increase in GDP' [*Australian Financial Review*]

remainder /rɪ'meɪndə/ *verb* □ **to remainder books** to sell new books off cheaply ○ *The shop was full of piles of remaindered books.*

remainder merchant /rɪ'meɪndə ˌmɜːtʃənt/ *noun* a book dealer who buys unsold new books from publishers at a very low price

remainders /rɪ'meɪndəz/ *plural noun* new books sold cheaply

reminder /rɪ'maɪndə/ *noun* a letter to remind a customer that they have not paid an invoice ○ *to send someone a reminder*

reminder advertising /rɪ'maɪndər ˌædvətaɪzɪŋ/ *noun* advertising designed to remind consumers of a product already advertised ○ *Reminder advertising is particularly important in a highly competitive market.*

reminder line /rɪ'maɪndə laɪn/ *noun* a little advertising gimmick, e.g. a give-away pen with the company's name on it

remnant /'remnənt/ *noun* an odd piece of a large item such as, a carpet or fabric sold separately ○ *a sale of remnants* or *a remnant sale*

remnant space /'remnənt speɪs/ *noun* odd unsold advertising space, which is usually available at a discount

render /'rendə/ *verb* □ **to render an account** to send in an account ○ *Please find enclosed payment per account rendered.*

rental list /'rentl lɪst/ *noun* a mailing list of names and addresses which can be rented

reorder /riː'ɔːdə/ *noun* a further order for something which has been ordered before ○ *The product has only been on the market ten days and we are already getting reorders.* ■ *verb* to place a new order for something ○ *We must reorder these items because stock is getting low.*

reorder level /riː'ɔːdə ˌlev(ə)l/ *noun* the minimum amount of stock of an item which must be reordered when stock falls to this amount

rep /rep/ *noun* same as **representative** (*informal*) ○ *to hold a reps' meeting* ○ *Our reps make on average six calls a day.*

repack /riː'pæk/ *verb* to pack again

repacking /riː'pækɪŋ/ *noun* the act of packing again

repeat /rɪ'piːt/ *verb* □ **to repeat an order** to order something again

repeat business /rɪˌpiːt 'bɪznɪs/ *noun* business which involves a new or-

der for something which has been ordered before

repeat order /rɪˌpiːt 'ɔːdə/ *noun* a new order for something which has been ordered before ○ *The product has been on the market only ten days and we are already flooded with repeat orders.*

repeat purchasing /rɪˌpiːt 'pɜːtʃɪsɪŋ/ *noun* the purchasing of the same product a second time ■ *verb* the frequent buying of a low-priced item that is for everyday use such as soap or bread

repertory grid technique /ˌrepət(ə)rɪ 'grɪd tekˌniːk/ *noun* a market-research technique in which a test is first run to discover what the respondents' main criteria are in judging product brands. This is followed by another test in which the respondents evaluate brands on the basis of these established criteria.

reply /rɪ'plaɪ/ *noun* an answer ○ *the company's reply to the takeover bid* ○ *There was no reply to my letter* or *to my phone call.* ○ *I am writing in reply to your letter of the 24th.* ○ *verb* to answer ○ *We forgot to reply to the solicitor's letter.* ○ *The company has replied to the takeover bid by offering the shareholders higher dividends.* (NOTE: **replies-replying- replied**)

reply coupon /rɪ'plaɪ ˌkuːpɒn/ *noun* a form attached to a coupon ad which has to be filled in and returned to the advertiser

report /rɪ'pɔːt/ *noun* **1.** a statement describing what has happened or describing a state of affairs ○ *to make a report* or *to present a report* or *to send in a report on market opportunities in the Far East* ○ *The accountants are drafting a report on salary scales.* ○ *The sales manager reads all the reports from the sales team.* ○ *The chairman has received a report from the insurance company.* **2.** an official document from a government committee ○ *The government has issued a report on the credit problems of exporters.* ■ *verb* **1.** to make a statement describing something ○ *The salesforce reported an increased demand for the product.* ○ *He reported*

the damage to the insurance company. ○ We asked the bank to report on his financial status. ○ Each manager reports on the progress made by the new recruits during their first six weeks in the department. **2.** □ **to report to someone** to be responsible to or to be under someone ○ She reports direct to the managing director. ○ The salesforce reports to the sales director.

'...a draft report on changes in the international monetary system' [*Wall Street Journal*]

'...responsibilities include the production of premium quality business reports' [*Times*]

'...the research director will manage a team of business analysts monitoring and reporting on the latest development in retail distribution' [*Times*]

'...the successful candidate will report to the area director for profit responsibility for sales of leading brands' [*Times*]

reposition /ˌriːpəˈzɪʃ(ə)n/ *verb* to change the position of a product or company in the market

'...it is thought that the company will reposition the range in the mass market or relaunch it' [*Marketing Week*]

repositioning /ˌriːpəˈzɪʃ(ə)nɪŋ/ *noun* a change or adjustment to the position of a product in the market, or the consumers' idea of it, by changing its design or by different advertising ○ If this spring's promotional campaign doesn't achieve a repositioning of the product, sales will continue to fall.

repossess /ˌriːpəˈzes/ *verb* to take back an item which someone is buying under a hire-purchase agreement, or a property which someone is buying under a mortgage, because the purchaser cannot continue the payments

represent /reprɪˈzent/ *verb* to work for a company, showing goods or services to possible buyers ○ He represents an American car firm in Europe. ○ Our French distributor represents several other competing firms.

representation /ˌreprɪzenˈteɪʃ(ə)n/ *noun* the act of selling goods for a company ○ We offered them exclusive representation in Europe. ○ They have no representation in the USA.

representative /reprɪˈzentətɪv/ *adjective* which is an example of what all others are like ○ We displayed a representative selection of our product range. ○ The sample chosen was not representative of the whole batch. ■ *noun* **1.** a company which works for another company, selling their goods ○ We have appointed Smith & Co our exclusive representatives in Europe. **2.** same as **sales representative**

resale /ˈriːseɪl/ *noun* the selling of goods which have been bought ○ to purchase something for resale ○ The contract forbids resale of the goods to the USA.

resale price maintenance /ˌriːseɪl ˈpraɪs ˌmeɪntənəns/ *noun* a system where the price for an item is fixed by the manufacturer and the retailer is not allowed to sell it at a lower price. Abbr **RPM**

research /rɪˈsɜːtʃ/ *noun* the process of trying to find out facts or information ■ *verb* to study or try to find out information about something ○ They are researching the market for their new product.

research and development /rɪˌsɜːtʃ ən dɪˈveləpmənt/ *noun* **1.** scientific investigation which leads to making new products or improving existing products ○ The company spends millions on research and development. Abbr **R&D 2.** activities that are designed to produce new knowledge and ideas and to develop ways in which these can be commercially exploited by a business (NOTE: Research and development activities are often grouped together to form a separate division or department within an organisation.)

'...drug companies must make a massive investment in research and development if they are to ensure their future, according to a recently published report' [*Marketing*]

research brief /rɪˈsɜːtʃ briːf/ *noun* the basic objectives and instructions concerning a market-research project

research department /rɪˈsɜːtʃ dɪˌpɑːtmənt/ *noun* the section of a company which carries out research

researcher /rɪˈsɜːtʃə/ *noun* a person who carries out research ○ Government statistics are a useful source of information for the desk researcher.

research unit /rɪ'sɜːtʃ ˌjuːnɪt/ *noun* a separate small group of research workers

research worker /rɪ'sɜːtʃ ˌwɜːkə/ *noun* a person who works in a research department

resell /riː'sel/ *verb* to sell something which has just been bought ○ *The car was sold in June and the buyer resold it to an dealer two months later.* (NOTE: **reselling- resold**)

reseller /riː'selə/ *noun* somebody in the marketing chain who buys to sell to somebody else such as wholesalers, distributors, and retailers

reseller market /riː'selə ˌmɑːkɪt/ *noun* a market in which customers buy products in order to resell them as wholesalers or retailers ○ *Fewer and fewer consumers are buying the product, so prices are falling in the reseller market.*

reserved market /rɪˌzɜːvd 'mɑːkɪt/, **restricted market** /rɪˌstrɪktɪd 'mɑːkɪt/ *noun* a market in which producers agree not to sell more than a specific amount in order to control competition

reserve price /rɪ'zɜːv praɪs/ *noun* the lowest price which a seller will accept, e.g. at an auction or when selling securities through a broker ○ *The painting was withdrawn when it failed to reach its reserve price.*

resistance /rɪ'zɪstəns/ *noun* opposition felt or shown by people to something ○ *There was a lot of resistance from the team to the new plan.* ○ *The chairman's proposal met with strong resistance from the banks.*

resources /rɪ'sɔːsɪz/ *plural noun* **1.** a source of supply of something □ **we are looking for a site with good water resources** a site with plenty of water available **2.** the money available for doing something □ **the cost of the new project is easily within our resources** we have quite enough money to pay for the new project

respond /rɪ'spɒnd/ *verb* to reply to a question

respondent /rɪ'spɒndənt/ *noun* a person who answers questions in a survey ○ *Some of the respondents' answers were influenced by the way the questions were asked.*

response /rɪ'spɒns/ *noun* a reply or reaction ○ *There was no response to our mailing shot.* ○ *We got very little response to our complaints.*

'...forecasting consumer response is one problem which will never be finally solved' [*Marketing Week*]

response booster /rɪ'spɒns ˌbuːstə/ *noun* anything that will help increase the response rate

response function /rɪ'spɒns ˌfʌŋkʃən/ *noun* a figure which represents the value of a particular quantity of advertising impressions on a person

response level /rɪ'spɒns reɪt/, **response rate** *noun* the proportion of people approached in a survey who agree to answer questions ○ *The response rate has been very disappointing.*

response marketing /rɪ'spɒns ˌmɑːkɪtɪŋ/ *noun* in e-marketing, the process of managing responses or leads from the time they are received through to conversion to sale

response mechanism /rɪ'spɒns ˌmekənɪz(ə)m/ *noun* a method of showing a response to an Internet advertisement, or the way in which a customer can reply to an advertisement or direct mailshot, such as sending back a coupon or a faxback sheet

response rate /rɪ'spɒns reɪt/ *noun* the proportion of people who respond to a questionnaire or survey

re-sticker /riː 'stɪkə/ *verb* to put new stickers on stock, e.g. when increasing the price

restock /riː'stɒk/ *verb* to order more stock ○ *to restock after the Christmas sales*

restocking /riː'stɒkɪŋ/ *noun* the ordering of more stock

restraint /rɪ'streɪnt/ *noun* control

restraint of trade /rɪˌstreɪnt əv 'treɪd/ *noun* **1.** a situation where employees are not allowed to use their knowledge in another company if they change jobs **2.** an attempt by companies to fix prices, create monopolies or re-

duce competition, which could affect free trade

restrict /rɪ'strɪkt/ *verb* to limit or to impose controls on ○ *to restrict credit* ○ *to restrict the flow of trade* or *to restrict imports* ○ *We are restricted to twenty staff by the size of our offices.*

restricted market *noun* same as **reserved market**

restriction /rɪ'strɪkʃən/ *noun* a limit or control ○ *import restrictions* or *restrictions on imports* □ **to impose restrictions on imports/credit** to start limiting imports or credit □ **to lift credit restrictions/import restrictions** to allow credit to be given freely or imports to enter the country freely

restrictive /rɪ'strɪktɪv/ *adjective* which limits

/rɪ,strɪktɪv 'treɪd ,præktɪsɪz/ *plural noun* an arrangement between companies to fix prices or to share the market in order to restrict trade

résumé /'rezjʊmeɪ/ *noun US* a summary of a person's life story with details of education and work experience (NOTE: British English is **curriculum vitae**)

retail /'riːteɪl/ *noun* the sale of small quantities of goods to the general public □ **the goods in stock have a retail value of £1m** the value of the goods if sold to the public is £1m, before discounts and other factors are taken into account ■ *adverb* □ **he sells retail and buys wholesale** he buys goods in bulk at a wholesale discount and sells in small quantities to the public ■ *verb* **1.** □ **to retail goods** to sell goods direct to the public **2.** to sell for a price □ **these items retail at/for £2.50** the retail price of these items is £2.50

'...provisional figures show retail sales dropped 1.5% in January but wholesale prices released this week reveal a 1% increase last month' [*Marketing*]

retail audit /'riːteɪl ,ɔːdɪt/ *noun* a market research method by which a research company regularly checks a sample of retailers for unit sales and stock levels of different brands ○ *Since subscribing to the retail audit we've been able to compare our performance with that of our competitors.*

retail cooperative /'riːteɪl kəʊ-,ɒp(ə)rətɪv/ *noun* an organisation whose business is the buying and selling of goods that is run by a group of people who share the profits between them (NOTE: Retail cooperatives were the first offshoot of the cooperative movement.)

retail dealer /'riːteɪl ,diːlə/ *noun* a person who sells to the general public

retailer /'riːteɪlə/ *noun* a person who runs a retail business, selling goods direct to the public

'...voucher schemes are very attractive from the retailers' point of view' [*Marketing Week*]

retailer cooperative /'riːteɪlə kəʊ-,ɒp(ə)rətɪv/ *noun* a group of retailers who buy together from suppliers so as to be able to enjoy quantity discounts

retailing /'riːteɪlɪŋ/ *noun* the selling of full-price goods to the public ○ *From car retailing the company branched out into car leasing.*

retail management /,riːteɪl 'mænɪdʒmənt/ *noun* managing the retail side of a business such as points of sale, stock control, and just-in-time purchasing

retail media /'riːteɪl ,miːdiə/ *noun* advertising media in retail outlets, e.g. ads on supermarket trolleys

retail outlet /'riːteɪl ,aʊtlet/ *noun* a shop which sells to the general public

retail price /'riːteɪl ,praɪs/ *noun* the price at which the retailer sells to the final customer

retail price(s) index /,riːteɪl 'praɪsɪz ,ɪndeks/ *noun* an index which shows how prices of consumer goods have increased or decreased over a period of time. Abbr **RPI**

retail trade /'riːteɪl treɪd/ *noun* all people or businesses selling goods retail

retention /rɪ'tenʃən/ *noun* keeping the loyalty of existing customers, as opposed to acquisition, which is the action of acquiring new customers (both can be aims of advertising campaigns)

'...a systematic approach to human resource planning can play a significant part in reducing recruitment and retention problems' [*Personnel Management*]

retrenchment /rɪ'trentʃmənt/ *noun* a reduction of expenditure or of new plans ○ *The company is in for a period of retrenchment.*

return /rɪ'tɜːn/ *noun* **1.** the act of sending something back □ **he replied by return of post** he replied by the next post service back **2.** the filling in of an official form ■ *verb* to send back ○ *to return unsold stock to the wholesaler* ○ *to return a letter to sender*

'Section 363 of the Companies Act 1985 requires companies to deliver an annual return to the Companies Registration Office. Failure to do so before the end of the period of 28 days after the company's return date could lead to directors and other officers in default being fined up to £2000' [*Accountancy*]

returnable /rɪ'tɜːnəb(ə)l/ *adjective* which can be returned ○ *These bottles are not returnable.*

return address /rɪ'tɜːn ə,dres/ *noun* the address to which you send back something

returns /rɪ'tɜːnz/ *plural noun* unsold goods, especially books, newspapers or magazines, sent back to the supplier

revenue /'revənjuː/ *noun* money received ○ *revenue from advertising* or *advertising revenue* ○ *Oil revenues have risen with the rise in the dollar.*

revenue accounts /'revənjuː ə,kaʊnts/ *plural noun* accounts of a business which record money received as sales, commission, etc.

reverse /rɪ'vɜːs/ *adjective* opposite or in the opposite direction

'…the trade balance sank $17 billion, reversing last fall's brief improvement' [*Fortune*]

reverse engineering /rɪ,vɜːs endʒɪ'nɪərɪŋ/ *noun* the taking apart of a product in order to find out how it was put together (NOTE: Reverse engineering can help a company redesign a product, but it can also enable competitors to analyse how their rivals' products are made.)

reverse takeover /rɪ,vɜːs 'teɪkəʊvə/ *noun* a takeover where the company which has been taken over ends up owning the company which has taken it over. The acquiring company's shareholders give up their shares in exchange for shares in the target company.

revocable /'revəkəbl/ *adjective* which can be revoked

revocable letter of credit /-,revəkəb(ə)l ,letər əv 'kredɪt/ *noun* a letter of credit that can be cancelled

revoke /rɪ'vəʊk/ *verb* to cancel ○ *to revoke a decision* or *a clause in an agreement* ○ *The quota on luxury items has been revoked.*

revolving credit /rɪ,vɒlvɪŋ 'kredɪt/ *noun* a system where someone can borrow money at any time up to an agreed amount, and continue to borrow while still paying off the original loan

risk /rɪsk/ *noun* **1.** possible harm or a chance of danger □ **to run a risk** to be likely to suffer harm □ **to take a risk** to do something which may make you lose money or suffer harm **2.** □ **at owner's risk** a situation where goods shipped or stored are insured by the owner, not by the transport company or the storage company ○ *Goods left here are at owner's risk.* ○ *The shipment was sent at owner's risk.* **3.** loss or damage against which you are insured **4.** □ **he is a good/bad risk** it is not likely or it is very likely that the insurance company will have to pay out against claims where he is concerned

'…remember, risk isn't volatility. Risk is the chance that a company's earnings power will erode – either because of a change in the industry or a change in the business that will make the company significantly less profitable in the long term' [*Fortune*]

risk analysis /'rɪsk ə,næləsɪs/ *noun* analysis of how much can be lost and gained through various marketing strategies ○ *After protracted risk analysis a very ambitious strategy was adopted.* ○ *Our risk analysis must concentrate on competitor activity.*

risk-averse /,rɪsk ə'vɜːs/ *adjective* not wanting to take risks

risk-free /,rɪsk 'friː/ *adjective* with no risk involved ○ *a risk-free investment*

'…there is no risk-free way of taking regular income from your money higher than the rate of inflation and still preserving its value' [*Guardian*]

'…many small investors have also preferred to put their spare cash with risk-free investments such as building societies rather than take chances on the stock market. The returns on a

host of risk-free investments have been well into double figures' [*Money Observer*]

risky /'rɪski/ *adjective* dangerous or which may cause harm ○ *We lost all our money in some risky ventures in South America.*

'…while the bank has scaled back some of its more risky trading operations, it has retained its status as a top-rate advisory house' [*Times*]

rival /'raɪv(ə)l/ *noun* a person or company that competes in the same market ○ *a rival company* ○ *to undercut a rival*

rival brand /,raɪv(ə)l 'brænd/, **rival product** /,raɪv(ə)l 'prɒdʌkt/ *noun* a brand or product that is competing for sales with another brand or product ○ *We are analysing the rival brands on the market.*

road /rəʊd/ *noun* a way used by cars, lorries, etc. to move from one place to another ○ *to send* or *to ship goods by road* ○ *The main office is in London Road.* ○ *Use the Park Road entrance to get to the buying department.* (NOTE: in addresses, **Road** is usually shortened to **Rd**) □ **on the road** travelling ○ *The salesforce is on the road thirty weeks a year.* ○ *We have twenty salesmen on the road.*

road haulage /rəʊd 'hɔːlɪdʒ/ *noun* the moving of goods by road

road haulage depot /rəʊd 'hɔːlɪdʒ ,depəʊ/ *noun* a centre for goods which are being moved by road, and the lorries which carry them

road haulier /rəʊd 'hɔːliə/ *noun* a company which transports goods by road

ROB *abbr* run of book

rock bottom /rɒk 'bɒtəm/ *noun* □ **sales have reached rock bottom** sales have reached the lowest point possible

'…investment companies took the view that secondhand prices had reached rock bottom and that levels could only go up' [*Lloyd's List*]

rocket /'rɒkɪt/ *verb* to rise fast ○ *Investors are rushing to cash in on rocketing share prices.* ○ *Prices have rocketed on the commodity markets.*

rolling /'rəʊlɪŋ/ *adjective* continuing with no break

rolling launch /,rəʊlɪŋ 'lɔːntʃ/ *noun* a gradual launch of a new product onto

the market by launching it in different areas over a period

rolling plan /,rəʊlɪŋ 'plæn/ *noun* a plan which runs for a period of time and is updated regularly for the same period

roll out /'rəʊl aʊt/ *verb* to extend a company's marketing of a product from its original test marketing area to the whole country

'…the company is expected to make a decision in the new year on whether to roll out the name through its electrical division' [*Marketing Week*]

rollout /'rəʊlaʊt/ *noun* **1.** extending the marketing of a product from the original test marketing area to the whole country **2.** same as **rolling launch**

roll over /,rəʊl 'əʊvə/ *verb* □ **to roll over credit** to make credit available over a continuing period □ **to roll over a debt** to allow a debt to stand after the repayment date

'…at the IMF in Washington, officials are worried that Japanese and US banks might decline to roll over the principal of loans made in the 1980s to Southeast Asian and other developing countries' [*Far Eastern Economic Review*]

RON *abbr* run of network

ROP *abbr* run of paper

ROS *abbr* **1.** run of site **2.** run of station

rough /rʌf/ *noun* the outline plan of an illustration for an advertisement ○ *The agency sent the rough to the advertisers for approval.* ○ *The advertising department will consider the rough carefully before telling the agency to go ahead and run the advertisement.*

rough out /,rʌf 'aʊt/ *verb* to make a draft or a general design ○ *The finance director roughed out a plan of investment.*

ROW *abbr* run of week

royalties /'rɔɪəltiz/ *plural noun* a proportion of the income from the sales of a product such as a new invention, a book, or a piece of music that is paid to its creator

royalty /'rɔɪəlti/ *noun* money paid to an inventor, writer or the owner of land for the right to use their property, usually a specific percentage of sales, or a specific amount per sale ○ *The country*

will benefit from rising oil royalties. ○ *He is still receiving substantial royalties from his invention.*

RPI *abbr* retail price(s) index

RPM *abbr* resale price maintenance

RRP *abbr* recommended retail price

run /rʌn/ *noun* to manage or to organise □ **a cheque run** a series of cheques processed through a computer

'…business is booming for airlines on the London to Manchester run' [*Business Traveller*]

'…applications for mortgages are running at a high level' [*Times*]

'…with interest rates running well above inflation, investors want something that offers a return for their money' [*Business Week*]

run down /ˌrʌn ˈdaʊn/ *verb* **1.** to reduce a quantity gradually ○ *We decided to run down stocks* or *to let stocks run down at the end of the financial year.* **2.** to slow down the business activities of a company before it is going to be closed ○ *The company is being run down.* (NOTE: **running- ran- has run**)

running total /ˌrʌnɪŋ ˈtəʊt(ə)l/ *noun* the total carried from one column of figures to the next

run of book /ˌrʌn əv ˈbʊk/, **run of paper** /ˌrʌn əv ˈpeɪpə/ *noun* an adver-

tiser's order to the advertising department of a publication that buys advertising space at the basic rate and does not specify the position of the advertisement in the publication. Abbr **ROB, ROP**

run of network /ˌrʌn əv ˈnetwɜːk/ *noun* banner advertising that runs across a network of websites. Abbr **RON**

run of site /ˌrʌn əv ˈsaɪt/ *noun* banner advertising that runs on one single website. Abbr **ROS**

run of station /ˌrʌn əv ˈsteɪʃ(ə)n/ *noun* TV advertising for which a particular time period has not been requested. Abbr **ROS**

run of week /ˌrʌn əv ˈwiːk/ *noun* an advertiser's order to the advertising department of a publication that buys advertising space at the basic rate and does not specify the issue it will appear in. Abbr **ROW**

run-on /ˈrʌn ɒn/ *noun* copies of a publication printed in addition to the original print order, as in the case of a leaflet whose setting-up costs have been covered. More copies of it can be printed at a relatively cheap unit cost.

S

sachet /'sæʃeɪ/ *noun* a small package or envelope containing a product in the form of liquid or powder ○ *If you are travelling, buy sachets of shampoo.* ○ *The magazine came with a free sachet of skin cream attached.* ○ *Sachets of coffee powder were provided.*

sack /sæk/ *noun* a large bag made of strong cloth or plastic ○ *a sack of potatoes* ○ *We sell onions by the sack.*

salability /ˌseɪləˈbɪlɪti/ *noun* another spelling of **saleability**

salable /'seɪləb(ə)l/ *adjective* another spelling of **saleable**

salary cheque /'sæləri tʃek/ *noun* a monthly cheque by which an employee is paid

salary package /'sæləri ˌpækɪdʒ/ *noun* same as **pay package**

salary structure /'sæləri ˌstrʌktʃə/ *noun* the organisation of salaries in a company with different rates of pay for different types of job

sale /seɪl/ *noun* **1.** an act of giving an item or doing a service in exchange for money, or for the promise that money will be paid □ **for sale** ready to be sold □ **to offer something for sale** *or* **to put something up for sale** to announce that something is ready to be sold ○ *They put the factory up for sale.* ○ *His shop is for sale.* ○ *These items are not for sale to the general public.* □ **sale as seen** a sale with no guarantee of quality ○ *If the equipment is for sale as seen, we shall have no comeback if it breaks down.* □ **sale by description** a sale on condition that the goods match the description of them given by the seller □ **sale or return** a system where the retailer sends goods back if they are not sold, and pays the supplier only for goods sold ○ *We*

have taken 4,000 items on sale or return. **2.** an act of selling goods at specially low prices ○ *The shop is having a sale to clear old stock.* ○ *The sale price is 50% of the normal price.*

'…many on Wall Street are suspicious of the recent sales and production gains posted by American Industry' [*Management Today*]

'…the latest car sales for April show a 1.8 per cent dip from last year's total' [*Investors Chronicle*]

saleability /ˌseɪləˈbɪlɪti/, **salability** *noun* a quality in an item which makes it easy to sell

saleable /'seɪləb(ə)l/, **salable** *adjective* which can easily be sold ○ *The company is not readily saleable in its present state.*

sale and lease-back /seɪl ən liːs/ *noun* the sale of an asset, usually a building, to somebody else who then leases it back to the original owner

saleroom /'seɪlruːm/ *noun* a room where an auction takes place

sales /seɪlz/ *plural noun* □ **the sales** period when major stores sell many items at specially low prices ○ *I bought this in the sales* or *at the sales* or *in the January sales.*

sales agent /'seɪlz ˌeɪdʒənt/ *noun* a person who sells for a business or another person and earns a commission ○ *How many sales agents do we have in this area?* ○ *She's a competent sales agent representing several non-competing companies.*

sales aids /'seɪlz eɪdz/ *plural noun* various tools used for selling, e.g. samples, display cases and sales literature ○ *The sales manager gave a talk on new sales aids which had just become available.* ○ *An exhibition of sales aids was held at the sales conference.*

sales analysis /'seɪlz ə,næləsɪs/ *noun* an examination of the reports of sales to see why items have or have not sold well

sales appeal /'seɪlz ə,piːl/ *noun* a quality in a product which makes customers want to buy it

sales assistant /'seɪlz ə,sɪstənt/ *noun* a junior person who sells goods in a retail shop

sales audit /'seɪlz ,ɔːdɪt/ *noun* an analysis of a company's sales in terms of such factors as product, revenue and area

sales book /'seɪlz bʊk/ *noun* a record of sales

sales budget /'seɪlz ,bʌdʒɪt/ *noun* a plan of probable sales

sales call /'seɪlz kɔːl/ *noun* a visit by a salesperson to a prospective customer in order to make a sale ○ *How many sales calls does the manager expect us to make each day?* ○ *She kept reports on all her sales calls.*

sales campaign /'seɪlz kæm,peɪn/ *noun* a series of planned activities to achieve higher sales

sales channel /'seɪlz ,tʃæn(ə)l/ *noun* any means by which products can be brought into the marketplace and offered for sale, either directly to the customer or indirectly through retailers or dealers

sales chart /'seɪlz tʃɑːt/ *noun* a diagram showing how sales vary from month to month

sales clerk /'seɪlz klɑːk/ *noun* US a person who sells goods to customers in a store

'…the wage agreement includes sales clerks and commission sales people in stores in Toronto' [*Toronto Star*]

sales contest /'seɪlz ,kɒntest/ *noun* an incentive scheme that rewards the salesperson who has the best results

sales contract /'seɪlz ,kɒntrækt/ *noun* a contract between a buyer and a seller, whereby the buyer agrees to pay money to the seller in return for goods ○ *The sales contract was signed after lengthy negotiations over price and delivery.* ○ *The sales contract commits us to the purchase.*

sales department /'seɪlz dɪ,pɑːtmənt/ *noun* the section of a company which deals in selling the company's products or services

sales director /'seɪlz daɪ,rektə/ *noun* a director who is responsible for an organisation's sales

sales drive /'seɪlz draɪv/ *noun* a vigorous effort to increase sales

sales executive /'seɪlz ɪg,zekjʊtɪv/ *noun* a person in a company or department in charge of sales

sales force /'seɪlz fɔːs/ *noun* a group of sales staff

sales forecast /'seɪlz ,fɔːkɑːst/ *noun* an estimate of future sales

salesgirl /'seɪlzɡɜːl/ *noun* a young woman who sells goods to customers in a store

sales incentive /'seɪlz ɪn,sentɪv/ *noun* something offered to encourage higher sales, e.g. paying the salespeople a higher commission or bonuses, or giving them prizes such as holidays for increased sales

sales interview /'seɪlz ,ɪntəvjuː/ *noun* a meeting between a salesperson and a prospective customer in which the customer obtains all information about a product necessary for them to be able to make a buying decision ○ *At the beginning of the sales interview, the salesperson established exactly what the prospective customer's needs were.*

saleslady /'seɪlzleɪdi/ *noun* a woman who sells goods to customers in a store (NOTE: plural is **salesladies**)

sales lead /'seɪlz liːd/ *noun* a piece of information about a potential customer which may lead to a sale ○ *It has been difficult approaching this territory with no sales leads to follow up.* ○ *I was given some useful sales leads by the sales rep who used to operate here.*

sales ledger /'seɪlz ,ledʒə/ *noun* a book in which sales to each customer are entered

sales ledger clerk /'seɪlz ledʒə ,klɑːk/ *noun* an office worker who deals with the sales ledger

sales letter /'seɪlz ˌletə/ *noun* a letter sent to prospective customers, especially as part of a direct-mail operation

sales literature /'seɪlz ˌlɪt(ə)rətʃə/ *noun* printed information which help sales, e.g. leaflets or prospectuses

salesman /'seɪlzmən/ *noun* **1.** a man who sells an organisation's products or services to customers ○ *He is the head salesman in the carpet department.* ○ *His only experience is as a used-car salesman.* **2.** a man who represents a company, selling its products or services to retail shops ○ *We have six salesmen calling on accounts in central London.* (NOTE: plural is **salesmen**)

sales manager /'seɪlz ˌmænɪdʒə/ *noun* a person in charge of a sales department

salesmanship /'seɪlzmənʃɪp/ *noun* the art of selling or of persuading customers to buy

sales network /'seɪlz ˌnetwɜːk/ *noun* the network of retailers, distributors, and agents who all contribute to selling a product

sales office /'seɪlz ˌɒfɪs/ *noun* a local office of a large organisation, which deals only with sales

sales outlet /'seɪlz ˌaʊtlet/ *noun* a shop which sells to the general public

salesperson /'seɪlz,pɜːs(ə)n/ *noun* **1.** a person who sells goods or services to members of the public **2.** a person who sells products or services to retail shops on behalf of a company (NOTE: plural is **salespeople**)

sales pitch /'seɪlz pɪtʃ/ *noun* a talk by a salesperson to persuade someone to buy

sales plan /'seɪlz plæn/ *noun* a plan that sets out the future aims of a sales department and shows ways in which it can improve its performance and increase sales

sales potential /'seɪlz pə,tenʃəl/ *noun* the maximum market share that can be achieved by a product

sales presentation /'seɪlz prez(ə)n,teɪʃ(ə)n/ *noun* a demonstration by a salesperson of a product

sales promotion /'seɪlz prə-,məʊʃ(ə)n/ *noun* promotional and sales techniques aimed at short-term increases in sales, e.g. free gifts, competitions and price discounts ○ *We need some good sales promotion to complement our advertising campaign.* ○ *Let's hope this sales promotion will help us sell off our stock.*

'…the novelty in the £1m sales promotion is that the consumer will know immediately if he or she has won a bottle of champagne' [*Marketing Week*]

sales promotion agency /'seɪlz prə,məʊʃ(ə)n ˌeɪdʒənsi/ *noun* an agency that specialises in the planning of promotions such as games, premium offers, and other incentives

sales promotion trap /'seɪlz prə-,məʊʃ(ə)n træp/ *noun* a problem that occurs when a number of competing firms use promotions, with the result that there is no advantage to any of them

sales quota /'seɪlz ˌkwəʊtə/ *noun* a sales target given to salespeople which is based on either unit sales or revenue ○ *The sales manager intends to introduce sales quotas, in order to put extra pressure on the sales force.*

sales representative /'seɪlz reprɪ-,zentətɪv/, **sales rep** /'seɪlz rep/ *noun* a person who sells an organisation's products or services ○ *We have six sales representatives in Europe.* ○ *They have vacancies for sales representatives to call on accounts in the north of the country.*

sales resistance /'seɪlz rɪ,zɪstəns/ *noun* a lack of willingness by the public to buy a product

sales response /'seɪlz rɪ,spɒns/ *noun* the degree to which customers buy a product in response to the promotion of it ○ *There was a very poor sales response to the advertising campaign.* ○ *Although the product was not spectacular, the sales response was enormous.*

sales revenue /'seɪlz ˌrevənjuː/ *noun* US the income from sales of goods or services (NOTE: British English is **turnover**)

sales statistics /'seɪlz stə,tɪstɪks/ *plural noun* figures relating a company's sales

sales target /'seɪlz ˌtɑːgɪt/ *noun* the amount of sales a sales representative is expected to achieve

sales team /'seɪlz tiːm/ *noun* all representatives, sales staff and sales managers working in a company

sales technique /'seɪlz tekˌniːk/ *noun* a method used by a salesperson to persuade customers to buy, e.g. presentation of goods, demonstrations and closing of sales

sales territory /'seɪlz ˌterɪt(ə)ri/ *noun* an area visited by a salesman

saleswoman /'seɪlzwʊmən/ *noun* **1.** a woman in a shop who sells goods to customers (NOTE: plural is **saleswomen**) **2.** a woman who sells products or services to retail shops on behalf of a company

salutation /ˌsæljʊ'teɪʃ(ə)n/ *noun* the way of addressing an email to a customer

sample /'sɑːmpəl/ *noun* **1.** a small part of an item which is used to show what the whole item is like ○ *Can you provide us with a sample of the cloth* or *a cloth sample?* **2.** a small group which is studied in order to show what a larger group is like ○ *We interviewed a sample of potential customers.* ■ *verb* **1.** to test or to try something by taking a small amount of it ○ *to sample a product before buying it* **2.** to ask a representative group of people questions to find out what the reactions of a much larger group would be ○ *They sampled 2,000 people at random to test the new drink.*

'…all firms in the sample received the same questionnaire along with a covering letter explaining the objectives of the study' [*International Journal of Advertising*]

sample size /'sɑːmpəl saɪz/ *noun* the number of individuals included in a statistical survey

sample survey /'sɑːmpəl ˌsɜːveɪ/ *noun* a statistical study of a selected group of individuals designed to collect information on specific subjects such as their buying habits or voting behaviour

sampling /'sɑːmplɪŋ/ *noun* **1.** the testing of a product by taking a small amount ○ *a sampling of European Union produce* **2.** the testing of the reac-

tions of a small group of people to find out the reactions of a larger group of consumers

sampling error /'sɑːmplɪŋ ˌerə/ *noun* the difference between the results achieved in a survey using a small sample and what the results would be if you used the entire population

sampling fraction /'sɑːmplɪŋ ˌfrækʃən/ *noun* a proportion of a group of people being surveyed that is chosen as a sample ○ *The sampling fraction will have to be small since we cannot afford many interviews with respondents.*

sampling frame /'sɑːmplɪŋ freɪm/ *noun* the definition of the group of people being surveyed out of which a sample is to be taken

sampling point /'sɑːmplɪŋ pɔɪnt/ *noun* a place where sampling is carried out ○ *The sampling point was just outside the main railway station.*

sandwich board /'sændwɪtʃ bɔːd/ *noun* a pair of boards with advertisements on them that is suspended from shoulder straps in front of and behind the person wearing them

sandwich man /'sændwɪtʃ mæn/ *noun* a man who carries a sandwich board

satellite television /ˌsæt(ə)laɪt 'telɪvɪʒ(ə)n/ *noun* a television service which is broadcast from a satellite, and which the viewer receives using a special aerial

satisfaction /ˌsætɪs'fækʃən/ *noun* a good feeling of happiness and contentment ○ *he finds great satisfaction in the job even though the pay is low*

satisfy /'sætɪsfaɪ/ *verb* **1.** to give satisfaction or to please □ **to satisfy a client** to make a client pleased with what they have purchased □ **a satisfied customer** a customer who has got what they wanted **2.** to fill (the requirements for a job, etc.) □ **to satisfy a demand** to fill a demand ○ *We cannot produce enough to satisfy the demand for the product.*

satisfying /'sætɪsfaɪɪŋ/ *noun* the act of making satisfactory profits and maintaining an acceptable market share

rather than making maximum profits at all costs

saturate /'sætʃəreɪt/ *verb* to fill something completely ○ *They are planning to saturate the market with cheap mobile phones.* ○ *The market for home computers is saturated.*

saturation /ˌsætʃə'reɪʃ(ə)n/ *noun* **1.** the process of filling completely □ **saturation of the market** *or* **market saturation** a situation where the market has taken as much of the product as it can buy □ **the market has reached saturation point** the market is at a point where it cannot buy any more of the product **2.** the fourth stage in a product's life cycle where sales level off

saturation advertising /ˌsætʃə'reɪʃ(ə)n ˌædvətaɪzɪŋ/ *noun* a highly intensive advertising campaign ○ *Saturation advertising is needed when there are large numbers of rival products on the market.*

savings account /'seɪvɪŋz əˌkaʊnt/ *noun* an account where you put money in regularly and which pays interest, often at a higher rate than a deposit account

SBU *abbr* strategic business unit

scale /skeɪl/ *noun* a system which is graded into various levels □ **scale of charges** *or* **scale of prices** a list showing various prices ■ *verb* □ **to scale down** to lower in proportion □ **to scale up** to increase in proportion

scaling technique /'skeɪlɪŋ tekˌniːk/ *noun* the use of a scale in questionnaires to make interpretation of results easier ○ *The scaling technique was so complicated that the respondents did not understand the questions.*

scarce /skeəs/ *adjective* not easily found or not common ○ *scarce raw materials* ○ *Reliable trained staff are scarce.*

scarceness /'skeəsnəs/, **scarcity** /'skeəsɪti/ *noun* the state of being scarce ○ *There is a scarcity of trained staff.*

scarcity value /'skeəsɪti ˌvæljuː/ *noun* the value something has because it is rare and there is a large demand for it

scatter /'skætə/ *noun* a strategy by which an advertising message is put out through several different vehicles at the same time

scattered market /ˌskætəd 'mɑːkɪt/ *noun* a market which is spread around a wide area, and therefore can only be reached by a company with an efficient distribution system

scenario /sɪ'nɑːriəʊ/ *noun* the way in which a situation may develop

'…on the upside scenario, the outlook is reasonably optimistic, bankers say, the worst scenario being that a scheme of arrangement cannot be achieved, resulting in liquidation' [*Irish Times*]

scenario planning /sɪ'nɑːriəʊ ˌplænɪŋ/ *noun* a planning technique in which the planners write down several different descriptions of what they think might happen in the future and how future events, good or bad, might affect their organisation (NOTE: Scenario planning can help managers to prepare for changes in the business environment, to develop strategies for dealing with unexpected events and to choose between alternative strategic options.)

schedule /'ʃedʒuːl/ *noun* **1.** a timetable, plan of time drawn up in advance □ **on schedule** at the time or stage set down in the schedule ○ *The launch took place on schedule.* **2.** a list, especially additional documents attached to a contract ○ *the schedule of territories to which a contract applies* ○ *See the attached schedule* or *as per the attached schedule.* ○ *Please find enclosed our schedule of charges.*

science /'saɪəns/ *noun* study or knowledge based on observing and testing

science park /'saɪəns pɑːk/ *noun* an area near a town or university set aside for technological industries

scientific /ˌsaɪən'tɪfɪk/ *adjective* referring to science

scientific management /ˌsaɪəntɪfɪk 'mænɪdʒmənt/ *noun* a school of management which believes in the rational use of resources in order to maximise output, thus motivating workers to earn more money

scope /skəʊp/ *noun* an opportunity or possibility ○ *There is considerable scope for expansion into the export market.* □ **there is scope for improvement in our sales performance** the sales performance could be improved

scrambled merchandising /ˌskræmbəld ˈmɜːtʃəndaɪzɪŋ/ *noun* the displaying and selling of products which are unrelated to most of the others in the store such as groceries in a newsagent's or sandwiches in a pharmacy

screen /skriːn/ *noun* **1.** a glass surface on which computer information or TV pictures can be shown ○ *She brought up the information on the screen.* ○ *I'll just call up details of your account on the screen.* **2.** a grid of dots or lines placed between the camera and the artwork, which has the effect of dividing the picture up into small dots, creating an image which can be used for printing ■ *verb* to examine something carefully to evaluate or assess it □ **to screen candidates** to examine candidates to see if they are completely suitable

screening /ˈskriːnɪŋ/ *noun* **1.** □ **the screening of candidates** examining candidates to see if they are suitable **2.** evaluating or estimating new product ideas ○ *Representatives from each department concerned will take part in the screening process.* ○ *Screening showed the product idea to be unrealistic for our production capacity.*

script /skrɪpt/ *noun* the written text of a commercial

SDRs *abbr* special drawing rights

seal /siːl/ *noun* **1.** □ **contract under seal** a contract which has been legally approved with the seal of the company **2.** a piece of paper, metal or wax attached to close something, so that it can be opened only if the paper, metal or wax is removed or broken ■ *verb* to close something tightly ○ *The computer disks were sent in a sealed container.*

sealed bid price /siːld ˈbɪd praɪs/ *noun* a price of goods or a service for which suppliers are invited to submit bids. The bids are considered together by the buyer who then chooses the lowest bidder.

sealed tender /siːld ˈtendə/ *noun* a tender sent in a sealed envelope which will be opened with others at a specific time

seal of approval /ˌsiːl əv əˈpruːv(ə)l/ *noun* a certificate from an organisation to show that a product has been officially approved

seaport /ˈsiːpɔːt/ *noun* a port by the sea

search /sɜːtʃ/ *noun* the facility that enables visitors to a website to look for the information they want

search engine /ˈsɜːtʃ ˌendʒɪn/ *noun* a website that enables users to conduct keyword searches of indexed information that is held on its database

search engine registration /ˈsɜːtʃ ˌendʒɪn redʒɪˌstreɪʃ(ə)n/ *noun* the process of registering a website with a search engine, so that the website is able to be selected when a user requests a search

season /ˈsiːz(ə)n/ *noun* **1.** one of four parts which a year is divided into, i.e. spring, summer, autumn, and winter **2.** a period of time when some activity usually takes place ○ *the selling season*

seasonal /ˈsiːz(ə)n(ə)l/ *adjective* which lasts for a season or which only happens during a particular season ○ *seasonal variations in sales patterns* ○ *The demand for this item is very seasonal.*

seasonal adjustment /ˌsiːz(ə)n(ə)l əˈdʒʌstmənt/ *noun* a change made to figures to take account of seasonal variations

seasonal business /ˌsiːz(ə)n(ə)l ˈbɪznɪs/ *noun* trade that varies depending on the time of the year, e.g. trade in goods such as suntan products or Christmas trees

seasonal demand /ˌsiːz(ə)n(ə)l dɪˈmɑːnd/ *noun* demand which exists only during the high season

seasonal discount /ˌsiːz(ə)n(ə)l ˈdɪskaʊnt/ *noun* a discount offered at specific times of the year during periods

of slack sales, such as by media owners to advertisers

seasonally adjusted /ˌsiːz(ə)nəli əˈdʒʌstɪd/ *adjective* referring to statistics which are adjusted to take account of seasonal variations

seasonal product /ˈsiːz(ə)n(ə)l ˌprɒdʌkt/ *noun* a product such as skis or New Year cards which is only bought for use at a specific time of year

seasonal variation /ˌsiːz(ə)n(ə)l veəriˈeɪʃ(ə)n/ *noun* variation in data that happens at particular times of the year, e.g. during the winter months or a tourist season

second /ˈsekənd/ *noun, adjective* (the thing) which comes after the first

secondary /ˈsekənd(ə)ri/ *adjective* second in importance

secondary audience /ˌsekənd(ə)ri ˈɔːdiəns/, **secondary readership** /ˌsekənd(ə)ri ˈriːdəʃɪp/ *noun* people who do not buy a newspaper or magazine themselves, but read a copy after the original purchaser has finished with it

secondary bank /ˈsekənd(ə)ri bæŋk/ *noun* a finance company which provides money for hire-purchase deals

secondary data /ˈsekənd(ə)ri ˌdeɪtə/ *noun* data or information which has already been compiled and is therefore found through desk research ○ *All this secondary data can be found in our files.* ○ *We found the secondary data in the embassy library.*

secondary industry /ˈsekənd(ə)ri ˌɪndəstri/ *noun* an industry which uses basic raw materials to produce manufactured goods

secondary meaning /ˌsekənd(ə)ri ˈmiːnɪŋ/ *noun* a nickname given to a brand deliberately by the producer or by the consumer

second-class /ˌsekənd ˈklɑːs/ *adjective, adverb* referring to a less expensive or less comfortable way of travelling ○ *The group will travel second-class to Holland.* ○ *The price of a second-class ticket is half that of a first class.*

second-generation product /-ˌsekənd dʒenəˈreɪʃ(ə)n ˌprɒdʌkt/ *noun* a product which has been developed from another

second half-year /ˌsekənd ˈhɑːf jɪə/ *noun* the six-month period from July to the end of December

secondhand /ˌsekəndˈhænd/ *adjective, adverb* which has been owned by someone before ○ *a secondhand car* ○ *the market in secondhand computers* or *the secondhand computer market* ○ *to buy something secondhand*

secondhand dealer /ˌsekəndhænd ˈdiːlə/ *noun* a dealer who buys and sells secondhand items

seconds /ˈsekəndz/ *plural noun* items which have been turned down by the quality controller as not being top quality ○ *The shop has a sale of seconds.*

second season /ˌsekənd ˈsiːz(ə)n/ *noun* the period when a second series of a network television programme is shown

sector /ˈsektə/ *noun* a part of the economy or the business organisation of a country ○ *All sectors of the economy suffered from the fall in the exchange rate.* ○ *Technology is a booming sector of the economy.*

'…government services form a large part of the tertiary or service sector' [*Sydney Morning Herald*]

'…in the dry cargo sector, a total of 956 dry cargo vessels are laid up – 3% of world dry cargo tonnage' [*Lloyd's List*]

secured loan /sɪˈkjʊəd ləʊn/ *noun* a loan which is guaranteed by the borrower giving assets as security

secure server /sɪˌkjʊə ˈsɜːvə/ *noun* a combination of hardware and software that makes e-commerce credit card transactions safe by stopping unauthorised people from gaining access to credit card details online

security /sɪˈkjʊərəti/ *noun* being protected against attack, etc.

seed /siːd/ *noun* details of the address of the person who owns a list, put into a rented mailing list to check if it is being used correctly ■ *verb* to put the names and addresses of the mailers into a

rented mailing list to check that it is being used correctly

see-safe /ˈsiː ˌseɪf/ *adverb* under an agreement where a supplier will give credit for unsold goods at the end of a period if the retailer cannot sell them ○ *We bought the stock see-safe.*

segment *noun* /ˈsegmənt/ a part of the sales of a large business defined by specific criteria ■ *verb* /segˈment/ to divide a potential market into different segments

'…like direct mail, telemarketing has assumed greater importance as consumer markets have become segmented' [*Financial Times*]

segmentation /ˌsegmənˈteɪʃ(ə)n/ *noun* the division of the market or consumers into categories according to their buying habits

'…different market segments and, ultimately, individual consumers, must be addressed separately' [*Financial Times*]

select /sɪˈlekt/ *adjective* of top quality or specially chosen ○ *The firm offers a select range of merchandise.* ○ *Our customers are a select group.* ■ *verb* to choose ○ *The board will meet to select three candidates for a second interview.* □ **selected items are reduced by 25%** some items have been reduced by 25%

selection /sɪˈlekʃən/ *noun* **1.** a choice **2.** a thing which has been chosen ○ *Here is a selection of our product line.*

selection procedure /sɪˈlekʃən prəˌsiːdʒə/ *noun* the general method of choosing a candidate for a job

selective /sɪˈlektɪv/ *adjective* choosing carefully

selective attention /sɪˌlektɪv əˈtenʃən/, **selective perception** *noun* an individual's tendency to unconsciously select what they want from an advertisement ○ *We must take selective perception into account when deciding what to stress in the advertising.*

selective demand /sɪˌlektɪv dɪˈmɑːnd/ *noun* demand for a particular brand

selective demand advertising /sɪˌlektɪv dɪˈmɑːnd ˌædvətaɪzɪŋ/ *noun* advertising that stimulates demand for a specific product or brand

selective distribution /sɪˌlektɪv dɪstrɪˈbjuːʃ(ə)n/ *noun* use by a producer of a limited number of wholesalers and retailers in a particular area ○ *This specialised product will need selective distribution.* ○ *Selective distribution may not enable the goods to reach consumers in sufficient quantities.*

selective exposure /sɪˌlektɪv ɪkˈspəʊʒə/ *noun* the process by which consumers decide whether they will watch or listen to advertising information

selective mailing /sɪˌlektɪv ˈmeɪlɪŋ/ *noun* the mailing out of promotional material to a selected address list

selective retention /sɪˌlektɪv rɪˈtenʃən/ *noun* the process by which people remember some information but not everything they hear

self- /self/ *prefix* referring to yourself

self-completion /self kəmˈpliːʃ(ə)n/ *noun* a type of questionnaire that can be filled in without an interviewer being present ○ *These self-completion questionnaires can be sent out through the post.* ○ *Self-completion is not a good idea if the respondents don't understand the questions.*

self-image /self ˈɪmɪdʒ/ *noun* an idea that a person has about his or her own character and abilities

self-liquidating offer /self ˈlɪkwɪdeɪtɪŋ ˌɒfə/ *noun* the offer of a free gift or the sale of another product at a discount, made when a product is bought, usually against proof of purchase. The intention is to encourage the customer to adopt the brand, and at the same time to cover the cost of the offer and reduce overall promotional costs for the product. ○ *Even with the self-liquidating offer our sales have not gone up very much.*

self-mailer /self ˈmeɪlə/ *noun* an item of promotional material sent through the post, which includes a postage-paid reply section which can be sent back without an envelope and on which customers can make an order ○ *Only 10% of the self-mailers we sent out have elicited any response.*

self-reference criterion /self 'refrəns kraɪˌtɪəriən/ *noun* the assumption that a product can successfully be sold abroad on the basis of its success in the home market (NOTE: plural is **criteria**)

self-regulation /self regjʊ'leɪʃ(ə)n/ *noun* the regulation of an industry by itself, through a committee which issues a rulebook and makes sure that members of the industry follow the rules (NOTE: For example, the Stock Exchange is regulated by the Stock Exchange Council.)

'…he blamed a tiny minority for breaking the codes and warned against agencies and clients trying to outwit the ASA. He called for honest dealings within the spirit of self-regulation and warned that the alternative to self-regulation was statutory restrictions' [*Marketing*]

self-regulatory /self regjʊ'leɪt(ə)ri/ *adjective* referring to an organisation which regulates itself

self-service petrol station /self ˌsɜːvɪs 'petrəl ˌsteɪʃ(ə)n/ *noun* a petrol station where the customers put the petrol in their cars themselves

self-service store /self 'sɜːvɪs stɔː/ *noun* a shop where customers take goods from the shelves and pay for them at the checkout

self-sticking label /self ˌstɪkɪŋ 'leɪb(ə)l/ *noun* a label with glue on it, ready to stick on an item

sell /sel/ *noun* an act of selling □ **to give a product the hard sell** to make great efforts to persuade customers to buy it ■ *verb* **1.** to give goods in exchange for money ○ *to sell something on credit* ○ *The shop sells washing machines and refrigerators.* ○ *They tried to sell their house for £100,000.* ○ *Their products are easy to sell.* **2.** to be sold ○ *These items sell well in the pre-Christmas period.* ○ *Those packs sell for £25 a dozen.* (NOTE: **selling – sold**)

sell-by date /'selbaɪ 'deɪt/ *noun* date on a food packet which is the last date on which the food is guaranteed to be good

seller /'selə/ *noun* **1.** a person who sells ○ *There were few sellers in the market, so prices remained high.* **2.**

something which sells ○ *This book is a steady seller.*

seller's market /ˌseləz 'mɑːkɪt/ *noun* a market where the seller can ask high prices because there is a large demand for the product

sell forward /ˌsel 'fɔːwəd/ *verb* to sell foreign currency, commodities, etc. for delivery at a later date

sell-in /'sel ɪn/ *noun* the amount of stock of a product taken by retailers when it is launched

-selling /'selɪŋ/ *suffix* □ **best-selling car** a car which sells better than other models

selling agent /'selɪŋ ˌeɪdʒənt/ *noun* a person who sells for a business or another person and earns a commission

selling costs /'selɪŋ kɒsts/ *plural noun* an amount of money to be paid for the advertising, reps' commissions, etc. involved in selling something

selling price /'selɪŋ praɪs/ *noun* the price at which someone is willing to sell something

selling space /'selɪŋ speɪs/ *noun* the amount of space in a retail outlet which is used for displaying goods for sale

sell off /ˌsel 'ɒf/ *verb* to sell goods quickly to get rid of them

sell out /ˌsel 'aʊt/ *verb* **1.** □ **to sell out of an item** to sell all the stock of an item ○ *to sell out of a product line* ○ *This item has sold out.* ○ *We have sold out of plastic bags.* **2.** to sell your business ○ *They sold out and retired to the seaside.*

sellout /'selaʊt/ *noun* □ **this item has been a sellout** all the stock of the item has been sold

semantic differential /sɪˌmæntɪk dɪfə'renʃəl/ *noun* a scaling technique which provides a range of possible answers between two opposite descriptive words

semi- /semi/ *prefix* half or part

semi-display advertisement /ˌsemi dɪ'spleɪ ədˌvɜːtɪsmənt/ *noun* an advertisement that has some of the features of a display advertisement such as a border and its own typeface or illustrations, but which is printed on the classified advertisement page

semi-finished product /ˌsemi ˈfɪnɪʃt ˌprɒdʌkt/ *noun* a product which is partly finished

semiotics /ˌsemiˈɒtɪks/ *noun* the use of such promotional tools as package design, logos and slogans in marketing (NOTE: takes a singular verb)

semi-solus /ˌsemi ˈsəʊləs/ *noun* an advertisement that shares a page with other advertisements, but is not immediately next to any of them

semi-structured interview /ˌsemi ˌstrʌktʃəd ˈɪntəvjuː/ *noun* an interview using some pre-set questions but allowing some questions that have been chosen by the interviewer as well ○ *Part of a semi-structured interview consists in respondents describing their first reactions to the advertisement.*

semi-variable cost /ˌsemi ˌveəriəb(ə)l ˈkɒst/ *noun* money paid to produce a product which increases, though less than proportionally, with the quantity of the product made ○ *Stepping up production will mean an increase in semi-variable costs.*

send away for /ˌsend əˈweɪ fɔː/ *verb* to write asking for something to be sent to you ○ *We sent away for the new catalogue.*

sender /ˈsendə/ *noun* a person who sends □ **'return to sender'** words on an envelope or parcel to show that it is to be sent back to the person who sent it

send off for /ˌsend ˈɒf fɔː/ *verb* to write asking for something to be sent to you ○ *We sent off for the new catalogue.*

sensitive /ˈsensɪtɪv/ *adjective* able to feel something sharply ○ *The market is very sensitive to the result of the elections.*

sequential sampling /sɪˌkwenʃəl ˈsɑːmplɪŋ/ *noun* the process of carrying on the process of sampling until enough respondents have been interviewed to provide the necessary information

serial number /ˈsɪəriəl ˌnʌmbə/ *noun* a number in a series ○ *This batch of shoes has the serial number 25–02.*

service /ˈsɜːvɪs/ *noun* **1.** payment for help given to the customer ○ *to add on 10% for service* □ **the bill includes service** the bill includes a charge added for the work involved ○ *Is the service included?* **2.** the act of keeping a machine in good working order ○ *the routine service of equipment* ○ *The machine has been sent in for service.* ■ *verb* **1.** to keep a machine in good working order ○ *The car needs to be serviced every six months.* ○ *The computer has gone back to the manufacturer for servicing.* **2.** □ **to service a debt** to pay interest on a debt ○ *The company is having problems in servicing its debts.*

service bureau /ˈsɜːvɪs ˌbjʊərəʊ/ *noun* an office which specialises in helping other offices

service centre /ˈsɜːvɪs ˌsentə/ *noun* an office or workshop which specialises in keeping machines in good working order

service charge /ˈsɜːvɪs tʃɑːdʒ/ *noun* US a charge which a bank makes for carrying out work for a customer (NOTE: the British equivalent is **bank charge**)

service department /ˈsɜːvɪs dɪˌpɑːtmənt/ *noun* the section of a company which keeps customers' machines in good working order

service engineer /ˈsɜːvɪs endʒɪˌnɪə/ *noun* an engineer who specialises in keeping machines in good working order

service history /ˈsɜːvɪs ˌhɪst(ə)ri/ *noun* a record of the times a machine has been serviced

service level /ˈsɜːvɪs ˌlev(ə)l/ *noun* a measurement of how efficient a producer is in distributing goods, e.g. the minimum number of back orders at any one time or delivery frequency to an area ○ *Service levels must be improved to fight competition.* ○ *The product is competitive in itself, but sales are affected by a low service level.*

service level agreement /ˈsɜːvɪs lev(ə)l əˌgriːmənt/ *noun* an agreement between a supplier and a customer which stipulates the level of services to be rendered. Abbr **SLA**

services /ˈsɜːvɪsɪz/ *plural noun* benefits which are sold to customers or clients, e.g. transport or education ○ *We*

give advice to companies on the marketing of services. ○ *We must improve the exports of both goods and services.*

service station /'sɜːvɪs ˌsteɪʃ(ə)n/ *noun* a garage where you can buy petrol and have small repairs done to a car

set /set/ *noun* a group of items which go together, which are used together or which are sold together ○ *a set of tools* ■ *adjective* fixed or which cannot be changed ○ *There is a set fee for all our consultants.* ■ *verb* to fix or to arrange ○ *We have to set a price for the new computer.* ○ *The price of the calculator has been set low, so as to achieve maximum unit sales.* □ **the auction set a record for high prices** the prices at the auction were the highest ever reached

set menu /set 'menjuː/ *noun* a cheaper menu in a restaurant where there are only a few choices

setting up costs /ˌsetɪŋ 'ʌp kɒsts/, **setup costs** /'setʌp 'kɒsts/ *plural noun* the costs of getting a machine or a factory ready to make a new product after finishing work on the previous one

settle /'setl/ *verb* □ **to settle an account** to pay what is owed

settlement /'setlmənt/ *noun* payment of an account □ **we offer an extra 5% discount for rapid settlement** we take a further 5% off the price if the customer pays quickly □ **settlement in cash** *or* **cash settlement** payment of an invoice in cash, not by cheque

'…he emphasised that prompt settlement of all forms of industrial disputes would guarantee industrial peace in the country and ensure increased productivity' [*Business Times (Lagos)*]

set up /ˌset 'ʌp/ *verb* to begin something, or to organise something new ○ *to set up an inquiry* or *a working party* □ **to set up a company** to start a company legally □ **to set up in business** to start a new business ○ *She set up in business as an insurance broker.* ○ *He set himself up as a freelance representative.*

'…the concern announced that it had acquired a third large tanker since being set up' [*Lloyd's List*]

share /ʃeə/ *noun* a part of something that has been divided up among several peoole or groups ■ *verb* to divide something up among several people or groups ○ *to share computer time* ○ *to share the profits among the senior executives* ○ *Three companies share the market.* □ **to share information** *or* **data** to give someone information which you have

'…falling profitability means falling share prices' [*Investors Chronicle*]

'…the share of blue-collar occupations declined from 48 per cent to 43 per cent' [*Sydney Morning Herald*]

share capital /'ʃeə ˌkæpɪtl/ *noun* the value of the assets of a company held as shares

shared mailing /ʃeəd 'meɪlɪŋ/ *noun* a mailing where two or more producers insert mailing pieces in the same envelope

shelf /ʃelf/ *noun* a horizontal flat surface attached to a wall or in a cupboard on which items for sale are displayed ○ *The shelves in the supermarket were full of items before the Christmas rush.*

shelf barker /'ʃelf ˌbɑːkə/, **shelf talker** /'ʃelf ˌtɔːkə/, **shelf wobbler** /'ʃelf ˌwɒblə/ *noun* a card placed on or hung from a shelf to promote an item for sale

shelf filler /'ʃelf ˌfɪlə/ *noun* a person whose job is to make sure that the shelves in a shop are kept full of items for sale

shelf life /'ʃelf laɪf/ *noun* the length of time during which a product can stay in the shop and still be good to use

shelf space /'ʃelf speɪs/ *noun* the amount of space on shelves in a shop

shift /ʃɪft/ *noun* a movement or change ○ *a shift in the company's marketing strategy* ○ *The company is taking advantage of a shift in the market towards higher-priced goods.*

ship /ʃɪp/ *noun* a large boat for carrying passengers and cargo on the sea □ **to drop ship** to deliver a large order direct to a customer's shop or warehouse, without going through an agent ■ *verb* to send goods, but not always on a ship ○ *to ship goods to the USA* ○ *We ship all our goods by rail.* ○ *The consignment of cars was shipped abroad last week.*

shipbroker /'ʃɪp ˌbrəʊkə/ *noun* a person who arranges shipping or transport of goods for customers on behalf of ship owners

ship chandler /ʃɪp 'tʃɑːndlə/ *noun* a person who supplies goods such as food to ships

shipment *noun* /'ʃɪpmənt/ goods which have been sent or are going to be sent ○ *Two shipments were lost in the fire.* ○ *A shipment of computers was damaged.* ■ an act of sending goods ○ *We make two shipments a week to France.*

shipper /'ʃɪpə/ *noun* a person who sends goods or who organises the sending of goods for other customers

shipping /'ʃɪpɪŋ/ *noun* the sending of goods ○ *shipping charges* ○ *shipping costs* (NOTE: **shipping** does not always mean using a ship)

shipping agent /'ʃɪpɪŋ ˌeɪdʒənt/ *noun* a company which specialises in the sending of goods

shipping confirmation /'ʃɪpɪŋ kɒnfəˌmeɪʃ(ə)n/ *noun* an email message informing the purchaser that an order has been shipped

shipping instructions /'ʃɪpɪŋ ɪnˌstrʌkʃənz/ *plural noun* the details of how goods are to be shipped and delivered

shipping note /'ʃɪpɪŋ nəʊt/ *noun* a note which gives details of goods being shipped

shop /ʃɒp/ *noun* **1.** a place where goods are stored and sold ○ *a computer shop* ○ *an electrical goods shop* ○ *She has bought a shoe shop in the centre of town.* ○ *All the shops in the centre of town close on Sundays.* ○ *She opened a women's clothes shop.* **2.** an advertising agency (NOTE: American English is usually **store**) ■ *verb* □ **to shop (for)** to look for things in shops

shop around /ˌʃɒp ə'raʊnd/ *verb* to go to various shops or suppliers and compare prices before making a purchase or before placing an order ○ *You should shop around before getting your car serviced.* ○ *He's shopping around for a new computer.* ○ *It pays to shop*

around when you are planning to get a mortgage.

shop audit /'ʃɒp ˌɔːdɪt/ *noun* a market-research method by which a research company regularly checks a sample of retailers for unit sales and stock levels of different brands ○ *Since subscribing to the shop audit we have seen how much better we're doing than our competitors.*

shopbot /'ʃɒpbɒt/ *noun* an automated device that searches the Internet for particular products or services, allowing the user to compare prices or specifications

shop floor /ʃɒp 'flɔː/ *noun* the space in a shop given to the display of goods for sale

shop front /'ʃɒp frʌnt/ *noun* a part of a shop which faces the street, including the entrance and windows

shopkeeper /'ʃɒpkiːpə/ *noun* a person who owns or runs a shop

shoplifter /'ʃɒplɪftə/ *noun* a person who steals goods from shops

shoplifting /'ʃɒplɪftɪŋ/ *noun* the practice of stealing goods from shops

shopper /'ʃɒpə/ *noun* a person who buys goods in a shop ○ *The store stays open to midnight to cater for late-night shoppers.*

shoppers' charter /ˌʃɒpəz 'tʃɑːtə/ *noun* a law which protects the rights of shoppers against shopkeepers who are not honest or against manufacturers of defective goods

shopping /'ʃɒpɪŋ/ *noun* **1.** the act of buying goods in a shop ○ *to go shopping* **2.** goods bought in a shop ○ *to buy your shopping* or *to do your shopping in the local supermarket*

shopping cart /'ʃɒpɪŋ kɑːt/ *noun* **1.** US a metal basket on wheels, used by shoppers to put their purchases in as they go round a supermarket (NOTE: British English is **shopping trolley** or **supermarket trolley**) **2.** a software package that records the items that an online buyer selects for purchase together with associated data, e.g., the price of the item and the number of items required

shopping centre /'ʃɒpɪŋ ˌsentə/ *noun* a group of shops linked together with car parks and restaurants

shopping experience /'ʃɒpɪŋ ɪk-ˌspɪəriəns/ *noun* the virtual environment in which a customer visits an e-merchant's website, selects items, places them in an electronic shopping cart and notifies the merchant of the order (NOTE: The shopping experience does not include a payment transaction, which is initiated by a message to a point-of-sale program when the customer signals that he or she has finished shopping and wishes to pay.)

shopping goods /'ʃɒpɪŋ gʊdz/ *plural noun* high-priced goods whose purchase has to be considered carefully by customers, who compare the good points of competing brands

shopping mall /'ʃɒpɪŋ mɒl/ *noun* an enclosed covered area for shopping, with shops, restaurants, banks and other facilities

shopping precinct /'ʃɒpɪŋ ˌpriːsɪŋkt/ *noun* a part of a town where the streets are closed to traffic so that people can walk about and shop

shopping trolley /'ʃɒpɪŋ ˌtrɒli/ *noun* same as **shopping cart**

shop-soiled /'ʃɒp sɔɪld/ *adjective* dirty because of having been on display in a shop ○ *These items are shop-soiled and cannot be sold at full price.*

shopwalker /'ʃɒpwɔːkə/ *noun* an employee of a department store who advises the customers and supervises the shop assistants in a department

shop window /ʃɒp 'wɪndəʊ/ *noun* a large window in a shop front, where customers can see goods displayed

shop window website /ʃɒp 'wɪndəʊ ˌwebsaɪt/ *noun* a website that provides information about an organisation and its products, but does not allow visitors to interact with it

shop-within-shop /ˌʃɒp wɪðɪn 'ʃɒp/ *noun* an arrangement in large department stores where space is given to smaller specialised retail outlets to trade

short /ʃɔːt/ *adjective* **1.** for a small period of time □ **in the short term** in the near future or quite soon **2.** not as much as should be ○ *The shipment was three items short.* ○ *My change was £2 short.* □ **when we cashed up we were £10 short** we had £10 less than we should have had □ **to give short weight** to sell something which is lighter than it should be □ **short of** with less than needed or not enough of ○ *We are short of staff* or *short of money.* ○ *The company is short of new ideas.*

shortage /'ʃɔːtɪdʒ/ *noun* a lack or low availability of something ○ *a shortage of skilled staff* ○ *We employ part-timers to make up for staff shortages.* ○ *The import controls have resulted in the shortage of spare parts.* □ **there is no shortage of investment advice** there are plenty of people who want to give advice on investments

short-change /ˌʃɔːt'tʃeɪndʒ/ *verb* to give a customer less change than is right, either by mistake or in the hope that it will not be noticed

short credit /ʃɔːt 'kredɪt/ *noun* terms which allow the customer only a little time to pay

shorthanded /ˌʃɔːt'hændɪd/ *adjective* without enough staff ○ *We're rather shorthanded at the moment.*

short lease /ʃɔːt 'liːs/ *noun* a lease which runs for up to two or three years ○ *We have a short lease on our current premises.*

short-range forecast /ˌʃɔːt reɪndʒ 'fɔːkɑːst/ *noun* a forecast which covers a period of a few months

short-staffed /ˌʃɔːt 'stɑːft/ *adjective* with not enough staff ○ *We're rather short-staffed at the moment.*

short-term /ˌʃɔːt 'tɜːm/ *adjective* for a period of weeks or months ○ *to place money on short-term deposit* ○ *She is employed on a short-term contract.* □ **on a short-term basis** for a short period

short-term debt /ˌʃɔːt tɜːm 'det/ *noun* a debt which has to be repaid within a few weeks

short-term forecast /ˌʃɔːt tɜːm 'fɔːkɑːst/ *noun* a forecast which covers a period of a few months

short-term gain /ˌʃɔːt tɜːm ˈɡeɪn/ noun an increase in price made over a short period

short-term planning /ˌʃɔːt tɜːm ˈplænɪŋ/ noun planning for the immediate future

shout /ʃaʊt/ noun a bold statement promoting a book, either printed on the cover or on posters and leaflets ○ *The author disliked the shout on the cover suggested by the publisher's promotional manager.*

show /ʃəʊ/ noun an exhibition or display of goods or services for sale ○ *a motor show* ○ *a computer show*

showcard /ˈʃəʊkɑːd/ noun a piece of cardboard with advertising material, put near an item for sale

showcase noun /ˈʃəʊkeɪs/ **1.** a cupboard with a glass front or top to display items **2.** the presentation of someone or something in a favourable setting ■ verb to present someone or something in a way that is designed to attract attention and admiration

showing /ˈʃəʊɪŋ/ noun a measurement of an audience's exposure to outdoor advertising

showroom /ˈʃəʊruːm/ noun a room where goods are displayed for sale ○ *a car showroom*

shrink /ʃrɪŋk/ verb to get smaller ○ *The market has shrunk by 20%.* ○ *The company is having difficulty selling into a shrinking market.* (NOTE: **shrinking – shrank – has shrunk**)

shrinkage /ˈʃrɪŋkɪdʒ/ noun **1.** the amount by which something gets smaller ○ *to allow for shrinkage* **2.** losses of stock through theft, especially by the shop's own staff (*informal*)

SIC abbr standard industrial classification

sideline /ˈsaɪdlaɪn/ noun a business which is extra to your normal work ○ *He runs a profitable sideline selling postcards to tourists.*

sight /saɪt/ noun the act of seeing □ **bill payable at sight** a bill which must be paid when it is presented □ **to buy something sight unseen** to buy something without having inspected it

'...if your company needed a piece of equipment priced at about $50,000, would you buy it sight unseen from a supplier you had never met?' [*Nation's Business*]

sight draft /ˈsaɪt drɑːft/ noun a bill of exchange which is payable when it is presented

sign /saɪn/ noun a board or notice which advertises something ○ *They have asked for planning permission to put up a large red shop sign.* ○ *Advertising signs cover most of the buildings in the centre of the town.*

signage /ˈsaɪnɪdʒ/ noun all the signs and logos which identify an organisation such as a retail group, chain of restaurants or motorway service area

'...if planning permission is granted and the Department of Transport is happy to grant motorway signage and access permission, you can buy or lease the land and start building' [*Caterer & Hotelkeeper*]

signature /ˈsɪɡnətʃə/ noun a special authentication code, such as a password, which a user must enter to prove his or her identity

signature file /ˈsɪɡnətʃə faɪl/ noun text at the end of an email message that identifies the sender and company name, address, etc. Abbr **sig file**

silver market /ˈsɪlvə ˌmɑːkɪt/ noun a market consisting of retired people (NOTE: also called **grey market**)

SINBAD abbr single income no boyfriend absolutely desperate

single column centimetre /ˌsɪŋɡəl ˌkɒləm ˈsentɪmiːtə/ noun a unit of measurement for newspaper and magazine advertisements, representing one column which is one centimetre in depth

single-currency /ˌsɪŋɡəl ˈkʌrənsi/ adjective using or shown as an amount in only one currency

single (European) market /ˌsɪŋɡ(ə)l ˌjʊərəpiːən ˈmɑːkɪt/ noun ◊ **European Union**

single sourcing /ˌsɪŋɡəl ˈsɔːsɪŋ/ noun the practice of obtaining all of a company's supplies from one source or supplier ○ *The buying department believes that single sourcing will lead to higher raw-material costs.* ○ *Single sourcing has simplified our purchasing plans.*

site /saɪt/ *noun* the place where something is located ○ *We have chosen a site for the new factory.* ○ *The supermarket is to be built on a site near the station.*

situation /ˌsɪtʃuˈeɪʃ(ə)n/ *noun* a state of affairs ○ *the financial situation of a company* ○ *the general situation of the economy*

situation analysis /ˌsɪtʃuˈeɪʃ(ə)n əˌnæləsɪs/, **situation audit** /ˌsɪtʃuˈeɪʃ(ə)n ˌɔːdɪt/ *noun* the stage in marketing planning concerned with investigating an organisation's strengths and weaknesses ○ *In the situation analysis particular attention was paid to existing production capacity.* ○ *It is clear from the situation analysis that distribution is our biggest problem.*

six-pack /ˈsɪks pæk/ *noun* a box containing six items, often bottles or cans

skim /ˈskɪmɪŋ/ *verb* to fix a high price on a new product in order to achieve high short-term profits. The high price reflects the customer's appreciation of the added value of the new product, and will be reduced in due course as the product becomes established on the market. ○ *We are skimming the market with a product that will soon be obsolete.*

skip scheduling /ˈskɪp ˌʃedʒuːlɪŋ/ *noun* the act of arranging for an advertisement to appear in every other issue of a publication

SKU *noun* a unique code made up of numbers or letters and numbers which is assigned to a product by a retailer for identification and stock control. Full form **stockkeeping unit**

SLA *abbr* service level agreement

slack season /ˈslæk ˌsiːz(ə)n/ *noun* a period when a company is not very busy

slash /slæʃ/ *verb* to reduce sharply ○ *We have been forced to slash credit terms.* ○ *Prices have been slashed in all departments.* ○ *The banks have slashed interest rates.*

sleeper /ˈsliːpə/ *noun* a product which does not sell well for some time, then suddenly becomes very popular

sleeper effect /ˈsliːpər ɪˌfekt/ *noun* an effect shown where a message becomes more persuasive over a period of time

slot /slɒt/ *noun* the period of time available for a TV or radio commercial ○ *They took six 30-second slots at peak viewing time.*

slot machine /ˈslɒt məˌʃiːn/ *noun* a machine which provides drinks or cigarettes, plays music, etc. when a coin is put in it

slow payer /sləʊ ˈpeɪə/ *noun* a person or company that does not pay debts on time ○ *The company is well known as a slow payer.*

slump /slʌmp/ *noun* **1.** a rapid fall ○ *the slump in the value of the pound* ○ *We experienced a slump in sales* or *a slump in profits.* **2.** a period of economic collapse with high unemployment and loss of trade ○ *We are experiencing slump conditions.* **3.** the world economic crisis of 1929 – 1933 ■ *verb* to fall fast ○ *Profits have slumped.* ○ *The pound slumped on the foreign exchange markets.*

small business /smɔːl ˈbɪznəs/ *noun* a little company with low turnover and few employees

small businessman /smɔːl ˈbɪznəsmæn/ *noun* a man who owns a small business

small print /ˈsmɔːl prɪnt/ *noun* details in an official document such as a contract that are printed in letters of a smaller size than the rest of the text and, consequently, may be overlooked even though they are often important

small-scale enterprise /ˌsmɔːl skeɪl ˈentəpraɪz/ *noun* a small business

SME *noun* an organisation that is in the start-up or growth phase of development and has between 10 and 500 employees, according to the UK Department of Trade and Industry definition. Full form **small and medium-sized enterprise**

smuggle /ˈsmʌg(ə)l/ *verb* to take goods illegally into a country or without declaring them to customs ○ *They had to smuggle the spare parts into the country.*

smuggler /ˈsmʌɡlə/ noun a person who smuggles

smuggling /ˈsmʌɡlɪŋ/ noun the practice of taking goods illegally into a country or without declaring them to customs ○ They made their money in arms smuggling.

snap up /ˌsnæp ˈʌp/ verb to buy something quickly ○ to snap up a bargain ○ She snapped up 15% of the company's shares. (NOTE: **snapping – snapped**)

snip /snɪp/ noun a bargain (informal) ○ These printers are a snip at £50.

social /ˈsəʊʃ(ə)l/ adjective referring to society in general

social audit /ˌsəʊʃ(ə)l ˈɔːdɪt/ an analysis of the social consequences of a particular marketing strategy ○ The social audit focused on the effects of pollution in the area. ○ The social audit showed that the factory could provide jobs for five per cent of the unemployed in the small town nearby.

social cost /ˈsəʊʃ(ə)l kɒst/ noun 1. a negative effect of a type of production on society ○ The report examines the social costs of building the factory in the middle of the town. ○ The industry's representative denied that any social cost was involved in the new development. 2. the way in which something will affect people

social marketing /ˌsəʊʃ(ə)l ˈmɑːkɪtɪŋ/ noun marketing with the purpose of contributing to society rather than just making a profit

social security /ˌsəʊʃ(ə)l sɪˈkjʊərɪti/, **social insurance** /ˌsəʊʃ(ə)l ɪnˈʃʊərəns/ noun a government scheme where employers, employees and the self-employed make regular contributions to a fund which provides unemployment pay, sickness pay and retirement pensions ○ He gets weekly social security payments.

social system /ˈsəʊʃ(ə)l ˌsɪstəm/ noun the way society is organised

societal /səˈsaɪət(ə)l/ adjective referring to society

societally conscious /səˌsaɪətəli ˈkɒnʃəs/ plural noun people who are successful in life and want to work with groups of people

societal marketing /səˌsaɪət(ə)l ˈmɑːkɪtɪŋ/ noun same as **social marketing**

society /səˈsaɪəti/ noun 1. the way in which the people in a country are organised 2. a club for a group of people with the same interests ○ We have joined a computer society.

socio-cultural research /ˌsəʊʃiəʊ ˌkʌltʃərəl rɪˈsɜːtʃ/ noun research into problems of society and culture, which gives insights into consumers and their needs

socio-economic /ˌsəʊʃiəʊ iːkə-ˈnɒmɪk/ adjective referring to social and economic conditions, social classes and income groups ○ We have commissioned a thorough socio-economic analysis of our potential market.

COMMENT: The British socio-economic groups are: **A: upper middle class:** senior managers, administrators, civil servants and professional people; **B: middle class:** middle-ranking managers, administrators, civil servants and professional people; **C1: lower middle class:** junior managers and clerical staff; **C2: skilled workers:** workers with special skills and qualifications; **D: working class:** unskilled workers and manual workers; **E: subsistence level:** pensioners, the unemployed and casual manual workers.

socio-economic groups /ˌsəʊʃiəʊ iːkəˌnɒmɪk ˈɡruːps/ plural noun groups in society divided according to income and position

socio-economic segmentation /ˌsəʊʃiəʊ iːkəˌnɒmɪk seɡmən-ˈteɪʃ(ə)n/ noun dividing the population into segments according to their incomes and social class

soft currency /sɒft ˈkʌrənsi/ noun the currency of a country with a weak economy, which is cheap to buy and difficult to exchange for other currencies

soft sell /sɒft ˈsel/ noun the process of persuading people to buy, by encouraging and not forcing them to do so

software /ˈsɒftweə/ noun computer programs

sole /səʊl/ adjective only

sole agency /səʊl 'eɪdʒənsi/ *noun* an agreement to be the only person to represent a company or to sell a product in a particular area ○ *He has the sole agency for Ford cars.*

sole agent /səʊl 'eɪdʒənt/ *noun* a person who has the sole agency for a company in an area ○ *She is the sole agent for Ford cars in the locality.*

sole distributor /səʊl dɪ'strɪbjʊtə/ *noun* a retailer who is the only one in an area who is allowed to sell a product

sole owner /səʊl 'əʊnə/ *noun* a person who owns a business on their own, with no partners, and has not formed a company

sole trader /səʊl 'treɪdə/ *noun* a person who runs a business, usually by themselves, but has not registered it as a company

solicit /sə'lɪsɪt/ *verb* □ **to solicit orders** to ask for orders, to try to get people to order goods

solus /'səʊləs/ *adjective* alone

solus (advertisement) /'səʊləs əd-ˌvɜːtɪsmənt/ *noun* an advertisement which does not appear near other advertisements for similar products

solus position /'səʊləs pə,zɪʃ(ə)n/ *noun* a position for an advertisement which is alone on a page, or not near advertisements for similar products

solus site /'səʊləs saɪt/ *noun* a shop which only carries products from one supplier

solution brand /sə'luːʃ(ə)n brænd/ *noun* a combination of a product and related services, e.g. a computer system plus installation and maintenance, that meets a customer's needs more effectively than the product on its own

sorting /'sɔːtɪŋ/ *noun* the process of organising a mailing list in a certain order (by name, by country, etc.)

source /sɔːs/ *noun* **1.** the place where something comes from ○ *What is the source of her income?* ○ *You must declare income from all sources to the tax office.* □ **income which is taxed at source** income where the tax is removed and paid to the government by the employer before the income is paid to the

employee **2.** the person who sends a message ■ *verb* to get supplies from somewhere ○ *We source these spare parts in Germany.*

source credibility /'sɔːs kredə-ˌbɪlɪti/ *noun* the image people have of someone which will determine that person's credibility

source power /'sɔːs ˌpaʊə/ *noun* the power derived by a source from being able to reward a customer

sourcing /'sɔːsɪŋ/ *noun* the process of finding suppliers of goods or services ○ *The sourcing of spare parts can be diversified to suppliers outside Europe.* ♦ **outsourcing**

space /speɪs/ *noun* an empty place or empty area □ **to take advertising space in a newspaper** to place a large advertisement in a newspaper

space buyer /'speɪs ˌbaɪə/ *noun* a person who buys advertising space in magazines and newspapers

spam /spæm/ *noun* articles that have been posted to more than one newsgroup, and so are likely to contain unsolicited commercial messages

spare parts /speə 'pɑːts/ *plural noun* a stock of components for a machine that are kept in case the machine breaks down and needs to be repaired

spatial segmentation /ˌspeɪʃ(ə)l segmən'teɪʃ(ə)n/ *noun* the segmentation or division of a market according to areas or regions

spec /spek/ *noun* same as **specification** □ **to buy something on spec** to buy something without being sure of its value

special /'speʃ(ə)l/ *adjective* better than usual ○ *He offered us special terms.* ○ *The car is being offered at a special price.* ■ *noun* a product which a retailer buys for a special purpose, e.g. a premium product

'…airlines offer special stopover rates and hotel packages to attract customers to certain routes' [*Business Traveller*]

special drawing rights /'speʃəl 'drɔːɪŋ 'raɪts/ *noun* a unit of account used by the International Monetary Fund, allocated to each member country for use in loans and other international

operations; their value is calculated daily on the weighted values of a group of currencies shown in dollars

specialisation /ˌspeʃəlaɪˈzeɪʃ(ə)n/, **specialization** *noun* the act of dealing with one specific type of product ○ *The company's area of specialisation is accounts packages for small businesses.*

specialise /ˈspeʃəlaɪz/, **specialize** *verb* to deal with one particular type of skill or product or service ○ *The company specialises in electronic components.* ○ *They have a specialised product line.* ○ *He sells very specialised equipment for the electronics industry.*

'...the group specializes in the sale, lease and rental of new and second-user hardware' [*Financial Times*]

specialist /ˈspeʃəlɪst/ *noun* a person or company that deals with one particular type of product or one subject ○ *You should go to a specialist in computers* or *to a computer specialist for advice.*

speciality /ˌspeʃiˈæləti/, **specialty** /ˈspeʃ(ə)lti/ *noun* the specific business interest or specific type of product that a company has ○ *Their speciality is computer programs.*

special offer /ˌspeʃ(ə)l ˈɒfə/ *noun* a situation where goods are put on sale at a specially low price ○ *We have a range of men's shirts on special offer.*

special position /ˌspeʃ(ə)l pəˈzɪʃ(ə)n/ *noun* an especially good place in a publication for advertising ○ *If we are prepared to invest the money we could choose a special position for the advertisement.*

specialty goods /ˈspeʃ(ə)lti ɡʊdz/ *plural noun* a special type of product which sells to a limited market ○ *We only deal in specialty goods.* ○ *These specialty goods require expert personal selling.* ○ *There's a high profit margin on specialty goods.*

specialty store /ˈspeʃ(ə)lti stɔː/ *noun US* a shop selling a limited range of items of good quality

specification /ˌspesɪfɪˈkeɪʃ(ə)n/ *noun* detailed information about what is needed or about a product to be supplied ○ *to detail the specifications of a computer system* □ **to work to standard**

specifications to work to specifications which are acceptable anywhere in an industry □ **the work is not up to specification** *or* **does not meet our specifications** the product is not made in the way which was detailed

specify /ˈspesɪfaɪ/ *verb* to state clearly what is needed ○ *to specify full details of the goods ordered* ○ *Do not include VAT on the invoice unless specified.* ○ *Candidates are asked to specify which of the three posts they are applying for.* (NOTE: **specifying- specified**)

specimen /ˈspesɪmɪn/ *noun* something which is given as a sample □ **to give specimen signatures on a bank mandate** to write the signatures of all the people who can sign cheques for an account so that the bank can recognise them

spend *verb* /spend/ **1.** to pay money ○ *They spent all their savings on buying the shop.* ○ *The company spends thousands of pounds on research.* **2.** to use time ○ *The company spends hundreds of person-hours on meetings.* ○ *The chairman spent yesterday afternoon with the auditors.* (NOTE: **spending – spent**) ∎ *noun* an amount of money spent ○ *What's the annual spend on marketing?*

spending /ˈspendɪŋ/ *noun* the act of paying money for goods and services ○ *Both cash spending and credit card spending increase at Christmas.*

spending money /ˈspendɪŋ ˌmʌni/ *noun* money for ordinary personal expenses

spending power *noun* /ˈspendɪŋ ˌpaʊə/ the fact of having money to spend on goods ○ *the spending power of the student market* ∎ the amount of goods which can be bought for a sum of money ○ *The spending power of the pound has fallen over the last ten years.*

sphere /sfɪə/ *noun* an area ○ *a sphere of activity* ○ *a sphere of influence*

spiff *noun* /spɪf/ special commission or special premium offers given to sales personnel or agents, based on sales over a specific period. Full form **special incentive for affiliates** ∎ *verb* □ **to spiff up a product** to enhance the sales of a

product by offering special incentives to sales personnel

spinner /'spɪnə/ *noun* a revolving stand on which goods are displayed in a shop ○ *There was a spinner with different types of confectionery at each checkout.*

spinoff /'spɪnɒf/ *noun* a useful product developed as a secondary product from a main item ○ *One of the spinoffs of the research programme has been the development of the electric car.*

split run /splɪt 'rʌn/ *noun* the printing of the same issue of a publication in several production runs, so that different advertisements may be placed in different printings, allowing the effects of the advertising to be compared

sponsor /'spɒnsə/ *noun* **1.** a person who recommends another person for a job **2.** a company which pays part of the cost of making a TV programme by taking advertising time on the programme ■ *verb* to act as a sponsor for something ○ *a government-sponsored trade exhibition* ○ *The company has sponsored the football match.*

sponsorship /'spɒnsəʃɪp/ *noun* the act of sponsoring ○ *the sponsorship of a season of concerts* ○ *The training course could not be run without the sponsorship of several major companies.*

spot /spɒt/ *noun* **1.** a place for an advertisement on a TV or radio show **2.** a place □ **to be on the spot** to be at a place ○ *We have a man on the spot to deal with any problems which happen on the building site.* **3.** the buying of something for immediate delivery **4.** done rapidly

spot cash /spɒt 'kæʃ/ *noun* cash paid for something bought immediately

spot check /'spɒt tʃek/ *noun* a rapid and unannounced check to see if things are working properly

spot colour /'spɒt ˌkʌlə/ *noun* one colour, apart from black, used in an advertisement

spot market /'spɒt ˌmɑːkɪt/ *noun* the market for buying oil for immediate delivery

'…with most of the world's oil now traded on spot markets, Opec's official prices are much

less significant than they once were' [*Economist*]

spread /spred/ *noun* two facing pages in a magazine or newspaper used by an advertiser for a single advertisement running across the two pages

SRDS *abbr* Standard Rate & Data Service

stabilisation /ˌsteɪbɪlaɪ'zeɪʃ(ə)n/, **stabilization** *noun* the process of making something stable, e.g. preventing sudden changes in prices □ **stabilisation of the economy** keeping the economy stable by preventing inflation from rising, cutting high interest rates and excess money supply

stabilise /'steɪbəlaɪz/, **stabilize** *verb* to make steady □ **prices have stabilised** prices have stopped moving up or down □ **to have a stabilising effect on the economy** to make the economy more stable

stability /stə'bɪlɪti/ *noun* the state of being steady or not moving up or down ○ *price stability* ○ *a period of economic stability* ○ *the stability of the currency markets*

stable /'steɪb(ə)l/ *adjective* steady or not moving up or down ○ *stable prices* ○ *a stable exchange rate* ○ *a stable currency* ○ *a stable economy*

stable market /ˌsteɪb(ə)l 'mɑːkɪt/ *noun* a market where sales do not change much in response to changes in price and where demand is therefore steady

staff appraisal /stɑːf ə'preɪz(ə)l/, **staff assessment** /stɑːf ə'sesmənt/ *noun* a report on how well a member of staff is working

stage-gate model /'steɪdʒ geɪt ˌmɒd(ə)l/ *noun* a business model for developing a new product from conception to its launch, where the development is divided into several stages at the end of which is a 'gate' where the management has to take a decision as to how to proceed to the next stage

stagflation /stæg'fleɪʃ(ə)n/ *noun* inflation and stagnation of an economy

stagnation /stæg'neɪʃ(ə)n/ *noun* the state of not making any progress, espe-

cially in economic matters ○ *The country entered a period of stagnation.*

stake /steɪk/ *noun* an amount of money invested □ **to have a stake in a business** to have money invested in a business □ **to acquire a stake in a business** to buy shares in a business ○ *He acquired a 25% stake in the company.* ■ *verb* □ **to stake money on something** to risk money on something

'...her stake, which she bought at $1.45 per share, is now worth nearly $10 million' [*Times*]

'...other investments include a large stake in a Chicago-based insurance company, as well as interests in tobacco products and hotels' [*Lloyd's List*]

stakeholder /'steɪkhəʊldə/ *noun* **1.** a person who has a stake in a business, e.g. a shareholder, an employee, or a supplier **2.** a person or body that is involved with a company or organisation either personally or financially and has an interest in ensuring that it is successful (NOTE: A stakeholder may be an employee, customer, supplier, partner, or even the local community within which an organisation operates.)

'...the stakeholder concept is meant to be a new kind of low-cost, flexible personal pension aimed at those who are less well-off. Whether it will really encourage them to put aside money for retirement is a moot point. Ministers said companies would be able to charge no more than 1 per cent a year to qualify for the stakeholder label' [*Financial Times*]

stakeholder theory /'steɪkhəʊldə ˌθɪəri/ *noun* the theory that a business organisation should base its policies on the interests of elements outside it such as suppliers, consumers and the general public, as well as on its own profit-making objectives

stall /stɔːl/ *noun* a small moveable wooden booth, used for selling goods in a market

stallholder /'stɔːlhəʊldə/ *noun* a person who has a stall in a market and pays rent for the site it occupies

stamp duty /'stæmp ˌdjuːti/ *noun* a tax on legal documents such as the sale or purchase of shares, the conveyance of a property to a new owner

stamp trading /'stæmp ˌtreɪdɪŋ/ *noun* the giving out of stamps or vouchers to customers according to the value of their purchases, the stamps being exchangeable for more goods or for cash. Compare **trading stamp**

stand /stænd/ *noun* an arrangement of shelves or tables at an exhibition for showing a company's products

standard /'stændəd/ *noun* the normal quality or normal conditions which other things are judged against □ **up to standard** of acceptable quality ○ *This batch is not up to standard* or *does not meet our standards.* ■ *adjective* normal or usual ○ *a standard model car* ○ *We have a standard charge of £25 for a thirty-minute session.*

Standard & Poor's rating /ˌstændəd ən 'pʊəz ˌreɪtɪŋ/ *noun* a share-rating service provided by the US agency Standard & Poor

standard costing /ˌstændəd 'kɒstɪŋ/ *noun* the process of planning costs for the period ahead and, at the end of the period, comparing these figures with actual costs in order to make necessary adjustments in planning

standard costs /ˌstændəd 'kɒsts/ *plural noun* planned costs for the period ahead

standard deviation /ˌstændəd diːviˈeɪʃ(ə)n/ *noun* the way in which the results of a sample deviate from the mean or average

standard error /ˌstændəd 'erə/ *noun* the extent to which chance affects the accuracy of a sample

Standard Industrial Classification /ˌstændəd ɪnˌdʌstriəl klæsɪfɪ-ˈkeɪʃ(ə)n/ *noun* the official listing and coding of industries and products. Abbr **SIC**

standardisation /ˌstændədaɪ-ˈzeɪʃ(ə)n/, **standardization** *noun* the process of making sure that everything fits a standard or is produced in the same way ○ *standardisation of measurements throughout the EU* ○ *Standardization of design is necessary if we want to have a uniform company style.* □ **standardisation of products** the process of reducing a large number of different products to a series which have the same measurements, design, packaging, etc.

standardise /'stændədaız/, **standardize** *verb* to make sure that everything fits a standard or is produced in the same way

standard letter /ˌstændəd 'letə/ *noun* a letter which is sent without change to various correspondents

standard rate /'stændəd reɪt/ *noun* a basic rate of income tax which is paid by most taxpayers

Standard Rate & Data Service /ˌstændəd reɪt ən 'deɪtə ˌsɜːvɪs/ an American publication listing advertising rates, circulation and other details of major American magazines, newspapers and other advertising media. Abbr **SRDS** (NOTE: the comparable British publication is **British Rate and Data**)

standing /'stændɪŋ/ *noun* a good reputation ○ *The financial standing of a company.* □ **company of good standing** very reputable company

standing order /ˌstændɪŋ 'ɔːdə/ *noun* an order written by a customer asking a bank to pay money regularly to an account ○ *I pay my subscription by standing order.*

standing room only /ˌstændɪŋ ruːm 'əʊnli/ *noun* a sales technique which suggests to the customer that the current offer will be available only for a very short time or may be changed in the near future

stand-out test /'stænd aʊt ˌtest/ *noun* a test designed to assess how well a package stands out or catches the eye on a shelf ○ *Stand-out tests were carried out to evaluate how effective the colour of the new product packaging was.*

staple commodity /ˌsteɪp(ə)l kə-'mɒdɪti/ *noun* a basic food or raw material

staple industry /ˌsteɪp(ə)l 'ɪndəstri/ *noun* the main industry in a country

staple product /ˌsteɪp(ə)l 'prɒdʌkt/ *noun* the main product

star /stɑː/ *noun* in the Boston matrix, a product which has a high market share and a high growth rate. It will need cash to finance its growth, but eventually should become a cash cow. ○ *We have*

only one star product but it's put our company on the map. ○ *They're hoping that at least two of their new product range will turn out to be stars.*

starch ratings /'stɑːtʃ ˌreɪtɪŋz/ *plural noun* US a method of assessing the effectiveness of an organisation's advertising

start /stɑːt/ *noun* the beginning

starting point /'stɑːtɪŋ pɔɪnt/ *noun* the place where something starts

start-up /'stɑːt ʌp/ *noun* **1.** the beginning of a new company or new product ○ *start-up costs* ○ *We went into the red for the first time because of the start-up costs of the new subsidiary in the USA.* **2.** a new, usually small business that is just beginning its operations, especially a new business supported by venture capital and in a sector where new technologies are used

state enterprise /ˌsteɪt 'entəpraɪz/ *noun* a company run by the state ○ *The bosses of state industries are appointed by the government.*

statement /'steɪtmənt/ *noun* □ **statement (of account)** a list of invoices and credits and debits sent by a supplier to a customer at the end of each month

state-of-the-art /ˌsteɪt əv ði 'ɑːt/ *adjective* as technically advanced as possible

'…each year American manufacturers increase their budget for state-of-the-art computer-based hardware and software' [*Duns Business Month*]

static market /ˌstætɪk 'mɑːkɪt/ *noun* a market which does not increase or decrease significantly over a period of time

statistical /stə'tɪstɪk(ə)l/ *adjective* based on figures ○ *statistical information* ○ *They took two weeks to provide the statistical analysis of the opinion-poll data.*

statistical discrepancy /stə-ˌtɪstɪk(ə)l dɪ'skrepənsi/ *noun* the amount by which sets of figures differ

statistical error /stəˌtɪstɪk(ə)l 'erə/ *noun* the difference between results achieved in a survey using a sample and what the results would be using the entire group of people surveyed. ♦ **law**

statistics /stə'tɪstɪks/ *plural noun* facts or information in the form of figures ○ *to examine the sales statistics for the previous six months* ○ *Government trade statistics show an increase in imports.*

steady demand /ˌstedi dɪ'mɑːnd/ *noun* demand for a product which continues in a regular way

sticker /'stɪkə/ *noun* a small piece of gummed paper or plastic to be stuck on something as an advertisement or to indicate a price ■ *verb* to put a price sticker on an article for sale ○ *We had to sticker all the stock.*

stickiness /'stɪkinəs/ *noun* a website's ability to retain the interest of visitors and to keep them coming back

sticky site /'stɪki saɪt/ *noun* a website that holds the interest of visitors for a substantial amount of time and is therefore effective as a marketing vehicle

stock /stɒk/ *noun* **1.** the available supply of raw materials ○ *large stocks of oil* or *coal* ○ *the country's stocks of butter* or *sugar* **2.** the quantity of goods for sale in a warehouse or retail outlet □ **in stock** available in the warehouse or store ○ *to hold 2,000 lines in stock* □ **out of stock** not available in the warehouse or store ○ *The item went out of stock just before Christmas but came back into stock in the first week of January.* ○ *We are out of stock of this item.* □ **to take stock** to count the items in a warehouse **3.** shares ■ *adjective* usually kept in stock ○ *Butter is a stock item for any good grocer.* ■ *verb* to hold goods for sale in a warehouse or store ○ *The average supermarket stocks more than 4500 lines.*

'US crude oil stocks fell last week by nearly 2.5m barrels' [*Financial Times*]

'…the stock rose to over $20 a share, higher than the $18 bid' [*Fortune*]

stockbroker /'stɒkbrəʊkə/ *noun* person who buys or sells shares for clients

stock control /'stɒk kənˌtrəʊl/ *noun* the process of making sure that the correct level of stock is maintained, to be able to meet demand while keeping the costs of holding stock to a minimum

stock controller /'stɒk kənˌtrəʊlə/ *noun* a person who notes movements of stock

stock depreciation /'stɒk dɪpriːʃiˌeɪʃ(ə)n/ *noun* a reduction in value of stock which is held in a warehouse for some time

stock figures /'stɒk ˌfɪgəz/ *plural noun* details of how many goods are in the warehouse or store

stocking agent /'stɒkɪŋ ˌeɪdʒənt/ *noun* a wholesaler who stocks goods for a producer, sells them and earns a commission

stocking filler /'stɒkɪŋ ˌfɪlə/ *noun* a small item which can be used to put into a Christmas stocking

stock-in-hand /ˌstɒk ɪn 'hænd/ *noun* stock held in a shop or warehouse

stock-in-trade /ˌstɒk ɪn 'treɪd/ *noun* goods held by a business for sale

stockist /'stɒkɪst/ *noun* a person or shop that stocks an item

stockkeeping /'stɒkˌkiːpɪŋ/ *noun* the process of making sure that the correct level of stock is maintained (to be able to meet demand while keeping the costs of holding stock to a minimum)

stockkeeping unit /'stɒkkiːpɪŋ ˌjuːnɪt/ *noun* full form of **SKU**

stock level /'stɒk ˌlev(ə)l/ *noun* the quantity of goods kept in stock ○ *We try to keep stock levels low during the summer.*

stocklist /'stɒklɪst/ *noun* a list of items carried in stock

stockout /'stɒkaʊt/ *noun* a situation where an item is out of stock

stockpile /'stɒkpaɪl/ *noun* the supplies kept by a country or a company in case of need ○ *a stockpile of raw materials* ■ *verb* to buy items and keep them in case of need ○ *to stockpile tinned food*

stockroom /'stɒkruːm/ *noun* a room where stores are kept

stock size /stɒk 'saɪz/ *noun* a normal size ○ *We only carry stock sizes of shoes.*

stocktaking /'stɒkteɪkɪŋ/, **stocktake** /'stɒkteɪk/ *noun* the count-

ing of goods in stock at the end of an accounting period ○ *The warehouse is closed for the annual stocktaking.*

stocktaking sale /ˈstɒkteɪkɪŋ seɪl/ *noun* a sale of goods cheaply to clear a warehouse before stocktaking

stock transfer form /ˌstɒk ˈtrænsfɜː fɔːm/ *noun* a form to be signed by the person transferring shares

stock turnover /ˌstɒk ˈtɜːnəʊvə/ *noun* the total value of stock sold in a year divided by the average value of goods held in stock

stock up /ˌstɒk ˈʌp/ *verb* to buy supplies of something which you will need in the future ○ *They stocked up with computer paper.*

stock valuation /ˌstɒl væljuˈeɪʃ(ə)n/ *noun* an estimation of the value of stock at the end of an accounting period

stop /stɒp/ *noun* not supplying □ **account on stop** an account which is not supplied because it has not paid its latest invoices ○ *We put their account on stop and sued them for the money they owed.* □ **to put a stop on a cheque** to tell the bank not to pay a cheque which you have written ■ *verb* □ **to stop an account** not to supply an account any more on credit because bills have not been paid □ **to stop payments** not to make any further payments

stoppage /ˈstɒpɪdʒ/ *noun* the act of stopping ○ *stoppage of payments* ○ *Bad weather was responsible for the stoppage of deliveries.* ○ *Deliveries will be late because of stoppages on the production line.*

'…the commission noted that in the early 1960s there was an average of 203 stoppages each year arising out of dismissals' [*Employment Gazette*]

stoppage in transit /ˌstɒpɪdʒ ɪn ˈtrænzɪt/ *noun* the legal right of sellers to stop delivery of goods that are in transit if they have reason to believe customers will not pay for them owing to insolvency

storage /ˈstɔːrɪdʒ/ *noun* **1.** the act of keeping something in store or in a warehouse ○ *We let our house and put the furniture into storage.* □ **to put a plan into cold storage** to postpone work on a

plan, usually for a very long time **2.** the cost of keeping goods in store ○ *Storage rose to 10% of value, so we scrapped the stock.* **3.** the facility for storing data in a computer ○ *a disk with a storage capacity of 100Mb*

storage capacity /ˈstɔːrɪdʒ kəˌpæsɪti/ *noun* the space available for storage

storage company /ˈstɔːrɪdʒ ˌkʌmp(ə)ni/ *noun* a company which keeps items for customers

storage facilities /ˈstɔːrɪdʒ fəˌsɪlɪtiz/ *plural noun* equipment and buildings suitable for storage

storage unit /ˈstɔːrɪdʒ ˌjuːnɪt/ *noun* a device attached to a computer for storing information on disk or tape

store /stɔː/ *noun* **1.** a place where goods are kept **2.** a quantity of items or materials kept because they will be needed ○ *I always keep a store of envelopes ready in my desk.* **3.** a large shop ○ *a furniture store* ○ *a big clothing store* ■ *verb* **1.** to keep in a warehouse ○ *to store goods for six months* **2.** to keep for future use ○ *We store our pay records on computer.*

store audit /ˈstɔːr ˌɔːdɪt/ *noun* a market-research method by which a research company regularly checks a sample of stores for unit sales and stock levels of different brands

store brand /ˈstɔː brænd/ *noun* a brand owned by the retailer and not by the manufacturer

store card /ˈstɔː kɑːd/ *noun* a credit card issued by a large department store, which can only be used for purchases in that store

storekeeper /ˈstɔːkiːpə/, **storeman** /ˈstɔːmən/ *noun* a person in charge of a storeroom

storeroom /ˈstɔːruːm/ *noun* a room or small warehouse where stock can be kept

store traffic /ˈstɔː ˌtræfɪk/ *noun* the number of customers who enter a store

storyboard /ˈstɔːribɔːd/ *noun* a series of drawings which give the outline of a film or TV advertisement ○ *If the*

advertiser likes the storyboard, the agency will go ahead with the idea.

straight line depreciation /streɪt 'laɪn dɪpriːʃiˌeɪʃ(ə)n/ *noun* depreciation calculated by dividing the cost of an asset, less its remaining value, by the number of years it is likely to be used

COMMENT: Various methods of depreciating assets are used; under the 'straight line method', the asset is depreciated at a constant percentage of its cost each year, while with the 'reducing balance method' the asset is depreciated at the same percentage rate each year, but calculated on the value after the previous year's depreciation has been deducted.

straight rebuy /streɪt 'riːbaɪ/ *noun* a type of organisational buying decision where the same product is bought as before from the same supplier

strategic /strə'tiːdʒɪk/ *adjective* based on a plan of action

strategic alliance /strəˌtiːdʒɪk ə'laɪəns/ *noun* an agreement between two or more organisations to co-operate with each other and share their knowledge and expertise in a particular business activity, so that each benefits from the others' strengths and gains competitive advantage (NOTE: Strategic alliances can reduce the risk and costs involved in relationships with suppliers and the development of new products and technologies and have been seen as a response to globalisation and the increasing uncertainty in the business environment.)

strategic business unit /strəˌtiːdʒɪk 'bɪznɪs ˌjuːnɪt/ *noun* a part or division of a large company which forms its own business strategy. Abbr **SBU**

strategic marketing /strəˌtiːdʒɪk 'mɑːkɪtɪŋ/ *noun* marketing according to a set strategy, which is developed after analysing the market, designing the advertising messages and launching the product

strategic partnering /strəˌtiːdʒɪk 'pɑːtnərɪŋ/ *noun* collaboration between organisations in order to enable them to take advantage of market opportunities together, or to respond to customers

more effectively than they could if each operated separately

strategic planning /strə'tiːdʒɪk 'plænɪŋ/ *noun* the process of planning the future work of a company

strategy /'strætədʒi/ *noun* a plan of future action ○ *a marketing strategy* ○ *a financial strategy* ○ *a sales strategy* ○ *a pricing strategy* ○ *What is the strategy of the HR department to deal with long-term manpower requirements?* ○ *Part of the company's strategy to meet its marketing objectives is a major recruitment and retraining programme.*

stratification /ˌstrætɪfɪ'keɪʃ(ə)n/ *noun* **1.** the structure of a questionnaire which should help to ensure reliable answers and make it easy to evaluate results ○ *The results of the survey are hard to interpret owing to poor questionnaire stratification.* ○ *Good stratification will streamline the whole process.* **2.** a framework for the selection of a sample that ensures that it adequately represents the entire group of people surveyed

streaming /'striːmɪŋ/ *noun* Web technology that enables a user who has to download a large amount of material to view or listen to part of it while the remainder is being downloaded

streamline /'striːmlaɪn/ *verb* to make something more efficient or more simple ○ *to streamline the accounting system* ○ *to streamline distribution services*

streamlined /'striːmlaɪnd/ *adjective* efficient or rapid ○ *We need a more streamlined production system.* ○ *The company introduced a streamlined system of distribution.*

streamlining /'striːmlaɪnɪŋ/ *noun* the process of making something efficient

street furniture /striːt 'fɜːnɪtʃə/ *noun* lamps, litter bins, bus shelters, etc., on which advertising can be placed

street vendor /striːt 'vendə/ *noun* a person who sells food or small items in the street

striver /'straɪvə/ *noun* in the VALS lifestyle classification, someone who likes spending money and wants to appear successful, rich and fashionable

structure /ˈstrʌktʃə/ *noun* the way in which something is organised ○ *the price structure in the small car market* ○ *the career structure within a corporation* ○ *The paper gives a diagram of the company's organisational structure.* ○ *The company is reorganising its discount structure.* ■ *verb* to arrange in a specific way ○ *to structure a meeting*

structured interview /ˌstrʌktʃəd ˈɪntəvjuː/ *noun* an interview using preset questions and following a fixed pattern. Compare **unstructured interview**

stuff /stʌf/ *verb* to put papers into envelopes ○ *We pay casual workers by the hour for stuffing envelopes* or *for envelope stuffing.*

stuffer /ˈstʌfə/ *noun* advertising material that is put in an envelope for mailing

style /staɪl/ *noun* a way of doing or making something ○ *a new style of product* ○ *old-style management techniques*

style obsolescence /ˈstaɪl ɒbsəˌles(ə)ns/ *noun* the redesign of a product in order to make previous models obsolete and therefore encourage buying of the latest one

suasionetics /sweɪʒəˈnetɪks/ *plural noun US* the techniques used to persuade people to adopt ideas or behaviour patterns (NOTE: takes a singular verb)

sub- /sʌb/ *prefix* under or less important

sub-agency /ˈsʌb ˌeɪdʒənsɪ/ *noun* a small agency which is part of a large agency

sub-agent /ˈsʌb ˌeɪdʒənt/ *noun* a person who is in charge of a sub-agency

subcontract *noun* /sʌbˈkɒntrækt/ a contract between the main contractor for a whole project and another firm who will do part of the work ○ *They have been awarded the subcontract for all the electrical work in the new building.* ○ *We will put the electrical work out to subcontract.* ■ *verb* /ˌsʌbkənˈtrækt/ (*of a main contractor*) to agree with a company that they will do part of the work for a project ○ *The electrical work has been subcontracted to Smith Ltd.*

subcontractor /ˌsʌbkənˈtræktə/ *noun* a company which has a contract to do work for a main contractor

subculture /ˈsʌbkʌltʃə/ *noun* a part or sector of society identifiable by factors such as lifestyle, religion and race ○ *Studies were made of spending in the student subculture.* ○ *Different subcultures have different buying priorities.*

subhead /ˈsʌbhed/, **subheading** /-ˈsʌbhedɪŋ/ *noun* a heading used to divide up text such as an email into separate sections

subject /ˈsʌbdʒɪkt/ *noun* the thing which you are talking about or writing about

subject line /ˈsʌbdʒɪkt laɪn/ *noun* the line at the top of an email which tells the recipient what it is about

sublease /ˈsʌbliːs/ *noun* a lease from a tenant to another tenant ○ *They signed a sublease for the property.*

subliminal advertising /sʌbˌlɪmɪn(ə)l ˈædvətaɪzɪŋ/ *noun* advertising that attempts to leave impressions on the subconscious mind of the person who sees it or hears it without that person realising that this is being done

subsample /ˈsʌbsɑːmpəl/ *noun* a subdivision of a sample

subscribe /səbˈskraɪb/ *verb* □ **to subscribe to a magazine or website** to pay for a series of issues of a magazine or for information available on a website

subscribed circulation /səbˌskraɪbd sɜːkjʊˈleɪʃ(ə)n/ *noun* circulation of a publication that is paid for in advance

subscriber /səbˈskraɪbə/ *noun* □ **subscriber to a magazine** *or* **magazine subscriber** a person who has paid in advance for a series of issues of a magazine or to have access to information on a website ○ *The extra issue is sent free to subscribers.*

subscription /səbˈskrɪpʃən/ *noun* money paid in advance for a series of issues of a magazine, for membership of a society or for access to information on a website ○ *Did you remember to pay the subscription to the computer magazine?*

○ *She forgot to renew her club subscription.* □ **to take out a subscription to a magazine** to start paying for a series of issues of a magazine □ **to cancel a subscription to a magazine** to stop paying for a series of issues of a magazine

subscription-based publishing /səb,skrɪpʃən beɪst 'pʌblɪʃɪŋ/ *noun* a form of publishing in which readers pay a subscription and in return have a magazine, book, or other publication delivered to them regularly by post or email

subscription process /səb'skrɪpʃən ,prəʊses/ *noun* the process by which users of a website sign up to receive specific information, content, or services from it

subscription rate /səb'skrɪpʃən reɪt/ *noun* the amount of money to be paid for a series of issues of a magazine

subsidiary /səb'sɪdiəri/ *adjective* which is less important ○ *They agreed to most of the conditions in the contract but queried one or two subsidiary items.* ■ *noun same as* **subsidiary company** ○ *Most of the group profit was contributed by the subsidiaries in the Far East.*

subsidiary company /səb,sɪdiəri 'kʌmp(ə)ni/ *noun* a company which is more than 50% owned by a holding company, and where the holding company controls the board of directors

subsidise /'sʌbsɪdaɪz/, **subsidize** *verb* to help by giving money ○ *The government has refused to subsidise the car industry.*

subsidised accommodation /,sʌbsɪdaɪzd əkɒmə'deɪʃ(ə)n/ *noun* cheap accommodation which is partly paid for by an employer or a local authority

subsidy /'sʌbsɪdi/ *noun* **1.** money given to help something which is not profitable ○ *The industry exists on government subsidies.* ○ *The government has increased its subsidy to the car industry.* **2.** money given by a government to make something cheaper ○ *the subsidy on rail transport* (NOTE: plural is **subsidies**)

substitute /'sʌbstɪtjuːt/ *noun* a person or thing that takes the place of someone or something else ■ *verb* to take the place of someone or something else

substitute product /'sʌbstɪtjuːt ,prɒdʌkt/ *noun* a product which may be bought instead of another when the price of the original product changes or if it becomes unavailable ○ *We must match our competitors since they produce substitute products to ours.* ○ *As the price of substitute products falls, they will be much in demand.*

substitution effect /,sʌbstɪ'tjuːʃ(ə)n ɪ,fekt/ *noun* the extent to which consumers will change from one product to another when the price of the product rises

suggestion /sə'dʒestʃən/ *noun* an idea which is put forward

suggestion box /sə'dʒestʃən bɒks/ *noun* a place in a company where members of staff can put forward their ideas for making the company more efficient and profitable

suggestion scheme /sə'dʒestʃən skiːm/ *noun* a scheme in which employees are asked to suggest ways in which the work they do or the way their organisation operates can be improved and receive a gift or cash reward for useful suggestions

suggestion selling /sə'dʒestʃən ,selɪŋ/ *noun* selling in such a way that the customer believes they really want the product ○ *Trainee salespeople learn the application of psychology to suggestion selling.*

sums chargeable to the reserve /sʌmz ,tʃɑːdʒəb(ə)l tə ðə rɪ'zɜːv/ *plural noun* sums which can be debited to a company's reserves

Sunday /'sʌndeɪ/ *noun* the seventh day of the week

Sunday closing /,sʌndeɪ 'kləʊzɪŋ/ *noun* the practice of not opening a shop on Sundays

Sunday supplement /,sʌndeɪ 'sʌplɪmənt/ *noun* a special extra section of a Sunday newspaper, usually on a special subject

supermarket /'suːpəmɑːkɪt/ *noun* a large store, usually selling food and household goods, where customers

serve themselves and pay at a checkout ○ *Sales in supermarkets* or *Supermarket sales account for half the company's turnover.*

supermarket trolley /'suːpəmɑːkɪt ˌtrɒli/ *noun* a metal basket on wheels, used by shoppers to put their purchases in as they go round a supermarket (NOTE: American English is **shopping cart**)

supernormal   profit /ˌsuːpənɔːm(ə)l 'prɒfɪt/ *noun* profit earned by a business through having a monopoly ○ *This company has survived the recession owing to supernormal profits.*

supersite /'suːpəsaɪt/ *noun* a particularly large poster site ○ *If we cannot afford a supersite we will have to settle for a site on an Underground station.* ○ *There are some key supersites at the side of the motorway.*

superstore /'suːpəstɔː/ *noun* a very large self-service store (more than 2,500 square metres) which sells a wide range of goods ○ *We bought the laptop at a computer superstore.*

supplement /'sʌplɪmənt/ *noun* a special addition to a magazine or newspaper which is given free to customers ○ *The colour supplement is mostly full of advertising.* ○ *The supplement contains special articles on recent marketing strategies.* ○ *What are the advertising rates in that paper's supplement?*

supplier /sə'plaɪə/ *noun* a person or company that supplies or sells goods or services ○ *We use the same office equipment supplier for all our stationery purchases.* ○ *They are major suppliers of spare parts to the car industry.*

supplier development /sə'plaɪə dɪˌveləpmənt/ *noun* the development of close and long-term relationships between customers and suppliers that are intended to benefit both

supplier   evaluation /sə'plaɪə ɪvælju,eɪʃ(ə)n/ *noun* the process of assessing potential suppliers of materials, goods, or services before placing an order, to find out which one of them will best satisfy the customer's requirements

(NOTE: When this process is undertaken after an order has been fulfilled, it is known as vendor rating.)

supplier rating /sə'plaɪə ˌreɪtɪŋ/ *noun* same as **vendor rating**

supply /sə'plaɪ/ *noun* **1.** the act of providing something which is needed **2.** □ **in short supply** not available in large enough quantities to meet the demand ○ *Spare parts are in short supply because of the strike.* **3.** stock of something which is needed ○ *Garages were running short of supplies of petrol.* ○ *Supplies of coal to the factory have been hit by the rail strike.* ○ *Supplies of stationery have been reduced.* ■ *verb* to provide something which is needed ○ *to supply a factory with spare parts* ○ *The finance department supplied the committee with the figures.* ○ *Details of staff addresses and phone numbers can be supplied by the HR department.*

supply and demand /sə,plaɪ ən dɪ'mɑːnd/ *noun* the amount of a product which is available and the amount which is wanted by customers

supply chain /sə'plaɪ tʃeɪn/ *noun* the manufacturers, wholesalers, distributors and retailers who contribute in turn to the process of making raw materials into finished goods and services and delivering them to consumers

supply chain management /sə'plaɪ tʃeɪn ˌmænɪdʒmənt/ *noun* the management of the movement of goods and the flow of information between an organisation and its suppliers and customers (NOTE: Supply chain management covers the processes of materials management, logistics, physical distribution management, purchasing, and information management.)

supply price /sə'plaɪ praɪs/ *noun* the price at which something is provided

supply-side economics /sə'plaɪ saɪd iːkə,nɒmɪks/ *noun* an economic theory that governments should encourage producers and suppliers of goods by cutting taxes, rather than encourage demand by making more money available in the economy (NOTE: takes a singular verb)

support advertising /səˈpɔːt ˌædvətaɪzɪŋ/ *noun* advertising which is designed to support other advertising in other media

support media /səˈpɔːt ˌmiːdiə/ *plural noun* non-traditional media which are used to reinforce messages sent to target markets through other more traditional media

surcharge /ˈsɜːtʃɑːdʒ/ *noun* an extra charge

surplus /ˈsɜːpləs/ *noun* more of something than is needed ○ *Profit figures are lower than planned because of surplus labour.* ○ *Some of the machines may have to be sold off as there is surplus production capacity.* ○ *We are proposing to put our surplus staff on short time.* □ **these items are surplus to our requirements** we do not need these items □ **to absorb a surplus** to take a surplus into a larger amount

'Both imports and exports reached record levels in the latest year. This generated a \$371 million trade surplus in June, the seventh consecutive monthly surplus and close to market expectations'
[*Dominion (Wellington, New Zealand)*]

survivor /səˈvaɪvə/ *noun* in the VALS lifestyle classification, someone with very little money who buys only what they need

suspect /ˈsʌspekt/ *noun* any individual taken from a database of prospective customers

swatch /swɒtʃ/ *noun* a small sample of a fabric ○ *The interior designer showed us swatches of the curtain fabric.*

sweep periods /ˈswiːp ˌpɪəriədz/ *plural noun* times of the year when television audiences are measured

sweepstake /ˈswiːpsteɪk/ *noun* a form of gambling promotion where customers put in their names for a draw and the lucky number wins a prize

switch /swɪtʃ/ *verb* to change from one thing to another ○ *to switch funds from one investment to another* ○ *The job was switched from our British factory to the States.*

switch selling *noun* /ˈswɪtʃ ˌselɪŋ/ a selling technique which involves trying to persuade customers to buy something

very different from what they wanted to buy in the first place ○ *Trainee sales staff are coached in switch selling.* ■ *verb* the practice of offering an apparently good bargain as bait in order to gain the attention of prospective customers then approaching them with a different offer which is more profitable to the seller

SWOT analysis /ˈswɒt əˌnæləsɪs/ *noun* a method of developing a marketing strategy based on an assessment of the Strengths and Weaknesses of the company and the Opportunities and Threats in the market

symbol /ˈsɪmbəl/ *noun* a sign, picture or object which represents something ○ *They use a bear as their advertising symbol.*

symbol group /ˈsɪmbəl gruːp/ *noun* a group to which symbol retailers belong

symbol retailer /ˈsɪmbəl ˌriːteɪlə/ *noun* a retailer that is a member of an independent group which secures favourable prices from suppliers through buying in bulk and has its own symbol or logo

synchro marketing /ˈsɪŋkrəʊ ˌmɑːkɪtɪŋ/ *noun* the practice of finding ways to use spare resources during periods of low demand ○ *Synchro marketing will stop wastage of our production and storage capacity in the off-season.*

syndicate /ˈsɪndɪkeɪt/ *verb* to produce an article, a cartoon, etc., which is then published in several newspapers or magazines

'…over the past few weeks, companies raising new loans from international banks have been forced to pay more, and an unusually high number of attempts to syndicate loans among banks has failed' [*Financial Times*]

syndicated programme /ˌsɪndɪkeɪtɪd ˈprəʊgræmz/ *noun* a programme which is sold to a range of different stations across the country

syndicated research /ˌsɪndɪkeɪtɪd rɪˈsɜːtʃ/ *noun* market research carried out by agencies and sold to several different companies

syndication /ˌsɪndɪˈkeɪʃ(ə)n/ *noun* an article, drawing, etc., which is pub-

lished in several newspapers or magazines at the same time

synectics /sɪˈnektɪks/ *plural noun* group discussions designed to elicit creative solutions to problems ○ *We are beginning to apply synectics to our strategy formulation.* ○ *Synectics is being encouraged as a method of approaching case-studies in business school.* (NOTE: takes a singular verb)

synergy /ˈsɪnədʒi/ *noun* the process of producing greater effects by joining forces than by acting separately ○ *There is considerable synergy between the two companies.*

synthetic materials /sɪnˈθetɪk məˈtɪərɪəlz/ *plural noun* substances made as products of a chemical process

system /ˈsɪstəm/ *noun* an arrangement or organisation of things which work together ○ *Our accounting system has worked well in spite of the large in-crease in orders.* □ **to operate a quota system** to regulate supplies by fixing quantities which are allowed ○ *We arrange our distribution using a quota system – each agent is allowed only a specific number of units.*

systems analysis /ˈsɪstəmz əˌnæləsɪs/ *noun* the process of using a computer to suggest how a company can work more efficiently by analysing the way in which it works at present

systems analyst /ˈsɪstəmz ˌænəlɪst/ *noun* a person who specialises in systems analysis

systems management /ˈsɪstəmz ˌmænɪdʒmənt/ *noun* the directing and controlling of all the elements in an organisation to achieve its basic objectives

systems selling /ˈsɪstəmz ˌselɪŋ/ *noun* the selling of an integrated system, not just separate products plus related services

table 265 takeover bid

T

table /'teɪb(ə)l/ *noun* a list of figures or facts set out in columns □ **table of random numbers** a table of numbers in no particular order or pattern, which is used for selecting samples in market research

table of discounts /ˌteɪb(ə)l əv 'dɪskaʊnts/, **discount table** /'dɪskaʊnt ˌteɪb(ə)l/ *noun* a table showing discounts for various prices and quantities ○ *According to the table of discounts, there was no discount for purchases involving less than 100 items of each product.*

tabloid /'tæblɔɪd/ *noun* a small size of newspaper, as opposed to a broadsheet ○ *We're advertising in three tabloids concurrently.*

tachistoscope /tə'kɪstəskəʊp/, **T-scope** /'tiː skəʊp/ *noun* a device used to measure the recognition level when a customer is exposed to a brand package or advertising material

tactic /'tæktɪk/ *noun* a way of doing things so as to be at an advantage ○ *Securing a key position at an exhibition is an old tactic which always produces good results* ○ *Concentrating our sales force in that area could be a good tactic.*

tactical /'tæktɪk(ə)l/ *adjective* referring to tactics

tactical campaign /ˌtæktɪk(ə)l kæm'peɪn/ *noun* a promotion that is planned according to a series of targets, in particular when attacking a competitor

tag /tæg/ *noun* a label ○ *a price tag* ○ *a name tag*

tailor /'teɪlə/ *verb* to design something for a specific purpose ○ *We mail out press releases tailored to the reader in-*terests of each particular newspaper or periodical.

tailor-made /ˌteɪlə 'meɪd/ *adjective* made to fit specific needs

tailor-made promotion /ˌteɪlə meɪd prə'məʊʃ(ə)n/ *noun* a promotion which is specifically made for an individual customer

take /teɪk/ *noun* the money received in a shop ○ *Our weekly take is over £5,000.* ■ *verb* to receive or to get □ **the shop takes £2,000 a week** the shop receives £2,000 a week in cash sales □ **he takes home £250 a week** his salary, after deductions for tax etc., is £250 a week

takeaway /'teɪkəweɪ/ *noun* **1.** a shop which sells food to be eaten at some other place ○ *There is no VAT on takeaway meals.* ○ *There's a Chinese takeaway on the corner of the street.* **2.** the food sold by a takeaway

take-ones /'teɪk wʌnz/ *plural noun* advertising leaflets or promotional cards which are delivered to shops where they are displayed in racks

takeover /'teɪkəʊvə/ *noun* an act of buying a controlling interest in a business by buying more than 50% of its shares

'…many takeovers result in the new managers/owners rationalizing the capital of the company through better asset management' [*Duns Business Month*]

takeover bid /'teɪkəʊvə bɪd/ *noun* an offer to buy all or a majority of the shares in a company so as to control it ○ *They made a takeover bid for the company.* ○ *He had to withdraw his takeover bid when he failed to find any backers.*

taker /'teɪkə/ *noun* a person who wants to buy ○ *There were very few takers for the special offer.*

takings /'teɪkɪŋz/ *plural noun* the money received in a shop or a business ○ *The week's takings were stolen from the cash desk.*

tannoy /'tænɔɪ/ *noun* a loudspeaker system for making public announcements

target /'tɑːgɪt/ *noun* something to aim for □ **to set targets** to fix amounts or quantities which employees have to produce or reach □ **to meet a target** to produce the quantity of goods or sales which are expected □ **to miss a target** not to produce the amount of goods or sales which are expected ○ *They missed the target figure of £2m turnover.* ■ *verb* to aim to sell to somebody □ **to target a market** to plan to sell goods in a specific market ○ *I'll follow up your idea of targeting our address list with a special mailing.*

'…in a normal leveraged buyout the acquirer raises money by borrowing against the assets of the target company' [*Fortune*]

'…the minister is persuading the oil, gas, electricity and coal industries to target their advertising towards energy efficiency' [*Times*]

'…he believes that increased competition could keep inflation below the 2.5 per cent target' [*Investors Chronicle*]

target audience /'tɑːgɪt ˌɔːdiəns/ *noun* consumers at whom an advertisement is aimed ○ *TV advertising will fail unless we have a clear idea of who the target audience is for our product.* ○ *What is the best media to reach our target audience?*

target market /'tɑːgɪt ˌmɑːkɪt/ *noun* the market in which a company is planning to sell its goods

target marketing /'tɑːgɪt ˌmɑːkɪtɪŋ/ *noun* the aiming of advertising or selling at a specific group of consumers who all have similar characteristics

target population /'tɑːgɪt pɒpjʊˌleɪʃ(ə)n/ *noun* a group of individuals or regions that are to be investigated in a statistical study

tariff /'tærɪf/ *noun* a rate of charging for something such as electricity, hotel rooms or train tickets

tariff barrier /'tærɪf ˌbæriə/ *noun* the customs duty intended to make imports more difficult ○ *to impose tariff barriers on* or *to lift tariff barriers from a product*

task *noun* /tɑːsk/ work which has to be done ○ *The job involves some tasks which are unpleasant and others which are more rewarding.* ○ *The candidates are given a series of tasks to complete within a time limit.* □ **to list task processes** to make a list of various parts of a job which have to be done ■ *verb* to give someone a task to do

task method /'tɑːsk ˌmeθəd/ *noun* the way of calculating an advertising appropriation by basing it on the actual amount needed to achieve the objectives

taste /teɪst/ *noun* a very small quantity of something taken to try it out

taste space /'teɪst speɪs/ *noun* different individuals or groups brought together into a database based on common interests

TAT *abbr* thematic apperception test

tax credit /'tæks ˌkredɪt/ *noun* the part of a dividend on which the company has already paid tax, so that the shareholder is not taxed on it

tax-exempt /tæks ɪgˈzempt/ *adjective* **1.** not required to pay tax **2.** (*of income or goods*) which are not subject to tax

tax-free /ˈtæksˈfriː/ *adjective* with no tax having to be paid ○ *tax-free goods*

TC *abbr* till countermanded

team /tiːm/ *noun* a group of people who work together and cooperate to share work and responsibility

team approach /'tiːm əˌprəʊtʃ/ *noun* a method of measuring the effectiveness of an advertising campaign when the evaluators are actually involved in the campaign

team-building /'tiːm ˌbɪldɪŋ/ *noun* training sessions designed to instil cooperation and solidarity in a group of workers who work together as a team

tear sheet /'teə ʃiːt/ *noun* a page taken from a published magazine or newspaper, sent to an advertiser as proof that their advertisement has been run

teaser /'tiːzə/, **teaser ad** *noun* an advertisement that gives a little information about a product in order to attract customers by making them curious to know more

technical /'teknɪk(ə)l/ *adjective* referring to a particular machine or process ○ *The document gives all the technical details on the new computer.*

'…market analysts described the falls in the second half of last week as a technical correction' [*Australian Financial Review*]

'…at the end of the day, it was clear the Fed had not loosened the monetary reins, and Fed Funds forged ahead on the back of technical demand' [*Financial Times*]

technical press /'teknɪk(ə)l pres/ *noun* newspapers and magazines on scientific or technical subjects ○ *We need to advertise this product in the technical press.*

technique /tek'niːk/ *noun* a skilled way of doing a job ○ *The company has developed a new technique for processing steel.* ○ *We have a special technique for answering complaints from customers.*

technology adoption life cycle /tek,nɒlədʒi ə,dɒpʃən 'laɪf ,saɪk(ə)l/ *noun* a method of describing when and how people and organisations start to use new technologies, typically classifying them as innovators, early adopters, early majority, late majority, and technology laggards, depending on whether they adopt the technologies sooner or later

technology laggard /tek'nɒlədʒi ,lægəd/ *noun* an individual or organisation that is very slow or reluctant to adopt new technology

telcos /'telkəʊz/ *plural noun* telecommunications companies (*informal*)

teleconferencing /'teli-,kɒnf(ə)rənsɪŋ/ *noun* the use of telephone or television channels to connect people in different locations in order to conduct group discussions, meetings, conferences, or courses

telemarketer /'teli,mɑːkɪtə/ *noun* a person who markets a product by telephone

telemarketing /'teli,mɑːkɪtɪŋ/ *noun* the selling of a product or service by telephone

telephone /'telifəʊn/ *noun* a machine used for speaking to someone over a long distance ○ *We had a new telephone system installed last week.*

telephone interview /'telifəʊn ,ɪntəvjuː/ *noun* same as **telephone survey**

telephone interview survey /,telifəʊn ɪntəvjuː 'sɜːveɪ/ *noun* a survey conducted by telephoning a selected group of people and asking them for their views on a particular subject

telephone kiosk /'telifəʊn ,kiːɒsk/ *noun* a shelter with a public telephone in it ○ *There are two telephone kiosks outside the post office.*

telephone order /'telifəʊn ,ɔːdə/ *noun* an order received by telephone ○ *Since we mailed the catalogue we have received a large number of telephone orders.*

telephone research /'telifəʊn rɪ-,sɜːtʃ/ *noun* same as **telephone survey**

telephone sales representative /,telifəʊn 'seɪlz repri,zentətɪv/ *noun* someone who sells to customers over the phone. Abbr **TSR**

telephone selling /'telifəʊn ,selɪŋ/ *noun* the practice of making sales by phoning prospective customers and trying to persuade them to buy

telephone survey /'telifəʊn ,sɜːveɪ/ *noun* an act of interviewing respondents by telephone for a survey ○ *How many people in the sample hung up before replying to the telephone survey?*

telesales /'teli,seɪlz/ *plural noun* sales made by telephone

teleshopping /'teli,ʃɒpɪŋ/ *noun* shopping from home by means of a television screen and a home computer

teletext /'telɪtekst/ *noun* a videotext broadcast by a TV company, e.g. Ceefax on BBC or Oracle on ITV

television /ˌtelɪ'vɪʒ(ə)n/ *noun* the broadcasting of moving images. Abbr **TV**

television consumer audit /ˌtelɪvɪʒ(ə)n kən'sjuːmə ˌɔːdɪt/ *noun* an act of questioning a sample of television viewers on their viewing and impressions

television network /ˌtelɪvɪʒ(ə)n 'netwɜːk/ *noun* a system of linked television stations covering the whole country

television ratings /telɪ'vɪʒ(ə)n ˌreɪtɪŋz/ *plural noun* statistics showing the size and type of television audiences at different times of day for various channels and programmes ○ *We will have to consult the TV ratings before buying a spot.* Abbr **TVR**

tender /'tendə/ *noun* an offer to do something for a specific price ○ *a successful tender* ○ *an unsuccessful tender* □ **to put a project out to tender** *or* **to ask for/invite tenders for a project** to ask contractors to give written estimates for a job □ **to put in/submit a tender** to make an estimate for a job □ **to sell shares by tender** to ask people to offer in writing a price for shares ■ *verb* □ **to tender for a contract** to put forward an estimate of cost for work to be carried out under contract ○ *to tender for the construction of a hospital*

tenderer /'tendərə/ *noun* a person or company that tenders for work ○ *The company was the successful tenderer for the project.*

tendering /'tendərɪŋ/ *noun* the act of putting forward an estimate of cost ○ *To be successful, you must follow the tendering procedure as laid out in the documents.*

terminal /'tɜːmɪn(ə)l/ *noun* the building where you end a journey

terminal poster /'tɜːmɪn(ə)l ˌpəʊstəz/ *noun* an advertising display in stations or airline terminals, etc.

termination clause /ˌtɜːmɪ'neɪʃ(ə)n klɔːz/ *noun* a clause which explains how and when a contract can be terminated

terms /tɜːmz/ *plural noun* the conditions or duties which have to be carried out as part of a contract, or the arrangements which have to be agreed before a contract is valid ○ *By* or *Under the terms of the contract, the company is responsible for all damage to the property.* ○ *to negotiate for better terms* ○ *He refused to agree to some of the terms of the contract.* □ **'terms: cash with order'** the terms of sale showing that payment has to be made in cash when the order is placed

'…companies have been improving communications, often as part of deals to cut down demarcation and to give everybody the same terms of employment' [*Economist*]

terms of payment /ˌtɜːmz əv 'peɪmənt/ *plural noun* the conditions for paying something

terms of sale /ˌtɜːmz əv 'seɪl/ *plural noun* the conditions attached to a sale

terms of trade /ˌtɜːmz əv 'treɪd/ *plural noun* the ratio of a country's import prices to export prices

territorial planning /ˌterɪtɔːriəl 'plænɪŋ/ *noun* the planning of a salesperson's calls, taking into account the best use of time in travelling and the priority of important customers ○ *The sales manager is giving the sales team some guidelines on territorial planning.* ○ *Bad territorial planning means time wasted in travelling.*

territorial rights /ˌterɪtɔːriəl 'raɪts/ *plural noun* the rights of a distributor, granted by the producer or supplier, to sell a product in a particular geographical area, often on condition that specific methods are used in the selling

territory /'terɪt(ə)ri/ *noun* an area visited by a salesperson ○ *We are adding two new reps and reducing all the reps' territories.* ○ *Her territory covers all the north of the country.*

tertiary industry /ˌtɜːʃəri 'ɪndəstri/ *noun* an industry which does not produce raw materials or manufacture products but offers a service such as banking, retailing, accountancy

tertiary readership /ˌtɜːʃəri 'riːdəʃɪp/ *noun* the people who do not buy a newspaper or magazine but come across it as a result of another activity such as waiting for an appointment with the dentist ○ *Many glossy magazines*

have a relatively small circulation but a high tertiary readership.

tertiary sector /'tɜːʃəri ˌsektə/ *noun* the section of the economy containing the service industries

test /test/ *noun* an examination to see if something works well or is possible ■ *verb* to examine something to see if it is working well ○ *We are still testing the new computer system.* □ **to test the market for a product** to show samples of a product in a market to see if it will sell well ○ *We are testing the market for the toothpaste in Scotland.*

test certificate /'test səˌtɪfɪkət/ *noun* a certificate to show that something has passed a test

test close /'test kləʊz/ *noun* an act of trying to obtain at least one immediate order from a buyer to see how promising a customer they are

test-drive /'test draɪv/ *verb* □ **to test-drive a car** to drive a car before buying it to see if it works well

testimonial /ˌtestɪ'məʊniəl/ *noun* a written report about someone's character or ability ○ *She has asked me to write her a testimonial.*

testimonial advertising /ˌtestɪ-'məʊniəl ˌædvətaɪzɪŋ/ *noun* advertising which makes use of testimonials from famous or qualified people, or from satisfied customers, to endorse a product

testing /'testɪŋ/ *noun* the act of examining something to see if it works well ○ *During the testing of the system several defects were corrected.*

testing bias /'testɪŋ baɪəs/ *noun* bias that occurs when respondents to questionnaires know they are being tested and change their responses accordingly

test-market /'test ˌmɑːkɪt/ *verb* □ **to test-market a product** to show samples of a product in a market to see if it will sell well ○ *We are test-marketing the toothpaste in Scotland.*

test marketing /'test ˌmɑːkɪtɪŋ/ *noun* marketing a product in a specific area or to a specific audience to test the

validity of the approach before launching a nationwide marketing campaign

test panel /'test ˌpæn(ə)l/ *noun* a group of people used to test a product or service

test run /'test rʌn/ *noun* a trial made on a machine

text /tekst/ *verb* to send a text message on a mobile phone or pager

text message /'tekst 'mesɪdʒ/ *noun* a message sent in text form, especially from one mobile phone or pager to another

T-group /'tiː gruːp/ *noun* a group of trainees following a training method, often used in training sales staff, which uses group discussions and activities to develop social skills and general self-awareness

thematic apperception test /θɪ-ˌmætɪk ˌæpə'seps(ə)n test/ *noun* a test used to find out attitudes or reactions to a brand, which consists of showing pictures to the subject who then constructs a story round them. Abbr **TAT**

thinker /'θɪŋkə/ *noun* in the VALS lifestyle classification system, a well-educated person with strong ideals who buys products that last a long time and are good value

threshold /'θreʃˌhəʊld/ *noun* the point at which something changes

ticket /'tɪkɪt/ *noun* a piece of paper or card which shows something

ticket counter /'tɪkɪt ˌkaʊntə/ *noun* a place where tickets are sold

tie /taɪ/ *verb* to attach or to fasten with string, wire, or other material ○ *He tied the parcel with thick string.* ○ *She tied two labels on to the parcel.* (NOTE: **tying – tied**)

tied shop /taɪd 'ʃɒp/ *noun* a business which has agreed to sell only a particular supplier's products ○ *The store felt constrained by the tied shop agreement and wanted to offer a wider range of brands.*

tie-in /'taɪ ɪn/ *noun* an advertisement linked to advertising in another media, e.g. a magazine ad linked to a TV commercial (NOTE: plural is **tie-ins**)

tie-up /'taɪ ʌp/ *noun* a link or connection ○ *The company has a tie-up with a German distributor.* (NOTE: plural is **tie-ups**)

till /tɪl/ *noun* a drawer for keeping cash in a shop

till countermanded /tɪl 'kaʊntəmɑːndɪd/ *noun* a clause in a contract which states that an advertisement will run until stopped by the advertiser. Abbr **TC**

time /taɪm/ *noun* **1.** a period during which something takes place, e.g. one hour, two days, fifty minutes, etc. **2.** a period before something happens □ **to keep within the time limits** *or* **within the time schedule** to complete work by the time stated

time and duty study /ˌtaɪm ən 'djuːti ˌstʌdi/ *noun* a study to see how effectively salespeople are using their time ○ *The time and duty study showed that 30% of time is wasted.* ○ *The aim of the time and duty study was to streamline our sales activities.*

time and motion expert /ˌtaɪm ən 'məʊʃ(ə)n ˌekspɜːt/ *noun* a person who analyses time and motion studies and suggests changes in the way work is done

time buyer /'taɪm ˌbaɪə/ *noun* a person who buys advertising time on radio or TV

timelength /'taɪmleŋkθ/ *noun* the length of a cinema, television or radio advertisement ○ *Find out the rates for the various timelengths before placing the commercial.*

time limit /'taɪm ˌlɪmɪt/ *noun* the maximum time which can be taken to do something ○ *to set a time limit for acceptance of the offer*

time limitation /'taɪm lɪmɪˌteɪʃ(ə)n/ *noun* the restriction of the amount of time available

time of peak demand /ˌtaɪm əv piːk dɪ'mɑːnd/ *noun* the time when something is being used most

time segment /'taɪm ˌsegmənt/ *noun* a period set aside for advertisements on television

time series analysis /'taɪm ˌsɪəriːz əˌnæləsɪs/ *noun* a method of assessing variations in data over regular periods of time such as sales per month or per quarter in order to try to identify the causes for the variations

time utility /'taɪm juːˌtɪlɪti/ *noun* the usefulness to a customer of receiving a product at a particular time ○ *Time utility has meant avoiding unreliable suppliers.* ○ *Some customers put time utility before place utility.*

tip /tɪp/ *noun* **1.** money given to someone who has helped you ○ *I gave the taxi driver a 10 cent tip.* ○ *The staff are not allowed to accept tips.* **2.** a piece of advice on buying or doing something which could be profitable ○ *The newspaper gave several stock market tips.* ○ *She gave me a tip about a share which was likely to rise because of a takeover bid.* ■ *verb* **1.** to give money to someone who has helped you ○ *She tipped the receptionist £5.* **2.** to say that something is likely to happen or that something might be profitable ○ *He is tipped to become the next chairman.* ○ *Two shares were tipped in the business section of the paper.* (NOTE: **tipping – tipped**)

tip sheet /'tɪp ʃiːt/ *noun* a newspaper which gives information about shares which should be bought or sold

TIR *abbr* Transports Internationaux Routiers

token /'təʊkən/ *noun* **1.** something which acts as a sign or symbol **2.** a device which involves the customer in an offer, e.g. a piece cut out of a newspaper which can be redeemed for a special premium offer **3.** a plastic or metal disk, similar to a coin, used in some slot machines

token charge /'təʊkən tʃɑːdʒ/ *noun* a small charge which does not cover the real costs ○ *A token charge is made for heating.*

token payment /'təʊkən ˌpeɪmənt/ *noun* a small payment to show that a payment is being made

top-down information /ˌtɒp daʊn ɪnfə'meɪʃ(ə)n/ *noun* a system of pass-

ing information down from management to the workforce

top-grade /'tɒp greɪd/ *adjective* of the best quality ○ *top-grade petrol*

top management /tɒp 'mænɪdʒmənt/ *noun* the main directors of a company

top-selling /tɒp 'selɪŋ/ *adjective* which sells better than all other products ○ *top-selling brands of toothpaste*

tort /tɔːt/ *noun* harm done to a person or property which can be the basis of a civil lawsuit

torture testing /'tɔːtʃə ˌtestɪŋ/ *noun* the act of pushing products to their limits during product testing ○ *Torture testing will show up any product deficiencies while changes can still be made.*

total /'təʊt(ə)l/ *adjective* complete or with everything added together ○ *The total amount owed is now £1000.* ○ *The company has total assets of over £1bn.* ○ *The total cost was much more than expected.* ○ *Total expenditure on publicity is twice that of last year.* ○ *Our total income from exports rose last year.*

total audience package /ˌtəʊt(ə)l 'ɔːdiəns ˌpækɪdʒ/ *noun* a media owner's arrangement or scheduling of advertisements across time segments on television and radio

total cost of ownership /ˌtəʊt(ə)l kɒst əv 'əʊnəʃɪp/ *noun* a method of calculating the costs of buying and using a product or service that, in addition to the purchase cost of the item, takes into account related costs such as ordering, delivery, subsequent usage and maintenance, supplier costs and after-delivery costs

total distribution system /ˌtəʊt(ə)l dɪstrɪ'bjuːʃ(ə)n ˌsɪstəm/ *noun* a system where all distribution decisions, including the purchasing of raw materials and parts, as well as the movement of finished products, are taken globally

total invoice value /ˌtəʊt(ə)l 'ɪnvɔɪs ˌvæljuː/ *noun* the total amount on an invoice, including transport, VAT, etc.

total offer /ˌtəʊt(ə)l 'ɒfə/ *noun* a complete package offered to the customer including the product or service itself, its price, availability and promotion

total quality management (TQM) /ˌtəʊt(ə)l 'kwɒlɪti ˌmænɪdʒmənt/ *noun* a philosophy and style of management that gives everyone in an organisation responsibility for delivering quality to the customer (NOTE: Total quality management views each production process as being in a customer/supplier relationship with the next, so that the aim at each stage is to define and meet the customer's requirements as precisely as possible.)

tracking /'trækɪŋ/ *noun* monitoring changes in the way the public sees a product or a firm, done over a period of years

trade /treɪd/ *noun* **1.** the business of buying and selling **2.** □ **to do a good trade in a range of products** to sell a large number of a range of products **3.** a particular type of business, or people or companies dealing in the same type of product ○ *He's in the secondhand car trade.* ○ *She's very well known in the clothing trade.*

'…a sharp setback in foreign trade accounted for most of the winter slowdown. The trade balance sank $17 billion' [*Fortune*]

'…trade between Britain and other countries which comprise the Economic Community has risen steadily from 33% of exports to 50% last year' [*Sales & Marketing Management*]

'Brazil's trade surplus is vulnerable both to a slowdown in the American economy and a pick-up in its own' [*Economist*]

trade advertising /'treɪd ˌædvətaɪzɪŋ/ *noun* advertising to trade customers and not to the general public

trade agreement /'treɪd əˌgriːmənt/ *noun* an international agreement between countries over general terms of trade

trade association /'treɪd əsəʊsiˌeɪʃ(ə)n/ *noun* a group which links together companies in the same trade

trade barrier /'treɪd ˌbæriə/ *noun* a limitation imposed by a government on the free exchange of goods between countries (NOTE: NTBs, safety stan-

dards and tariffs are typical trade barriers.)

trade counter /'treɪd ˌkaʊntə/ *noun* a shop in a factory or warehouse where goods are sold to retailers

trade cycle /'treɪd ˌsaɪk(ə)l/ *noun* a period during which trade expands, then slows down, then expands again

trade debtor /'treɪd ˌdetə/ *noun* a debtor who ows money to a company in the normal course of that company's trading

trade delegation /'treɪd delə-ˌɡeɪʃ(ə)n/ *noun* a group of official delegates on a commercial visit

trade description /treɪd dɪ-'skrɪpʃən/ *noun* a description of a product to attract customers

Trade Descriptions Act /ˌtreɪd dɪ-'skrɪpʃənz ækt/ *noun* an act which limits the way in which products can be described so as to protect customers from wrong descriptions made by manufacturers

trade directory /'treɪd daɪˌrekt(ə)ri/ *noun* a book which lists all the businesses and business people in a town

trade down /ˌtreɪdɪŋ 'daʊn/ *verb* to move to selling at lower prices to increase sales volume ○ *We're trading down now because too many customers were put off by our high prices.*

trade fair /'treɪd feə/ *noun* a large exhibition and meeting for advertising and selling a specific type of product ○ *There are two trade fairs running in London at the same time – the carpet manufacturers' and the mobile telephones.*

trade gap /'treɪd ɡæp/ *noun* the difference in value between a country's imports and exports

trade in /ˌtreɪd 'ɪn/ *verb* **1.** to buy and sell specific items ○ *The company trades in imported goods.* ○ *They trade in French wine.* **2.** to give in an old item as part of the payment for a new one ○ *The chairman traded in his old Rolls Royce for a new model.*

trade-in /'treɪd ɪn/ *noun* an old item, e.g. a car or washing machine, given as part of the payment for a new one ○ *She*

bought a new car and gave her old one as a trade-in.

trade-in price /'treɪd ɪn praɪs/, **trade-in allowance** /'treɪd ɪn ə-ˌlaʊəns/ *noun* an amount allowed by the seller for an old item being traded in for a new one

trade magazine /'treɪd mæɡəˌziːn/ *noun* a magazine aimed at working people in a specific industry

trademark /'treɪdmɑːk/, **trade name** /'treɪd neɪm/ *noun* a particular name, design, etc. which has been registered by the manufacturer and which cannot be used by other manufacturers (it is an 'intangible asset') ○ *You can't call your beds 'Softn'kumfi' – it is a registered trademark.*

trade mission /'treɪd ˌmɪʃ(ə)n/ *noun* a visit by a group of businesspeople to discuss trade ○ *He led a trade mission to China.*

trade-off /'treɪd ɒf/ *noun* an act of exchanging one thing for another as part of a business deal (NOTE: plural is **trade-offs**)

trade-off analysis /'treɪd ɒf ə-ˌnæləsɪs/ *noun* same as **conjoint analysis**

trade paper /treɪd 'peɪpə/ *noun* a newspaper aimed at people working in a specific industry

trade price /'treɪd praɪs/ *noun* a special wholesale price paid by a retailer to the manufacturer or wholesaler

trade promotion /'treɪd prə-ˌməʊʃ(ə)n/ *noun* the promotion of products to distributors ○ *The new trade promotion campaign is designed to attract wholesalers in all our areas of distribution.*

trader /'treɪdə/ *noun* a person who does business

trade route /'treɪd ruːt/ *noun* a route along which goods are transported for trade ○ *The main trade routes were studied to see which areas of the country were most accessible.* ○ *When the Suez Canal was closed some vital trade routes were affected.*

trade show /'treɪd ʃəʊ/ *noun* same as **trade fair**

tradesman /'treɪdzmən/ *noun* a shopkeeper (NOTE: plural is **tradesmen**)

tradespeople /'treɪdz,pi:p(ə)l/ *plural noun* shopkeepers

trade terms /'treɪd tɜ:mz/ *plural noun* a special discount for people in the same trade

trade up /,treɪd 'ʌp/ *verb* to move to selling more expensive goods or to offering a more up-market service

trading /'treɪdɪŋ/ *noun* the business of buying and selling

trading account /'treɪdɪŋ ə,kaʊnt/ *noun* an account of a company's gross profit

trading area /'treɪdɪŋ ,eəriə/ *noun* a group of countries which trade with each other

trading channel /'treɪdɪŋ ,tʃæn(ə)l/ *noun* a series of purchases and sales from company to company which are made until the finished product is purchased by the customer

trading company /'treɪdɪŋ ,kʌmp(ə)ni/ *noun* a company which specialises in buying and selling goods

trading estate /'treɪdɪŋ ɪ,steɪt/ *noun* an area of land near a town specially for building factories and warehouses

trading loss /'treɪdɪŋ lɒs/ *noun* a situation where a company's receipts are less than its expenditure

trading partner /'treɪdɪŋ ,pɑ:tnə/ *noun* a company or country which trades with another

trading profit /'treɪdɪŋ ,prɒfɪt/ *noun* a result where the company' receipts are higher than its expenditure

trading stamp /'treɪdɪŋ stæmp/ *noun* a special stamp given away by a shop, which the customer can collect and exchange later for free goods

Trading Standards Office /,treɪdɪŋ 'stændədz ,ɒfɪs/ *noun* a UK government department responsible for such matters as making sure that advertisements are true or that weighing machines are correct

traffic /'træfɪk/ *noun* illegal trade ○ *drugs traffic* or *traffic in drugs*

traffic builder /'træfɪk ,bɪldə/ *noun* a software programme which increases traffic to a website, by linking with search engines, etc.

training levy /'treɪnɪŋ ,levi/ *noun* a tax to be paid by companies to fund the government's training schemes

tramp ship /'træmp ʃɪp/ *noun* a ship with no fixed schedule or itinerary that can be chartered by a company to transport goods

transaction /træn'zækʃən/ *noun* a piece of business □ **fraudulent transaction** a transaction which aims to cheat someone

'…the Japan Financial Intelligence Office will receive reports on suspected criminal transactions from financial institutions, determine where a probe should be launched and provide information to investigators' [*Nikkei Weekly*]

transaction e-commerce /træn,zækʃən 'i: kɒmɜ:s/ *noun* the electronic sale of goods and services, either business-to-business or business-to-customer

transfer *noun* /'trænsfɜ:/ an act of moving an employee to another job in the same organisation ○ *He applied for a transfer to our branch in Scotland.* ■ *verb* /træns'fɜ:/ to move someone or something to a new place ○ *The accountant was transferred to our Scottish branch.* ○ *He transferred his shares to a family trust.* ○ *She transferred her money to a deposit account.*

transferable skill /træns,fɜ:rəb(ə)l 'skɪl/ *noun* a skill that is not related to the performance of a particular job or task (NOTE: The skills that make people good at leadership, communication, critical thinking, analysis or organisation are among those thought of as transferable skills.)

transfer pricing /'trænsfɜ: ,praɪsɪŋ/ *noun* prices used in a large organisation for selling goods or services between departments in the same organisation; also used in multinational corporations to transfer transactions from one country to another to avoid paying tax

transformational advertising /ˌtrænsfəmeɪʃ(ə)n(ə)l ˈædvətaɪzɪŋ/ *noun* a form of emotional advertising that aims to relate emotional experiences to the product or service being advertised, and then tries to change these emotions into an active interest in purchasing

tranship /trænˈʃɪp/ *verb* to move cargo from one ship to another (NOTE: **transhipping – transhipped**)

transient advertisement /ˌtrænziənt ədˈvɜːtɪsmənt/ *noun* an advertisement which the target audience cannot keep to look at again, e.g. a cinema advertisement, as opposed to an intransient one in a newspaper or magazine

transit /ˈtrænsɪt/ *noun* the movement of passengers or goods on the way to a destination ○ *Some of the goods were damaged in transit.* □ **goods in transit** goods being transported from warehouse to customer

transit advertising /ˈtrænsɪt ˌædvətaɪzɪŋ/ *noun* advertisements on or inside buses, taxis, trains, etc.

transnational corporation /trænz ˌnæʃ(ə)n(ə)l kɔːpəˈreɪʃ(ə)n/ *noun* a large company which operates in various countries

transport *noun* /ˈtrænspɔːt/ the moving of goods or people ○ *air transport* or *transport by air* ○ *rail transport* or *transport by rail* ○ *road transport* or *transport by road* ○ *the passenger transport services into London* ○ *What means of transport will you use to get to the factory?* ■ *verb* /trænsˈpɔːt/ to move goods or people from one place to another in a vehicle ○ *The company transports millions of tons of goods by rail each year.* ○ *The visitors will be transported to the factory by air* or *by helicopter* or *by taxi.*

transport advertising /ˈtrænspɔːt ˌædvətaɪzɪŋ/ *noun* advertising appearing on or in forms of transportation such as buses or trains ○ *Transport advertising will reach too broad a public for our product.* ○ *Is your transport advertising on the sides of buses or in Underground trains?*

transportation /ˌtrænspɔːˈteɪʃ(ə)n/ *noun* **1.** the moving of goods or people from one place to another **2.** vehicles used to move goods or people from one place to another ○ *The company will provide transportation to the airport.*

transporter /trænsˈpɔːtə/ *noun* a company which transports goods

Transports Internationaux Routiers /ˌtrɔːnspɔːz ænteˌnæsjəˈnəʊ ˌruːtieɪ/ *noun* a system of international documents which allows dutiable goods to cross several European countries by road without paying duty until they reach their final destination. Abbr **TIR**

transsship /trænsˈʃɪp/ *noun* another spelling of **tranship**

travel /ˈtræv(ə)l/ *verb* to go from one place to another, showing a company's goods to buyers and taking orders from them ○ *She travels in the north of the country for an insurance company.* (NOTE: **travelling – travelled**. The American spelling is **traveling – traveled**)

traveller /ˈtræv(ə)lə/ *noun* a person who travels (NOTE: the American spelling is **traveler**)

traveller's cheques /ˈtræv(ə)ləz tʃeks/ *plural noun* cheques bought by a traveller which can be cashed in a foreign country

travelling expenses /ˈtræv(ə)lɪŋ ekˌspensɪz/ *plural noun* money spent on travelling and hotels for business purposes

travelling salesman /ˌtræv(ə)lɪŋ ˈseɪlzmən/ *noun* a salesman who travels around an area visiting customers on behalf of his company ○ *Travelling salesmen must make regular contact with company headquarters by phone.*

travel magazine /ˈtræv(ə)l mægəˌziːn/ *noun* a magazine with articles on holidays and travel

travel organisation /ˈtræv(ə)l ɔːgənaɪˌzeɪʃ(ə)n/ *noun* a body representing companies in the travel business

treaty /ˈtriːti/ *noun* **1.** an agreement between countries ○ *The two countries signed a commercial treaty.* **2.** an agree-

ment between individual persons □ **to sell a house by private treaty** to sell a home to another person not by auction

trend /trend/ *noun* a general way things are going ○ *a downward trend in investment* ○ *There is a trend away from old-established food stores.* ○ *The report points to inflationary trends in the economy.* ○ *We notice a general trend towards selling to the student market.* ○ *We have noticed an upward trend in sales.*

'…the quality of building design and ease of accessibility will become increasingly important, adding to the trend towards out-of-town office development' [*Lloyd's List*]

trend analysis /'trend ə,næləsɪs/ *noun* analysis of particular statistics over a period of time in order to identify trends ○ *Trend analysis has shown how soon major competitors begin to copy innovations.*

trial *noun* /'traɪəl/ a test to see if something is good □ **on trial** in the process of being tested ○ *The product is on trial in our laboratories.* ■ *verb* to test a product to see how good it is (NOTE: **trialling- trialled**)

trial balance /'traɪəl ,bæləns/ *noun* the draft calculation of debits and credits to see if they balance

trial offer /'traɪəl ,ɒfə/ *noun* a promotion where free samples are given away

trial period /'traɪəl ,pɪəriəd/ *noun* the time when a customer can test a product before buying it

trial sample /'traɪəl ,sɑːmpəl/ *noun* a small piece of a product used for testing

triplicate /'trɪplɪkət/ *noun* □ **invoicing in triplicate** the preparing of three copies of invoices

troll /trəʊl, trɒl/ *verb* to search websites for Internet addresses which are then added to an email address list for promotional purposes

trolley /'trɒli/ *noun* a small metal cart which is used by customers in supermarkets to carry their shopping (NOTE: American English is **shopping cart**)

truck /trʌk/ *noun* **1.** a large motor vehicle for carrying goods **2.** an open railway wagon for carrying goods

truckage /'trʌkɪdʒ/ *noun* the carriage of goods in trucks ○ *What will the truckage costs be for these goods?*

truck distributor /'trʌk dɪ-,strɪbjʊtə/, **truck jobber** /'trʌk ,dʒɒbə/ *noun US* a wholesaler who usually only delivers goods directly by truck to retailers

trucking /'trʌkɪŋ/ *noun* the carrying of goods in trucks ○ *a trucking firm*

trust /trʌst/ *noun US* a small group of companies which control the supply of a product

trustbusting /'trʌstbʌstɪŋ/ *noun US* the breaking up of monopolies to encourage competition

T-scope /'tiː skəʊp/ *noun* same as **tachistoscope**

TSR *abbr* telephone sales representative

tube card /'tjuːb kɑːd/ *noun* a card with an advertisement on which is either put on the walls of Underground stations or inside Underground trains ○ *Half the tube cards in one carriage were advertising the same product.* ○ *The Underground railway system uses tube cards to advertise its own services.*

turnkey contract /'tɜːnkiː ,kɒntrækt/ *noun* an agreement by which a contractor undertakes to design, construct and manage something and only hand it over to the client when it is in a state where it is ready for immediate use

turn over /,tɜːn 'əʊvə/ *verb* to have a specific amount of sales ○ *We turn over £2,000 a week.*

'…a 100,000 square foot warehouse can turn its inventory over 18 times a year, more than triple a discounter's turnover' [*Duns Business Month*]

turnover /'tɜːnəʊvə/ *noun* **1.** *GB* the amount of sales of goods or services by a company ○ *The company's turnover has increased by 235%.* ○ *We based our calculations on the forecast turnover.* (NOTE: the American equivalent is **sales volume**) **2.** the number of times something is used or sold in a period, usually one year, expressed as a percentage of a total

turn round /,tɜːn 'raʊnd/ *verb* to make a company change from making a

loss to become profitable □ **they turned the company round in less than a year** they made the company profitable in less than a year

turnround /'tɜːnraʊnd/ *noun* **1.** the value of goods sold during a year divided by the average value of goods held in stock (NOTE: American English is **turnaround**) **2.** the action of emptying a ship, plane, etc., and getting it ready for another commercial journey (NOTE: American English is **turnaround**) **3.** the act of making a company profitable again (NOTE: American English is **turnaround**)

'…the US now accounts for more than half our world-wide sales; it has made a huge contribution to our earnings turnround' [*Duns Business Month*]

TV *abbr* television

TVR *abbr* television ratings

TV spot /tiː 'viː spɒt/ *noun* a short period on TV which is used for commercials ○ *We are running a series of TV spots over the next three weeks.*

twenty-four-hour trading /ˌtwenti fɔː aʊə 'treɪdɪŋ/ *noun* trading in bonds, currencies or securities that can take place at any time of day or night (NOTE: Twenty-four-hour trading does not involve one trading floor being open all the time, but instead refers to the possibility of conducting operations at different locations in different time zones.)

twin-pack /'twɪn pæk/ *noun* a banded pack of two items sold together

24/7 /ˌtwenti fɔː 'sev(ə)n/ *adverb* twenty-four hours a day, every day of the week (NOTE: Businesses often advertise themselves as being 'open 24/7'.)

24-hour service /ˌtwenti fɔːr aʊə 'sɜːvɪs/ *noun* help which is available for the whole day

two-sided message /ˌtuː saɪdɪd 'mesɪdʒ/ *noun* a message which presents two arguments for purchasing a product or service

tying contract /'taɪɪŋ ˌkɒntrækt/ a contract under which a producer sells a product to a distributor on condition that the distributor also buys another product ○ *Tying contracts are used to get wholesalers acquainted with lesser-known products.*

typological analysis /taɪpə-ˌlɒdʒɪk(ə)l ə'næləsɪs/ *noun* a categorisation of households based on socio-economic factors and buying habits ○ *Typological analysis helped the company clarify what market segments the new product should be aimed at.*

tyrekicker /'taɪəˌkɪkə/ *noun* a prospective customer who wants to examine every option before making up his or her mind about a purchase (as opposed to a 'first choice' who chooses the first option available) (NOTE: The usual US spelling is **tirekicker**.)

U

ultimate /'ʌltɪmət/ *adjective* last or final

ultimate consumer /ˌʌltɪmət kən-'sjuːmə/ *noun* the person who actually uses the product

umbrella advertising /ʌm'brelə ˌædvətaɪzɪŋ/ *noun* the advertising of an organisation or an association of companies rather than a single product

umbrella organisation /ʌm'brelə ˌɔːɡənaɪzeɪʃ(ə)n/ *noun* a large organisation which includes several smaller ones

unaided recall /ʌnˌeɪdɪd 'riːkɔːl/ *noun* same as **unprompted recall**

unavailability /ˌʌnəveɪlə'bɪlɪti/ *noun* the fact of not being available ○ *The unavailability of any reliable sales data makes forecasting difficult.*

unavailable /ˌʌnə'veɪləb(ə)l/ *adjective* not available ○ *The following items on your order are temporarily unavailable.*

uncontrollable /ˌʌnkən'trəʊləb(ə)l/ *adjective* which cannot be controlled ○ *uncontrollable inflation*

uncontrollable variable /ʌnkən-ˌtrəʊləb(ə)l 'veəriəb(ə)l/ *noun* a variable or factor in marketing that cannot be controlled, e.g. legislation or the state of the country's economy ○ *There are too many uncontrollable variables for any real planning.* ○ *Changes in fashion constitute a dangerous uncontrollable variable for a clothes shop.*

uncrossed cheque /ˌʌnkrɒst 'tʃek/ *noun* a cheque which does not have two lines across it, and can be cashed anywhere (NOTE: They are no longer used in the UK, but are still found in other countries.)

under- /ʌndə/ *prefix* less important than or lower than

underbid /ˌʌndə'bɪd/ *verb* to bid less than someone (NOTE: **underbidding – underbid**)

underbidder /'ʌndəbɪdə/ *noun* a person who bids less than the person who buys at an auction

undercharge /ˌʌndə'tʃɑːdʒ/ *verb* to ask for too little money ○ *She undercharged us by £25.*

underclass /'ʌndəklɑːs/ *noun* a group of people who are underprivileged in a way that appears to exclude them from mainstream society

undercut /ˌʌndə'kʌt/ *verb* to offer something at a lower price than someone else ○ *They increased their market share by undercutting their competitors.* (NOTE: **undercutting- undercut**)

underdeveloped /ˌʌndədɪ'veləpt/ *adjective* which has not been developed ○ *Japan is an underdeveloped market for our products.*

underdeveloped countries /ˌʌndədɪveləpt 'kʌntriz/ *plural noun* countries which are not fully industrialised

underdeveloped market /ˌʌndədɪveləpt 'mɑːkɪt/ *noun* a market which has not been fully exploited ○ *Japan is an underdeveloped market for our products.*

underlease /'ʌndəliːs/ *noun* lease from a tenant to another tenant

underline /'ʌndəlaɪn/ *noun* a short description printed underneath an illustration

underpayment /ˌʌndə'peɪmənt/ *noun* a payment of less than the correct invoiced amount

underpricing /ˌʌndəˈpraɪsɪŋ/ *noun* the charging of a lower price than is justified by demand ○ *The company's underpricing is due to ignorance of the growing market.* ○ *Underpricing can be used as a strategy to increase market share.*

undersell /ˌʌndəˈsel/ *verb* to sell more cheaply than ○ *to undersell a competitor* □ **the company is never undersold** no other company sells goods as cheaply as this one

under-the-counter sales /ˌʌndə ðə ˌkaʊntə ˈseɪlz/ *plural noun* black-market sales

undervaluation /ˌʌndəvæljʊˈeɪʃ(ə)n/ *noun* the state of being valued at less than the true worth

undervalued /ˌʌndəˈvæljuːd/ *adjective* not valued highly enough ○ *The dollar is undervalued on the foreign exchanges.* ○ *The properties are undervalued on the company's balance sheet.*

'…in terms of purchasing power, the dollar is considerably undervalued, while the US trade deficit is declining month by month' [*Financial Weekly*]

underweight /ˌʌndəˈweɪt/ *adjective* □ **the pack is twenty grams underweight** the pack weighs twenty grams less than it should

undifferentiated /ˌʌndɪfəˈrenʃieɪtɪd/ *adjective* which has no unique feature

undifferentiated marketing strategy /ˌʌndɪfəˌrenʃieɪtɪd ˈmɑːkɪtɪŋ ˌstrætədʒi/ *noun* a marketing strategy which seeks to present a product to the public without stressing any unique feature of the product, thus appealing to all segments of the market. ♦ **concentrated marketing, differentiated marketing strategy**

undifferentiated product /ʌndɪfəˌrenʃieɪtɪd ˈprɒdʌkt/ *noun* a product which has no feature to set it apart from others on the market ○ *Only an extra-low price will sell an undifferentiated product in a market where there is already a wide choice of brands.*

undue influence /ˌʌndjuː ˈɪnfluəns/ *noun* unfair pressure put on someone to sign a contract ○ *The* salesforce were discouraged from exerting undue influence on prospective buyers.

uneven /ʌnˈiːv(ə)n/ *adjective* not smooth or flat

uneven playing field /ʌnˌiːv(ə)n ˈpleɪɪŋ fiːld/ *noun* a situation where the competing groups do not compete on the same terms and conditions (NOTE: The opposite is a 'level playing field'.)

unfair /ʌnˈfeə/ *adjective* not just or reasonable

unfair competition /ˌʌnfeə kɒmpəˈtɪʃ(ə)n/ *noun* the practice of trying to do better than another company by using techniques such as importing foreign goods at very low prices or by wrongly criticising a competitor's products

unfavourable /ʌnˈfeɪv(ə)rəb(ə)l/ *adjective* not favourable (NOTE: the American spelling is **unfavorable**) □ **unfavourable balance of trade** a situation where a country imports more than it exports □ **unfavourable exchange rate** an exchange rate which gives an amount of foreign currency for the home currency which is not good for trade ○ *The unfavourable exchange rate hit the country's exports.*

unfulfilled /ˌʌnfʊlˈfɪld/ *adjective* (*of an order*) which has not yet been supplied

unilateral /ˌjuːnɪˈlæt(ə)rəl/ *adjective* on one side only or done by one party only ○ *They took a unilateral decision to cancel the contract.*

unilaterally /ˌjuːnɪˈlæt(ə)rəli/ *adverb* by one party only ○ *The decision was taken to cancel the contract unilaterally.*

unique /juːˈniːk/ *adjective* unlike anything else

unique selling point /juːˌniːk ˈselɪŋ pɔɪnt/, **unique selling proposition** /juːˌniːk ˈselɪŋ prɒpəˌzɪʃ(ə)n/ *noun* a special quality of a product which makes it different from other goods and is used as a key theme in advertising ○ *A five-year guarantee is a USP for this product.* ○ *What's this product's unique selling proposition?* Abbr **USP**

unit /ˈjuːnɪt/ *noun* **1.** a single product for sale **2.** a separate piece of equipment or furniture **3.** a group of people set up for a special purpose

unit cost /ˈjuːnɪt kɒst/ *noun* the cost of one item, i.e. the total product costs divided by the number of units produced

United Nations /juːˌnaɪtɪd ˈneɪʃ(ə)nz/ *plural noun* an organisation which links almost all the countries of the world to promote good relations between them

unit pack /ˈjuːnɪt pæk/ *noun* a pack containing only one unit of a product ○ *Will the product be sold in unit packs, or in packs of ten or twenty units?*

unit price /ˈjuːnɪt praɪs/ *noun* the price of one item

unit pricing /ˈjuːnɪt ˌpraɪsɪŋ/ *noun* the pricing of items by showing how much each costs per unit of measurement, e.g. per metre or per kilo

Universal Product Code /juːnɪˌvɜːs(ə)l ˈprɒdʌkt kəʊd/ *noun* the code which identifies an article for sale, usually printed as a bar code on the packet or item itself. Abbr **UPC**

universe /ˈjuːnɪvɜːs/ *noun* the total population which is being studied in a survey and out of which a sample is selected ○ *Is this sample really representative of the universe?* ○ *In the survey, the universe is all British men between the ages of forty and fifty.* ○ *From a universe of two million, a sample of two thousand was chosen by random selection.*

unladen /ʌnˈleɪdn/ *adjective* without a cargo ○ *The ship was unladen when she arrived in port.*

unlimited /ʌnˈlɪmɪtɪd/ *adjective* with no limits ○ *The bank offered him unlimited credit.*

unlimited liability /ʌnˌlɪmɪtɪd laɪəˈbɪlɪti/ *noun* a situation where a sole trader or each partner is responsible for all a firm's debts with no limit on the amount each may have to pay

unload /ʌnˈləʊd/ *verb* **1.** to take goods off a ship, lorry etc. ○ *The ship is unloading at Hamburg.* ○ *We need a fork-lift truck to unload the lorry.* ○ *We*

unloaded the spare parts at Lagos. ○ *There are no unloading facilities for container ships.* **2.** to sell stock which is no longer needed at a lower price than usual ○ *They tried to unload some unsellable items onto the Far Eastern market.*

unloading /ʌnˈləʊdɪŋ/ *noun* the act of selling off goods at a lower price than usual, often when they are no longer being produced and the producers merely want to get rid of remaining stock ○ *Many customers are taking advantage of our unloading and are buying in bulk.*

unprofitable /ʌnˈprɒfɪtəb(ə)l/ *adjective* not profitable
'…the airline has already eliminated a number of unprofitable flights' [*Duns Business Month*]

unprompted recall /ʌnˌprɒmptɪd ˈriːkɔːl/, **unprompted awareness test** /ʌnˌprɒmptɪd əˈweənəs test/ *noun* an advertising research test to see how well a respondent can remember an advertisement when he or she is given no help in remembering it ○ *A disappointing number of respondents did not remember the advertisement at all in an unprompted recall.* Compare **prompted recall**

unseen /ʌnˈsiːn/ *adverb* not seen

unsold /ʌnˈsəʊld/ *adjective* not sold ○ *Unsold items will be scrapped.*

unsolicited /ʌnsəˈlɪsɪtɪd/ *adjective* which has not been asked for ○ *an unsolicited gift*

unsolicited testimonial /ʌnsəˌlɪsɪtɪd ˌtestɪˈməʊniəl/ *noun* a letter praising someone or a product, without the writer having been asked to write it

unstructured interview /ʌnˌstrʌktʃəd ˈɪntəvjuː/ *noun* an interview which is not based on a series of fixed questions and which encourages open discussion ○ *Unstructured interviews are effective in eliciting original suggestions for product improvement.* ○ *Shy respondents often perform well in unstructured interviews where they have more freedom of expression.* Compare **structured interview**

unsubsidised /ʌnˈsʌbsɪdaɪzd/, **unsubsidized** *adjective* with no subsidy

unused /ʌn'juːzd/ *adjective* which has not been used ○ *We are trying to sell off six unused computers.*

UPC *abbr* Universal Product Code

update *noun* /'ʌpdeɪt/ information added to something to make it up to date ○ *Here is the latest update on sales.* ■ *verb* /ʌp'deɪt/ to revise something so that it is always up to date ○ *The figures are updated annually.*

up front /ʌp 'frʌnt/ *adverb* in advance

uplift /'ʌplɪft/ *noun* an increase ○ *The contract provides for an annual uplift of charges.*

upmarket /ˌʌp 'mɑːkɪt/ *adverb, adjective* more expensive or appealing to a wealthy section of the population □ **the company has decided to move upmarket** the company has decided to start to produce more luxury items

'…up market companies which are doing well need a conference venue to reflect this' [*Marketing Week*]

'…prices of up market homes (costing $350,000 or more) are falling in many areas' [*Economist*]

upscale /'ʌpskeɪl/ *adjective* aimed at customers at the top end of the socio-economic ladder, who are well-educated and have higher incomes

upselling /'ʌpselɪŋ/ *noun* selling extra products to go with the one the customer is planning to buy

upset price /'ʌpset praɪs/ *noun* the lowest price which the seller will accept at an auction

up-to-date /ˌʌp tə 'deɪt/ *adjective, adverb* current, recent or modern ○ *an up-to-date computer system* □ **to bring something up to date** to add the latest information or equipment to something □ **to keep something up to date** to keep adding information to something so that it always has the latest information in it

○ *We spend a lot of time keeping our mailing list up to date.*

upturn /'ʌptɜːn/ *noun* a movement towards higher sales or profits ○ *an upturn in the economy* ○ *an upturn in the market*

usage /'juːsɪdʒ/ *noun* how something is used

usage pull /'juːsɪdʒ pʊl/ *noun US* the degree to which those who see or hear advertisements for a product buy more of it than those who do not ○ *We're only able to assess usage pull some time after the advertising campaign.*

usage segmentation /'juːsɪdʒ segmenˌteɪʃ(ə)n/ *noun* the dividing of a market into segments according to the type of use which customers will make of the product

use-by date /'juːz baɪ ˌdeɪt/ *noun* a date printed on a packet of food showing the last date on which the contents should be used. Compare **best-before date, sell-by date**

user /'juːzə/ *noun* a person who uses something

user-friendly /ˌjuːzə 'frendli/ *adjective* which a user finds easy to work ○ *These programs are really user-friendly.*

user's guide /'juːzəz gaɪd/ *noun* a book showing someone how to use something

utility /juː'tɪlɪti/ *noun* the usefulness or satisfaction that a consumer gets from a product ○ *The price charged depends on the product's utility.*

utility goods /juː'tɪlɪti gʊdz/ *plural noun* basic goods that are necessary for everyday life ○ *Even some utility goods can be considered luxuries during a depression.* ○ *Consumers say that shopping for utility goods is routine and boring.*

V

valorem /vəˈlɔːrəm/ noun ◊ **ad valorem duty**

VALS noun a system of dividing people into segments according to their way of living. Full form **Values and Lifestyles**

valuation /ˌvæljʊˈeɪʃ(ə)n/ noun an estimate of how much something is worth ○ *to ask for a valuation of a property before making an offer for it* □ **to buy a shop with stock at valuation** when buying a shop, to pay for the stock the value as estimated by the valuer □ **to purchase stock at valuation** to pay for stock the price it is valued at

value /ˈvæljuː/ noun the amount of money which something is worth ○ *the fall in the value of sterling* ○ *He imported goods to the value of £2500.* ○ *The valuer put the value of the stock at £25,000.* □ **good value (for money)** a bargain, something which is worth the price paid for it ○ *That restaurant gives value for money.* ○ *Buy that computer now – it is very good value.* ○ *Holidays in Italy are good value because of the exchange rate.* □ **to rise/fall in value** to be worth more or less ■ *verb* to estimate how much money something is worth ○ *He valued the stock at £25,000.* ○ *We are having the jewellery valued for insurance.*

value added /ˌvæljuː ˈædɪd/ noun **1.** the difference between the cost of bought-in materials and the eventual selling price of the finished product **2.** the amount added to the value of a product or service, being the difference between its cost and the amount received when it is sold **3.** the features that make one product or service more desirable than others as far as the customer is concerned and make it worth a higher price

value-added reseller /ˌvæljuː ˈædɪd ˈriːselə/ noun a merchant who buys products at retail prices and packages them with additional items for resale to customers

value-added services /ˌvæljuː ˈædɪd ˈsɜːvɪsɪz/ plural noun services which add value to a service or product being sold

Value Added Tax /ˌvæljuː ædɪd ˈtæks/ noun full form of **VAT**

value-adding intermediary /ˌvæljuː ædɪŋ ɪntəˈmiːdiəri/ noun a distributor who adds value to a product before selling it to a customer, e.g., by installing software or a modem in a computer

value analysis /ˈvæljuː əˌnæləsɪs/ noun analysis by a producer of all aspects of a finished product to determine how it could be made at minimum cost ○ *Value analysis showed an excessive amount of rubber was used in manufacturing the product.*

value chain /ˈvæljuː tʃeɪn/ noun **1.** the sequence of activities a company carries out as it designs, produces, markets, delivers, and supports its product or service, each of which is thought of as adding value **2.** the pattern that people traditionally have in mind when considering their career prospects, which involves them identifying at each stage in their careers what the next, most obvious, upward move should be

valued impression per pound /ˌvæljuːd ɪmˌpreʃ(ə)n pə ˈpaʊnd/ noun a method of showing how many readers are reached by advertising for a given sum of money. Abbr **VIP**

value engineering /ˈvæljuː endʒɪˌnɪərɪŋ/ noun analysis by a producer of

all aspects of a product at the design stage to determine how it could be made at minimum cost ○ *Value engineering allows very economical production and competitive prices at every stage in the distribution channel.*

value map /'vælju: mæp/ *noun* the level of value that the market recognises in a product or service and that helps to differentiate it from competitors

value proposition /'vælju: prɒpə-ˌzɪʃ(ə)n/ *noun* a statement by an organisation of the way in which it can provide value for a customer

valuer /'væljʊə/ *noun* a person who estimates how much money something is worth

Values and Lifestyles /ˌvælju: ən 'laɪfˌstaɪlz/ *noun* full form of **VALS**

van /væn/ *noun* a small goods vehicle

van ship /'væn ʃɪp/ *noun* a ship designed to carry goods in containers

VAR *abbr* value-added reseller

variable /'veəriəb(ə)l/ *adjective* which changes

variable costs /ˌveəriəb(ə)l 'kɒsts/ *plural noun* production costs which increase with the quantity of the product made, e.g. wages or raw materials

variable pricing /ˌveəriəb(ə)l 'praɪsɪŋ/ *noun* the practice of giving a product or service different prices in different places or at different times

variance /'veərɪəns/ *noun* the difference between what was expected and the actual results □ **at variance with** which does not agree with ○ *The actual sales are at variance with the sales reported by the reps.*

variation /ˌveəri'eɪʃ(ə)n/ *noun* the amount by which something changes □ **seasonal variations** variations in sales which take place at different times of the year ○ *seasonal variations in buying patterns*

variety /və'raɪəti/ *noun* different types of things ○ *The shop stocks a variety of goods.* ○ *We had a variety of visitors at the office today.*

variety chain store /və'raɪəti 'tʃeɪn stɔː/ *noun* a chain store which sells a large range of goods ○ *The vari-*

ety chain stores sell everything from jewellery to electrical products.*

variety store /və'raɪəti stɔː/ *noun* US a shop selling a wide range of usually cheap items

VAT /ˌvi: eɪ 'ti:, væt/ a tax on goods and services, added as a percentage to the invoiced sales price ○ *The invoice includes VAT at 17.5%.* ○ *The government is proposing to increase VAT to 22%.* ○ *Some items (such as books) are zero-rated for VAT.* Full form **Value Added Tax**

'…the directive means that the services of stockbrokers and managers of authorized unit trusts are now exempt from VAT; previously they were liable to VAT at the standard rate. Zero-rating for stockbrokers' services is still available as before, but only where the recipient of the service belongs outside the EC' [*Accountancy*]

VAT declaration /'væt dekləˌreɪʃ(ə)n/ *noun* a statement declaring VAT income to the VAT office

VAT inspector /'væt ɪnˌspektə/ *noun* a government official who examines VAT returns and checks that VAT is being paid

VAT invoice /'væt ˌɪnvɔɪs/ *noun* an invoice which includes VAT

VAT invoicing /'væt ˌɪnvɔɪsɪŋ/ *noun* the sending of an invoice including VAT

VATman /'vætmæn/, **vatman** *noun* a VAT inspector

VAT office /'væt ˌɒfɪs/ *noun* the government office dealing with the collection of VAT in an area

VDU *abbr* visual display unit

Veblenian model /ve'bleɪniən ˌmɒd(ə)l/ *noun* a theory of buying behaviour proposed by Veblen, which explains consumption mainly in terms of social influences or pressures rather than economic ones ○ *A Veblenian model helps to illustrate the non-rational side of consumer behaviour.*

vehicle /'viːɪk(ə)l/ *noun* a machine with wheels, used to carry goods or passengers on a road

vending /'vendɪŋ/ *noun* selling

vending machine /'vendɪŋ mə‚ʃiːn/ *noun* same as **automatic vending machine**

vendor /'vendə/ *noun* **1.** a person who sells something, especially a property ○ *the solicitor acting on behalf of the vendor* **2.** person who sells goods

vendor rating /'vendə ‚reɪtɪŋ/ *noun* an assessment of a vendor by a buyer on the basis of the vendor's reliability and the quality and price of the goods on offer ○ *Vendor rating has already disqualified three suppliers on the grounds of price.* ○ *A good reputation for quick delivery is a key factor in the buying department's vendor ratings.*

venture /'ventʃə/ *noun* a commercial deal which involves a risk ○ *They lost money on several import ventures.* ○ *She's started a new venture – a computer shop.* ■ *verb* to risk money

venture capital /‚ventʃə 'kæpɪt(ə)l/ *noun* capital for investment which may easily be lost in risky projects, but can also provide high returns

'…the Securities and Exchange Board of India allowed new companies to enter the primary market provided venture capital funds took up 10 per cent of the equity. At present, new companies are allowed to make initial public offerings provided their projects have been appraised by banks or financial institutions which take up 10 per cent of the equity' [*The Hindu*]

venture team /'ventʃə tiːm/ *noun* a group of people from different departments in a company who work together on a new product-development project ○ *The venture team met regularly to monitor progress in the product's development.*

version /'vɜːʃ(ə)n/ *verb* to adapt a website for different categories of customer by maintaining different versions of it

vertical /'vɜːtɪk(ə)l/ *adjective* upright, straight up or down

vertical communication /‚vɜːtɪk(ə)l kəmjuːnɪ'keɪʃ(ə)n/ *noun* communication between senior managers via the middle management to the workforce

vertical industrial market /‚vɜːtɪk(ə)l ɪn'dʌstriəl ‚mɑːkɪt/ *noun* a market in which a product is used by only one industry

vertical marketing system /‚vɜːtɪk(ə)l 'mɑːkɪtɪŋ ‚sɪstəm/ *noun* a distribution system that is a co-ordinated integrated unit involving the manufacturer, the wholesaler and the retailer, where marketing decisions are taken globally

vertical publication /‚vɜːtɪk(ə)l pʌblɪ'keɪʃ(ə)n/ *noun* a publication for people working at different levels in the same industry. Compare **horizontal publication**

vessel /'ves(ə)l/ *noun* a ship

viable /'vaɪəb(ə)l/ *adjective* which can work in practice □ **not commercially viable** not likely to make a profit

videoconferencing /'vɪdiəʊ‚kɒnf(ə)rənsɪŋ/ *noun* the use of live video links that enable people in different locations to see and hear one another and so to discuss matters and hold meetings without being physically present together in one place

videotape /'vɪdiəʊteɪp/ *noun* a magnetic tape for recording sound and vision, used for making original recordings or taping existing television material ○ *The advertiser studied the videotape of the advertisement and sent comments to the agency.* ■ *verb* to record something on videotape ○ *The reactions of respondents trying the product for the first time were videotaped.*

view /vjuː/ *verb* to watch a TV programme

viewer /'vjuːə/ *noun* a person who watches television

viewing figures /'vjuːɪŋ ‚fɪgəz/ *plural noun* figures showing the numbers of people watching a TV programme

viral /'vaɪrəl/ *adjective* acting in the same way as a virus ■ *noun* a message spread by viral marketing

viral design /'vaɪrəl dɪ‚zaɪn/ *noun* the design of a message that encourages recipients to forward the message on to others

viral effect /ˈvaɪrəl ɪˌfekt/ *noun* the number of recipients of a message who forward the message on to others

viral forwards /ˌvaɪrəl ˈfɔːwədz/ *plural noun* the number of messages forwarded

viral marketing /ˈvaɪrəl ˌmɑːkɪtɪŋ/ *noun* marketing by word of mouth or by spreading advertising messages on the Internet

virtual office /ˌvɜːtʃuəl ˈɒfɪs/ *noun* a workplace that has no physical location but is created when a number of employees use information and communications technologies to do their work and collaborate with one another (NOTE: A virtual office is characterised by the use of teleworkers, telecentres, mobile workers, hot-desking, and hotelling.)

virtual team /ˌvɜːtʃuəl ˈtiːm/ *noun* a group of employees working in different locations who use communications technologies such as groupware, email, an intranet, or videoconferencing to collaborate with each other and work as a team

VISA /ˈviːzə/ a trademark for international credit card system

visible /ˈvɪzɪb(ə)l/ *adjective* which can be seen

vision statement /ˈvɪʒ(ə)n ˌsteɪtmənt/ *noun* a statement that sets out in general terms what an organisation is aiming or hoping to achieve in the future (NOTE: Vision statements express corporate vision, and are related to mission statements.)

visual /ˈvɪʒuəl/ *adjective* which can be seen ■ *noun* a photograph, picture, chart, or graph used to display information or promotional material

visual display terminal /ˌvɪzjuəl dɪˈspleɪ ˌtɜːminəl/, **visual display unit** /ˌvɪʒuəl dɪˈspleɪ ˌjuːnɪt/ *noun* a screen attached to a computer which shows the information stored in the computer. Abbr **VDT, VDU**

visualizer /ˈvɪʒuəlaɪzə/ *noun* a person who produces visual ideas for advertisements or advertising campaigns

voicemail /ˈvɔɪs meɪl/ *noun* an electronic communications system which stores digitised recordings of telephone messages for later playback

voiceover /ˈvɔɪs ˌəʊvə/ *noun* the commentary for a TV or cinema advertisement, spoken by an actor who does not appear in the advertisement

volume /ˈvɒljuːm/ *noun* a quantity of items □ **low/high volume of sales** a small or large number of items sold

volume discount /ˈvɒljuːm ˌdɪskaʊnt/ *noun* the discount given to a customer who buys a large quantity of goods

volume of output /ˌvɒljuːm əv ˈaʊtpʊt/ *noun* the number of items produced

volume segmentation /ˈvɒljuːm segmenˌteɪʃ(ə)n/ *noun* the segmentation or division of a market on the basis of the quantity of the product bought

volumetrics /ˌvɒljuːˈmetrɪks/ *noun* analysis of the relative influence of various media by considering the number of people who are exposed to them, and their importance as buyers ○ *Volumetrics has been our most useful tool in media buying.* ○ *The marketing department consulted an expert in volumetrics to help plan the advertising campaign.* (NOTE: takes a singular verb)

voluntarily /ˈvɒlənt(ə)rəlɪ/ *adverb* without being forced or paid

voluntary /ˈvɒlənt(ə)ri/ *adjective* **1.** done freely without anyone forcing you to act **2.** done without being paid

voluntary chain /ˈvɒlənt(ə)ri tʃeɪn/, **voluntary group** /ˈvɒlənt(ə)ri gruːp/ *noun* a group of distributors who join together to buy from suppliers so as to enjoy quantity discounts ○ *After joining the voluntary chain the shop saved up to 20% in buying.*

voluntary control /ˌvɒlənt(ə)ri kənˈtrəʊl/ *noun* a system adopted by the advertising industry for controlling possible abuses which involves following guidelines laid down for the industry as a whole ○ *If voluntary controls are not effective, the government will have to bring in legislation.*

voluntary organisation
/ˈvɒlənt(ə)ri ɔːgənaɪˌzeɪʃ(ə)n/ *noun*
an organisation which does not receive
funding from the government, but relies
on contributions from the public

voucher /ˈvaʊtʃə/ *noun* **1.** a piece of
paper which is given instead of money
2. a written document from an auditor to
show that the accounts are correct or
that money has really been paid

W

wage differential /ˈweɪdʒ dɪfə-ˌrenʃəlz/ *noun* a difference in salary between employees in similar types of jobs

waggon jobber /ˈwægən ˌdʒɒbə/ *noun US* a limited function wholesaler, usually one who delivers goods by truck to retailers

wagon /ˈwægən/ *noun* a goods truck used on the railway

want /wɒnt/ *noun* a need felt by a person, which is formed by that person's education, culture, and character

WAP /wæp/ *noun* a technical language and set of processing rules that enables users of mobile phones to access websites (NOTE: WAP stands for Wireless Application Protocol and is the equivalent of HTML for mobile phones.)

warehouse /ˈweəhaʊs/ *noun* a large building where goods are stored □ **price ex warehouse** the price for a product which is to be collected from the manufacturer's or agent's warehouse and so does not include delivery ■ *verb* to store goods in a warehouse ○ *Our offices are in London but our stock is warehoused in Scotland.*

warehouse capacity /ˈweəhaʊs kəˌpæsɪti/ *noun* a space available in a warehouse

warehouseman /ˈweəhaʊsmən/ *noun* a person who works in a warehouse (NOTE: plural is **warehousemen**)

warehousing /ˈweəhaʊzɪŋ/ *noun* the act of storing goods in a warehouse ○ *Warehousing costs are rising rapidly.*

warranty /ˈwɒrənti/ *noun* a legal document which promises that a machine will work properly or that an item is of good quality ○ *The car is sold with a twelve-month warranty.* ○ *The warranty covers spare parts but not labour costs.*

waste /weɪst/ *noun* an unnecessary use of time or money

waste coverage /ˈweɪst ˌkʌv(ə)rɪdʒ/ *noun* media coverage which goes beyond the target audience

waybill /ˈweɪbɪl/ *noun* a list of goods being transported, made out by the carrier

wealth management /ˈwelθ ˌmænɪdʒmənt/ *noun* investment services offered by banks to people with more than a specific amount of money in liquid assets

wear and tear /ˌweər ən ˈteə/ *noun* damage to a product through use over a period of time

web /web/ *noun* the thousands of websites and webpages within the Internet, which users can visit

webcast /ˈwebkɑːst/ *noun* a broadcast made over the web that enables an event to be viewed by a large number of people who are all connected to the same website at the same time (NOTE: Webcasts often use rich media technology.)

web commerce /ˈweb ˌkɒmɜːs/ *noun* same as **e-commerce**

web marketing /ˈweb ˌmɑːkɪtɪŋ/ *noun* marketing that uses websites to advertise products and services and to reach potential customers

web marketplace /ˈweb ˌmɑːkɪpleɪs/ *noun* a network of connections that enables business buyers and sellers to contact one another and do business on the web (NOTE: There are three types of web marketplace: online catalogues, auctions, and exchanges.)

webmaster /'webmɑːstə/ *noun* the person who looks after a website, changing and updating the information it contains and noting how many people visit it (NOTE: Several different people within an organisation may share the job of webmaster.)

webpage /'webpeɪdʒ/ *noun* a single file of text and graphics, forming part of a website

website /'websaɪt/ *noun* a position on the web, which is created by a company, organisation or individual, and which anyone can visit ○ *How many hits did we have on our website last week?*

weekly /'wiːkli/ *noun* a newspaper or magazine which is published each week ○ *The clothes were advertised in the fashion weeklies.* (NOTE: plural is **weeklies**)

weight /weɪt/ *noun* a measurement of how heavy something is □ **to sell fruit by weight** the price is per pound or per kilo of the fruit □ **to give short weight** to give less than you should

weighted average /ˌweɪtɪd 'æv(ə)rɪdʒ/ *noun* an average which is calculated taking several factors into account, giving some more value than others

weighted index /ˌweɪtɪd 'ɪndeks/ *noun* an index where some important items are given more value than less important ones

weighting /'weɪtɪŋ/ *noun* a statistical process which gives more importance to some figures or results than others in the process of reaching a final figure or result

weight limit /'weɪt ˌlɪmɪt/ *noun* the maximum weight ○ *The packet is over the weight limit for letter post, so it will have to go by parcel post.*

wet goods /'wet gʊdz/ *plural noun* goods that are sold in liquid form ○ *Special plastic containers have to be used for wet goods.* ○ *Inflammable wet goods are the most dangerous type of product to transport.*

wheel of retailing /ˌwiːl əv 'riːteɪlɪŋ/ *noun* a model which explains changes in the evolution of the retailing trade

COMMENT: This model explains that retailers start as low-price downmarket stores and gradually trade up, and sometimes eventually go out of business, being replaced by new downmarket stores.

white coat rule /waɪt 'kəʊt ruːl/ *noun* a rule for advertising on TV stating that doctors or actors in white coats cannot promote medical products

white goods /'waɪt gʊdz/ *plural noun* **1.** machines which are used in the kitchen, e.g. refrigerators, washing machines **2.** household linen, e.g. sheets and towels

wholesale /'həʊlseɪl/ *adjective, adverb* referring to buying goods from manufacturers and selling in large quantities to traders who then sell in smaller quantities to the general public ○ *I persuaded him to give us a wholesale discount.* □ **he buys wholesale and sells retail** he buys goods in bulk at a wholesale discount and then sells in small quantities to the public

wholesale dealer /'həʊlseɪl ˌdiːlə/ *noun* a person who buys in bulk from manufacturers and sells to retailers

wholesale price /'həʊlseɪl praɪs/ *noun* a price charged to customers who buy goods in large quantities in order to resell them in smaller quantities to others

wholesale price index /ˌhəʊlseɪl 'praɪs ˌɪndeks/ *noun* an index showing the rises and falls of prices of manufactured goods as they leave the factory

wholesaler /'həʊlseɪlə/ *noun* a person who buys goods in bulk from manufacturers and sells them to retailers

wholesale trade /'həʊlseɪl treɪd/ *noun* trade that involves buying goods in large quantities at lower prices in order to resell them in smaller quantities and at higher prices to others

WIIFM *noun* the basic thoughts that affect the decision taken by a prospective customer. Full form **what's in it for me?**

win /wɪn/ *verb* to be successful □ **to win a contract** to be successful in tendering for a contract ○ *The company announced that it had won a contract worth £25m to supply buses and trucks.*

window /'wɪndəʊ/ *noun* an opening in a wall, with glass in it

window display /'wɪndəʊ dɪˌspleɪ/ *noun* the display of goods in a shop window

window dressing /'wɪndəʊ ˌdresɪŋ/ *noun* the practice of putting goods on display in a shop window, so that they attract customers

window shopping /'wɪndəʊ ˌʃɒpɪŋ/ *noun* the practice of looking at goods in shop windows, without buying anything

windscreen sticker /'wɪndskriːn ˌstɪkə/ *noun* an advertising sticker put onto the windscreen of a car

win-win situation /wɪn 'wɪn sɪtjuˌeɪʃ(ə)n/ *noun* a situation in which, whatever happens or whatever choice is made, the people involved will benefit

women's magazine /'wɪmɪnz mægəˌziːn/ *noun* a magazine aimed at the women's market

word /wɜːd/ *noun* something spoken

word-of-mouth communications /ˌwɜːd əv maʊθ kəmjuːnɪ'keɪʃ(ə)nz/ *plural noun* informal channels of communication such as friends and neighbours, colleagues and members of the family

working capital /'wɜːkɪŋ ˌkæpɪt(ə)l/ *noun* capital in the form of cash, stocks and debtors (less creditors) used by a company in its day-to-day operations

work in progress /ˌwɜːk ɪn prəʊ'gres/ *noun* the value of goods being manufactured which are not complete at the end of an accounting period ○ *Our current assets are made up of stock, goodwill and work-in-progress.* Abbr **WIP** (NOTE: American English is **work in process**)

works /wɜːks/ *noun* a factory ○ *There is a small engineering works in the same street as our office.* ○ *The steel works is expanding.* (NOTE: takes a singular or plural verb)

workshop /'wɜːkʃɒp/ *noun* a small factory

world /wɜːld/ *noun* **1.** the earth □ **the world market for steel** the possible sales of steel throughout the world **2.** people in a specific business or people with a special interest ○ *the world of big business* ○ *the world of lawyers* or *the legal world*

'…the EU pays farmers 27 cents a pound for sugar and sells it on the world market for 5 cents' [*Duns Business Month*]

'…manufactures and services were the fastest growing sectors of world trade' [*Australian Financial Review*]

world enterprise /wɜːld 'entəpraɪz/ *noun* an advanced form of international marketing

world rights /wɜːld 'raɪts/ *plural noun* he has the right to sell the product anywhere in the world

worldwide /'wɜːldwaɪd/ *adjective*, *adverb* everywhere in the world ○ *The company has a worldwide network of distributors.* ○ *Worldwide sales* or *Sales worldwide have topped two million units.* ○ *This make of computer is available worldwide.*

World Wide Web /ˌwɜːld ˌwaɪd 'web/ *noun* same as **web**

wrap /ræp/, **wrap up** /ˌræp 'ʌp/ *verb* to cover something all over in paper ○ *He wrapped (up) the parcel in green paper.* □ **to gift-wrap a present** to wrap a present in attractive paper

wrapper /'ræpə/ *noun* a piece of material which wraps something ○ *The biscuits are packed in plastic wrappers.*

wrapping paper /'ræpɪŋ ˌpeɪpə/ *noun* a special type of coloured paper for wrapping presents

X Y Z

yard /jɑːd/ *noun* a measure of length (same as 0.91 metres) (NOTE: can be written **yd** or **yds** after numbers: **10 yd**. Yards are no longer in official use in the UK.)

yearbook /ˈjɪəbʊk/ *noun* a reference book which is published each year with updated or new information

yellow goods /ˈjeləʊ ɡʊdz/ *plural noun* high-priced goods which are kept in use for a relatively long time and so are not replaced very frequently. Compare **orange goods, red goods**

Yellow Pages /ˌjeləʊ ˈpeɪdʒɪz/ *trademark* a section of a telephone directory printed on yellow paper which lists businesses under various headings such as computer shops or newsagents

young old /jʌŋ ˈəʊld/ *noun* the market sector consisting of people aged between 60 and 75, that is with a median age of around 66

yuppies /ˈjʌpiz/ *plural noun* young professional people with relatively high incomes (NOTE: short for **young upwardly-mobile professionals**)

zero-rated /ˌzɪərəʊ ˈreɪtɪd/ *adjective* referring to item which has a VAT rate of 0%

zero-rating /ˈzɪərəʊ ˌreɪtɪŋ/ *noun* the rating of an item at 0% VAT

ZIP code /ˈzɪp kəʊd/ *noun US* numbers in an address that indicate a postal delivery area (NOTE: British English is **postcode**)

zone /zəʊn/ *noun* an area of a town or country for administrative purposes ■ *verb* to divide a town into different areas for planning and development purposes □ **land zoned for light industrial use** land where planning permission has been given to build small factories for light industry

SUPPLEMENT

VALS Lifestyle Segmentation

Social group	*Description of members*
Innovators	Successful, sophisticated people, often leaders in their profession, who are interested in new ideas and products and who buy a lot of expensive things
Thinkers	Well-educated and well-informed people, often idealistic, who buy things that last a long time and are good value for money
Achievers	Successful people with traditional tastes and values who buy expensive products that have a good reputation or that save them time
Experiencers	Young people who like new and unusual things and spend a lot of money on fashion and on their social life and hobbies
Believers	Conventional people with strong morals and ideals who like traditional, well-known products and are loyal customers
Strivers	People who want to appear successful, rich and fashionable, who enjoy shopping and would like to have more money to spend
Makers	Practical people who like to be independent and control their own lives and who buy goods that are good value for money but are not expensive or fashionable
Survivors	People without much money who cannot afford expensive things and buy only what they need, often at reduced prices

SWOT Analysis

Organisation

Strengths
The services or products
or skills which the
organisation is good at
doing or making

Weaknesses
The services or products
or skills which the
organisation can't do or
doesn't do well

Market

Opportunities
Segments of the market
which are attractive, and
where changes in the
market might work in
favour of the
organisation

Threats
Segments of the market
or changes taking place
in the market which
make it difficult for the
organisation to work
there

Social Classes in the UK

This classification of social classes is based on the one used by National Statistics, the UK government service that provides statistical information on many areas of British life.

Code	*Description of members of group*
I	senior managers, administrators, senior civil servants, leading professional people (doctors, lawyers, architects, etc.)
II	middle managers and administrators, middle-level civil servants and professional people
III N (= non-manual)	junior managers and administrators, clerical staff
III M (= manual)	workers with skills and qualifications
IV	unskilled workers, such as manual workers, in permanent jobs
V	pensioners, unemployed people, casual manual workers

Advertising Rates for a Periodical

RATE CARD

ADVERTISEMENT RATES: DISPLAY

Size	Number of Insertions		
	1	2	3
Black and White			
Full page	£1100	£1050	£1000
Half page	700	675	650
Third page	550	525	500
Quarter page	450	425	400
Four colour			
Full page	£1700	£1600	£1450
Half page	900	800	700
Two Colour			
Full page	£1350	£1200	£1100
Half page	900	800	700
Inside covers full colour	£2000	£1600	£1350
Facing editorial:	Basic card rate plus 10%		
Full page bleed:	Basic card rate plus 10%		

Inserts

Preprinted inserts can be accepted folded

Rates (per 1000):		Full print run	Targeted
	one issue:	£88	£98
	three issues:	£220	£245
	six issues:	£396	£441

ADVERTISEMENT RATES: CLASSIFIED

Recruitment:

Full page	£800
Half page	£450
Single column centimetre	£12.50
Double column centimetre	£20.00
Three column centimetre	£27.00

Classified under headings:

For Sale	Wanted	Property
Freelance offered	Technical Services	Marketing
Business Supplies	Personal	Educational

Single Column Centimetre	£10.00
Double Column Centimetre	£17.00

All advertisements must be pre-paid

Box numbers £5.00 per insertion

Copy required by 5pm four working days before publication

Technical Information for a Periodical

MECHANICAL DATA

Circulation:	25,000
Frequency:	Monthly
Publication day:	First Thursday in month
Printing process:	Offset litho
Binding:	Wire-stitched
Trim size:	285 x 210mm
Screen:	Black & White 120/48 line per cm
	Colour 150/60 lines per cm
Bleeds:	Bleed trim on all trimmed edges is 3mm
Materials required:	
Colour:	Screened positives, emulsion-side down, right-reading, with progressives
Black & White:	Screened positives, emulsion-side down, right-reading
Copy for setting:	Double space typed
Artwork:	Digital artwork only, following file formats accepted: Quark Express, EPS with embedded fonts, TIFF, JPEG